Connecticut's Pennsylvania "Colony" 1754-1810

Susquehanna Company Proprietors, Settlers and Claimants

Volume I
The Proprietors

Donna Bingham Munger

HERITAGE BOOKS
2007

HERITAGE BOOKS

AN IMPRINT OF HERITAGE BOOKS, INC.

Books, CDs, and more—Worldwide

For our listing of thousands of titles see our website
at
www.HeritageBooks.com

Published 2007 by
HERITAGE BOOKS, INC.
Publishing Division
65 East Main Street
Westminster, Maryland 21157-5026

International Standard Book Number: 978-0-7884-4238-4

Contents

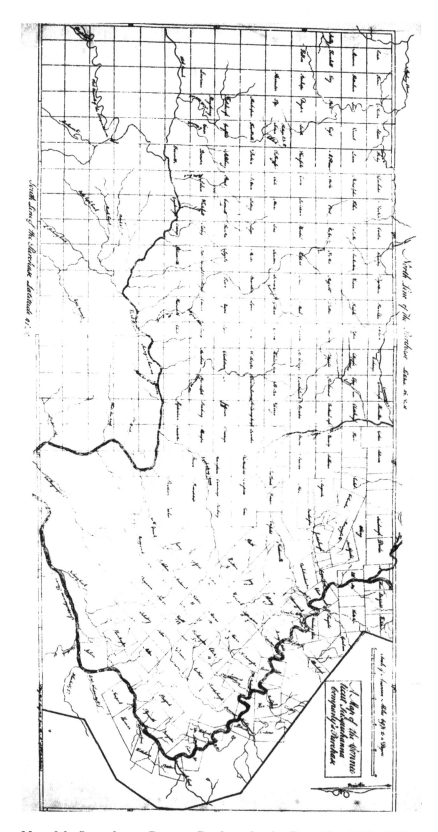

Map of the Susquehanna Company Purchase showing Townships, 1753 - 1800
Original in Leffingwell Collection, New Haven Colony Historical Society

Introduction, with Acknowledgments

Between 1762 and 1800, a steady stream of settlers from Connecticut and to a lesser extent Rhode Island, Massachusetts and New York moved west, settled in northeastern Pennsylvania and disappeared from written records. Most of the settlers had bought shares from the Connecticut based Susquehanna Company, a self-proclaimed land company whose aim was to wrest control of the East Branch of the Susquehanna River from Pennsylvania. Each share entitled the subscriber to a proportional share of land in a Company township. Company clerks recorded sales of shares, conveyances of deeds, township grants and other miscellaneous documents in the Minute Book of meetings and ten volumes of Account Books.

Sequestered in a private Pennsylvania collection for years, then donated to the Connecticut Historical Society, the original Minute and Account Books languished in corners and over the years were used by only a few local historians. In the late 1920s when Julian Boyd was editor of the multi-volume *Susquehanna Company Papers* he had the Account Books Photostatted. Although he, and later editor Robert Taylor, collected and published eleven volumes of Susquehanna Company papers, neither editor incorporated any material from the Account Books and rarely cited them in footnotes.

Wanting to use the Account Books for a research project of my own and mystified as to their whereabouts, I enlisted the help of the Connecticut Historical Society, the Wyoming Historical and Geological Society, and the Pennsylvania Historical and Museum Commission. The late Ruth Blair of the Connecticut Historical Society graciously helped me locate eight of the ten Account Books and later she located the misplaced two volumes. William H. Siener kindly let me and Roland Baumann of the Pennsylvania State Archives search the attic storeroom at the Wyoming Historical and Geological Society where we found six Photostat volumes that had survived the Susquehanna River flood of 1936. In the attic we also found, much to our surprise, a nearly complete every name card file. Margaret Craft, librarian, let us borrow the cards which we duplicated to form an alphabetical surname index. But, since the page numbers referred to the Photostat copy pagination and not the original pagination, the index was of use only as a second opinion when surname spelling was in question. For a more detailed discussion of the Account Books see the author's earlier article, "Following Connecticut Ancestors to Pennsylvania: Susquehanna Company Settlers," *The New England Historical and Genealogical Register*, Volume 139, April 1985, p. 112-25

After studying the Account Books, their value for historical and genealogical purposes became apparent. In a more personal way than the collected *Susquehanna Company Papers*, the Account Books brought to life the Susquehanna Company's efforts at settlement in northeastern Pennsylvania. Thus, I decided to create a database of proprietors using fields common to all deeds, that is: grantor, grantor residence, grantee, grantee residence, description, amount, location, deed date, recording date, page, and notes. By moving from grantor to grantee, it is possible to trace a chain of title.

For preservation's sake, the Pennsylvania State Archives copied the Photostat copies of the Account Books that we thought were missing. That enabled the Connecticut Historical Society to produce a complete microfilm version of the Account Books from which I have worked.

This entire project would not have been possible, however, without the commitment of Hertha Williams, my AARP volunteer at the Pennsylvania State Archives when I was Chief of the Division of Land Records. She used her private time to make printouts and prepare handwritten abstracts of every deed following a database format. I owe her my profound gratitude and only wish she were alive to see the results. I, myself, reread every deed as I entered details in the computer database. Thus, the errors, and there are undoubtedly some, are mine and mine alone. If you as a user detect an error kindly contact me so that I can make a correction in the master computerized database.

When this volume documenting *Susquehanna Company Proprietors* was nearly finished, I realized that only one-third of the story was told. To tell the other two-thirds meant continuing the database, thus two more volumes materialized. Volume II documents the actual Susquehanna Company settlers and has the title *Connecticut's Pennsylvania "Colony," Susquehanna Company Settlers*. Volume III documents the settlers that remained to claim title to their land under Pennsylvania law and has the title *Connecticut's Pennsylvania "Colony," Susquehanna Company Claimants*. Users will want to consult those volumes for the rest of the story.

Donna G. Bingham Munger
Former Chief, Pennsylvania Division of Land Records
Yelm, Washington

SECTION 1   THE HISTORICAL SETTING

Historical Setting: The Proprietors

A large group of people, one source guesses 250 citizens (Brewster), assembled at Windham, Connecticut on July 18, 1753 and pledged to pay two Spanish milled dollars each to send a journeying committee to view a tract of land on the Susquehanna River. Eager to promote their need for more land, several of these citizens had already petitioned the Connecticut General Assembly for title to this tract heedless to the fact that it lay within the colony of Pennsylvania. Located near *Chiwaumuck*, meaning "Large Plain" in the Delaware language, English speaking colonists called the place *Wyomock, Wyomink* or *Wyoming*. Without regard to colonial boundaries, the journeying committee had authority to purchase title from the Indians and to receive a deed in the name of each subscriber in equal proportion. So was born the Susquehanna Company.

Organizers envisioned apportioning their land among as many subscribers or shareholders as was necessary to support the project. At first this number was relatively small. Subscribers only wanted a tract about ten by twenty miles along the Susquehanna River. They envisioned eight townships five miles square each containing 16,000 acres. Shareholders had until September 1, 1753 to pay their $2.00 directly to the journeying committee.

Minutes of this first meeting and most of the ensuing meetings were copied into one of two Minute Books, later sewn together to form one book. Until 1770, lists of share purchasers were simply incorporated within or between the minutes. This database contains the names of all proprietors entered in the Minute Book as well as those in the Account Books.

An alphabetized list of 306 subscribers, 313 counting duplicate names, follows the minutes of the first meeting. The list, probably prepared seven years later in 1760 as per a Company vote requiring the Clerk to "make an Alphabetical roll of all the proprietors" (Minute Book, March 12, 1760), documents the amount that many, but not all, proprietors paid. Only 49 purchasers on this alphabetical list are noted as paying the journeying committee $2.00 by the end of 1753.

> **1753, July 18, Windham - 1st meeting, Minute Book 1: 1-21;** *Papers*, **I: 28-39, No. 13;** *PA (2)*, *18*: **3-12.** [Author's notes: (1) an alphabetized list of subscribers containing 306 different names follows these minutes and is entered in the database with deed date as July 18, 1753; (2) for a more detailed discussion of the Minute Book see under Short Titles: Munger (1)].

Before the journeying committee left for the Susquehanna River, the Company held a second meeting, mainly to admit a group of subscribers from Colchester, Connecticut that had similar interests. The Colchester people agreed to the $2.00 subscriber fee and other terms. Of equal importance, the Company voted to sell half shares for $1.00. Voters also decided not to admit minors and to extend the journeying committee departure deadline to October 1.

> **1753, September 6, Canterbury - 2nd meeting, Minute Book 1: 22-23;** *Papers*, **I: 40-1, No. 15;** *PA (2)*, *18*: **12-13.**

Sometime during the designated month of October the journeying committee viewed the "Lands of Wyoming" where they succeeded in creating a "great disturbance" according to Richard Peters, Secretary of the Pennsylvania Land Office. Peters reported that the people from Connecticut told the Wyoming inhabitants that the British Crown's Connecticut Grant predated the Pennsylvania Grant, that the Grant extended from "Sea to Sea," and that Wyoming was within the latitude of Connecticut. To make matters worse, added Peters, the journeying committee announced that "a Thousand Men" would come in the spring to settle. ("Richard Peters to the Pennsylvania Proprietaries." *Papers*, I: 42, No.17)

Clearly, the Pennsylvania Land Office from this early date was aware of the Susquehanna Company interest in the Wyoming region. But the Pennsylvania Proprietors had not yet purchased the area from the Indians, as was their policy, before making the land available for legal settlement. Connecticut people saw the region as unsettled and ripe for the taking.

Word of the journeying committee's successful viewing circulated in Connecticut and by the end of 1753 a total of 171 men had paid their $1.00 for a half share or $2.00 for a whole share. In response, the Company formed a committee of six to collect money and admit shareholders from Windham and the nearby towns of Hebron, Colchester, New London, and Norwich.

Interest spread across the colony so rapidly that in January 1754 shareholders voted to add 240 new subscribers to the existing 306 original subscribers. Recruitment shifted to the county level. To apportion the new shares fairly, the Company placed a limit on how many could be sold in each county. New Haven and Fairfield were permitted forty shares each, but the remaining four counties already had several subscribers so that Hartford was permitted only thirty more, New London and Litchfield twenty more, and Windham ten more. New committee members for each county were selected to solicit and take the names and money of new subscribers. This system created havoc with record keeping as most committee members were slow to return their accounts.

At this third meeting, the Company also increased the cost of a whole share to $4.00 for all newly admitted subscribers and levied a tax of $1.00 on every $2.00 and $4.00 shareholder. Thus, the price of a new whole share rose to $5.00 and a new half share to $2.50. Individuals who had pledged to become subscribers, but had not yet paid were permitted to pay at the old rate of $2.00. The Minute Book lists thirty-two such persons, nine of whom were noted as paid. The remaining twenty-three persons paid before July 11, 1754 and their names are on the deed, but not all are on the list of original subscribers.

> **1754, January 9, - 3rd meeting, Minute Book 1: 24-9;** *Papers*, **I: 43-50, No.19;** *PA (2), 18*: **13-16.** [Author's note: three accountings follow these minutes. First, a list of 76 shareholders that paid the new $1.00 tax to Samuel Gray, clerk, by April 30, 1754, p. 30 (the *PA* version omits many names that are in the original). Second, a list of 9 more that paid the tax by May 29, 1754, p. 31. Third, a list of 34 newly enlisted persons that paid Samuel Gray by January 9, 1754, p. 32-3 (The *PA* version omits one person)].

Originally scheduled for April 17, the next Company meeting got under way in Windham on May 1, 1754. The real purpose was to clarify the quota for each county and to appoint new county representatives. To reach the number of 500 subscribers, Hartford, New Haven, Fairfield, New London and Windham counties were allowed eighty shareholders each while Litchfield was limited to forty. Middlesex and Tolland counties did not exist at this time. The remaining sixty shares were to form a reserve for "particular persons". Thomas Stantly and Stephen Gardner were new committeemen for Hartford, Thomas Darling for New Haven, Captain Samuel Adams for Fairfield, John Elderkin for New London, and Captain Uriah Stevens for Litchfield. A committee composed of Captain John Fitch, Jedediah Elderkin and Samuel Gray was to admit people from Windham. Lists of shareholders obtained by each committeeman were copied into the Minute Book.

The database, combining information from all lists in the Minute Book, shows that the Susquehanna Company had 416 subscribers by July 1, 1754. Of these, 278 held whole shares and 89 held half shares. For 49 subscribers no share amount was noted. Payment records exist for 239 of the whole shares and all 89 of the half shares.

> **1754, April 17 adjourned to May 1, Windham - 4th meeting, Minute Book 1: 33-4; *Papers*, I: 86-90, No. 49; *PA (2), 18*: 16-22.** [Author's note: A list of thirty-six Windham subscribers admitted by Jedediah Elderkin all of whom presumably paid follows these minutes. Next is a list of four subscribers from Hartford County who paid Charles Dewey and Charles Bulkley in September 1753. Bulkley and Dewey were former committeemen who had not turned in their accounts. Third is the list of the forty-seven subscribers that Thomas Stantly took in from Hartford County. Of these, eight qualified as "particular persons". The final list is of persons for whom Stantly paid the $1 tax, Minute Book 1: pp. 34-7.]

An opportunity to approach the Indians with a request to purchase the tract at Wyoming on the Susquehanna River came in July 1754 at the Albany Congress. The Congress, held at the outbreak of the French and Indian War to discuss unified action between the seven northern British colonies and the Six Nations, gave other groups a chance to meet and discuss various issues with the Indian Chiefs. Representing the Susquehanna Company fell to John Henry Lydius, an influential frontier trader. Lydius took on the task after the Company's chosen delegate, Rev. Timothy Woodbridge of the Stockbridge Indian School entrusted it to him.

With little difficulty, Lydius negotiated a deed whereby the Six Nations relinquished their rights to a large tract of land extending 10 miles to the east of the Susquehanna River between the forty-first and forty-second parallels and 120 miles west of the east line. This included much of the East Branch of the Susquehanna River and extended west as far as present day Clearfield, Pennsylvania. The deed claimed that the tract lay within the charter bounds of Connecticut. The Indians, of course, would have had no way of knowing whether that statement was true or not. Most unfortunately, the deed was not discussed in open Council and mistakes, erasures, and corrections clouded the wording. Worse yet, not all of the Indian Chief's pictographs were obtained on the deed date of July 11, 1754. The last four Chiefs drew their symbols on March 4, 1755.

According to the deed, the Company paid two thousand pounds for the tract, but Julian Boyd states that a note in the *Sir William Johnson Papers* says "that only £200 currency was paid in hand." (*Papers*, I: 103 footnote 18) Testimony Lydius gave in 1761 in "Confirmation of the Truth and Authtickness" of the deed, claims that he dispensed $1,705 Spanish milled dollars among the Indian Sachems. (*Papers*, I: 120; No. 57.) None of these amounts was accurate. At any rate, most of the money was given to the Indians after the deed date. For example, voters at the November 20, 1754 meeting agreed to send Lydius $1000.00 to complete the purchase.

Included in the deed were the names of the original Company proprietors. Stated to be 534 whole-share owners and 136 half-share owners, this number by actual count was 542 whole-share owners and 157 half-share owners. After entering all names in this database and correcting the list as per instructions in the Minute Book and eliminating names entered twice, the number of whole-share owners turned out to be 533 and half-share owners 156.

The terms of the deed entitled each whole-share owner to 2/1224 parts of the purchase and each half-share owner to 1/1224 parts of the purchase. This allocation suggests those 1068 portions were allocated to whole share owners, leaving 156 portions for half shareholders. Thus the database number of 533 whole-share owners is off by only 1 and the number of half-share owners at 156 is accurate.

Deed from Indians of the Six Nations to the Susquehanna Company [including affidavits dated 1761], Liber B1-15; *Papers*, **I: 101-117, No. 57;** *PA* **(2), II: 147-58. Other copies in (1) Records of the State of Connecticut, Book 4, Patents, Deeds, and Surveys of Land. This copy sent to the Connecticut Assembly by George Wyllys, Company Secretary in 1782; (2)** *Connecticut Archives, Susquehanna Settlers***; (3) Connecticut Claims collection, I: 1, HSP; (4)** *Sir William Johnson Papers***, I, 405; (5) the** *John Franklin Papers***, Pennsylvania State Archives.** [Author's note: 699 names, 5 removed as per minutes of November 20, 1754 and 5 duplicates for 689 different names. Many names appear on the deed but not elsewhere in the Company records.]

While John Lydius was dealing with the Indians on behalf of the Susquehanna Company, Pennsylvania representatives, also at the Albany Congress, were negotiating a similar deed with the same Chiefs. The resulting agreement, known in Pennsylvania as the Purchase of 1754, opened to white settlement almost all of the land on the west side of the Susquehanna River from a mile north of the mouth of Penn's Creek in present day Snyder County northwest to the provincial border. However, due to Indian dissatisfaction, the purchase boundaries were redrawn in 1758 with far shorter western and northwestern boundaries. The resulting area did not overlap any land that the Indians intended to be included in the treaty with the Susquehanna Company. For a map showing Pennsylvania's purchase treaties with the Indians see the *Genealogical Map of the Counties* published by the Pennsylvania Historical and Museum Commission (*Munger (2)*, inset and elsewhere).

When Susquehanna Company proprietors met next, they sought additional funds by offering 300 more shares at the increased price of $7.00 a share or $9.00 including tax. This brought the number of possible shareholders to 800. Shareholder David Phelps wrote in his conveyance to William Willcockson, dated December 25, 1755, that his share was "supposed to Contain about one eight Hundreth part of the whole tract..." (Account Book E87). Some of the money raised was to go toward the expense of seeking a grant from Britain confirming the purchase.

1754, November 20, Hartford - 5th meeting, Minute Book 1: 38-42; *Papers*, **I: 166-180, No. 84;** *PA* **(2), 18: 22-32** [Author's notes: (1) the second paragraph of the original is missing in *PA*; (2) Corrections and additions to the names in the Indian deed follow the main business of the meeting. Next is a list of 97 paid proprietors that Captain Uriah Stevens, *MB*: 42, admitted and were already named in the deed. Then follows several accountings of money received for the payment of taxes since November 1753. Some of these were noted as certified in 1755. The last list, perhaps added in an empty space at a later time, is of four new proprietors of 1762. All new shareholders are entered in this database.]

Daniel Edward's Roll Book. Connecticut Claimants Loose Papers, Pennsylvania State Archives. [Author's note: Also included in the database are the names of ninety-three new half and whole shareholders that Daniel Edwards admitted after the November 20, 1754 meeting when share costs were increased. Each paid $4.50 for a half share or $9 for a whole share. Since the Roll Book in which the names appear does not include dates and none of the names are on the Indian deed, the database uses 5/1/1755 as the deed date unless a duplicate entry in the Account Books gives a specific date. The page is entered as RB].

The Susquehanna Company was not the only Connecticut group interested in Pennsylvania land. Calling themselves the Delaware Company, another group negotiated three separate purchases with the Delaware Indians in December 1754 and May, 1755. Forming two companies called the First and Second Delaware Companies, but later the Delaware and Lackawack Companies, these companies held deeds to all the land located between forty-one and forty-two degrees north latitude west of the Delaware River and east of the Susquehanna Company lands.

Seeking official government approval for actions taken so far, Susquehanna Company proprietors petitioned the Connecticut General Assembly during the May 1755 session. (The Public Records of the Colony of Connecticut, 1636-1776, X, 378,) Essentially, proprietors asked for assistance in receiving Crown approval "to erect and settle a colony" on the tract purchased from the Six Nations. In response, the Assembly indicated that it would approve the venture provided His Majesty would grant the lands. Attached to the petition were the names of about 850 Company proprietors. This number compares with Minute and Account

Book records for 528 paid shareholders and 382 shareholders for which no clear record of payment exists through May 1, 1755. Of those who had paid, 354 were whole-share owners, 170 were half-share owners and 4 were not indicated.

A day before the General Assembly had begun its May 1755 session, the Susquehanna Company had held its own spring meeting and had voted to send settlers to Wyoming. The rationale was to protect Company interests by erecting corner markers in the northeast and southeast corners of the purchased land, and by laying out a township and building a fort, gristmill, and sawmill. Plans quickly changed, however, when the French and Indian war broke out and word reached Connecticut of General Braddock's defeat in western Pennsylvania in July 1755. Instead of incorporating as planned and before asking His Majesty for confirmation of title and a Royal grant, Company activities came to a stand still. The only one to go to Wyoming was the Company surveyor. No more meetings were held until March 12, 1760.

1755, May 1, Hartford -6th meeting, not in the Minute Book; Jonathan Trumbull Papers, XXI: 88, CSL; *Papers*, I: 283-84, No. 136; *PA (2), 18*: 32-33

Committee members did continue to sell shares, however. Thomas Darling admitted 48 proprietors between May 2 and December 31, 1755. (March 12, 1760 minutes) Twenty-eight others claimed to have bought shares during the same time according to the Account Books. In all, entries in the Minute Book, the Indian Deed, and Daniel Edward's Roll Book (see above ff. Nov. 20, 1754 meeting.) show that the Susquehanna Company had met its 800-member goal before recessing for the French and Indian war.

Company activity began to pick up in March 1760 when proprietors met again following their five-year recess. The first order of business was to attempt to straighten out the Company records by calling for outstanding accounts and preparing an alphabetical roll of all proprietors. This roll is probably the list of subscribers in the Minute Book following the minutes of the first Company meeting July 18, 1753. Copies of the alphabetical roll were to go to county committeemen.

About this same time and in keeping with the need to maintain better Company records, the clerk began a series of account books. The first account book was labeled Liber A, Liber meaning Book. To date, all that has been found of Liber A is an index, but from references and duplicate entries in other account books and the Minute Book, we know that Liber A mainly contained deeds conveying shares between shareholders from 1762 to 1773. For example, Liber B210 identifies Liber A as "The first Book of Records of Deeds" when referring to a deed from Zephaniah Perkins to Nathan Carpenter recorded on page A443 while the index to Liber A references the same names and page. Many of the 495 deeds in Liber A were dated as early as 1754 and while most of the deeds were conveyances between individuals, other deeds duplicated Minute Book entries by re-recording the sale of shares from the Company to an individual. A few pages originally left blank at the end were later filled with deeds entered in 1796. Every grantee and grantor name from Liber A is entered in the database.

At their March 1760 meeting, proprietors also decided to approach the Delaware Company about a joint application to the British government for grants covering the territory both companies had purchased from the Indians. Although the Susquehanna Company had purchased land in Pennsylvania before the Delaware companies, Delaware shareholders were the first to settle on their tract. By 1760 and possibly as early as 1757, First Delaware Company settlers had surveyed three townships near *Cushietunck*, now Cochecton, on the upper Delaware River, built several cabins, a saw mill and a grist mill. Leaders of all three companies saw a benefit in working together. Nothing materialized immediately, however, and proprietors ended their meeting by replacing all "Receivers of Money" with two new committee members for each county.

1760, March 12, Hartford - 7th **meeting, Minute Book 1: 49-50;** *PA (2), 18*: **33-35.** [Author's note: Includes list of 48 paid proprietors admitted by Thomas Darling between May 2 and December 31, 1755.]

1761, February 25, Windham - 8th **meeting, Minute Book 1: 53-5;** *Papers,* **II: 62-3. No. 43;** *PA (2), 18*: **35-6.** [Author's note: first meeting held at Windham since 1754; no list of subscribers follows the minutes]

Meeting in Windham again on April 9, 1761 proprietors finally decided to let the Delaware companies participate in a joint application to the Crown and appointed Eliphalet Dyer to be their representative in England. The Susquehanna Company agreed to pay two thirds of Dyer's expenses and salary of £150 per annum while the Delaware Company was to pay one-third. To raise money, proprietors voted to sell 200 more whole shares at £8 or $25 each. Purchasers, as before, were to be apportioned among the six Connecticut counties.

1761, April 9, Windham - 9th **meeting, Minute Book 1: 55-8;** *Papers,* **II: 72-6, No. 53;** *PA (2), 18*: **36-9.** [Author's note: several lists of subscribers dated 1761 with notations such as entered here in 1761 or 1762 follow this meeting.]

Dyer's trip to England did not happen as planned. Committee members who were to prepare the case that Dyer was to argue failed to complete the presentation. So instead of Dyer traveling to England, the Company found an agent in England who would plead their case.

Another startling change of tactic was the Company decision to hire 100 men to go to Wyoming "to prepare the minds of the Indians" for white settlers. For some time the Delaware Indians, complaining that they had not been involved in the deed, had opposed white settlement. At the same time, certain sachems of the Six Nations denied that they had sold land to the Delaware companies and expressed unhappiness with the settlements at *Cushietunk*. (Letter from New York Governor to Penna on word of Thos Nottingham. Special Applications, Oct 14, 1760 - Oct 4, 1765, Vol. 166, Records of the land Office (RG-17), microfilm 17.27, Pennsylvania State Archives, Harrisburg.) Pennsylvania's Governor James Hamilton took advantage of the Indian dissatisfaction and in September 1761 issued a dire warning to all whites settled on land not purchased from the Indians.

1762, January 5, Hartford - 10th **meeting, Minute Book, 1: 60-2;** *Papers,* **II: 119-21. No 85;** *PA (2), 18*: **39-41.** [Author's note: one list of proprietors taken in 1755]

Deciding to honor Hamilton's warning, the Susquehanna Company changed plans once again. In place of employing 100 men to intimidate the Indians, the Company temporized and asked the Reverend Timothy Woodbridge of the Stockbridge Indian School to intercede. Using his expertise and friendship with certain chiefs, Woodbridge simply demanded that the Indians confirm the deed and practice restraint in the spring of 1762 when up to one hundred white families would come to settle.

With the Indians forewarned, the Susquehanna Company voted to permit 50 to 100 shareholders, no substitutes, to settle and improve a ten-mile tract of land on the East Side of the Susquehanna River within their purchase. This tract was to be a gratuity of an extra 640 acres per person over and above each settlers' respective shares in the rest of the purchase, provided they arrive within four months, that is by September, 1762, and remain for five years.

1762, May 19, Hartford- 11th **meeting, Minute Book, 2: 3;** *Papers,* **II: 130-33, No. 98;** *PA (2), 18*: **41-3.** [Author's note: These minutes begin a second minute book with new numbering, but sewed together with the first minute book.]

Concerned about the danger of an Indian uprising should the Company press settlement plans, Connecticut's Governor Thomas Fitch brought the issue of government support before the Connecticut Assembly. Not wanting to alienate prominent leaders and businessmen who were also active in the Susquehanna Company, the Assembly authorized a proclamation that neither prohibited not supported settlement. Julian Boyd claimed that the Company's reaction to the proclamation was contemptuous and prompted the decision to increase the number of settlers to 200. *(Papers, 2: xxvii)* As an incentive, proprietors approved a second gratuity tract of ten square miles on the opposite or West Side of the river from the first tract. Settlers were given three months to arrive.

1762, July 27, Windham - 12th meeting, Minute Book, 2: 4-6; *Papers* **II: 145-47, No. 112;** *PA* **(2), 18: 43-4**
[Author's note: an accounting of Proprietors admitted Sept 4, 1761 and Nov 4, 1762 follows these minutes.]

In early September 1762, ninety-three armed Connecticut settlers joined sixteen men from Cushetunk and followed the rough road from the Delaware River to Mill Creek on the Susquehanna River. Equipped with a few farm implements, they began their first settlement. Upon learning of the settlers' presence the Indians complained to Pennsylvania authorities. Daniel Brodhead, a young deputy surveyor who later became Pennsylvania Surveyor General was sent to investigate. Boldly, the settlers told Brodhead to expect 1,000 more Connecticut people with two pieces of artillery in the spring of 1763 and insisted that they had the support of the Connecticut Governor. *(Papers, II, 166-170, No. 27.).* The settlers also talked of a forthcoming meeting with the Six Nations. After listening to their comments Brodhead convinced the settlers to withdraw and avoid further difficulties. The Connecticut men returned home. For the names of seventy-three of the settlers see *Connecticut's Pennsylvania "Colony": Susquehanna Company Settlers,* list *2.*

As soon as news of the settlers' withdrawal reached Connecticut, Company leaders extended their offer of gratuity acreage to those who would return to Mill Creek the following spring. To raise money to fund the return venture, the Company offered 50 to 100 more special shares at £15 or $50.00 per whole share. The database shows that between November 16, 1762 and June 1, 1763 when settlers were to have returned to Mill Creek, the Company sold 51 whole shares and 32 half shares. Of those shares whose price was recorded, 13 whole shares sold at £15, 1 whole share at $50.00 and 8 half shares at $25.00. If all new shareholders had paid at that rate the Company could have raised $3,350.00

1762, November 16, Windham - 13th meeting, Minute Book, 2: 7-9; *Papers,* **II: 177-80, No. 136;** *PA* **(2), 18: 45-7.**
[Author's note: three lists of shares sold 1762-63 follow this meeting.]

In the spring of 1763, Susquehanna Company plans changed for a third time. Despite prior arrangements, the meeting with the Six Nations did not take place and the Company lost one more opportunity to procure official recognition of its purchase. Rather than continue to risk their interest, shareholders decided to take control of the soil and developed a blueprint for settlement. They would begin by surveying eight townships of five miles square as close to the gratuity townships as possible. To be viable, each township would ultimately need forty settlers, but could begin to organize with as few as twenty settlers. Each township was to be surveyed in the New England pattern, that is fifty-three parts, reserving three for public use. The other fifty parts would go to shareholders in 300-acre amounts split among three, four, or even five divisions. To ensure an even quality of land, each 300-acre tract was to be allocated among town, meadow and woodland plots. Settlement was further encouraged by permitting sons to settle in place of their fathers. For their first community leader, the Company hired Rev. Timothy Woodbridge at a salary of £20 per month for six months. Settlement was to take place by September 15, 1763.

1763, April 7, Windham - 14th meeting, Minute Book 2: 11-16; *Papers,* **II: 204-08, No.155, PA (2), 18: 47-51.**
[Authors notes: (1) several lists of proprietors from 1762 and 1763 follow these minutes; (2) The Company reserved all beds of iron ore and coke.]

Learning of the impending white settlement, certain leaders of the Six Nations demanded a hearing before the Connecticut Assembly. Traveling to Hartford, the Indian Chiefs delivered innocuous pronouncements. Assembly members followed suit. The only accomplishment was the tacit understanding that both the Susquehanna Company and the Chiefs who signed the deed were acting independently of their respective governments. Meanwhile, the first group of settlers set out from Connecticut about the first of May 1763.

Shortly after the first of May, Governor Thomas Fitch received a letter from the British government advising him to prevent the Susquehanna Company from settling at Wyoming until the King-in-Council could review the issue. Fitch took no direct action, but did notify Company leaders who called for a meeting in Hartford on May 18 where they voted to suspend further settlement. Boyd commented that this decision merely meant that the Company agreed not to authorize settlement beyond that already approved and settler Parshall Terry stated in his 1794 deposition that about 150 settlers were present throughout the summer but not that many on the ground at any one time. (*Papers*, 2: xxviv, note 91; 10: 200-08, No. 118; *PA (2)*, 18, 700-08; HSP, Connecticut Claims in Pennsylvania, III, signed by Terry) As Boyd goes on to point out, on the same day that the Company voted not to send more settlers, Pennsylvania's Governor Hamilton noted that fourteen settlers were already at Wyoming and more were expected daily.

> **1763, May 18, Hartford - 15th meeting, Minute Book 2: 17-18;** *Papers*, **II: 219, No. 169;** *PA (2), 18*: **51.** [Author's note's: the letter from the British Government was from Charles Wyndham, Lord Egremont, Secretary of State for the Southern Department and brother-in-law of George Grenville who became First Lord in April 1763. Egremont died in August 1763 and Grenville in November 1770.]

The King's official order-in-council prohibiting settlement took affect on June 15, 1763. Designed to protect the rights of the Indians, the order called for the removal of the Connecticut people from lands belonging to the Six Nations and the Delaware Indians. However, Connecticut's Governor Fitch did not receive instructions accompanying this order until September and by then Eliphalet Dyer had left for England to lobby for support.

The Indians could not be bothered with such political maneuverings and took matters into their own hands. Attacking the settlers at Wyoming on October 15, 1763, the Indians killed about twenty settlers and captured several more. Not one word about this first Indian "massacre" appears in the Minute Book, but the Company held no meetings and sold no shares in 1764. Dyer was the only Company leader to publicly acknowledge the Indian problems when he wrote from England saying that the massacre at Wyoming in October had made his arrival "most Inoppertune" and given the Company cause a great disadvantage. (*Papers*, II: 291-3, No. 232)

Dyer remained in England for more than a year, but failed in his efforts to influence the Crown. Reporting to the Company on January 16, 1765 after he returned home, Dyer stated that he could not find an influential person in Great Britain willing to represent the Company. Nevertheless, the Committee did appoint John Gardiner of Inner Temple, London as their representative in England. Of equal importance at this time was the need for more income. Another Company meeting on April 24th in Windham called upon all proprietors to settle their accounts so funds could be sent to England.

> **1765, January 16, Windham - 16th meeting, Minute Book, 2: 19;** *Papers*, **II: 307-08, No. 245;** *PA (2), 18*: **52-3.**

> **1765, Apr 24, Windham- 17th meeting, Minute Book, 2: 20-1;** *Papers*, **II, 309, No. 246;** *PA (2), 18*: **53.**

When that approach did not work and with more than £500 outstanding on unpaid shares, the Company voted on May 16, 1765 to borrow money from a few wealthy supporters. To attract lenders, Ezra Stiles developed a financial report. A copy he sent to Peletiah Webster in November, 1766 showed an initial offering of 400 proprietors @ $5, followed by 300 proprietors @ $7 and 150 proprietors @ $9 for a total of 850 proprietors bringing in $5450 or £1635. Added to these were 200 additional proprietors @ £8 and 50 special proprietors at $50 each bringing in £2350. Thus in 1766 the Company claimed an offering of 1100 whole shares which if all sold would have brought in £3985 or £3000 Sterling. *(Papers, II: 318, No. 262)*

A side-by-side comparison of these figures with actual Company records is not possible due to the very poor Company bookkeeping. Information on fully half of the shares the Company claimed it sold is incomplete and lacks amount paid, deed date, or description. However, after converting two half shares to a whole share, the database shows payment records for 349 whole shares sold up to and including November 9, 1754. These qualify as the initial offering and at $5 a whole share brought in $1745 or £528. Likewise converting two half shares to a whole share, between November 9, 1754 and April 9, 1761, 121 shares sold @ $9 for a total of $1089 or £330. After April 9, 1761, 38 proprietors paid £8 for a whole share and 54 proprietors paid £4 for a half share for a total of £520. Of the special proprietors, 18 or 20 paid £15 or $50 for whole shares and 8 paid $25 for half shares for a total of £360. Adding the totals together we get £1738, certainly not the amount Stiles declared. No shares sold at $7 as voters changed that amount to $9 at the same meeting.

> **1765, May 16, Hartford - 18th meting, Minute Book, 2: 21-22;** *Papers,* **II: 310, No. 247; PA (2), 18: 54.** [Author's note: Three lists of proprietors follow this meeting; one is dated 1766 and two are dated July, 1769 in original, but 1767 in *PA*.]

To add to the Company's financial problems word arrived from England that their agent was unable to pursue their petition as he had moved from London. Needing to raise additional funds for a new agent, proprietors voted on January 6, 1768 to assess $2.00 on each share. Of the amount collected, $1.50 was to go toward prosecuting the case in England and $.50 was to go to John Lydius for money owed him. Voting to send Dyer to Great Britain for a second time rather than hire an unknown as agent, the Company later changed its mind and appointed Samuel Johnson who was already in England. Finally, the Committee agreed to sell all remaining and forfeited shares at £15 each as one more attempt at raising money

> **1767, September 16 adjourned to November 11, Windham - 19th meeting, Minute Book 2: 23-4;** *Papers* **II: 322-23, No. 270;** *PA (2), 18:* **55.**

> **1768, January 6, Windham - 20th meeting, Minute Book, 2: 24-5;** *Papers,* **III: 1-2, No. 1;** *PA (2), 18:* **55-7.**

> **1768, April 6, Hartford and June 8, Windham - 21st meeting, Minute Book, 2: 26-7;** *Papers,* **III: 14-18, No. 17;** *PA (2), 18:* **57-8.** [Author's notes: Minute Book pages 2: 27-29 contains copies of receipts dating 1755 - 1767 recorded December 28, 1768]

Welcome news arrived with the summer of 1768. The Crown, after years of pressure, finally agreed to run the Indian boundary line so eagerly awaited by colonial governments, land companies, and settlers alike. Meeting at Fort Stanwix, near present day Rome, New York in June and July, the Iroquois released their claim to all land east of Fort Stanwix. In effect, this established a settlement line in Pennsylvania following river courses from Tioga Point, now Athens, on the East Branch of the Susquehanna River to the point where the Ohio River crossed Pennsylvania's western boundary. Calling this, in Pennsylvania, the New Purchase or the Purchase of 1768, the Treaty of Fort Stanwix opened a huge amount of land to anyone willing to follow Pennsylvania's warrant and patent procedures. *(Munger (2), 62, 79-84)* Included in the purchase was the land at the forks of the Susquehanna River and much but not all of the Susquehanna Company tract.

Immediately, the Pennsylvania colonial government surveyed two proprietary manors in the Wyoming Valley as was their usual policy before opening a region to legal settlement. *(Munger (2): 23, 84)* These manors, Stoke and Sunbury, were located on opposite sides of the Susquehanna River where the Connecticut settlers intended to lay out townships and where Wilkes-Barre, Kingston, and Plymouth are today *(Harvey, 455-56)*. John Penn, then Proprietary Governor of Pennsylvania, granted one-hundred acres within the Manor of Stoke to Amos Ogden, John Jennings, and Charles Stewart with the proviso that they build a trading house and defend themselves against all enemies, in particular Connecticut intruders.

To protect its purchase, the Susquehanna Company planned to have 240 settlers at Wyoming before Pennsylvania's land office was ready to accept applications for warrants. Meeting at Hartford on December 28, 1768 the Company voted to send 40 proprietors over the age of 21 to Wyoming by February 1, 1769. These first forty were to be joined by 200 more proprietors not later than May 1. The Company agreed to pay for building a convenient road to the Susquehanna River and appropriated £200 to cover costs that might be incurred if any settlers were apprehended, sued or prosecuted. To help defray expenses all proprietors that had not yet paid were told to pay at least £6 toward their share by April 12 or be removed from the Company Rolls.

To ensure true settlement, the 240 settlers needed to fulfill certain tasks. They were to survey five townships, three on one side of the Susquehanna River and two on the other side. Each township was to extend five miles along the River and five miles back and was to belong to the settlers over and above their regular shares provided they occupy and improve their land for five years. The first forty were to have the first choice of township. As an added incentive to settlement, the Company planned to send a minister. Almost as an after thought, proprietors granted Dr. Eleazar Wheelock a tract six by ten miles for the use of an Indian school, but Wheelock declined the offer.

To gain support, the Company voted to approach the Connecticut General Assembly once again for a grant confirming ownership of the entire tract purchased from the Six Nations. Such support became all the more important given the impossibility of placing any request before the King-in-Council. By now, Company leaders began to understand that the British Government had no intention of creating any inland colonies in North America. Hope for the Susquehanna Company came only through controlling the Connecticut Assembly. For the time being, however, the Company could garner only Upper House support. In January 1768, the Lower House voted down the Company's petition for the Colony's deed to the land.

1768, December 28, Hartford - 22nd meeting, Minute Book 2: 30-5; *Papers*, **III: 43-47, No. 40;** *PA (2), 18*: **58-62.** [Author's note: Minute Book 2: 35-7 contain copies of receipts 1754-55 and proprietors admitted 1779. The PA version page 63 is out of sequence with the original.]

As scheduled, the first forty setters arrived at Mill Creek, the old settlement on the Susquehanna River north of the Wyoming Valley, early in February, 1769. Having prior knowledge of their arrival, John Jennings, the Northampton County Sheriff was there to meet them. He arrested three of the forty, Isaac Tripp, Benjamin Follet, and Jedediah Elderkin, and warned the others that their fate would be the same if they did not leave. Tripp, Follet, and Elderkin spent four days in the Easton jail before joining the others at their temporary camp near the Delaware River. The entire contingent then returned Mill Creek.

About two weeks later, on March 13, Sheriff Jennings, accompanied by an even larger posse, showed up and arrested thirty-one of the forty settlers. On the way to Easton jail eleven of the thirty-one escaped. The twenty who arrived in Easton were formally arraigned and jailed, then bailed out. Most of the men had returned to Connecticut by the first week in April. (Joseph Chew to Sir William Johnson, N. London, Ap 6th 1769, *Papers*, III: 94, No. 76.) For the names of the first forty and those who were arrested see *Connecticut's Pennsylvania "Colony": Susquehanna Company Settlers*, lists 3 and 4 or *Papers* or *Harvey*.

Quickly responding to Pennsylvania's surprise arrests, Company proprietors met at Hartford on April 12, 1769 and voted to send 300 more settlers to Wyoming. To qualify, prospective settlers needed to be an original proprietor or to have purchased a share from an original proprietor and agree to arrive by May 10. These settlers were assigned to the West Branch where the Company authorized three more townships.

Their job was to provide a protective barrier near the recently surveyed Pennsylvania proprietary manors of Pomfret, Muncy and Job's Discovery and the French and Indian War officers' tracts. (*Munger (2)*, 80). Although the townships were never officially surveyed, the Company's strategy was to force an ejectment suit followed by a trial and an appeal as the only way to approach the King-in-Council. ("Eliphalet Dyer to William Samuel Johnson." *Papers*, III: 159-60, No 135.)

To raise needed funds, the Committee placed a new assessment of $2.00 on each share and offered 100 new shares for sale at £12 each. Twenty of the £12 shares were designated for sale in the frontier areas of New York, New Jersey and Pennsylvania and thirty shares were to be sold by the Committee of Settlers at Wyoming. Although the Company had now authorized eight townships, one for the first forty, four for the next 200, and three for the 300 on the West Branch, settlers were to live together in one place, fortify themselves, be governed as one unit and apportion jobs among all.

At the same time, the Company agreed to send at least two of their three strongest representatives, Eliphalet Dyer, Samuel Talcott and/or Jedediah Elderkin to defend the twenty settlers who had been arrested and were scheduled for trial at Easton. As the April, 1769 meeting closed, leaders expressed fear that many proprietors had no intention of paying for their shares until the Company received some sort of official approbation. ("Samuel Gray to Gershom Breed." *Papers*, III: 107, No. 84) Therefore, as their last piece of business, proprietors approved another warning to unpaid shareholders and set June 1 as a deadline for paying or forfeiting their shares.

1769, April 12, Hartford - 23rd meeting Minute Book, 2: 37-9; *Papers*, III: 96-8, No. 79; *PA (2), 18*: 63-6.

Settlers continued to leave Connecticut for Wyoming. Led by Major John Durkee, over 100 settlers arrived at the Susquehanna on May 12 and a few days later another 150 settlers loaded with provisions and a few cattle and horses joined them. Everyone set to work building log cabins placed to form a stockade and named their enclave Fort Durkee. On May 24th the Sheriff of Northampton County appeared once again, this time to read a proclamation from Governor Penn. About 150 settlers politely assembled the next day only to be told that they were in violation of the law and should evacuate immediately. In response, the Connecticut people defiantly fired a gun over the Sheriff's head. He withdrew and the settlers went back to their usual tasks. For a list of settlers at Wyoming on June 2 see *Susquehanna Company Settlers* list 5.

Attention then shifted to Easton where the trial of the twenty arrested settlers was to occur during the June term of the Northampton County court. Eliphalet Dyer and Jedediah Elderkin and their sons traveled from Connecticut via Wyoming to represent the defendants while Major Durkee and most of the defendants came directly from Wyoming. But the case was rescheduled for the September term and bail was renewed at the staggering sum of £4000. Durkee and the majority of defendants returned to Wyoming; the rest went home to Connecticut. For a list of Wyoming settlers at the end of August see *Susquehanna Company Settlers*, list 6.

While Major John Durkee was in Easton, a militia company of Pennsylvanians from Philadelphia, in full military array under the command of Colonel Turbot Francis, approached Fort Durkee and demanded surrender. After delivering many unsuccessful threats, Francis withdrew rather than initiate armed confrontation.

Still, the Company proprietors at their July 26, 1769 meeting in Windham began to ask the question, should the people currently at Wyoming be recalled? Responding in the negative, proprietors went on to approve the sale at public auction of all shares that were not fully paid by September 1, 1769.

1769, July 26, Windham - 24th meeting, Minute Book 2: 40-1; *Papers*, III: 155-56, No. 130; PA (2), 18: 66-7.
[Author's note: three short lists of shares sold follow this meeting, but lists in PA version out of order from original.]

Despite the repeated threats to sell unpaid shares, money still did not flow into the Company treasury fast enough. Rather than taking action on reselling pledged shares, proprietors continually voted to extend the deadline. Thus, at the September 6, 1769 meeting, the September 1 deadline for selling shares at auction was extended to October 20. Voters also approved funds for defraying the expense of traveling "the Distance of the way Each one lives from sd Court" for the twenty that were to go to trial in Easton later in the month.

1769, September 6, Windham - 25th meeting, Minute Book 2: 42-3; *Papers*, III: 174-76, No. 151, PA (2), 18: 67-8.

The outcome of the trial was no surprise. Convicted and fined, eight defendants somehow made payment and were released while the remaining twelve were jailed, but not for long. Since the jail was very small and lacked facility to care for more than twenty to thirty inmates, officials arranged for the eight to escape. As soon as the prisoners were safely away, the Sheriff posted a reward for their capture. But since each had fled Pennsylvania jurisdiction, this was a hopeless gesture.

Meanwhile, settlers at Wyoming had surveyed the boundaries of their five gratuity or settling townships. Wilkesbarre (later Wilkes-Barre), surveyed first, included the Mill Creek and Fort Durkee settlements on the East Side of the Susquehanna River. Nanticoke (renamed Hanover) and Pittstown (later Pittston) were also on the East Side of the River. Forty (renamed Kingston) and Plymouth were on the West Side of the Susquehanna River.

Once again, however, before the townships could be subdivided into lots, the settlers were forced from Wyoming. On the same November 8 day that the Executive Committee of the Susquehanna Company voted to make up 50 barrels of pork for the 240 settlers, Colonel Francis arrived at Wyoming, this time from Fort Augusta at the forks of the Susquehanna, with about twenty men and a small canon. On the 11th, his men captured Major John Durkee and on the 12th Sheriff Jennings and about 200 Pennsylvania men arrived. On the 14th, the settlers surrendered and agreed to depart within three days. To protect their cattle and crops, fourteen settlers and their families were permitted to remain. For names of the settlers involved see *Susquehanna Company Settlers*, lists 7 and 8. (Harvey: 629; *Papers*, III, 201-02, No. 179 Frederick Spyer who stayed the winter not on either list 7 or 8.)

Major John Durkee was jailed in Philadelphia, but was released on bail after ten to twelve days and returned to his home in Norwich, Connecticut. Consequently, he was able to attend the December 6, 1769 Susquehanna Company meeting in Windham where he and Samuel Gray, the clerk, were asked to collect evidence relating to the events since May. Proprietors voted to give Durkee the money to pay all bills from the trial at Easton, but cash was short and money was available only by collecting on delinquent accounts, selling forfeited shares and borrowing from proprietors.

1769, November 8, Hartford and December 6, Windham- 26thmeeting, Minute Book 2: 44-6, Susquehanna Company Records; *Papers*, III: 206-07, No. 184, PA (2), 18: 68-70.

More significantly, in January 1770 the Company accepted help from the Paxtang Boys, a group of Lancaster County, Pennsylvania frontiersmen led by Lazarus Stewart. Apparently sometime in December the Paxtang Boys had taken over Fort Durkee and the Wyoming lands on behalf of the withdrawing settlers. Stewart and his followers offered to take care of the settlers' houses and effects and to help retain possession of the land in return for the grant of a township six miles square. By accepting the township, Stewart and his followers agreed to the same regulations as the other settlers. (Extract From the *Connecticut Courant. Papers*, IV: 4, No. 3; "The Executive Committee to John Montgomery and Lazarus Young." *Papers*, IV: 5, No. 4.)

In order to "keep and maintain possession" of their purchase on the Susquehanna River, the Company in January also augmented its own leadership at Wyoming by appointing two additional senior men, Captain Robert Durkee and Captain Zebulon Butler, to the Committee of Settlers. And, since the Company was still short of funds, they sought another loan and again threatened proprietors with forfeiture if they did not pay all delinquent accounts by March 1, 1771.

1770, January 10, Windham - 27th meeting, Minute Book 2: 46-7; *Papers*, IV: 4, No. 2; PA (2), 18: 70-?

Captain Zebulon Butler arrived at Wyoming on the twelfth of February 1770 and took command of Fort Durkee. As head of the Settlers' Committee, Butler was responsible for admitting new settlers, for surveying and distributing land and for organizing resistance. (Memorandum Book of Zebulon Butler, February - May, 1770. *Papers*, IV: 79, No. 58; original in Sheldon Reynolds MSS, WHGS.) He was also to prepare full and timely reports for the Executive Committee in Connecticut.

Under Butler's leadership, skirmishes between Connecticut and Pennsylvania settlers escalated. Each side took prisoners then set them free, but this game ended on April 23 when Connecticut settlers laid siege to Amos Ogden's Fort, formerly the Pennsylvania Trading House in the Manor of Stoke. After six days, Ogden and his men gave up and withdrew. Butler and his people burned the fort. In its stead, Butler had orders to set up a Company trading house where all settlers were to make their purchases.

The serious work of settlement now began. At its June 6, 1770 meeting in Hartford, the Susquehanna Company approved the surveys for the five settling townships. Voters also approved a sixth township to be six miles square instead of the usual five and to be located either at "Laccawanna" or south of Nanticoke. The Company also gave the Settling Committee at Wilkesbarre authority to lay out more townships at their discretion as more settlers applied.

1770, June 6, Hartford - 28th meeting, Minute Book 2: 47-50; *Papers*, IV: 84-86, No. 60, PA (2), 18: 71-2.
[Author's note: two conveyances within the minutes]

During the summer, work began on subdividing the townships into lots. Major Durkee hired a Pennsylvania surveyor to plot Wilkesbarre while the company surveyor, David Mead, assisted by several other proprietors, subdivided the other four townships. Before drawing individual lots, the Settler's Committee made a "List of the Proprietors of the Five Townships" presumably present at Wyoming. Their 282 names are in list 9, *Susquehanna Company Settlers*. Settlers assigned to Wilkesbarre drew their lots at the end of June, but many months elapsed before proprietors in the other townships drew their lots.

As Connecticut settlers continued to stream into the Wyoming Valley new and serious problems developed. Governor John Penn issued a proclamation urging Pennsylvania magistrates and sheriffs to prosecute and bring to justice all intruders on Pennsylvania land. Armed with this authority, Sheriff Jennings deputized Nathan Ogden and gave him a warrant for the arrest of ninety-one of the Connecticut settlers that had burned Ogden's fort. With about 140 Pennsylvanians, Ogden set out from Easton in mid September. When he and his men arrived at Fort Durkee on the 22nd they attacked and captured several settlers including Major John Durkee and Captain Zebulon Butler. Ogden marched the prisoners to the small Easton jail. After three weeks of confinement, the judge released everyone except Durkee, Butler and Major Simeon Draper. He sent all three to Philadelphia to be arraigned, Durkee for the second time. Most of the settlers returned to Connecticut.

As soon as the Susquehanna Company proprietors in Windham learned of the settlers' imprisonment at Easton they met at Windham and decided to approach the Connecticut Assembly once again. Ostensibly, proprietors wanted the Assembly to ask the Governor to intervene in the release of the prisoners, but as important, they hoped the Assembly would claim Wyoming as part of Connecticut and grant governmental powers to the settlers.

Continuing the meeting at Hartford on November 27, the Company voted to send £50 to Easton and Philadelphia for the maintenance and support of Major Durkee and the other Connecticut prisoners. Company proprietors also encouraged the displaced settlers to return to Wyoming and/or the West Branch townships by May 15, 1771 by setting that date as the deadline for retaining settling rights in a township. Thereafter, new settlers could take up any vacant right.

1770, October 17, Windham and November 27, Hartford - 29th meeting, Minute Book 2: 51-3; *Papers*, IV: 131, No. 108 and 135-36, No. 116; *PA (2), 18*: 73-4. [Author's note: The last few lines are missing in the original.]

Recapturing Fort Durkee, however, fell not to returning settlers, but to Lazarus Stewart and his Paxtang Boys. Stewart and a handful of his followers returned to Wyoming in the middle of December and took back the Fort with little effort. With Stewart in control of Fort Durkee, the Susquehanna Company met in January, 1771 and rescinded the May 15 return date for settlers and instead called upon all 240 approved settlers to return immediately or forfeit their settling rights. Each settler who returned was asked to sign a statement agreeing to perform and support the settlement. In the margin of the Minutes beside this provision is a note in a different handwriting stating that the Company would pay each man $5.00 to arm and equip himself. Captain Zebulon Butler and Major John Durkee who were still in jail and John Smith Esq. were to continue as their leaders and Lazarus Stewart and one representative from each of the five Wyoming townships were to join this Settlers' Committee. As promised, in return for their assistance and despite mustering less than the required 50 settlers, the Company deeded Nanticoke Township to Stewart and his men who promptly renamed the township, Hanover.

At about the same time, proprietors also approved Lackawanna Township for the 35 settlers that had been living there since 1769. This was the sixth township on the East Branch and was located at Capouse Meadows where the first path from the Delaware River met the Lackawanna River.

1771, January 9, Windham - 30th meeting, Minute Book, 2: 53-6; *Papers*, IV: 146-50, No. 149; *PA (2), 18*: 74-7. [Author's notes: Minute Book minutes followed by list of shares sold 1773, p. 56; list of 8 of the 200 to go in spring 1769, p. 57; one short list of receipts given 1755, 1761, 1762, p. 58. This marks the end of the lists of proprietors in the Minute Book]

Just twelve days later, before settlers began to return, Fort Durkee fell to Pennsylvania once again. On Friday, January 18 the Ogden brothers, Amos of the former Pennsylvania Trading Post and Nathan the deputy sheriff, arrived in Wyoming with a contingent of nearly 100 men and a warrant for the arrest of Lazarus Stewart. Hostilities broke out and Stewart apparently killed Nathan Ogden. Realizing the possible consequences, Stewart evacuated the Fort in the night of January 21 and fled to Connecticut, but the Pennsylvanians managed to take several Connecticut prisoners. Some prisoners were sent to join Major Durkee and Captain Butler in the Philadelphia jail while others were incarcerated at Easton. For the fifth time Pennsylvania had driven Susquehanna Company settlers from Wyoming.

In March when Susquehanna Company proprietors met in Windham they defiantly labeled the Pennsylvanians "a gang of lawless and wicked men" and voted to send the 240 settlers plus Lazarus Stewart and his men back to Wyoming. And if any of the 240 refused to go, then anyone going in their place was eligible for a settling right. Furthermore, each one going would receive $5.00. To pay for this the Company levied a new tax of $2.00 on each share. Twenty-one proprietors were then chosen to take the names of settlers volunteering to go. In addition, the 300 settlers approved for the West Branch were free to go and collect their settling right provided they left by June 1, 1771.

1771, March 13, Windham - 31st meeting, Minute Book 2: 59-60; *Papers*, IV: 180-81, No. 151; *PA (2), 18*: 77-78.

However, the Susquehanna Company completely changed tactics before anyone could return to Wyoming. Virtually unable to collect the $2.00 tax, the Company decided on April 4 to suspend all settlement. The rationale was to create a favorable image of itself in anticipation of the May General Assembly meeting when it was hoped that Connecticut would announce its claim to western lands including the Susquehanna Purchase. Money was so short that proprietors were still trying to raise the £50 to send to Major John Durkee and others in the Philadelphia jail and to reimburse those who had boarded Lazarus Stewart and his six men when they had fled to Connecticut.

1771, April 4, Windham - 32nd meeting, Minute Book 2: 61-5; *Papers*, IV: 200-04, No. 159; *PA (2), 18*: 78-82.

As predicted, the Connecticut Assembly, in May, did produce an official yet vague statement about Connecticut's claim to western land. Encouragingly, they also appointed a committee to collect substantive evidence for the claim and send the material to England for a legal opinion. (*The Public Records of Connecticut*, May 1771, pg. 427-28.) Viewing the Assembly's action as official support, the Susquehanna Company decided to send all 540 settlers to Wyoming immediately. Anticipating a rush of settlers, proprietors in Connecticut gave the Settler's Committee at Wyoming power to admit new settlers on the rights of defaulting proprietors.

1771, May 19, Windham and May 23 and June 12, Hartford- 33rd meeting, Minute Book, 2: 66-8; *Papers*, IV: 216, No. 169; *PA (2), 18*: 82-3.

Almost immediately, an advance group of 50 shareholders led by Captain Zebulon Butler set out from Connecticut. Each one had been at Wyoming previously. Rendezvousing with Lazarus Stewart and his Paxtang Boys in northern New Jersey, they marched as a combined force and arrived at the old Mill Creek blockhouse about July 6. More settlers arrived daily. Soon, enough settlers were present to begin to build fortifications near Fort Wyoming where the Pennsylvanians were holding out. By August 10 Zebulon Butler had a force large enough to attack the Pennsylvanians. For five days the fighting continued until Fort Wyoming surrendered on August 15 and the Pennsylvanians withdrew. This marked the end of what later came to be called the First Yankee-Pennamite War, Pennamite being the derogatory term Connecticut settlers used for Pennsylvanians holding land within the Susquehanna Company Purchase. Settlers at Wyoming held their first peaceful meeting on August 22nd and continued to meet regularly during the fall of 1771 conducting the business necessary in setting up a new community. For names of settlers present from July through October see *Susquehanna Company Settlers*, lists 10 and 11.

While the settlers were busy developing their new community, the Executive Committee was grappling with the problem of collecting the new $2.00 tax. Having recently increased the number of collectors, the Committee now asked each collector to submit the money collected along with a written accounting. Knowing there would be a shortfall, the Committee authorized the sale of another 10 of the 100 special shares at £12 each. This database shows that up to October, 1771 the Company had managed to sell only 8 special shares at £12 each and of the 10 shares now authorized, only 9 were sold and those over the next six years, 1772-1778.

1771, October 9, Windham - 34th meeting, Minute Book 2: 69; *Papers*, IV: 274, No. 232; *PA (2), 18*: 83-4.

Settlers at Wyoming felt the same monetary pinch and in December 1771 voted exorbitant fees for settlers purchasing new shares. For example, Kingston (originally Forty) charged new settlers who were neither original proprietors nor under purchasers $60 for a share. Wilkesbarre and Plymouth charged new settlers $50, and in Lackawanna (Pittstown) new settlers paid $40. (Town Book of Wilkes-Barre, Westmoreland Records, 1054; *Harvey*, 717.)

A huge number of settlers arrived in the Wyoming Valley in 1772. To accommodate the increase, proprietors appointed a new committee with broad authority to locate new townships. Their first assignment was to lay out a township at Capouse Meadows for any 40 shareholders that had lost settling rights due to imprisonment or forced withdrawal. Another township could be located on the West Branch at Muncy Creek if more "aggrieved" settlers came forward. In fact, whenever twenty proprietors applied and could show certificates verifying that they had paid their taxes, the committee could authorize other townships.

With the number of newcomers increasing rapidly, settlers began to agitate for local government. Returning to Connecticut to conduct legal business was difficult and when Pennsylvania formed Northumberland County in March, 1772 Company settlers perceived their need for local government to be all the more urgent. Although they were never assessed Northumberland County taxes, Susquehanna Company settlers were excluded from all county services such as deed recording and probate proceedings. In April, proprietors voted to apply to the Connecticut Assembly for the establishment of their own civil government.

1772, April 1, Norwich - 35th meeting, Minute Book, 2: 70; *Papers*, IV: 314-16, No. 279; *PA (2)*, 18: 84-6.

During the rest of 1772, settlement continued at a rapid and peaceful pace. Between May and December at least 328 settlers arrived as shown on list 12, *Susquehanna Company Settlers*. Near the end of April, settlers had been allowed to leave the area of the Company fort and move into their own settling townships where they were admonished to fortify and guard themselves by forming town militias. Well settled by October 1772 list 13 *Susquehanna Company Settlers* shows that 243 men petitioned the Connecticut General Assembly that month for legal status for Wyoming. By November so many new settlers had arrived that the township committee authorized a seventh township. Named Exeter, the new township was located on both sides of the Susquehanna River immediately north of Kingston and Pittston. (Liber B, page 296) Difficulties continued on the West Branch, however, and settlers were driven away in June when they attempted to survey the recently authorized township at Muncy Creek.

The issue of self-government dominated Company business in 1773. At its annual April meeting, proprietors in Connecticut acknowledged an abundance of complaints and grievances from settlers at Wyoming. In June they issued a lengthy code of conduct binding on all settlers. Proprietors also acknowledged problems with the method of assigning individual lots. Settlers who disliked their location were permitted to find new lots. To appease everyone, each whole share proprietor was permitted to increase his holdings from one fifty-third part to two fifty-third parts in one township or one fifty-third part in two townships.

As new settlers continued to arrive in 1773, the Company formed new townships on the East Branch. Both Salem and Newport townships, authorized in April and May were located south of the five settling townships, one on each side of the Susquehanna River.

Settlement on the West Branch remained a contentious issue. Four years earlier, in 1769, the Company had authorized three gratuity townships on the West Branch and anxious proprietors had formed committees and named and even surveyed at least six townships, but the Company had not given proprietors authorization to settle. ("Minutes of a Meeting of the Proprietors of New Wethersfield," P.S.L., Provincial *Papers*, XLII, 33 in *Papers*, V: 78-9, No. 91; see also *Papers*, V: xxvii note 26 re Butler *Papers*, WHGS.) However, the shift in power from Easton to Ft Augusta at Sunbury, the Northumberland county seat located at the forks of the Susquehanna River, promised to make it more difficult for the Susquehanna Company to survey and settle townships on the West Branch. Anxious proprietors petitioned the Company for the right to settle and protect their interests.

Cautiously, the Company gave approval in April 1773 for 120 men to settle anytime within the next five years at New Weathersfield [Sic.] as one centrally located Gratuity Township and rescinded the grants of the other two gratuity townships.

Still agitating for local government, the Company also approved a more detailed petition to the Connecticut General Assembly asking that Wyoming be formed into a separate county. Two hundred eighty-eight different names in two handwritings were attached to the petition. For the names of the petitioners see list 14 *Susquehanna Company Settlers.*

1773, April 22, Hartford - 36th meeting, Minute Book 2: 73; *Papers,* **V: 119-120, No. 100;** *PA (2), 18:* **86-8.**

Despite the West Branch problems, the Company approved individual grants at Warrior's Run, near present day Watsontown in Northumberland County, for Governor Jonathan Trumbull and five other proprietors for losses sustained and also a township opposite the mouth of Pine Creek to include the Long Island which would be in present day Lycoming County opposite Jersey Shore. These West Branch grants and this unnamed township were never settled. In fact, a party of settlers did head toward the West Branch in June 1773 intending to build a fort. Intercepted near Chillisquaque on the 8th by William Plunket and about 100 men, sixty or so of the settlers turned back while thirty-nine surrendered their arms. When two men offered themselves as hostages, Plunket released the rest and returned their arms. (*Papers,* V: 146-49, Nos. 117 - 121; *Harvey,* 768-69.)

1773, June 2, Hartford - 37th meeting, Minute Book 2: 76-85, Papers, V: 138-45, No. 115: *PA (2), 18:* **88-95.** [Author's notes: (1) The Warrior's Run grant was for 3200 acres, 1,100 acres to Gov. Jonathan Trumbull and 125 acres each for Maj. John Durkee, Vine Elderkin, Ebenezer Gray Jr., Andrew French and Capt. Ebenezer Backus (Liber F32 and F92). The Company re-granted the same in 1796 on the East Branch as Trumbull Township (Liber F110). (2) The grant opposite Pine Creek on the West Branch went to Capt. Judah Woodruff and Assoc. to be 5 mi. sq., but along the river as far as land fit for improvement extended].

The Connecticut Assembly finally granted local government to the settlers in January 1774 by creating the Town of Westmoreland. Despite the intervening portion of New York, the Assembly attached the Town of Westmoreland to Litchfield County, Connecticut. Encompassing all of the Delaware Company lands, the town's boundary extended west only fifteen miles from Wilkesbarre. Since West Branch townships were not included, settlers soon petitioned the Assembly for an extension of the boundary west. Pointing out that 126 families lived within the town boundaries, while 200 more families lived west of the town, the petition asked that the western boundary be relocated along the 1768 Fort Stanwix Treaty line. A year and a half later in May 1775 the Assembly approved the change to include all of the townships granted so far on the north side of the West Branch of the Susquehanna River. ("Petition of Zebulon Butler and Others to the Connecticut General Assembly." Susquehanna Settlers, I, 57 a-d; *Papers,* VI: 285-88, No. 105. For a map of the new western boundary see The Purchase of 1768 (New Purchase) on *The Genealogical Map of the Counties.* For a written description see *Munger (2),* 62.)

By creating the Town of Westmoreland, the Assembly had finally accepted an active role in defending the Susquehanna Company purchase. In return, proprietors agreed to levy a tax of 24 shillings on a whole share and 12 shillings on a half share to be used by the Connecticut treasury to defray expenses that might arise in defense of their purchase. Shareholders that did not pay the tax within the year were to forfeit their shares. To provide a military presence for the Town of Westmoreland, the following year in May 1775 the Assembly created the 24th Regiment and appointed Zebulon Butler Colonel. Every settler between the ages of sixteen and fifty needed to participate.

Inactive shareholders now felt more confident in their investment and began to consider settlement. Those who's names appeared on the Indian Deed or were enrolled in the records of the Company but had never paid taxes were offered the opportunity to activate their shares by paying all back taxes with interest and an additional sum of £10. To sweeten the offer, the Company extended from two to three years the time required for townships to acquire twenty proprietors or be forfeited.

1774, March 9, Windham - 38th meeting, Minute Book 2: 85-90, *Papers*, V: 325-29, No. 259; *PA (2)*, 18: 95-9.

In May 1774, the last meeting prior to the outbreak of the American Revolutionary War, the Executive Committee met by adjournment at Hartford. In addition to examining and redressing individual settler's complaints and grievances, they formally accepted the irregular survey of the town of Warwick granted in November 1773 and located near Nescopeck Falls. Pitches made outside of township limits they declared invalid, however, unless granted by the Company. Decisions such as this indicate that the Executive Committee in Connecticut realized the danger of loosing control to squatters. Thus, they asked that every town send a list of settlers to the Committee of Settlers at Wyoming.

1774, May 24, Hartford - 39th meeting, Minute Book 2: 90-4; *Papers*, VI: 252-55, No. 78; *PA (2)*, 18: 99-102.

Interest in the West Branch still ran out of control. Against Company wishes, West Branch settlers formed an association and pledged to adhere to peaceable ways although determined to protect their purchase. Setting out from Wilkesbarre, the West Branch men arrived at Warrior's Run on September 23, 1775. Five days later they were attacked by an overwhelming force of Northumberland County militia under the command of Colonel William Plunket. One settler was killed and several were wounded before they surrendered. All the horses and furniture were stolen. Three of the leaders were jailed in Sunbury and two in Philadelphia. Everyone else was released

Encouraged by his success at Warrior's Run, Colonel William Plunket believed that he could drive the settlers from the East Branch as well. Leading his Northumberland County militia upstream in December 1775, Plunket and his men met surprising opposition from Westmoreland's recently completed 24th regiment and were soundly defeated. The Connecticut settler's victory marked the end of the Second Yankee-Pennamite War and gave the Susquehanna Company firm control of the East Branch. For more detail see *Connecticut's Pennsylvania "Colony": Susquehanna Company Settlers.*

After the Declaration of Independence in July 1776, the new Continental Congress asked Pennsylvania to raise six military companies. Either with irony or with malice Pennsylvania announced that two of the companies would be from the Town of Westmoreland. To avoid serving under Pennsylvania authority, settlers petitioned the Connecticut Assembly for county status. Granted in the fall of 1776, the new county boundaries were coterminous with the Town. Congress had other ideas for the two military companies, however, and assigned them independent status. In January 1777 General Washington ordered the two Westmoreland Independent Companies to New Jersey leaving the Wyoming Valley poorly protected from British and Indian attack. For settlers present in Westmoreland in 1776 and 1777 see lists 15 and 16 *Susquehanna Company Settlers.*

Six months later on the second anniversary of the Declaration of Independence, Major John Butler, leading his Iroquois and British troops, attacked the unprotected Wyoming Valley settlements. Defeating the small Westmoreland home guard, the invaders pillaged and burned virtually every cabin. Settlers fled to New Jersey, New York and home to Connecticut. At least seventy-eight male settlers were killed during the battle. Some reporters called this episode the Wyoming Massacre and the name remains. For settlers present in 1778 see list 17 *Susquehanna Company Settlers.* For a list of men killed in the battle of July 3, 1778 see list 18, *Susquehanna Company Settlers.*

Settlers trickled back to their homes over the next two years. Only 113 had returned by August 1780 as shown on list 19, *Susquehanna Company Settlers.* List 20 in *Susquehanna Company Settlers* indicates that another forty or so had returned by August 1781. An inhabitants' bill of losses reported to the Connecticut General Assembly in October, 1781, list 21 in *Susquehanna Company Settlers*, shows that 286 men and women property owners suffered losses between July 3, 1778 and May, 1780. Most of these families had returned by 1783.

Using the greatly reduced number of settlers as an opportunity to exert control, the newly formed Pennsylvania State legislature began to push for a resolution to the land controversy with Connecticut. Ratification of the Articles of Confederation on March 1, 1781 brought the proper legal machinery and Pennsylvania asked for a trial under Article IX. Ultimately, the case between Pennsylvania and Connecticut became the only case tried under Article IX. Pennsylvania made preliminary statements to Congress in November 1781 and Connecticut made statements in June 1782. The trial was scheduled for the end of November 1782.

Meeting for the first time in eight and one half years proprietors in Connecticut gathered to make preparations for the trial. Company stalwarts Eliphalet Dyer and William Samuel Johnson joined by Jesse Root agreed to present the Company case at the trial and were to be paid a whole share each for their efforts. To pay for the trial, committeemen for each county agreed to collect the $4.00 tax on each whole share that had been levied in 1774 and to sell 50 new whole shares at whatever price they could get. Shareholders who did not pay by the end of 1782 ran the risk of forfeiting their shares. Samuel Gray, clerk, and William Judd agreed to make all other preparations for the trial. For his efforts the Company paid Judd with a grant of a triangular tract of land between the townships of Kingston, Plymouth, Bedford, and Northmoreland.

> **1782, November 13-14, Hartford- 40th meeting, Minute Book 2: 95-9; *Papers*, VII: 139-42, No. 125; *PA* (2), 18: 102-04.**

Convening at Trenton, New Jersey, the trial lasted only a few weeks. Each side presented opening arguments at the end of November and the court announced its decision on December 30. No one showed surprise when the court awarded jurisdiction over the entire Susquehanna Purchase to Pennsylvania. Completely discouraged, Eliphalet Dyer wrote home that the cause was lost. He did not again act as agent for the Susquehanna Company.

Yet the decision, as simple as it was, did not solve the major issue for most settlers. More concerned with the title to their own land than to which county they would pay taxes and in which state they would vote, settlers at Wyoming vowed to pursue their own individual claims. Following suit, proprietors in Connecticut voted to use all lawful means in their power to help settlers maintain possession of their tracts. Another trial under Article IX to determine individual property ownership became their goal.

> **1783, May 21, Hartford - 41st meeting, Minute Book 2: 99; *Papers*, VII: 293-94, No. 161; *PA* (2), 18: 104-05.**

But instead of action, proprietors in Connecticut did virtually nothing while the settlers at Wyoming engaged in war with the Pennsylvania landowners for their very existence. Mainly speculators, the Pennsylvanians with the support of the state legislature tried to enforce the Trenton Decree by using military force to remove the Susquehanna settlers. Violence consumed the Wyoming Valley until the end of 1784 when the Pennsylvania militia withdrew bringing an end to the Third Yankee-Pennamite War.

John Franklin now emerged as leader of the settlers. Determined to see the issue of property rights solved, Franklin tried to rekindle congressional action on Zebulon Butler's November 1783 petition requesting a new trial. (Papers, VII, Nos. 187, 203, 204) After meeting with Connecticut delegates at the Continental Congress in New York, Franklin traveled to Connecticut to meet with Susquehanna Company proprietors.

His goal was to fill up the land with as many settlers as possible and he convinced Company leaders to let him try this approach.

Holding a meeting at Hartford in July with Franklin in attendance, proprietors made three far-reaching decisions. First, they agreed to support the settlers' petition to Congress for a trial of the right of soil. Although perfunctory after Congress denied the petition in October, the vote gave legitimacy to their second and third decisions. They voted to dispose of all non-resident proprietors' rights and to replace them with 400 new half shares that would go to settlers who simply met residency requirements. These settlers were to arrive by October 1, 1785, remain on their tracts for three years and not leave without permission, although the October 1 deadline was never enforced. John Franklin, Zebulon Butler and ten others formed a committee to oversee the half-share program. Henceforth, very few shares were sold for actual money.

A half-share eventually came to be worth 1,000 acres distributed through three divisions in one township or one division in two or three townships. Lots were allocated on the basis of sixteen 300 acre tracts per division. This was in line with the normal 300-acre Pennsylvania tract rather than the New England method that the Company had used heretofore of smaller lots in several different divisions. Usually, half-share holders kept their first division lots and sold their right to the remaining 700 acres often called "after division" land and infrequently laid out. This database documents 80 of these half shares by number followed by the phrase - of the 400. The Account Book labeled Liber A, Volume 2 contains a spreadsheet showing that Franklin actually granted 143 of the 400 half shares. For some reason, Franklin did not grant the half shares in numerical order and some half shares he granted to teams of two individuals.

Franklin also devised a new whole share program with no settlement restrictions. He wanted to attract speculators who would take up entire townships, then subdivide and resell smaller tracts. These shares were not as difficult to peddle and Franklin used them to justify the township grants that burgeoned from 1794 to 1796. Franklin even offered many of these 600 whole shares as two half shares. By specific number, the Account Books mention only 89 of the 600 shares, but the spreadsheet in Account Book Liber A, Volume 2 shows at least 231 of the 600 shares accounted for. Speculators such as Caleb Benton, Elihu Chauncey Goodrich and Seth Turner held multiple shares and several townships each. Proprietors ended the July meeting by voting a $1.00 tax on each whole share and $.50 on each half share.

1785, July 13, Hartford - 42nd meeting, Minute Book 2: 101-5; *Papers*, **VIII: 247-50, No. 141;** *PA (2), 18*: **105-08.**

As soon as Franklin returned to the Wyoming Valley he rallied settlers and offered the new half shares to long time as well as new residents. To keep track of his grants, Franklin started his own account book. Later labeled Liber I of the Susquehanna Company Account Books, Franklin dated the first entry June 3, 1786. Between then and 1799 Franklin recorded 80 half shares and 36 whole shares in Liber I, partly of the 400 and partly of the 600. The Company clerks recorded others of the 600 in Libers C15, D1, E8. F4, and H11.

Franklin returned to Connecticut in May 1786 for the next meeting of the Susquehanna Company. His scheme this time involved the creation of a new state out of the Susquehanna Purchase and he brought Col. Ethan Allen with him to help promote the idea. But the Connecticut proprietors were disinterested and instead appointed Franklin clerk of a new committee with authority to form new townships. As clerk, Franklin was directed to keep fair records and send copies as reports. So out went the old township committee and in came Franklin's new committee of John Jenkins, Zebulon Butler, Ethan Allen and, of course, himself.

At Wilkesbarre in July 1786, the committee approved the re-grant and survey of Ulster originally laid out in 1775. By this time the Susquehanna Company had authorized and approved all of the seventeen townships that were later to compose the certified townships as well as several other townships on both the East and West Branches of the Susquehanna River. For more detailed information about townships see volume III of this series: *Connecticut's Pennsylvania "Colony": Susquehanna Company Claimants.*

1786, May 17 , Hartford - 43rd meeting, Minute Book 2: 105-6; Liber I: 30; *Papers*, VIII: 330-32, No. 198; *PA (2), 18*: 108-09.

Franklin, now recognized as the leader of a more militant faction of the Susquehanna Company, united the settlers behind a petition for a new Pennsylvania county that would encompass the Susquehanna Company townships located along the East Branch of the Susquehanna River. In their own county, settlers could elect their own local officials and be sure of representation in the Pennsylvania legislature. Realizing that this might be the only solution to a peaceable settlement of the land dispute, the Pennsylvania legislature acquiesced and formed Luzerne County in September 1786. To oversee the transition to Pennsylvania government, the legislature hired Timothy Pickering, a New England native and Philadelphia resident with land interests in the new county.

Franklin next maneuvered to identify the bona fide Susquehanna Company settlers and where their lots were located so that this information could be legally recorded. Returning to Connecticut in December 1786, Franklin convinced the Executive Committee to appoint a twenty-one man commission, himself included, to make a list from the Company records of all proprietors and their land. Franklin and his associates would hold hearings in Wilkes-Barre using the list to determine the authenticity of the settler's right. If valid, the commissioners would do a survey or approve the existing survey and record the deed in Company records. Hence, many deeds in the Account Books were recorded years after they were actually written. Franklin also saw to it that the half-share men were protected by ensuring that they were entitled to a survey of 200 acres within a township or 600 acres in the mountainous areas outside a township. The Connecticut proprietors gave the commissioners other broad powers such as granting new townships and confirming or disallowing settlements made contrary to Company regulations. For all intents and purposes, the Connecticut proprietors passed all Company authority to the new commission and made any three of them together with their secretary a quorum to do business. No more Company meetings were held in Connecticut.

1786, December 26-7, Hartford - 44th meeting, Minute Book 2: 106-10; *Papers*, VIII: 425-29, No. 268; *PA (2), 18*: 109-12.

John Franklin now had secure control of the Susquehanna Company and he transferred the entire operations to Pennsylvania. Company meetings were no longer held in Connecticut and minutes were no longer recorded in the Minute Book. When he returned to Wilkes-Barre shortly after February 8, 1787 Franklin undoubtedly had the Company Minute Book and the three existing Account Books with him. Although extant records make no specific comment about the move, evidence is persuasive. Franklin needed the Company records in Wilkes-Barre on March 6, 1787 when the newly appointed commissioners began hearings on land claims. Samuel Gray, the long-time Company clerk in Connecticut made his final entry on page 108 of Account Book C on January 30, 1787. David Paine, the new Company clerk made his first entry on page 109 of Account Book C in 1794 after Franklin moved the office to Athens. Between 1787 and 1794 Franklin recorded deeds in his own Account Book, Liber I.

While Franklin maneuvered in Connecticut, Timothy Pickering and Zebulon Butler arranged for elections in Luzerne County. Unbeknownst to Franklin, the settlers elected him their representative to the Pennsylvania State Assembly. Angered and not wanting the position, Franklin refused to take his seat. Settlers also petitioned the Pennsylvania Assembly to confirm deeds granted before the Trenton decree in the original seventeen townships and in the township of Athens and certain detached tracts. Franklin was even more upset when the Assembly passed the Confirming Act on March 28, 1787. By this act, Pennsylvania agreed to recognize Connecticut claimants' rights to lots occupied or acquired before December 30, 1782, the date of the Trenton Decree. To receive a regular title, the act required that lots be resurveyed and patented at the individual settler's expense. Franklin was totally opposed to the law for many reasons and rallied behind him followers who were also opposed. For the names of eighty of Franklin's supporters see list 28 in volume II of this series: *Susquehanna Company Settlers*.

Discord now erupted between moderate and militant settlers and came to a head in the fall of 1787 when commissioners working under the Confirming Act began to accept settlers' claims. Franklin retaliated by organizing a September meeting at Athens for sixty-seven of his supporters and a few New York land speculators who agreed to invest in shares. Desperate to remove Franklin, Pennsylvania named him "a pernicious and seditious man …" and issued a warrant for his arrest. Authorities apprehended him in October and sent him to jail in Philadelphia. (*Papers*, IX, No. 101; *PA*(1): XI, 179; *Harvey*, 1582)

Two more years of dissension ensued, but Franklin's ideas eventually prevailed. While he languished in jail, Franklin's supporters, termed "Wild Yankees" by some, kidnapped Timothy Pickering in hopes of securing Franklin's bail. When that failed his supporters released Pickering and a few days later lost a skirmish with the militia, now composed of the moderate settlers. Lord Butler, sheriff and son of Zebulon Butler, arrested several of the "Wild Yankees" and jailed them in Easton. From jail in Philadelphia Franklin wrote to the Pennsylvania Assembly claiming to be determined to put a stop to the disturbances. So persuasive was his statement and so fearful of a backlash was Pennsylvania that his case never came to trial. Instead, Franklin moved in and out of jail over the next two years until his final released in September 1789. In the meantime, the Confirming Act commissioners had fled the Wyoming Valley and the Legislature suspended the act on March 29, 1788. Final repeal came in 1790. Susquehanna Company settlers were left without a resolution to the validity of their deeds.

Many changes occurred in the next five years. Pickering left in 1791 to become Postmaster General of the United States. Franklin settled down to the life of a farmer and Pennsylvania's Governor Mifflin pardoned him in 1792. In 1793, Luzerne County voters elected him sheriff and Mifflin appointed him lieutenant colonel of militia.

Despite his new, apparently law-abiding life, Franklin managed to keep the Susquehanna Company alive and operating. In the later part of 1789, shortly after his release from jail, he shifted the Company operations to Athens, Pennsylvania. Closer to New York State and away from Wilkes-Barre, Athens presented a better location for Franklin's associates. Several of his New York land speculator friends employed men living near Athens as agents to travel about the countryside buying shares from disillusioned proprietors. Twenty shares would convert to a grant of a whole township which could be subdivided and sold in small lots.

Most active of the speculators at this time was Elihu Chauncey Goodrich. His business associates were Chester Bingham, John Dorrance, Major William Wynkoop, and Major William Brown. ("Elihu Chauncey Goodrich to John Jenkins, Claverack 22nd Septr 1794 in *Papers*, X: 208-09, No. 119.) The "Wild Yankees" joined these efforts. To accommodate everyone, Franklin reactivated the Susquehanna Company township committee composed of Zebulon Butler, John Jenkins and himself and granted new townships. In November 1793 they granted Columbia on Sugar Creek, followed by sixteen more townships in 1794. All told, the Susquehanna Company granted 325 Townships and Pitches. So brisk was business that Franklin hired as assistant clerk, David Paine, and set him up in the fall of 1794 with an office at Athens. Soon thereafter, Franklin, himself, moved to Athens.

Using their old authority as commissioners, Franklin, John Jenkins, Simon Spalding and Peter Loop called a Company meeting for February 1795 at the dwelling house of James Irwin in Athens on Tioga Point. Breaking with past regulations, attendees drastically altered Company policy in order to aid speculators and half-share men. From here on each whole share was to be worth 2,000 acres of land which meant that only 8 shares were needed to claim a 16,000 acre township. Since shares needed to be held in the names of original proprietors, speculators sent agents throughout New England buying up shares.

Appointing a new Executive Committee of nine members with only one former Connecticut proprietor, Franklin made himself clerk and John Jenkins became surveyor. To maintain a semblance of authenticity they decided to reclaim all shares not exhibited to them by March 1796. Franklin was well on his way to filling up the Susquehanna Company purchase with half-share men and whole townships.

1795, February 18-20, Athens - 45th meeting, Liber C399-404; *Papers*, X: 213-19, No. 125; *PA (2), 18*: 112-17.

The Pennsylvania Attorney General launched an investigation. By April 9, 1795 Pennsylvania had an Intrusion Law in place. It provided for a fine and imprisonment for anyone taking land under a half-share right or other pretended title, but did not affect the rights of settlers who had obtained their land before the Trenton Decree. Enforcement was another matter. Everyone seemed to be waiting for a decision in the test case of Van Horne's Lessee vs. Dorrance. However, the verdict in May in this intrusion case gave no one satisfaction. Although finding in favor of the plaintiff, the jury awarded only 7 cents in damages and sidestepped the main issue of valid land titles.

Franklin finally took his seat as Luzerne County's representative in the Pennsylvania House of Representatives in December 1795 despite having authorized 168 new townships including a few re-grants and 10 pitches that year. Susquehanna Company townships now covered almost the entire area purchased from the Six Nations. Space remained for only thirteen new townships and three pitches and the Company granted them between 1796 and 1800. As a legislator, Franklin played a less militant role and used his influence to pursue the old goal of Congressional intervention.

As a ploy to gain support from the Connecticut General Assembly, Company proprietors met at Athens in June 1796 and voted to suspend the use of half-shares. They agreed that only proprietors with a recorded deed in one of the Account Books were eligible to act on the share. They also chose Chester Bingham, one of Goodrich's men and a resident of Ulster Township, as an acting commissioner to replace Colonel Zebulon Butler who had died recently.

1796, June 6, Tioga Point - 46th meeting; Liber E222; *Papers*, X: 348-9, No. 157; *PA (2), 18*: 117-18.

Proprietors met again on September 13 and 14, 1796 at Athens. Business conducted at the meeting authorized Company commissioners to dispose of four new townships, to sell the remaining whole shares of the 600, and to take all legal means to collect money due the Company.

1796, September 13-4, Tioga Point - 47th meeting Liber E390-91; *Papers*, X, 383-84, No. 174; *PA (2), 18*: 118-19.

September 13, 1796 was also the date of the "Petition of the Connecticut Settlers to the Connecticut General Assembly" asking that the State of Connecticut approach the federal government on behalf of the settlers to obtain a resolution to the problem of land titles. Actually seven petitions circulated in different regions of Luzerne County. The entire number of signatures amounted to 690 names as shown on list 30, *Susquehanna Company Settlers*. Still, the Connecticut upper house refused to support the petition.

Pennsylvania finally grew tired of waiting for the federal government to intervene. In his annual address of 1798, Governor Mifflin told the legislature to resolve the problem reasonably and decisively. In April 1799 the legislature passed the Compromise Act. This act required settlers in the townships settled before the Trenton Decree of December 1782 to prove a chain of title from before that date and pay for their land according to quality and quantity. Commissioners appointed to administer the act were to certify both the townships and the individual lot claims based upon Company records. The law also required Pennsylvania landholders to release surveys that overlapped settlers' claims in return for reimbursement. The catch was that the Connecticut settler's claim could not be honored unless the Pennsylvania landholder had released his survey. These provisions were actually more stringent than those of the earlier Confirming Act, but did succeed in removing most of the Pennsylvania landowners. The Company's effort to blanket its purchase with townships inhabited by half-share settlers seemed to have been for naught. The database shows that the Susquehanna Company commissioners made only nine grants in 1799, but 184 proprietors sold shares to others.

Implementation of the Compromise Act stalled under two sets of inexperienced commissioners. The main problem centered on how to handle overlapping claims of Connecticut settlers and Pennsylvania landholders. Another issue was lack of documentation to prove a claim since none of the Connecticut settlers' deeds had been obtained using Pennsylvania's warranting and patenting procedure. Meanwhile, speculators in Susquehanna Company shares frantically sought buyers for their worthless shares.

Finally, in 1801 Thomas Cooper took over as lead commissioner. Under his guidance, the legislature amended the law to enable Connecticut claimants to obtain clear title to all of their land even though the overlapping Pennsylvania owner had not released their entire claim. Borrowing the Susquehanna Company Minute Book from Franklin, Cooper made a copy to use in his deliberation. Years later, the Pennsylvania State Archives placed the copy in the Franklin *Papers* collection. Cooper also borrowed and copied the minutes of settlers' meetings at Wilkes-Barre interspersed in the Westmoreland Records. He needed these records to certify the dates of the first seventeen townships and to understand Company rules and regulations. As soon as he and his fellow commissioners certified a township, claimants could submit their chain of title for approval.

Disgruntled Company stalwarts were not satisfied and met again in October 1801 to propose yet one more scheme to circumvent the law. Trying to resolve issues of overlapping claims outside of the seventeen townships, they suggested that five proprietors including Franklin and Jenkins meet with a committee of Pennsylvania landholders. If the Pennsylvanians refused to cooperate, the Company planned an appeal directly to the United States Congress asking for a special trial of private rights of soil. Pennsylvania landholders, virtually all speculators, completely discounted the idea.

1801, October 20, 22-23, Athens - 48th meeting, Minute Book 2: 111-14 (not numbered); *Papers***, XI, Nos. 99 and 100;** *PA (2), 18***: 120-22**

Company proprietors met for the last time in May 1802. Despite their failure to reach a compromise with the Pennsylvania landholders, proprietors voted to continue their attempt to collect back taxes and to draw up rules and regulations for protecting the property that proprietors had purchased through the Susquehanna Company. Proprietors also decided to proceed with their petition to Congress. Dated November 1, 1802 and signed by 1,150 settlers as shown on list 31, *Susquehanna Company Settlers,* the petition plainly asked Congress to provide some means whereby all Connecticut claimants could continue to hold possession of their individual tracts of land. Congress read the petition on January 5, 1802 and referred it to committee. Two months later the committee reported that the Trenton Decree and the case of Van Horne's Lessee v. Dorrance had settled all issues. Susquehanna settlers who had land in any one of the 300 or so townships authorized after 1782 had no hope of securing title under the Compromise Law of 1799. The Susquehanna Company held no more meetings and sold no more shares.

1802, May 17 -19, - 49th meeting, Minute Book 2: 115-20 (not numbered); *Papers*, **XI: 323-26, No. 151.**

Land problems related to Susquehanna Company settlers continued for years. Near the end of 1802, Thomas Cooper removed the townships of Bedford and Ulster from the list of seventeen certified townships and it was not until 1810 that new legislation gave settlers in those townships an opportunity to obtain legal title. Legislation passed in 1807 gave settlers one more year to apply under the original Compromise Law. By 1811 the vast majority of conflicting land claims had been resolved, but individual court cases continued until 1827 and later. For more detail on the problems of Bedford and Ulster and a more complete discussion of Connecticut claimants and related records see *Susquehanna Company Claimants*.

Abbreviations, Vocabulary, Short Titles

Brewster
William Brewster. *History of the Certified Township of Kingston, Pennsylvania 1769-1929*. School District of the Borough
of Kingston, 1930.

Cmte
Committee

CHS
Connecticut Historical Society, Hartford

CSL
Connecticut State Library, Hartford

Decd, decd
deceased

Dela
Delaware

DP
Delaware Purchase, also called the First Delaware Purchase

div/divs
division, divisions

Ex or exec.
Executor or executrix

ex
except

gore
a triangular piece of land wedged between other tracts

Harvey
Oscar Jewell Harvey. *A History of Wilkes-Barre*. 3 volumes, Raeder Press, 1909-1930. Reprint, 1998. Micro film, Family History Library.

HSP
Historical Society of Pennsylvania, Philadelphia

LCHS
Luzerne County Historical Society, formerly The Wyoming Historical and Geological Society, Wilkes-Barre

Liber
Book

LP
Lackawack Purchase also called the Second Delaware Company

MB
Susquehanna Company Minute Book (see Susquehanna Company Records Location Table)

Minute Book
Articles of Agreement and Minutes of Meetings. Susquehanna Company Records. CHS.

Munger (1)
Donna Bingham Munger. "Following Connecticut Ancestors to Pennsylvania: Susquehanna Company Settlers." *The New England Historical and Genealogical Register*, 139, April 1985, 112-25.

Munger (2)

Donna Bingham Munger. *Pennsylvania Land Records: A History and Guide for Research*. Scholarly Resources, Wilmington, DE, 1991; since 2004, see SR Books, Rowman-Littlefield, Lanham, MD.

No.

Number

OP

Original Purchaser

p

perch = 1 pole or 1 rod = 16.5 feet; 160 square perches, rods or poles = 1 acre

PA (1)

Samuel Hazard, ed. *Pennsylvania Archives*. 1st ser. 12 vols. Philadelphia, 1856.

PA (2)

John B. Linn and William H. Egle, eds. *Pennsylvania Archives*. 2d ser. 19 vols., Harrisburg, 1874-1893

Papers

Boyd, Julian P. and Taylor, Robert, eds. *The Susquehanna Company Papers*. Vols. 1-4, 1932, reprint. Ithaca, NY, 1962. Vols. 5-11, Ithaca, NY, 1967-1971.

Pct

Precinct

Pitch -

a tract granted to an individual and located outside of any surveyed township

PSA

Pennsylvania State Archives, Harrisburg

pt

part

Pwr. Att.

Power of Attorney

RB

Daniel Edward's Roll Book. Connecticut Claimants Loose Papers, Pennsylvania State Archives.

SP

Susquehanna Purchase

Susq

Susquehanna, originally spelled Susquehannah

Twp

township

val con

valuable consideration

WHGS

Wyoming Historical and Geological Society, now Luzerne County Historical Society, Wilkes-Barre

WPR

"The Records of the Probate Court of Westmoreland ...." S. Judson Stark, trans. Proceedings and Collections of the Wyoming Historical and Geological Society, Vol. XVIII, Wilkes-Barre, 1923.

Susquehanna Company Records   Location Table

Description	Location	Paging
MINUTE BOOK Articles of Agreement and Minutes of Meetings, 1753-1774, 1782-1802	Original copy CHS Compromise Commissioners copy, PSA. printed in *PA* *(2)*, XVIII, 1-123 Copy passim, *Papers* Microfilm	

ACCOUNT BOOKS
Liber A - Records of Deeds 1762 - 1773 ("The first Book of Records of Deeds")
  Index to a volume paged 1 - 492: names and page numbers only
  Deed dates 1754 - 1775.
  Recording dates 1762 - 1773 (see text for Explanation)
  495 Deeds
    128 with Susquehanna Co. grantor (51 also recorded in Minute Book)
    367 conveyances between individuals
	Original missing 1862
	Index loosely placed in
	  Liber I and microfilmed
	  as if index to I	

Liber B - Records of Deeds with Index, 1773 - 1778 ("Copy of original deed of sale by Indians and Records of Deeds")
  Deed dates 24 August 1753 - 1 June 1778
  Recording dates 12 February 1763 - 11 November 1782
  Recording year and number of deeds: 1763 - 1, 1769 - 4, 1771 - 5, 1772 -19,
    1773 - 179, 1774 - 362, 1775 - 79, 1776 - 23, 1777 - 38, 1778 - 34,
    1779 - 1, 1780 - 0, 1781 - 2, 1782 - 1, 1796 - 4, 1798 - 1;
  758 Deeds
    287 with Susquehanna Co. grantor
    471 conveyances between individuals (a few duplicate entries)
	Original CHS
	Photostat WHGS
	Microfilm
		1-387
		1-195
		1-15

Liber C - Records of Deeds with Index, 1779 - 1795. ("This Book Contains The Records of Deeds and Transfers of Land belonging To The Susquehanna Company. Anno Domini 1779")
  Deed dates 6 September 1753 - 20 October 1798
  252 deeds dated before January 18, 1787; 165 deeds dated 1794; 302 deeds dated 1795
  Recording dates 15 January 1762 - 2 September 1799
  Recording year and number of deeds: 1762 - 1; 1773 - 1; 1774 - 2;
    1775 - 2; 1778 - 3; 1779 - 20; 1780 - 14; 1781 - 7; 1782 - 67; 1783 - 5;
    1784 - 5; 1785 - 9; 1786 - 19; 1787 - 3; 1788 - 2; 1790 - 1; 1794 - 24;
    1795 - 531; 1796 - 4; 1797 - 1; 1798 - 3; 1799 - 2.
  862 deeds
    70 Susquehanna Company to individual
    669 conveyances between individuals
    123 townships and pitches
	Original CHS
	Photostat WHGS
	Microfilm
		1 - 651
		196 - 525

Description	Location	Paging

Liber D - Records of Deeds 1795 - 1798
  Deed dates 11 February 1754 - 30 July 1798; 117 dated 1794, 1795, 1796
  Recording dates 28 Jany 1795 - 28 August 1798; 1795 - 106; 1796 - 32;
    1798 - 4
  191 deeds
  13 Susquehanna Company to individual
  130 conveyances
  48 townships and pitches
	Original CHS
	No Photostat, see Paging
	Microfilm
		1-180

Liber E - Records of Deeds, 1795 - 1798 (Book begun March 1796)
  Deed dates 6 September 1753 - 7 March 1798; 1795 - 237; 1796 - 333
  Recording dates 15 Jan 1762 - 13 February 1801; 1796 - 712
  907 deeds
  112 Susquehanna Company grantor
  722 conveyances
  73 townships and pitches
	Original CHS
	Photostat, WHGS, PSA
	Microfilm
		1-557
		526-802

Liber F   Records of Deeds, 1795 - 1802 (Book begun 1 March 1796)
  Deed dates 6 September 1753 - 15 January 1803: 1794 - 9; 1795 - 55;
    1796 - 72; 1797 - 23; all other years 1 to 5
  Recording dates 15 January 1762 - 17 January 1803; 1762 - 1; 1772 - 1;
    1789 - 1; 1793 - 1; 1794 - 3; 1795 - 7; 1796 - 120; 1797 - 72; 1798 - 31;
    1803 - 1
  261 deeds
  34 Susquehanna Company grantor
  211 conveyances
  16 townships and pitches
	Original CHS
	Photostat WHGS, PSA
	Microfilm
		1-278
		804-943

Liber G - Records of Conveyances 1766 - 1778 ??? (Book kept by
    Settlers' Committee?)
  Deed dates 18 July 1753 - 21 February 1786; no date 102; 1772 - 11;
    1773 - 29; 1774 - 44; 1775 - 11; 1776 - 11; 1777 - 9; 1786 - 1
  Recording dates; 20 April 1771 - 1786; no date 169; 1773 - 12; 1774 -
    20; 1775 - 21; 1776 - 6; 1777 - 7; 1778 - 1; 1786 - 1
  238 records
  13 Susquehanna Company grantor
  225 conveyances
	Original CHS
	No Photostat, see paging
	Microfilm
		GC-GN

Liber H   Records of Deeds, 1798 - 1803 (Book begun 13 October 1798
  Deed dates 26 Jan 1754 - 10 November 1802; 1794 - 9; 1795 - 17; 1796
    - 35; 1797 - 26; 1798 - 38; 1799 - 69; 1800 - 59; 1801 - 19; 1802 - 13;
    other years 1 - 5
  Recording dates 9 August 1774 - 1803; 1798 - 43; 1799 - 111; 1800 -
    83; 1801 - 54; 1802 - 24; 1803 - 3; other years 1 - 5
  354 deeds
  37 Susquehanna Company grantor
  299 conveyances
  18 townships and pitches
	Original CHS
	Photostat WHGS, PSA
	Microfilm
		1-349
		944-1118

Description	Location	Paging

Liber I   Records of Deeds by John and Billa Franklin. 1786-1799
(Book begun June 1786; also called the Wyoming Cmte Book see Exeter
   Folder 7, LRO)
Deed dates 8 February 1754 - 19 June 1799: 1785 - 44; 1786 - 34; 1793
   - 30; 1795 - 54; other years 1 - 10
Recording dates 25 May 1774 - 15 Aug 1799: 1786 - 79; 1794 - 84;
   1795 - 114; other years 1 - 10
385 deeds
  129 Susquehanna Company grantor: 83 half shares, 28 are of the 600,
    8 of the 400, 44 of one or the other - CHECK ORIGINAL; 44 whole
    shares, 24 of the 600
  212 conveyances
  44 townships and pitches
	Original CHS
	No Photostat
	Microfilm
		1-276

Liber A (Volume 2)   Records of Conveyances 1754 - 1798
[Labeled Liber A by Edward Herrick, 1863]
Spreadsheet as follows:
  Part 1. Of the 400 half shares opened to settlers
  Part 2. Of the 600
  Part 3. Original Proprietor's Conveyances alpha by first letter of Surname
  Part 4. Original Proprietor's Conveyance's for S - W, share numbers
    1236 - 1428; remaining W - Y not numbered
  Part 5. Corrections or Addenda A - Y in John Franklin's handwriting
	Original CHS
	Microfilm	

SECTION 2   THE DATABASE

Guide to the Database

This database of 5008 records contains 1768 deeds from the Susquehanna Company to original proprietors and 3240 conveyances between individuals. All records are from the Company Minute Book and Account Books. The Minute Book contains lists of subscribers, also called proprietors, who purchased shares from 1753 through 1770. Some lists state how much a subscriber paid and to whom. About 1762, the Company clerk began a series of deed books that eventually came to be called Account Books. The Account Books begin with Liber A and continue through Liber I. These volumes record in a more formal way than a list, the sale of shares from the Company to an individual and between individuals.

Database fields are: grantor (the Susquehanna Company or conveyor along the chain of title), grantor residence, grantee, grantee residence, amount paid in dollars or pounds, description such as amount of share, location, date of deed or list, date deed was recorded and notes. Tracking the payment of Company taxes is not included in the database since taxes were frequently assessed and poorly collected and recorded. Neither are the names of witnesses included.

The Account Books are extant except for Liber A. However, the grantor-grantee index to Liber A does exist although it is filed and filmed with Liber I. From the index, from duplicate entries in other Liber and from information in other deeds, this database reconstructs much of Liber A. Another volume labeled Liber A, Volume 2 is an attempt to compile in spreadsheet form a chain of title for every share sold. It is incomplete, and microfilmed at the beginning of reel one as if it were the first Liber A.

Many shareholders became settlers, but others did not. Those who did not either sold their shares or gave them by Will to their heirs. Many sons and daughters became settlers in their father's right. Information in this database may indicate that a shareholder became a settler, but for more complete information about settlers see volume II, *Susquehanna Company Settlers*. Shareholders that became settlers may also have become claimants. For information about claimants see volume III, *Susquehanna Company Claimants*.

How to search
The database is arranged in alphabetical order by grantor and then by grantee. Begin by doing a surname search under Susquehanna Company as grantor and the surname under grantee. Next, look for the grantee's surname as a grantor. Note that many shareholders who were Susquehanna Company grantees became grantors more than once. Continue to search the chain of title by going from grantee to grantor.

If the chain of title for a surname is incomplete or broken, search the database for alternate spellings or other possibilities, but be aware that not all chains are complete.

Do not be concerned if the number of shares an individual purchased does not always mesh with the number of shares an individual sold because record keeping was lax. Often a shareholder sold his share long before the transaction was recorded. Likewise, speculators who bought up shares en masse seldom kept accurate records. Near the end, as the Company approaches its demise, the account books make it obvious that speculators are assisted by assigning them outstanding shares in order to grant townships and blanket the entire area purchased from the Indians.

Spelling

Surname and place name spelling as it appears in the actual deed is retained in most cases, thus variations of the same name occur. In a few instances, if the accurate spelling is known and used in other deeds with regularity, the variant spelling may have been changed.

Database Fields (reading across)

Grantor - the seller (heirs may be grantors on behalf of the shareholder or in their own right.)

Grantor Residence - place recorded in the deed; may change as grantor relocates. If no residence is given for a particular deed, use residence from another deed for same person.

Description - what is being transferred (such as 1 share, power of attorney, acres, lots). If a description field contains entries separated by a semicolon, then the location field will contain entries separated by a semicolon. The first entries relate to each other, the next entries relate to each other and so on.

Amount - the cost of the item described. Amounts for shares where the Susquehanna Company is grantor reflect actual price. Amounts for shares and townships after 1794 may be greatly inflated. During most of this period £1 equaled $3.33.

Deed Date - date stated in the deed

Grantee - the buyer

Grantee Residence - place recorded in the deed; may change as grantee relocates. If no residence is given for a particular deed, use residence from another deed for same person.

Location - where the item described is physically located or was located at a later date (such as a lot or acres). To find the location of townships see volume III, *Susquehanna Company Claimants* or the maps inserted in volumes 1 and 2 of *The Susquehanna Company Papers*.

Page - the letter refers to the account book, also called Liber (Latin for book); the number refers to the page of the account book, eg. C120 is Liber C, page 120. (See the Susquehanna Company Records Location Table). If page numbering was missing in the original, pages in the database are numbered as a subset of the last numbered page, eg. C120 is followed by C120.1.)

Date Recorded - date the clerk received the deed to record

Notes - explanatory comments included in the deed

Asterisk * - refers to an entry in the notes field

Empty Fields - the deed contains no information

Witnesses - names of witnesses to deeds and the names of court officers who witnessed grantors' signatures, although part of many entries in the Account Books are not included in this database. Almost all of these individuals lived where the deed was drawn.

grantor grantee notes	grantor residence grantee residence	description location	amount acct bk page	deed date record date
Abbe, John				
Skiff, Benjamin			A11	
Abbe, John heirs*	Windham, Windham, CT	1/4 share	£3	1/5/1775
Wales, Elisha	Ashford, Windham, CT		B284	1/15/1775
Charles Ripley & Tabitha Abbe, wf				
Abbe, Peter	Enfield, Hartford, CT	mortgage for 500 A	$200	11/18/1796
Dana, Daniel	Enfield, Hartford, CT	Westminster Twp	E504	2/6/1797
Abbott, Abiel	Windham, Windham, CT	1/2 share	Love	2/11/1772
Abbott, Phillip			B54	8/28/1772
Abbott, Joel		1/2 share	$50	5/2/1796
Tinkham, Samuel			E166	5/2/1796
Ackley, Joseph	East Haddam, Hartford, CT	1 share	£3	4/4/1774
Durkee, Robt & Farnum, Ruben	Windham & Canterbury, CT		B204	4/5/1774
Ackley, Joseph	East Haddam, Hartford, CT	1/2 share	£12.18	3/24/1774
Farnam, Ruben	Canterbury, Windham, CT		B196	3/25/1774
Ackley, Joseph	East Haddam, Hartford, CT	1/2 share	£12.18	3/24/1774
Pearl, David	Windham, Windham, CT		B197	3/25/1774
Ackley, Joseph	East Haddam, Hartford, CT	1/2 share	£3	3/25/1774
Pearl, Phillip	Windham, Windham, CT		B196	2/25/1774
Ackley, Joseph	East Haddam, Hartford, CT	1/2 share	£30.10	4/24/1780
Percival, Francis	East Haddam, Hartford, CT		C22	11/20/1780
Adams, David, Doct	Pomfret, Windham, CT	1/2 share	£30	9/18/1786
Ensworth, Jedediah	Pomfret, Windham, CT		C101	9/29/1786
Adams, David Dr., Execs*	Mansfield, Windham, CT	Pwr Att to dispose of shares		11/1/1792
Adams, Jabez Dr.	Mansfield, Windham, CT		C469	2/20/1795
Lucy Adams & Experience Storrs				
Adams, Jabez Dr.	Mansfield, Windham, CT	Pwr Att in Susq affairs		2/22/1795
Paine, David	Luzerne Co, PA		C470	2/20/1795
Adams, Jabez Dr.		Pwr Att*		2/22/1795
Paine, David			C464	2/20/1795
to sell 1 share of Jedidiah Ensworth's				
Adams, Jabez Dr.	Mansfield, Windham, CT	1/2 share	$42	8/15/1800
Park, Reuben	Canterbury, Windham, CT		H315	
Adams, John Jr.	Canterbury, Windham, CT	1 share	£20	7/24/1777
Utley, John	Woodstock, Windham, CT	Salem Twp	B365	9/19/1777
Adams, Josiah			$200	3/18/1801
Moore, John			H288	3/19/1801
Ailsworth, Jedediah				
Beats, Joshua			A247	
Ailsworth, Phillip Jr.	Coventry, Kent, RI	1/4 share	£3	10/25/1773
Sabin, Jesse	Dudley, Worcester, MA		B131	1/20/1774
Aim, George of Norwich	Windham, Windham, CT	1/2 settling right and 1/4 share	£7	3/13/1770
Badger, Edmund	Windham, Windham, CT		B130	1/17/1774
Samuel Badger & Daniel Hebard's settling right; 1/4 share fr E. Badger				
Alden, Mason F.		1/2 share		
Marcy, Zebulon			GM	
Alden, Mason Fitch	Harlem, Luzerne, PA	8,000 A	$2,500	4/30/1796
Hammond, Elisha	Chenango, Tioga, NY	Harlem Twp, East 1/2	E156	5/4/1796
Alden, Mason Fitch	Harlem, Luzerne, PA	500 A	£80	3/9/1795
Kingsbury, Phinehas	Granby, Hartford, CT	Harlem Twp	E428	9/24/1796
Alden, Mason Fitch	Harlem, Luzerne, PA	4 half shares	$80	3/9/1795
Street, Caleb	Catskill, Albany, NY	Harlem Twp	E269	
Alden, Mason Fitch	Harlem, Luzerne, PA	2.5 shares & crtf for 200 A	£30	3/23/1795
Street, Caleb	Catskill, Albany, NY		E270	6/6/1796
Alden, Prince		Lot 10*		7/18/1792
Dyke, Nathaniel		Athens Twp	E118	3/1/1796
nearly opposite dwelling of James Irwin, 6 p on street & back to Tioga R.				
Alexander, David	Tioga, Luzerne, PA	10 A: 1/3 2nd Div Lots 44 & 45	5s	1/10/1797
Paine, David	Tioga, Luzerne, PA	Athens Twp	E540	1/10/1797
Allen, Benjamin	Hudson, Columbia, NY	1/2 share, Lots 5, 10, 30 + undiv land	£20	5/2/1792
Shepard, John	Tioga, Luzerne, PA	Athens, Luzerne, PA	E324	4/10/1796
Allen, Benjamin Capt	Providence, RI	1 share, No. 72 of 400		3/1/1795
Platner, Henry			D52	11/9/1795

grantor grantee notes	grantor residence grantee residence	description location	amount acct bk page	deed date record date
Allen, Ira, surveyor	Salisbury, Litchfield, CT	1 share	5s	3/5/1774
Allen, Levi	Salisbury, Litchfield, CT		B216	5/17/1774
Allen, John	Kingston, Luzerne, PA	1/3 Lot 7(100 A) + 300 A	$200	6/28/1796
Arnold, Nehemiah	Providence, RI	Smithfield Twp	E219	7/2/1796
Allen, John				
Norton, Ebenezer			A262	
Allen, Joseph estate*	Salisbury, Litchfield, CT	1 share	£15	1/13/1772
Baker, Ephriam	Woodbury, Litchfield, CT		B161	3/9/1774
heirs Ethan, Heber, Heman, Levi, Zimri, Lucy and Ira Allen				
Allen, Joseph estate*	Cornwall, Litchfield, CT	1 share	£15	3/31/1763
Baker, Ephriam	Woodbury, Litchfield, CT		C64	11/13/1782
Ethan & Heman Allen heirs				
Allen, Levi		1/2 share		
Cady, Jeremiah			GH	
Allen, Levi	Salisbury, Litchfield, CT	1 share	£40	6/28/1777
Dean, Ezra	West Greenwich, Kent, RI		B363	9/15/1777
Allen, Levi	Salisbury, Litchfield, CT	1/2 share	£20	7/28/1775
Hall, Asa	Gageborough, Berkshire, MA		B363	3/26/1777
Allen, Levi	Salisbury, Litchfield, CT	1 share	£40	1/2/1777
Horsemore, Timothy	Farmington, Hartford, CT		B360	7/2/1777
Allen, Levi	Northeast Precinct, Dutchess,	1 share	£100	2/28/1779
Hosmer, Timothy	Farmington, Hartford, CT		C647	5/10/1779
Written on this page upside down, in a different handwriting, pen and ink and numbered "Page 100"				
Allen, Levi	Salisbury, Litchfield, CT	1/2 share	£10	12/26/1774
Kilburn, Joseph	Litchfield, Litchfield, CT		B326	2/24/1775
Allen, Levi	Salisbury, Litchfield, CT	1 share	£10	12/26/1774
Kilburn, Joseph	Litchfield, Litchfield, CT		B327	2/24/1775
Allen, Levi	Salisbury, Litchfield, CT	1 share	£10	10/27/1774
Kilburn, Joseph	Litchfield, Litchfield, CT		B328	2/24/1775
Allen, Levi	Salisbury, Litchfield, CT	1/2 share	1/2 share	1/3/1775
Merril, Isaac	Hartford, Hartford, CT		B287	1/19/1775
Allen, Levi	Salisbury, Litchfield, CT	1/2 share	£20	7/28/1775
Safford, Elisha	Gageborough, Berkshire, MA		B367	3/26/1777
Allen, Levi	Salisbury, Litchfield, CT	1 share	£5	3/22/1775
Sheppard, Willard	Gageborough, Berkshire, MA		B385	4/8/1778
Allen, Levi	St. Albans, Chittenden, VT	9 shares	$375	2/6/1796
Wadsworth, Elijah/Bryon, Richard	Litchfield, Litchfield, CT		E226	7/2/1796
Allen, Levi	Salisbury, Litchfield, CT	1 share	20s	10/6/1774
West, Jabez, merchant	Norwich, New London, CT		C81	10/10/1782
Allen, Nathaniel	Catskill, Albany, NY	600 A, No. 197 of 600		3/11/1795
Everest, Noah		Burlington Twp	C570	5/20/1795
Allen, Nathaniel	Catskill, Albany, NY	300 A, No. 393 of 600		3/12/1795
Everest, Noah		Burlington Twp	C570	6/29/1795
Allen, Nathaniel	Catskill, Albany, NY	No. 388 of 600		3/11/1795
Everest, Noah			C570	5/20/1795
Allen, Nathaniel	Catskill, Albany, NY	No. 198 of 600		3/11/1795
Everest, Noah			C570	5/20/1795
Allen, Nathaniel	Catskill, Albany, NY	No. 387 of 600		3/11/1795
Everest, Noah			C571	5/20/1795
Allen, Nathaniel	Catskill, Albany, NY	No. 383 of 600		6/1/1795
Hamilton, Samuel			C571	5/20/1795
Allen, Nathaniel		1/2 share No. 389 of 600		12/15/1794
Lay, John			E271	6/6/1796
Allen, Nathaniel		1/2 share No. 398 of 600		12/15/1794
Lay, John			E270	6/6/1796
Allen, Nathaniel	Catskill, Albany, NY	1/2 share No. 394 of 600		4/14/1794
Murray, Noah			C285	9/7/1795
Allen, Nathaniel		1/2 share	$50	3/15/1796
Stephens, Ira			E490	6/20/1796
Allen, Nathaniel	Catskill, Albany, NY	1/2 share No. 395, 300 A*		4/13/1794
Thompson, Caleb		Burlington Twp	I229	9/6/1795
laid out 6/18/1795				

grantor grantee notes	grantor residence grantee residence	description location	amount acct bk page	deed date record date
Allen, Nathaniel	Catskill, Albany, NY	1/2 share No. 396, 300A*		4/13/1794
Thompson, Caleb		Burlington Twp	I229	9/6/1795
laid out 6/18/1795				
Allen, Roger Jr.				
Strong, Return			A42	
Allen, Stephen				
LeHommedieu, Ezra			A356	
Allen, Stephen	Plymouth, Luzerne, PA	1 share	£20	6/4/1796
Manville, Ira	Plymouth, Luzerne, PA		E267	7/18/1796
Allen, Timothy	Pawlett, Rutland, VT	1 share	$20	6/4/1795
Mosely, Nathaniel J.	Pawlett, Rutland, VT		C567	6/20/1795
Alling, Ichabod	Hamden, New Haven, CT	2 1/2 shares	good consideration	12/3/1794
Osborn, Elisha	Derby, New Haven, CT		I158	1/16/1795
Alling, Nathan	New Haven, New Haven, CT	1/2 share	£10	9/1/1774
Clark, William, Jr.	Gageborough, Berkshire, MA		H90	8/19/1799
Allyn, John B.	Berlin, Hartford, CT	200 A	valuable sum	3/11/1797
Johnson, Bethel	Berlin, Hartford, CT	Brookfield Twp	F238	6/1/1797
Anderson, Ebenezer	East Haddam, Hartford, CT	1 share	£15	3/21/1774
Ackley, Joseph	East Haddam, Hartford, CT		B195	3/25/1774
Andrews, John	East Haddam, Hartford, CT	all rights	£10	3/30/1774
Ackley, Joseph	East Haddam, Hartford, CT		B206	4/5/1774
Andrews, Samuel	Stamford NY	all right	£2.11	10/14/1794
Jessup, Ebenezer Jr.	Fairfield, Fairfield, CT		C526	5/1/1795
Andrews, Simon, decd.*	Fairfield, Fairfield, CT	1/6 share	42s	11/3/1794
Jessup, Ebenezer Jr.	Fairfield, Fairfield, CT		C518	5/1/1795
Andrews, Abraham adm, probate court ordered sale				
Andrews, Thomas*	Fairfield, Fairfield, NY	1/12 share	20s	11/3/1794
Jessup, Ebenezer Jr.	Fairfield, Fairfield, CT		C525	5/1/1795
John Andrews of Fairfield, grandfather, OP				
Andrus, Epiphras				
Hitchcock, John			A465	
Andrus, Joseph				
Whittlesey, Eliphalet			A463	
Andrus, Miles	Weathersfield, Hartford, CT	1/2 share	£10	10/26/1774
Starkweather, Stephen	Kent, Litchfield, CT		B311	2/10/1775
Andrus, William				
Andrus, Joseph			A467	
Andrus, William				
Andrus, Miles			A466	
Angar, August	Bartic, Lincoln, Upper Canada	Pwr Att to recover and receive		2/4/1797
House, John	Bartic, Lincoln, Upper Canada		E537	3/3/1797
Angar, Frederick, husbandman	Bartic, Upper Canada	Pwr Att to recover and receive		4/21/1795
Angar, August, trusted friend	Bartic, Upper Canada		E535	3/3/1797
Arnold, Benedict heirs*	Norwich, New London, CT	2 shares	val con	11/4/1763
Avery, Christopher	Norwich, New London, CT		B30	8/30/1773
Benedict and Hannah Arnold, son & dau.				
Arnold, Joseph				
Rider, Samuel			A476	
Arnold, Joseph heirs*	East Haddam, Hartford, CT	1/2 share; 1/2 suffering right	£100	8/19/1783
Enos, Joab	East Windsor, Hartford, CT		C91	12/14/1785
Joseph, Ephriam, John				
Arnold, Josiah	West Greenwich, Kent, RI	1/4 share	£7 10s	6/11/1795
Whitford, George	West Greenwich, Kent, RI		E463	11/18/1796
Arnold, Nehemiah	RI	eight 300 A tracts	$1,200 in $400/3 yr	6/30/1796
Dixon, Nathaniel	Putnam, Luzerne, PA	Smithfield Twp	E335	7/14/1796
Arnold, Nehemiah*	Providence, Providence, RI	300 A	$300	8/9/1796
Gould, James	Providence, Providence, RI	Smithfield Twp	H135	9/14/1799
one of 8 lots Arnold purchased from Dixson - Dickson				
Arnold, Stephen		Lot 10, possession began April 1787		1/7/1796
Blanchard, Andrew		Hanover Twp	D138	1/28/1795
Atwood, Elijah	Woodbury, Litchfield, CT	1/2 share		2/17/1796
Martin, Reuben	Woodbury, Litchfield, CT		D170	7/2/1796

grantor	grantor residence	description	amount	deed date
grantee	grantee residence	location	acct bk page	record date
notes				
Atwood, Elisha/Judson, Gideon	Woodbury, Litchfield, CT	Pwr Att 2 shares*		5/13/1795
Leavensworth, Asa			C633	7/10/1795
Philo Stoddard 1, Reuben Martin 1, Oliver & Jonah Sanford 1, Jonah Sanford 1				
Atwood, Gideon	Bethlehem, Litchfield, CT	1 share	£17	12/27/1794
Fabrique, John	Bethlehem, Litchfield, CT		E402	9/15/1796
Augur, Abraham & Sarah wf*	New Haven, New Haven, CT	all right	good cause	12/30/1794
Pope, Robert	Derby, New Haven, CT		C419	4/4/1795
maiden name Ingraham				
Augusta Proprietors	Fairfield, Fairfield, CT	500A		3/9/1795
Morgan, Nath. 1 of 8 proprietors*		Augusta Twp	C534	5/7/1795
Nathaniel Morgan to settle Augusta with 8 settlers to secure twp to sd proprietors				
Austin, Aaron	Torrington, Litchfield, CT	1/2 share	£14.8	2/8/1774
Ensign, Otis	New Hartford, Litchfield, CT		B183	3/10/1774
Austin, Aaron	Farmington, Litchfield, CT	1/2 share	£17	4/29/1777
Waters, Elihu	Westmoreland, Litchfield, CT		C449	2/21/1795
Austin, David	New Haven	1/2 share	$40	2/11/1796
Goodrich, Benjamin	Canaan		E406	9/15/1796
Austin, John Jr.	Simsbury, Hartford, CT	1 share		5/4/1769
Hovey, Daniel	Herton, NS		B249	5/4/1769
Austin, Samuel heirs*	New Haven, Hartford, CT	agents to obtain a survey of 1 share		4/28/1795
Crary, Oliver & Throop, Benjamin	Preston/Bozrah, CT		C113	9/1/1795
Lydia Austin, wid of New Haven; Rev. Samuel Austin of Worcester; William of New Haven; Lydia, wf of Rev. David Hale of Lisbon				
Avered, Seth and Eunice, wf	Woodbury, Litchfield, CT	1/4 share	£3.10	5/27/1772
Crissy, John 3rd	Woodbury, Litchfield, CT		C86	5/26/1784
Avery, Bebee D.	Rutland, Rutland, VT	150 A, 1/2 Lot 15	$160	5/8/1801
Bird, Michael	Rutland, Rutland, VT	Smithfield Twp	H301	5/26/1801
Avery, Christopher	Norwich, New London, CT	1 share		8/30/1773
Avery, Humphrey	Norwich, New London, CT		B25	8/30/1773
Avery, Christopher	Norwich, New London, CT	1 share	£30	12/2/1762
Avery, Humphrey	Norwich, New London, CT		B28	8/30/1773
Avery, Christopher	Westmoreland, Litchfield, CT	1/2 share	£18	9/29/1775
Tripp, Job 2nd	Westmoreland, Litchfield, CT		B350	10/30/1776
Avery, Elisha	Groton, New London, CT	1/2 share	£15	1/6/1775
Hall, Ruben	Stonington, New London, CT		B325	4/13/1775
Avery, Humphrey	Norwich, New London, CT	2 shares*	competent sum	4/21/1769
Avery, Aaron	Norwich, New London, CT		B85	11/9/1773
1/2 share Susq Co; 1/2 share First Dela Co; 1 share Second Dela Co also called Lackawacksen Co				
Avery, Humphrey	Norwich, New London, CT	4 shares	£144	8/5/1762
Avery, Samuel	Groton, New London, CT		E394	9/20/1796
Avery, Humphrey	Norwich	1 share, Lot 35	love	1/23/1777
Avery, Solomon		Putnam Twp	C18	3/16/1780
Avery, Humphrey	Norwich	1 share, Lot 36	love	1/23/1777
Avery, Solomon		Putnam Twp	C18	3/16/1780
Avery, Humphrey				
Brewster, John			A224	
Avery, Humphrey	Norwich, New London, CT	1 share	£30	10/5/1761
Hallock, William, Blacksmith	Southaven, Suffolk, NY		B190	3/17/1774
Avery, Humphrey, decd*	Norwich, New London, CT	1 share	£30	1/5/1780
Avery, Palmer	Norwich, New London, CT		I173	2/22/1795
Solomon Avery, adm				
Avery, Isaac	Norwich, New London, CT	1 share	£35	9/5/1762
Avery, Samuel	Groton, New London, CT		E398	9/20/1796
Avery, James	Norwich, New London, CT	1 share	£8	8/3/1766
Clements, Jeremiah	Norwich, New London, CT		C79	12/25/1782
Avery, Jonathan	Wyoming	1 share	£10	3/2/1787
Fanning, James	Wyoming	Muncy Creek 400 A	I39	3/2/1787
Avery, Latham	Groton, New London, CT	1 share		2/20/1796
Burrows, Roswell	Stonington, New London, CT		E240	7/4/1796
Avery, Latham	Groton, New London, CT	Pwr Att to lay and locate 1 share		5/27/1796
Downer, Joshua	Preston, New London, CT		E240	7/6/1796
Avery, Palmer	Norwich, New London, CT	1 share		8/20/1773
Avery, Humphrey	Norwich, New London, CT		B24	8/30/1773

grantor grantee notes	grantor residence grantee residence	description location	amount acct bk page	deed date record date
Avery, Palmer	Norwich, New London, CT	1 share	£30	3/7/1769
Avery, Humphrey	Norwich, New London, CT		B28	8/30/1773
Avery, Palmer	Preston, New London, CT	1 share	£60	2/7/1795
Tracy, Elisha	Norwich, New London, CT		I172	2/22/1795
Avery, Samuel	Norwich, New London, CT	1 share	£8	6/3/1771
Clements, Jeremiah	Norwich, New London, CT		B240	8/20/1774
Avery, Samuel	Norwich, New London, CT	1 share	£18	6/1/1771
Clements, Jeremiah	Norwich, New London, CT		B242	8/20/1774
Avery, Samuel				
Stoddard, Mortimer			A360	
Avery, Siball	Groton, New London, CT	1 share	£36	8/30/1762
Avery, Samuel	Groton, New London, CT		E393	9/20/1796
Avery, Siball	Groton, New London, CT	1 share	£30	5/9/1762
Avery, Samuel	Groton, New London, CT		E395	
Avery, Solomon		2 shares, Lots 35 & 36	£40	6/13/1796
Hunt, Bensly		Putnam Twp	C38	9/17/1796
Avery, Solomon	Wilkesbarre, PA	1 Town Lot, 3 1/2 A	val con	10/18/1786
Neill, Thomas	Wilkesbarre, PA	Wilkesbarre, Front St	I1	10/19/1786
Avery, Solomon		1/2 share*		8/18/1786
Williams, William	Wyoming	Putnam Twp	I35	11/22/1786
orig deed 11/1/1778				
Avery, Solomon estate*	Norwich, New London, CT	3 shares	£90	1/5/1780
Avery, Samuel			E393	9/20/1796
Humphrey Avery, adm				
Avery, Stephen 2nd & Luther	Stonington, New London, CT	1/2 share	£100	2/1/1796
Kingsberry, Joseph	Enfield, Hartford, CT		F124	7/27/1796
Avery, Thomas		agent for a Twp survey	1/2 share	7/20/1795
Throop, Benjamin			C120.1	9/1/1795
for fifteen owners, including Throop, who pay Throop 6s per day for his time and horse; total of 8 shares; T. Avery 1/2 share				
Avery, Waitstill	Norwich, New London, CT	1 share	£20	8/12/1773
Avery, Latham			B83	11.9.1773
Avery, William	Norwich, New London, CT	1 share	£37	12/2/1762
Avery, Samuel	Groton, New London, CT		E398	9/20/1796
Avery, William	Sharon, Litchfield, CT	all right	£10	3/19/1795
King, George & Mills, Eli	Sharon, CT & Amenia, NY		C573	6/22/1795
Avery, Wm et al*		1 share	pd Isaac Tracy	10/20/1761
Avery, Humphrey			A21	
Solomon, James & Christopher				
Ayer, John & Ayer, Squire	Franklin, New London, CT	1 share	£20	4/20/1795
Tracy, Elisha	Norwich, New London, CT		C597	7/9/1795
Babcock, Elisha	Willingburough, Luzerne, PA	1/2 share	£30	5/11/1795
Marther, Abner	Willingburough, Luzerne, PA		F71	5/24/1796
Babcock, Gameliel heirs*	Windham, Windham, CT	1/2 share & 100 A + 370 A, Lot 2	$300	2/17/1798
Drake, Nathaniel Jr.	East Windsor, Hartford, CT	Providence Twp	F265	3/12/1798
Beriah Babcock of Windham CT & David and Mary Rockwell of East Windsor, Hartford, CT				
Babcock, Isaiah	Partridgefield, Berkshire, MA	1 share, 600 A	£40	10/24/1794
Kinne, Daniel	New Milford, Litchfield, CT	New Milford Twp	C331	2/26/1795
Babcock, Oliver	Stonington, New London, CT		£50	1/1/1755
Rian, John & Arthur, Bartholomew	Voluntown, Windham, CT		B344	3/27/1776
Backus, Ebenezer	Windham, CT	1/2 share	£10	2/22/1774
Backus, Sylvanus/Silvenus	Windham, CT		C19	1/10/1775
Backus, Ebenezer	Tioga	all rights		10/1/1794
Rositter, Samuel	Claverack		C443	2/21/1795
Backus, Ebenezer				
Rowland, Henry			A329	
Backus, Ebenezer sisters Eunice,	Norwich, New London, CT	1 share, 3298 A	£60	2/10/1795
Morgan, Charles	Freehold, Albany, NY		C343	2/10/1795
quit claim; Eunice wf of Jonathan Trumbull, Sally wf of David Trumbull , Abigail single*				
Backus, Elijah	Norwich, New London, CT	1 share	£30	10/7/1795
Tracy, Elisha	Norwich, New London, CT		E41	2/22/1796
Backus, Elijah & Backus, John	Norwich, New London, CT	1 share	£20	10/7/1795
Tracy, Elisha	Norwich, New London, CT		E41	2/22/1796

grantor grantee notes	grantor residence grantee residence	description location	amount acct bk page	deed date record date
Backus, John				
Backus, Sylvanus			A233	
Backus, John	Hudson, Columbia, NY	1 share, No. 42 of 600		7/13/1785
Booth, Stephen			C571 - E542	7/7/1795
Backus, Simon	Guilford, New Haven, CT	1 share	£50	4/6/1795
Hale, George	Catskill, Albany, NY		D16	9/18/1795
Backus, Sylvanus				
Backus, Ebenezer			A232	
Backus, Sylvanus	Windham, Windham, CT	1/4 share	£6.10	2/21/1774
Badger, Edmund	Windham, Windham, CT		B145	2/21/1774
Backus, Sylvanus	Windham, CT	1/2 share	£9	1/18/1775
Gray, Ebenezer & Samuel Jr.	Windham, CT		C34	1/18/1775
Bacon, Andrew	Canaan	1/2 share*		11/27/1786
Hutchinson, John			I17	11/27/1786
taxes pd to date				
Bacon, Daniel	Farmington, Hartford, CT	1/2 share: 75 A pitch; 20 A pitch	£100	10/21/1774
Bacon, Moses	Farmington, Hartford, CT	Yale Town; New Weathersfield Twp	B352	3/8/1777
Bacon, Moses*	Bristol, Hartford, CT	1/2 share and 2 settling rights*	valuable sum	2/23/1795
Bacon, Seth	Woodbury, Litchfield, CT		F152	11/1/1796
brother Daniel bought 1/2 share fr Stephen Hungerford				
Badger, Edmund				
Aim, George			A322	
Badger, Edmund	Windham, Windham, CT	1/4 share	£7.10	3/9/1774
Andruss, William	Norwich, New London, CT		B178	3/9/1774
Badger, Edmund				
Huntington, Hezekiah			A372	
Badger, Edmund	Windham, Windham, CT	1 1/2 shares*	£5	2/5/1795
Larrabee, Libbeus	Windham, Windham, CT		C366	3/2/1795
1 share Samuel Badger settling right as 1 of 200; 1/2 share Samuel Badger OP				
Badger, Edmund				
Post, Eldad			A350	
Badger, Samuel	Chelsea, Orange, VT	1/2 share and 1 settling right	£5	1/26/1795
Badger, Edmund	Windham, Windham, CT		C363	3/2/1795
Badger, Samuel				
Badger, Edmund & Flint, James Jr.			A326	
Bagley, James	Providence, Luzerne, PA	350 A	£93.6	8/10/1795
Rossell, John	West Chester, NY	Lackawanna River*	E488	12/6/1796
btw Picket's Pitch and Moses Scoville				
Bailey, Benjamin	Shemung [Chemung], Tioga,	1/2 share	£20	9/2/1795
Irwin, James	Tioga Point, Luzerne, PA		E435	9/20/1796
Bailey, Benjamin, Black Smith	Newtown, Tioga, NY	2 shares inc. 600 A laid out*	$3,000	10/26/1796
Teall, Nathan	Newtown, Tioga, NY	Newport Twp	E460	11/10/1796
shares granted to Bailey for services				
Bailey, Richard				
Warren, Moses			A241	
Baker, Elisha		1771 tax on 1/2 share	6s	3/6/1773
Rood, Robert			E363	9/5/1796
Baker, Ephriam	Washington, Litchfield, CT	Pwr Att locate, lay out, div 1/2 share*		1/26/1795
Baker, Samuel	Luzerne Co, Susq Purchase		D55	11/10/1795
share recd from heirs of Joseph Allen: Heber, Ethan, Heman, Levi, Zimry, Lucy, Ira. see B161				
Baker, Ephriam	Woodbury, Litchfield, CT	1/2 share	£9.10	9/5/1774
Guthrie, William	Kent, Litchfield, CT		B318	3/16/1775
Baker, Erastus		2 shares		4/1/1796
Holt, Jacob			F58	4/23/1796
Baker, John	Watertown, Litchfield, CT	1 share	£3.10	3/3/1795
Brown, David	Brookfield, Fairfield, CT		C640	8/9/1795
Baker, John		1/2 share		
Bullard, Josiah			GM	
Baker, Jonathan				
Sumner, Edward Jr.			A18	
Baker, Jonathan	Ashford	1 share		1/1/1761
Sumner, Edward Jr.	Ashford		C321	4/7/1782

grantor grantee notes	grantor residence grantee residence	description location	amount acct bk page	deed date record date
Baker, Samuel	NY	5,000 A, 1/50th pt [300 A]	£40	6/18/1796
Cole, Benjamin	Lycoming, PA	Hamilton, Lycoming, PA	E532	11/10/1796
Baker, William	Ontario, NY	1/2 share	£60	9/29/1794
Biles, Joseph	Tioga, NY		E371	9/10/1796
Baker, William	Oblong, Dutchess, NY	1/4 share	£12.10	2/15/1755
Paine, Joshua	Oblong, Dutchess, NY		E115	3/17/1796
Baldwin, Caleb	New Town, Fairfield, CT	1/2 share	$7	3/14/1755
Smith, Joseph	New Town, Fairfield, CT		B88	10/28/1773
Baldwin, Caleb Jr. & Daniel	New Town, Fairfield, CT	1/2 share	£3	2/3/1773
Jones, Benjamin	South Precinct, Dutchess, NY		B375	1/10/1778
Baldwin, Ebenezer	Coventry, CT now Fairlie, VT	1 share	£6.10	4/14/1795
Barrett, Jonathan & Rathburn, Wait	Norwich & Middletown, VT		C645	8/10/1795
Baldwin, Ebenezer	Mansfield, Windham, CT	1 share	$5	1/27/1795
Larrabee, Libbeus	Windham, Windham, CT		C362	3/2/1795
Baldwin, Henry	Newtown, Tioga, NY	1/2 share	£20	3/6/1796
Baldwin, Thomas	Newtown, Tioga, NY		E356	7/20/1796
Baldwin, Isaac		1 share		8/14/1774
Ransom, Samuel			GC	9/4/1774
Baldwin, Isaac	Newtown, Tioga. NY	100 A of Lot 23, 2nd Div*	£150	6/30/1795
Saterlee, Elisha	Luzerne Co PA	Pittstown, Luzerne, PA	C608	7/9/1795
certified 8/17/1797 Court of Common Pleas, Luzerne Co.				
Baldwin, Isaac Jr.	Litchfield, Litchfield, CT	3 shares*	£30	12/5/1794
Street, Caleb	Catskill, Albany, NY		E399	9/15/1796
Street is to take "at his own risque & Hazzard" as all Baldwin's papers destroyed by the enemy at Wyoming				
Baldwin, John	Norwich, New London, CT	1 share	£8	6/27/1768
Scovell, Elisha	Colchester, Hartford, CT		B198	4/1/1774
Baldwin, John	Branford, New Haven, CT	Pwr Att *	1/2 share or £300	4/2/1795
Steel, John 2nd	Bethlehem, Litchfield, CT	Watertown Twp	C620	7/1/1795
to locate 1 share & pay taxes & costs by 1/1/1797; 300 A laid out in Watertown Twp.				
Baldwin, Reuben*	Darby, New Haven, CT	1/2 share	£3	3/1/1796
Pope, Robert	Darby, New Haven, CT		E497	12/17/1796
James Baldwin willed 1/2 share to chr: Silas, Reuben, Jesse. Jesse died without chr.				
Baldwin, Samuel	W. Stockbridge, Berkshire, MA	500 A: Lots 6 & 7, 3rd Range	$500	12/9/1796
Andrews, Benajah	W. Stockbridge, Berkshire, MA	Baldwinsville Twp	H336	5/20/1802
Baldwin, Samuel	West Stockbridge, Berkshire,	500 A: two 250 acre lots	£84	11/29/1795
Bennet, Benajah & Daniel	Stockbridge, Berkshire, MA	Baldwinsville Twp	D143	5/28/1796
Baldwin, Samuel	West Stockbridge, Berkshire,	250 A	$150	4/9/1796
Bennet, Benajah & Daniel	Stockbridge, Berkshire, MA	Baldwinsville Twp	D144	6/10/1796
Baldwin, Samuel		16,000 A	$2,000	2/1/1796
Tiffany, Isaiah & Whiting, Wm B.		Fairfax Twp	E512	2/10/1796
Baldwin, Samuel and Tiffany, Isaiah	W. Stockbridge, Berkshire, MA	16,000 A	$16,000	5/6/1796
Henshaw, Joshua	New Hartford, Litchfield, CT	Mount Pleasant, Northumberland, PA	E309	8/8/1796
Baldwin, Samuel & Tiffany, Isaiah	W. Stockbridge, Berkshire, MA	16,000 A	$16,000	6/1/1796
Clark, Samuel & Bulkley, James	Middletown, Middlesex, CT	Gilford Twp	E307	8/8/1796
Baldwin, Silas	Derby, New Haven, CT	1/6 share	£23.10	12/19/1780
Keeler, Nathaniel	Salem, Westchester, NY		C103	9/30/1786
Baldwin, Simon*		1 share of Ebenezer Baldwin's*	$55	12/31/1795
Goodrich, Benj. & Munson, Joshua			E255	7/1/1796
son of Ebenezer; except 600 A in Bachelor's Adventure Twp				
Baldwin, Simon		1/2 share	$35	12/31/1795
Goodrich, Benj. & Munson, Joshua			E255	7/1/1796
Baldwin, Thomas	Ulster, Luzerne, PA	Lot 1*	£100	7/7/1786
Bingham, Chester	Ulster, Luzerne, PA	Up. end Old Sheshequin, Ulster Twp	C499	2/21/1795
Begin at stake by side of road, W 1.5 mi, N 1 mi, E 1.5 mi, S on bank of [Susq] river to beginning				
Baldwin, Thomas	Chemung, Tioga, NY	3 Lots	£8	1/14/1792
Cole, Stephen	Chemung, Tioga, NY	Athens Twp	E106	3/1/1796
Twp Lot 26; 2nd Div Lot 25; 3rd Div Lot 19				
Baldwin, Water./Newman, Jonthn	Luzerne, PA	16,000 A	$3,500	4/18/1796
Morgan, Asa	New Milford, Litchfield, CT	Beavertown Twp	E533	1/21/1797
Baldwin, Waterman	Luzerne Co PA	Lot 50, 2nd Div, abt 10A	£20	10/28/1795
Bedlock, Stephen	Athens, Luzerne, PA	Athens Twp	D47	11/6/1795
Baldwin, Waterman	Luzerne Co PA	Lot 19, 1st Div, abt 1A	£4.10	10/13/1795
Bedlock, Stephen	Athens, Luzerne, PA	Athens Twp	D48	11/6/1795

grantor grantee notes	grantor residence grantee residence	description location	amount acct bk page	deed date record date
Baldwin, Waterman		1/2 of 1/2 share of the 400*	$20	3/29/1796
Ellis, Thomas		Harlem Twp	F186	3/3/1798
500 A certified and entered in Harlem 8/18/1797				
Baldwin, Waterman		1 share*		3/22/1796
Irwin, James		Athens Twp	E437 - I161	
"all right to within" & "recorded in Committee Book p. 61" written on back of certificate; see I61				
Baldwin, Waterman	Pittstown, Luzerne, PA	Lot 49*	£20	6/7/1788
Patterson, Benjamin	Athens, Luzerne, PA	Athens Twp	D142	11/17/1795
East Side Susquehanna River opposite the Island by survey Second of May				
Baldwin, Waterman		1/2 share	$20	1/15/1796
Stephens, Ira		Allensburgh Twp	E366	4/1/1796
Baldwin, Waterman	Pittstown, Luzerne, PA	16,600 A	$6000	12/17/1794
Street, Caleb / Kingsbury, Phineas	Catskill, NY and Granby, CT	Pleasant Valley Twp*	D25	9/28/1795
Regranted to C. Street and P. Kingsbury under name of Easton, see E188				
Baldwin, Waterman	Chemung, Tioga, NY	273 A	$400	12/30/1799
Thayer, Levi	Athens, Luzerne, PA	Athens Twp	H176	1/1/1800
Baldwin, William	New Haven, New Haven, CT	1 share	$70	12/31/1795
Goodrich, Benj. & Munson, Joshua	Canaan, Litchfield, CT		E257	7/1/1796
Baldwin, William		1/2 share	value received	3/27/1795
Kenney, Thomas			E330	4/10/1796
Baldwin, William	Newtown, Tioga, NY	16,000 A	$6,000	2/9/1795
Street, Caleb	Catskill, Albany, NY	Franklin Twp	E175	6/2/1796
Baldwin, William	Newtown, Tioga, NY	16,000 A	$6,000	2/9/1795
Street, Caleb	Catskill, Albany, NY	Otterstown Twp	E175	6/2/1796
Ballard, Joseph	Fairhaven, Rutland, VT	1/2 share	£60	8/30/1782
Bewell, Ephriam	Castleton, Rutland, VT		C84	2/12/1783
Ballard, Steph /Chamberlain, S. C*	Tioga, PA & Colebrook, CT	Pwr Att to locate shares		1/15/1795
Spalding, John	Tioga, Luzerne, CT	Watertown Twp	C627	7/1/1795
Stephen Ballard & Samuel Clark Chamberlain				
Ballard, Stephen	Jusdburgh, Luzerne, PA	100 acres in Lot 15	£50	7/9/1796
Bull, Nathan	Luzerne, PA	Juddsburgh Twp	E276	7/10/1796
Ballau, Noah	Cumberland, Providence, RI	1/2 share	£12	3/17/1775
Clark, Stephen	Hoosic, Berkshire, MA		B321	3/22/1775
Bancroft, Azariah, heirs*	Granville, Hampshire, MA	1 share	£20	2/9/1795
Brown, Sanford	Sanderfield, Berkshire, MA		F8	3/1/1796
Samuel and Enoch Bancroft				
Banks, Ebenezer	Fairfield, Fairfield, CT	1/2 share	£7.10	12/14/1773
Bradley, Increase	Fairfield, Fairfield, CT		B128	1/20/1774
Banks, Ebenezer, heirs*	Fairfield, Fairfield, CT	quit claim as heirs to 1/2 share		1/23/1795
Banks, Ebenezer	Fairfield, Fairfield, CT		E171	5/31/1796
Elisha Bradley & Eunice, h & w; Ebenezer Wakeman& Anne, h & w; Joseph Banks; John Wilson Jr. & Sarah, h & w				
Barber, David	Hebron, Tolland, CT	Pwr Att to locate & lay out		1/23/1795
Pratt, Isaac	Braintrim, Luzerne, PA		D55	11/10/1795
Barber, David				
Root, Jonathan & Sarah, wf			A481 - GM	
Barber, David	Hebron CT	1 share		8/31/1794
Turner, Seth	New Haven CT		C220	2/28/1795
Barber, Thomas, Ex*		1/2 share	£10	3/2/1796
Gage, Amos			E148	4/22/1796
Elisha Barber				
Barker, John	Wallingford, New Haven, CT	1/3 of 1/2 share	love	6/14/1770
Barker, Edward son			E124	3/1/1796
Barker, John	Wallingford, New Haven, CT	1/3 of 1/2 share	love	6/14/1770
Beadles, Eunice *	Wallingford, New Haven, CT		E123	3/1/1796
dau of John Barker & wf of John Beadles				
Barker, John	Wallingford, New Haven, CT	1/3 of 1/2 share	love	6/14/1770
Johnson, Mary	Wallingford, New Haven, CT		E122	3/1/1796
dau of John Barker& wf of Solomon Johnson				
Barlow, Nathan	Luzerne Co PA	1 share No. 193 of 600, Lots 29, 48	£11	1/11/1794
Bates, Caleb	PA	Putnam Twp	I96	5/26/1794
Barnes, Benoni		1 share		
Pond, Thomas	Sharon		GJ	

grantor grantee notes	grantor residence grantee residence	description location	amount acct bk page	deed date record date
Barnes, Ebenezer	Windsor, Hartford, CT	1/2 share	£17	3/4/1774
Wells, Asahel	Hartford, Hartford, CT		F151	1/28/1795
Barnes, Ebenezer	Windsor, Hartford, CT	1/2 share	£17	3/5/1764
Wells, Ashbell	Hartford, Hartford, CT		B237	8/24/1774
Barnes, Nathaniel	New Haven	1/2 share	£12	10/24/1774
Thompson, John	Branford		C31	2/2/1782
Barnes, Titus	New Haven	1/2 share	£12	11/14/1773
Thompson, John	Branford		C30	2/6/1782
Barnet, Moses				
Satterly, Benedict			A13	
Barnet, Moses		1/2 share		
Shephard, Abraham			GD	
Barney, Henry		1/2 share, of the 400		10/14/1795
Holt, Jacob			F57	4/23/1796
Barney, Henry	Plymouth, Luzerne, PA	16,000 A	$5,000	11/18/1795
Holt, Jacob	Canaan, Litchfield, CT	Wallingham Twp	F126	11/23/1796
Barns, Samuel	New Haven	1/2 share	£12	9/4/1773
Thompson, John	Branford, New Haven, CT		B36	9/15/1773
Barnum, Jehiel	Kent, Litchfield, CT	1 share	£60	1/17/1755
Holloway, John	Cornwall, Litchfield, CT		C531	5/1/1795
Barrett, Jonathan	Norwich, Windsor, VT	1/2 of all rights	£3	5/18/1795
Rathburn, Wait	Middletown, Rutland, VT		C645	8/9/1795
Barrit, John		1 share	val con	5/2/1795
Paine, David	Athens, Luzerne, PA		E77	3/2/1796
Bartlet, John	Cabot, Orange, VT	all right	$50	2/15/1796
Wheeler, Preserved	Charlotte, Chittenden, VT		E131	3/28/1796
Bass, Henry				
Frink, Matthew			A325	
Bates, Caleb	Luzerne Co PA	100 A of Lot 23*	£25	12/26/1788
Hopper, Cornelius	Luzerne Co PA	Pittstown, Luzerne, PA	C609	7/9/1795
certified 4/11/1791 in Court Common Pleas, Luzerne Co				
Bates, Caleb	Coventry, Kent, RI	1/2 share	£50	8/30/1757
Ide, Nicholas	Coventry, Kent, RI		B191	3/9/1774
Bates, Jonathan	New Haven, New Haven, CT	1/2 share	£5	9/16/1794
Lester, Eliphalet	Saybrook, Middlesex, CT		D10	9/18/1795
Bates, Luke	Hudson, Columbia, NY	1/2 of share No. 54 of 600*	£100	10/14/1786
Moder, John J.A.	Hudson, Columbia, NY	Franklin Twp*	E454	10/28/1796
Lot 24 1st div, Lot 47 home & water, and one lot not drawn; lots drawn at meeting held at Gabriel Esseltine's in Claverack, 7 Aug 1786				
Battle, James	Tyringham, Berkshire, MA	1000 A	£100	11/11/1795
Hatch, Timothy	Blanford, Berkshire, MA	Sharon Twp	D67	12/4/1795
Battle, James	Tyringham, Berkshire, MA	300 A	£37.10	11/11/1795
Knox, William	Blanford, Hampshire, MA	Sharon Twp	D70	12/4/1795
Battle, Thiel	Tyringham, Berkshire, MA	1/4 twp	$5	9/19/1795
Bacon, Reuben	Stockbridge, Berkshire, MA	Nankin Twp	D68	12/4/1795
Battle, Thiel	Tyringham, Berkshire, MA	8000 A	$1000	11/10/1795
Battle, James	Tyringham, Berkshire, MA	Sharon Twp, 1/2	D66	12/4/1795
Beach, Zerah	Amenia Precinct, NY	1/2 share, No. 362 of 600 inc. 300 A		2/22/1794
Calkins, Moses		Burlington Twp	I77	9/7/1795
Beach, Zerah	Amenia Precinct, NY	1/2 share, No. 363 of 600 inc. 300 A		2/22/1794
Calkins, Moses		Burlington Twp	I77	9/7/1795
Beadle, Thomas				
Buck, Asahel			A77	
Beal, Matthew	Norwalk, Fairfield, CT	1/2 share	£7	11/16/1779
Whitelsey, John	Washington, Litchfield, CT		C32	2/18/1782
Beardslee, Hall	Huntington, Fairfield, CT	1/2 share	£8	1/27/1795
Lewis, LeGrand M.	Huntington, Fairfield, CT		C611	6/9/1795
Beardslee, Josiah	Newtown	1/2 share		4/2/1761
Beardslee, Samuel, bro.			C611	6/9/1795
Beardslee, Samuel Jr.*	Huntington, Fairfield, CT	1/2 share		3/26/1795
Beardslee, Hall	Huntington, Fairfield, CT		C611	6/9/1795
heir of Samuel Beardslee, Sr.				
Beardslee, Silas		700 A on 1/2 share		10/9/1800
Kinney, Daniel		Springhill Twp, 2nd division	H256	10/13/1800

grantor grantee notes	grantor residence grantee residence	description location	amount acct bk page	deed date record date
Beardsley, John	Branford, New Haven, CT	1/3 5,900 A (1,966 A)	$3,290	10/19/1796
Tyler, Peter & Rose, Ameriah	Branford, New Haven, CT	Fairfax, Luzerne, PA	F159	4/24/1797
Beckwith, George	Litchfield, Litchfield, CT	1 share*	£20	9/9/1774
Olcott, Elisha	Hartford, Hartford, CT		C112	4/1/1790
1/2 George Beckwith, 1/2 Nathaniel Brown Beckwith, bro.				
Beckwith, Stephen	Springfield, Luzerne, PA	300 A, Lot 6	£225.10	2/7/1795
Eno, Erasmus	Athens, Luzerne, PA	Springfield Twp	C310	2/28/1795
Beckwith, Stephen				
Wells, Amos			A480	
Beebe, Solomon	Luzerne Co, PA	Lot No. 48	£20	5/10/1795
Shepherd, John	Luzerne Co, PA	Murraysfield Twp	C583	6/26/1795
Beebee, Samuel	Southold, Suffolk, NY	1/2 share	£10	3/10/1774
Lester, Eliphalet	New London		D7	9/18/1795
Beecher, Burke & Bristol	Woodbridge & New Haven, CT		$26.25	2/17/1796
Pope, Robert	Darby, New Haven, CT		E482	11/15/1796
Sarah Beecher, Mary Burke, Eunice Bristol				
Beecher, Burke & Bristol	Woodbridge & New Haven,	1 share	$52.50	2/17/1796
Pope, Robert	Darby, New Haven, CT		E483	11/15/1796
Sarah Beecher, Mary Burke, Eunice Bristol				
Beecher, David	New Haven, New Haven, CT	1/2 share	£8	10/4/1773
Morris, Amos	New Haven, New Haven, CT		B88	10/21/1773
Beecher, Joseph N.	Woodbridge, New Haven, CT	1 share	good cause	12/27/1794
Osburn, Elisha	Derby, New Haven, CT		I161	2/16/1795
Beeman, Ebenezer	Warren, Litchfield Co, CT	1/2 share	£24	12/25/1795
Beeman, Timothy	Warren, Litchfield Co, CT		E54	2/24/1796
Beers, Nathan		1 share*		12/31/1755
Brunson, Timothy	New Haven		MB	
pd Thomas Darling				
Belcher, Andrew	Patridgefield, Berkshire, MA		£15	6/26/1785
Burnham, Elias	Patridgefield, Berkshire, MA		C99	6/26/1786
Belden, Jonathan	Berlin, Hartford, CT	3/4 share	18d	1/4/1796
Smith, Lemuel & Allyn, John B.	Berlin, Hartford, CT		E140	2/25/1796
Beldin, Ezra	Luzerne Co PA	1 A, Lot No., upper div meadow	£3.15	11/21/1786
Myers, Lawrence		Plymouth Twp	I36	10/4/1786
Belding, Chester	Claverack, Columbia, NY		£1,200	1/4/1797
Burroughs, William Y.	Claverack, Columbia, NY	Hector Twp	E515	2/17/1797
Belding, Chester	Claverack, Columbia, NY	1/3 Twp	£566	4/7/1796
Frost, Elisha		Jay Twp	E160	5/17/1796
Belding, Chester	Claverack, Columbia, NY	8,000 A	£1066.13.4	9/25/1795
Lombard, Roswell	Stockbridge, Berkshire, MA	Lebanon Twp, east 1/2	F62	4/23/1796
Belding, Chester	Claverack, Columbia, NY	12 1/2 lots of 160 A each*	$1,000	2/25/1797
Maxwell, Anthony	Kinderhook, Columbia, NY	Eastham Twp	H280	9/1/1800
Nos. 93, 46, 45, 89, 98, 74, 83, 21, 8, 19, 42, 56, and 1/2 44				
Belding, Chester	Claverack, Columbia, NY	1/4 part	$2,000	10/14/1795
Myers, Jacob and Gregory,	Tyringham, Berkshire, MA	Hancock Twp	E478	11/20/1796
Belding, Chester	Claverack, Columbia, NY	1/3 Twp	£566	4/7/1796
Ransom, Theophilus		Jay Twp	E161	5/17/1796
Belding, Chester	Claverack, Columbia, NY	1/4 Twp	£800	10/22/1795
Williams, Ebenezer	Stockbridge, Berkshire, MA	Hancock Twp	F323	11/1/1797
Belding, Simeon	Hartford, Hartford, CT	Pwr Att to locate	1/2 land	2/26/1796
Strong, Jabin	Glastonbury, Hartford, CT		E426	9/16/1796
Belding, Thomas, decd.*	Weathersfield, Hartford, CT	1 or more shares	$10	5/13/1794
Hale, George	Catskill, Albany, NY		C369	2/28/1795
Ezekiel P. Belding, adm				
Belknap, Abel	Cherry Valley, Otsego, NY	1/2 share	£80	3/25/1796
Butler, Josiah	Cherry Valley, Otsego, NY		E136	4/11/1796
Bellamy, Matthew	Wallingford, New Haven, CT	1/2 share		
Platner, Henry			D52	11/9/1795
Bellamy, Moses	Wallingford, New Haven, CT	all right	£2.10	1/3/1769
Bellamy, Matthew	Wallingford, New Haven, CT		D52	11/9/1795
Benjamin, Isaac		1/2 share		3/1/1776
Bennet, Ishmael			GF	4/9/1776

grantor / grantee / notes	grantor residence / grantee residence	description / location	amount / acct bk page	deed date / record date
Benjamin, Nathan	Sheffield, Berkshire, MA	12,000 A	$6,000	3/14/1799
Bradley, Lemuel & Timothy	Sunderland, Bennington, VT	Middlesex Twp	H293	4/28/1801
Bennet, Ephriam	New Town, Fairfield, CT	1/2 share	£6.10	2/26/1763
Baldwin, Daniel	Sharon, Litchfield, CT		C55	11/11/1782
Bennet, Ephriam	Newtown, Fairfield, CT	1/3 share	13s	3/18/1760
Terril, George	Newtown, Fairfield, CT		C23	3/29/1781
Bennet, Isaac				
Bennet, James			A54	
Bennet, Joseph, Plat & Ezra	Fairfield, Reading, Weston, CT	700 A	$80	9/20/1798
Morgan, Nathaniel	Weston, Fairfield, CT	Granby Twp	H7	10/13/1798
Bennet, Joshua		1/2 share	value recd	6/4/1796
Manville, Ira			E266	7/8/1796
Bennet, Thomas	Kingston, Northumberland, PA	1/2 share	$20	10/17/1785
Bennet, Solomon, son	Kingston, Northumberland, PA		C93	2/7/1786
Bennet, William				
Powers, Stephen			A283	
Bennett, Amos		2nd div lot on 1/2 share*		3/18/1795
Beardsley, Silas		Standing Stone Twp	D91 - H256	8/28/1798
keep 1st div lot on 1/2 share for self				
Bennett, Banks*	Halifax, Windham, VT	1/2 share	£7	10/11/1782
Terrey, John	Halifax, Windham, VT		E376	9/13/1796
heir of Samuel Banks, decd father, late of Tolland CT				
Bennett, Edward & Canfield, Joel	New Milford, Litchfield, CT	2 shares	10s	9/2/1794
Terrill, Job & Brownson, Isaac	New Milford, Litchfield, CT	New Milford Twp	I154	12/6/1794
Bennett, Elisha	Newport, Luzerne, PA	1/2 share	$70	7/1/1794
Jackson, Silas	Luzerne, PA		H285	1/13/1801
Bennett, Ishmael				
Inman, Elijah			GF	
Bennett, John	Preston, New London, CT	1/2 share	6s	3/30/1769
Larrabe, John	Plainfield, Windham, CT		B62	10/9/1773
Benton, Caleb	Hillsdale, Columbia, NY	Town Lot 45	$10	2/20/1796
Burroughs, William G.	Columbia, NY	Athens Twp	E165	5/16/1796
Benton, Caleb	Hillsdale, Columbia, NY	16,000 A	$2,000	11/14/1797
Franklin, John	Athens, Luzerne, PA	Dallas Twp	H22	
Benton, Caleb	Columbia, NY	Mifflin Twp	$8,000	8/8/1796
Pixley, Ephriam	Columbia, NY		C165	8/8/1796
Benton, Caleb	Hillsdale, Columbia, NY	16,000 A	$8,000	3/7/1795
Pixley, Ephriam	Hillsdale, Columbia, NY	Goresburgh Twp	E348	8/24/1796
Benton, Caleb		8,000 A*		10/20/1798
Wood, Nathaniel		Cato Twp	C425	10/20/1798
Lots 20, 21, 22, 23 of 600 later withdrawn fr Cato & entered in Cumberland				
Benton, Caleb	Columbia, NY	16,000 A	$9,000	6/27/1795
Wynkoop, William	Tioga, NY	Cato Twp	C156	10/20/1798
Benton, Nathaniel	Litchfield, Litchfield, CT	Pwr Att to sell 1/2 share		11/19/1795
Bostwick, Benjamin	Brookfield, Fairfield, CT		D92	12/4/1795
Benton, Samuel	Cornwall, VT	security & note for 2 lots	£120	9/17/1794
Bingham, Chester	Ulster, Luzerne, PA	Murraysfield Twp	H94	10/1/1794
Bertell, Peter Jr.		four 1/2 shares to sell or return		9/26/1794
Maxwell, Guy	Canadaigua, Ontario, NY		C317	9/26/1794
Bertell, Peter Jr.	Seneca, Ontario, NY	four 1/2 shares*		12/14/1794
Stevens, Phineas	Ontario, NY		C316	3/9/1795
Stevens gives Guy Maxwell to sell for not less than £10 each David Woodward, No 70; Jeptha Earl, No 81; Daniel Earl, No 80; Quit Claim fr Enos Tubbs				
Bestwick, Bushnell				
Brownson, Roger			A71	
Bibbins, Ebenezer	Windham, Windham, CT	all right	5s	
Elderkin, Joshua	Windham, Windham, CT		B136	1/29/1774
Bicknel, Zachariah Jr.	Ashford, Windham, CT	1 share	£50	12/26/1794
Adams, Jabez Dr.	Canterbury, Windham, CT		C467	2/20/1795
Bicknell, Samuel	Ashford, Windham, CT	all right	£6	8/16/1774
Edgerton, Asa	Norwich, New London, CT	Salem Twp	F205	8/14/1797
Bicknell, Zachariah	Ashford, Windham, CT	1/2 of 1 share inc. 50 A Lot No. 8*	£20	8/16/1774
Edgerton, Asa	Norwich, New London, CT	Salem Twp	F206	8/14/1797
taxes pd for Town of Salem 10/5/1773				

grantor	grantor residence	description	amount	deed date
grantee	grantee residence	location	acct bk page	record date
notes				
Bidlack, Benjamin		1/2 share to locate		5/3/1794
Satterlee, Elisha			E438	10/1/1796
Bidlack, Philemon		2/3 of 1/2 share	$25	11/13/1795
Irwin, James			E438	10/1/1796
Bidlack, Stephen	Athens, Luzerne, PA	Town Lot 19 1st Div. abt 1 A	£10	3/15/1796
Baldwin, Waterman	Athens, Luzerne, PA	Athens Twp	E111	3/17/1796
Bidwell, Bidwell & Morehouse*	Stillwater, Saratoga, NY	all right	£48	2/13/1795
Dunning, Dillino, Ramsey, Baldwin			E113	3/1/1796
David Bidwell heirs: Ebenezer, Phillip, David & Jacob Bidwell; Phineas Bidwell, David Morehouse to E. Dunning, P.Dillino, D. Ramsey, J. Baldwin				
Bidwell, Daniel	Stillwater, Albany, NY	shares inherited fr David Bidwell*	£5	12/18/1795
Givens, Joseph	Ballston, Saratoga, NY		E109	3/1/1796
Biedleman, Samuel		1/2 share, 300 A Lot 36		3/3/1795
Paine, David		Murraysfield Twp	C318	3/15/1795
Bigelow, David	Glastonbury, Hartford, CT	1 share	$20	5/9/1795
Hale, George	Catskill, Albany, NY		C377	2/28/1795
Bigelow, David Jr.	Glastonbury, Hartford, CT	1/2 share	$20	5/9/1795
Hale, George	Catskill, Albany, NY		C378	2/28/1795
Bigelow, John				
Bigelow, John 3rd			A319	
Biles, Joseph	Luzerne, PA	150 A to be laid out	$10	6/27/1798
Jones, Benjamin	Luzerne, PA		H24	8/20/1798
Biles, Joseph, surveyor	Athens, Luzerne, PA	12,000 A	$5,000	3/6/1797
Benjamin, Nathan	Sheffield, Berkshire, MA	Middlesex Twp	H292	4/28/1801
Bill, Benajah	Hartford, Windsor, VT	1 share	£5	12/5/1795
Swift, Silas	Lebanon, Windham, CT		E95	3/8/1796
Billings, Increase*		1/2 share	val con	4/16/1796
Thayer, Levi			E338	5/15/1796
Pwr Att given 12/10/1795 to attorney Joseph Bennight				
Billings, Joseph	Preston, New London, CT	1/2 share	Love	4/20/1763
Hewet, Jonas, son-in-law	Preston, New London, CT		B86	11/8/1773
Billings, Stephen				
Billings, Increase			A312	
Billings, Stephen*		1000 A		5/23/1796
Billings, Increase		Bowdoin Twp	E168	5/23/1796
by Att. Joseph Bennight				
Bingham, Chester*	Ulster, Luzerne, PA	520 A	$260 & good causes	10/9/1798
Basset, John	Pitsfield, Otsago, NY	Durkee Twp, W adj. John Swain	H43	3/20/1799
witnessed by sons Augustus and Joseph Bingham				
Bingham, Chester	Ulster, Luzerne, PA	8000 A	£1200	9/7/1794
Hale, George & Brown, Daniel	Catskill & Freehold, Albany,	Fairfield, east 1/2	D19	9/22/1795
Bingham, Chester	Ulster, Luzerne, PA	Lot 6, 150 A & 150 A undiv.	£80	2/8/1796
Olmsted, David	Catskill, Albany, NY	Columbia Twp	E173	6/1/1796
Bingham, Chester	Ulster, Luzerne, PA	Lot 8, 150 A & 150 A undiv.	£80	11/13/1795
Olmsted, David	Catskill, Albany, NY	Columbia Twp	E174	6/1/1796
Bingham, Chester	Luzerne Co PA	Lot 22, 300 A	£150	3/3/1795
Paine, Clement	Rensselaerville, Albany, NY	Murraysfield Twp	C257	3/4/1795
Bingham, Chester	Luzerne, PA	8,000 A	$3000	9/22/1795
Paine, David		Fairfield Twp, west 1/2*	D24	9/22/1795
except NW corner sold to Henry VanRensaelaer and Henry Platner				
Bingham, Chester		1,550 A		11/5/1794
Platner, Henry		Fairfield Twp, NW corner	F149	
Bingham, Chester*	Tioga, Luzerne, PA	Lot 5, 150 A & 150 A undivided	£80	1/15/1796
Ritter, Henry & Olmsted, David	Catskill, Albany, NY	Columbia Twp	E172	6/1/1796
for John Fuller				
Bingham, Chester	Ulster, Luzerne, PA	800 A	$400 & good causes	10/9/1798
Swain, John	Luzerne, PA	Durkee Twp	H44	3/20/1799
Bingham, Chester	Luzerne, PA	4,000 A*	$6,000	11/20/1796
Thayer, Levi	Luzerne, PA	Fairfield Twp, east	H155	12/26/1799
Nos.,1-4, 6-7, 9-1, 13 400 A each				
Bingham, Chester	Ulster, Luzerne, PA	880 A*	$1,500	6/15/1799
Thayer, Levi	Luzerne, PA	Ulster Twp	H160	12/30/1799
on Susq R btw Isaac Trask and Benj Dorrance except 150 A fr S.E. corner				

grantor grantee notes	grantor residence grantee residence	description location	amount acct bk page	deed date record date
Bingham, Chester	Ulster, Luzerne, PA	500 A*	$1,000	6/15/1799
Thayer, Levi	Athens, Luzerne, PA	Ulster	H165	12/30/1799
A good mill seat on waters of Sugar Creek				
Bingham, Chester	Ulster, Luzerne, PA	10,000 A*	$8,000	8/1/1799
Thayer, Levi	Athens, Luzerne, PA	Durkee Twp, south part	H166	12/30/1799
except assigned lots of actual settlers				
Bingham, Chester	Ulster, Luzerne, PA	2,350 A	$255	11/15/1794
Van Rensselaer, John H.	Hudson Bush, Columbia, NY	Fairfield Twp	F147	11/12/1796
Bingham, Chester	Tioga, Luzerne, PA	16,000 A	$8,000	11/21/1795
Wallace, Uriah	Northsalem, West Chester, NY	Hexham Twp	E468	11/6/1796
Bingham, Chester	Tioga, Luzerne, PA	16,000 A	$9,000	11/30/1795
Worthington, William	Catskill, Albany, NY	Durkee Twp	F78	6/3/1796
Bingham, Chester & Martha	Ulster, Luzerne, PA	Lot 37, 300 A	£120	6/17/1794
Paine, David	Rensselaerville, Albany, NY	Murraysfield Twp	I81	6/21/1794
Bingham, Chester & Martha	Ulster, Luzerne, PA	1139 A adj. Jedediah Shaw	$500	6/21/1794
Paine, David	Rensselaerville, Albany, NY	Ulster Twp	I83	6/21/1794
Bingham, Chester & Martha	Ulster, Luzerne, PA	16,000 A	$8,000	6/20/1794
Paine, David	Rensselaerville, Albany, NY	Fairfield Twp	I85	6/21/1794
Bingham, Chester & Martha	Ulster, Luzerne, PA	Lot 35, 300 A	£120	6/14/1794
Paine, David	Rensselaerville, Albany, NY	Smithfield Twp	I87	6/21/1794
Bingham, Elijah				
Bingham, Silas			A105	
Bingham, Elijah				
McColly, Joseph			A455	
Bingham, Gideon, heir John	Windham, Windham, CT	1/2 share	£5	1/12/1795
Dorrance, Benjamin	Kingston, Luzerne, CT		C539	5/7/1795
Bingham, Joseph	Mansfield, Windham, CT	1/2 share	£6	4/11/1773
Bingham, Chester & Ozias, sons	Sheffield, Berkshire, MA;		B56	4/12/1773
Bingham, Joseph	Windham, Windham, CT	1/2 share*	£10	12/6/1791
Bingham, Wheelock	Windham, Windham, CT		C601	7/10/1795
other 1/2 share to sons Chester and Ozias previously; witness Samuel Gray, Sarah Bingham				
Bingham, Silas	Windham, Windham, CT	1/2 share	£10	2/17/1774
Gray, Ebenezer & Samuel Jr.	Windham, Windham, CT		B141	8/17/1774
Birchard, Jesse, son	Bozrah, New London, CT	1 share	$100	11/22/1794
Hyde, Elisha; Tracy, Elisha	Norwich, New London, CT		I170	2/22/1795
Birchard, Jesse son	Bozrah, New London, CT	1/2 share	$100	11/22/1794
Hyde, Elisha; Tracy, Elisha	Norwich, New London, CT		I170	2/22/1795
Birchard, John	Norwich, New London, CT	1/2 share	£14	3/3/1761
Hollister, Timothy	Glastonbury, Hartford, CT		B269	11/11/1774
Birchard, John		1/2 share*		3/17/1793
Morgan, John, now decd	Groton		A447 - F46	4/23/1796
taxes pd 3/17/1773 by Stephen Hurlbut on behalf of heirs of Capt John Morgan				
Birchard, John 3rd				
York, Amos			A36	
Birchard, John heirs*	New London, New London, CT	1/2 share	£10	2/3/1795
Tracy, Elisha	Norwich, New London, CT		I171	
Nathaniel Birchard; Elizabeth Birchard gdau; Abigail Birchard gdau & hus George Hallam				
Birchard, John Jr.	Granby, Hampshire, MA	1/2 share	21s	4/26/1774
Winchester, Andrew	Canterbury, Windham, CT		B214	5/20/1774
Bird, Joseph	Tyringham, Berkshire, MA	1 share	£6	11/11/1794
Stone, Ethan	Landerfield, Berkshire, MA		C446	2/21/1795
Bird, Joseph estate	Salisbury, Litchfield, CT	1 share	valuable sum	6/5/1769
Phelps, Elijah			B311	2/23/1775
Bird, Michael	Smithfield Twp (late Rutland,	160 A, 1/2 Lot 15	$60	2/23/1802
Lester, Simeon	Rutland, Rutland, VT	Smithfield Twp	H330	2/26/1802
Bird, Thomas & Isaac	Salisbury, Litchfield, CT	1 share*	£20	3/21/1795
Stone, Ethan	Sanderfield, Berkshire, MA		F6	
pd £16. 5s taxes 1/31/1754				
Bishop, Samuel Jr.	New Haven, New Haven, CT		£6.15.2	3/24/1772
Hopkins, Stephen	Waterbury, New Haven, CT		B66	6/2/1773
Bissell, Hezekiah	Hartford, CT	4,000 A (1/4 pt)	$500	2/8/1796
Hyde, Ezekiel	Norwich, New London, CT	Stephensburgh Twp	F36	4/23/1796

grantor / grantee / notes	grantor residence / grantee residence	description / location	amount / acct bk page	deed date / record date
Blackman, Eleazer		300 A		9/17/1796
Blackman, Elizabeth et al*		Claverack Twp	F105	9/17/1796
& heirs of Jehadbad Blackman				
Blackman, Eleazer	Wilkesbarre, Luzerne, PA	4,050 A on Great Mahoping Creek	$1,500	11/30/1795
Dana, Daniel	Enfield, Hartford, CT	Westminster Twp	F216	10/26/1797
Blackman, Eleazer/Tuttle, Steph	Wilkesbarre, Luzerne, PA	16,000 A	$5,000	6/18/1796
Clark, Samuel & Buckley, James	Middletown, Middlesex, CT	Venus Twp	H105	9/3/1799
Blackman, Mary	Huntington, Fairfield, CT	1 share	$5	1/1/1795
Lewis, Walker			E279	6/8/1796
Blackslee, Tilly				
Hopkins, Stephen			A397	
Blanchard, Jedediah	Enfield, Hartford, CT	1/2 share	£16.10	3/10/1779
Rogers, Ichabod	Brimfield, Hampshire, MA		C63	11/13/1782
Bliss, Ebenezer	Lebanon, Grafton, NH	1/2 share*	£5	6/8/1795
Horton, John	Brandon, Rutland, VT		E48	
$10 tax pd 12/30/1782				
Bliss, John	Norwich, New London, CT	1 share	£12	11/30/1794
Tracy, Elisha	Norwich, New London, CT		I144	12/25/1794
Blodget, James	Dresden, Hampshire Grants,	1/2 share	£100 bond dated	2/28/1783
Hatfield, William et al			C432	4/14/1795
Jonathan Mason & Nathan Howard				
Bohennen: William, Thomas, Mikal	Tioga, Luzerne, PA	1 1/2 shares	£60	12/29/1794
Hutchinson, John	Tioga, Luzerne, PA	Murraysfield 1; Columbia 1/2	C305	2/28/1795
Bolles, John	New London, New London, CT	1/2 share	30s	9/4/1794
Elliot, William	Saybrook, Middlesex, CT		C122	10/1/1794
Bolles, John estate				
Bolles, Stephen			A302	
Bolles, Stephen		agent for a Twp survey	1 share	7/20/1795
Throop, Benjamin			C120.1	9/1/1795
for fifteen owners, including Throop, who pay Throop 6s per day for his time and horse; total of 8 shares; S. Bolles 1 share				
Bolls, David	Ashford, Windham, CT	1/2 share	£2	6/10/1773
Wickwise, James	East Haddam, Hartford, CT		B71	6/14/1773
Booth, Elisha	Farmington, Hartford, CT	1 share	20s	4/5/1773
Belding, Ezra	Farmington, Hartford, CT		B159	3/9/1774
Booth, John	Hudson, Columbia, NY	16,000 A	$1,000	11/27/1795
Judd, William	Farmingtown, Hartford, CT	Millsbury Twp	F20	4/23/1796
Booth, Jonathan				
Seeley, Benjamin			A39	
Booth, Nathan	Farmington, Hartford, CT	1 share	£6	7/30/1773
Morris, Amos	New Haven, New Haven, CT		B87	10/21/1773
Booth: Nathan Jr. & Fransa	Berlin, Hartford, CT	1/6 share	£3	2/1/1796
Smith, Lemuel & Allyn, John B.	Berlin, Hartford, CT		E138	2/25/1796
Booth, Stephen		1 share, No. 42 of the 600		3/4/1797
Burroughs, William Y.			E542	10/24/1797
Bostwick & Beardsley*		1/4 share each		
Bostwick, Dimon	New Milford, Litchfield, CT	New Milford Twp	I153	12/6/1794
Bostwick, Elnathan H. & Beardsley, Mehitable				
Bostwick, David	Courtwright, Otsego, NY	16,000 A	$4,000	2/10/1796
Curtiss, Peter	Freehold, Albany, NY	Springhill Twp	E206	6/20/1796
Bostwick, David	Otsego, NY	16,000 A	$4,000	2/8/1795
Pepoon, Silas	Stockbridge, Berkshire, MA	Springhill Twp	E214	
Bostwick, Joseph	New Milford, Litchfield, CT	1/2 share	good cause	4/15/1793
Beardsley, Mehitable wf of Elisha	New Milford, Litchfield, CT		I148	12/6/1794
Bostwick, Joseph	New Milford, Litchfield, CT	all right	love	9/22/1794
Bostwick, Elnathan, son	New Milford, Litchfield, CT		I149	12/6/1794
Bott, William	Wilsborough, Clinton, NY	1 share	$10	4/30/1795
Douglass, Zebulon	Canaan, Columbia, NY		C591	7/7/1795
Boutel, Ezra*	Ashford, Windham, CT	Pwr Att to lay out 1 right		2/4/1795
Larrabee, Libbeus	Windham, Windham, CT		C607	7/9/1795
John Williams heir in law married 3/25/1790 to Cynthia Williams, dau John of Williams killed in the action at Susquehanna with the Indians, 1778; certified 6/5/1795 by Ashford Town Clerk				
Bowman, Samuel	Norwich, New London, CT	300 A	£60	3/22/1797
Osgood, Jeremiah	Norwich, New London, CT	Smithfield Twp	H137	9/14/1799

grantor grantee notes	grantor residence grantee residence	description location	amount acct bk page	deed date record date
Bowmen, Eliezer		1/2 share		4/5/1774
Ross, Jeremiah			WPR	
Boyd, John		three 1/2 shares	£23	10/23/1794
Eno, Erasmus			C447	10/23/1794
Bradford, James	Plainfield, Windham, CT	1 share	£5	9/10/1776
Wall, Henry	North Kingstown, Kings, RI		B348	10/1/1776
Bradley, Abraham	Litchfield, Litchfield, CT	two 1/2 shares	good cause	5/27/1782
Strong, Solomon, Capt	Claverack, Albany, NY		F197	8/2/1797
Bradley, Elisha	Fairfield, CT	1/2 share, part laid out	£14	2/25/1796
Bradley, Walter	Fairfield, CT	Augusta Twp	H2	10/13/1798
Bradley, Erastus, adm*	New Haven, Hartford, CT	1 share	good consideration	12/19/1794
Bishop, John	New Haven, New Haven, CT		E80	3/2/1796
Timothy Alling				
Bradley, Joel	North Haven, Hew Haven, CT	3/4 share*	£9	9/10/1794
Fowler, William	Guilford		C120	10/1/1794
1/2 self as OP & 1/4 John Spencer				
Bradley, Josiah				
Bradley, Samuel			A30	
Bradley, Timothy	Sunderland, Bennington, VT	1/2 twp in common	$2,200	3/25/1801
Pratt, Joel	Manchester, Bennington, VT	Beavertown Twp	H291	4/28/1801
Bradley, Timothy	Sunderland, Bennington, VT	4,724 A	$2,000	3/25/1801
Pratt, Joel 2nd	Manchester, Bennington, VT	Middlesex Twp	H294	4/28/1801
Bradley, Walter	Fairfield, CT	1400 A 2nd division land*	$5	9/29/1798
Morgan, Nathaniel			H3	10/13/1798
remainder after two half shares of 1st division land, 300 A each, laid out in Augusta Twp				
Bragg, Nicholas				
Arnold, Joseph			A108	
Bragg, Nicholas	Easton, Washington, NY	1 share	£6	3/12/1795
Janes, Eljh; Dole, Jas; Rathbun,	Troy, Rensselaer, NY		C127	8/9/1795
Janes and Dole merchants; Rathbun innkeeper				
Branch, Thomas	Preston, New London, CT	1 share	£100	12/8/1794
Hyde, Elisha	Norwich, New London, CT	Salem Twp 1/2; Cabot Twp 1/2	I132	12/25/1794
Brassett, James	Luzerne, PA	300 A	$100	9/18/1797
Wilcox, Symorris	Luzerne, PA	Sugar Creek	E547	12/8/1797
Breed, Gershom				
Bradley, Josiah			A221	
Breed, Gershom				
Millington, Samuel			A219	
Breed, Gershom				
White, William			A220	
Brett, Cornelius		1 share*	5s	8/28/1773
Parke, James			F239	12/5/1794
pt taxes pd by Benjamin Covey 12/5/1794				
Brewer, Daniel		1/2 share		2/7/1774
Allen, Joseph			GL	10/31/1774
Brewster, Jonah	Worthington, Hampshire, MA	1/2 share	$40	4/11/1796
Kenne, John			E294	6/20/1796
Brewster, Jonathan	Worthington, Hampshire, MA	1/2 share	$50	4/16/1796
Woodbridge, Stephen	Stockbridge, Berkshire, MA		E293 - B282	6/20/1796
Brockney, Bemen	Catskill, Albany, NY	3900 A, 2100 A, 900 A*	$1,950	5/3/1797
Livingston, John	Livingston, Columbia, NY	Athens, Burlington, Murraysfield	E544	10/24/1797
3900 A gore adj. Athens; 2,100 A Burlington; 900 A Lots 6, 26, 38, Murraysfield 300 A each				
Brockway, Reed	Athens, Luzerne, PA	1 1/4 shares (2,500 A)	$200	9/9/1799
Alger, George	Chatham, Columbia, NY		H95	9/11/1799
Brockway, Richard	Westmoreland, Westmrld, CT	1 share	£12	12/26/1776
Buck, Asahel	Westmoreland, Westmrld, CT		B359	6/19/1777
Brown, Abraham, son	Mount Pleasant, West Chester,	1,000 A +/ -	£400	5/9/1796
Rossell, John	West Chester, NY	Lackawanna R. SE of Providence	E488	12/6/1796
Brown, Abraham, son	Mount Pleasant, West Chester,	500 A	£52.10	5/9/1796
Russell, John	West Chester, NY	E side Lackawanna R	E489	12/6/1796
Brown, Benjamin	Southhold, Suffolk, NY	1/2 share	£10	9/20/1773
Lee, Joseph	Southold, Suffolk, NY		C22	10/17/1780

grantor grantee notes	grantor residence grantee residence	description location	amount acct bk page	deed date record date
Brown, Charles	New Fairfield, Fairfield, CT	1 share	£20	12/4/1794
Brush, Jonas	New Fairfield, Fairfield, CT		I194	3/29/1795
Brown, Daniel		16,000 A, except 1,000 A	$8,000	8/31/1795
Barney, Luke & Stone, John	Chesterfield, Hampshire, MA	Pittsfield Twp	C163	7/1/1797
Brown, Daniel	Freehold, Albany, NY	500 A (1/4 of 1/2 share)*		5/25/1797
Cowles, Ebenezer	Norfolk, Litchfield, CT	Brownington Twp	H100	9/3/1799
1/2 share Ebenezer Cowles to Daniel Brown 10/23/1794, see E505				
Brown, Daniel		Pwr Att revoked*		5/16/1795
Gardiner, John			E103	10/13/1796
Gardiner to sell and dispose 2 Twps of land, but sold only 1/4 Watertown Twp to Levi Thayer				
Brown, Daniel		1/2 share No. 12 of 400		12/9/1794
Harris, Thomas			E271	6/6/1796
Brown, Daniel	Freehold, Albany, NY	250 A (1/2 of 1/4 share)*		5/25/1797
Mills, Samuel	Norfolk, Litchfield, CT	Brownington Twp	H103	9/3/1799
1/4 share Samuel Mills to Daniel Brown 10/23/1794				
Brown, Daniel	Freehold, Albany, NY	500 A (1/4 of 1/2 share)*		5/18/1797
Riggs, Miles	Norfolk, Litchfield, CT	Rutland Twp	H102	9/3/1799
1/2 share Miles Riggs to Daniel Brown 10/23/1794				
Brown, Daniel Jr.	Freehold, Albany, NY	1,000 A (1/16 part undivided)	£150	5/13/1795
Cornwell, Ashbel	Mayfield, Montgomery, NY	Alba Twp	H317	10/26/1801
Brown, Daniel Jr.	Freehold, Green, NY	1,000 A (1/2 share)	$1,000	11/2/1801
Cornwell, Ashbell	Montgomery, NY	Orange Twp	H337	6/11/1802
Brown, Daniel Jr.	Freehold, Albany, NY	16,000 A	£100	11/8/1794
Hale, George	Catskill, Albany, NY	Fairfield Twp	C474	2/24/1795
Brown, Daniel Jr.	Freehold, Albany, NY	1/2 Rutland Twp	$3,000	11/27/1795
Moseley, Nathaniel T.	Pollot [Pawlet], Rutland, VT		E304	8/8/1796
Brown, Daniel Jr.	Freehold, Albany, NY	1 share	$100	6/14/1796
Pitkin, Elisha Jr.	East Hartford, Hartford, CT		E245	7/1/1796
Brown, David	Brookfield, Fairfield, CT	3 shares	£24	4/27/1795
Janes, Dole & Rathbun*	Troy, Rensselaer, NY		C641	8/9/1795
Elijah Janes & James Dole merchants; Wait Rathbun innkeeper				
Brown, Michael		1 share		8/6/1770
Weitman, Abraham			B197	3/28/1774
Brown, Samuel				
Davis, Benj & Joshua			A297	
Brown, Samuel				
Frishnet, Samuel			A471	
Brown, Samuel Jr.				
Hopkins, Noah			A282	
Brown, Solomon	Patridgefield, Berkshire, MA	2 shares*	$60	1/28/1796
Grant, Josiah	Poultney, Rutland, VT		E334	3/24/1796
"at the Risk of the said Josiah whether said Company's title is good or not"				
Brown, Thomas	Hebron, Tolland, CT	1/2 share	£10	1/23/1795
Swift, Silas	Lebanon, Windham, CT		I207	4/1/1795
Brown, William by Caleb Taylor		agent for a Twp survey	1/2 share	7/20/1795
Throop, Benjamin			C120.1	9/1/1795
for fifteen owners, including Throop, who pay Throop 6s per day for his time and horse; total of 8 shares; W. Brown 1/2 share				
Brownson, Abel	Woodbury, Litchfield, CT	150 A, Lot 17; 300 A	good cause	2/28/1795
Reed, Henry	Woodbury, Litchfield, CT	New Milford Twp; Wyalusing Cr.	C512	8/22/1795
Brownson, Benjamin & Matthew	New Milford, Litchfield, CT	1 share	48s	6/28/1794
Turrell/Terrill, Job Jr.	New Milford, Litchfield, CT	New Milford & Jenkinsboro*	C336	2/26/1795
New Milford Twp 600A; Jenkinsboro Twp 1400A				
Brownson, Isaac	Luzerne, PA	1/2 Lot 23	$150	1/19/1797
Terrill, Job	New Milford, CT	New Milford Twp	H25	9/5/1798
Brownson, Isaac and Terril	New Milford	750 A	1/4 share	1/19/1797
Wanzer, Abraham	New Fairfield, CT	Footsburgh Twp	H36	9/8/1798
Brownson, Josiah				
French, Thomas			A255	
Buck, Asahel	Westmoreland, Westmrld, CT	1/2 share	£10	5/27/1777
Beach, Zerah	Salisbury, Litchfield, CT		B358	6/19/1777
Buck, Asahel	Westmoreland, Litchfield, CT	1 share	£24	8/30/1774
Lothrop, Ebenezer Jr.	Norwich, New London, CT		B246	8/30/1774

grantor grantee notes	grantor residence grantee residence	description location	amount acct bk page	deed date record date
Buck, Jonathan	Amenia, Dutchess, NY	1/4 share, but not his settling right	Love	2/18/1774
Buck, Zadoc	Amenia, Dutchess, NY		C574	6/22/1795
Buck, William			A282	
Hopkins, Noah				
Buck, William	Tioga Co NY	4,900 A or 3 1/2 2nd Div rights*	£367	3/6/1795
Spalding, John	Luzerne Co PA		C614 - D33	7/1/1795
1 share David Pixley, B245; 1 share Elijah Buck, B247; 1 share William Buck, B244, 1/2 share Uriah Stevens to Gamaliel . Whiting to Wm Buck see "First Book of Deeds, page 66 [A66].				
Buck, William		rights Buck recd fr Spalding		10/6/1795
Wynkoop, William			D33 - C647	10/5/1795
Buckley, Eliphalet, Col., heir	Colchester, New London Co CT	1 share	1 share	1/22/1795
Turner, Seth	New Haven, New Haven CT		C216	2/25/1795
Bucklin, David	Herkimer, Herkimer, NY	all right*		3/8/1796
Bucklin, Benjamin, son	German Flatts, Herkimer, NY		E431	10/15/1796
Note appended dated Windham March 27, 1775 claims Bucklin entitled to 1/2 share in conflict with pervious records				
Bucklin, John	Coventry, Kent, RI	1/2 share	£9	4/5/1767
Belcher, Andrew, house wright	Providence, Providence, RI		B242	8/27/1774
Bucklin, Joseph	Coventry, Kent, RI	1/2 share	Love	3/11/1775
Nichols, Nathan & Philip, gsons	MA & NY*		B320	3/22/1775
New Providence MA; Socialbery, Otter Creek, NY				
Bull, David	Hartford, Hartford, CT	Pwr Att to locate 2 shares in 2 years	1/2 of located lands	1/12/1795
Ballard, Stephen/Chamberlain, S.	Judsboro, PA & Colebrook, CT	Union Twp and others	C625	7/1/1795
Bull, David			A378	
Goss, Phillip				
Bull, Isaac, estate*	Kent, Litchfield, CT	1 share	£5	9/10/1768
Skiff, Benjamin	Kent, Litchfield, CT		B343	2/7/1776
Swift, Elisha & Hubbel, Ephriam Jr. adms				
Bull, Isaac trustees			A285	
Swift, Elisha				
Bull, Thomas			A407	
Hooker, William				
Bull, Thomas	Woodbury, Litchfield, CT			
Hunt, John	Woodbury, Litchfield, CT		A50	
Bullard, Josiah		1/2 share		
Alden, Mason F.			GM	
Bullard, Josiah	Kingston Twp	1/2 share	£6	7/24/1773
Drake, Nathaniel	East Windsor, Hartford, CT		B142	2/21/1774
Bullard, Josiah	Kingston Twp	1/2 share	£6	7/24/1773
Lothrop, Lothrop & Rockwell*	East Windsor, Hartford, CT		B180	3/15/1774
Thatcher & Grant Lothrop; Samuel Rockwell				
Bullard, Josiah	S. Brimfield, Hampshire, MA	1/2 share	£37	2/7/1779
Parks, Oliver	S. Brimfield, Hampshire, MA	Fishing Creek	C6	4/15/1779
Bullard, Josiah		1/2 share		8/16/1773
Ross, Timothy			GH	
Bullard, Josiah		1/2 share		8/16/1774
Ross, Timothy			GM	
Bullard, Josiah				
Staples, John			GH	
Bullock, Nathaniel			A305	
Camp, William				
Bump, James	Amenia, Dutchess, NY	1/4 share	£1.10	7/5/1792
Hunt, Samuel	Kinderhook, Dutchess, NY		E99	3/1/1796
Burge, Daniel	Hebron, Hartford, CT		valuable sum	6/3/1755
Root, Jonathan	Hebron, Hartford, CT		B46	5/23/1772
Burgess, Joshua	Summer, Hartford, CT	1/2 share	£20	2/24/1775
Belding, Simeon	Hartford, Hartford, CT		C65	11/14/1782
Burghart, Henry	Kinderhook, Albany, NY	1 share	£40	6/10/1775
Hogeboom, Jeremiah	Claverack, Albany, NY		F270	3/14/1798
Burke, Edmund*		all right	$30	5/31/1796
Pope, Robert	Darby, New Haven, CT		E485	11/15/1796
husband of Mary Burke				
Burnham, Asahel		1/2 share of 400		6/28/1794
Marshall, Josiah			I97	6/28/1794

grantor grantee notes	grantor residence grantee residence	description location	amount acct bk page	deed date record date
Burnham, Elizer	Patridgfield, Berkshire, MA	1/2 share	£30	8/16/1786
Walker, William	Lenox, Berkshire, MA		E64	2/26/1796
Burnham, Elizur	Partridgefield, Berkshire, MA	1 share	£170	7/9/1782
Franklin, Gideon	Windsor, Berkshire, MA		C66	12/14/1782
Burnham, Elizur	Glastonbury	1 share	£60	4/9/1777
Leffingwell, Christopher	Norwich		C38	2/25/1782
Burnham, Elizur	Glastonbury, Hartford, CT	1/2 share	£6	3/27/1772
Loveland, Jonathan	Glastonbury, Hartford, CT		B47	4/3/1772
Burnham, Elizur	Glastonbury, Hartford, CT	1 share	£30	3/10/1774
Martin, William	Colchester, Hartford, CT		B180	3/10/1774
Burnham, Elizur	Glastonbury, Hartford, CT	1/2 share	£40	6/1/1774
Newcomb, Zachary	Great Nine Partners, Dutchess,		B274	11/11/1774
Burnham, Kenney*		1/2 share No. 212 of 400		6/28/1794
Marshall, Josiah		White Haven Twp	I97	6/28/1794
Asahel Burnham signing for Kenney Burnham				
Burr, John	Fairfield, Fairfield, CT	1/2 share	40s	5/16/1769
Hull, Cornelius	Fairfield, Fairfield, CT		B108	12/23/1773
Burr, Jonathan	Lansingburgh, Rensselaer, NY	3 shares	£320	1/17/1797
Grant, Josiah			E532	1/17/1797
Burrett, Stephen	Hanover, Luzerne, PA	15,000 A*	£1,550	2/10/1796
Lewis, Walker	Brookfield, Fairfield, CT	Burrettsfield Twp	E317	8/8/1796
Burrett reserves 1,000 A				
Burrough, Wm Y./ Magdalena, wf	Hudson, Columbia, NY	10 A, Lot 39, 2nd Div	$150	3/7/1798
Clarkson & Stratfield*	Livingston Manor, NY	Athens Twp	E553	5/1/1798
General Matthew Clarkson& Thomas Stratfield in trust for Catherine Livingston wf of John Livingston				
Burrows, Roswell	Stonington, New London, CT	1 share	$5	5/9/1796
Downer, Joshua	Preston, New London, CT		E241	7/4/1796
Burt, Henry	Taunton, Bristol, MA	Pwr Att to locate land		1/14/1795
Dorrance, Saml & Ward, Ichabod	Windham, Windham, CT		C389	2/22/1795
Burt, Joseph				
Perkins, James			A421	
Burwell, Jonathan	Tioga, NY	700 A in 2nd division*	£15	9/14/1796
Stephens, Ira	Athens, Luzerne, PA	Athens Twp	E442	9/16/1796
remainder of 1/2 share after 300 A in Athens				
Bush, Jonathan	Enfield, Hartford, CT	1 share	£12	9/11/1795
Brown, Daniel	Freehold, Albany, NY		F1	3/1/1796
Butler, Josiah	Cherry Valley, Otsego, NY	1/2 share	£10	6/10/1796
Bebee, Solomon	Athens, Luzerne, PA		E322	
Butler, Malachi	Woodbury, Litchfield, CT	1/4 share	£3	4/22/1772
Hende, Barzilla	Woodbury, Litchfield, CT		B132	1/20/1774
Butler, William		1/2 share		
Cole, Samuel			GM	
Byenton, Robert	Wallingford	1/8 share	£30	3/15/1755
Kirkum, John	Branford, New Haven, CT		B35	9/15/1773
Cady, Abijah	Canterbury, Windham, CT	1/2 share	£10	4/9/1774
Abbot, James	Windham, Windham, CT		B207	4/9/1774
Cady, Abijah				6/15/1773
Gallop, Wm & Smith, Tim			A214 - G	10/22/1774
Cady, Abijah	Canterbury, Windham, CT	1 share	£10	4/14/1795
Ward, Ichabod	Windham, Windham, CT		E55	2/24/1796
Cady, Jeremiah	Gageborough, Berkshire, MA	1/2 share	£30	3/12/1778
Dean, Ezra	West Greenwich, Kent, RI		B385	4/8/1778
Cady, Jeremiah	Gageborough, Berkshire, MA	1/2 share	£40	4/7/1774
Hall, John	Canaan, Litchfield, CT		B207	4/15/1774
Cady, Jeremiah	Gageborough	1/2 share	£25	9/10/1774
Norton, Zebulon	Ashueloit Equivalent		C1	9/11/1779
Cady, Jeremiah		1/2 share		4/6/1777
Owen, Samuel			GH	
Cady, John, estate*	Plainfield, Windham, CT	Pwr Att to locate right		1/10/1795
Spalding, John	Ulster, Luzerne, PA		C614	7/1/1795
Joanna Cady, adm				
Cady, William	Ashulot, Berkshire, MA	1/2 share	£9	9/15/1773
Clark, Ezekiel & Heath, Joseph	Noble Town, Albany, NY		B152	3/8/1773

grantor / grantee / notes	grantor residence / grantee residence	description / location	amount / acct bk page	deed date / record date
Cady, William		1/2 share		
Morgan, Roswell			A237 - G	
Cady, William Jr.	Plainfield, Windham, CT	1/4 share	£3.10	2/16/1770
Cady, John	Plainfield, Windham, CT		B203	4/6/1774
Calkin, Moses		all right except 300 A in Burlington	value received	6/8/1796
Beebe, Solomon			E332	4/10/1796
Calkin, Moses		1/2 share No. 362 of 600	$20	1/19/1796
Shepard, John			E331	4/10/1796
Camp, Amos	Wallingford, New Haven, CT	2 shares	£2	5/9/1782
Halls, Joseph Doct	Wallingford, New Haven, CT		C48	9/25/1782
Camp, Enos	New Milford, Litchfield, CT	1 share	£50	1/18/1774
French, Isaac; Foster, Samuel	Voluntown, CT; Scituate, RI		B124	1/21/1774
Campbell, James	Hanover, Luzerne, PA	all right	$8,000	5/6/1796
Bulkley, James & Clark, Samuel	Middletown, Middlesex, CT	Spring Gardens Twp	D180	8/9/1796
Campbell, James		1 share, No. 93 of 600 ex 600 A		
Spalding, William		Juddsburgh Twp	H118	11/25/1799
Campbell, James, estate*	Milton, Chittenden, VT	1/2 share	$10	5/12/1795
Douglass, Zebulon	Canaan, Columbia, NY		C592	7/7/1795
Nathan Campbell, adm				
Campbell, Samuel & Anna, wf	Athens, Luzerne, PA	306 A*	$300	6/14/1799
Roberts, Gilbert	Walkill, Orange, NY	Litchfield, Luzerne, PA	H70	6/14/1799
Campbell reserves choice of mill seat in tract with road to and from and 1/2 A adj. for lumber yard and privilege of building 15 ft dam				
Campbell, William	South Hero, Chittenden, VT	2 shares	valuable sum	2/26/1795
Stoddard, Philo	Woodbury, Litchfield, CT		C631	7/10/1795
Canfield, Joseph	New Milford, Litchfield, CT	1/2 share	£20	12/2/1773
Wheeler, Joseph	Woodbury, Litchfield, CT		B133	1/20/1774
Canfield, Samuel				
Canfield, Joseph			A69	
Canfield, Samuel				
Rundel, Joseph			A85	
Canfield, Samuel	New Milford, Litchfield, CT	2 shares	10s	9/2/1794
Terrill, Job & Brownson, Isaac	New Milford, Litchfield, CT	New Milford Twp	I151	
Canfield, Seba		700 A 2nd division land	$30	3/1/1795
Brown, Daniel		Burlington Twp	E354	7/20/1796
Canfield, Seba	Luzerne, PA	1/2 of 2 half shares after first division	$30	3/1/1795
Brown, Daniel		Murraysfield & Juddsburgh Twps	E355	7/20/1796
Canfield, Seba, blacksmith	Luzerne Co, PA	300 A, Lot 27	£100	9/5/1795
Caulkins, Moses	Luzerne Co, PA	Juddsburgh Twp	I230	9/7/1795
Canfield, Thomas				
Eaton, Joseph			A335	
Canfield, Thomas				
Hicock, Nathaniel			A336	
Carew, Simeon	Norwich	1 share	£12.10	7/18/1771
Clements, Jeremiah	Norwich		C80	12/25/1782
Carey, Samuel				
Bailey, Richard			A240	
Carey, William				
Utley, John			A441	
Carney, William	Tunkhannock, Luzerne, PA	1 share No. 87 of 600*	$20	12/23/1795
Shepard, John	Athens, Luzerne, PA		E328	4/10/1796
except 600 A in Mahoopen; see Kerney				
Carpenter, Carel				
Kasson, William			A267	
Carpenter, Comfort A.	Cranston, Providence, RI	400 A	$300	12/11/1800
Arnold, Ephriam	Warwick, Kent, RI		H302	6/9/1801
Carpenter, Comfort A.	Providence, Providence, RI	1/2 share	$90	10/10/1799
Satterlee, Elias	Athens, Luzerne, PA		H304	6/1/1800
Carpenter, Comfort A.	Providence, Providence, RI	8,000 A	$4,000	5/12/1800
Thayer, Levi	Athens, Luzerne, PA	Bloomfield Twp	H305	6/24/1801
Carpenter, Nathan		1/2 share		
Clark, William Jr.			GC	
Carpenter, Nathan	Hardwick, Worcester, MA	1 share	£12	3/8/1774
Washburn, Joseph	New Braintree, Worcester, MA		B210	4/25/1774

grantor grantee notes	grantor residence grantee residence	description location	amount acct bk page	deed date record date
Carpenter, Zenas	Bolton, Tolland, CT	1/16 of 4,000 A [250 A]	$200	2/18/1797
Loomis, Silas	Bolton, Tolland, CT	Bowdoin Twp	H97	9/20/1799
Carr, Robert		1/2 share		2/10/1776
Shaw, Daniel			GH	2/16/1776
Carver, David	Hebron, Hartford, CT	1/2 share & 1/12 share*	£6	4/20/1769
Carver, Samuel	Bolton, Hartford, CT		B193	3/23/1774
Amos Stiles, OP				
Carver, Samuel	Bolton, Tolland, CT	1/2 share & 1/12 share*	£40	9/25/1795
Pitkin, Elisha Jr.	East Hartford, Hartford, CT		E284	6/6/1796
Carver pd 12s taxes on Amos Stiles share 4/27/1772				
Cary, Comfort, heir*	Hanover, Luzerne, PA	1 proprietor's right*	£18.15	7/9/1795
Perry, Ben	Wilkesbarre, Luzerne, PA		E301	6/8/1796
Eleazer Cary OP; certified by Zebulon Butler 5/18/1795				
Cary, Jabez	Mansfield, Windham, CT	1/2 share	£15	3/12/1776
Allen, Eleazar	Stafford, Hartford, CT		C59	11/11/1782
Case, Benjamin	Simsbury, Hartford, CT	Pwr Att to locate 1/4 share in 2 years	1/2 of located lands	1/15/1795
Ballard, Steph & Chamberlain, S C	Judsboro, PA & Colebrook, CT		C626	7/1/1795
Case, Caleb	Simsbury, Hartford, CT	Pwr to locate 1/2 share	1/2 of land located	1/15/1795
Ballard, Steph & Chamberlain, S C	Judsboro, PA & Colebrook, CT		C625	7/1/1795
Case, Chloe et al*	Landisfield, Berkshire, MA	3/12 of 1 share	£6	12/26/1794
Benton, Elihu	Guilford, New Haven, CT		D56	11/16/1795
Griswold, Wealthy & Oliver				
Case, Daniel	Simsbury, Hartford, CT	1 share	$60	10/22/1795
Hyde, Ezekiel	Norwich, New London, CT		I253	12/4/1795
Case, James estate*	Simsbury, Hartford, CT	1/4 share	£7.10	10/29/1773
Ensign, Samuel	New Hartford, Litchfield, CT		B184	3/10/1774
Josiah Case 2nd, Isaac Fuller, Phebe Fuller, heirs				
Case, James, heir of James Case	London, Berkshire, MA	1 share	£15	12/13/1794
Twining, William Jr.	Granville, Hampshire, MA		F9	3/1/1796
Case, James, heirs*	Simsbury, Hartford, CT	1/2 share	£15	10/29/1773
Ensign, Otis	New Hartford, Hartford, CT		B119	1/11/1774
Jeremiah Case, Francis Garrat, Ruth Garret				
Case, Joseph	Norfolk, Orange, VT	all right	$30	6/14/1793
Bartlet, John	Cabot, Orange, VT		E131	3/28/1796
Case, Joseph	Simsbury, Hartford, CT	all right	£8	4/4/1781
Case, Joseph Jr. et al	Simsbury & Norfolk CT		C149	2/24/1794
Solomn, Hosia, Jedediah, Benajah, Ashael Case				
Case, Roger	Simsbury, Hartford, CT	Pwr to locate 1/4 share	1/2 of land located	1/16/1795
Ballard, Steph & Chamberlain, S C	Judsboro PA & Colebrook, CT		C624	7/1/1795
Case, Stephen	Ulster Co, NY	1/2 share	£50	2/5/1773
Lawyer, Johanas H.	Schoharie, Albany, NY		B227	7/6/1774
Case, Zacheus				
Woodruff, Judah			A472	
Catlin, Jonathan	Harwinton, Litchfield, CT	rights of a $9 purchase	£10.10	2/12/1774
Austin, Aaron	Torrenton, Litchfield, CT		B182	3/10/1774
Caulfield, Samuel	New Milford, Litchfield, CT	1 share	certain sum	5/9/1775
Brownson, Josiah	Woodbury, Litchfield, CT		B329	6/23/1775
Center, Jonathan		1/2 share, No. 170 of 400	£5	
Pixley, David	Owego, NY		E67	2/26/1796
Center, Robert & Williams, Elisha	Richmond & Hillsdale	1/2 share	$100	1/2/1797
Spencer, Nehemiah & Segar,	Kinderhook & Chatham	Rutland Twp	E526	3/14/1797
laid out in Rutland 7/27/1798; removed from Rutland and entered in Alba 12/5/1800				
Chaffe, Jonathan Jr.	Ashford, Windham, CT	1/2 share	£20	9/20/1773
Rogers, Joseph	Ashford, Windham, CT		B347	6/15/1776
Chalker, Daniel	Colebrook, Litchfield, CT	Pwr Att to lot out my right	1/2 all charges	1/27/1795
Ballard, Stephen	Judsborough, Luzerne, PA	Union Twp, on Towandee Cr.	C622	7/1/1795
Chalker, Daniel	Saybrook, New London, CT	1/2 share	£100	10/16/1781
Harley, Thomas	Saybrook, Middlesex, CT	Winchester Twp	F49	5/1/1796
Chamberlain, John	Thetford, Albany, NY	1/2 share	£8	5/17/1772
Porter, Jonah	Lebanon, Windham, CT		B41	5/23/1772
Chamberlain, John		1/2 share		
Spafford, Josiah			GC	

grantor	grantor residence	description	amount	deed date
grantee	grantee residence	location	acct bk page	record date
notes				
Chapman, Caleb	Stockbridge, Berkshire, MA	1/2 share	$30	11/5/1795
Chapman, James	Stockbridge, Berkshire, MA		F189	7/19/1797
Chapman, James	Stockbridge, Berkshire, MA	Pwr Att to locate 1/2 share		9/24/1796
Tucker, John	Stockbridge, Berkshire, MA		F189	7/19/1797
Chapman, Joseph et al	Norwalk and Fairfield,	1/2 share except lot in Augusta Twp	$10	9/29/1798
Morgan, Nathaniel	Weston, Fairfield, CT		H8	10/13/1798
Albert, James, John, Phinehas Chapman				
Chapman, Nathaniel	Weston, Fairfield, CT	3/4 twp	$5,000	11/5/1798
Chapman: Jos, James, John, Joshua	Fairfield, CT	Granby Twp	H31	1/24/1798
Chapman, Noah estate*	New London, New London, CT	1/2 share	£6	9/3/1794
Lester, Eliphalet	Saybrook, Middlesex, CT		D9	9/18/1795
Jason Chapman, adm				
Chase, Benjamin	Hudson, NY	1 share, No. 56 of 600		4/28/1795
Whitaker, Ephriam	Hudson, NY	Richmond Twp	H319	10/26/1802
Chase, Benjamin	Hudson, NY	4 shares, Nos. 63,64, 67, 68 of the		4/28/1795
Whitaker, Ephriam		Richmond Twp	H333	5/21/1802
Chase, Benjamin	Hudson, Columbia, NY	1 share, No. 55 of 600	val recd	4/28/1795
Whitaker, Ephriam	Hudson, Columbia, NY	Richmond Twp	H319	10/26/1802
Chase, Solomon*	Amenia, Dutchess, NY	Lot 10, 340 A*	£15	3/26/1773
Rice, Stephen	Canaan, Litchfield, CT	Plymouth Twp	B64	6/3/1773
heir of Joseph Chase, decd; 30 A lower tier lot and 210 A to be laid out				
Chatfield, Joseph		1/2 share		
Yale, Benjamin			A86 - E408	
Chauncey, Worthington G.	Durham, New Haven, CT	1/2 share	$50	2/21/1795
Brown, Daniel	Freehold, Albany, NY		C444	2/21/1795
Chauncey, Worthington Gallop	Durham, New Haven, CT	1/2 share	$50	2/24/1795
Brown, Daniel	Freehold, Albany, NY		C442	2/21/1795
Cheney, Ebenezer		1 share*		
Moriss, David	Sturbridge, Hampshire, MA		C440 - A434	4/14/1795
all taxes pd to June 17, 1772				
Chew, Joseph				
DeNoyelles, John			A296	
Chick, John	Simsbury, Hartford, CT	1 share	£20	8/3/1776
Howard, Peter	Surry, Chester, NH		B351	2/6/1777
Chittenden, Daniel Jr.	Guilford, New Haven, CT	1/2 share	£12	9/18/1794
Fowler, William	Guilford, New Haven, CT		C119	10/1/1794
Chittenden, James	Freehold, Albany, NY	1/4 share	£40	8/15/1794
Brown, Daniel Jr.	Freehold, Albany, NY		C380	2/28/1795
Choate, John Jr.	Norwich, New London, CT	1/7 share	£6	7/28/1777
Witter, Ebenezer Capt			C58	11/11/1782
Choate, William	Norwich, New London, CT	1 share*		2/27/1775
Gore, Obadiah Capt	Westmoreland, Litchfield, CT	Ulster Twp	I42 - I44	8/17/1786
Originally 1/2 Cabbanashanna 8/9/1773; 1/2 Northmoreland Twp				
Choate, William	Norwich, New London, CT	1/7 share	£7.5	9/18/1782
Witter, Ebenezer, Jr. Capt.	Preston, CT	New Groton Twp	C56	11/11/1782
Church, Almond	Kingston, Luzerne, PA	16,000 A	$5,000	11/14/1795
Booth, John	Hudson, Columbia, NY	Millsbury Twp	F16	4/23/1796
Church, Joseph	Hartford, Hartford, CT		£3	6/28/1794
Brown, Daniel	Freehold, Albany, NY		C477	2/1/1795
Church, Silas	New London, New London, CT	Lots 4 & 11*	1/2 Lot 4 & house	4/6/1775
Hamilton, Gurdon	Colchester, Hartford, CT	Allfield Twp	C459	2/21/1795
Hamilton agrees to build 2 log dwellings 16' x 18' with shingle roofs on 5 A each & to fence & till. Hamilton has use and income for 3 years then all but 1/2 lot 4 except the house goes to Church.				
Church, Silas estate*	New London, New London, CT	all right	£3	7/4/1794
Elliot, William	Saybrook, Middlesex, CT		C450	2/21/1795
Marvin Waite, adm				
Church, William	Cambridge, Washington, NY	1 share	$5	6/15/1795
Church, Alanson	Cambridge, Washington, NY		C555	8/10/1795
Churchel, William		all right	£15	1/8/1796
Terrel, Job			E128	3/1/1796
Churchill, Benjamin	Bristol, Hartford, CT	1/2 share	good cause	8/29/1794
Robards [Roberts], Seth	Paris, Herkimer, NY		C637	7/29/1795
Churchill, Jessee	Weathersfield, Hartford, CT	1/2 share	£20	8/25/1794
Robards [Roberts], Seth	Whitestown NY		C640	7/29/1795

grantor grantee notes	grantor residence grantee residence	description location	amount acct bk page	deed date record date
Clapp, Elijah	Hartford, Hartford, CT	1 share	£25	8/18/1774
Bull, David	Hartford, Hartford, CT		B234	8/19/1774
Clark, Abel	Killingsworth, Middlesex, CT		£15	9/15/1794
Lester, Eliphalet	Saybrook, Middlesex, CT		D11	9/18/1795
Clark, Abel	Windham, Windham, CT	1 share	£5	2/3/1795
Swift, Silas	Lebanon, Windham, CT		I206	4/1/1795
Clark, Abner		1/2 share		5/6/1775
Bullard, Josiah			GM	
Clark, Benjamin		1/2 share		1/27/1773
Pratt, Samuel			GM	
Clark, Benjamin of Hebron	Wilkes Barre Twp	1/4 share	£5	2/11/1773
Post, Thomas Jr.	Hebron, Hartford, CT		B95	12/1/1773
Clark, Ezekiel	Claraden, Bennington, VT	1/2 share	£50	6/28/1780
White, Simpson	Claraden, Bennington, VT		C23	2/28/1781
Clark, Gamaliel	Stockbridge, Berkshire, MA	4,000 A	$1,000	11/19/1795
Wynkoop, William	Chemung, Tioga, NY	Cato Twp, NE 1/4	F219	11/1/1797
Clark, James, Nathan & Zachariah	Huntington, Fairfield, CT	Pwr Att*		3/12/1795
Bostwick, Dimon	New Milford, Litchfield, CT		E473	11/28/1796
to locate 1 share & to collect father's fee for selling 33 whole shares				
Clark, John	Juddsburgh, PA	700 A		6/26/1793
Scovell, Champion		Juddsburgh Twp, 2nd division	C397	8/24/1795
Clark, John estate	Colchester, Hartford, CT	1/2 share	£12	12/23/1773
Wells, Amos	Colchester, Hartford, CT		B188	3/9/1774
Clark, John Sr., insolvent debtor	Colchester, Hartford, CT	2 parcels: 63 A and 20 A*		9/17/1772
Clark, John Jr., trustees		Colchester, Hartford, CT	B192	3/9/1774
Clark, Oliver	Montgomery, Hampshire, MA	1/2 share	£16	4/11/1796
Squire, Amasa	Montgomery, Hampshire, MA		F44	4/23/1796
Clark, Samuel	Middletown, Middlesex, CT	4,000 A*	$400	1/14/1797
Canfield, Samuel & Foot, William	Middletown and E Haddam, CT	Hannibal Twp	E527	2/7/1797
deed void if Canfield and Foot cannot collect on court case involving payment for watches which Clark sold for them.				
Clark, Samuel & Buckley, James	Middletown, Middlesex, CT	16,000 A	$8,000	6/25/1796
Lathrop, Benjamin	Worthington, Hampshire, MA	Venus Twp	H28	9/13/1798
Clark, Stephen	New Providence, Berkshire,	1/2 share	£30	1/22/1776
Ballard, Joseph	East Hoosick, Berkshire, MA		C83	2/12/1783
Clark, Stephen	Berkshire, MA	all rights	$5	1/10/1795
Sherman, Daniel & Co.	Adams, Berkshire, MA		I152	1/18/1795
Clark, Stephen	Clarkesborough, Berkshire, MA	1/2 share, 1,000 A	$4	1/15/1802
Taylor, David	Wilmington, Windham, VT		H339	6/14/1802
Clark, William	Gageborough, Berkshire, MA	1 share	£40	1/31/1777
Dean, Ezra	West Greenwich, Kent, RI		B369	3/26/1777
Clark, William	Middletown, Ontario, NY	1/2 share	£10	12/5/1795
Hann, Michael	Southbury, Litchfield, CT		H91	8/19/1799
Clark, William, Capt		1/2 share		
Walker, Edward			GC	
Clark, William Jr.		1/2 share		3/1/1774
Lee, Jonathan			GC	
Clark, Zachariah		Pwr Att		9/13/1794
Lester, Eliphalet			D10	9/18/1795
Cleaveland, Josiah				
Lawrence, Isaac			A461	
Cleaveland, Josiah				
Whitney, Joshua			A474	
Cleaveland, Moses	Canterbury, Windham, CT	Pwr Att*		5/14/1796
Larrabee, Lebbeus	Windham, Windham, CT		H312	8/11/1801
to locate and lay out 1/2 share Capt Aaron Cleaveland and 1/2 share William Foster, Sr. both late of Canterbury, CT				
Clefts, Wells & Mary, wife*	Fairfield, Fairfield, CT	all right	$40	5/10/1796
Sherwood, Moses	Fairfield, Fairfield, CT		E180	6/1/1796
Heirs of John Hazzard				
Clemence, Thomas	Johnston, Providence, RI	1/5 share undivided land	£1.9	4/21/1797
Carpenter, Nicholas	Johnstown, Providence, RI		H264	6/17/1799
Clement, Jeremiah	Norwich, New London, CT	1/2 share	£16	5/18/1760
Clark, Oliver	Norwich, New London, CT		F43	4/23/1796

grantor grantee notes	grantor residence grantee residence	description location	amount acct bk page	deed date record date
Clement, Jeremiah		1 share and 300 A		4/20/1775
Dellano, Richard		Berlin Twp*	GC	
no record as a granted twp but mentioned B267, C530				
Clement, Jeremiah				
Hall, Joshua			A107	
Clement, Jeremiah				
Lester, Eliphalet			A364	
Clement, Jeremiah		1 share to be "paid the old way"	£20*	8/10/1779
Lester, Eliphalet			F30	4/23/1796
Clement, Jeremiah				
Whitman, Zerubabel			A106	
Clements, Jeremiah	Norwich, New London, CT	1/2 share	£12	6/3/1771
Avery, Christopher	Norwich, New London, CT		B27	8/30/1773
Clements, Jeremiah	Norwich, New London, CT	3500 A*	£75	4/12/1775
Egery, Daniel	Dartmouth, Bristol, MA	Berlin Twp	C530	5/1/1795
300 A laid out as ff: 100 A, Lot 11, Div 1; 100 A, No. 11 Tier 8; 100 A, No. 8, 3rd Div, Tier 4; no record as a granted twp but mentioned B267; shows that Berlin was surveyed before 4/12/1775				
Clements, Jeremiah	Norwich, New London, CT	1 share	£12	3/15/1770
Robertson, Patrick	New London, New London, CT		C359	3/2/1795
Clements, Jeremiah	Norwich	1 share	£46	2/23/1780
Winship, Jabez	New London		C15	3/7/1780
Clerk, John		1/2 share		1/1/1774
Fitch, Samuel			GC	
Clerk, William		1/2 share		2/24/1774
Walker, Edward			GC	
Cleveland, Aaron	Norwich, New London, CT	two 1/2 shares*	$150	11/19/1798
Dodge, David. L.	Norwich, New London, CT	Seeleysborough Twp & DP	H141	9/14/1799
1/2 share inc. 300 A Seeleysborough Twp, remainder exchanged for land in Delaware Purchase				
Cleveland, Aaron	Norwich, New London, CT	Pwr Att for two 1/2 shares*		2/13/1796
Hyde, Ezekiel	Norwich, New London, CT	Seelysboro Twp	F38	4/23/1796
to rent and/or sell 2,000 A				
Cleveland, Clark		Minister's or Parsonage Lot 4th Div	$500	4/29/1800
Redington, John		Athens Twp adj. school lot	H215	5/16/1800
Cluckston, John estate*	Reading, Fairfield, CT	1/2 share, abt 900 A	£4.10	8/4/1794
Morgan, Nathaniel	Reading, Fairfield, CT		C532	5/1/1795
William Hamilton, adm				
Cmte to Lease Public Lots,		909 yr lease to Minister's Lot	1¢ yr for 6 yrs*	8/15/1797
Cleveland, Clark or leasee		Athens Twp adj. school lot	H214	5/16/1800
John Franklin, Elisha Satterlee, Elisha Matthewson; $10.00 annual after 6 yrs				
Cockson, James		1/2 share		
Thayer, David			GC	
Cockson, Samuel		1 share		12/6/1774
Cockson, James [son]			GC	1/9/1775
Cockson, Samuel		1/2 share		
Cockson, James, son			GC	
Cogshall, John	Alford, Berkshire, MA	1 share	£15	2/28/1775
Spencer, Asa	Salisbury		C26	11/19/1781
Cogswell, Daniel	Sandgate, Bennington, VT	3 shares	£9	4/9/1795
Tuttle, Joseph	Sandgate, Bennington, VT		C643	8/9/1795
Cogswell, John	Sandgate, Bennington, VT	1 share	s40	3/2/1795
Cogswell, Daniel	Sandgate, Bennington, VT		C642	8/9/1795
Cole, David	Waterbury, New Haven, CT	1 share	£15	11/4/1767
Barnes, Ebenezer & Amos	Farmington, Hartford, CT		A78 - B238	8/24/1774
Cole, David				
Frisby, Zebulon			A79	
Cole, David				
Tibbel, Thomas			A449	
Cole, David				
Yale, Job			A96	
Cole, Ebenezer		1 share		
Dodge, Rufus			GC	
Cole, Leonard	Awago, Tioga, NY	1/2 share*	£6	3/2/1795
Stephens, Ira	Athens, Luzerne, PA		E327	4/10/1796
granted by Susq Co in 1784 for services, certificate given 1785				

grantor	grantor residence	description	amount	deed date
grantee	grantee residence	location	acct bk page	record date
notes				
Cole, Samuel Jr.		1/2 share*		3/7/1774
Mills, John			GC	
taxes pd by John Mills to Z. Butler				
Cole, Stephen	Athens, Luzerne, PA	Lot 46	$26	12/3/1795
Hyde, Ezekiel	Norwich, New London, CT	Athens, Luzerne, PA	I255	12/4/1795
Cole, Stephen	Athens, Luzerne, PA	Town Lot 26 and Meadow Lot 25*	£80	3/16/1796
Paine, David	Athens, Luzerne, PA	Athens Twp	E117	3/17/1796
all land purchased from Thomas Baldwin 1/14/1792 except Lot 19				
Colegrove, Francis	Voluntown, Windham, CT	1 share	£10	11/8/1791
Colegrove, Samuel	Stephentown, Albany, NY		C271	3/3/1795
Coleman, Josiah & Elihu	Sharon, Litchfield, CT	two 1/2 shares*	£8	12/22/1795
Hunt, Salmon	Canaan, Litchfield, CT		E248	7/1/1796
Gawn Miller & Peter Swetland, OP; Coleman pd taxes 1783, 1785 on Swetland 1/2				
Coleman, Niles	Colchester, Hartford, CT	1/2 share	£7	4/2/1768
Porter, Amos	Lebanon, Windham, CT		B42	5/23/1772
Coleman, Thomas		1/2 share. 300 A	val con	9/1/1795
Brown, George		Enfield Twp	I231	9/9/1795
Coleman, Thomas		Pwr Att to locate	1/3 part land	11/4/1795
Gordon, Samuel			F52	5/1/1796
Coley, David Jr.	Bolton, Fairfield, CT	1/2 share	$21	4/17/1795
Lacy, Josiah & Burr, Ozias	Fairfield Co CT		C516	5/1/1795
Colgrove, Samuel	Irwin, Ontario, NY	1 share	£50	3/13/1795
Teal, Nathan	Newtown, Tioga, NY		C307	3/14/1795
Collins, Ambrose	Tioga, Luzerne, PA	3,480 A	£50	12/18/1799
Hutchinson, John	Ulster, Luzerne, PA	Graham Twp, south part	H177	1/1/1800
Collins, Ambrose	Farmington, Hartford, CT	1/2 share	£30	5/17/1774
Judd, Enoch	Westmoreland, Litchfield, CT		B307	1/28/1775
Collins, Benjamin				
Collins, Zerubbabel			A383	
Collins, Jedediah	Luzerne, PA	1/2 share	val con	2/2/1796
Smith, Benjamin			E321	4/10/1796
Collins, John	Mayfield, Tryon, NY	1/2 share	£13.6.8	12/3/1773
Mallery, Samuel	Claverack, Albany, NY		B150	3/8/1774
Collins, Josiah	Windham	1/4 share	£40	12/1/1779
Griffin, Benjamin	Windham		C11	12/6/1779
Collins, Josiah	Hampton, Windham, CT	1/4 share*	10s	1/27/1795
Larrabee, Libbeus	Windham, Windham, CT		C364	3/2/1795
except 50 A lot in Salem sold to Jabez Adams				
Collins, Zerubbabel	Lebanon, Windham, CT	1/2 share, equal parts	£3	4/15/1771
Collins: Benj, Josiah, Saml, Julius	Mansfield, Windham, Hanover,		B21	4/16/1773
Colt, Harris	Lyme, New London, CT	1 share	£3	3/10/1794
Elliot, William	Saybrook, Middlesex, CT		C451	2/21/1795
Colt, Harris	Lyme, New London, CT	1/2 share	£3	3/10/1794
Elliot, William	Saybrook, Middlesex, CT		C460	2/2/1795
Colt, Harrison				
Colt, Joseph			A366	
Colt, Harrison	Lyme	1/2 share		10/12/1770
Morgan, Samuel			A366	
Colver, Samuel				
McNeal, Archibald			A250	
Colver, Zebulon				
McNeal, Archibald			A249	
Colvin, Benjamin				
Colvin, Caleb			A280	
Colvin, Benjamin	?ington, Albany, NY	1/2 share	£18	1/8/1777
Dean, Ezra	West Greenwich, Kent, RI		B368	3/26/1777
Committee of Settlers*		1 settling right, 400 A*		2/20/1775
Williams, Peter		Six Mile Township*	H119	7/6/1800
Zebulon Butler, Ezekiel Peirce, Stephen Fuller, Obadiah Gore, Jr.; recd WR 2/27/1775; originally planned for Muncey Cr. on West Branch, but relocated and named Huntington Twp				
Conant, Shubal	Mansfield, Windham, CT	1 share	£30	3/8/1774
Gray, Ebenezer	Windham, Windham, CT		B250	3/21/1774

grantor	grantor residence	description	amount	deed date
grantee	grantee residence	location	acct bk page	record date
notes				
Cone, John Sr., estate*	East Haddam, Hartford, CT	1/2 share	£10	3/16/1774
Ackley, Joseph	East Haddam, Hartford, CT		B186	3/19/1774
John Cone Jr. and Alamander Cone, heirs				
Cook, Abel	Harwinton, Litchfield, CT	400 A settling right	£200	1/6/1774
Sedgwick, Benjamin	Canaan, Litchfield, CT	Hanover Twp	B116	1/12/1774
Cook, John	Hebron, Tolland, CT	1 share	£5	1/24/1795
Swift, Silas	Lebanon, Windham, CT		C345	2/27/1795
Cook, Nathaniel	Tunkhannock, Luzerne, PA	two 1/2 shares	£50	4/9/1795
Shepard, John	Tioga, Luzerne, PA		E329	4/10/1795
Cook, Reuben	Tioga, Lycoming, PA	500 A undivided	$50	1/24/1799
Wheeler, Walter	Ulster, Luzerne, PA	Suttonfield Twp	H29 - H61	1/7/1799
Cook, Samuel				
Cook, Samuel, son			A483	
Cook, Samuel	New Haven, New Haven, CT	1/2 share	val sum	11/5/1773
Dorchester, Benjamin	New Haven, New Haven, CT		B111	12/16/1773
Cook, Samuel		1/2 share		8/27/1773
Edmons, Robert			GC	12/7/1774
Cook, William & Cook, Margaret	NY City and New Haven CT		£30	11/26/1794
Worthington, William, Col.	New Haven, New Haven CT		C298	3/4/1795
Cooke, Nathaniel	Southington, Hartford, CT	1 share	good cause	8/21/1794
Robards [Roberts], Seth	Paris, Herkimer, NY		C636	7/29/1795
Coon, James	Salisbury, Litchfield, CT	1/2 share	£18	3/2/1775
Fellows, Ephriam & Nathan	Canaan, Litchfield, CT		I9	6/5/1786
Coon, John heirs*	Salisbury, CT	1/4 & 1/8 share	£18	4/30/1774
Steavens, Ebenezer	Salisbury, CT		C3	7/27/1779
Elizabeth and James Coon				
Cooper, Jemima	Stockbridge, Berkshire, MA	1 share	$20	5/20/1796
Woodbridge, Stephen	Stockbridge, Berkshire, MA		E295	6/20/1796
Cooper, Thomas				
Robert, Jabez			A88	
Corey, Benjamin	Tioga, Luzerne Co PA	1/2 share	$50	2/20/1795
Platt, Daniel	Durham, Albany Co NY		C197	2/28/1795
Cornish, Jabez				
Spaulding, Deliverence			A425	
Cornwell, Ashbell	Mayfield, Montgomery, NY	100 A	$40	6/2/1802
Canary, James	Mayfield, Montgomery, NY	Litchfield Twp	H337	6/11/1802
Cortwright, Cornelius	Wilkesbarre, Luzerne, PA	1 share*	£30	1/15/1795
Hutchinson, John	Tioga, Luzerne, PA		D49	9/2/1795
original share to William Ladley for service to Susquehanna Company				
Cory, Benjamin	Athens, Luzerne, PA	1/2 share	$35	5/14/1795
Shepard, John	Tioga, Luzerne, PA		E323	4/10/1796
Cory, Jabez		1/2 share		3/12/1774
Allen, Ebenezer			GG	
Cory, Joseph	Salem, Luzerne, PA	1/2 share	$20	4/17/1795
Hyde, William & Blackman,			F86	9/17/1795
Cotgrove, Jonathan		Pwr Att to locate	1/3 part land	11/27/1795
Gordon, Samuel			F52	5/1/1796
Cotton, Henry	Longmeadow, Hampshire, MA	1/2 share	$40	2/2/1795
Kingsbury, Lemuel	Enfield, Hartford, CT		C589	6/25/1795
Couch, Benoni & Elizabeth, bro/sis	Sandfield, Berkshire, MA	1 share	£12	12/5/1794
Twining, William Jr.	Granville, Hampshire, MA		C430	2/1/1795
Couch, Gideon	Greenfield, Fairfield, CT	1/5 share*	£4.16	1/25/1795
Sherwood, Moses	Fairfield Co CT		C521	5/1/1795
Thomas Couch, OP, father, decd.				
Cowles, Ebenezer		1/2 share		
Cowles, Samuel			GC	
Cowles, Samuel		1/2 share		7/13/1774
Williams, Timothy			GC	2/14/1775
Cowls, Ebenezer*	Norfolk, Litchfield, CT	1/2 share	bond received	10/23/1794
Brown, Daniel	Freehold, Albany, NY		E505	6/1/1796
by will to Ebenezer fr Samuel Cowles, father				
Coye, Joseph	Windham, Windham, CT	1/2 share	£16	3/18/1778
Roberts, Elias	Farmington, Hartford, CT		B379	3/13/1778

grantor	grantor residence	description	amount	deed date
grantee	grantee residence	location	acct bk page	record date
notes				
Crandell, Nathaniel	Stonington	1/2 share	$4	11/17/1794
Minor, Saxton	Stonington		C28	9/1/1795
Crane, John & Hannah	Nobletown NY	1/3 share	£3	4/24/1773
Bixley, Elias & James: Squire, Zach	Nobletown NY		B23	9/16/1773
Crane, Silas	Lebanon, Windham, CT	1/2 share	£12	1/5/1774
Thomas, James	Lebanon, Windham, CT		B121	1/20/1774
Crary, Aaron	Preston, New London, CT	all interest	£3	4/7/1761
Parks, William	Plainfield, Windham, CT		B80	10/11/1773
Crary, Benjamin	Voluntown, Windham CT	1 share	£3.8	11/14/1757
Fuller, Joshua	Newton, Middlesex, MA		B204	4/7/1774
Crary, Benjamin	Plainfield, Windham, CT	1/2 share	£12	2/22/1775
Palmer, Zebulon	Voluntown, Windham, CT		B329	6/1/1775
Crary, Christopher	Voluntown, Windham, CT	1/2 share	£1.19	9/17/1770
Crary, Benjamin	Plainfield, Windham, CT		B78	10/17/1773
Crary, Ezra	Clarendon, Rutland, VT	Pwr Attorney	1/2 the lands	3/10/1795
Ward, Ichabod			E56	2/24/1796
Crary, John		agent for a Twp survey*	1/4 share	7/20/1795
Throop, Benjamin			C120.1	9/1/1795
for fifteen owners, including Throop, who pay Throop 6s per day for his time and horse; total of 8 shares; J. Crary 1/4 share				
Crary, Oliver		agent for a Twp survey*		7/20/1795
Throop, Benjamin			C120.1	9/1/1795
for fifteen owners, including Throop, who pay Throop 6s per day for his time and horse; total of 8 shares; O. Crary 1 share				
Crary, Robert*	Preston, New London, CT	1 share	£12	11/20/1794
Hyde, Elisha	Norwich, New London, CT	Cabot Twp	I129	12/25/1794
eldest son and heir of Robert Crary				
Crary, Robert 2nd		all right		7/27/1795
Downer, Joshua Doctr	Preston, New London, CT		C24	9/1/1795
Crary, Robert, decd	Preston, New London, CT	all right by will		7/28/1795
Crary children*			C24	9/1/1795
John, Robert 2nd, Huldah & Eunice; Huldah wf Dr. John Downer; Eunice wf John Morgan				
Crery, Oliver	Preston	Agent		7/28/1795
Throop, Benjamin			C9	9/1/1795
Crery, William	Voluntown, Windham, CT	1/2 share	£6	10/25/1773
Brewster, Jonathan	Preston, New London, CT		B282	12/30/1774
Crissey, John Jr.	Woodbury, Litchfield, CT	1/2 share	£15	8/4/1774
Avreed, Timothy	Woodbury, Litchfield, CT		B351	1/23/1777
Crissey, William Truman	Hanover, Luzerne, PA	2,400 A laid out on 1 1/2 shares*	$500	12/1/1795
Dana, Daniel	Enfield, Hartford, CT	Burlington Twp	F217	10/26/1797
on Whapwallopee & Nescopack Creeks				
Crissy, John	Landaff, Grafton, NH	1/4 share	£50	3/17/1783
Crissy, Gould	Southington, Hartford, CT		C86	5/26/1784
Crocker, John	Richmont, Berkshire, MA	1 share*	love	5/23/1778
Crocker, John, son	Weathersfield, Hartford, CT		C88	5/30/1778
2/3 bought fr Nathaniel Rushman; 1/3 bought fr John Crocker & Rowland Smith				
Crofoot, David	Reading, Fairfield, CT	all right	£2	1/18/1796
Crofoot, Ebenezer	Redding, Fairfield, CT		H4	10/13/1798
Crofoot, David heir James	Reading	Pwr Att to sell share		11/14/1795
Morgan, Nathaniel			I271	1/2/1796
Crofoot, Ebenezer	Reading, Fairfield, CT	all right	$10	10/30/1797
Morgan, Nathaniel	Weston, Fairfield, CT		H4	10/13/1798
Crouch, William	Groton, New London, CT	1/2 share	£20	3/13/1775
Tozer, Samuel Jr.	Colchester, Hartford, CT		B346	4/23/1776
Culver, Edward	Springfield, Luzerne, PA	1 share	£112 s10	1/2/1795
Eno, Erasmus	Athens, Luzerne, PA	Allensburgh Twp Lots 14 & 15	C309	2/28/1795
Culver, Edward	Springfield, Luzerne, PA	Lots 14 & 15	$300 in goods*	1/2/1795
Eno, Erasmus	Athens, Luzerne, PA	Allensburgh Twp	C342	3/10/1795
Deliver to John Hutchinson's in Sheshequin: $100 with 1/3 in West India goods at cash price by 2/10/1796; $200 in merchant's goods with 1/3 in West India goods at cash price by 5/1/1796				
Curtis, Jabez & Betty, wf*	Stratford, Fairfield, CT	1 share	$30	4/8/1795
Strong, Joseph	Fairfield, Fairfield, CT		C529	5/1/1795
Betty Curtis, only surviving child of John Wells				
Curtis, John Jr.	Hampton, Windham, CT	1/2 share	£3	12/31/1794
Dorrance, Samuel	Windham, Windham, CT		C391	2/22/1795

grantor grantee notes	grantor residence grantee residence	description location	amount acct bk page	deed date record date
Curtis, Nathan Jr. heirs*	Huntington, Fairfield, CT	1 share	val con	3/18/1795
Lewis, Edmund	Stratford, Fairfield, CT		C576	6/19/1795
Eunice wf & exec; William, Samuel, Charity Southworth; Benjamin Wells & Elizabeth, wf; John McEvers & Anne, wf; Joseph Whiting, &				
Jerusha, wf				
Curtis, Peter	Freehold, Albany, NY	1 share	£20	8/1/1794
Brown, Daniel Jr.	Freehold, Albany, NY		C385	2/28/1795
Curtis, Peter Jr.	Freehold, Albany, NY	4,000 A	$4,000	3/23/1796
Pratt, Noah	Danby, Rutland, VT	Springhill Twp	E208	6/20/1796
Curtiss, Agur & Samuel	Woodbury, Litchfield, CT	1/2 share	£10	1/3/1774
Richards, Joseph	Woodbury, Litchfield, CT		B163	3/9/1774
Curtiss, Daniel Jr.	Chatham, Columbia, NY	Lots 40, 44, 45 & west 2/3 Lot 34*	£800	3/10/1800
Curtiss, Seth	Chatham, Columbia, NY	Watertown Twp	H300	6/3/1801
Each lot 300 A; 2/3 Lot 34 is 200 A				
Curtiss, Josiah				
Hitchcock, John			A468	
Curtiss, Matthew	New Town, Fairfield, CT	1/2 share	$7	4/14/1755
Gun, Joseph Jr.	New Town, Fairfield, CT		B89	11/23/1773
Curtiss, Nathan				
Allen, Amos			A417	
Curtiss, Peter Jr.	Freehold, Albany, NY	1/4 part	$4,000	3/23/1796
Buell, William	New York, New York, NY	Springhill Twp	E463	11/21/1796
Curtiss, Peter Jr.	Freehold, Albany, NY	4,000 A (1/4 township)	$4,000	4/1/1796
Fuller, Sylvester, merchant	Providence, RI	Springhill Twp	D159	6/20/1796
Curtiss, Samuel	Wethersfield, Hartford, CT	1/2 share	£15	11/29/1773
Ensign, Otis	New Hartford, Hartford, CT		B119	1/11/1774
Cushman, Nathaniel				
Crocker, John & Swift, Rowland			A286	
Cutler, Beach		1/2 share		
Dunlap, Joshua			GC	
Cutler, Beach	Plainfield, Windham, CT	1 share	£7.10	6/9/1769
Dunlap, Joshua & Dean, Nathan	Plainfield, Windham, CT		B113	12/22/1773
Cutler, William	Plainfield, Windham, CT	1/2 share*	£10	9/9/1794
Peirce, Abel	Luzerne, PA		E367	4/1/1796
Cutler pd taxes on Miller's share 6/10/1769 (E368)				
Cutright, Orry	Luzerne, PA	1/2 share	$20	12/9/1795
Shepard, John	Athens, Luzerne, PA		E327	4/10/1796
exec for John Cutright, father				
Dana, Jacob	Ashford, Windham, CT	1/8 of 1/2 share		4/2/1774
Tenney, Pricilla, dau	Ashford, Windham, CT		B199	4/2/1774
Danford, Thomas				
Gore, Obadiah			A427	
Danforth, Thomas estate*	Norwich, New London, CT	1/2 share	£60	12/9/1794
Hyde, Elisha	Norwich, New London, CT	Cabot Twp	I138	12/25/1794
John Danforth, adm				
Danihu, Daniel	Castleton, Rutland, VT	3 shares	$120	5/20/1795
Stevens, Levi	Castleton, Rutland, VT	In tract disputed between PA and CT	C560	6/20/1795
Darby, Phinehas	Poultney, Rutland, VT	1/2 share	$1,000	9/29/1800
Fellows, Nathan	Poultney, Rutland, VT		H259	10/18/1800
Darby, Phinehas	Poultney, Rutland, VT	Pwr Att to survey and lot out 1,000 A		9/29/1800
Fellows, Nathan	Poultney, Rutland, VT		H260	10/18/1800
Darby, Phinehas*	Poultney, Rutland, VT	all right	£10	10/21/1796
Kingsberry, Lemuel	Canaan, Litchfield, CT		H228	8/8/1800
Phinehas is only male heir of Reuben Darby, OP				
Darby, Shadra	Woodstock, Windsor, VT	1/2 of 2 shares*	£30	4/10/1795
Douglass, Zebulon	Canaan, Columbia, NY		F66	4/23/1796
1/2 the original right of William Cady and 1/2 the original right of William Williams				
Darby, Shadrach	Woodstock, Windsor, VT	two 1/2 shares	£30	4/9/1795
Douglass, Zebulon	New Canaan, Columbia, NY		F63	4/23/1795
Darby, Shadrack		1/2 share		7/26/1776
Anderson, Dana			GG	8/28/1776
Darby, William		1/2 share		12/5/1777
Darby, Shadrack			GD	
Darling, Thomas				
Canfield, Samuel			A68	

grantor grantee notes	grantor residence grantee residence	description location	amount acct bk page	deed date record date
Darrow, Zadoc	New London, New London, CT	1 share	£20	7/21/1779
Lester, Eliphalet	New London, New London, CT		C42	5/27/1782
Dart, Joseph	Chatham, Hartford, CT	3/4 share	£2	3/10/1770
Dart, Thomas	Bolton, Hartford, CT		B261	10/20/1774
Dart, Thomas	Gilsum, Cheshire, NH	Pwr Att to locate 1 share	1/2 of land	4/6/1795
Strong, Jabin	Glastonbury, Hartford, CT		E88	3/4/1796
Dart, William	East Hartford, Hartford, CT	1 share	£10	4/21/1795
Pitkin, Elisha Jr.	East Hartford, Hartford, CT		D26	9/28/1795
Davenport, John*	New York City	Pwr Att to locate 1 share	1/3 of lands	4/9/1795
Spalding, John*	Luzerne Co PA	Watertown Twp	C617	7/1/1795
Elizabeth is wid and heir of John Davenport, minister of the gospel; Spalding is to pay taxes due and costs				
Davis, Benajah, decd, father*	Montville, New London, CT	1/2 share	£5	12/31/1795
Lester, Eliphalet	Say Brook, New London, CT		E343	6/15/1796
Heirs are Jephthat Davis, Ransford Comstock, Azubah Comstock, Elihu Lester, Nancy Lester				
Davis, Henery		1/2 share		12/14/1774
Thayer, David Capt			GD	
Davis, Henry	Sheffield, Berkshire, CT	1 share	£10	2/17/1767
Borghardt, Hendrick	Great Barrington, Berkshire,		F269	3/14/1798
Davis, Isaac	Lee, Berkshire, MA	1 share	£20	11/25/1795
Pixley, David	Owego, Tioga, NY		D134	12/25/1795
Davis, Joseph/Tomlinson, Henry	Derby, New Haven, CT	1 share	val con	3/30/1795
Plumb, Joseph	Huntington, Fairfield, CT		C575	6/19/1795
Davis, Samuel	Lebanon, Windham, CT	1/2 share	$5	1/16/1795
Yong, William Jr.	Windham, Windham, CT		I202	4/1/1795
Davis, Urian		1/2 share		
Owens, Daniel			GC	
Daviss, Benj & Joshua				
LeHommedieu, Ezra			A298	
Day, Thomas	Canaan, Litchfield, CT	1/2 share	£17	9/9/1760
Parris, Elkanah	Canaan, Litchfield, CT		B134	2/1/1774
Dean, Benjamin	Athens, Luzerne, PA	Lot 40, 3rd Div about 100 A*	£100	1/9/1795
Livingston, John Esqr	Livingston, Columbia, NY	Athens Twp	C542	4/1/1795
Bounds: E Susq R 40 rods, N Julius Gaylord, S John Franklin				
Dean, Eleazar				
Hebard, Moses			A56	
Dean, Ephriam	Taunton, Bristol, MA	1 share	£5	3/15/1769
Dean, Simeon son	Ashford, Windham, CT		B51	2/29/1772
Dean, Ezra	West Greenwich, Kent, RI	1/2 share	£25	1/15/1777
Aborn, James	Warwick, Kent, RI		B366	3/26/1777
Dean, Ezra	West Greenwich, Kent, RI	1 share	£50	2/11/1777
Aborn, James	Warwick, Kent, RI		B371	3/26/1777
Dean, Ezra	West Greenwich, Kent, RI	1 share	£100	3/26/1778
Aborn, John	Warwick, Kent, RI		B386	4/8/1778
Dean, Ezra	West Greenwich, Kent, RI	1/2 share	£25	2/11/1777
Aborn, Samuel	Warwick, Kent, RI		B364	3/26/1777
Dean, Ezra	West Greenwich, Kent, RI	1 share	£55	8/5/1777
Aborn, Samuel	Warwick, Kent, RI		B370	9/15/1777
Dean, Ezra	West Greenwich, Kent, RI	1/2 share	£25	3/20/1777
Aborn, Samuel	Warwick, Kent, RI		B370	3/29/1777
Dean, Ezra	West Greenwich, Kent, RI	1/2 share	£25	2/11/1777
Aborn, Samuel	Warwick, Kent, RI		B371	3/26/1777
Dean, Ezra	West Greenwich, Kent, RI	2 shares	£180	4/4/1778
Aborn, Samuel	Warwick, Kent, RI		B382	4/8/1778
Dean, Ezra	West Greenwich, Kent, RI	1/2 share	£45	4/4/1778
Aborn, Samuel	Warwick, Kent, RI		B383	4/8/1778
Dean, Ezra	Cranston, Providence, RI	1 share	£30	4/1/1782
Aborns, Samuel	Warwick, Kent, RI		C45	6/3/1782
Dean, Ezra				
Dean, Jonathan			A387	
Dean, James heirs		1 1/2 share	£100	1/27/1795
Throop, Benjamin		Warwick Twp	CB	9/1/1795
Dean, Jameson	Ashford, Windham, CT	Pwr Att to locate three 1/2 shares		1/14/1795
Chauncey, Worthington G.	Durham, New Haven, CT		C323	2/26/1795

grantor grantee notes	grantor residence grantee residence	description location	amount acct bk page	deed date record date
Dean, John	Spencer Town, Albany, NY	1 share	£16	12/9/1774
Allen, Levi	Salisbury, Litchfield, CT		B386	4/8/1778
Dean, Josiah				
Jones, William			A246	
Dean, Josiah		1/2 share		9/14/1773
Millard, Thomas			GD	11/23/1773
Dean, Josiah Jr.		1/2 share		
Dean, Josiah			GD	
Dean, Nathan	Plainfield, Windham, CT	1/2 share	£5	1/12/1774
Gore, Elijah	Voluntown, Windham CT		I93	7/7/1794
Dean, Nathaniel		1/2 share		
Shephard, Abraham			GD	
Dean, Silas		16,000 A	$6,000	3/22/1796
Lombard, Roswell and Plumb, Saml		Hannibal Twp	E320	8/8/1796
Deans, James	Lebanon, Windham, CT	1/2 share	£20	4/11/1774
Williams, Vetch & Lothrop, David	Lebanon/Norwich CT		B208	3/19/1774
Decker, Junis	Kingston, Luzerne, PA	16,000 A	£2,600	12/22/1795
Tuttle, John & Swetland, Joseph	Kingston, Luzerne, PA	Mount Pleasant Twp	E550	12/20/1797
Decker, Tunis, Blacksmith	Kings[ton], Luzerne, PA	16,000 A*	$4,000	9/22/1796
Phelps, Beriah	Hillsdale, Columbia, NY	Oston Twp	F171	6/26/1797
except 1,300 A now occupied by actual settlers				
Deforest, Nehemiah heir	Huntington, Fairfiald, CT	Pwr Att to lay out 1 share		1/18/1796
Bostwick, Dimon	New Milford, Litchfield, CT		E125	3/1/1796
Heir is Samuel Deforest				
Delano, Elisha	Hanover, Luzerne, PA	1/2 twp	$6,000	7/20/1796
Brown, Daniel Jr.	Freehold, Albany, NY	Orange Twp	E551	2/6/1798
Deming, Ebenezer	Weathersfield, Hartford, CT	2 half shares	Love	11/4/1782
Deming children*			I101	10/7/1794
2/3 equally to sons Ebenezer Jr., John, Simeon, Jesse and 1/3 equally to dau Amy,and Rebecca's heirs Jerusha, Elizabeth, Hester				
Deming, Gideon	Hartford, Hartford, CT	1/2 share	£16	12/9/1773
Bidwell, Amos	Hartford, Hartford, CT		B286	1/17/1775
Denham, James		1/2 share		
Smith, Elisha			GD	
Denison, Isaac	Stonington, New London, CT	1/2 share	18s	7/15/1794
Miner, Daniel, 2nd, in-law	Stonington, New London, CT		C151	2/24/1795
Denison, Joseph 2nd*		1/2 share		5/19/1774
Niles, Sands & Ells, Edward			CB	
deed recorded Stonington, CT, Bk. 9, folio 447				
Denison, Nathan				
Denison, Nathan Jr.			A102	
Denison, Nathan*	Kingston, Luzerne, PA	1 share	£5	12/8/1789
Franklin, John	Wilkesbarre, Luzerne, PA	Athens Twp	F254	12/8/1789
also signed by Elizabeth Denison				
Denniss, George		1/2 share		
Gore, Obadiah			A429	
Dewey, Aaron	Colchester, New London, CT	1 share		10/13/1794
Turner, Seth	New Haven, New Haven, CT		C292	3/4/1795
Dewey, Azariah	Poultney, Rutland, VT	1/2 Lots 7, 13, 23, 500 A each	$50	3/8/1802
Moseley, Moseley	Rutland, VT	Armenia Twp	H341	6/13/1802
Dewey, David	Hebron, Tolland, CT	2 shares	£10	8/13/1794
Dewy, Adijah	Freehold, Albany, NY		C476	2/1/1795
Dewey, David	Berlin, New Haven, CT	1/2 share	$25	1/7/1796
Smith, Lemuel & Allyn, John B.	Berlin, Hartford, CT		E142	2/25/1796
Dewey, Noah	Lebanon, Windham, CT	1/2 share	£6	3/8/1760
Barber, David	Hebron, Hartford, CT		B165	3/10/1774
Dewey, Noah	Fairlee, Glouster, NY	1/2 share	£40	11/18/1773
Paine, John	Fairlee, Glouster, NY		B135	2/2/1774
Dewey, Stephen	Sheffield, Berkshire, MA	1/4 Twp [4000 A]	$6,260	11/3/1795
Henshaw, Daniel	Middletown, Middlesex, CT	Dunkirk Twp	E32	2/10/1796
Dewey, Thomas	Rutland, Rutland, VT	1 share	$120	6/20/1796
Bryan, Richard	Watertown,Litchfield, CT		E487	11/15/1796

grantor grantee notes	grantor residence grantee residence	description location	amount acct bk page	deed date record date
Dewitt, Paul		1 share, No. 100 of the 600*		8/4/1795
Spalding, John	Luzerne Co PA		C528	9/30/1795
minus 1200 A laid out				
Dewitt, William	Juddsburgh PA	700 A		8/17/1795
Scoville, Champion	Tioga Twp PA	Juddsburgh Twp, 2nd div	C398	8/17/1795
Dike, Nathaniel	Ontario Co NY	Pwr Att to sell Lot 46		10/10/1795
Cole, Stephen	Athens, Luzerne, PA	Tioga Point [Athens, Luzerne, PA]	I255	12/4/1795
Dilingfries, Anna*	Norwich, New London, CT	1 share	£60	11/24/1794
Tracy, Elisha; Hyde, Elisha	Norwich, New London, CT		I144	12/25/1794
dau of Col. John Durkee, decd.				
Dimmick, Israel				
Carey, William			A439	
Dimock, David		all rights		12/18/1795
Dimock, Asa			F168	6/26/1797
Dimock, David		1 share		10/30/1792
Ousterhout, Gideon			I219	7/8/1795
Dixon, Archibald	Underhill, Chittenden, VT	1/2 share	val sum	2/26/1795
Stoddard, Philo	Woodbury, Litchfield, CT		C635	7/10/1795
Dixon, Barnet		1 share		
Dean, Ezra			A80	
Dixon, Barnet, son	Voluntown, Windham, CT	1/2 share	£7.10	10/4/1773
Dorrance, George	Voluntown, Windham, CT		B68	10/8/1773
Dixon, Curtis		1/2 share		
MacGregor, John			GD	
Dixon, James				
Baldwin, Sylvester			A26	
Dixon, John		1/2 share		
Dixon: Jn Jr., Robt, Thomas, Sister			GG	
Dixon, John	Voluntown, Windham, CT	1/2 share	Love	6/18/1770
Dixon, Robert Jr., son	Voluntown, Windham, CT		B57	8/28/1772
Dixon, John	Sterling, Windham, CT	1/2 share	£10	1/15/1795
Dorrance, Benjamin	Kingston, Luzerne, PA		C540	5/7/1795
Dixon, John Jr.		1/2 share		5/5/1774
Pierce, Abel			GG	5/9/1774
Dixon, Robert		1/2 share		
Dixon, Curtis			GD	
Dixon, Robert	Voluntown, Windham, CT	1/2 share	£16	3/4/1774
Stevenson, James	Voluntown, Windham, CT		B181	3/10/1774
Dixon, Robert Jr.	Voluntown, Windham, CT	1/2 share	£30	2/25/1775
Dow, Benjamin	Voluntown, Windham, CT		B330	6/29/1775
Dixon, Robert, Thomas & Sister		1/2 share		
Dixon, John Jr.			GG	
Dixon/Dickson, Nathaniel	Pittston - Putnam, Luzerne, PA	eight 300 A lots	$12	6/30/1796
Arnold, Nehemiah	Providence, RI	Smithfield Twp	E219	7/2/1796
Dixson, Barnet	Voluntown, Windham, CT	1/2 share	8£	6/4/1782
Aborn, Samuel	Warwick, Kent, RI		H131	11/30/1799
Dobbin, William		1 share except 600 A 1st div,	val recd	6/5/1795
Spalding, John			E135	3/29/1796
Dodd, Benjamin	Hartford, Hartford, CT	1/2 share	£15	2/14/1774
Sedgwick, Abraham	Hartford, Hartford, CT		B217	5/25/1774
Dodd, Bishop	New Haven, New Haven, CT	1 share		12/18/1794
Munson, Eneas Jr.	New Haven, New Haven, CT		C294	3/4/1795
Dodd, Thomas heirs*	New Haven, New Haven, CT	1/2 share	£1. 19	1/8/1795
Spalding, John	New Haven, New Haven, CT		C411	4/4/1795
Heirs are Newman, Rebekah, Joseph Eason, and Sarah Trowbridge and Guy Dodd				
Dodge, Rufus		1/2 share		3/17/1774
Cole, Samuel Jr.			GC	
Doneghy, John	New York, New York, NY	1/2 share	£15	4/22/1772
Case, Stephen	Providence, Ulster, NY		B228	7/6/1774
Dorchester, Abigail	New Haven, New Haven, CT	all right	£2. 4	5/30/1796
Pope, Robert	Darby, New Haven, CT		E484	11/15/1796
Dorrance, Benjamin	Kingston, Luzerne, PA	all right	$8,000	5/6/1796
Bulkley, James and Clark, Samuel	Middletown, Middlesex, CT	Sterling Twp	D180	8/9/1796

grantor	grantor residence	description	amount	deed date
grantee	grantee residence	location	acct bk page	record date
notes				
Dorrance, Benjamin	Luzerne, PA	1/2 share		9/3/1795
Lockwood, Ephriam			C307	9/6/1795
Dorrance, Benjamin	Kingston, Luzerne, PA	1 share	$50	3/9/1795
Shepard, John	Tioga, Luzerne, PA		E323	4/10/1796
Dorrance, Benjamin	Luzerne, PA	1/2 share	$20	2/15/1796
Stephens, Ira	Luzerne, PA		E368	4/1/1796
Dorrance, Benjamin	Kingston, Luzerne, PA	1 share, 300 A	£20	7/16/1794
Terrill, Job	New Milford, Litchfield, CT	Northmoreland, Luzerne, PA*	I150	12/6/1794
entered in Northmoreland for Capt Joseph Park by Zebulon. Butler				
Dorrance, George		1/4 share		8/25/1773
Taylor, Lemuel			GM	
Dorrance, George, Alexander,	Foster, Providence, RI	1 share	£12	1/9/1795
Dorrance, Samuel	Windham, Windham, CT		C396	2/22/1795
Dorrance, Gersham & Polly wf	Lebanon, Windham, CT	all right to twp	$10000	10/17/1795
Paine, David	Luzerne Co PA	Dorrancebough Twp	D61	12/1/1795
Dorrance, Gershom	Windham, Windham, CT	1/2 share	$23	1/20/1795
Dorrance, Benjamin	Kingston, Luzerne, CT		C539	5/7/1795
Dorrance, James	Sterling, Windham, CT	1/2 share	£5	1/2/1795
Dorrance, Samuel	Windham, Windham, CT		C387	2/22/1795
Dorrance, John	Kingston, Luzerne, PA	1100 A not yet laid out	£8. 5	1/29/1796
Stephens, Ira	Luzerne, PA		E370	4/1/1796
Dorrance, John		1/4 share		1/23/1774
Walker, Samuel			GH	
Dorrance, Samuel	Windham, Windham, CT	two 1/6 shares	£15	6/4/1794
Brown, Daniel	Freehold, Albany, NY		C481	2/1/1795
Dorrance, Samuel				
Dorrance, George			A492	
Dorrance, Samuel	Voluntown, Windham, CT	1/2 share	Love	8/11/1773
Dorrance, James, son			B59	8/12/1773
Dorrance, Samuel	Voluntown, Windham, CT	1/2 share	Love	8/10/1773
Dorrance, Lemuel, son	Voluntown, Windham, CT		B69	8/12/1773
Dorrance, Samuel				
Dorrance, Samuel 3rd			A238	
Douglas, Asa		1/2 share		12/3/1754
Whitemarsh, Nicholas			GD	
Douglas, Ebenezer	New London	1 share *	£3	9/21/1794
Ely, Elisha	Saybrook		C114	10/1/1794
1/2 share by deed from father, 1/2 share in father's estate				
Douglass, Asa	Canaan, Columbia, NY	1 1/2 shares	$10	6/16/1795
Douglass, Zebulon	Canaan, Columbia, NY		C591	7/7/1795
Douglass, Asa	Canaan, Litchfield, CT	1/4 share	£4	7/7/1763
Wheeler, Eunice	Grt Nine Partners, Dutchess,		B384	6/19/1778
Douglass, Daniel & Israel	Saybrook, Middlesex, CT	1/2 share + 1 share No. 159 of 600		3/27/1794
Elliot, William		Johnstown Twp	C352	3/2/1795
Douglass, Samuel		1/2 share		
Marvin, David			A253	
Douglass, Thomas	Voluntown CT	1 share	£10	9/12/1769
Campbell, Samuel	Voluntown, Windham, CT		B37 - B260	3/29/1771
Douglass, Thomas	Voluntown, Windham, CT	1 share	£10	10/12/1774
Campbell, Samuel	Voluntown, Windham, CT		B260 - B37	10/13/1774
Douglass, Zebulon	Canaan, Columbia, NY	4 shares, 8,000 A	$400	9/25/1795
Lombard, Roswell	Stockbridge, Berkshire, MA		F64	4/25/1796
Downer, Andrew				
Porter, Josiah			A485	
Downer, Andrew	Sharon, Windsor, VT	1/2 share except 1/4 pt 2nd div land	£50	9/30/1782
Simmons, Reuben	Sharon, Windsor, VT		C49	10/22/1782
Downer, Ezra	Wall Kill Town, Ulster, NY	1/2 share	$18	12/15/1793
Campbell, Samuel	Wall Kill Town, Ulster, NY		H262	11/16/1799
Downer, Joshua		agent for a Twp survey	1/2 share	7/20/1795
Throop, Benjamin			C120.1	9/1/1795
for fifteen owners, including Throop, who pay Throop 6s per day for his time and horse; total of 8 shares; J. Downer 1/2 share				
Downer, Joshua	Preston, New London, CT	1/4 twp, i.e. 1/4 interest in 8 shares	$500	6/9/1796
Woodbridge, Joseph	Hartford, Hartford, CT	Stephensburgh Twp	E237	7/4/1796

grantor / grantee / notes	grantor residence / grantee residence	description / location	amount / acct bk page	deed date / record date
Downer, Richard	Norwich, New London, CT	1/2 share	$10	3/25/1774
Harris, Phillip	Lebanon, Windham, CT		C88	8/16/1785
Downer, Samuel	Lebanon, CT	300 A	£50	9/9/1782
Newcomb, James	Lebanon, CT	Westmoreland Co., CT	C47	9/9/1782
Downing, David		1/4 share		
Stark, William			GD	
Downing, Henry	Chelsea, Windsor, VT	1/2 share	£6	2/28/1796
Park, Reuben	Canterbury, Windham, CT		H315	
Downing, Perrigo	Canterbury, Windham, CT	1/2 share	£6	4/1/1773
Utley, John	Windham, Windham, CT		B324	4/8/1775
Drake, Asahel		1/2 share		3/19/1773
Lyons, Asa			GD	
Drake, Asahel		2/4 share		6/9/1774
Willerds, Dubartius			GD	6/9/1774
Drake, Francus		3/4 share		
Hopkins, Noah			GD	
Drake, John		1 share	£60	11/12/1774
Allen, Levi	Salisbury, Litchfield, CT		E227	
Drake, Nathaniel Jr.				
Drake, Nathaniel			A462	
Draper, Amos	Union, Tioga, NY	1/4 Lot 19 with full iron mine rights*	£100	5/11/1795
McMaster, James	Union, Tioga, NY	Claverack, Wisocks Great Marsh*	D37 - E424	10/20/1795
1/4 to McMaster 4/24/1795 and 1/2 to Samuel Hepburn and Guy Maxwell of Tioga Point on 4/7/1795; NW side Wisocks Cr.				
Draper, Amos	Union, Tioga, NY	1/4 Lot 19 with full iron mine rights*	£200	10/20/1795
Wattles, Mason	Union, Tioga, NY	Claverack, Wisocks Great Marsh*	D36	10/20/1795
1/4 to Wattle and 2/4 to McMaster, James previously; NW side Wisocks Cr.				
Draper, Amos*	Union, Tioga, NY	lease 1/4 Lot 19, full iron mine rights	$5 yr rent*	9/7/1795
Wattles, Mason	Union, Tioga, NY	Claverack, Wysocks Great Marsh*	D39	10/21/1795
Draper leased from Henry Tuttle and Isaac Strope. Rent to begin 1799, if demanded. Wattles paid Draper in advance £25 for 19/20ths part of rent. Great Marsh located NW side Wysocks Cr.				
Dresser, Jacob & Sarah*	Killingly, Windham, CT	1 share	20s	3/13/1782
Walcott, Nathaniel	Windham, Windham, CT		C87	3/23/1784
Sarah, was 1st wf of Joseph Walden, OP				
Dudley, Gideon & William; Wait,	Canandaigua, Ontario, NY	quit claim to all rights	£50	12/29/1794
Dudley, Martin	Canandaigua, Ontario, NY	Susquehanna lands	C311	2/28/1795
Dudley, Martin	Canadaigua, Ontario, NY	600 A (3/4 of 800 to French,	£100	1/7/1795
Saterlee, Elisha; Hutchinson, John	Tioga, Luzerne, PA	Lackawack R btw	C303	2/28/1795
Dudley, Martin, trader	Canadahey, Ontario, NY	all right*	val sum	1/7/1795
Saterlee, Elisha; Hutchinson, John	Tioga, Luzerne, PA		C301	2/28/1795
except 1/2 in Col. Franklin's hands that I bought of him				
Dudley, Oliver	Guilford, New Haven, CT	1/2 share	£3	2/5/1770
Burnham, Elizur	Glastonbury, Hartford, CT		B53	4/3/1772
Dudley, Oliver Cap't	Guilford, New Haven, CT	1/2 share	36s	4/13/1768
Jocelin, Simeon	Guilford, New Haven, CT		B23	4/15/1773
Dunlap, Joshua		1/2 share		2/21/1774
Pierce, Phinehas			GC	
Dunlap, Joshua	Plainfield, Windham, CT	Pwr Att to locate 1/2 share*, 300 A	1/2 of lands or £100	1/9/1795
Spalding, John	Sheshequin, PA	Watertown, but withdrawn 1796	C616	7/1/1795
Spalding pays taxes due and costs				
Dunning, Elias				
Strong, Timothy			A412	
Durkee, Andrew				
Howard, John			A446	
Durkee, Jeremiah Sr. heir	Hampton, Windham, CT	1/2 share	24s	12/17/1794
Chauncey, Worthington G.	New Haven, New Haven, CT		C441	2/21/1795
Durkee, John	Norwich, New London, CT	1/2 share	£6	1/27/1774
Ross, Jeremiah	New London, New London, CT		B185 - GD	3/11/1774
Durkee, John				
Stark, Nathan			A89	
Durkee, John Col.	Norwich, New London, CT	1 share	love	7/20/1774
Durkee, Anna dau	Norwich, New London, CT	Lackawack, Westmoreland, CT*	I145	12/25/1794
Lackawack. was another name for the Second Delaware Purchase				
Durkee, Robert	Windham, Windham, CT	1/2 share	£24	10/29/1774
Downing, Jonathan Jr.	Canterbury, Windham, CT		B334	3/15/1775

grantor	grantor residence	description	amount	deed date
grantee	grantee residence	location	acct bk page	record date
notes				
Durkee, Robert	Westmoreland, Westmrld, CT	250 A	Love	4/23/1778
Durkee, Sarah, dau	Westmoreland, Westmrld, CT	Wilkes Barre, Lot 36, third division	B381	8/27/1779
Dyer, Eliphalet		1 share* + 1 settling right		7/9/1773
Dyer, Thomas			B75	7/12/1773
repossessed for non payment of loan to Bowen				
Dyke, Nathaniel	Luzerne, PA	Lot 10*	£2. 12	5/14/1793
Maxwell, Guy	Luzerne, PA	Athens opposite James Irwin	E118	3/1/1796
6 perches wide fronting the street and running back to the Tioga R.				
Earl, Benjamin	Putnam, Luzerne, CT	1/4 share	good cause	5/28/1795
Gaylord, Lemuel	Luzerne, PA		C607	7/9/1795
Earl, Benjamin	Luzerne, PA	1 Lot	£25	11/5/1791
Stafford, John		Putnam Twp. adj. river and Joseph	I98	5/26/1794
Earle, Jeptha		1/2 share, No. 81 of 400		4/4/1794
Bartell, Peter Jr.			C315	3/9/1795
Easton, Ashbel and Sarah, wf*	East Hartford, Hartford, CT	1/2 share	£7	10/16/1795
Pitkin, Elisha Jr.	East Hartford, Hartford, CT		E287	6/6/1796
dau & only heir of Henry Arnold, OP, who paid 6s of 24s taxes 10/25/1782				
Easton, Joseph	Washington, Litchfield, CT	1/4 share	val con	6/14/1782
Graham, James	Kent. Litchfield, CT		C51	10/28/1782
Eaton, Joseph				
Jackson, Robert			A269	
Edgerton, Asa				
French, Andrew			A231	
Edgerton, Asa	Mansfield	1/2 share, 50 A Lot 8 and 200 A	£500	10/23/1779
Waterman, Luther	Norwich	Salem Twp.	C4	11/2/1779
Edmons, Robert		1/2 share		1/27/1775
McKardehan, William			GC	1/29/1775
Edmunds, Robert				
Mitchell, Timothy			A62	
Edwards, Daniel heirs*	Hartford, Hartford, CT	1 share	£3	6/28/1794
Brown, Daniel	Freehold, Albany, NY		C480	2/1/1795
Charles Caldwell & Mary Caldwell				
Edwards, Timothy	Stockbridge, Berkshire, MA	deposition*		6/2/1796
			E300	6/20/1796
Heirs of Joseph Woodbridge: Jahiel, Jemima Cooper, Mabel Jones, wid, all Stockbridge; Isabel Persons wf of Zinus Persons, Springfield, Hampshire, MA, Inn holder; Jahiel entitled to double share; daughters to single share				
Edwards, Timothy	Stockbridge, Berkshire, MA	Pwr Att to locate & sell all rights*		5/28/1796
Woodbridge, Stephen	Washington, Berkshire, MA		E297	6/20/1796
Rights belonging to Rev. Jonathan Edwards, decd and Timothy Edwards; see E300 for deposition				
Elderkin, Jedediah				
Elderkin, Vine			A103	
Elderkin, John	Windham, Windham, CT	1/2 share	£15	1/4/1774
Crouch, William & Rogers, John	Groton, New London, CT		B114	1/4/1774
Elderkin, John				
Elderkin, John, son			A490	
Elderkin, John				
Elderkin, Joshua			A489	
Elderkin, John Jr.	Windham, Windham, CT	1/2 share	£6	10/7/1773
Lothrop, Ebenezer Jr.	Norwich, New London, CT		B55	10/7/1773
Elderkin, Joshua	Chelsea, Orange, VT	all share	£3	3/24/1795
Barrett, Jonathan	Norwich, Windsor, VT		C644	8/10/1795
Elderkin, Joshua				
Elderkin, John			A491	
Elderkin, Joshua				
Hull, Stephen			A59	
Elderkin, Joshua				
Linkon, Hezekiah			A230	
Elderkin, Joshua	Windham CT	1 share	£3	8/9/1762
Parke, Joseph	Voluntown CT		C192	2/27/1795
Eley, Joseph				
Eley, Elihu			A300	
Ellery, Benjamin		1/4 share*		
Stiles, Ezra			A293	
Stiles pd taxes on 1/4 share 5/31/1769				

grantor / grantee / notes	grantor residence / grantee residence	description / location	amount / acct bk page	deed date / record date
Elliot, Christopher	Pawling, Dutchess, NY	1 share	£10	12/13/1785
Osterhouse, Gideon	Pawling, Dutchess, NY		C92 - E442	12/14/1785
Elliot, John				
Austin, Samuel			A321	
Elliot, William	Saybrook, Middlesex, CT	6 whole shares & 3 half shares*	£2400	11/8/1794
Brown, David Jr.	New Durham, Albany, NY		C461-2	2/21/1795
Deed receipts chain of each share				
Elliot, William	Killingsworth, Middlesex, CT	Lot 20	$900	12/27/1798
Elliot, Richard	Kent, Litchfield, CT	Elliotsburg Twp*	H198	12/9/1799
granted as Johnstown Twp				
Elliot, William	Killingsworth, Middlesex, CT	Lot 19, 2/3 Lot 23, 2/3 of 100 A*	$800	12/27/1798
Elliot, Richard and Spencer, Urich	Kent, Litchfield, CT and Tioga,	Elliotsburg Twp*	H200	12/9/1799
includes 2/3 privilege of streams of water and erecting of mills; granted as Johnstown Twp				
Elliot, William	Saybrook, Middlesex, CT	3 shares	£30	10/4/1794
Fowler, William	Guilford, New Haven, CT		C123	10/4/1794
Elliot, William	Saybrook, Middlesex, CT	2 shares No. 157, 158 of 600	£60	5/28/1796
Frothingham, Saml & Winship, Tim	Middletown, Middlesex, CT		F120	6/6/1796
Elliot, William	Killingsworth, Middlesex, CT	200 A, N end Lot 12	60£	9/12/1798
Geer, Benjamin	Groton, New London, CT	Elliottsburgh Twp*	H88	8/16/1799
granted as Johnstown Twp				
Elliot, William	Saybrook, Middlesex, CT	3,000 A, Lots	£5	2/1/1797
Gregory, Uriah M.	Saybrook, Middlesex, CT	Johnstown Twp	E552	4/10/1798
Elliot, William	Saybrook, Middlesex, CT	Lot No. 17, 300 A	£90	2/7/1795
Grissing, John & Pratt, Reuben	Saybrook, Middlesex, CT	Elliotsburgh Twp*	C219	2/28/1795
granted as Johnstown Twp				
Elliott, Aaron	Killingsworth, Middlesex, CT	1 share and three 1/2 shares	£41.2	12/1/1795
Lester, Eliphalet	Say Brook, Middlesex, CT		E346	6/15/1796
Ells, Edward	Stonington	Pwr Attorney		3/23/1795
Ells, Cushing	Norwich		CC	
Ells, Edward by Ells, Cushing		agent for a Twp survey	1/2 share	7/20/1795
Throop, Benjamin			C120.1	9/1/1795
for fifteen owners, including Throop, who pay Throop 6s per day for his time and horse; total of 8 shares; E. Ells 1/4 share				
Elster, Casper	Pauling Town, Dutchess, NY	two 1/2 shares*	£15	4/21/1795
Gilbert, Warner	Warner, Litchfield, CT		E63	2/26/1796
1/2 share from father-in-law Giddeon Draper of Dutchess Co; 1/2 share by resolve of Susq Co 7/13/1785				
Ely, Elijah	Lyme, New London, CT	1 share	£5	8/23/1794
Waterhouse, Saml & Harris,	Saybrook, Middlesex, CT		C113 - 117	10/3/1794
Ely, Elisha	Saybrook, Middlesex, CT	3 lots, 300 A each No. 24, 36, 38	£120	9/15/1796
Clark, Beaumont	Saybrook, Middlesex, CT	Elysium Twp	E526	3/15/1797
Ely, Elisha	Saybrook, Middlesex, CT	Lot 12, 300 A	£60	2/7/1795
Grissing, John & Pratt, Reuben	Saybrook, Middlesex, CT	Elysium Twp	C218	2/28/1795
Ely, Elisha	Saybrook, Middlesex, CT	Lot 1, 300 A	£10	4/30/1795
Hill, William	Saybrook, Middlesex, CT	Ely Twp	H11	10/19/1798
Ely, Elisha	Say Brook, Middlesex, CT	1 share	$100	6/10/1796
Walworth, Danl and Winship, Tim	Middletown, Middlesex, CT		E342	6/15/1796
Ely, John	Saybrook, Middlesex, CT	No 60 & 1/2 No 53 & 59 of 600	£66	2/6/1795
Chalker, Moses & Oliver	Saybrook, Middlesex, CT		D140	3/2/1795
Ely, John	Saybrook, Middlesex, CT	1/2 No. 59 of 600	£17	2/5/1795
Clerk, Nathan	Saybrook, Middlesex, CT		D139	3/2/1795
Ely, John	Saybrook, Middlesex, CT	2 shares	£6	8/14/1794
Elliot, William	Saybrook, Middlesex, CT		C121.1	10/1/1794
Ely, Marsh	Lyme, New London, CT	1 1/2 share*	£3	10/29/1794
Ely, Elisha	Saybrook, Middlesex, CT		D141	3/2/1795
1 share orig Samuel Ely; 1/2 share orig Timothy Tiffany				
Ely, Samuel, Nathaniel Ely Ex				10/29/1794
Ely, Elisha	Saybrook, Middlesex, CT		C340	3/2/1795
Emerick, Andrew		1/2 share		12/24/1773
Aurand, John			B176	3/14/1774
Emerson, Nathaniel				
Perkins, James			A422	
Eno, Erasmus	Luzerne Co PA	Lot 39, 300 A	£50	1/9/1795
Dailey, Solomon	Luzerne Co PA	Murraysfield Twp	C300	2/11/1795

grantor grantee notes	grantor residence grantee residence	description location	amount acct bk page	deed date record date
Eno, Erasmus	Luzerne Co PA	1/2 share	$60 inc. other shares	12/6/1794
Satterlee, Elisha	Luzerne Co PA		I261	12/6/1794
Eno, Samuel	Windsor, Hartford, CT	Pwr Att to locate 1/2 share		2/9/1795
Brown, Daniel et al	Freehold, Albany, NY;		F2	3/1/1796
Daniel Brown, Jr., Selby Brainard & Ethan Stone				
Enos, Ebenezer	Oxford, Tioga, NY	1/2 share No. 46 of the 400	£10	5/22/1795
Irwin, James	Athens, Luzerne, PA		E437	10/1/1796
Enos, Erasmus		1/2 share No. 136 of 400		9/25/1796
Dutcher, Christopher		Newtown Point	E495	12/17/1796
Enos, Erasmus		1/2 share		11/12/1794
Satterlee, Elisha			H261	6/1/1800
Enos, Joab		1/2 share		9/23/1794
Hollenback, Isaac			E338 - C91	5/15/1796
Ensign, Ezekiel	Stillwater, Saratoga, NY	Pwr Att to locate and survey 1,000 A		10/8/1800
Fellows, Nathan	Poultney, Rutland, VT		H261	10/18/1800
Ensign, Zerah/Hayden, Jonathan	Tioga, PA & Cummington, MA	1 1/2 shares		8/21/1795
Kingsbury, Joseph	Tioga, Luzerne, PA		C398	8/23/1795
Ensworth, Jedediah	Pomfret, Windham, CT	Pwr Att 1 share		11/21/1792
Adams, Jabez Dr.	Mansfield, Windham, CT		C463	2/20/1795
Evans, Zeba	Murraysfield, Luzerne, PA	1/2 share No. 275 of 400, Lot 11	£50	6/30/1795
Ransom, Samuel	Tioga, NY	Murraysfield Twp	E439	10/1/1796
deed actually dated June 31, 1795				
Eveland, Frederick	Plymouth	22 A Meadow Lot 36, River Tier	$160	4/10/1787
Hervey, Benjamin	Plymouth	Plymouth Twp, Shawanese Flat	I48	4/11/1787
Evelyn, Frederick		1/2 share, No. 45 of 400	£5	8/13/1795
Pixley, David	Owego, NY		E65	8/27/1774
Evelyn, Frederick		1/2 share No. 322 of 400	5£	8/12/1795
Pixley, David	Owego, NY		E66	8/27/1774
Evens, Edward		1/2 share		
Smith, Abel			GE	
Everest, Noah	Catskill, Albany, NY	16,000 A	£2000	9/22/1795
Morgan, Asa	Catskill, Albany, NY	Guilford Twp	F208	1/27/1797
Everet, Josiah	Litchfield, Litchfield, CT	1/4 share	£3.10	4/26/1773
Guthrie, Joseph	Kent, Litchfield, CT		B16	9/15/1773
Eyers		1/2 share	£6. 6s note	11/4/1772
Follet, Benjamin			GE	
Fabrique, John	Bethlehem, Litchfield, CT	1 1/2 shares	$50	10/19/1795
Moseley, William	Woodbury, Litchfield, CT		E403	9/15/1796
Fabrique, John	Bethlehem, Litchfield, CT	1/2 share	£18	1/1/1795
Sanford, Daniel	Newtown, Fairfield, CT		E403	9/15/1796
Fanning, James			A270	
Gaylord, Samuel				
Farlan, Hutchinson*	Plainfield, Windham, CT	Pwr Att to locate 1 share		3/31/1796
Peirce, John	Plainfield, Windham, CT		E273	7/15/1796
son and exec of Samuel Farlan [see McFarland], claims OP 2 shares but only 1 found				
Farlan, Hutchinson	Plainfield, Windham, CT	1 share	$200	9/11/1797
Young, William Jr.	Windham, Windham, CT		H243	9/20/1800
Farnam, Robert	Windham	1/2 share*	£10	11/18/1777
Morris, Amos	New Haven		C29	2/6/1782
except pitch in twp that Capt Durkee & Esqr Simons laid out				
Farnam, Ruben	Windham	2/3 suffering right	£10	3/8/1779
Cleaveland, Ephriam & Griffin,	Ashueliot Equivalent/Windham	Muncy Creek Twp	C10	4/27/1779
Farnam, Ruben	Windham	1/2 share	£10	3/8/1779
Cleaveland, Ephriam & Griffin,	Ashueliot Equivalent/Windham		C10	4/27/1779
Farnam, Ruben	Canterbury, Windham, CT	1/4 share	£3	4/9/1773
Utley, Joseph	Windham, Windham CT		B72	4/12/1773
Farnam, Zebadiah*	Windham, Windham, CT	1/2 share	love	2/17/1772
Farnam, Levi, son	Windham, Windham, CT		B45 - F204	2/18/1772
see F204 for alt deed date 3/8/1774				
Farnam, Zebulon			A478	
Farnam, Ebenezer				
Farnham, Ebenezer		1/2 share except 300 A laid out	val recd	4/20/1794
Blackman, Eleazer			F98	9/15/1796

grantor / grantee / notes	grantor residence / grantee residence	description / location	amount / acct bk page	deed date / record date
Farnham, Ebenezer	Wilkes Barre, Luzerne, PA	1/2 share	£50	12/31/1793
Farnham, Elisha	Hudson, Columbia, NY		C585	6/28/1795
Farnham, Ebenezer	Bennington, Bennington, VT	three 1/2 shares*	$100	2/16/1797
Tilden, Joel	Lebanon, Grafton, NH		F205	8/14/1797
1/2 of 1 share in Susq Purchase and 1/2 of 1 share in first Delaware Purchase and 1/2 of 1 share in second Delaware Purchase called the Lackawack Purchase				
Farnham, Elisha	Cazenova, Herkimer, NY	1/4 share	£100	2/12/1795
White, Solomon	Hudson, Columbia, NY		C585	6/28/1795
Farnham, Elisha	Hudson, Columbia, NY	1/4 share	£200	4/8/1794
White, Solomon	Hudson, Columbia, NY		C586	6/28/1795
Farnham, Levi heir Levi	Lebanon, Windham, CT	1/2 share	£3	5/6/1795
Larrabee, Lebbeus	Windham, Windham, CT		C602	7/9/1795
Farnham, Levi [Sr.] died a prisoner in the late war btw Gr. B and America and Levi and Samuel are only children; certified by Ebenezer Moseley, JP, Windham Co, CT				
Farnham, Stephen		1/2 share		
Benjamin, Isaac			GF	
Farnham, William		1/2 share		3/12/1774
Farnham, Stephen			GF	4/2/1776
Farnum, Levi of Windham	S.Brimfield, Hampshire, MA	1/2 share	£30	6/12/1775
Farnam, Zebadiah, father	Windham, Windham, CT		B332	7/1/1775
Farnum, Ruben	Canterbury, Windham, CT	1/2 share	good cause	4/5/1774
Faulkner, Caleb	Canterbury, Windham, CT		B276	11/14/1774
Faulkner, Caleb	Canterbury, Windham, CT	1/2 share	good cause	11/12/1774
Fish, Joseph	Canterbury, Windham, CT		B277	11/14/1774
Fellows, Abiel		1/2 share		2/15/1774
Whitney, Joshua			GF	
Fellows, Abiel		1 share		
Whitney, Joshua			GF	
Fellows, Nathan	Poultney, Rutland, VT	1,000 A	$333.33	10/4/1801
Ashley, John and Noah	Poultney, Rutland, VT		H296	5/21/1801
Fellows, Nathan	Putney, Rutland, VT	1 share	$400	5/19/1796
Batman, Zadoc	Putney, Rutland, VT		E379	9/15/1796
except 1/3 to Jabin Strong and 700 A to Daniel Beman				
Fellows, Nathan	Putney, Rutland, VT	1 share and 1/2 share with	$400	5/19/1796
Batman, Zadoc	Putney, Rutland, VT		E379	9/15/1796
except 1/3 sold to Jabin Strong and 700A to Daniel Beman; except 1/2 to heirs John Koon and 100 A to Ashbel Paine				
Fellows, Nathan	Poultney, Rutland, VT	200 A	6s	2/19/1796
Beeman, Daniel	Addison, VT		F46	4/25/1796
William Cook has 500 A of this share and first choice of location out of the 700 A total				
Fellows, Nathan	Poultney, Rutland, VT	500 A	£150	2/9/1796
Cook, William	New Haven, Addison, VT		F47	4/25/1796
Fellows, Nathan	Putney, Rutland, VT	Pwr Attorney for 1 share	1/3 land to Strong	4/30/1795
Strong, Jabin	Glastonbury, Hartford, CT		E68	2/28/1796
Fellows, Stephen	Canaan, Litchfield, CT	1/3 (2/3 of 1/2) share		7/13/1774
Harrison, Steven	Canaan, Litchfield, CT		I5	6/6/1786
Fenn, Roswell	Luzerne, PA	500 A undivided from 11,000 A	$500	5/20/1800
Elwell, Dan		Gore of land adj. W of Athens Twp	H216	5/28/1800
Ferry, John & Ferry, John Jr.	Sheffield, Berkshire, MA	100 A, Lot 19	1 lot of land	7/15/1776
Franklin, John	Canaan, Litchfield, CT	Huntington, Westmoreland, PA	I3	6/3/1786
Field, John	Watertown, Litchfield, CT	1 share	£100	3/30/1795
Field, Samuel & Noah	Waterbury, New Haven, CT &		C636	7/10/1795
Field, Samuel	Saybrook, CT	1/2 share	£9	9/5/1794
Waterhouse, Saml & Harris,	Saybrook, CT		C116	9/6/1794
Firch, Rufus	Pawlet, Rutland, VT	1 share	£9	6/5/1795
Mosely, Nathaniel J.	Pawlet, Rutland, VT		C565	6/20/1795
Fish, Jabez	Wilkesbarre, Luzerne, PA	1 1/2 shares	$90	11/21/1795
Hyde, Ezekiel	Norwich, New London, CT		I254	12/4/1795
Fish, John	Lower Smithfield Twp, PA*	1/5 share*	$3	4/1/1775
Brookes, James	Lower Smithfield Twp, PA*		I165	2/21/1795
Northampton Co, PA; see record at Hartford CT				
Fish, Moses	Voluntown, Windham, CT	1/2 share	£5	11/14/1782
Boardman, David	Preston, New London, CT		C67	12/16/1782
Fish, Moses	Voluntown, Windham, CT	1 share	£10	11/14/1782
Kenney, Ezra	Preston, New London, CT		C68	12/16/1782

grantor grantee notes	grantor residence grantee residence	description location	amount acct bk page	deed date record date
Fish, Thomas*	Groton, New London, CT	Pwr Att 1 1/2 shares		10/28/1795
Fish, Jabez*	Wilkesbarre, Luzerne, PA		I254	12/4/1795
bros. and sons of Capt Thomas Fish				
Fisk, Moses				
Robins, Caleb			A315	
Fitch, Abel				
Dean, James			A457	
Fitch, Daniel	Pawlet, Rutland, VT	1 share	£20	4/14/1795
Fitch, Rufus	Pawlet, Rutland, VT		C565	6/20/1795
Fitch, Ebenezer	Lebanon, Windham, CT*	1 share	£40	4/29/1775
Trumbull, David	Lebanon, Windham, CT		F32	4/23/1796
now New Amherst, Cumberland, NS				
Fitch, Eleazar				
Conant, Shubal			A62	
Fitch, Eleazer	Windham, Windham, CT	1 share	£10	1/1/1795
Fitch, Eleazer Jr.	Windham, Windham, CT		C615	7/1/1795
Fitch, Eleazer Esqr		1 share		
Gray, Ebenezer & Lee, Samuel			MB	
Fitch, Eleazer Jr.	Windham, Windham, CT	Pwr Att to locate 1 share		1/20/1795
Spalding, John	Ulster, Luzerne, PA		C615	7/1/1795
Fitch, Jabez	Canterbury, Windham, CT	1/2 share	£5	9/26/1755
Curtis, John	Canterbury, Windham, CT		C390	2/22/1795
Fitch, Jabez	Canterbury, Windham, CT	1/2 share	10£	2/28/1770
Fitch, James	Windham, Windham, CT		B304	1/20/1775
Fitch, Jabez	Vergennes, Addison, VT	1 share SP; 1 share DP	$50	4/8/1795
Fitch, Samuel	Vergennes, Addison, VT		E73	3/1/1796
Fitch, Jabez	late Jr. of Canterbury, CT*	1 share	$50	11/10/1795
Grant, Josiah	Poultney, Rutland, VT		F70	5/24/1796
now of Vergennes, Addison, VT				
Fitch, James				
Backus, Ebenezer			A328	
Fitch, James				
Guild, Samuel			A294	
Fitch, James Jr.	Windsor, Hartford, CT	1/2 share	40s	11/4/1774
Allen, Levi	Salisbury, Litchfield, CT		B304	1/20/1775
Fitch, James Jr.	East Windsor, Hartford, CT	1/2 share	£4	11/14/1774
Allen, Levi	Salisbury, Litchfield, CT		B335	4/24/1775
Fitch, James Jr.	East Windsor, Hartford, CT	1/2 of 1 share; 1 share; 1 share*		11/4/1774
Allen, Levi	Salisbury, Litchfield, CT		E226	7/2/1796
1/2 share Susquehanna Purchase; 1 share First Delaware Purchase; 1 share Second Delaware Purchase				
Fitch, John, distribution				
Fitch, James			A280	
Fitch, John heirs*	Windham, Windham, CT;	1/2 share	£7.10	9/28/1785
Hall, Joshua	Colchester, New London, CT		C89	10/24/1785
John Fitch; Ellie & Jonathan Marsh				
Fitch, John heirs*	Windham & Norwich, CT	1/2 share	£7.10	9/28/1785
Kellog, Martin	East Haddam, Middlesex, CT		C90	10/24/1785
John Fitch; Ellie & Jonathan Marsh				
Fitch, Jonathan	Bridport, Addison, VT*	1 share	$15	5/18/1795
Grant, Josiah	Poultney, Rutland, VT		C564	8/9/1795
formerly of Norwich, CT				
Fitch, Rufus	Pawlett, Rutland, VT	1 share	$35	6/3/1795
Hooker, James	Poultney, Rutland, VT		C566	6/20/1795
Fitch, Samuel Sherwood	Montville, New London, CT	2 shares	£30	11/29/1794
Tracy, Elisha	Norwich, New London, CT	Cabot Twp	I136	12/25/1794
Fitch, William		1 share		4/25/1774
Fitch, Jabez			GF	
Fitch, William	New Town, Fairfield, CT	1/2 share	£20	2/20/1781
Taylor, Ruben	New Town, Fairfield, CT		C54	11/11/1782
Fitch, William Capt	Pawlett, Rutland, VT	all shares*	£150	3/4/1795
Fitch, Rufus	Pawlett, Rutland, VT		D30	10/5/1795
Susquehanna, Delaware and Lackaway purchases				

grantor grantee notes	grantor residence grantee residence	description location	amount acct bk page	deed date record date
Fletcher, Cotten and Ebenezer		1/2 share		12/13/1773
Pell, John			GF	
Fletcher, Cotten and Ebenezer		1/2 share		12/14/1773
Ransom, Samuel			GF	8/20/1774
Fletcher, Ebenezer, Doct		1 share		
Fletcher, Cotten & Ebenezer, heirs			GF	
Flint, James	Windham, Windham, CT	150 A*	$25	1/19/1796
Elderkin, Alfred	Windham, Windham, CT		E192	6/11/1796
1/2 of 300 A of a half share				
Flint, James	Windham, Windham, CT	1/3 of 1/2 share	40s	5/14/1795
Larrabee, Lebbeus	Windham, Windham, CT		C603	7/9/1795
Flint, James	Windham, Windham, CT	Pwr to locate 300 A	150 A	1/20/1795
Spalding, John			E192	6/11/1796
Flint, James Jr.	Windham, Windham, CT	1/4 share	£7	3/9/1774
Andruss, William	Norwich, New London, CT		B179	3/9/1774
Flint, James Jr.		1/2 share as per C363		
Badger, Samuel Jr.			A225	
Flint, James Jr.	Windham, Windham, CT	800 A pitch on Lackawanna R.	£150	9/5/1777
Flint, James	Windham, Windham, CT	between Providence & Pittston	B361	9/5/1777
Flint, James Jr.	Windham, Windham, CT	200 A of 1/2 share	£5	6/24/1769
Gilbert, Jesse	Windham, Windham, CT		C82	1/13/1783
Follet, Charles Att	Bennington, Bennington, VT	300 A near Standing Stone	£20	6/26/1786
Fitzgerald, Darrick [spld Fitch	Wyoming	adj. Fitzgerald on west side Susq R.	I166	2/20/1795
for Elizabeth Follet, mother				
Follet, Elizabeth	Bennington, Bennington, VT	Pwr Att		2/5/1786
Follett, Charles, son	Bennington, Bennington, VT		I166	2/20/1795
Follet, Joseph				
Bennet, William			A283	
Follette, Charles	Worthington, Hampshire, MA	16,000 A each	$10,666.66*	7/8/1796
Bostwick, Benjamin	Brookfield, Fairfield, CT	Benjamin Twp, Starsboro Twp	E352	8/29/1796
terms = £5 earnest money, $1500 in 25 days and equal pts. in 8, 16, 24 mos.				
Foot, Charles	Colchester, New London, CT	1 share		4/15/1794
Turner, Seth	New Haven, New Haven, CT		C290	3/4/1795
Foot, Daniel	Colchester, New London, CT	Pwr Att 1 share		10/26/1793
Foot, Isaac	Stafford, Tolland, CT		E378	9/13/1796
Ford, Bethiah Estate*	Branford, New Haven, CT	1/2 share	$10	3/29/1796
Pope, Robert	Derby, New Haven, CT		D172	7/2/1796
John Ford (husband), exec.				
Forsey, James				
Butler, Zebulon			A444	
Forward, Abel		1/4 share*		9/7/1791
Forward, Jesse			I157	2/19/1795
Deed recorded in Granby CT				
Forward, Abel		1/4 share*		9/7/1791
Forward, Samuel			I157	2/19/1795
Deed recorded in Granby CT				
Forward, Joseph	Granby, Hartford, CT	1/2 share	£12	9/20/1794
Lamb, Ezekiel	Enfield, Hartford, CT		C327	3/1/1795
Foster, John late of Wilkesbarre	West Chester Co, NY	5 A Lot adj. Nathan Chapman mill	£15	11/20/1786
Baker, Nehemiah	Wilkesbarre	Wilkesbarre Twp	I13	11/20/1786
Foster, William	Canterbury, Windham, CT	Pwr Att to sell 1 share		12/20/1788
Cleaveland, Moses	Canterbury, Windham, CT		H312	8/11/1801
Foster, William Jr.	Whitehall, NY*	1/2 share	£3	1/26/1795
Larrabee, Lebbeus	Windham, Windham, CT		C367	3/2/1795
late of Canterbury, Windham, CT				
Fowler, Daniel	Bethlehem, Berkshire, MA	1/4 twp	900£	8/29/1796
Hulbert, Stephen	Bethlehem, Berkshire, MA	Eastham Twp	E457	10/31/1796
Fowler, Dijah	Lebanon, Windham, CT	1/2 share	£20	12/31/1794
Adams, Jabez	Canterbury, Windham, CT		C463	2/2/1795
Fowler, Reuben	Killingsworth, Middlesex, CT	all 1st division rights	$15,000	7/16/1796
Baker, Daniel M.	Arlington, Bennington, VT	Alba and Weathersfield Twps	E347	8/24/1796
Fowler, Reuben	Killingworth, Middlesex, CT	3 shares	£20	9/24/1794
Fowler, William	Guilford, New Haven, CT		C119	10/1/1794

grantor grantee notes	grantor residence grantee residence	description location	amount acct bk page	deed date record date
Fowler, Reuben	Killingsworth, CT	16,000 A	$5,000	6/1/1796
Tiffany, Isaiah/Baldwin, Saml,	W Stockbridge, Berkshire, MA	Armenia Twp	F180	7/16/1797
Fowler, William	Guilford, New Haven, CT	8 1/2 shares	£400	10/15/1795
Prescott, Benj & Sherman, Roger	New Haven, New Haven, CT		E216	
Fox, Benjamin	New London, New London, CT	1/2 share		12/21/1773
Jerom, Augustus	New London, New London, CT		C559	6/20/1795
Francis, Elijah	Berlin, New Haven, CT	1 share	£12	1/29/1796
Smith, Lemuel & Allyn, John B.	Berlin, Hartford, CT		E143	2/25/1796
Frank, William	Williamsboro, Duddas, Up CAN	Pwr Att to recover and receive		9/9/1795
Angar, August, trusted friend	Bartic, Upper Canada		E536	3/3/1797
Franklin, Jehiel	Woodbury, Litchfield, CT	1/2 share	£15	11/10/1773
Backus, Delicina	Woodbury, Litchfield, CT		B143	2/21/1774
Franklin, Jehiel		all right		2/27/1795
Foster, Isaac & Rufus		Warcorlack, Tioga Twp	I190	3/19/1795
Franklin, Jehiel		300 A, 1/2 share No. 205 of 400		12/6/1794
Terries, Job		New Milford Twp	C116	2/26/1795
Franklin, John	Athens, Luzerne, PA	Lot 1 of Little Meadow or Point Lots*	affection	3/9/1799
Beebe, Hezia, dau	Athens, Luzerne, PA	Tioga Point, Athens, Luzerne, PA	H48	3/9/1799
Franklin, John	Athens, Luzerne, PA	Lot 2: Ten Acre or Little Meadow	$200	3/9/1799
Beebe, Solomon	Athens, Luzerne, PA	Tioga Point, Athens, Luzerne, PA	H45	3/9/1799
Franklin, John	Athens, Luzerne, PA	Lots 16, 17: Ten Acre or Mdow Lots	affection	3/9/1799
Beebe, Solomon, Doct & wf	Luzerne, PA	Tioga Point, Athens, Luzerne, PA	H46	3/9/1799
Daughter of John Franklin				
Franklin, John	Canaan, Litchfield, CT	1/2 share inc. Lot 47, 100A	£45	2/3/1778
Fellows, Obil	Canaan, Litchfield, CT	Huntington Twp	I56	6/4/1787
Franklin, John	Canaan, Litchfield, CT	1/2 Lot 19, 50 A	love	2/3/1778
Harrison, Sussanah, dau	Canaan, Litchfield, CT	Huntington Twp	I7	6/6/1786
Franklin, John		1000 A*		6/20/1795
Hebard, Jonathan		anywhere unappropriated*	C580	7/20/1795
Hebard in Wilkesbarre, 1769 for greater part of two years. Conrad Baker took his duty and drew a right in the twp; Baker taken prisoner, right reassigned; Hebard could never regain his right.				
Franklin, John	Canaan, Litchfield, CT	1/2 share	£30	5/25/1778
Hooker, Hezekiah	Sheffield, Berkshire, MA		I10	6/6/1786
Freeman, Nathaniel	Chatham, Middlesex, CT	1/2 share	£12	12/30/1795
Hosmer, Zachariah	Chatham, Middlesex, CT		E426	9/16/1796
Freese, John & Desire*	Lee, Berkshire, MA	3/4 share	£15	11/6/1794
Twining, William Jr.	Granville, Hampshire, MA		E507	6/1/1796
& Hannah Williams, wid, of Great Barrington, Berkshire, MA				
French, Andrew	Windham, Windham, CT	800 A pitch Lackawanna R.	£150	1/9/1776
Flint, James Jr.	Windham, Windham, CT	between Providence & Pittstown	B340	1/9/1776
French, Francis and Burrett, Wm	Darby, New Haven, CT	1 share	good cause	1/25/1796
Pope, Robert	Darby, New Haven, CT		E407	9/15/1796
French, Jonathan, painter	Providence, Providence, RI	600 A, all of French's right	$70.00	3/15/1800
Larcher, James, hatter	Providence, Providence, RI	Durkee Twp	H225	6/2/1800
Frink, Elias				
Frink, Joseph			A112	
Frink, Elias, heir Frink, Andrew	Windham, Windham, CT	1/2 share	20s	6/19/1795
Larrabee, Lebbeus	Windham, Windham, CT		C602	7/9/1795
Frink, Elias Jr., decd,	Windham, Windham, CT	1 share	15s	12/11/1794
Chauncey, Worthington G.	Durham, New Haven, CT		C322	12/11/1794
Hezekiah Manning, adm				
Frink, John				
Flint, James Jr.			A217	
Frink, Joseph				
Forsey, James			A362	
Frink, Joseph	Windham, Windham, CT	1/2 share	£6	4/24/1773
Larrabe, Timothy	Windham, Windham, CT		B73	5/10/1773
Frink, Mathias/Matthew	Sterling, Windham, CT	1/4 share	£3	1/14/1796
Peirce, John	Plainfield, Windham, CT		E274	7/15/1796
Frisbe, Jacob	Bethlehem, Litchfield, CT	1/4 share, 300 A	£3	6/18/1796
Moseley, Nathaniel T.	Pawlet, Rutland, VT	Smithfield Twp adj. Solomon Morse	H74	5/20/1799
Frisbe, James	Bethlehem, Litchfield, CT	1/2 share	$20	6/7/1796
Moseley, Nathaniel T.	Pawlet, Rutland, VT		H73	5/20/1799

grantor	grantor residence	description	amount	deed date
grantee	grantee residence	location	acct bk page	record date
notes				
Frisbie, James	Woodbury, Litchfield, CT	1/4 share	£3	4/7/1773
Frisbie, Jacob	Woodbury, Litchfield, CT		B169	3/9/1774
Frisby, James	Branford, New Haven, CT	1 share	£13. 10	10/17/1787
Doty, David	Sharon, Litchfield, CT		D53	11/18/1795
Frisby, Zebulon	Farmington, Hartford, CT	1 share	£25	12/4/1777
Roberts, Elias	Farmington, Hartford, CT		B378	3/13/1778
Frost, Elisha	Plymouth, Litchfield, CT	1/3 Twp, undivided	£586	6/17/1796
Clark, Samuel	Middletown, Middlesex, CT	Jay Twp	D176	8/9/1796
Frotheringham, Samuel	Middletown, Middlesex, CT	Pwr Att 1/2 share, survey &		2/15/1796
Wallworth, Daniel	Middletown, Middlesex, CT		E341	6/15/1796
Condition: if E. Frotheringham attorneys have laid out 1/2 share already this Pwr null; see C625				
Frothingham, Ebenezer	Middletown, Middlesex, CT	Pwr to locate 1 share within 2 yrs		1/8/1796
Ballard, Step & Chamberlain, S C.	Judsboro, PA & Colebrook, CT		C625	7/1/1795
Frothingham, Samuel	Middletown, Middlesex, CT	1 share, No 158 of 600 & 1/2 share	$1,000	2/7/1799
Winship, Tim and Walworth, Danl	Middletown, Middlesex, CT		H99	9/14/1799
Fuller, John	New Sheshequin	1 share, No. 132 of 600 except 300	£16	12/9/1795
Irwin, James	Tioga	Columbia Twp	E438	10/1/1796
Fuller, John and Reuben	Ulster, Luzerne, PA	1,100 A Towanda Creek	$1,100	1/4/1800
Thayer, Levi	Tioga, Luzerne, PA	adj. south of Stephen Fuller	H192	1/4/1800
Fuller, Stephen	Wilkesbarre, Westmoreland,	1/2 share	£20	12/14/1782
Chelsey, Abner	Pittstown, Westmoreland, CT		I49	7/4/1786
Fuller, Stephen	Ulster, Luzerne, PA	4,000 A except 300 A	$3,000	12/30/1799
Thayer, Levi	Tioga, Luzerne, PA	Fuller Pitch	H179	1/1/1800
Fuller, Stephen Jr.	Windham, Windham, CT	1/2 share	£5	1/6/1762
Abbott, Joseph	Pomfret, Windham, CT		B57	3/29/1773
Fuller, Sylvester	Providence, Providence, RI	1350 acres	$1750	5/20/1796
Whitman, George	Providence, Providence, RI	Springhill, Luzerne, PA	D161	6/20/1796
Gale, Benjamin				
Colt, Harris			A359	
Gale, Benjamin	Wallingford, New Haven, CT	1/2 share inc. 1 pitch	love	5/4/1780
Gale, Thomas, son	Derby, New Haven, CT	Yalmouth Twp	C72	11/14/1782
Gallop, Isaac	Sterling, Windham, CT	1/3 share and Pwr Att*	£5	4/22/1795
Larrabee, Lebbeus	Windham, Windham, CT		C603	7/9/1795
to lay out 2/3 share for Gallop and split taxes due				
Gallop, William	Groton, New London, CT	1/2 share	£6	4/27/1770
Breed, Gershom	Norwich, New London, CT		B173	3/12/1774
Gallop, William				
French, Solomon			A402	
Gallup, William	Groton, New London, CT	1 share	£36	12/5/1762
Avery, Samuel	Groton, New London, CT		B241	8/20/1774
Gallup, William	Groton, New London, CT	1 share	£30	10/26/1762
Avery, Samuel	Groton, New London, CT		E395	9/20/1796
Gardiner, Caleb	Norwich, New London, CT	1/3 share	£20	3/29/1777
Carr, Robert	Westmoreland, Litchfield, CT		B354	4/5/1777
Gardiner, John	St.Johnsbury, Orange, VT	all right	$25	5/12/1795
Horton, Hiram	Brandon, Rutland, VT		E53	2/25/1796
Gardner, Benjamin	Genesse Dist, Ontario, NY	1/2 share: 3 Lotts*	£100	11/25/1795
Hutchinson, John	Athens, Luzerne, PA	Athens Twp	E159	5/16/1796
Lots given to Gardner for service				
Gardner, Benoni				
Case, Joseph			A303	
Gardner, Benoni		1/2 share		10/1/1773
Gardner, Benoni heirs			GG	11/1/1774
Gardner, Benoni		1/2 share		
Thayer, David			GG	
Gardner, Benoni heirs				
Carrier, Thomas			GG	
Gardner, John	Catskill, Albany, NY	4,000A (2 1/2 mi.sq.)	£1600	11/11/1794
Thayer, Nathan	Hudson, Columbia, NY	Watertown Twp	C551	6/10/1795
Gardner, Jonathan estate*	Bozrah, New London, CT	1 share	£15	11/25/1794
Hyde, Elisha; Tracy, Elisha	Norwich, New London, CT	Cabot Twp, 1/2	I134	12/25/1794
Lemuel Gardner, adm				

grantor grantee notes	grantor residence grantee residence	description location	amount acct bk page	deed date record date
Gardner, Jonathan estate,	Bozrah, New London, CT	1 share*	£20	11/5/1794
Tracy, Elijah Capt	Norwich CT	Exeter Twp	I109	12/6/1794
Lemuel Gardner, Adm; auctioned at court order				
Gardner, Peregrine		1/4 share		
Buck, Phillip			GG	
Gardner, Peregrine		1/4 share		2/23/1775
Vincent, Cornelius			GH	9/13/1775
Gardner, Sanford	Providence, Providence, RI	1 share	$30	1/16/1795
Ward, Ichabod	Windham, Windham, CT		C395	2/22/1795
Gardner, Stephen	Colchester, Hartford, CT	1 share	£36	4/28/1760
Fitch, Sherwood	Norwich, New London, CT		I183	2/22/1795
Gardner, Stephen	Colchester, Hartford, CT	1 share	£1,000	3/6/1780
Raymond, Christopher Jr.	New London, CT		C17	3/7/1780
Gardner, Stephen Jr.		1 share		5/2/1774
Scoville, Nathan			GG	5/12/1774
Garner, Libbeus	Wilusink	1/2 share of 400		12/5/1794
Whitcomb, Joel		Allensberg Twp	C199	2/19/1795
Garnsey, Ebenezer	Woodbury, Litchfield, CT	1 share	£4.10	9/20/1766
Cole, David	Waterbury, New Haven, CT		B377	3/13/1778
Garnsey, Ebenezer	Woodbury, Litchfield, CT	1 share	£4.10	9/20/1766
Cole, David	Waterbury, New Haven, CT		F198	8/2/1797
Garnsey, Joseph	Waterbury, New Haven, CT	1/2 share	val sum	4/21/1774
Barns, Titus	Waterbury, New Haven, CT		B160	3/9/1774
Garnsey, Joseph	Watertown, Litchfield, CT	1 share	$30	10/27/1795
Taylor, John	Schodack, Rensselaer, NY		E291	6/20/1796
Gaskill, Silas & Jonathan	Union, NY	1 share ex 600 A	$27	10/20/1795
Shepard, John		Murraysfield Twp	E329	4/10/1795
Gaston, Alexander	Salisbury, Litchfield, CT	1/2 share	£5	10/12/1763
Dixon, John	Voluntown, Windham, CT		B106 - GG	12/15/1773
Gaston, Alexander Jr.	Richmond, Berkshire, MA	all land in Susquehanna Purchase	£15	6/29/1796
Center, Robert & Williams, Elisha	Richmond, MA & Hillsdale, NY		E354	8/24/1796
Gaston, Alexander, last will	Richmond, Berkshire, MA	all lands		1/22/1781
Gaston, Alexander Jr.			E353	7/20/1796
Gaylord, Aaron	Westmoreland, Westmrld, CT	1/2 share	£42.10	12/31/1777
Brockway, Richard	Westmoreland, Westmrld, CT		B387	2/25/1778
Gaylord, Ambrose		1/2 share ex 300 A		3/1/1795
Shepard, John		Allensburgh Twp	E330	4/10/1795
Gaylord, Edmund		1/2 No. 121 of 400, Lot 12 1st Div		4/12/1794
Hutchinson, John		Columbia Twp	D50	11/6/1795
Gaylord, Eleazer	Braintrim, Luzerne, PA	700 A 2nd division land	$20	5/26/1795
Shepard, John	Tioga, Luzerne, PA	[Columbia Twp]	E322	4/10/1796
Gaylord, Joseph				
Gaylord, Eleazar			A99	
Gaylord, Justin Jr.		1/2 share No. 86 of 400	$20	3/2/1795
Shepard, John			E331	4/10/1796
Gaylord, Lemuel	Luzerne Co PA	Lot 12; Lot 15	good cause	12/25/1795
Hitchinson, John	Luzerne Co PA	Columbia; Murraysfield Twps	C533	5/1/1795
Gaylord, Lemuel		1 share, No. 187 of 600		7/23/1795
Hutchinson, John		Murraysfield Twp	D50	11/6/1796
Gaylord, Lemuel	Athens, Luzerne, PA	1 acre, pt of house lot*	£7. 10	6/4/1791
Root, Jared	Athens, Luzerne, PA	Plymouth Twp	E44	2/23/1796
now occupied by Rufus Lawrence				
Gaylord, Lemuel		1/2 share, No. 133 of 400		5/30/1794
Stow, Polly		Juddsborough Twp*	D24	9/24/1795
entered 300 A for Polly Stow on Lot No. 36, 4/1/1795				
Geer, Amos	Groton, New London, CT	1 share	£60	2/6/1795
Hyde, Elisha	Norwich, New London, CT		I181	2/22/1795
Gennings, Jonathan				
Gore, Obadiah			A432	
Gere, Robert	Groton, New London, CT	1/2 share	£6	2/6/1795
Hyde, Elisha	Norwich, New London, CT		I180	2/22/1795

grantor grantee notes	grantor residence grantee residence	description location	amount acct bk page	deed date record date
Gibbs, Zebulon	Litchfield South Farms,	Deposition re James Morris*		2/17/1796
			E405	9/15/1796
Gibbs lived South Farms 70 yrs. James Morris, decd, the only James Morris ever lived there and James Morris now living has no bros and sisters alive and James Morris did own 1/2 or 1 share.				
Gilbert, Elisha	Mansfield, Windham, CT	1/2 share	£12	4/14/1773
Blanchard, Jedediah Cap't	Ashford, Windham, CT		B70	4/14/1773
Gilbert, Elisha				
Lane, Samuel			A340	
Gilbert, Elisha		1 share		
Lane, Samuel			GG	
Gilbert, Noah		1 share		
Gilbert, Elisha, heir by will			GG	
Gilbert, Samuel				
Mitchel, Peter			A51	
Giles, Benjamin	Norwich	1 share inc. 1 lot	£40	5/15/1775
Clements, Jeremiah	Norwich	Berlin Twp	C80	12/25/1782
Giles, Benjamin				
Randal, Sylvester			A456	
Giles, Benjamin				
Reynolds, Jedediah			A236	
Giles, Thomas	Groton, New London, CT	2 share	£100	2/5/1795
Hyde, Elisha	Norwich, New London, CT		I179	2/22/1795
Gillet, Hezekiah				
Gaylord, Samuel			A271	
Gillet, John	Norfolk, Litchfield, CT	1/10 of 1 share	15s	2/10/1795
Strong, Jabin	Glastonbury, Hartford,CT		E81	3/2/1796
Gillet, John		1/2 share		
Whitney			GG	
Gold, Hezekiah				
McCoy, Ephriam			A341	
Gonegal, James H.	Voluntown, Windham, CT	1/4 share	£5	7/12/1774
Jameson, John	Westmoreland, Litchfield, CT		B230	7/13/1774
Goodrich, Benjamin	Canaan, Litchfield, CT	29 3/4 shares*	3s and agreement	4/24/1796
Pitkin, Elisha	Catskill, Albany, NY		E263	7/1/1796
original proprietors named but most have intermediate conveyors; agreement dated 12/ 22/1795				
Goodrich, Charles W.	Alford, Berkshire, MA	250 A from 6 Lots 9, 10 two, 12 two,	$250	4/15/1797
Thomson, Silas & Church, Rufus	Salem, Washington, NY	Baldwinville, Luzerne, PA	F160	5/13/1797
Goodrich, Craft		1/2 share		1/19/1773
Downer, Samuel			A475	
Goodrich, E. C./Hogeboom, Peter	Claverack, Columbia, NY	1 twp	5s	8/25/1795
Turner, Seth		WashingtonTwp	E179	6/1/1796
Goodrich, Elihu C.	Claverack, Columbia, NY	750 A 1st div & 1/2 land remaining*	Stanley's right*	1/12/1798
Stanley, Lot	Berlin, Hartford, CT	Hudson Twp	H208	
Stanley's right one of several on which Goodrich granted twp. In return, Goodrich grants Stanley 750 A 1st div & 1/2 land remaining on right				
Goodrich, Elihu C.	Claverack, Columbia, NY	16,000 A	5s	8/25/1795
Turner, Seth		Canton Twp	E178	6/1/1796
Goodrich, Elihu C. and Hogeboom,	Claverack, NY	16,000 A	5s	8/25/1795
Turner, Seth		Clinton Twp	E177	6/1/1796
Goodrich, Elihu C., Attorney	Claverack, Columbia, NY	16,000 A	5s	10/17/1796
Hogeboom, Peter	Hudson, Columbia, NY	Hudson Twp	F130	11/12/1796
Goodrich, Elihu C. & Turner, Seth	Claverack, Columbia, NY	16,000 A	5s	8/25/1795
Hogeboom, Peter	Hudson, Columbia, NY	Adams Twp	F132	11/12/1796
Goodrich, Elihu C. & Turner, Seth	Claverack, Columbia, NY	16,000 A	5s	8/25/1795
Hogeboom, Peter	Hudson, Columbia, NY	Jay Twp	F134	11/12/1796
Goodrich, Elihu Chauncey*	Claverack, Columbia, NY	all right	5s	9/7/1795
Battle, Thiel	Tyringham, Berkshire, MA	Richmond Twp	D72	12/4/1795
Master in Chancery, Columbia, NY				
Goodrich, Elihu Chauncey	Claverack, Columbia, NY	8000 A*	£800	10/22/1795
Belding, Chester	Claverack, Columbia, NY	Hancock Twp, 1/2	E385	9/10/1796
Turner and Hogeboom released to Goodrich				
Goodrich, John, Abigail Goodrich,	Glastenbury, Hartford, CT	1/2 share	£100	4/23/1795
Hale, George	Catskill, Albany, NY		D16	9/18/1795
Goodwin, Daniel				
Marshal, Noah			A94	

grantor	grantor residence	description	amount	deed date
grantee	grantee residence	location	acct bk page	record date
notes				
Goodwin, Samuel			A376	
Goss, Phillip				
Goodwin, Samuel heirs*	Hartford, Hartford, CT	Pwr Att to survey and locate 1 share	1/2 surveyed land	1/14/1795
Ballard, Steph & Chamberlain, S.	Judsborough, Luzerne, PA &		C623	7/1/1795
Samuel, James, George, David Goodwin, et al				
Gordon, Alexander	Bethlehem, Litchfield, CT	1/2 share, 300 A	£9	1/26/1795
Hannah, Robert	Bethlehem, Litchfield, CT	Watertown Twp	C619	7/1/1795
Gordon, James A.	Athens, Luzerne, PA	1/4 pt Lot 8, 2nd division, undivided	$100	3/25/1799
Thayer, Levi	Athens, Luzerne, PA	Athens Twp	H162	12/30/1799
Gordon, John	Woodbury, Litchfield, CT	1/2 share	£8. 5	1/16/1786
Lewis, Judah	Woodbury, Litchfield, CT		C333	2/26/1795
Gordon, Robert	Woodbury, Litchfield, CT	1/2 share, 300 A	£9	1/26/1795
Gordon, Alexander	Bethlehem, Litchfield, CT	Watertown Twp	C618	7/1/1795
Gordon, Samuel	Luzerne, PA	16,000 A	£700	5/9/1795
Barney, Henry	Plymouth, Luzerne, PA	Walsingham Twp	D136	12/20/1795
Gordon, Samuel	Voluntown, Windham, CT	1 share	£19	1/9/1795
Dorrance, Benjamin	Kingston, Luzerne, PA		I211	4/1/1795
Gore, John	Kingston, Luzerne, PA	1/2 share, 4 Lots*		2/24/1789
Farnham, Ebenezer	Kingston, Luzerne, PA	Northmoreland Twp	C584	6/28/1795
Lot No. 8, 4th tier; No. 9, 2nd tier; No 18, 5th tier; No 13, 5th tier				
Gore, John heir of Gore, Obadiah		1/2 share ex 300 A	$20	3/1/1795
Shepard, John	Tioga, Luzerne, PA	Northmoreland Twp	E330	4/10/1796
Gore, Obadiah	Wilkesbarre	Lot No 5, 3 1/2 A house lot	£15	3/20/1787
Cleveland, Aaron	Wilkesbarre	Wilkesbarre Twp	I47	11/8/1786
Gore, Obadiah		1/2 share		
Pierce, Hannah			GH	
Gore, Robert 2nd	Groton, New London, CT	1/2 share	£3	9/8/1794
Elliot, William	Saybrook, Middlesex, CT		C354	3/2/1795
Gore, Samuel	Voluntown, Windham, CT	1 share	love	1/11/1789
Gore, Elijah son	Halifax, Windham, VT		I92	7/7/1794
Gorham, Jabez	Fairfield, Fairfield, CT	1/2 share	£10	1/5/1774
Hull, John	Fairfield, Fairfield, CT		B128	1/20/1774
Gorham, Jabez	Romulus, Onondaga, NY		£11	2/16/1796
Sherwood, Stephen			E75	3/1/1796
Gorton, Othniel & Theodosia	Warwick, Kent, RI	1/2 share	£28. 9. 3	3/10/1774
Garnder, John	Exeter, Kings, RI		B212	5/5/1774
Goss, Nathaniel	Huntington, Luzerne, PA	1/2 proprietor's rgt inc. Lot 31, 300 A	20£	6/5/1795
Seaward, Enos	Huntington, Luzerne, PA	Huntington Twp	F122	11.21.1796
Goss, Philip	Huntington, Luzerne, PA	300 A*	$40	11/21/1796
Long, John	Huntington, Luzerne, PA		H284	8/26/1799
out of right of David Bull of Hartford; Long may survey 300 A where he now lives, i.e. Huntington Twp				
Goss, Prudence, dau and heir	Berkshire, MA	1/2 share	50£	5/25/1779
Squire, Zachariah	Albany, NY		F270	3/14/1798
Goss, William		1 share		4/17/1770
Gallon, Francis			GL	1/1/1774
Gott, Daniel	Hebron, Tolland, CT	Pwr Att to locate 1 share	1/3 part of land	3/23/1795
Strong, Jabin	Glastonbury, Hartford,CT		E84	3/2/1796
Gould, James	Providence, Providence, RI	300 A*	$200	2/22/1797
Bowman, Samuel	Norwich, New London, CT	Smithfield Twp	H136	9/14/1799
choice of location in one of 8 lots Gould purchased from Arnold				
Gould, John, heir*	Lebanon, Windham, CT	1 share	£5	2/2/1795
Swift, Silas	Lebanon, Windham, CT		I208	4/1/1795
Augustin Gould heir and adm				
Graham, Andrew	Woodbury, Litchfield, CT	1/2 share	$20	1/1/1757
Ives, Jesse	Wallingford, New Haven, CT		B115	1/6/1774
Graham, Andrew				
Rose, Timothy			A409	
Graham, Andrew				
Tweedy, John & Samuel			A40	
Graham, Andrew, Pract. in Physic	Woodbury, Litchfield, CT	1/3 share	£5	2/8/1759
Graham, Chauncy	Kumbout, Dutchess, NY		B42	6/3/1773
Graham, Sheldon & Platt, Daniel	Albany and Columbia, NY	buy shares to procure grants of twps	$240	3/1/1795
Gordon, Saml and Hutchinson, John	Luzerne, PA		E265	7/1/1796

grantor	grantor residence	description	amount	deed date
grantee	grantee residence	location	acct bk page	record date
notes				
Granger, Simeon	Sanderfield, Berkshire, MA	1/4 of 1 share	£20	1/23/1797
Kingsbery, Danl Jr.& George*	Sanderfield, Berkshire, MA		F210	8/16/1797
Clothiers				
Grant, John				
Bicknal, Samuel			A442	
Grant, John				3/10/1770
Chaffee, Jr.			A330	
Grant, John				
Lampshire, Isaac			A276	
Grant, John	Ashford, Windham, CT	1/2 share	£6	10/15/1771
Pratt, Jacob	Saybrook, New London, CT		B48	4/1/1772
Grant, Josiah	Graham, Luzerne, PA	160 A with 8 A reserved for roads	$205	5/9/1799
Barnes, Joel	Granville, Hampshire, MA	Graham Twp	H212	2/11/1800
Grant, Josiah	Poultney, Rutland, VT	3 shares	$180	6/20/1795
Burr, Jonathan	Lansingburgh, Rensselaer, NY		C569	6/22/1795
Grant, Josiah	Poultney, Rutland, VT	4,000 A	$840	3/9/1796
Cook, John & Patterson, Robert	Poultney, Rutland, VT	Bowdoin Twp	E418	9/16/1796
Grant, Josiah	Graham, Luzerne, PA	160 A Lot 24 reserving 8 A for roads	$130	1/2/1800
Darling, Theron	Graham, Luzerne, PA	Graham, Luzerne, PA	H209	2/5/1800
Grant, Josiah	Graham, Luzerne, PA	1,200 A*	$700	6/30/1800
Fellows, Nathan	Poultney, Rutland, VT		H225-226	1/30/1800
300 A entered in Lot 36, Smithfield for Nathan Fellows by John Franklin				
Grant, Josiah	Poultney, Rutland, VT	176 A, Lot 29	$160	9/5/1798
Gregory, Elijah	Castleton, Rutland, VT	Graham Twp	H258	10/18/1800
Grant, Josiah	Poultney, Rutland, VT	1,200 A*	$60	10/12/1796
Hutchinson, John & Gordon, Saml	Luzerne, PA	Standing Stone Twp	H13 - C569	11/10/1798
600 A on Jabez Fitch Jr., OP; 600 A on Robert Park, OP, entered in Standing Stone by John Franklin				
Grant, Josiah	Poultney, Rutland, VT	4,000 A, SE 1/4, 2.5 mi. sq.	$4,000	7/2/1796
Paine, David	Athens, Luzerne, PA	Bowdoin Twp	E229	
Grant, Josiah	Poultney, VT	1/2 share	$50	6/15/1796
Pitkin, Elisha	Catskill, Albany, NY		E258	7/1/1796
Grant, Josiah	Polton [Poultney], Rutland, VT	7,400 acres	$400	6/15/1796
Pitkin, Elisha	Catskill, Albany, NY		E264	7/1/1796
Grant, Josiah	Poultney, Rutland, VT	2,540 A*	good cause	5/25/1786
Thayer, Levi	PA		E332	7/2/1796
OP: Joseph Follett 600, Thomas Little 300, Nathan Patrick 300, Benjamin Brown 150, Benjamin Green 300, Benjamin Fox 300, Daniel Fitch 300, Jonah Fitch 300				
Grant, Josiah	Poultney, Rutland, VT	4,000 A	$500	10/12/1796
Thayer, Levi	Athens, Luzerne, PA	Graham Twp, south half	E427	10/14/1796
Grant, Josiah	Graham, Luzerne, PA	140 A off the SE corner Lot 23	good cause	9/9/1799
Wheeler, Peter	Graham, Luzerne, PA	Graham Twp	H313	7/20/1801
Grant, Noah		1/2 share		7/1/1776
Landon, John			GG	
Grant, Solomon		1/2 share		
Grant, Noah, heir			GG	
Gray, Ebenezer	Windham, Windham, CT	1/2 share	£15	3/23/1774
Lee, Samuel	Windham, Windham, CT		B194	3/24/1774
Gray, Samuel Esq., decd	Windham, Windham, CT	1/2 share	gift	5/7/1795
Gray, Lucy, dau.			E50	2/24/1796
Gray, Samuel Esq., decd*	Windham, Windham, CT	1/2 settling right, about 200 acres	gift	5/7/1795
Huntington, Enoch Jr., et al*		Town of Lawrence*	E49	2/24/1796
Samuel Gray & Esther chr of Wm & Mary Huntington, by Will; No Town of Lawrence, possibly meant Luzerne?				
Gray, Samuel Esq., decd	Windham, Windham, CT	1/2 share	gift	5/7/1795
Huntington, Mary wf of Rev. Wm		Warwick Twp, first division	E49	
Green, Benjamin	Grenville, Washington, NY	1/2 share	£10	3/17/1795
Janes, Elijah, merchant, et al	Troy, Rensselaer, NY		C128	8/9/1795
James Dole, merchant & Wait Rathbun, innkeeper				
Green, Benjamin	Canaan, Litchfield, CT	1/2 share	£25	11/30/1754
Paine, Joshua and Baker, William	Oblong, Dutchess, NY		E114	3/17/1796
Green, Benjamin heirs	Poultney, Rutland, VT	1 share	£9. 12	5/25/1795
Hooker, James Major	Poultney, Rutland, VT		C562	8/9/1795
thru Robert Green: Oliver Sanford and Catharine Sanford; Amasa Thatcher and Phebe Thatcher; Huldah Green and Ellis Green				

grantor / grantee / notes	grantor residence / grantee residence	description / location	amount / acct bk page	deed date / record date
Green, John	Coventry, Kent, RI	3/4 of 2 half shares, Lots 23, 26, 600	£9	2/1/1795
Green, Lodowick	Coventry, Kent, RI	Warwick, transferred to Smithfield	H230	8/21/1800
entered in Warwick 1774, but falling out of the Purchase was reentered in Smithfield				
Green, John	Coventry, Kent, RI	1/4 of 2 half shares, Lots 23, 26, 300	$5	4/2/1799
Green, Martha, spinster	Coventry, Kent, RI	Warwick, transferred to Smithfield	H231	8/21/1800
Green, Thomas	Warwick, Kent, RI	1/2 share	love	12/9/1794
Hill, Sarah, dau, wf of Caleb Hill	North Kingston, Washington, RI		H17	11/15/1798
Green, Timothy	New London, New London, CT	1/2 share	£5	2/2/1773
Hurlbut, John	Groton CT		B158	3/9/1774
Greene, Joshua				
Updike, Lodowick			A244	
Greene, Nathaniel estate	Boston, Suffolk, MA	quit claim to 1 share	5s	11/4/1773
Greene, Joseph, merchant	Boston, Suffolk, MA		B137	11/24/1773
Annabelle, widow & exec.				
Greene, Thomas				
Greene, Job Jr.			A311	
Gregory, Ebenezer B./Myer,	Tyringham, Berkshire, MA	1/4 undivided part	2000s	7/16/1796
Northrop, Isaac	Hudson, Columbia, NY	Hancock Twp	E335	8/10/1796
Gregory, Elijah	Castleton, Rutland, VT	Lot 29, 126 A*	$200	4/14/1800
Roberts, Lebius	Castleton, Rutland, VT	GrahamTwp	H224	5/31/1800
reserve 1 A every 20 for public roads				
Griffen, Ebenezer		Pwr Att to locate & lay out 1/2 share	1/4 pt	5/6/1795
Young, William Jr.			C599	7/9/1795
Griffin, John				
Marsh, Elihu			A74	
Griswold, Abel	Norwich, New London, CT	1 share	£10	2/7/1795
Hyde, Elisha; Tracy, Elisha	Norwich, New London, CT		I178	2/7/1795
Griswold, Elijah	Claverack, Albany, NY	1/2 share	£11	11/4/1773
Hagaman, John, Trader	Claverack, Albany, NY		F202	8/2/1797
Griswold, Gideon	Berlin, Hartford, CT	2 shares*	£20	4/10/1795
Smith, Joel	Berlin, Hartford, CT		D166	6/24/1796
1 share Gideon Griswold; 1 share father David Griswold, decd				
Griswold, Joseph	Norwich, New London, CT	1 share	£7	11/24/1794
Hyde, Elisha; Tracy, Elisha	Norwich, New London, CT		I140	12/25/1794
Griswold, Noah		1/2 share		1/22/1774
Oster, Caleb			GG	
Griswold, Samuel et al				1/1/1794
Benton, Elihu	Guilford, New Haven, CT		D58	11/16/1795
Scoville, Bela & Chloe Griswold; incomplete deed				
Griswould, Elijah	Chemung, Tioga, NY	1 share	val con	3/28/1796
Baldwin, Thomas	Newtown, Tioga, NY		E356	7/20/1796
Grosvenor, Ebenezer	Pomfret, Windham, CT	all rights	6s	7/14/1771
Grosvenor, Thomas	Pomfret, Windham, CT	Susquehanna Purchase	B19	7/19/1773
Grosvenor, John	Pomfret, Windham, CT	1 share	£12	1/12/1795
Adames, Jabez & Adams, Asahel	Canterbury, Windham, CT		C468	2/20/1795
Grosvenor, Thomas	Pomfret, Windham, CT	all right*	£12	1/9/1795
Adams, Asahel & Adams, Jabez	Canterbury, Windham, CT	Susquehanna Purchase	C465	2/20/1795
1 share				
Grover, Ebenezer		300 A		2/26/1777
Forsyth, James			GG	
Grover, Isaiah	Ulster, Luzerne, PA	300 A, Lot 32*	$150	4/17/1797
Couch, David	Ulster, Luzerne, PA	Smithfield Twp	H329	12/29/1801
adj. S Capt. Adriel Simmons				
Grover, Isaiah	Luzerne, PA	300 A, Lot 23	$500	12/2/1796
Mitchell, Reuben	Luzerne, PA	Smithfield Twp	E480	12/2/1796
Grover, Sarah*	Norwich, New London, CT	1 share & 2 half shares	£100*	11/17/1794
Hyde, Elisha	Norwich, New London, CT	1 SP, 1/2 DP; 1/2 LP	I133	12/25/1794
dau of Ebenezer Grover, decd.; 1/2 share of SP laid out in Cabot Twp				
Grover, Sarah dau	Norwich, New London, CT	1/2 share	£100*	11/17/1794
Hyde, Elisha	Norwich, New London, CT	Delaware Purchase	I133	12/25/1794
amt. inc. other shares				

grantor grantee notes	grantor residence grantee residence	description location	amount acct bk page	deed date record date
Grover, Sarah dau	Norwich, New London, CT	1 share	£100*	11/17/1794
Hyde, Elisha	Norwich, New London, CT	Lackawack Purchase	I133	12/25/1794
amt. inc. other shares				
Guiteau, Francis Jr.	Lanesborough, Berkshire, MA	1/2 share	£6	7/20/1772
Parmelee, Thomas Jr.	Woodbury, Litchfield, CT		B174	3/9/1774
Guitteau, Ephriam				
Minor, Elizabeth			A43	
Guitteau, Ephriam	Norfolk, Litchfield, CT	1/2 share	£20	12/20/1781
Minor, John Jr.	Norfolk, Litchfield, CT		C87	9/29/1784
Guitteau, Joshua				
Atwood, Elijah			A406	
Guitteau, Joshua	Woodbury, Litchfield, CT	1/2 share	val con	6/21/1760
Mitchel, John	Woodbury, Litchfield, CT		B127	1/18/1774
Guitteau, Sarah & Phebe				
Guittean, Joshua			A46	
Gunn, Joseph	Brookfield, Fairfield, CT	1/2 share	10s	5/16/1794
Gunn, Abel	Brookfield, Fairfield, CT		I94	6/7/1794
Gunn, Joseph	Brookfield, Fairfield, CT	1/2 share	10s	5/16/1794
Host, Daniel & Anna	Danbury, Fairfield, CT		I94	6/7/1794
Gunsales [Gonzales], Manuel		1 share		1/1/1757
Depui, Nicholas			E105 - F237	3/1/1796
Gurney, Bezaleel	Paris, Herkimer, NY	1/2 share	val sum	9/11/1794
Robards [Roberts], Seth	Paris, Herkimer, NY		C638	7/29/1795
Guthrie, Ephriam	Kent, Litchfield, CT	1/4 share	£5	3/25/1774
Palmer, William	Kent, Litchfield, CT		B218	5/24/1774
Guthrie, Joseph	Washington, Litchfield, CT	1/4 share	£100	12/22/1779
Graham, James	Kent, Litchfield, CT		C46	6/7/1782
Guthrie, Joseph	Washington, Litchfield, CT	1/4 share	£100	12/22/1779
Kelsey, Heth	Kent, Litchfield, CT		C45	6/7/1782
Guthrie, Joseph	Washington, Litchfield, CT	two 1/2 shares	£10	6/27/1794
Turrell/Terrill, Job	New Milford, Litchfield, CT	New Milford Twp	C339	2/26/1795
Hagaman, John	Claverack, Albany, NY	1/2 share	£15	9/10/1776
Hogeboom, Jeremiah	Westmoreland on Susquehanna		F203	8/2/1797
Hail, Elisha				
Hungerford, Benjamin			A76	
Hale, Curtis	Harwinton, Litchfield, CT	1/2 share	val sum	8/23/1794
Roberts, Seth	Paris, Herkimer, NY		C638	7/29/1795
Hale, David	Glastonbury, Hartford, CT	1/4 share	£1	5/13/1794
Hale, George	Catskill, Albany, NY		C372	2/28/1795
Hale, David		agent for a Twp survey	Throop share	7/20/1795
Throop, Benjamin			C120.1	9/1/1795
for fifteen owners, including Throop, who pay Throop 6s per day for his time and horse; total of 8 shares; D. Hale unspecified share				
Hale, Elisha	Glastonbury, Hartford, CT	3/4 share	£6	5/19/1794
Hale, George	Catskill, Albany, NY		C373	2/28/1795
Hale, George	Catskill, Albany, NY	10 Lots 1-4, 6-7, 9-11, 13 400 A ea.	£100	10/30/1796
Paine, David	Athens, Luzerne, PA	Fairfield Twp, east half, 4,000 A	E540	11/1/1796
Hall, Asa	Gageborough, Berkshire, MA	1/2 share	£16	2/1/1777
Dean, Ezra	West Greenwich, Kent, RI		B364	2/1/1777
Hall, Joash	Wallingford, New Haven, CT	1 share	£30	11/21/1782
Hall, Brenton	Wallingford, New Haven, CT		C61	12/5/1782
Hall, Joash	Wallingford, New Haven, CT	1/2 share	£15	11/21/1782
Hall, Phineas Jr.	Wallingford, New Haven, CT		C61	12/5/1782
Hall, John	Canaan, Litchfield, CT	1/2 share, 109 A plus A in later Divs.	£10	4/26/1774
Farnam, Levi	Brimfield, Hampshire, MA	Chillisquake Twp	B331	7/1/1775
Hall, Joshua	Colchester, Hartford, CT	1/2 share	£12	10/22/1773
Dean James	Lebanon, Windham, CT		B92	11.30.1773
Hall, Joshua	Colchester, New London, CT	all shares	£30	7/5/1795
Dorrance, Gershom	Windham, Windham Co CT		C537	5/7/1795
Hall, Joshua				
Perkins, John			A355	
Hall, Reuben	Stonington, New London, CT	1/2 share	£15	1/6/1775
Avery, Elisha	Groton, New London, CT		H349	1/12/1803

grantor grantee notes	grantor residence grantee residence	description location	amount acct bk page	deed date record date
Hall, Reuben	Stoningtown, New London, CT	1 share	£30	4/2/1795
Dorrance, Gershom	Lebanon, Windham, CT		E96	3/6/1796
Hall, Reuben		all right		11/12/1793
Minor, Saxton			E364	7/7/1799
Hall, Thomas & Sarah*		Pwr Att locate, apportion 1 share		2/10/1796
Walworth, Daniel			E342	6/15/1796
heirs of Josiah Robinson				
Hall, William	Union Twp, NY	1/2 share No. 59 of 400	£1	4/16/1792
Bates, Caleb	Putnam, Luzerne, PA		I162	5/26/1794
edge note: William Hall received 5s fr Capt Caleb Bates for deed on this certificate 29 Feb 1788				
Hallsted, Richard Jr.	Luzerne Co PA	4,000 A	$2,000	1/6/1796
Wood, Nathaniel	Hillsdale, Columbia, NY	Hallsted Twp, NE corner	E24	2/9/1796
Halstead, Samuel of the 400	Luzerne Co PA	1/2 share	£12	2/28/1795
Smith, Jonas	Sugar Creek, Luzerne, PA		C271	3/10/1795
Halsted, Richard Jr.	Exeter, Luzerne, PA	16,000 A	$2,000	9/16/1796
Decker, Tunis, Blacksmith	Kingstown, Luzerne, PA	Oston Twp	F175	6/26/1797
Hamilton, Dudley	Schenectady, Albany, NY	Promissory deed for payment	$2,275*	11/13/1795
Rankin, George	Newtown, Tioga, NY	Dorchester Twp	E433	4/1/1796
$650 in 90 days; $1625 in 9 mo.				
Hamilton, Dudly	Schenectady, Albany, NY	16,000 A	$3,250	11/13/1795
Booth, John, merchant	Hudson, Columbia, NY	Dorchester Twp	D148	6/10/1796
Hamilton, Ezekiel	Canaan, Litchfield, CT	1/2 share	£12	12/15/1774
Guitteau, Ephriam	New Marlboro, Berkshire, MA		B297	12/21/1774
Hamilton, Joseph	Hudson, NY	2,750 A	£400	3/1/1797
Belknap, Ebenezer	Durham, CT	Hamilton Twp	F259	3/2/1798
Hamilton, Joseph	Hudson, Columbia, NY	5,000 A	£125	12/18/1795
Satterlee, Elisha	Athens, Luzerne, PA	Hamilton Twp, NE corner	E357	6/1/1796
Hamilton, Patrick, Dr.	Canaan, Columbia, NY	16,000 A	$2000	10/5/1795
Battle, Thiel	Tyringham, Berkshire, MA	Sharon Twp*	D64	12/4/1795
granted to Patrick Hamilton on 8 certificates 46, 59, 60, 73, 73, 74, 74, 69 fr Joseph Hamilton				
Hamilton, Samuel		1 share, No. 383 of 600		6/16/1795
Betts, Ebenezer			C571	5/20/1795
Hamilton, Silas	Wilmington, Windham, VT	1,000 A	$1,000	9/10/1800
Hamilton, John	Hampshire, MA	Kingsberry Twp	H295	5/6/1801
Hamilton, Solomon	Norwich, New London, CT	1 share	val con	10/22/1794
Kingsbery, Joseph	Enfield, Hartford, CT		I112	12/6/1794
Hamilton, Solomon, ship carpenter	Norwich, New London, CT	1/2 of 1 share*	£2. 8	3/5/1760
Davis, Benajah	New London, CT		E343	6/15/1796
Davis heirs pd $2 tax 12/31/1782				
Hamilton, Walter	Hudson, Columbia, NY	1/2 share No. 75 of 600, Lot 49,	£100	3/31/1795
Booth, John	Hudson, Columbia, NY	Murraysfield Twp	C534	5/7/1795
Hamilton, Walter	Hudson, Columbia, NY	150 A undivided	$40	10/1/1794
Button, Peter	Oxford, Chenango, NY	Burlington, Luzerne, PA	H298	5/19/1801
Hamilton, Walter	Athens, PA/Hudson, NY	16,000 A*	£800	7/20/1795
Paine, David	Athens, PA	Salisbury Twp	C508	9/7/1795
Nos. 45-48, 1400 A each; Nos. 49-50, 53-54; 2000 A each; Nos. 75, 357, 700 A each; Nos. 159, 1000 A				
Hamilton, Walter	Hudson, Columbia, NY	Eastham Twp	£800	8/17/1795
White, Solomon, taylor	Hudson, Columbia, NY		D146	6/10/1796
Hammond, Elisha	Chenango, Tioga, NY	4,000 A	$1,250	5/4/1796
Hitchcock, Joseph	Chenango, Tioga, NY	Harlem Twp, 1/4 of E half	E157	5/4/1796
Hammond, Elnathan*	Middlebury, Addison, VT	1/2 share*	£10	3/7/1795
Ward, Ichabod	Windham, Windham, CT		E57	2/25/1796
heir & grandson of Elnathan Hammond of Newport; pd taxes 2/18/1768; 5/27/1769; 11/5/1786				
Hanks, Uriah	Mansfield, Windham. CT	1/2 share	$11.00	1/29/1795
Kingsberry, Joseph	Enfield, Hartford, CT		F123	7/29/1796
Hann, Michael	Southbury, Litchfield, CT	1/2 share	£12	1/27/1796
Adams, Ezra	Fairfield, Fairfield, CT		H92	8/19/1799
Hannah, James	Woodbury, Litchfield, CT		£34	5/20/1755
Parmelee, Jonathan	Middletown, Hartford, CT		C349	9/1/1795
Hannah, Robert	Bethlehem, Litchfield, CT	two 1/2 shares*	val sum	4/13/1795
Wheeler, Abner	Bethlehem, Litchfield, CT		C619	7/1/1795
1/2 share Robert Hannah, father, OP; 1/2 Robert Gordon, OP, to Alexander Gordon, son, to Robert Hannah; 300 A on half share Robert Hannah laid out in Watertown Twp to John Spalding 6/1/1795				

grantor / grantee / notes	grantor residence / grantee residence	description / location	amount / acct bk page	deed date / record date
Hard, James				
Hurlbut, Nathan			A96	
Harden, Abraham				
Spencer, Jared			A8	
Harding, Abraham	Westmoreland, Litchfield, CT	1/2 share & right in the 2 ten mi	£20	10/28/1776
Strong, Solomon	Westmoreland, Litchfield, CT		F200	8/2/1797
The 2 ten mile tracts were intended for the first 200 settlers. These tracts became Wilkes-Barre and Forty later Kingston Twp				
Harret, Thomas		1/2 share		4/7/1796
Hollenback, Isaac		Murraysfield Twp	E338	5/15/1796
Harrington, Jeremiah	Owego, Tioga, NY	1/2 share, Lot 33	£30	12/23/1795
Hutchinson, John	Tioga, Luzerne, PA	Columbia Twp	C306	2/28/1795
Harrington, Jeremiah Jr.	Glastonbury, Hartford, CT	1500 acres	$1,500	3/4/1796
Randall, Joseph	Wallingford, Rutland, VT	Plato Twp	E283	7/15/1796
Harris, Alpheus		1 share, No 187 of the 600		7/1/1795
Gaylord, Lemuel			D50	7/1/1795
Harris, Alpheus	Athens, Luzerne, PA	300 A, Lot 17	$100	1/2/1800
Satterlee, Elias	Athens, Luzerne, PA	Murraysfield Twp	H190	1/4/1800
Harris, Charles	Kingston Twp	1/2 share		11/26/1794
Baldwin, Waterman	Newtown	Allensburgh Twp*	E366	4/1/1796
asks John Franklin and others on Committee to relocate share from Allensburgh Twp				
Harris, Lebbeus				
Spencer, Jared			A33	
Harriss, Jedediah				
Harriss, James, Joseph & Nicholas			A90	
Haskel, Gideon				
Gore, Obadiah			A431	
Haskel, Gideon		1/2 share		
Gore, Obadiah			GH	
Hatch, John				
Bull, Thomas			A50	
Haughton, James	Montville, New London, CT	all right	£6	1/28/1796
Peirce, John	Plainfield, Windham, CT		E272	7/15/1796
Hawkins, Samuel	Schenectady, Albany, NY	1/16 undivided land	$800	1/28/1799
Barnaby, Ambrose	Franklin, Delaware, NY	Sheffield Twp	H116	11/28/1799
Hawkins, Samuel	Schenectady, Albany, NY	1/16th undivided land	$500	11/14/1796
Dunlap, William, sadler	Schenectady, Albany, NY	Sheffield Twp	H233	9/11/1800
Hawley, Francis	Huntington, Fairfield, CT	1 share	val con	1/31/1795
Hawley, Elijah, son	Huntington, Fairfield, CT		E277	6/8/1796
Hawley, Francis	Stratford	1/2 share		
Hinman, Ebenezer	Woodbury, Litchfield, CT		B73	5/24/1773
Hawley, Milton		1/2 share		
Bostwick, Dimon	New Milford, Litchfield, CT	New Milford Twp	I153	12/6/1794
Hawley, Ruth	Huntington, Fairfield, CT	all right to my share	£1.10	1/1/1796
Lewis, Walker			E279	6/8/1796
Hays, David		1 share		1/1/1774
Brown, John			GH	
Hayward, Benjamin				3/9/1770
Grant, John			A331	
Hayward, Joseph		1/2 share		2/17/1756
Dean, Ephriam			B51	4/29/1772
Hazzard, Stephen	South Kingston, Washington, RI	amount not stated*	ten hundred dollars	7/17/1800
Knowles, Joseph M.	South Kingston, Washington, RI		H234	9/19/1800
land bought with Lodowick Updike & Sylvester Robinson; no acreage stated				
Hazzard, Stephen	South Kingston, Kings, RI	1/2 share	6s	11/26/1773
Wait, John, goldsmith	South Kingston, Kings, RI		B168	3/11/1774
Hazzen, Howlet	Norwich, New London, CT	1/2 share	£10	10/8/1773
Hyde, Azel	Lebanon, Windham, CT		E525	1/1/1797
Hazzen, Joseph				
Clements, Jeremiah			A107	
Heard, Thomas				
Robinson, William			A257	
Heath, Joseph	Claverack, Columbia, NY	Lot 24, 300 A	£100. 10	2/16/1795
Arms, Samuel	Claverack, Columbia, NY	Smithfield Twp	D164	6/18/1796

grantor grantee notes	grantor residence grantee residence	description location	amount acct bk page	deed date record date
Heath, Joseph	Noble Town, Albany, NY	1/4 share	£15	5/2/1778
Hogeboom, Jeremiah	Claverack, Albany, NY		F276	3/19/1798
Heath, Joseph		1/4 share		5/5/1774
Pixley, Elias			GH	9/19/1775
Heath, Joseph	Lanenburgh, Albany, NY	1/2 twp	£1000	11/7/1794
Rositer, Samuel	Claverack, Columbia, NY	Lebanon Twp, E 1/2	I113	12/8/1794
Heath, Joseph and Clark, Ezekiel	Noble Town, Albany, NY	1/2 share	£25	10/10/1778
Hogeboom, Jeremiah	Claverack, Albany, NY		F276	3/19/1798
Heath, Thomas		1/4 share, 300 A		7/3/1795
Heath, Adolph		Bedford Twp	I221	7/4/1795
Hebard, Augustus	Windham, Windham, CT	100 A	$100	10/30/1798
Bleight, Samuel	Windham, Windham, CT		H62	5/15/1799
Hebard, Gideon	Windham, Windham, CT	1/2 share	10s	12/11/1794
Chauncey, Worthington G.	Durham, New Haven, CT		C324	2/26/1795
Hebard, Jonathan	Windham, Windham, CT	100 A undivided	$50	2/1/1796
Hebard, Augustus	Windham, Windham, CT	Athens, near	E184	6/7/1796
Hebard, Jonathan	Windham, Windham, CT	4,000 A	£200	3/26/1796
Hunt, Walter	Lebanon, Windham, CT	Hebard Gore	E192	6/11/1796
Hebard, Moses	Sturbridge, Worcester, MA	all shares & Pwr att to recover shares val con		4/10/1788
Parsons, Theodosius	Windham, Windham Co CT		C538	5/7/1795
Hende, Barzilla	Woodbury, Litchfield CT	1/2 share	£10	3/19/1773
Guthrie, Ephriam	Kent, Litchfield, CT		B16	9/15/1773
Hende, Barzilla Jr.	Colebrook, Litchfield, CT	Pwr Att to locate share	1/2 located lands	2/21/1795
Martin, Reuben	Woodbury, Litchfield, CT		C627	7/15/1795
Hendee, Shubal	Woodbury, Litchfield, CT	3/4 share	£9	1/1/1795
Martin, Reuben	Woodbury, Litchfield, CT		C634	7/10/1795
Henderson, James	New Hartford, Litchfield, CT	1/2 share	£13	1/4/1774
Kellog, Solomon	New Hartford, Litchfield, CT		B122	1/20/1774
Hepburn, Samuel and Maxwell,		2/3 Lot 44 and pt Lot 45*	5s	3/1/1795
Alexander, David		Athens, Luzerne, PA	E337	8/1/1796
to be taken from upper pt, i.e. end adjoining town plot				
Hepburn, Samuel and Maxwell,		1/3 Lot 44 and pt Lot 45	5s	3/1/1795
Paine, David		Athens, Luzerne, PA	E337	8/1/1796
to be taken from lower end				
Herrick, Cyprian, heirs*	Claremont, Hampshire, MA*	1/2 share	£20	7/12/1762
Hollister, Timothy	Glastonbury, Hartford, CT		B271	11/11/1774
chr Samuel, Margaret & Sylvia; (Margaret & Ephriam Ingraham Jr. of Norwich, New London, CT; Sylvia & Josiah Reed of Kinderhook, Albany, NY				
Hervey, Thomas		1/2 share		9/23/1794
Harret, Thomas		Murraysfield Twp	E338	5/15/1796
Hewett, Walter	Stillwater, Saratoga, NY	1 share	£12	4/3/1795
Janes, Elijah, merchant et al*	Troy, Rensselaer, NY		C126	8/9/1795
James Dole, merchant; Wait Rathbun, innkeeper				
Hibbard, Jabez*	Windham, Windham, CT	1/2 share	10s	12/11/1794
Chauncey, Worthington G.	Durham, New Haven, CT		C313	2/26/1795
heir of father Zebulon Hibbard of Windham				
Hickox, Wm & Abraham, John				
Yale, Benjamin			A98	
Hide, Eli	Huntington, Fairfield, CT	1/2 share	£15	2/9/1796
Lewis, Walker	Brookfield, Fairfield, CT		E282	6/8/1796
Hide, Eliakim		1/2 share		
Hide, John			A35	6/8/1796
Hide, Elijah Sr.	Lebanon, Windham, CT	1/2 share	love	10/8/1773
Hide, Eliphalet & Ebenezer, sons	Lebanon, Windham, CT		B60	10/9/1773
Hide, Elijah Sr.	Lebanon, Windham, CT	1/2 share	love	12/4/1782
Hide, Moses & Lina, sons	Lebanon, Windham, CT		C69	12/7/1782
Hide, Elisha	Norwich, New London, CT	2 lots 150 A each + 300 A	$80	2/23/1795
Baker, Joab	Coeymans, Albany, NY	Columbia Twp	C141	2/23/1795
Hide, Ephriam chr and heirs*	Huntington, Fairfield, CT;	1/2 share	val con	2/12/1796
Hyde, Eli	Huntington, Fairfield, CT		E281	6/8/1796

William Niles and Abigail, wf; Anna Nichols; Samuel D. Hide all of Huntington, Fairfield CT; Ebenezer Dorman and Salena, wf; Phinehas Judson and Amelia, wf all of Charlotte, Chittenden, VT

grantor grantee notes	grantor residence grantee residence	description location	amount acct bk page	deed date record date
Hide, James				
Blackman, Elisha & Elliot, Thomas			A420	
Hide, Joseph & Nash, Thomas	Fairfield, Fairfield, CT	1/4 share Hide's; 1/4 share Nash's	£10	12/10/1794
Coley, Ebenezer	Weston, Fairfield, CT		C520	5/1/1795
Hide, Matthew	East Windsor, Hartford, CT	1/2 share	£10	11/14/1774
Fitch, James Jr.	East Windsor, Hartford, CT		B334	4/24/1775
Hill, Charles		Pwr Att to locate 1 share		7/9/1796
Hyde, Ezekiel			F90 - F91	8/31/1796
Hill, Thomas				
Gorham, Jabez			A242	
Hill, Thomas		1/3 share		
Sprague, Theodore			GH	
Hill, Thomas		1/4 share		
Sprague, Theodore			GH	
Hillard, Jonathan*	Voluntown, Windham, CT	Pwr Att to lay out 1/4 pt of right		4/10/1795
Larrabee, Lebbeus	Windham, Windham, CT		C605	7/9/1795
for Temperance Hillard, wf				
Hills, John	Charlotte, Chittenden, VT	all rights	$1	3/1/1796
Wheeler, Preserved	Charlotte, Chittenden, VT		E129	3/28/1796
Hills, Jonathan	East Hartford, Hartford, CT	all right	£3	10/13/1794
Pitkin, Elisha Jr.	East Hartford, Hartford, CT		E245	7/1/1796
Hills, Jonathan	East Hartford, Hartford, CT	1 share	£12	10/14/1795
Pitkin, Elisha Jr.	East Hartford, Hartford, CT		E289	7/1/1796
Hinchman, Joseph		1/2 share		1/20/1795
Tower, Henry			E302	6/20/1796
Hinckley, Hannah & Jared*	Lebanon, Windham, CT	1 share	1/4 land	2/28/1795
Strong, Jabin	Glastonbury, Hartford, CT		E89	3/5/1796
Hannah, wf and Jared heirs of Joseph Sluman, East Haddam, Middlesex, CT				
Hinkley, Gershom, Hinkley, Jared*	Lebanon, Windham, CT	1 share	£5	2/12/1795
Young, William, Jr.	Windham, Windham, CT		C598	7/10/1795
Mary Hinkley, Jared Hinkley, Charles Hinkley were the only executors of Gershom Hinkley Last Will and Testament				
Hinman, Ebenezer	Woodbury, Litchfield, CT	1/2 share	£5.7	4/21/1772
Wooster, Arthur	Derby, New Haven, CT		B73	5/24/1773
Hinman, Jonas, John, Eleazar,				
Hooker, William			A416	
Hinman, Titus	Woodbury, Litchfield, CT	1/4 share	£3	2/10/1772
Northrup, Samuel	Woodbury, Litchfield, CT		B172	3/9/1774
Hinman, Truman	Woodbury, Litchfield, CT	1/2 share	£25	11/15/1773
Curtiss, Gideon	Woodbury, Litchfield, CT		B167	3/9/1774
Hinman, Truman				
Galor, Joseph			A97	
Hinman, Truman		1/2 share		
Moseley, Increase			A404 - C338	
Hinsdale, Elijah	Berlin, New Haven, CT	1 share	$50	1/6/1796
Smith, Lemuel & Allyn, John B.	Berlin, Hartford, CT		E144	2/25/1796
Hinsdale, Joseph	New Milford, Litchfield, CT	1/2 share	5s	12/22/1794
Kinne, Daniel	Canaan, Litchfield, CT		C609	7/9/1795
Hinton, George		1/4 share		3/18/1777
Hamington, Ruben			GD	3/18/1777
Hitchcock, Ebenezer	Derby, New Haven, CT	1 share	val sum	3/24/1795
Davis, Joseph	Derby, New Haven, CT		C575	6/19/1795
Hitchcock, John	Pitsford, Rutland, VT	six 1/4 shares	£9	4/1/1795
Douglass, Zebulon	Canaan, Columbia, NY		C592	7/7/1795
Hitchcock, John	Pitsford, Rutland, VT	1/4 of each of 3 shares	£24	12/27/1788
Roberts, Duran/Ganson, Benjamin	Newhaven, VT/Petersham, MA		E79	3/1/1796
Hitchcock, John	Kent, Litchfield, CT	1/2 share	£7	5/11/1773
Wadham, Noah	New Milford		C106	12/27/1786
Hitchcock, Samuel		1/2 share, taxes pd to date		11/27/1786
Hutchinson, John/Auston, Nathaniel			I17	11/27/1786
Hogeboom, Jeremiah	Claverack, Albany, NY	Last Will and Testament	estate division	12/21/1782
Hogeboom:Annalee, Christina,			E448 - E449	10/25/1796
Annalee, wf, £50 and my part of estate of Jerrian & David Van Hoeson, decd; Christina, day & wf of Gideon N. Hubbard, £100 two yrs after my death; Peter Hogeboom, son, all rest; proved 1/16/1784 Albany, NY				

grantor grantee notes	grantor residence grantee residence	description location	amount acct bk page	deed date record date
Hogeboom, Jeremiah		1/2 share		4/5/1773
Hogeboom, Peter			GH	4/7/1773
Hogeboom, Jeremiah		1/2 share		4/5/1773
Storom, Thomas			GH	4/7/1773
Hogeboom, Peter	Hudson, Columbia, NY	16,000 A	£1600	9/18/1796
Belding, Chester	Claverack, Columbia, NY	Jay Twp	E383	9/16/1796
Hogeboom, Peter	Hudson, Columbia, NY	16.000 A	5s	11/19/1795
Goodrich, Elihu Chauncey		Claverack Twp*	E448	10/25/1796
inc. all papers, maps, surveys, receipts				
Hogeboom, Peter		16,000 A	5s	10/17/1796
Goodrich, Elihu Chauncey	Claverack, Columbia, NY	Adams Twp	F142	11/12/1796
Hogeboom, Peter	Hudson,Columbia, NY	16,000 A	5s	1/4/1798
Goodrich, Elihu Chauncey	Columbia, NY	Hudson Twp	F260	3/2/1798
Hogeboom, Peter	Hudson,Columbia, NY	16,000 A	5s	7/12/1797
Goodrich, Elihu Chauncey	Columbia, NY	Claverack Twp	F262 - F263	3/8/1798
Hogeboom, Peter & Turner, Seth		16,000 A	5s	8/25/1795
Goodrich, Elihu Chauncey	Claverack, Columbia, NY	Hancock Twp	F137	11/12/1796
Hogeboom, Peter & Turner, Seth		16,000 A	5s	8/25/1795
Goodrich, Elihu Chauncey	Claverack, Columbia, NY	New Haven Twp	F141	11/12/1796
Hogskis, Samuel		1/2 share		
Strong, Solomon			GL	
Holbrook, David Wales	Stratford, Grafton, NH	400 A	$100	1/15/1803
Burr, Labin & Printis, Levi	Claremont, Cheshire, NH	Addison Twp	Fl	1/17/1803
Holbrook, Joseph	Bethlehem, Litchfield, CT	3,000 A	$3,000	11/10/1802
Holbrook, David W.	Stratford, Grafton, NH	Addison Twp	H348	1/7/1803
Holbrook, Joseph				
Wilmot, Daniel			A67	
Holcomb, James	Freehold, Albany, NY	4000 A	£400	9/12/1795
Brown, Daniel		Amsterdam Twp	E104	3/10/1796
Holden, Phineas	Norwich, New London, CT	1/2 share	$2.50	4/24/1760
Danforth, Thomas	Norwich, New London, CT	Cabot Twp	I137	12/25/1794
Holden, Phineas	Norwich, New London, CT	1/2 share already laid out	£20	5/12/1777
Hayward, Caleb	Lebanon, Windham, CT	Newport Twp	B360	8/18/1777
Holden, Phinehas	Norwich, New London, CT	1/2 share	£10	4/20/1769
Story, Jonathan & Story, Samuel	Norwich, New London, CT		F41	4/23/1796
Holister, Ephriam				
Goodwin, Thomas			A27	
Holland, William	Westmoreland, Litchfield, CT		£15	4/25/1774
Hollenback, John	Wilkes Barre Twp		B306	1/25/1775
Hollenback, Isaac		Pwr to locate two 2nd div half		4/29/1796
Thayer, Levi			E338	5/15/1796
1/2 Thomas Hervey; 1/2 Joseph Arnold, OP				
Hollenback, Matthew	Westmoreland, Litchfield, CT	1 share	£50	2/7/1776
Carr, Robert	Westmoreland, Litchfield, CT		B353 - GH	4/5/1777
Hollenback, Matthew		1/2 share		
Carr, Robert			GH	
Hollister, Charles	Glastonbury, Hartford, CT	1/2 share	£15	4/11/1763
Hollister, Timothy	Glastonbury, Hartford, CT		MB - B272	11/11/1774
Hollister, Charles	Glastonbury, Hartford, CT	1/2 share*	£6	5/15/1772
Talcott, Elizar for Susq Co			B91	11/4/1773
bought for bro. Francis Hollister, decd, never paid so returned to Susquehanna Company				
Hollister, Ephm & Goodwin, Thos	Farmington & Middleton, CT	1/2 share	£6. 7	9/15/1773
Yale, Stephen	Wallingford, New Haven, CT		B221	5/16/1774
Hollister, Gideon Jr.	Glastonbury, Hartford, CT	1/2 share*	£12	2/9/1765
Hollister, Timothy	Glastonbury, Hartford, CT		MB - B270	1/12/1774
sold by Elizer Talcott				
Hollister, Isaac	Dutchess, NY	1/2 share	£20	5/9/1774
Newcomb, Zacheus	Dutchess, NY		B275	11/11/1774
Hollister, Nathaniel	Glastonbury, Hartford, CT	1/2 share	£8	5/17/1774
Burnham, Elizur	Glastonbury, Hartford, CT		B272	11/11/1774
Hollister, Nathaniel				
Newcomb, Zach			MB	

grantor grantee notes	grantor residence grantee residence	description location	amount acct bk page	deed date record date
Hollister, Nathaniel	Glastenbury, Hartford, CT	Pwr Att to locate 1/2 share	1/2 all land	2/20/1796
Strong, Jabin	Glastenbury, Hartford, CT		E420	9/16/1796
Hollister, Theodore	Glastenbury, Hartford, CT	Pwr Attorney 1 share	1/3 land	3/16/1795
Strong, Jabin	Glastenbury, Hartford, CT		E72	2/29/1796
Hollister, Timothy	Glastonbury, Hartford, CT	1/2 share	£12	8/6/1761
Chittenden, Simeon	Guilford, New Haven, CT		B66	6/3/1773
Hollister, Timothy		1/2 share		3/24/1763
Chittenden, Simeon			MB	
Holmes, Sanford	Woodstock, Windham, CT	two 1/2 shares	£40	1/18/1796
Tucker, John	Stockbridge, Berkshire, MA	Hebard Gore & Bedford Twp*	F193 - 195	7/19/1797
300 A laid out in Bedford, rest not located, expenses and taxes yet to be pd				
Holmes, Stephen	Stephentown, Rensselaer, NY	1/2 share	12s	10/18/1794
Ely, Elisha	Saybrook, Middlesex, NY		C340	3/2/1795
Holt, Ammi	Athens, Luzerne, PA, formerly	1,200 A, 1st division land*	$90	6/20/1799
Brockway, Reed	Athens, Luzerne, PA		H78	6/20/1799
(Andrew Robe, 600; Richard Loomis, 300; Hezekiah Phelps, 300)				
Holt, Jacob	Canaan, Litchfield, CT	4 shares & 4,000A	$200	2/25/1799
Holt, Ammi	Norfolk, Litchfield, CT	Lebanon Twp, 1/4	H42	2/25/1799
Holt, Jacob	Canaan, Litchfield, CT	2,000 A	300£	1/5/1796
Ide, Nehemiah	Stockbridge, Berkshire, MA	Baldwin Twp	E388	9/19/1796
Holt, Jacob	Canaan, Litchfield, CT	$5,000		4/4/1796
Lombard, Roswell, sadler	Stockbridge, Berkshire, MA	Wallingham Twp	F183	7/16/1797
Holt, Paul	Hampton, Windham, CT	1/2 share	£3	1/4/1795
Dorrance, Gershom & Swift, Silas	Windham, CT		C536	5/7/1795
Holt, Paul	Windham, Windham, CT	1/2 share	£5	1/10/1769
Griffin, Ebenezer Jr.	Windham, Windham, CT		B75	10/11/1773
Homes, James		1/4 share		
Gardner, Peregrine			GH	
Hooker, Elnathan	Farmington	1/2 share	£12.10	8/20/1774
Whitelsey, Abner	Weathersfield		C33	2/18/1782
Hooker, Hezekiah	Great Barrington, Berkshire,	two 1/2 shares ex 600A Huntington	£20	12/15/1794
Brown, Sanford & Twining, Wm Jr.	Sandisfield & Grandville, MA		C433	2/1/1795
Hooker, James	Poultney, Rutland, VT	1/2 share	£9	6/9/1795
Grant, Josiah	Poultney, Rutland, VT		C563	8/9/1795
Hooker, James Jr.	Poultney, Rutland, VT	2 1/2 shares	$100	5/9/1795
Grant, Josiah Capt	Poultney, Rutland, VT		C566	6/20/1795
Hooker, Joseph			A414	
Hooker, Wm & Jahel et al				
Waitstill Goodrich, Seth Bird				
Hooker, Roger	Farmington, Hartford, CT	1/2 share	£7	4/19/1773
Collens, Ambrose	Farmington, Hartford, CT		B307 [308]	2/6/1775
Hooker, Roger	Farmington, Hartford, CT	1/3 share	diverse con	6/8/1773
Hooker, Elijah	Farmington, Hartford, CT		C326	2/20/1795
Hooker, Roger		1/2 share		
Judd, Enoch			GH	
Hooker, William	Woodbury, Litchfield, CT	1/2 share	£15	9/23/1773
Crisey, John Jr.	Woodbury, Litchfield, CT		B164	3/9/1774
Hooker, William	Washington, Litchfield, CT	1/2 share	£50	4/19/1779
Hazen, John	Washington, Litchfield, CT		C5	5/15/1779
Hooker, William				
Rose, Timothy			A408	
Hooker, William	Litchfield, CT	1/2 share	£50	6/23/1778
Strong, Ebenr Jr. & Wagner, David	Woodbury & Litchfield, CT		C7	5/15/1779
Hooker, William				
Strong, Timothy			A415	
Hopkins, David	Hebron, Washington, NY	Revoke Pwr Att to recover and lay		7/15/1800
Grant, Josiah			H259	10/18/1800
Hopkins, James & David	West Greenwich, Kent, RI	1/2 share	£9	1/17/1772
Eaton, Joseph	Plainfield, Windham, CT		B373	10/21/1777
Hopkins, John B.	Waterbury, New Haven, CT	all right		1/26/1796
Allyn, John B.	Berlin, Hartford, CT		E141	2/25/1796
Hopkins, Noah		3/4 share		7/5/1774
Pain, John			GD	7/5/1774

grantor grantee notes	grantor residence grantee residence	description location	amount acct bk page	deed date record date
Hopkins, Roswell* Strong, Jabin *heir and exec of Stephen Hopkins*	Amenia, Dutchess, NY Glastenbury, Hartford, CT	Pwr Att to locate 1 share	1/2 all land E421	8/7/1796
Hopkins, Stephen, decd* Canfield, Judson *Samuel Hopkins, exec. Stephen Hopkins pd all prior taxes on 3/6/1774 and pd $2 taxes toward $4 total 7/13/1785.*		1/2 share	val con E406	9/15/1796
Hopkins, Stephen estate* Hamilton, Joseph *Roswell Hopkins adm*	Amenia, Dutchess, NY Sharon, Litchfield, CT	1/4 share	£10 B357	10/25/1773 6/19/1777
Hopkins, Timothy Hopkins, Dorcas			A479	
Hopkins, William of Harwinton Tiffany, Consider	Windsor, Hartford, CT Hartland, Litchfield, CT	1/2 share	£10 B323	3/28/1775 3/29/1775
Hopson, Jordan Staples, John		1/2 share	GH	5/30/1772 5/10/1777
Horsford, Daniel Wheeler, Preserved	Charlotte, Chittenden, VT Charlotte, Chittenden, VT	all right	$1 E129	2/19/1796 3/28/1796
Hosford, Josiah Huxley, Jared			A472	
Hosmer, Timothy Allen, Levi	Farmington, Hartford, CT Northeast Precinct, Dutchess,	1 share	£40 E497	4/14/1779 12/17/1796
Hough, David & Jabez Hyde, Elisha & Tracy, Elisha	Bozrah, New London, CT Norwich, New London, CT	2/3 share Cabot Twp	£100 I130	12/9/1794 12/25/1794
Hough, John Stark, Benajah, grandson	Norwich, New London, CT Fairfield, Fairfield, CT	1/4 share Warwick Twp	love B265	10/31/1774 11/5/1774
Hough, Walter & Hough, Erastus Tracy, Elisha	Canterbury, Windham, CT Norwich, New London, CT	1/3 share	£20 I169	1/26/1795 2/23/1795
Houghton, Lemuel Allen, Levi	East Windsor, Hartford, CT Salisbury, Litchfield, CT	1/2 share	£10 E225	1/27/1775 7/2/1796
House, John for August Angar Paine, David *Angar 300 A E side Susq R, 3-4 mi S Tankawannah Cr. where John Fitch now lives & Frank Lot near mouth of Tankawannah Cr. where Newman now lives*	Bartic, Lincoln, Upper Canada Tioga, Luzerne, PA	1 share* Tankawannah Cr. area	$200 E538	3/3/1797 3/3/1797
Hovey, Daniel Gray, Ebenezer	Mansfield, Windham, CT Windham, Windham, CT	1 share	£20 B249	2/21/1774 2/22/1774
Hovey, Nathaniel Hovey, James	Orring, Grafton, NH Lime, Grafton, NH	1/2 of 1 share	$150 E387	5/30/1795 9/10/1796
Hovey, Nathaniel Leavenworth, Asa	Landoff, Grafton, NH Waterbury CT	1/2 of 1 share	£15 D47	12/15/1774 11/6/1795
Hovey, Nathaniel Jr. Griffin, Benjamin	Windham Windham	1/4 share	£5 C12	3/8/1779 4/27/1779
How, James How, Nehemiah	Ashton, Windham, CT Ashton, Windham, CT	all rights	6s C365	2/2/1795 3/2/1795
How, Samuel Kellogg, Stephen	Canaan, Litchfield, CT Sheffield, Hampshire, MA	1/8 share	£10 E108	4/17/1761 2/17/1796
How, Samuel Spaulding, Deliverence			A426	
How, Samuel, estate, John Gilbert, Elderkin, Joshua	Mansfield, Windham, CT Windham, Windham, CT	1 share	£8 B178	3/14/1763 3/11/1774
Howard, Calvin & Howard, Elias* Strong, Jabin *only heirs of Peter Howard; Deed actually refers to A351, 2/6/1777*	Surry, Cheshire, NH Glastonbury, Hartford,CT	Pwr Att to locate 1 share	1/3 part of land E82	4/4/1795 3/2/1796
Howard, Isaac* Howard, Thomas *Extract of Will of Isaac Howard*		1/2 share	H289	4/8/1777 3/19/1801
Howard, John Durkee, Andrew			A278	
Howard, John Howard, John Jr.			A235 - B321	3/21/1769
Howard, John Jr. Howard, John, Capt., father	Windham, Windham, CT Windham, Windham, CT	1/4 share	£4 B321	3/16/1775 3/23/1775
Howard, Joseph Barrett, Jonathan	Lime, Grafton, NH Norwich, Windsor, VT	all share	£7 C644	4/14/1795 8/10/1795

grantor grantee notes	grantor residence grantee residence	description location	amount acct bk page	deed date record date
Howard, Thomas		1/2 share		3/17/1801
Adams, Josiah			H288	3/19/1801
Howard, Thomas	Sturbridge, Worcester, MA	1/2 share		6/20/1774
Blodget, James	Monson, Hampshire, MA		C437	4/14/1795
Howard, Thomas	Sturbridge, Worcester, MA	1/2 share	£30	12/27/1774
Howard, Nathan et al	Sturbridge, Worcester, MA		C77	12/10/1782
William Hatfield, Jonathan Mason				
Howard, Thomas		1/2 share		
Whitmore, Josiah			GH	
Howard, Thomas		1 share		
Whittemore, Josiah			GH	
Howard, William		1/4 share except lands in Salem Twp		2/4/1795
Larrabee, Lebbeus			C193	2/27/1795
Howell, Josiah		1/4 share	10s	10/5/1796
Earl, Benjamin			C531	5/1/1795
Hoxsey, Zebulon		1/2 share		9/20/1773
Hicks, Levi			GH	
Hubbard, Daniel estate*	New Haven, New Haven CT	all rights	20s	10/8/1774
Allen, Levi	Salisbury, Litchfield, CT		B289	1/20/1775
Stephen Ball, adm				
Hubbard, Ebenezer		1/2 share		5/25/1772
Robertson, Thomas			GH	
Hubbard, John		1/2 share	$2	12/30/1782
Susq Co [for tax on 1/2 share]			E27	1/9/1796
Hubbard, Leverett, Col./gentleman	New Haven, New Haven, CT	1/2 share	£10	3/23/1774
Allen, Levi, merchant	Salisbury, Litchfield, CT		B257	10/5/1774
Hubbard, Leverett, Doctor	New Haven, New Haven, CT	1 share*		
Stiles, Ezra, Rev.			A291	11/15/1796
Stiles pd taxes on 2 3/4 shares 5/31/1769 (1 fr Leveret Hubbard, 1 from Nathaniel Hubbard, 1/2 in own name, 1/4 from 1/2 John Rice original half share, see E480)				
Hubbard, Nathaniel, Doctor, decd*	New Haven, New Haven, CT	1 share		
Stiles, Ezra, Rev.			A292	11/15/1796
"at the Island of Cuba"; Stiles pd taxes on 2 3/4 shares 5/31/1769 (1 fr Leveret Hubbard, 1 from Nathaniel Hubbard, 1/2 in own name, 1/4 from 1/2 John Rice original half share, see E480)				
Hubbard, Sarah wid of Daniel	New Haven, New Haven CT	all right	good con	1/1/1795
Goodyear, Asa Jr.	Hamden, New Haven, CT		I158	1/16/1795
Hubbard, Watts Jr.	Wallingford, New Haven, CT	1/2 share	£3. 12	1/10/1795
Spalding, John Jr.	New Haven, New Haven, CT		C413	4/4/1795
Hubbard, William Capt	Colchester, New London, CT	all shares	£10	12/30/1794
Adams, Jabez	Canterbury, Windham, CT		C466	2/20/1795
Hukley, John		1/2 share		
Hukley, John, son			GH	
Hukly, John, son		1/2 share		
Spalding, Simon			GH	
Huling, Marcus*		1/2 share		8/20/1770
Gorden, Samuel			GH	1/13/1775
"a proprietor on condition of paying £6 NY"; "conditions do not appear to be complyed with"				
Hull, Bradley	Fairfield, Fairfield, CT	all right except lot in Augusta Twp	$10	11/1/1797
Morgan, Nathaniel			H6	10/13/1798
Hull, John heirs	Fairfield, Fairfield, CT	1/2 share	£7. 10	12/2/1794
Banks, Ebenezer	Fairfield, Fairfield CT		C522	5/1/1795
Hull: Eleanor, John, Benjamin, Eliphalet 2, Lyman, Sarah, Mable				
Hull, Stephen	Stonington, New London, CT	2 settling rights from 1769	£3	6/27/1794
Fowler, Reuben	Killingworth, Middlesex, CT		C117	6/27/1794
Humfrevele, Benjamin				
LeHommedieu, Ezra			A384	
Humperville, Ebenezer & Lemuel	New Haven, New Haven, CT	1 share	val con	2/18/1796
Pope, Robert	Derby, New Haven, CT		D169	7/2/1796
Humphrey, Charles Jr. & Benajah	Simsbury, Hartford, CT	1/4 of 1 share	$12.50	4/13/1796
Kingsbury, Phinehas Jr.	Granby, Hartford, CT		E441	9/16/1796
Humphrey, John				
Humphrey, Michael			A368- A389	

grantor grantee notes	grantor residence grantee residence	description location	amount acct bk page	deed date record date
Humphrey, Jonathan	Simsbury, Hartford, CT	1/2 share*	£8.12	7/4/1772
Case, Reuben	Simsbury, Hartford, CT		B63	6/3/1773
1/53 in Twp which Noah Phelps has gone to lay out and not in Col. Eleazer Talcott's which is for myself, rest at Susq Co. direction.				
Humphrey, Michael				
Perkins, John			A369	
Humphrey, Thomas				
Milles, Peletiah Jr.			A100	
Humphreys, Hezekiah	Simsbury, Hartford, CT	1/2 share	£7	1/3/1775
Allen, Levi	Salisbury, Litchfield, CT		E224	7/2/1796
Humphry, Abigail*	East Hartford, Hartford, CT	Pwr Att to locate 1/2 share	1/4 part of land	6/12/1795
Strong, Jabin	Glastonbury, Hartford, CT		E86	3/4/1796
heir of Henry Arnold dec'd				
Humphry, Jonathan	Simsbury, Hartford, CT	1/2 share	$5	5/19/1795
Hale, George	Catskill, Albany, NY		C376	2/28/1795
Hungerford, Benjamin	Farmington, Hartford, CT	1/2 share	£20	11/3/1777
Gaylord, Aaron	Westmoreland, Westmrld, CT		B387	2/25/1778
Hungerford, Benjamin				
Hungerford, Stephen			A252	
Hungerford, Benjamin Sr.	Farmington, Hartford, CT	1/2 share	love	1/21/1769
Hungerford, Benjamin Jr.	Woodbury, Hartford, CT		B265	11/5/1774
Hungerford, Stephen	Farmington, Hartford, CT	1/2 share	£10	4/27/1773
Bacon, Daniel	Farmington, Hartford, CT		B116	1/11/1774
Hunn, Samuel				
Edgerton, Asa			A234	
Hunt, Bensley		2 shares*	$1,100	9/20/1800
Hunt, Samuel		Putnam Twp	H347	4/28/1802
with all the buildings and improvements				
Hunt, Ephriam				4/26/1769
Brown, Daniel			GM	1/1/1774
Hunt, John	Woodbury, Litchfield, CT	1/2 share		4/17/1765
Hunt, Seth & John, sons	Woodbury, Litchfield, CT		E163	5/19/1796
Hunt, John	Roxbury/Woodbury, Litchfld,	Pwr Att to locate		5/28/1796
Reed, Hezekiah			E411	9/15/1796
Hunt, John heirs	Woodbury, Litchfield, CT	Pwr Att over 1/2 share		9/11/1796
Hunt, John (brother)	Woodbury, Litchfield, CT		E163	5/20/1796
Seth, Gideon, Simon, & Thomas Judson Hunt				
Hunt, Salmon		two half shares*	$60	1/20/1796
Goodrich, Benjamin			E248	7/1/1796
1/2 Gain Miller, OP; 1/2 Peter Swetland, OP				
Hunt, Salmon		all right to 2 deeds*	$100	1/20/1796
Goodrich, Benjamin			E260	7/1/1796
William Avery, John Williams				
Hunt, Samuel	Kinderhook, Columbia, NY	1/4 of 1 share	£6	11/2/1792
Hunt, Bensle	Putnam. Luzerne, PA		F236	12/12/1797
Hunt, Samuel		2 shares*	$700	1/25/1802
Varborough, Abraham		Putnam Twp	H347	4/28/1802
with all the buildings and improvements				
Hunt, Thomas	Stockbridge, Berkshire, MA	1/4 interest	$2,000	2/9/1796
Cone, Ashbel & Crocker, William	W Stockbridge, Berkshire, MA	Richmond Twp	E494	11/15/1796
Hunt, Walter	late Lebanon, Windham, CT*	50 A (1 undivided 80th of 4000 A)	$12.85*	4/2/1798
Fitch, Miller		Hebard Gore	H144	9/14/1799
now Hartford, Hartford, CT; if same amount pd by Hunt to Fitch by 4/2/1799 deed is void				
Hunt, Walter	Lebanon, Windham, CT	1,000 A, Lots 11-20, 100 A each	£120	4/21/1796
Gray, Eliphalet	Lebanon, Windham, CT	Hebard Gore	H143	9/14/1799
Hunter, John				
Franklin, George			A4	
Hunter, Robert*	New Lebanon, Albany, NY	1/3 share		1/28/1793
Miller, Gain			I100	
for Samuel Hunter Sr. heirs: Robert Hunter, son; Gain Miller and heirs; Rebecca, widow of John Hunter and heirs; Samuel Hunter Jr., heirs				
Hunter, Robert et al*	Still Water, Saratoga, NY	1 share	£10	5/5/1795
Hunter, Andrew			E381	7/1/1795
Jehiel Parke & Mary Parke, heirs of Samuel Hunter				

grantor / grantee / notes	grantor residence / grantee residence	description / location	amount / acct bk page	deed date / record date
Huntington, Hezekiah	Windham, Windham, CT	2 1/2 shares	10s	9/12/1794
Chauncey, Worthington G.	Durham, New Haven, CT		C320	2/26/1795
Huntington, Hezekiah		1/2 share		
Kilborn, Benjamin*			GK	
Kilborn has pd taxes to 2/11/1773				
Huntington, Hezekiah				
Post, Eldad			A349	
Deed Post to Jabin Strong, E67, refers to this Deed Liber A349 as proof that Post was a proprietor and is one proof among many that index inserted in Liber I belongs to lost Liber A.				
Huntington, Hezekiah		1/2 share		
Spencer, Caleb			A351	
Huntington, Nathan		300 A of 1/2 share		1/10/1795
Flint, James	Windham, Windham, CT		E192	6/11/1796
Huntington, Samuel et al*		1 share	$50	2/18/1796
Hyde, Elisha & Tracy, Elisha	Norwich, New London, CT		F31	4/23/1796
Fanny Huntington, Devisees and Residuary Legatees				
Huntington, Sarah	Windham	1 share	£20	2/25/1778
Huntington, Jabez et al*	Windham		C14	7/8/1778
Ann Huntington, Lucy Storrs, Jabez H. Hamilton				
Huntington, Simon	Norwich, New London, CT	1 share and 1/4 share*	£15	4/7/1795
Tracy, Elisha	Norwich, New London, CT		E363	9/6/1796
belonging to late mother Sarah Huntington				
Hurd, Ephriam heir*	Huntington, Fairfield, CT	1/2 share	val con	3/12/1795
Bostwick, Dimon	New Milford, Litchfield, CT		C610	7/9/1795
Hurd, Elnathan				
Hurlbert, Nathan		1/4 share		
Heath, Joseph			GH	
Hurlbert, Nathan		1/2 share		
Hurlbert, Simeon			GH	
Hurlbert, Nathan		1/2 share		
Mason, David			GH	
Hurlbert, Simeon		1/2 share		
Allen, Levi			GH	
Hurlburt, Sarah	Berlin, Hartford, CT	1/2 share	$25	1/26/1796
Allyn, John B,	Berlin, Hartford, CT		E140	2/25/1796
Hurlbut, Christopher	Hanover, Luzerne, PA	Lot 17 Athens, W side Tioga R*	£30	12/11/1792
Root, Jared	Plymouth, Luzerne, PA	Tioga, otherwise called Athens, Twp	E45	2/23/1796
N by Oliver Bigelow; S by Sylvenus Traverse; E by Tioga R				
Hurlbut, George Battolps*	New London, New London, CT	1/2 share	good cause	8/26/1794
Turner, Seth	New Haven, New Haven, CT		C456	2/21/1795
heir & adm Mrs. Mary Hurlbut				
Hurlbut, Joseph, decd, heirs	New London, New London, CT	all right	£50	1/28/1796
Tracy, Elisha	Norwich, New London, CT	First Delaware Company	F26	4/23/1796
chr. Samuel Hurlbut, Anna Welch, Hannah Hurlbut, Mary Hulbut, Mary Taber, Job Taber				
Hurlbut, Nathan	Ashford, Berkshire, MA	1 share	£13	9/26/1773
Heath, Joseph & Clark, Ezekiel	Noble Town, Albany, NY		B149	3/8/1774
Hurlbut, Nathan	Alford, Berkshire, MA	2 shares	£80	12/20/1773
Hurlbut, Simeon	Alford, Berkshire, MA		B295	5/25/1774
Hurlbut, Nathan				
McNeal, John			A264	
Hurlbut, Nathan	Sharon, Litchfield, CT	1 share	£8	4/20/1763
Seely, Ephriam	Amenia, Dutchess, NY		B313	3/7/1775
Hurlbut, Nathan, gentleman	Alford, Berkshire, CT	1 share	£25	12/20/1773
Kellogg, Daniel, yeoman	Sheffield, Berkshire, MA		B294 - E97	3/1/1796
Hurlbut, Simeon	Alford, Berkshire, MA	2 shares	£80	3/9/1796
Baker, Erastus	Salisbury, Litchfield, CT		F57	4/23/1796
Hurlbut, Thomas	Washington, Litchfield, CT	all right (by Will)	val sum	2/23/1795
Royce, Mark	Washington, Litchfield, CT		E254	7/1/1796
Hutchings, William	Luzerne, PA	1 share	£15	1/15/1796
Stephens, Ira	Luzerne, PA	Southold Twp [unknown]	E378	9/14/1796
Hutchins, Charles	Chenango, Tioga, NY	16,000 A	$8,000*	10/18/1796
Hart, Elihu	Freehold, Albany, NY	Plainfield Twp	F158	4/24/1797
Indenture terms: $4,000 by 7/1797 or sell at public auction				

grantor	grantor residence	description	amount	deed date
grantee	grantee residence	location	acct bk page	record date
notes				
Hutchinson, Ezra	Sharon, Litchfield, CT	1/3 share	£3	4/17/1773
Hutchinson, Samuel	Sharon, Litchfield, CT		F255	3/19/1798
Hutchinson, John	Sheffield, Berkshire, MA	1/2 share, taxes pd	£25	11/15/1786
Baldwin, Thomas	Wyoming		I46	11/1/1786
Hutchinson, John	Luzerne, PA	1 share	£30	12/10/1795
Beebe, Solomon	Luzerne, PA		E321	4/10/1796
Hutchinson, John	Ulster, Luzerne, PA	100 A	$1,500	1/3/1800
Carpenter, Comfort A.	Providence, Providence, RI	Ulster Twp	H191	1/4/1800
my home lot adjoining S, Josiah Marshall, N, Joseph Hitchcock, W, Susq R.				
Hutchinson, John	Ulster, Luzerne, PA	4,500 A	£50	7/8/1796
Collins, Ambrose	Ulster, Luzerne, PA	Graham Twp, south part	E267	7/18/1796
Hutchinson, John	Ulster, Luzerne, PA	16,000 A	full value	6/10/1795
Everett, Noah		Guilford Twp	C506	8/1/1796
Hutchinson, John	Westmoreland on Susq R.	four 1/2 shares	£122.15	8/25/1781
Hogeboom, Jeremiah	Claverack, Albany, NY		F255	3/19/1798
Hutchinson, John	Tioga, Luzerne, PA	6 Lots; 5 Lots*	£440	12/25/1794
Linley, Erastus, merchant	Newtown, Tioga, NY	Murraysfield Twp; Columbia Twp	C142	7/23/1795
6 Lots Murraysfield: 2, 7, 15, 20, 28, 47 & 5 Lots Columbia: 12, 12, 24, 31, 33 + undivided rights of said lots.				
Hutchinson, John	Athens, Luzerne, PA	1 share	$100	2/20/1796
Street, Caleb	Catskill, Albany, NY		E268	7/6/1796
Hutchinson, John	Ulster, Luzerne, PA	3000 A	$3,000	12/28/1799
Thayer, Levi, Capt	Athens, Luzerne, PA	Graham Twp	H177	1/1/1800
Hutchinson, John	Tioga, Luzerne, PA	300 A, Lot 2 plus undivided land	$300	12/27/1799
Thayer, Levi & Satterlee, Elias*	Tioga, Luzerne, PA	Columbia Twp	H163	12/30/1799
Capt. Levi Thayer & Doct. Elias Satterlee, traders				
Hutchinson, John & Gordon,	Luzerne, PA	8,000 A	£300	6/16/1796
Grant, Josiah	Poultney, Rutland, VT	Graham Twp	E217	7/2/1796
Hutchinson, Samuel decd		1 share, taxes pd to date		11/27/1786
Hutchinson, John			I17	11/27/1786
Huxley, Dan	New Marlboro, Berkshire, MA	1/2 share	£15	9/19/1774
Hubbard, John	Sheffield, Berkshire, MA		E26	1/9/1796
Huxley, Jared				
Huxley, Dan			A470	
Hyde, Caleb	Bethlehem, Litchfield, CT	1 share	£9	9/28/1795
Grigg, Jacobs	Watertown		D58	11/27/1795
Hyde, Ebenezer; Hyde, James	Norwich, New London, CT	Pwr Att		10/19/1795
Hyde, Ezekiel	Norwich, New London, CT		I253	12/4/1795
Hyde, Elisha	Norwich, New London, CT	16,100 A left on 9 full & 4 half	$1,200	2/24/1796
Brown, Daniel Jr.	New Durham, Albany, NY		F14	3/1/1796
conveyors named in deed and entered individually in database				
Hyde, Ezekiel	Norwich, New London, CT	agent for my allotted land*	$60	9/10/1796
Backus, Ebenezer	Tioga, NY		E427	9/11/1796
1400 A, pt of Nos. 274 & 275 of the 400; 700 A fr Joseph Reynolds; 1000 A fr Joseph Tracy Jr.; 580 A fr Asa Waterman				
Hyde, Ezekiel	Norwich, New London, CT	8,000 A	$6,000	1/2/1796
Kingsberry, Joseph	Enfield, Hartford, CT	Rittenhouse Twp, 1/2	H182	1/4/1800
Hyde, Ezekiel	Norwich, New London, CT	300 A, Lot 17	$90	4/3/1797
Mason, Daniel	Lebanon, Windham, CT	Smithfield Twp	F212	10/21/1797
Hyde, Isael & Joseph	Darby, New Haven, CT	1/2 share, 700 A laid out* +	£15	3/1/1796
Bostwick, Dimon	New Milford, Litchfield, CT	New Milford & New Preston Twps	E475	11/28/1796
300 A New Milford, 400 A New Preston				
Hyde, James & Hyde, Eliab	Norwich, New London, CT	all lands	£10	2/12/1796
Cleveland, Aaron	Norwich, New London, CT	Selasborough [Seeleysburgh] Twp	F40	4/23/1796
Hyde, Jonathan & Nathaniel	Lebanon, Windham, CT	1/2 share	30s	2/6/1795
Dorrance, Gershom	Windham, Windham, CT		I204	4/1/1795
Hyde, Moses Ex of Zina Hyde, decd		Pwr Att to locate 1/2 share*		4/20/1796
Throop, Benjamin	Bozrah, New London, CT		E234	
at Zina Hyde's expense unless Gen. Hyde lays out land				
Hyde, William	Hanover, Luzerne, PA	7,300 A	£1,000	11/28/1795
Blackman, Eleazer & Dane, Daniel	Enfield, CT	Westminster Twp	E503	2/6/1797
Hyde, William	Hanover, Luzerne, PA	about 160 A, all right to 4th division	40s	11/2/1793
Franklin, John	Athens, Luzerne, PA	Athens Twp	F251	11/2/1796
Hyde, William		1/2 share; 300 A		8/28/1795
Irwin, James		Athens Twp	E437	10/1/1796

grantor	grantor residence	description	amount	deed date
grantee	grantee residence	location	acct bk page	record date
notes				
Hyde, William	Hanover, Luzerne, PA	5 A, Lot 40, 2nd Div	$30	9/5/1795
Satterlee, Elisha	Athens, Luzerne, PA	Athens Twp	E520	
Ingersol, Jared				
Seely, Ephriam			A37	
Inman, Edward, order		1/2 share replacement*		12/23/1794
Franklin, John			F53	5/1/1796
John Hyde took share and Inman can't recover it				
Inman, John	Hanover, Luzerne, PA	1/2 share	£200	12/19/1795
Tuttle, Steph Jr. & Blackman,	Wilkesbarre, Luzerne, PA		E300	6/8/1796
Irwin, James	Athens, Luzerne, PA	Lot 3, meadow & 50 A of Lot 8	£100	5/19/1795
Gorden, James A.	Wilkesbarre, Luzerne, PA	Athens Twp	E419	10/8/1795
Irwin, James	Athens, Luzerne, PA	Lot 11, 300 A	$200	2/4/1796
Hutchinson, John	Athens, Luzerne, PA	Murraysfield Twp	E158	5/15/1796
Irwin, James	Tioga Point, Luzerne, PA	Lots 1, 4, 5, 6	£16	5/5/1794
Livingston, John	Columbia, NY	Athens Twp	C542	4/1/1795
Irwin, James	Tioga, Luzerne, PA	300 A, 1st Div on No. 231 of 400	10s	9/1/1796
Ross, Daniel	Tioga, Luzerne, PA	New Milford Twp	E362	9/8/1796
Irwin, James	Luzerne, PA	16,000 A	£3200	9/23/1795
Wood, Nathaniel	Hillsdale, Columbia, NY	Litchfield Twp	E15	
Irwin, James	Luzerne, PA	16,000 A	£3000	10/10/1795
Wood, Nathaniel	Hillsdale, Columbia, NY	Cumberland Twp	E17	2/1/1796
Ives, Jesse	Monson, Hampshire, MA	Pwr Att to defend claim		6/26/1799
Ives, Jesse, Jr., my eldest son			H203	6/2/1800
Jackays, Jackways, William		1/2 share No. 139 of 400		6/17/1794
Sawyer, Daniel		Athens Twp	E152	4/25/1796
Jackson, Robert				
Hopkins, David & James			A314	
Jackson, Silas		1/2 share No. 267 of 400 ex 150 A		
Stewart, Enos & Levi			H285	1/13/1801
Jackway, William	Ontario, NY	2 half shares, all divisions	$20	1/26/1795
Shepard, John	Athens, Luzerne, PA		E328	4/10/1796
Jacobs, John	Hanover, Luzerne, PA	1/2 share for service to Susq Co	$20	5/14/1795
Gordon, Samuel	Springfield, Luzerne, PA		C594	7/9/1795
Jearom, Zerubabel	Farmington, Hartford, CT	1/2 share	£16	3/18/1778
Roberts, Elias	Farmington, Hartford, CT		B378	3/13/1778
Jenkins, John	Exeter, Luzerne, PA	14 A of Lot 53, 2nd Div	£10	2/17/1794
Bidlack, Stephen	Luzerne Co PA	Athens Twp adj. I. Stevens&	I91	9/20/1794
Jenkins, John	Exeter, Luzerne, PA	100 A, Lot 40, 3rd Div*	£50	10/9/1793
Dean, Benjamin	Tioga, Luzerne, PA	Athens Twp*	I90	9/20/1793
drawn by Phineas Stephen; adj. Loftus, Gaylord & John Franklin				
Jenkins, John	Exeter, Luzerne, PA	1 share	$50	
Kerny, William			F237	1/12/1797
Nicholas Depue's share from Manuel Gansals [Gonzales]				
Jenkins, John	Luzerne Co PA	100 A, Lot No. 23, 4th Div*	$20	11/6/1794
Livingston, John	Livingston, Columbia, NY	Athens Twp	C544	11/7/1794
E on Susq R; N Col. John McKinstry; W Highway; S Elisha Saterlee				
Jenkins, John	Luzerne, PA	6400 A	$6,000	3/17/1796
Murray, Noah	Luzerne, PA	Jenkins Pitch	E110	3/17/1796
Jenkins, John		1/2 share		2/21/1795
Platt, Daniel	Kinderhook, NY		C199	2/28/1795
Jenkins, John		1/2 share No. 227 of 400		11/10/1794
Platt, Daniel			I192	3/19/1795
Jenkins, John	Luzerne, PA	Lots 1 and 25, 150 A each	$200	12/12/1801
Satterlee, Samuel	Luzerne, PA	Columbia Twp	H328	12/23/1801
Jenkins, John		6,400 A*	$10,000	12/29/1799
Thayer, Levi & Carpenter, Comfort		Jenkin's Pitch	H168	12/30/1799
reserving 1400 A which is to be in common				
Jenkins, Stephen		1 share		
Johnson, David			GJ	
Jenkins, Stephens	Luzerne Co PA	1/2 share	£5	3/3/1795
Parks, John	Luzerne Co PA		I235	10/24/1795
Jenkins, Thomas	Exeter, Luzerne, PA	Lot 45, 300 A	$150	6/28/1796
Arnold, Nehemiah	Providence, RI	Smithfield Twp	E218	7/2/1796

grantor grantee notes	grantor residence grantee residence	description location	amount acct bk page	deed date record date
Jennings, John		1 share		
Jennings, Josiah			GJ	
Jennings, Joshua	Fairfield, Fairfield, CT	1/2 share	$21	10/18/1794
Cooley, David Jr.	Weston, Fairfield, CT		C524	12/23/1773
Jennings, Josiah		1 share		6/19/1775
Cochran, James			GJ	6/5/1775
Jennings, Solomon				6/7/1775
Jennings, John, heir			GJ	
Jerom, Augustus	Little Hosack, Albany, NY	1/2 share		4/19/1785
Torrey, John	Little Hosack, Albany, NY		C559	6/20/1795
Jerom, Benjamin	New London, New London, CT	1/2 share		10/28/1773
Chapman, Caleb			D33	10/6/1795
Jessup & Hyde*	Fairfield, Fairfield, CT	all shares	£9	2/11/1795
Sherwood, Moses	Fairfield, Fairfield, CT	Fairfield Twp	C526	5/1/1795
Ebenezer Jessup Jr.; Joseph Hyde Jr.& Arete, wf				
Jewell, Eliphalet	Ashford, Berkshire, MA	1 share	£15	7/23/1794
Brown, Daniel	Freehold, Albany, NY		C479	2/1/1795
Jewett, David H. Doctr.	Montville, New London, CT	1 share		10/2/1794
Turner, Seth	New Haven, New Haven, CT		C293	3/4/1795
Johnson, Abraham	Luzerne Co, PA	300 A Lot	£10	12/30/1788
Roberts, Daniel	Luzerne Co, PA	Athens Twp	I262	3/3/1795
Johnson, Daniel	Farmington	1/2 share		1/20/1775
Allen, Levi	Salisbury		E227	7/2/1796
Johnson, David		1 share		5/5/1774
Vincent, John			GJ	
Johnson, Ebenezer	Mudd Creek, Ontario, NY	two 1/2 shares	£8	11/27/1795
Hutchinson, John	Athens, Luzerne, PA		E160	5/16/1796
Johnson, Elizabeth, heir	Bristol, Hartford, CT	1/2 share	£15	10/4/1796
Roberts, Seth	Bristol, Hartford, CT		E529	11/1/1796
Johnson, Jehoida		1/2 share No. 227 of 400		11/10/1794
Jenkins, John			I192	3/19/1795
Johnson, Job				
Borden, Samuel			A437	
Johnson, John		1 share		9/9/1773
Barnes, Benoni			GJ	11/29/1774
Johnson, John				
Huntington, Hezekiah			A375	
Johnson, John	Southbury, Litchfield, CT	Pwr Att to locate 1 share	1/2 share	8/13/1794
Towsey, Zerah	Freehold, Albany, NY		C382	2/28/1795
Johnson, John 2nd	Colchester, New London, CT	1 share	£3	7/17/1794
Elliot, William	Saybrook, Middlesex, CT		C121	10/1/1794
Johnson, John et al*	Southbury, Litchfield, CT	1/2 share	val con	1/27/1795
Tousey, Zerah	Freehold, Albany, NY		D51	11/6/1795
Anna Johnson, Wait Hinman, Joseph Post, Betty Post				
Johnson, Solomon	Wilkesbarre, Luzerne, PA	2 half shares		2/27/1795
Franklin, Jehiel Capt		Warrior Lock, Tioga Twp, PA	I190	3/19/1795
Johnson, Truman	Mindon, PA*	160 A, Lot 86	$60	2/24/1802
Benham, Josiah	New Hartford, Litchfield, CT	Minden Twp*	H316	2/25/1803
Minden was a Delaware Company Township located in present day Susquehanna County, PA.				
Johnson, Turner		1/2 share	$20	2/25/1795
Stephens, Ira			E366	4/1/1796
Johnson, Ward, Exec*	Wallingford, New Haven, CT	1/2 share	£5	10/8/1794
Street, Caleb	Catskill, NY		I168	12/29/1794
Mecock Ward, OP				
Johnston, Daniel	Farmington, Hartford, CT	1/2 share	£10	9/30/1774
Allen, Levi	Salisbury, Litchfield, CT		B288	1/20/1775
Jones, Abijah	E. Windsor, Hartford, CT	1/2 share	£20	4/8/1780
Damon, Aaron	E. Windsor, Hartford, CT		C20	6/2/1780
Jones, Abijah	Kingsborough, Washington, NY	Pwr Att to locate 1 share		4/24/1795
Dewey, Thomas	Rutland, VT		E486	11/15/1796
Jones, Abijah	Kingsborough, Washington, NY	Pwr Att to sell 1 share		
Dewey, Thomas	Rutland, VT		E487	11/15/1796

grantor grantee notes	grantor residence grantee residence	description location	amount acct bk page	deed date record date
Jones, Asahel*	Westmoreland, CT	1 share	£30	1/21/1777
Carr, Robert	Westmoreland, CT		B355	4/5/1777
late of Colchester, Hartford, CT				
Jones, Asahel		1/2 share		1/23/1777
Depew, Nicholas			GJ	1/23/1777
Jones, Benjamin	Turbutt, Northumberland, PA	1/2 share	£6	6/14/1774
Vreeland, Garardus [Garet]	Turbutt, Northumberland, PA		I199	4/1/1795
Jones, Israel	Lyme, New London, CT	1 share +3 lots*	150¢	1/21/1779
Gardner, Stephen	Colchester, Hartford, CT	Wilkes Barre Twp	C17	3/7/1780
Lot 30, 1st div; Lot 10, 2nd div; Lot 45, 3rd div.				
Jones, James		1/2 share		
Jones, Asahel, heir			GJ	
Jones, Josiah	Stockbridge, Berkshire, MA	1 share inc. 100 A Lot 47	£45	1/16/1778
Franklin, John	Canaan, Litchfield, CT	Huntington Twp	I55	6/12/1787
Jones, Josiah Jr.	Stockbridge, Berkshire, MA	1 share	£25	4/15/1795
Baldwin, Samuel	West Stockbridge, Berkshire,		C501	5/1/1795
Jones, Justus		1 share No. 120 of 600*		11/26/1795
Miller, William			H15	11/17/1798
share number not recorded in Susq Co grant to Justin Jones, I276				
Jones, Mabel, widow	Stockbridge, Berkshire, MA	1 share	$20	6/1/1796
Woodbridge, Stephen	Washington, Berkshire, MA		E298	6/20/1796
Jones, Nathan		1/2 share	val recd	1/19/1795
Towland, Levey			I219	6/22/1795
Jones, Thomas	Claremont, NH	1 share	£43	12/12/1768
Jones, Israel	Colchester, Hartford, CT		C16	3/7/1780
Jordan, Miles	Voluntown, Windham, CT	1/2 share	£45	5/6/1755
Dorrance, James	Voluntown, Windham, CT		B157	3/9/1774
Jordan, Miles	Voluntown, Windham, CT	1/2 share	£60 Bills Credit O.T.	1/22/1755
Smith, John	Voluntown, Windham, CT		B219	6/3/1774
Judd, Anthony	Tioga, NY	1 share	£10	10/25/1795
Pixley, David	Owego, Tioga, NY		D135	12/25/1795
Judd, Bela & Judd, John	Berlin, Hartford, CT	1/2 share	2s	1/15/1796
Smith, Lemuel & Allyn, John B.	Berlin, Hartford, CT	Allynsgrove Twp	E150	9/20/1781
Judd, Enoch		1/2 share		
Kingsley, Nathan			GJ	
Judd, Enoch		1/2 share		1/12/1775
Smith, Isaac			GH	1/13/1775
Judd, Enoch	Wilkes Barre Twp	1/2 share	£24	11/23/1773
Spafford, Darius			B202	4/6/1774
Judd, Enoch	Westmoreland, Litchfield, CT	1/2 share	£24	6/11/1774
Spafford, Darius	Windham, Windham, CT		B232	6/20/1774
Judd, William*	Middlesex, CT			11/1/1795
Huntington, Enoch			E95	2/24/1796
certified OP by Matthew T. Russel, Notary Public Middlesex Co, CT				
Judd, William	Farmingtown, Hartford, CT	20,000 A, about	$1,000 = £300	12/10/1795
Keeler, Hezekiah	Catskill, Albany, NY	Millsbury Twp	F21	4/23/1795
Judge of Probate*	Fairfield, CT	Letters Adm		4/20/1765
Mills, Elisha	Stratford, Fairfield, CT		E280	6/8/1796
David Rowland, Esq.; on estate of Isaac Mills of Darby, son and purchaser of Rev. Jedidiah Mills' share				
Judson, Augar	Stratford, Fairfield, CT	1 share	£10	8/9/1774
Atwood, Gideon*	Bethlehem, Woodbury,		E402	
Atwood pd $4 taxes 12/20/1782				
Judson, David, decd.	Washington, Litchfield, CT	Pwr att to locate, lay out, div 1/2		1/26/1795
Baker, Samuel	Luzerne Co, Susq Purchase		D54	11/10/1795
Gideon Hollister & David Judson, exec; recd fr Jonathan Smith see C60				
Judson, John	Huntington, Fairfield, CT	1 share	val con	2/9/1796
Judson, John 3rd	Huntington, Fairfield, CT		E278	6/8/1796
Judson, Jonathan	Huntington, Fairfield, CT	1/7 share	$7	5/26/1796
Hawley, Moses	Warren, Litchfield, CT		E278	6/8/1796
Kasson, Adam	Coventry, Kent, RI	1/4 share	love	11/3/1795
Bailey, Adonijah & Elizabeth, dau	Sterling, Windham, CT		E183	6/7/1796

grantor	grantor residence	description	amount	deed date
grantee	grantee residence	location	acct bk page	record date
notes				
Kasson, Adam	Coventry, Kent, RI	1/2 of father's 1 share	paternal affection	12/31/1773
Kasson, Archibald			F4	3/1/1796
Kasson, Adam	Coventry, Kent, RI	1/4 share	love	11/3/1795
Kelly, Nancy, dau & wid	Coventry, Kent, RI		E182	6/7/1796
Kasson, Alexander	Bethlehem, Litchfield, CT	600 A of 1 share	val sum	4/13/1795
Wheeler, Abner	Bethlehem, Litchfield, CT	Watertown Twp*	C621	7/1/1795
1/2 by deed, 1/2 by will; , later Pitkin Twp				
Kasson, Archibald	Granby, Hartford, CT	1/2 share	£7. 10	1/28/1795
Selby, Brainard	Sanderfield, Berkshire, MA		F5	3/1/1796
Kasson, James	Bethlehem, Litchfield, CT	1/3 share	love for son	5/4/1795
Kasson, Myron	Bethlehem, Litchfield, CT		E161	5/17/1796
Kasson, Samuel	Voluntown, Windham, CT	1/2 share	£6	4/16/1773
Jameson, Robert	Voluntown, Windham, CT		B71	4/16/1773
Kasson, Samuel		1/4 share		
Murphey, John			GK	
Kasson, Samuel				
Murphy, John & Ray, James			A111	
Kasson, William	Voluntown, Windham, CT	1/3 share	£7	3/5/1774
Dorrance, Samuel 4th	Voluntown, Windham, CT		B226	6/28/1774
Keeler, Hezekiah	Catskill, Albany, NY	8 shares*	$900	11/9/1795
Clark, Samuel	Middletown, Middlesex, CT		E50	2/24/1796
1 ea. fr Bishop Dodd, Col. William Worthington, Samuel Cook, John Sheen, Christopher Palmer, Charles Bulkley, Samuel Cook, Charles Foot				
Keeler, Hezekiah	Catskill, Albany, NY	2 whole shares and 13 half shares	$1000	11/4/1795
Clark, Samuel	Middletown, Middlesex, CT		E52	2/24/1796
Nos. 169 & 170 of the 600 and Nos. 316, 317, 320, 321, 324, 325, 328, 329, 334, 335, 338, 339, 308, 309 also of the 600, recorded only in Liber A, Volume 2.				
Keeler, Hezekiah	Catskill, Albany, NY	Nos. 342, 343 of the 600	$200	11/7/1795
Morgan, John	Hartford, Hartford, CT		E51	2/24/1796
Keeler, Hezekiah	Catskill, Albany, NY	16,000 A	$5,000	12/23/1795
Turner, Seth	Catskill, Albany, NY	Millsbury Twp	F22	4/23/1796
Keeler, Nathaniel	Salem, Westchester, NY			3/7/1783
Roland, David Jr.	Sharon, Litchfield, CT		C103	9/30/1786
Keeler, Timothy Jr.	Ridgefield, Fairfield, CT	4,000 A	5s	3/22/1796
Mead, Jasper	Ridgefield, Fairfield, CT	West Fairfield Twp, 1/4	E380	9/15/1796
Kegwin, John	Voluntown, Windham, CT	1 share	£30	9/13/1774
Avery, Elisha	Groton, New London, CT		B251	9/14/1774
Kegwin/Kagwin, James				
Ailsworth, Jedediah			A248	
Kellog, Abrahm				
Perkins, John			A338	
Kellog, Daniel	Hebron, Tolland, CT	Pwr Att to locate 1/2 share	1/4 part of land	3/23/1795
Strong, Jabin	Glastonbury, Hartford,CT		E83	3/2/1796
9s taxes pd 3/9/1773; $1 taxes pd 6/1/1772				
Kellogg, Amos	Sheffield, Berkshire, MA	Extract fr Will Bk. No. 1, p. 130*		
Kellogg, Prudence, wife & chr	Sheffield, Berkshire, MA		F256	3/19/1798
sons Ebenezer, Jesse, and three younger; daus. Abigail, Prudence, Mary, Thankful, Joanna; see for more details and see Kellogg, Prudence to Hogeboom, Jeremiah				
Kellogg, Eldad	Athens, Luzerne, PA	190 A, Lot 13, 4th division	£30	6/7/1796
Burrough, William Y.	Livingston, Columbia, NY	Athens Twp	E444	10/25/1796
Kellogg, Eldad	Athens, Luzerne, PA	100 A, Lot 45, 3rd division	$300	5/26/1801
Holmes, James, farmer	Wayne, Mifflin, PA	Athens Twp	H297	5/26/1801
bounded W by Susq R, N by Elisha Matthewson, E by 1st division lots, S by Benedict Satterlee				
Kellogg, Eldad		all right ex 300 A Athens Twp	$35	8/8/1795
Shepard, John			E331	4/10/1796
Kellogg, Jesse, adm Kellog, Daniel	Sheffield, Berkshire, MA	1 share	£40	10/10/1781
Hogeboom, Jeremiah	Claverack, Albany, NY		F273	3/14/1798
Kellogg, Josiah		1/2 share No. 88 of 400	Val recd	
Kingsley, Warham			E136	3/29/1796
Kellogg, Prudence*	Sheffield, Berkshire, MA	1 share	£35	5/6/1780
Hogeboom, Jeremiah	Claverack, Albany, NY		F256	3/19/1798
executrix for Amos Kellogg				
Kenne, John	Worthington, Hampshire, MA	1/2 share	$40	4/14/1796
Woodbridge, Stephen	Stockbridge, Berkshire, MA		E294	6/20/1796

grantor grantee notes	grantor residence grantee residence	description location	amount acct bk page	deed date record date
Kennedy, Benjamin	Gageborough, Berkshire, MA	1/2 share	£20	3/20/1775
Hanks, Silas	Mansfield CT		C48	10/18/1782
Kennedy, Benjamin	Gageborough, Berkshire, MA	1/2 share	£25	10/27/1774
Hanks, Uriah	Mansfield, Windham, CT		C65	11/22/1782
Kennedy, Benjamin	Gageborough, Berkshire, MA	2 shares	£40	12/26/1774
Law, Samuel	New Providence, Berkshire,		B384	4/8/1778
Kennedy, Benjamin	Gageborough	1/2 share	£20	4/1/1777
Olcott, James	Harrington CT		C25	6/21/1781
Kennedy, Isaac	Windham, Windham, CT	1/4 share	£10	6/10/1774
Grey, Thomas	Windham, Windham, CT		B262	6/11/1774
Kenney, Asa	Preston, New London, CT	1/2 share	£6	4/3/1761
Wedge, William	Stonington, New London, CT		B175	3/9/1774
Kenney, John	Worthington, late Voluntown	1/2 share		9/19/1795
Brewster, Jonah	Worthington, Hampshire, MA		E294	6/20/1796
Kenney, John	Worthington, late Voluntown	1/2 share		7/7/1762
Robins, Moses*			E294	10/12/1774
taxes pd to 3/9/1774				
Kenney, Joseph		700 A of 1/2 share ex 300 A in		6/19/1799
Wells, Samuel		Graham Twp	I21	6/19/1799
Kenney, Joseph	Ulster, Luzerne, PA	700 A in 2nd division*	$15	6/10/1799
Wells, Samuel	Ulster, Luzerne, PA	Gore btw Graham Twp, purchase	H72	6/19/1799
remainder of 1/2 share after 300 A in Ulster				
Kenney, Spencer	Preston, New London, CT	all rights	£9	1/20/1774
Pellet, John Jr.	Canterbury, Windham, CT		B182	3/10/1774
Kenney, Thomas		1/2 share		10/11/1794
Baldwin, William			E330	4/10/1796
Kenney, Thomas	Preston, New London, CT	his right*	£50	8/24/1762
Fish, Moses	Voluntown, Windham, CT		B189	3/10/1774
in the "discreted" Susquehanna Co. tract				
Kenney, Thomas		1/2 share ex 300 A in Whitehaven	$20	3/22/1796
Shepard, John			E331	4/10/1796
Kent, Samuel				
Canfield, Samuel			A72	
Kent, Seth				
Guthrie, Joseph			A474	
Kerny, William		300 A, Lot 53*		
Kerny, John		Putnam Twp	F237	1/12/1797
on Nicholas Depue's share from Manuel Gansals [Gonzales]				
Keyes, Timothy		1/2 share		
Staples, John			GK	
Kilborn, Aaron, carpenter	Ontario Co, NY	all shares	£30	12/29/1794
Dudley, Martin	Canadaigua, Ontario, NY		C304	2/28/1795
Kilborn, Benjamin	East Hartford, CT, late Bolton	3 half shares	£20	10/13/1795
Pitkin, Elisha Jr.	East Hartford, Hartford, CT		E285	6/6/1796
Kilborn, Benjamin	Bolton, Hartford, CT	1/2 share	val amt.	4/3/1769
Root, Sarah	Hebron, Hartford, CT		B40	5/23/1772
Kilborn, Benjamin		1/2 share fr Saml Gray		2/15/1773
Root, Sarah			GK	
Kilborn, Joseph	Litchfield, Litchfield, CT	1/2 share	£30	11/26/1781
Bradley, Abraham	Litchfield, Litchfield, CT		C70	11/13/1782
Kilbourn, Timothy	Seneca, Ontario, NY	1/2 share, orig certificate lost		2/28/1795
Whitcomb, Joel			I189	3/9/1794
Kilburn, Joseph		1/2 share, see WR, Ledger A: 128		12/5/1782
Schott, John Paul			C330	9/3/1795
Kimball, Jacob				
Gore, Obadiah			A430	
King, Apollo		16,000 A		10/24/1796
Clark, Gamaliel	Stockbridge, Berkshire, MA	Jefferson Twp	F240	11/9/1797
King, George	Sharon, Litchfield, CT	5 quit claim deeds	good cause	6/5/1795
Mills, Eli	Amenia, Dutchess, NY		C586 - C573 - C574	6/30/1795
John Reed 4/6/1795; John Gardner 4/6/1795; John Williams 4/4/1795; Samuel Cole 4/25/1795; William Avery 3/19/1795				
King, Solomon, heir	Becker, Berkshire, MA	1 share	$100	2/29/1796
Woodbridge, Stephen; Hunt, Thos	Stockbridge, Berkshire, MA		E292	6/20/1796

grantor grantee notes	grantor residence grantee residence	description location	amount acct bk page	deed date record date
Kingsberry, Joseph	Ulster, Luzerne, PA	16,000 A	$16,000	1/3/1800
Thayer, Levi & Carpenter, Comfort		Rittenhouse Twp	H182	1/4/1800
Kingsberry, Joseph	Ulster, Luzerne, PA	17 Lots*	$2,700	1/3/1800
Thayer, Levi & Carpenter,	Athens, Luzerne, PA and	Bachelor's Adventure Twp	H184	1/3/1800
lots 4-5, 8, 9-10, 12-15, 18, 19, 21, 29, 33-36				
Kingsberry, Lemuel	Canaan, Litchfield, CT	1/2 share	£15	4/8/1786
Fanning, James	Canaan, Litchfield, CT		I38	8/1/1786
Kingsberry, Phinehas	Granby, Hartford, CT	1,000 A	$1,000	12/19/1797
Hamilton, Silas	Wilmington, Windham, VT	Kingsberry Twp, Northumberland,	H295	5/6/1801
Kingsberry, Phinehas	Ulster, Luzerne, PA	2,000 A; 1,200 A	$4,000	1/4/1800
Thayer, Levi & Carpenter,	Athens, Luzerne, PA and	Enfield Twp; Harlem Twp	H195	1/4/1800
Kingsberry, Phinehas	Granby, Hartford, CT	4000 A	£400	4/21/1796
Wood, Nathaniel	Hillsdale, Columbia, NY	Hartford Twp, Northumberland, PA	H51	4/14/1798
Kingsbery, Phinehas	Granby, Hartford, CT	1,000 A	$1,000	10/9/1797
Scott, Matthew	Woodford, Bennington, VT	Kingsbery Twp	F257	6/22/1798
Kingsbery, Phinehas Jr.	Granby, Hartford, CT	1000 A to be divided	£100	11/14/1796
Robbins, Joshua	Sanderfield, Berkshire, MA	Kingsbery Twp	F209	8/16/1797
Kingsbery, Phinehas Jr.	Granby, Hartford, CT	2.000 A	£200	9/17/1796
Rogers, Nathaniel and Asa	Granville, Hampshire, MA	Kingsbury, Northumberland, PA	E400	9/17/1796
Kingsbury, John	Waterbury, New Haven, CT	all right	good cause	1/18/1796
Hopkins, Jesse	Waterbury, New Haven, CT		E145	2/25/1796
Kingsbury, Lemuel	Canaan, Litchfield, CT	3 shares; 1/2 share	£10	7/25/1794
Brown, Daniel	Freehold, Albany, NY		C445	2/21/1795
Kingsbury, Phineas	Granby, Hartford, CT	1 share	£30	8/26/1795
Bates, John	Grenville, Hampshire, MA		D27	9/29/1795
Kingsbury, Phineas	Granby, Hartford, CT	1 tract	£250	9/5/1794
Street, Caleb	Catskill, Albany, NY	Enfield Twp, Luzerne, PA	C473	2/20/1795
Kingsbury, Phinehas	Granby, Hartford, CT	4 twps	£6,000	3/9/1795
Street, Caleb	Catskill, Albany, NY	Federal, Sullivan, Pleasant Vly, Fame	E176	6/1/1796
Kingsley, Nathan		1/2 share		1/14/1774
Spalding, Simon			GJ	
Kingsley, Warham		1/2 share, No. 88 of 400		
Phelps, Jesse			E136	3/29/1796
Kinne, Jeremiah	Voluntown, Windham, CT	1/2 share	love	3/29/1770
Palmer, Joseph 4th, son-in-law	Voluntown, Windham, CT		C603	7/9/1795
Kinne, John	Preston, New London, CT	1/2 share	£3	7/7/1762
Robbins, Moses	Voluntown, Windham, CT		B352	12/20/1776
Kinne, Joseph	Plainfield, Windham, CT	1/2 share	Love	3/20/1775
Kinne, Experience, dau	Preston, New London, CT		B348	10/4/1776
Kinne, Moses, Blacksmith	Voluntown, Windham, CT	1/2 share	love	4/17/1772
Kinne, Cyrus, son			B338	11/1/1775
Kinney, Nathan	Lebanon, Windham, CT	1 share	£10	2/2/1795
Dorrance, Gershom	Windham, Windham, CT		I205	4/1/1795
Kirtland, Constant	Wallingford, New Haven, CT	1/2 share	£5	8/31/1772
Johnson, Israel	Wallingford, New Haven, CT		E121	3/1/1796
Knap, Ebenezer	Canaan, Litchfield, CT	1 share	£20	4/23/1778
Franklin, John	Canaan, Litchfield, CT		I4	6/3/1786
Knap, Luke	Canaan, Litchfield, CT	1/2 share	£5	7/12/1773
Guittau, Ephriam	New Marlboro, Berkshire, MA		B281	12/21/1774
Knowles, Joseph M.	South Kingston, Washington, RI	1/2 share bot fr Stephen Hazzard	$50	9/19/1800
Overton, Thomas	Tioga, Luzerne, PA		H241	9/20/1800
Knowlton, Abraham	Ashford, Windham, CT	Pwr Att to locate 1/2 share		3/12/1795
Young, William, Jr.	Windham, Windham, CT		C600	7/9/1795
Laboree, John	Stratford, Fairfield, CT	1/4 share	full con recd	3/16/1763
Clark, Nathan	Stratford, Fairfield, CT		B126	1/18/1774
Laboree, John	Stratford, Fairfield, CT	1/4 share		3/16/1763
Levensworth, Edmund	Stratford, Fairfield, CT		B110	12/21/1773
Laboree, John Doctr, estate*	Stratford, Fairfield, CT	1/2 share	£10 + $1 tax	11/11/1773
Hawley, Milton	Stratford, Fairfield, CT		B107	12/18/1773
Samuel Adams & Deborah Laboree, heirs				
Lamb, Ezekiel	Enfield, Hartford, CT	1/2 share	£12	2/5/1795
Kingsbury, Lemuel	Enfield, Hartford, CT		C328	3/1/1795

grantor grantee notes	grantor residence grantee residence	description location	amount acct bk page	deed date record date
Lamson, King William	Woodbury, Litchfield, CT	16,000 A*	val sum	11/19/1798
Morgan, Nathaniel	Weston, Fairfield, CT	Granby Twp	H30	1/24/1799
original deed Morgan to Lamson 6/13/1796 lost so Morgan taking twp back				
Lancton, Jonathan	Farmington, Hartford, CT	1/2 share		6/5/1754
Lancton, Samuel			B15 - A399	9/20/1781
Landon, John		1/2 share		1/2/1777
Pierce, Phinehas			GG	
Lane, Benjamin	Claverack, Columbia, NY	1/12 part	£100	2/27/1796
Chauncey, Worthington Gallup	Durham, New Haven, CT	Calcutta Twp	E529	11/1/1796
Lane, Benjamin	Hudson, Columbia, NY	10,000 A	$5,312	7/7/1795
Heath, Joseph	Esperanza, Albany, NY	Amsterdam Twp	C579	7/20/1795
Lane, Samuel	Mansfield, Windham, CT	1/2 share	£40	9/14/1770
Carey, Jabez	Mansfield, Windham, CT		B112	12/22/1773
Lane, Samuel		1/2 share		3/3/1774
Cory, Jabez			GG	5/14/1774
Langton, Jonathan	Berlin, New Haven, CT	1/2 share	$25	1/1/1796
Allyn, John B.	Berlin, Hartford, CT		E143	2/25/1796
Lansing, Abraham	Lansinghborough, NY	1 share	£20	10/10/1777
Hogeboom, Jeremiah	Claverack		E446	10/25/1796
Lansing, Abraham Jacob	Lansinghborough, Albany, NY	4 shares	£40	8/8/1796
Hogeboom, Jeremiah	Lackawanna, Westmoreland,	Claverack Twp	E445	10/25/1796
Larabee, Lebbeus		all right		10/17/1795
Paine, David		Larabee Twp	E78	
Larchar, James	Tioga, Luzerne, PA	150 A, 1/2 Lot 48	$150	11/3/1800
Thornton, Elihu	Johnston, Providence, RI	Smithfield Twp	H268	11/3/1800
Larrabe, John	Norwich, New London, CT	1 share	£16	2/5/1773
Baldwin, Isaac	Norwich, New London, CT		B61 - B67 - G	10/9/1773
Larrabe, John				
Carey, Jabez			A3	
Larrabee, Libbeus	Windham, Windham CT	1 share*, 300 A; 1700 A	$70	2/27/1795
Dorrance, Benjamin	Kingston, Luzerne, PA	Salem Twp; Lindsley Twp	C347	2/27/1795
L. Larrabee purchased from Prince Tracy				
Larrabee, Libbeus	Windham, Windham, CT		£6	2/25/1795
Lindsley, Eleazer	Ontario Co NY		C349	2/25/1795
Larrance, Daniel		1/2 share		
Hogskis, Samuel			GL	
Lassell, James				
Skiff, Benjamin			A388	
Lassley, James Jr.	Hanover, Luzerne, PA	1/2 share for service to Susq Co	$20	5/14/1795
Gordon, Samuel	Springfield, Luzerne, PA		C594	7/9/1795
Lathrop, Benjamin	Worthington, Hampshire, MA	8,000 A, 1/2 twp	$4,000	10/29/1799
Dunkin, Frebrin	Beekman, Dutchess, NY	Weathersfield Twp	H112	11/12/1799
Lathrop, Benjamin	Worthington, Hampshire, MA	all right	$23,000	5/6/1796
Henshaw, Joshua	New Hartford, Litchfield, CT	Moab Twp	D175	8/9/1796
Lathrop, Benjamin	Worthington, Hampshire, MA	16,000. A	$9,000	11/1/1796
Root, Azariah	Sheffield, Berkshire, MA	Venus Twp	H26	9/3/1796
Lathrop, Zachariah	Norwich, New London, CT	1/2 share	£60	2/6/1795
Tracy, Elisha	Norwich, New London, CT		I176	2/22/1795
Lattimer, Henry*	Montville, New London, CT	all right	£6	2/2/1796
Peirce, John	Plainfield, Windham, CT		E275	7/15/1796
heir of Jonathan Lattimer				
Lattimer, Henry Jr.	Montville, New London, CT	all right	£12	1/18/1796
Peirce, John	Plainfield, Windham, CT		E275	7/15/1796
Law, Samuel	New Providence, Berkshire,	2 shares	£120	3/11/1778
Dean, Ezra	West Greenwich, Kent, RI		B383	4/8/1778
Lawrence, Daniel				
Vannist, Isaac			A347	
Lawrence, Gideon				
Taylor, Ebenezer Jr.			A411	
Lawrence, Isaac	Canaan, Litchfield, CT	1/2 share	love	12/6/1774
Lawrence, Jonas, son	Canaan, Litchfield, CT		C62	11/14/1782

grantor grantee notes	grantor residence grantee residence	description location	amount acct bk page	deed date record date
Lawrence, Joseph et al*	Plainfield, Windham, CT	3/8 share	£10	3/30/1786
Lawrence, Josiah	Dalton, Berkshire, MA		E90	3/4/1796
Thomas Lawrence, Plainfield, CT; Porsilar and Benjamin Gallup, Dalton, Berkshire, MA				
Lawrence, Josiah	Dalton, Berkshire, MA	Pwr Att 3/8 share plus 1/8 share	1/2 land	5/12/1795
Strong, Jabin	Glastenbury, Hartford, CT		E91	3/5/1796
Lawrence, Josiah	Dalton, Berkshire, MA	Pwr Att 1/2 share	1/2 land	5/12/1795
Strong, Jabin	Glastenbury, Hartford, CT		E92	3/5/1796
Lawrence, Josiah	Dalton, Berkshire, MA	1/2 Lot 2, all Divs.	£6	4/5/1787
Underwood, Isaac	Dalton, Berkshire, MA	White Haven Twp	I241	12/1/1795
Lawrence, Stephen	Canaan, Litchfield, CT	1/2 share	£7	8/21/1762
Baldwin, Daniel	Sharon, Litchfield, CT		C53	11/11/1782
Lay, John	Catskill, Albany, NY	1 share	£40	10/15/1795
Hamilton, Ira	Harpersfield, Otsego, NY		E268	6/6/1796
Lay, John		1/2 share No. 398 of 600		12/15/1794
Hamilton, Ira			E271	6/6/1796
Lay, John		1/2 share No. 389 of 600		12/15/1794
Hamilton, Ira			E271	6/6/1796
Leavensworth, Asa		1/2 share No. 202 of 600		2/20/1795
Murray, Reuben			C571	7/10/1795
Leavensworth, Asa		1/2 share No. 208 of 600		2/20/1795
Murray, Reuben			C571	7/10/1795
Leavensworth, James, heir*	Huntington, Fairfield, CT	grantor's % of 1 share	good cause	3/11/1795
Lewis, Edmund	Huntington, Fairfield, CT		C577	6/19/1795
Daniel Leavensworth				
Leavensworth, James, heir	Huntington, Fairfield, CT	grantor's % of 1 share	6s	4/2/1795
Lewis, Edmund	Huntington, Fairfield, CT		C577	6/19/1795
Samuel L. Hurd, heir of James Leavensworth				
Leavensworth, James, heirs*	Huntington, Fairfield, CT	grantor's % of 1 share	£2. 2	3/12/1795
Lewis, Edmund	Huntington, Fairfield, CT		C577	6/19/1795
Mehitable Leavensworth Wetmore and Josiah Wetmore, husband				
Lee, Ebenezer	Luzerne, PA	1/2 share No. 287 of 600*	$40	3/17/1795
Pease, Jonathan	Luzerne, PA		E339	5/15/1796
except the 1st division portion laid out on Sugar Creek between Ulster & Juddsburgh on 12/16/1793				
Lee, Samuel	Canaan, Litchfield, CT	1/2 share	£50	3/31/1755
Douglas, Ira	Canaan, Litchfield, CT		B233	8/20/1774
Lee, Samuel	Poultney, Rutland, VT	1/4 share	$20	9/25/1795
Grant, Josiah	Poultney, Rutland, VT		D32	9/5/1795
Lee, Samuel	Windham, Windham, CT	1/2 share	£6	4/27/1787
Gray, Ebenezer	Windham, Windham, CT		C581	6/20/1795
Lee, Samuel		1/2 share		11/5/1771
Ransom, Samuel			GL	4/20/1771
Lee, Stephen	Farmington, Hartford, CT	1/2 share	val con	6/4/1755
Holmes, David, Dr.	Woodstock, Windham, CT		MB - B283	12/31/1774
Lee, Stephen				
Yale, Benjamin			A87	
Leffingwell, Christopher	Norwich, New London, CT	1 share	£20	11/17/1794
Tracy, Elisha	Norwich, New London, CT	Cabot Twp	I139	12/25/1794
LeHommedieu, Ezra	Southhold NY	1/2 share, SP; 1/2 share DP	val con	10/12/1762
Avery, Humphrey	Norwich, New London, CT		B29	8/30/1773
Lester, Eliphalet	Saybrook, Middlesex, CT	1/2 share	£20	12/23/1785
Bushnell, John H.	Saybrook, Middlesex, CT		C111	8/19/1788
Lester, Eliphalet	Saybrook, Middlesex, CT	4 1/2 shares	£40	8/14/1794
Elliot, William	Saybrook, Middlesex, CT		C356	3/2/1795
No. 160, 151, 152 of the 600; 1 share Timothy Morgan; 1/2 share self				
Lester, Eliphalet		Pwr Att for Zachariah Clark		9/24/1794
Hale, George & Thomas			D10	9/18/1795
Lester, Eliphalet	Saybrook, Middlesex, CT	6 shares	£800	9/24/1794
Hale, George & Thomas	Catskill, Albany, NY		D15	9/18/1795
Lester, Eliphalet	Saybrook, New London, CT	1 share	£40	6/27/1782
Hurlbut, Joseph	New London, New London, CT		F30	4/23/1796
Lester, Eliphalet	Saybrook	1 share	£20	9/20/1779
Morgan, Theophilus	Killingsworth		C43	5/27/1782

grantor	grantor residence	description	amount	deed date
grantee	grantee residence	location	acct bk page	record date
notes				
Lester, Eliphalet	Saybrook, Middlesex, CT	1/2 share	£20	1/6/1786
Reeve, John	Saybrook, Middlesex, CT		H96	9/17/1799
Lester, Eliphalet	Saybrook, New London, CT	1/2 share	£20	11/14/1782
Stark, Lawrence	Westfield, Hampshire, MA		C104	11/8/1786
Lester, Eliphalet				
Stuart, John			A365	
Lester, Eliphalet	New London, New London, CT	1/2 share	£8	10/13/1794
Tuthill, Rufus	Plumb Island, Suffolk, NY		C358	3/2/1795
Lester, Eliphalet				
Tuttle, Daniel			A364	
Lester, Eliphalet	Killingsworth, Middlesex, CT	Lot 48	£40	2/6/1798
Warner, Phinehas	Saybrook, Middlesex, CT	Elliotsburg Twp granted as	H19	11/27/1798
Levensworth, Asa	Canaan, Columbia, NY	7 shares* & 1 share Simeon Smith	$800	5/18/1795
Murray, Reuben			H212	2/10/1800
James Woodward 1; Samuel Brown 1; James Babcock 1; Nathan T. Moseley 1; Sarah and James Babcock 1; Archibald Dickson 1/2; Stephen Starkweather 1/2; Jonathan Parker 1				
Levensworth, Asa	New Canaan, NY	two 1/2 shares ex 300 A in	val con	11/1/1798
Ransom, Samuel	Owego, NY		H14	11/1/1798
1,700 A in Halestown for Samuel Ransom on this right				
Levingsworth, Asa	New Canaan, NY	1/2 share	$50	10/10/1798
Hamlin, Salmon	Athens, Luzerne, PA		H116	11/19/1799
Lewis, Adonijah	Berlin, Hartford, CT	1/2 share	$30	3/28/1796
Smith, Lemuel & Allen, John B.	Berlin, Hartford, CT		F250	6/1/1797
Lewis, Benjamin	Union, NY	1/2 share ex 300 A Murraysfield		2/23/1796
Shepard, John	Tioga, Luzerne, PA		E330	4/10/1795
Lewis, Elihu	Goshen, Litchfield, CT	4 full shares; 2 half shares*	val sum	11/2/1795
Wheeler, Abner	Bethlehem, Litchfield, CT		E250	7/1/1796
3 shares from OP John Norton, Nehemiah Lewis, Samuel Osborn; two half shares from OP Timothy Everett, John Curtiss; and the share of Ebenezer Lewis as heir				
Lewis, Ethan	Westmoreland, CT	1/2 share	£15	11/15/1775
Wainwright, David	Sheffield, Berkshire, MA		F274	3/19/1798
Lewis, Griffin, heir of Wm		1 share		4/30/1796
Shaw, Ichabod			E266	7/8/1796
Lewis, Joseph & Lewis, Thomas	Stratford & Huntington, CT	1/2 share	£7	12/17/1794
Lewis, LeGrand M.	Huntington, Fairfield, CT		C610	6/9/1795
Lewis, Joseph & Lewis, Thomas	Stratford and Huntington, CT	1/2 of a whole share	£7	12/17/1794
Lewis, Walker	Brookfield, Fairfield, CT		H217	2/1/1795
Lewis, Judah	Goshen, Litchfield, CT	1/2 share inc. 300 A	£6	1/9/1795
Wheeler, Abner	Bethlehem, Litchfield, CT	New Milford Twp	C334	2/26/1795
Lewis, Legrand M.	Huntington, Fairfield, CT	2 half shares	$1	3/1/1796
Lewis, Walker	Brookfield, Fairfield, CT		E283	6/8/1796
Lewis, Nehemiah	Goshen, Litchfield, CT	1 share	val sum	10/6/1795
Lewis, Elihu	Hartford Co CT		E250	7/1/1796
Lewis, Nehemiah Jr., heirs*	New Haven, New Haven, CT	1/2 share	20s	10/8/1774
Allen, Levi	Salisbury, Litchfield, CT		B305	1/20/1775
Isaac & Lois Bradley,				
Lewis, Thomas		1/2 share	$2.50	12/19/1754
Hurd, Ephriam			C610	7/9/1795
Lewis, Walker	Brookfield, Fairfield, CT	16,000 A	$5354.99	5/20/1796
Lombard, Roswell & Plumb,	Stockbridge, Berkshire, MA	Burrettsfield Twp	E318	8/8/1796
Lewis, Walker	Brookfield, Fairfield, CT	1000 A; 2 half shares inc. 300 A	£50	10/3/1798
Morgan, Nathaniel	Weston, Fairfield, CT	Granby Twp; Bedford Twp	H10	10/13/1798
Lidwell, Thomas, tailor	Tioga, Luzerne, PA	1/2 share inc. Lot 2	$40	12/18/1794
Hutchinson, John	Tioga, Luzerne, PA	Murraysfield Twp	C305	2/28/1795
Lillie, Silas				
White, William			A374	
Lindsley, Aaron	Bristol, Hartford, CT	1/2 share	val sum	8/25/1794
Roberts, Seth	Paris, Herkimer, NY		C638	7/29/1795
Ling, Thomas	Middleborough, Plymouth, MA	1/2 share	val sum	8/25/1773
Broughton, Thaddeus	Woodbury, Litchfield, CT		B139	2/5/1774
Linkon, Hezekiah	Lempster, NH	1/4 share	£5	1/1/1774
Flint, James Jr.	Windham, Windham, CT		B137	1/31/1774
Linkon, Hezekiah				
Huntington, Hezekiah			A381	

grantor grantee notes	grantor residence grantee residence	description location	amount acct bk page	deed date record date
Linsley, Aliel	Cornwall, Addison, VT	1 share	£4.16	2/23/1795
Stoddard, Philo	Woodbury, Litchfield, CT		C631	7/10/1795
Linsly, Erastus	Catskill, Albany, NY	300 A Lots 20, 15; 300 A Lot 24	$45	11/2/1796
Dewey, Stephen	Sheffield, Berkshire, MA	Murraysfield Twp; Columbia Twp	E505	2/7/1797
Lippert, Thomas	Warwick, Kent, RI	1/2 share	£9	4/7/1795
Carpenter, Comfort A., Physician	Warwick, Kent, RI		H303	6/1/1800
Lippit, John		1/2 share		
Sprague, Theodore			GL	
Little, Thomas	Litchfield, CT	all shares in SP, DP, LP	$5	9/1/1795
Grant, Josiah	Poultney, Rutland, VT		D31	10/5/1795
Livingston, John	Livingston, Columbia, NY	misc. acres and lots*	£234.4.8	8/16/1797
Burroughs, William Y.	Claverack, Columbia, MY	Athens Twp	E555	5/1/1798
100 A 3rd Div N Denison; Lot 21, 22 4th Div J Franklin; 100 A 1/2 lot 23 4th Div; 340 A 1/3 Lot 2, 3 4th Div J Kellogg & J Jenkins; 1/2 4th Div lots Z Beach & J Gaylord; 1/2 Town Lot 40 B Dean				
Livingston, John	Livingston, Columbia, NY	376 A Lot 41 with exceptions*	£326	12/24/1796
Conklin, Ananias	Athens, Luzerne, PA	Athens Twp	E522	2/21/1796
grantor retains right to erect and repair and ingress and egress to Grist Mill and Distillery on Creek that runs through and to dam the creek and to grind for the distillery only				
Lloyd, John	West Stockbridge, Berkshire,	1 share	£30	12/23/1794
Baldwin, Samuel	West Stockbridge, Berkshire,		C502	5/1/1795
Loghry, William, farmer	Tioga, Luzerne, PA	175 A	$40	10/25/1796
Miller, Johnson, joiner	Tioga, Luzerne, PA	Tioga, Luzerne, PA	H39	1/25/1799
Lois Douglas, widow of Daniel	Norwich, New London, CT	3 shares	£100	12/10/1794
Hyde, Elisha	Norwich, New London, CT	1 each Susquehanna, First & Second	I142	12/25/1794
as per D. Douglas will recorded Norwich Probate District				
Lombard, Boswell, saddler	Hillsdale, Columbia, NY	8,000 A	$2,000	7/30/1798
Phelps, Beriah	Hillsdale, Columbia, NY	Armenia Twp, E half	D131	8/28/1798
Lombard, Roswell	Northbridge, Berkshire, MA	12,000 A	$4,000	7/13/1796
Battle, Thiel	Tyringham, Berkshire, MA	Lewistown Twp, E 3/4	E477	11/20/1796
Lombard, Roswell	Stockbridge, Berkshire, MA	Pwr Att, lay out Lombard's land in SP		4/6/1796
Holt, Jacob	Canaan, Litchfield, CT		F61	4/23/1796
Lombard, Roswell	Stockbridge, Berkshire, MA	250 A	$150	10/18/1797
Lincoln, Jedediah	Stockbridge, Berkshire, MA	Lovisa Twp	E549	11/5/1797
Lombard, Roswell	Stockbridge, Berkshire, MA	250 A	$125	9/2/1797
Whittlesey, Eliphalet	Stockbridge, Berkshire, MA	Lovisa Twp	F230	11/1/1797
Lombard, Roswell & Plumb,		entire Twp	$8,000	5/7/1796
Bulkley, James & Clark, Samuel		Hannibal Twp	E320	8/8/1796
Lombard, Roswell, Sadler	Hillsdale, Columbia, NY	1,750 A	$200	8/24/1798
Bacon, Stephen, farmer	Stockbridge, Berkshire, MA	Lovisa Twp	F95	9/11/1798
Lomis, Richard	Plymouth, Luzerne, PA	1/2 share of 400	$20	4/4/1795
Barney, Henry	Plymouth, Luzerne, PA		F56	4/23/1796
Loomis, Ezra				
Downer, Andrew			A479	
Loomis, Ezra				
Spencer, Edward			A478	
Loomiss, Ebenezer				
Hurlbut, Nathan			A101	
Loomiss, Seth				
Gillet, Jonathan			A469	
Loop, Peter Jr.	Newtown, Tioga, NY	300 A Pt of No. 82 of 600*	£30	3/4/1795
Birney, Henry	Standing Stone, Luzerne, PA	Standing Stone Twp	I187	3/4/1795
now occupied by Henry Birney				
Loop, Peter Jr.	Newtown, Tioga, NY	270 A Pt of No. 82 of 600*	£25	3/4/1795
Moger, Theophilus		Claverack Twp	I186	3/4/1795
now occupied by Theo. Moger				
Loop, Peter Jr.	Newtown, Tioga, NY	Lot No. 11	£120	3/3/1795
Moger, Theophlilus		Standing Stone Twp	I185	3/4/1795
Loovens, John		1 share		
Loovens, Peter			GL	
Loovens, Peter		1 share		10/25/1774
Skinner, Ebenezer			GL	2/5/1775
Lothrop, Abiel		agent for a Twp survey	1/2 share	7/20/1795
Throop, Benjamin			C120.1	9/1/1795
for fifteen owners, including Throop, who pay Throop 6s per day for his time and horse; total of 8 shares; A. Lathrop 1/2 share				

grantor grantee notes	grantor residence grantee residence	description location	amount acct bk page	deed date record date
Lothrop, Azariah	Norwich, New London, CT	1 share	£10	11/7/1794
Tracy, Elijah Capt	Norwich CT		I111	12/6/1794
Lothrop, Daniel				
Walsworth, John			A275	
Lothrop, Ebenezer	Colchester, New London, CT	1 share; 2 half shares*	£30	4/11/1795
Hide, Elisha	Norwich, New London, CT		C597	7/9/1795
except land laid out in Warwick & Salem Twps				
Lothrop, Ebenezer Jr.	Norwich, New London, CT	1/2 share	£7. 10	6/16/1774
Adams, David	Pomfret, Windham, CT		B187	3/17/1774
Lothrop, Rufus				
Mason, Jeremiah			A304	
Lothrop, Thacher/Grant,	East Windsor, Hartford, CT	1/2 share	$6	10/18/1797
Drake, Nathaniel Jr.	East Windsor, Hartford, CT		F267	3/12/1798
Lothrop, William	Norwich, New London, CT	1/2 part	£20	2/27/1775
Griste, John	Norwich, New London, CT	Berlin Twp	C93	2/9/1786
Lothrup, Rufus		1 share		
Mason, Jeremiah			GL	
Loveland, John	Durham, New Haven, CT	all shares	15s	1/27/1795
Chauncey, Worthington G.	Durham, New Haven, CT		C314	2/26/1795
Loveland, Jonathan				
Birge, Jonathan			A487	
Loveland, Jonathan	Brandon, Rutland, VT	1/2 share	£3	5/23/1795
Mosely, Nathaniel J.	Pawlett, Rutland, VT		C567	6/20/1795
Lowe, Cornelius	New Town, Tioga, NY	1/4 tract*	£94. 10	1/18/1797
Livingston, John & Burroughs, Wm	Columbia, NY	Claverack, Luzerne, PA	E517 - E424	2/20/1797
Wysock Great Marsh containing the beds of iron ore				
Ludlow, Peter R.	Goshen, Orange, NY	4 lots*	£140	11/11/1796
Burroughs, William Y.	Claverack, Columbia, NY	Athens Twp	E516	2/17/1797
1 house lot with log store house erected or finished by Wiese & Hollenback; Lots 1 & 39; 1 undiv 4th div Lot; all drawn in right of Daniel McDowell				
Lusk, John & Mary	Berlin, Hartford, CT	1/4 share	£3. 15	1/16/1796
Smith, Lemuel	Berlin, Hartford, CT		E147	2/25/1796
Lusk, Seth & Goodrich, Isaac	Berlin, Hartford, CT	all right	£6	2/1/1796
Smith, Lemuel & Ally, John B.	Berlin, Hartford, CT		E147	2/25/1796
Lydias, John H. & Lydias, Beleazer		all right	$100	12/20/1772
Winders, William	Albany, Albany, NY		E130	3/28/1796
Lyman, Elihu*	New Haven, New Haven, CT	4 shares	$280	12/29/1795
Munson, Joshua	Canaan, Litchfield, CT		E256	7/1/1796
son and heir of Daniel Lyman; Daniel Lyman pd taxes of £20. 14. 6 and 9s more on 7/29/1768 on 4 shares				
Lyman, Phineas	Suffield, Hartford, CT	all rights	£24	12/4/1773
Kent, Benajah	Suffield, Hartford, CT		B347	5/16/1776
Lyndon, Josias trustees*	Newport, Newport, Middletown	1 share	£12	1/9/1795
Dorrance, Samuel	Windham, Windham, CT		C394	2/22/1795
Benjamin Hall, Joseph Pike, William Pike				
Lyon, Ebenezer	Weston, Fairfield, CT	1 share	£15	8/18/1794
Morgan, Nathaniel	Reading, Fairfield, CT		C532	5/1/1795
MacClure [McClure], Thomas		1/2 share		
Clark, Benjamin			GM	
MacGregor, John		1/2 share		
Barnet, Moses			GD	
MacNeal, Archibald		1/4 share		11/17/1773
Marshall, Gad			GM	
Man, Nathan	Hebron, Hartford, CT	1/2 share	£2	7/31/1758
Stiles, Nathan	Lebanon, Windham, CT		B20 - GM	5/6/1773
Manley, William	Simsbury, Hartford, CT	1/2 share	18s	4/30/1755
Goodwin, Stephen	Simsbury, Hartford, CT		B96	11/2/1773
Manning, Hezekiah				
Murdock, Daniel			A277	
Manning, John Jr.	Windham, Windham, CT	1/2 share	£9	12/14/1762
Walker, Sylvanius	Brookfield, Worcester, MA		B90	11/17/1773
Mansfield, John	Sterling, Windham, CT	1 share	$20	1/2/1795
Dorrance, Samuel	Windham, Windham, CT		C386	2/22/1795
Mansfield, Richard				
Holbrook, Joseph			A68	

grantor grantee notes	grantor residence grantee residence	description location	amount acct bk page	deed date record date
Mansfield, Samuel			A357	
LeHommedieu, Ezra				
Mansfield, Thomas		1/4 share		
Mansfield, Thomas, Jr.			GM	
Mansfield, Thomas, Jr.		1/4 share		
Milk, Job			GM	
Manson, Eneas Jr.*	New Haven, New Haven, CT	1, 1/4, 1/2 of 1/4 shares	$100	7/2/1796
Wise, Samuel P.	Watertown		E479	11/15/1796
shares deeded to Manson by Abiel Holmes, adm of estate of Ezra Stiles, decd.				
Manvill, Ira	Plymouth, Luzerne, PA	16,000 A	$2,000	8/18/1796
Halsted, Richard Jr.	Exeter, Luzerne, PA	Oston Twp	F174	6/26/1797
Markham, Joseph				
Witham, Joshua			A459	
Marsh, David		1/2 share		4/28/1774
Clark, Abner			GM	
Marshall, Josiah	Tioga/Athens, Luzerne, PA	Lot 9 on Headwaters of Sugar Creek	$150	4/23/1794
Hutchinson, John	Athens, Luzerne, PA	Murraysfield Twp	E158	5/16/1796
Marshall, Josiah	Ulster, Luzerne, PA	2,500 A	$2,500	12/26/1799
Thayer, Levi	Athens, Luzerne, PA	Fullersville Twp	H164	12/30/1799
Marshall, Seth	Farmington, Hartford, CT	1/2 share	£7. 10	4/15/1763
Barber, Thomas	Simsbury		E148	4/22/1796
Marshall, Seth & Preserved	Farmington, Hartford, CT	1 share	£1.10	7/29/1794
Fowler, Reuben	Killingworth, Middlesex, CT		C118	10/1/1794
Marther, Abner	Freehold, Albany, NY	1 share; 1/2 share	£60	10/29/1795
Grant, Josiah	Poultney, Rutland, VT		F72	5/24/1796
Marther, Eleazer	Lyme, Middlesex, CT	1 share	val con	6/4/1794
Elliot, William	Saybrook, Middlesex, CT		C455	2/21/1795
Martin, Reuben	Woodbury, Litchfield, CT	1/2 share	val sum	4/2/1795
Deforest, Curtis	Woodbury, Litchfield, CT		C634	7/10/1795
Martin, Reuben	Woodbury, Litchfield, CT	pt of a share	£4.10	5/11/1795
Judson, Gideon & Elisha			C628	7/15/1795
Martin, Reuben	Woodbury, Litchfield, CT	Pwr Att on Barzilla Hende share		5/16/1795
Leavensworth, Asa			C627	7/15/1795
Martin, Reuben	Woodbury, Litchfield, CT	1/2 share	val sum	4/2/1795
Messer, Daniel	Newfield, Fairfield, CT		C633	7/10/1795
Martin, William	Jamestown, Norfolk, RI	1 share + 36 A	5s	1/18/1787
Martin, Anderson, son	Lebanon, Windham, CT	Susq R adj. Peter Harris	C107	1/30/1787
Mason, David		1/2 share		11/13/1773
Kinne, James			GH	
Mason, David		agent for a Twp survey*	1/2 share	7/20/1795
Throop, Benjamin			C120.1	9/1/1795
for fifteen owners, including Throop, who pay Throop 6s per day for his time and horse; total of 8 shares; D. Mason 1/2 share				
Mason, Jeremiah			A222	
Mason, David & Huntington,				
Mason, Jeremiah			A343	
Pendleton, Benajah				
Mason, Jeremiah		1 share		
Pendleton, Benajah			GL	
Mason, Jeremiah	Lebanon, Windham, CT	Pwr Att to layout share		6/6/1796
Throop, Benjamin	Bozrah, New London, CT		E235	7/1/1796
Mason, Jeremiah			A82	
Walsworth, Nathan				
Mason, Jonathan	Sturbridge, Worcester, MA	interest in 1/2 share	£14	1/5/1795
Howard, Nathan	Sturbridge, Worcester, MA		C439	4/14/1795
Massachusetts, State of		Ltrs Adm, estate of Daniel Kellogg		1/5/1779
Kellogg, Jesse	Sheffield, Berkshire, MA		F272	3/14/1798
Matterson, Thomas	Coventry, Kent, RI	1/2 share	£16	3/17/1777
Dean, Ezra	West Greenwich, Kent, RI		B372	3/26/1777
Matterson, Thomas Jr.	Scituate, Providence, RI	1/2 share	£7. 17. 3	4/13/1774
Matterson, Israel	Johnston, Providence, RI		B264	11/4/1774
Matteson, Thomas	Coventry, Kent, RI	1/2 share	$25	10/20/1773
Dorrance, Lemuel	Voluntown, Windham, CT		B94	11/4/1773

grantor / grantee / notes	grantor residence / grantee residence	description / location	amount / acct bk page	deed date / record date
Matteson, Thomas	East Greenwich, Kent, RI	1/2 share		5/29/1754
Dorrance, Lemuel			B211	5/15/1774
Matthews, Henry *		1 share except 300 A*		
Hyde, William & Blackman,			F87	9/19/1796
named changed from Gameliel Maltar; where Henry Matthews now lives; no date on deed				
Matthews, Peter		1/4 share		4/1/1773
Kimberly, Nathan			GD	4/16/1773
Matthewson, Betsey	Athens, Luzerne, PA	300 A, Lot 20	$300	12/21/1799
Satterlee, Elias	Athens, Luzerne, PA	Columbia Twp	H153	12/26/1799
Matthewson, Thomas		1/2 share		12/1/1774
Matthewson, Israel			GM	12/2/1774
Maxwell, Guy		4 half share rights*	$75	9/26/1794
Paine, David			C317	3/9/1795
David Wood, No. 70; Jeptha Earl, No. 81; Daniel Earl, No. 80; Enos Tubbs No. 82				
Maxwell, Guy		Lot 10*	$12	3/1/1795
Paine, David		Athens (Tioga Pt) nearly opposite	E118	3/1/1796
6 perches wide fronting the street and running back to the Tioga R.				
Maxwell, Guy	Luzerne, PA	Town Lot 9*	$12	3/1/1795
Paine, David	Luzerne, PA	Athens Twp	E119	3/1/1796
6 perches on street and running back to Tioga R.				
Maxwell, John	Lebanon, Windham, CT	1/2 share	£5	12/29/1794
Dorrance, Gershom	Windham, Windham, CT		C538	5/7/1795
May, Eleazer	Haddam, Middlesex, CT	1/2 share	$5	2/11/1795
Selby, Brainard	Sanderfield, Berkshire, MA		F3	3/1/1796
May, Hezekiah				
Roberts, Seth			A254	
May, Samuel, William May, Ex	Weathersfield, Hartford, CT	1/2 share	$10	5/13/1794
Hale, George	Catskill, Albany, NY		C383	2/28/1795
Mayhew, Elisha	Shewfells Flatts, Luzerne, PA	about 300 A*	£25	1/22/1793
Satterlee, Benedict	Athens, Luzerne, PA	Athens Twp	H202	12/27/1799
Town Lot 60; Ten Acre Lot 18; Hundred Acre Lot 46; 1/53 of the undivided land				
McClure, Thomas	Tioga NY	100 A Lot 15*	£45	12/2/1794
Gaylord, Lemuel	Luzerne Co PA	Athens Twp	C590	12/2/1794
50 rods W side Tioga R; S Noah Murray; N Sylvester Travis				
McClure, Thomas	Tioga, NY	Lot 44 and part Lot 45*	£50	4/25/1794
Hepburn, Samuel and Maxwell,	Tioga (Athens), Luzerne, PA	Athens, Luzerne, PA	E336	8/1/1796
inc. house and garden occupied by Hofflebeam				
McClure, Thomas	Tioga Co, NY	Town Lot 11, near Tioga Point	£2. 10	2/24/1795
Paine, David	Luzerne, PA	Athens Twp	E120	3/1/1796
McDowel, Daniel	Athens, Luzerne, PA	Lots No 15, 16; 1, 39 all undiv land	£100	5/9/1787
Moder, John Jay A.	Hudson, Columbia, NY	Athens, on Tioga R.	E451	10/28/1796
15 & 16 each 3/4 A house lots subject to PA and CT claim; Lots No 1 & 39 under CT claim;				
McDowel, Daniel		1/2 share No. 269 of 600	$15	3/1/1795
Shepard, John			E331	4/10/1796
McKarnehan, William		1/2 share		
Thayer, David			GC	
McKinstry, John	Livingston, Columbia, NY	1/2 share	5s	9/5/1796
Burrough, William Y.		Athens, Luzerne, PA	E429	10/14/1796
McKinstry, John	Hudson, NY	Lot 47, 3rd divi*, Lot 15, 4th div	deed to Athens tract	10/12/1793
Franklin, John	Athens	Athens Twp	F253	10/12/1793
W by Susq. R, S by J Franklin, N by Benedict Satterlee, E fr river 1 mi;				
McKinstry, John	Livingston, Columbia, NY	300 A of 1/2 share	£120	12/23/1794
Livingston, John	Livingston, Columbia, NY	Athens, Luzerne, PA	C543	4/1/1795
McMaster, James	Union, Tioga, NY	1/4 tract*	£100	11/25/1795
Lowe, Cornelius	Newtown, NY	Claverack, Luzerne, PA	E424 - D37	10/11/1795
Wysock Great Marsh containing the beds of iron ore				
McMaster, James	Union, Tioga, NY	1/4 Lot 19*	100£	10/17/1795
Wattles, Mason	Union, Tioga, NY	Claverack Twp*	D38	10/20/1795
with full iron mining rights; Wisocks Great Marsh, NW side Wisocks Cr.				
McNeal, Archibald				
Reynolds, James			A258	
McNiel, Archibald	Litchfield, Litchfield, CT	1/2 share	£19	11/29/1773
Olcot, James Jr.& Mary	Harwinton, Litchfield, CT		B177	3/6/1774

grantor grantee notes	grantor residence grantee residence	description location	amount acct bk page	deed date record date
McNiele, Alexander	Litchfield, Litchfield, CT	1/2 share	£8	4/27/1773
Dixon, Archibald	Woodbury, Litchfield, CT		B99	12/8/1773
McWhorter, Thomas	Tioga, Luzerne, PA	1/2 share inc. Lot 47	£20	12/19/1794
Hutchinson, John	Tioga, Luzerne, PA	Murraysfield Twp	C312	2/28/1795
Meeker, Amos		1/2 share, No. 133 of 400	for value	3/27/1794
Gaylord, Lemuel			D24	9/24/1795
Merrell, Joseph 2nd	New Hartford, Litchfield, CT	1/2 share	£6	5/3/1763
Douglas, Samuel			B80	10/11/1773
Merrill, Isaac	Thetford, Orange, VT	1/2 share	40s	4/21/1795
Barrett, Jonathan & Rathburn, Wait	Norwich, VT; Middletown, VT		C646	8/10/1795
Metcalf, Andrew				
Fitch, Abel			A419	
Metcalf, Andrew				
Newton, James			A398	
Milk, Job		1/4 share		
Pettibone, Noah, Jr.			GM	
Miller, Abraham	Newtown, Tioga, NY	1 share	$100	2/16/1796
Teal, Nathan	Newtown, Tioga, NY		H50	1/10/1799
Miller, Gain		1/2 share		3/5/1773
Frisbe, Benjamin			GM	
Miller, Gam	Sharon, Litchfield, CT	1 share	£1. 1. 7	9/22/1794
Coleman, Elihu, Jesse, Amasa			I99	10/2/1794
Miller, Johnson	Shemung [Chemung], Tioga,	175 A*	£70	5/8/1798
Mathewson, Oliver	Athens, Luzerne, PA	Tioga [Athens], Luzerne, PA	H40	1/25/1799
adjacent to Ulster and Susq R				
Miller, Johnston		300 A, 1/4 of 1/2 of No. 95 of 600		5/11/1793
Alexander, David		2 mi W Athens Twp sur. 12/25/1792	I68	5/30/1793
Miller, Peter		1/2 share, all rights of P Miller*		4/12/1769
Butler, William			GM	
Butler says deed date was 4/19/1774				
Miller, Peter	Standing Stone, Luzerne, PA	all right to improvements on land*		5/23/1797
Gordon, Samuel	Luzerne, PA	Standing Stone Twp	H14	11/10/1798
reserving right for Miller's wife to live in house until 1 Oct 1797				
Miller, William		1520 A of 1 share, No. 120 of 600		8/1/1798
Jones, Justus		on main branch Buttermilk Cr.*	H15	11/17/1798
in present day Falls Twp, Wyoming Co., PA				
Miller, William & Dimock, Asa	Pittstown, Luzerne, PA	8,000 A	$2,000	7/7/1796
Davenport, Jonathan	Hillsdale, Columbia, NY	Btw Exeter and Greenfield Twps	F169	6/26/1797
Miller, William & Dimock, Asa	Pittstown, Luzerne, PA	16,000 A	£1,600	2/26/1795
Wynkoop, Wm & Spelman,	Chemung, Tioga, NY; Catskill,	Greenfield Twp	C139	2/23/1795
Mills, Alexander & Lydia Yale wf	Frederick Town, Dutchess, NY	1/2 share	$23	2/3/1795
Kimberly, Israel; Kimberly, Liberty	Derby, New Haven, CT		C409	4/4/1795
Mills, Betsey Riggs	Derby, New Haven, CT	all right	36s	12/6/1794
Pope, Robert	Derby, New Haven, CT		C418	4/4/1795
Mills, Eli	Armenia, Dutchess, NY	all right to 2 deeds*	love and good will	10/19/1795
Hunt, Salmon	Canaan, Litchfield, CT		E260	7/1/1796
William Avery C573 & John Williams C574; see King to Mills C586				
Mills, Elisha	Huntington, Fairfield, CT	1/2 share*	£15	1/16/1796
Lewis, Walker	Brookfield, Fairfield, CT		E279	
other half share owned by heirs John Moose, decd				
Mills, Elisha		1/2 share		2/12/1754
Morse, John			E474	11/28/1796
Mills, Elisha	Stratford, Fairfield, CT	1/2 share	30s	11/11/1773
Moss, John Lt.	Stratford, Fairfield, CT		B107	12/10/1773
Mills, Jedediah		1 share	val sum	11/28/1765
Mills, Isaac	Darby		E280	6/8/1796
Mills, Philo Jr.	Killingsworth, Middlesex, CT	all right	val con	12/11/1794
Riggs, Joseph	Derby, New Haven, CT		C417	4/4/1795
Mills, Reuben		1/2 share		6/4/1794
Ross, Daniel			E362	
Mills, Saml & Abigail Cowls Mills	Norfolk, Litchfield, CT	1/4 share	bond recd	10/23/1794
Brown, Daniel	Freehold, Albany, NY		E506	6/1/1796

grantor grantee notes	grantor residence grantee residence	description location	amount acct bk page	deed date record date
Miner, Daniel	Stonington, New London, CT	1/2 share	18s	11/22/1794
Kingsbury, Joseph	Enfield, Hartford, CT		C151	2/24/1795
Miner, Henry	Stonington, New London, CT	1/2 share	£40	8/27/1755
Rathbun, John	Stonington, New London, CT		E347 - GM	8/24/1796
Miner, Manasseh	Voluntown, Windham, CT	1/4 all right after 1st div is made	love	12/8/1778
Hillard, Temperance dau	Voluntown, Windham, CT		C604	7/9/1795
Minor, Elizabeth				
Hurd, Nathan Jr.			A45	
Minor, Manasseh	Voluntown, Windham, CT	1/4 all right after 1st div is made	love	12/8/1778
Gilmore, Sarah, dau	Keene NH		C605	7/9/1795
Minor, Manasseth	Voluntown, Windham, CT	1/4 share	love	12/8/1778
Robins, Keziah, dau	Voluntown, Windham, CT		C82	10/26/1782
Minor, Mannaseth	Voluntown	600 A 1st Div	Love	12/8/1778
York, Lucretia dau. & York gchr.*		Springfield Twp	C13	3/18/1779
Ester, Welthia, Manasah Minor, Beranthia, Keziah, Sarah, Temperance, Hannah, Lucretia Buck				
Minor, Mannaseth	Voluntown	1/4 part all right	love	12/8/1778
York, Manassah Minor &	Susquehannah	Susquehanna Purchase	C13	3/18/1779
100 A of 1/4 part to grandson Manassah Minor York, rest to daughter Lucretia Minor York				
Minor, Saxton	Stonington	1/2 share	£5	11/29/1794
Brown, William	Preston, New London, CT		C28	9/1/1795
Minor, Saxton	Stonington, New London, CT	Pwr Att* and own 1/2 share fr Robin		2/20/1796
Hyde, Ezekiel	Norwich, New London, CT		F37	4/23/1796
to locate on behalf of heirs of Henry Minor, decd				
Mitchel, Peter		Pwr to take and act upon 1/2 share		10/27/1794
Martin, Reuben			E225	
Mitchel, Timothy	Woodbury, Litchfield, CT	1/8 share	£2	3/23/1768
Root, Jesse	Woodbury, Litchfield, CT		I122	
Mix, John & Bradley, Erastus*	New Haven, Hartford, CT	all Mix's right	good con	12/19/1794
Bishop, John	New Haven, New Haven, CT		E80	3/2/1796
heirs of Wm Phineas Bradley				
Moder, John J. A.	Hudson, Columbia, NY	1/2 of No. 54 of 600*	£100	3/5/1787
Ludlow, Peter R.	Claverack, Columbia, NY	Franklin Twp	E454	10/28/1796
No. 24 1st div; No 47 home and water lot; one lot not yet drawn				
Moder, John J. A.	New York City, NY	1 share		9/28/1786
Raston, Edward R.			E166	5/14/1796
Moder, John J. Ac	Claverack, Columbia, NY	Lots No. 15, 16; 1, 39 & all undiv	£111. 10	9/23/1787
Ludlow, Peter R.	Claverack, Columbia, NY	Athens Twp.	E452	10/28/1796
15 & 16 each 3/4 A house lots subject to PA and CT claim; Lots 1 & 39 under CT claim.				
Moffatt, Thomas	Stephen Town, Rensselaer, NY	1 share	£40	1/23/1795
Murray, Reuben	Canaan, Columbia, NY		E166	5/20/1796
Moffett, Joseph, Physician	Brimfield, Hampshire, MA	Pwr Att to locate	1/2 land	1/22/1796
Tucker, John	Stockbridge, Berkshire, MA		F204	7/19/1797
Mohamedieu, Ezra L.	Southark, Suffolk, NY	two 1/4 shares	£15	7/26/1762
Reeve, James	Southold, Suffolk, NY	Delaware Co and Susq Co	F28	4/23/1796
Montgomery, Elijah, eldest son	Stillwater, Saratoga, NY	1 share	£12	3/26/1795
Janes, Elijah, merchant et al*	Troy, Rensselaer, NY		C125-6	8/10/1795
James Dole, James; Wait Rathbun, innkeeper				
Montgomery, James	Albany Co NY	take possession of 1/2 of 1 share	2/3 of the 1/2 share	1/20/1787
Flowers, Zephen	Albany Co NY		D49	9/2/1795
Montgomery, John		1 share		12/22/1794
Barrit, John			E77	3/2/1796
Montgomery, John Jr.				
Gordon, George			A61	
Montgomery, Robert*	Voluntown, Windham, CT	1/3 share	£4	4/18/1769
Dorrance, George	Voluntown, Windham, CT		B53	8/12/1773
by will of John Montgomery, father				
Montgomery, Robert		1/4 share		
Dorrance, George			GM	
Morehouse, David & wf	Stillwater, Saratoga, NY	all right	5s	11/8/1795
Dunning, Ebenezer et al			E112	3/1/1796
heirs of David Bidwell; Philip Dillino/Delano; David Ramsey; Jacob Baldwin				
Morehouse, Nathan Jr.	Weston, Fairfield, CT	1/2 share	£12	1/6/1795
Strong, Joseph	Fairfield, Fairfield, CT		C517	5/1/1795

grantor grantee notes	grantor residence grantee residence	description location	amount acct bk page	deed date record date
Morey, Jonathan				
Moor, David			A1	
Morgan, Asa	Litchfield, Litchfield, CT	16,000 A	$4,300	12/29/1795
Bradly, Timothy	Sunderland, Bennington, VT	Beavertown Twp	H270	12/3/1800
Morgan, Jacob & Pardee, Samuel	New Haven	certification		4/5/1796
Humperville, Ebenezer & Samuel*			E530	11/1/1796
Ebenezer and Samuel are only heirs of Benjamin Humperville				
Morgan, John		1/4 share		3/23/1774
Morgan, John, Jr.			GN	9/9/1774
Morgan, John		agent for a Twp survey*	1/4 share	7/20/1795
Throop, Benjamin			C120.1	9/1/1795
for fifteen owners, including Throop, who pay Throop 6s per day for his time and horse; total of 8 shares; J. Morgan 1/4 share				
Morgan, Nathaniel	Weston, Fairfield, CT	320 A, Lot 2	£30	3/9/1797
Bradley, Walter	Fairfield, Fairfield, CT	Augusta Twp	H9	10/13/1798
Morgan, Nathaniel	Weston, Fairfield, CT	320 A, Lot 6	$320	4/4/1798
Lyon, Zachariah & Andrew	Weston, Fairfield, CT	Augusta Twp	H80	7/27/1799
120 A to Zachariah and 200 A to Andrew				
Morgan, Nathaniel	Reading, Fairfield, CT	1/2 share	$50	4/1/1795
Morgan, Stephen	Luzerne Co PA	Augusta Twp, 1/49th pt	C535	5/7/1795
Morgan, Roswell	Plainfield, Windham, CT	1 share	£6	6/7/1769
Larrabe, John	Norwich, New London, CT		B67 - GC	10/9/1773
Morgan, Samuel	Colchester, Hartford, CT	1/2 Morgan's share	£3. 10	12/11/1772
Ackley, Joseph	East Haddam, Hartford, CT		B184	3/10/1774
Morgan, Samuel	Colchester, Hartford, CT	1/2 share	£3.10	12/11/1772
Bigelow, John Jr.	Colchester		C44	5/27/1782
Morgan, Samuel	New London, New London, CT	1/2 share	£3	9/2/1794
Elliot, William	Saybrook, Middlesex, CT		C350	3/2/1795
Morgan, Samuel				
Lester, Eliphalet			A367	
Morgan, Samuel				
Morgan, Timothy			A266	
Morgan, Sylvia	Vergenne, Addison, VT	1/2 share	$25	2/20/1796
Fitch, Samuel	Vergenne, Addison, VT		E76	3/1/1796
Morgan, Theophilus		1/4 share		
Morgan, John			GN	
Morgan, Timothy				
Lester, Eliphalet			A367	
Morgan, William	Norwich, New London, CT	1 share	val con	9/9/1762
Avery, Humphrey	Norwich, New London, CT	Second Delaware Co	B84	11/9/1773
Morgan, William	Norwich, New London, CT	1/2 share	val con	9/9/1762
Avery, Humphrey	Norwich, New London, CT	First Delaware Company	B84	11/9/1773
Morgan, William	Norwich, New London, CT	1/2 share	val con	9/9/1762
Avery, Humphrey	Norwich, New London, CT	Susquehanna Company Purchase	B84	11/9/1773
Morris, Daniel	Attford, Berkshire, MA	1/2 share		2/27/1775
Morris, Eleazer, son		Starlingtown Twp	E46	2/24/1796
Morris, Daniel	Fairfield, Fairfield, CT	1/4 share	£3. 15	
Sherwood, Albert & Daniel Jr.	Fairfield, Fairfield, CT		C520	5/1/1795
Morris, James	Litchfield, Litchfield, CT	1 share	£15	12/29/1794
Fabrique, John	Bethlehem, Litchfield, CT		E404	9/15/1796
Morriss, Daniel	Fairfield, Fairfield, CT	1/4 share	£3.15	3/5/1774
Sherwood, Jeremiah	Fairfield, Fairfield, CT		B153	3/8/1774
Morse, Barnabas				4/26/1769
Hunt, Ephriam			GM	1/1/1774
Morse, Barnabas				
Hunt, Ephriam			GM	
Morse, David		1/2 share		
Osborn, John			GM	
Morse, John, decd		Elihu Morse agent to lot out 1/2 share		3/16/1795
Morse, Wm, Jos, Isaac, Elihu, sons	Huntington, Fairfield, CT	New Milford 300 A; Millsburg 700	E474	11/28/1795
Morse, Joseph	Poultney, Rutland, VT	all right to inherited Lots 11, 14,	$15	4/27/1799
Morse, Solomon	Poultney, Rutland, VT	Smithfield Twp	H75	5/20/1799

grantor grantee notes	grantor residence grantee residence	description location	amount acct bk page	deed date record date
Morse, Solomon, decd	Cheshire and Waterberry CT	certificate of entitlement to share		2/9/1799
Morse, Solomon et al*			H75	6/22/1799
Joseph Morse, William Morse; Elizabeth wf of Josiah Hart, Sarah, wf of Capt. Israel Harris, chr of decd dau Eunice wf of Amasa Holcomb; $13 taxes paid				
Moseley, Abishai	Pawlett, Rutland, VT	1/2 share	£7. 10	2/17/1795
Stoddard, Philo	Woodbury, Litchfield, CT		C635	7/10/1795
Moseley, Abner	Woodbury, Litchfield, CT	1/4 share	£5	1/8/1774
Wheeler, Consider, wf of Benjamin	Woodbury, Litchfield, CT		B280	10/31/1774
Moseley, Increase	Woodbury, Litchfield, CT	1/2 share	£20	6/29/1774
Lamb, Joseph	Woodbury, Litchfield, CT		B328	5/17/1775
Moseley, Increase	Woodbury, Litchfield, CT	1/2 share	£6	4/20/1772
Moseley, Abisha	Woodbury, Litchfield, CT		B103	12/13/1773
Moseley, Nathan	Rutland, Rutland, VT	1,500 A	$100	5/2/1801
Ethridge, John	Smithfield Twp	Homerstown Twp	H324	7/21/1801
Moseley, Nathaniel	Pawlett, Rutland, VT	14,000 A*	$3,000	5/21/1796
Stoddard, Philo	Woodbury, Litchfield, CT	Homerstown Twp	F213	10/25/1797
Moseley, Nathaniel T.	Pawlett, Rutland, VT	1/2 Township	$3,000	6/13/1796
Clark, Samuel & James Bulkley		Rutland Twp	E303	8/8/1796
Moseley, Nathaniel T.	Rutland, VT	100 A in Lot 13	$60	3/8/1802
Farmer, Minott	Rutland, VT	Armenia Twp	H340	6/13/1802
Moseley, Nathaniel T.	Brandon, Rutland, VT	2 3/4 shares*	$50	4/10/1799
Morse, Solomon	Poultney, Rutland, VT		H73	5/20/1799
1/4 Jacob Frisbe; 1/2 James Frisbe; 1 Ephriam Loomis; 1 Simian Edgerton				
Moseley, Nathaniel T.	Pawlett, Rutland, VT	1/2 share	$25	2/17/1795
Stoddard, Philo	Woodbury, Litchfield, CT		C634	7/10/1795
Moseley, William	Woodbury, Litchfield, CT	2 shares	$160	2/11/1796
Taylor, Augustine	Sharon, Litchfield, CT		E401	9/15/1796
Moseley, William & Hale, Joseph	Glastonbury, Hartford, CT	1 share	$20	5/19/1794
Hale, George	Catskill, Albany, NY		C370	2/28/1795
Mosely, Abner	Washington, Litchfield, CT	2 1/4 shares inc. 300 A laid out		7/1/1794
Turrell/Terrill, Job Jr.	New Milford, Litchfield, CT	New Milford Twp	C338	2/26/1795
Mosely, Increase	Woodbury, Litchfield, CT	1/4 share	£5	9/18/1773
Hooker, William	Woodbury, Litchfield, CT		B173	3/9/1774
Mosely, Increase	Woodbury, Litchfield, CT	1/2 share	£6	1/3/1772
Northrop, Samuel	Woodbury, Litchfield, CT		B163	3/9/1774
Mosely, Increase	Woodbury, Litchfield, CT	1/4 share	£10	9/27/1773
Starkweather, Stephen	Kent, Litchfield, CT		B171	3/9/1774
Mosely, Joseph	Glastonbury, Hartford, CT	1 share	$20	5/9/1795
Hale, George	Catskill, Albany, NY		C374	2/28/1795
Mosely, Nathaniel J.	Pawlet, Rutland, VT	1 1/2 share	$60	6/6/1795
Hooker, James Jr.	Poultney, Rutland, VT		C565	6/20/1795
Moss, Solomon	Smithfield, Twp	1/2 Lots 7, 13, 23 - 500 A each	$750	2/16/1801
Dewey, Azariah	Poultney, Rutland, VT	Armenia Twp	H341	6/13/1802
Mott, Edward	Preston, New London, CT	1 share•	£15	11/21/1794
Hyde, Elisha	Norwich, New London, CT		I141	12/25/1794
except settling right and 5/600 A fr PA Assembly				
Moulton, Samuel, heir, son Heman	Casselton, Rutland, VT	1 share	$10	3/1/1796
Burr, Jonathan	Lansingburgh, Rensselaer, NY		F75	5/24/1796
Mowry, George	Smithfield, Providence, RI	1 1/2 shares	£6	1/18/1796
Peirce, John	Plainfield, Windham, CT	Bald Eagle Twp* (1 share)	E272	7/15/1796
not a granted Twp; Bald Eagle Cr. flows into Susq R at Lock Haven on W Branch				
Moy, Deion		1/4 share		
Roberts, Seth			GM	
Munson, Baszel	Hamden, New Haven, CT	1 share	good cause	8/27/1794
Roberts, Seth	Paris, Herkimer, NY		C639	7/29/1795
Munson, Eneas	New Haven, New Haven, CT	1 share		1/19/1795
Turner, Seth	New Haven, New Haven, CT		C295	3/4/1795
Munson, Joshua		1 share	$90	1/15/1796
Goodrich, Benjamin			E252	7/1/1796
Munson, Joshua		4 shares	$100	1/15/1796
Goodrich, Benjamin			E256	7/1/1796
Munson, Walter	New Haven, New Haven, CT	500 A	$50	11/3/1800
Munson, Mansfield, Betsey, Pauline	New Haven, New Haven, CT	Cabot Twp	H273	1/10/1801
children				

grantor grantee notes	grantor residence grantee residence	description location	amount acct bk page	deed date record date
Murdock, Dan	Windham, Windham, CT	1/2 share	£17. 10	4/6/1774
Downing, Levi	Canterbury, Windham, CT		B202	4/6/1774
Murdock, John	Amenia, Dutchess, NY	1/4 share	£6	4/28/1763
Smith, Oliver	Amenia, Dutchess, NY		B310 - G	2/9/1775
Murphey, John		1/4 share		9/25/1772
Swetland, Caleb			GK	
Murphy, John		1/4 share		
Swetland, Caleb			GM	
Murray, Joel	Athens, Luzerne, PA	320 A, Lot 24	$300	12/25/1799
Thayer, Levi	Athens, Luzerne, PA	Smithfield Twp	H156	12/26/1799
Murray, Noah		all interest in 1/2 share*		3/11/1796
Allen, Nathaniel			E114	3/17/1796
formerly belonging to Barnabas Paine				
Murray, Noah	Tioga, Luzerne, PA	Lot 6, 300 A	$150	9/6/1794
Bingham, Chester	Tioga, Luzerne, PA	Murraysfield Twp	D30	9/22/1795
Murray, Noah	Tioga, Luzerne, PA	Lot 3, 150 A + 150 A undivided	$150	5/20/1794
Gansey, D. Philo	Watertown, Litchfield, CT	Columbia Twp*	E180	6/4/1796
Murray called it "Tioga Twp on Sugar Creek known by the name of Columbia."				
Murray, Noah	Tioga, Luzerne, PA	Lot 19, 150 A + 150 A undivided	$150	5/20/1794
Garnsey Jr., Abijah	Watertown, Litchfield, CT	Columbia Twp*	E181	6/4/1796
Murray called it "Tioga Twp on Sugar Creek known by the name of Columbia."				
Murray, Noah	Athens, Luzerne, PA	500 A	$500	6/23/1796
Garnsey, Philo	Watertown, Litchfield, NY	John Jenkins pitch	D167	6/23/1796
Murray, Noah	Athens, Luzerne, PA	6,400 A*	$4,000	12/29/1799
Jenkins, John	Exeter, Luzerne, PA	Jenkin's Pitch	H167	12/30/1799
reserving 1000 A which is to be in common				
Murray, Noah		700 A of 1/2 share*		9/5/1795
Lockwood, Ephriam			C283	9/7/1795
300 A, Lot 6 in Murraysfield reserved				
Murray, Noah		700 A of 1/2 of No. 394 of 600*		9/5/1795
Lockwood, Ephriam			C285	9/7/1795
300 A, Lot 19 Murraysfield reserved				
Murray, Reuben	Columbia, NY	1 share	5s	1/25/1795
Wynkoop, William	Tioga, NY		E167	5/20/1796
Nash, Robert W.	Foster, Providence, RI	500 A, 1/32 pt all undivided land	$706.16	10/22/1796
Dean, Calvin, tanner and currier	Providence, Providence, RI	Springhill, Luzerne, PA	F247	2/13/1798
Neill, Thomas	Wilkesbarre, PA	1 Town Lot, 300 A* & 1/2 A	£62.10	10/18/1786
Fridley, Jacob	Dauphin Co, PA	Wilkesbarre Twp	I2	10/19/1786
orig Christopher Avery decd; 1 frame house; 2600 brick; 2000 ft boards; 2000 pine shingles 3 ft long all to be delivered to said lot				
Nevins, David	Norwich CT	350 A +/-	£9	11/5/1794
Tracy, Elijah Capt	Norwich CT	Bedford Twp	I108	12/6/1794
Nevins, David	Norwich, New London, CT	1 share	£6	11/5/1794
Tracy, Elisha	Norwich, New London, CT		I197	4/1/1795
Nevins, David Capt*	Norwich, New London, CT	1 share	£30	12/10/1794
Hyde, Elisha	Norwich, New London, CT		I177	2/22/1795
eldest son David Nevins Sr.				
Newcomb, James	St Town Dist, Albany, NY	1/2 share	love	10/16/1787
Newcomb, James & Tipper	St Town Dist, Albany, NY		C110	
Newton, John				
Morgan, Theophilus			A448	
Newton, John		1/4 share		
Morgan, Theophilus			GN	
Nichols, Benjamin estate*	Newport, RI	all right	£50	6/9/1791
Douglas, William shopkeeper	Newport, RI		C595	7/8/1795
Joseph B. Nichols, cordwainer, adm.				
Nichols, Robert		1 share		5/1/1774
Vreeland, Grant			GN	
Nichols, Robert		1 share		
Woodbridge, Timothy			GN	
Niles, Sands	Stonington, New London, CT		£13.5	3/18/1795
Ells, Edward	Stonington, New London, CT		CB	9/1/1795
Nisbitt, Abram		all right	value recd	12/15/1795
Manville, Ira			E267	7/8/1796

grantor	grantor residence	description	amount	deed date
grantee	grantee residence	location	acct bk page	record date
notes				
Noble, Sylvanus	New Milford, Litchfield, CT	Pwr Att to locate, layout, sell 1/3		11/23/1795
Bostwick, Benjamin	Brookfield, Fairfield, CT		D94	12/4/1795
Noble, Sylvanus	New Milford, Litchfield, CT	Pwr Att to locate, layout, sell 1 share		11/23/1795
Bostwick, Benjamin	Brookfield, Fairfield, CT		D94	12/4/1795
Noble, Sylvanus	New Milford, Litchfield, CT	Pwr Att to survey, sell 1 1/3 shares		11/23/1795
Bostwick, Benjamin	Brookfield, Fairfield, CT		D94	12/4/1795
Noble, Sylvanus	New Milford, Litchfield, CT	Pwr Att to locate, layout, sell 1 share		11/23/1795
Bostwick, Benjamin	Brookfield, Fairfield, CT		D94	12/4/1795
Noble, Sylvanus	New Milford, Litchfield, CT	Pwr Att to locate, layout, sell 1 share		11/23/1795
Bostwick, Benjamin	Brookfield, Fairfield, CT		D94	12/4/1795
North, James & Rhoda	Berlin, Hartford, CT	1/4 share	2s	1/15/1796
Smith, Lemuel & Allyn, John B.	Berlin, Hartford, CT	Allynsgrove Twp	E151	9/20/1781
Northrop, Enoch	Weathersfield, Hartford, CT	all right	£4	2/12/1795
Strong, Jabin	Glastonbury, Hartford, CT		D46	11/3/1795
Northrop, Richard	Athens, Luzerne, PA	Town Lot 45	$16.00	2/20/1795
Benton, Caleb	Hillsdale, Columbia, NY	Athens Twp	E165	3/14/1796
Northrop, Samuel	Woodbury, Litchfield, CT	1/4 share	£3.15	2/16/1773
Hooker, William	Woodbury, Litchfield, CT		B162	3/9/1774
Northrup, Amos	New Milford, Litchfield, CT	all rights	£7	4/1/1763
Camp, Enos	New Milford, Litchfield, CT		B122	1/20/1774
Northrup, Isaac	Brookfield, Fairfield, CT	1/2 share; & the sixth part of a right	20s	7/19/1793
Gunn, Joseph	Brookfield, Fairfield, CT		I95	6/7/1794
Norton, Ebenezer	Farmington, Hartford, CT	1/2 share	£8	8/13/1773
Yale, Stephen	Wallingford, New Haven, CT		B220	5/26/1774
Norton, George, Zebulon, Agnis Jr.				
Norton, Agnis			A410	
Norton, Isacher				
Pitcher, Benjamin			A47	
Norton, Jedediah, decd	Berlin, Hartford, CT	all right and title to all land*		1/29/1796
Norton, Josiah, son		Susquehanna Purchase	E152	4/25/1796
Extract from Will recorded Farmington Probate District, CT				
Norton, Ruben	Guilford, New Haven, CT	1/2 share	£12	10/22/1761
Brown, Samuel	Guilford, New Haven, CT		B22	9/15/1773
Norton, Samuel	Salisbury, Litchfield, CT	1/2 share	£8	9/6/1760
Parish, Elkhanah	Canaan, Litchfield, CT		I37	
Noyes, William	Lyme, New London, CT	1 share	£12	12/1/1795
Hyde, Elisha & Tracy, Elisha	Norwich, New London, CT		F23	4/23/1796
Ogden, Humphrey	Paulington, Dutchess, NY	1/2 share	£20	10/9/1794
Ogden, Joseph	Weston, Fairfield, CT		C523	5/1/1795
Ogden, Joseph	Weston, Fairfield, CT	tract	£6	10/11/1794
Cooley, David Jr.	Weston, Fairfield, CT	Augusta, Luzerne, PA	C524	5/1/1795
Ogden, Joseph	Weston, Fairfield, CT	1/2 share	£6	4/12/1796
Sherwood, Samuel	Weston, Fairfield, CT		E169	5/31/1796
Olcot, Samuel	Norfolk, Litchfield, CT	1 share	good cause	10/23/1794
Brown, Daniel	Freehold, Albany, NY		C436	2/1/1795
Olcott, Elisha	East Hartford, Hartford, CT	1 1/2 share*; 1 share*; 1 share*	£60	10/4/1795
Pitkin Jr., Elisha	East Hartford, Hartford, CT		E244	7/1/1796
fr Nathaniel Olcott; fr Reuben Stockin; fr Samuel Flagg,				
Olcott, James & Mary	Litchfield, Litchfield, CT	two 1/2 shares	good cause	8/21/1794
Robards [Roberts], Seth	Paris, Herkimer, NY		C637	7/29/1795
Olcott, Nathaniel	East Hartford, Hartford, CT	1 1/2 shares, taxes paid	bond of equal date	9/28/1795
Olcott, Elisha	East Hartford, Hartford, CT		E246	7/1/1796
Olcott, Thomas, decd, Olcott, Jas,	Pompey, Onondaga, NY	Pwr Att to locate 1 share	1/3 land	9/8/1796
Hill, Thomas	Cazenovia, Herkimer, NY		F87 - F88	9/15/1796
Olmsted, David Jr.	Catskill, Albany, NY	Lot 5, 1/2 of 1/2 share	£60	1/2/1798
Ritter, Henry	Catskill, Albany, NY	Columbia Twp	D129	2/7/1798
Olmsted, John	Colchester, New London, CT	Pwr Att to lay out 1 share		8/5/1795
Olmsted, Zachariah, son	Colchester, New London, CT		C340	9/1/1795
Olmsted, William	East Hartford, Hartford, CT	1/2 share, pd $2 tax Mar 1774	£6	10/13/1794
Pitkin, Elisha Jr.	East Hartford, Hartford, CT		E288	6/6/1796
Orcutt, John	Mansfield, Windham, CT	1 share		2/5/1754
Austin, John Jr.	Mansfield, Windham, CT		B248	4/1/1769

grantor	grantor residence	description	amount	deed date
grantee	grantee residence	location	acct bk page	record date
notes				
Orton, Azuriah	Litchfield, Litchfield, CT	1/2 share		6/3/1796
Bradley, Phinehas, Doct	Litchfield, Litchfield, CT		E223	7/2/1796
Orton, Darius, decd*	Litchfield, CT	all right	£5	11/4/1797
Butler, Amos	Springfield, Otsego, NY		E545	11/23/1797
Azariah Orton, Exec.				
Orton, Eliada	Springfield, Otsego, NY	all right	£5	11/4/1797
Butler, Amos	Springfield, Otsego, NY		E545	11/23/1797
Orton, Eliada	West Haven, Rutland, VT	1 share	love	2/8/1797
Orton, Eliada Jr., son	Cherry Valley, Otsego, NY		E546	11/23/1797
Orton, Hezekiah	Litchfield, Litchfield, CT	1/2 share	£15	11/2/1773
Orton, Sedgwick, son	Litchfield, Litchfield, CT		B213	5/12/1774
Orton, John	Sharon, Litchfield, CT	1 share	£12	11/24/1768
Buck, Asahel	Amenia, Dutchess, NY		B242	8/30/1774
Orton, John	Litchfield, Litchfield, CT	9/10 of 1/2 share	54s	12/30/1794
Sanford, Jonah	Litchfield, Litchfield, CT		C628	7/15/1795
Orton, Lemuel		1 share		
Moseley, Increase			A411	
Orton, Samuel, decd.	Litchfield, CT	all right*		11/17/1763
Orton, Gideon & Azariah,	Litchfield, CT		E217	7/2/1796
extract from Will				
Osborn, Elisha	Woodbridge, New Haven, CT	1/2 share	30s	3/23/1795
Loveland, Lewis	Derby, New Haven, CT		C416	4/4/1795
Osborn, Jeremiah	New Haven, New Haven, CT	1/2 share	£4	11/3/1772
Osborn, Jonathan	New Haven, New Haven, CT		B100	10/21/1773
Osborn, John		1/2 share		
Baker, John			GM	
Osborn, Samuel		1 share*		8/8/1794
Towsey, Zerah			C482	2/1/1795
Towsey will locate 1 share and deed 1/2 back to Osborn				
Osborne, Jonathan heirs*	New Haven, New Haven, CT	2 1/2 shares	£3.12	11/1/1794
Elliott, Aaron	Middlesex, CT		E344	6/15/1796
Mehitable wf, Jonathan, Mehitable 2nd, Anna; John Peck and Lois, wf, quit claim to both shares				
Osburn, Elisha	Derby, New Haven, CT	2 1/2 shares	val con	12/22/1794
Goodyear, Jared	Hamden, New Haven, CT		I160	1/16/1795
Osburn, Elisha	Derby, New Haven, CT	1 share	good con	1/16/1795
Person, Isaac	Derby, New Haven, CT		I163	2/16/1795
Ossencup, Jacob		1/2 share		2/21/1795
Vanfleet, Joshua			C447	2/21/1795
Osterhout, Gideon	Pauling Precinct, Dutchess, NY	1/4 share	£10	3/18/1786
Bump, James	Amenia Precinct, Dutchess, NY		E98	3/1/1796
Osterhout, Gideon	Putnam, Luzerne, PA	1/4 of 1 share	£5	11/1/1792
Hunt, Bensle	Putnam. Luzerne, PA		F237	12/12/1797
Otis, Jonathan & Bigelow, Asa*		Pwr Att to locate 1/2 share	1/4 part of land	3/23/1795
Strong, Jabin	Glastonbury, Hartford,CT		E85	3/2/1796
heirs of Asa Bigelow of Colchester, New London, CT				
Owen, Solomon	Gloucester, Providence, RI	1 share	$20	1/23/1796
Owen, Daniel et al	Gloucester, Providence, RI		F102	9/15/1796
Owen, Thomas 3rd; Gadcomb, Amy wid				
Ozgood [Osgood], Jeremiah	Norwich, New London, CT	300 A, Lot 31	$200	3/22/1798
Tyler, Samuel and Pascal	Norwich, New London, CT	Smithfield Twp	H138	9/22/1799
Paddock, Nathan	Catskill, Albany, NY	16,000 A	$6,666	9/9/1796
Cadwell, Phinehas	New Hartford, Litchfield, CT	Falmouth Twp	H322	9/1/1791
Pain, John		3/4 share		2/1/1775
Hogeboom, Jeremiah			GD	7/1/1775
Paine, Barnabas heir of Paine,		Pwr Att to locate	1/2 land	3/11/1796
Murray, Noah			E114	3/17/1796
Paine, David	Luzerne, PA	16,000 A	$3,000	9/7/1795
Ashman, Phinehas, merchant	Stockbridge, Berkshire, MA	Solon Twp	C144	9/7/1795
Paine, David	Rensselaer Ville, Albany, NY	16,000 A*; 1.139 A*; Lots 35, 37*	$8,000	9/4/1794
Bingham, Chester	Ulster, Luzerne, PA	Fairfield Twp and others*	C471	9/4/1794
Fairfield Twp; 1.139A Ulster (Old Sheshequin Lot 1, upper end); Murraysfield Lot No. 37; Smithfield Lot No. 35				
Paine, David	Luzerne Co PA	all right	$2500	11/19/1795
Brown, Elisha	Stockbridge, Berkshire, MA	Dorranceborough Twp	D62	12/1/1795

grantor	grantor residence	description	amount	deed date
grantee	grantee residence	location	acct bk page	record date
notes				
Paine, David	Luzerne, PA	8,000 A	$4,000	12/31/1799
Carpenter, Comfort A.	Providence, Providence, RI	Bloomfield Twp	H185	1/3/1800
Paine, David	Luzerne, PA	choice of lots to make 7,000 A*	$3,500	12/31/1799
Carpenter, Comfort A. and Thayer,	Providence, RI and Luzerne,	Bloomingdale Twp	H186	1/3/1800
except lots 1, 4, 9, 15, 22				
Paine, David		1,500 A undivided	$750	12/10/1799
Fenn, Roswell	Kent, Litchfield,CT	in a gore of 11,000 A adj. W Athens*	H132	12/23/1799
no name given but may be Durkee Twp				
Paine, David	Athens, Luzerne, PA	four 1/2 shares		2/20/1795
Maxwell, Guy			C319	2/20/1795
Paine, David	Luzerne, PA	2 townships of 16,000 A each	$6,000	9/7/1795
Pepoon, Silas & Whitney, Silas	Stockbridge, Berkshire, MA	Salisbury & Roxbury Twps	C134	9/7/1795
Paine, David	Athens, Luzerne, PA	16,000 A	$4,006	3/1/1796
Scott, Matthew	Columbia Co, NY	Larabee Twp	E78	3/1/1796
Paine, David		4,000A*		9/13/1796
Strong, Jabin			E377	9/15/1796
amt. and location not given in deed, but see J. Grant to D. Paine, SE 1/4 Bowdoin Twp				
Paine, David	Luzerne, PA	8,000 A	$4,000	12/31/1799
Thayer, Levi	Luzerne, PA	Bloomfield Twp	H187	1/4/1800
Paine, David	Luzerne, PA	7,000 A undivided	$1,000	9/10/1796
Young, William Jr.	Windham, CT	Bloomingdale Twp	H334	5/20/1802
Paine, William	Wallingford	1/4 share	£2	4/23/1772
Thompson, John	Branford, New Haven, CT		B34	9/15/1773
Palmer, Christopher	Lebanon CT	1 share		8/26/1794
Turner, Seth	New Haven CT		C221	2/28/1795
Palmer, David				
Gore, Obadiah			A432	
Palmer, David	Norwich	1/2 share		6/9/1772
Gore, Obadiah Capt	Norwich		E124	3/1/1796
Palmiteer, Joseph	Hopkinton/Amenia, Dutch., NY	1 share	£20	4/20/1780
Lloyd, John	Amenia, Dutchess, NY		C503	5/1/1795
Park, Benajah estate, Seth Smith,	Stonington, New London, CT	1/2 share	£12.15	5/19/1777
Gore, Obadiah	Westmoreland	Ulster Twp	I40	8/17/1786
for Hannah Gore, widow of Obadiah				
Park, Benajah estate	Stonington, New London, CT	1/2 share	£12	3/20/1775
Sisson, Oliver	Preston, New London, CT		B342	2/5/1776
Park, James				
LeHommedieu, Ezra			A350	
Park, Reuben		1/2 share		3/15/1797
Adams, Jabez			H315	9/12/1797
Park, Thomas	Athens, Luzerne, PA	160 A	$30	6/11/1799
Brown, Elisha, Jr.	Litchfield, Luzerne, PA	Litchfield, Luzerne, PA	H67	6/11/1799
Park, Thomas	Litchfield, Luzerne, PA	4 half shares	$60	3/1/1796
Shepard, John	Tioga, Luzerne, PA		E325	4/10/1796
Parke, Benjamin of Voluntown	Plainfield, Windham, CT		$4.50	6/1/1758
Parke, Joseph	Voluntown, Windham CT		B104	12/13/1773
Parke, Christopher & Sarah	Stockbridge, Berkshire, MA	1/2 share	£6	3/15/1774
Morris, Daniel	Alford, Berkshire, MA		B292 - I54	5/25/1774
Parke, Robert	Corinth, Orange, VT	1 share	$36	4/15/1795
Danihu, Daniel	Castleton, Rutland, VT		C560	6/20/1795
Parke, William	Plainfield, Windham, CT	1 share	love	4/27/1773
Parke, William, son	Kent, Litchfield, CT		C105	12/20/1786
Parker, Cardee*	Coventry, Tolland, CT	Pwr Att for 1 share		2/13/1795
Young, William Jr.	Windham, Windham, CT		C601	7/9/1795
son of James & Elizabeth Parker born Coventry Feb 22, 1737; certified by John Hale Town Clerk, Coventry, Mar 5, 1795				
Parker, Elijah	Belchertown, MA	discharge all claims on estate	£70	12/29/1777
Parker, James, father	Coventry, Tolland, CT		C601	7/9/1795
Parker, John*	Franklin, New London, CT	1 share	£5	1/6/1795
Dorrance, Gershom	Windham, Windham, CT		I209	4/1/1795
by John Parker, heir & adm				
Parker, John	Coventry, Tolland, CT	1/2 share	£2	2/16/1795
Parker, Cardee	Coventry, Tolland, CT		C600	7/9/1795

grantor	grantor residence	description	amount	deed date
grantee	grantee residence	location	acct bk page	record date
notes				
Parker, Joshua	Phillips Patent, NY	1/2 share	£30	8/21/1763
Hollister, Timothy	Glastonbury, CT		B268	1/12/1774
Parker, Josiah				
Parker, Benajah			A245	
Parkhurst, Calvin	Royalton, VT	1 share	£15	12/24/1781
Tyler, Caleb	Preston, New London, CT		C27	6/17/1782
Parkhurst, Joseph				
Parkhurst, Calvin, son			C27	6/17/1782
Parks, John		Pwr Att for 1 share		11/18/1795
Morgan, Nathaniel			I271	1/2/1796
lay out 1/2 share and sell 1/2 share at not less than £12				
Parks, John	Woodbury, Litchfield, CT	1 share	val con	4/27/1785
Parks, John Jr.	Woodbury, Litchfield, CT	Hanover Twp	I270	12/28/1795
Parks, John Jr.	Southberry, Litchfield, CT	2 shares	£12	4/15/1796
Morgan, Nathaniel	Reading, Fairfield, CT		H5	10/13/1798
Parks, Nathaniel				
Morgan, Samuel			A265	
Parks, Robert	Russell, Hampshire, MA	1 share	$20	4/5/1796
Parks, Reuben	Russell, Hampshire, MA		E375	9/12/1796
Parmalee, Hezekiah 2nd	New Haven, New Haven, CT	1/2 share	£1.10	10/31/1794
Elliott, Aaron	Middlesex, CT		E345	6/15/1796
Parmelee, Bryan	Chatham, Middlesex, CT	Pwr Att to locate 1 share		9/1/1795
Olmstead, Zachariah	Colchester, New London, CT		C331	9/1/1795
Parmelee, Thomas Sr.*	Washington, Litchfield, CT	2 half shares inc. land laid out*		7/2/1794
Turrell/Terrill, Job	New Milford, Litchfield, CT	New Milford & Jenkins Twp	C335	2/27/1795
by Thomas Jr., heir & Ex; 300 A in New Milford on Gitteau's 1/2 share & 700 A in Jenkins on Gould's 1/2 share				
Parris, Elkhanah	Williamstown, Berkshire, MA	1st division rights on 2 half shares	£6.12	1/24/1774
Bidwell, David	Stillwater, Albany, NY		B134	2/1/1774
Paterson, John				
Holmes, Stephen			A20	
Patrick, Jacob	Voluntown, Windham, CT	1/2 share	£1	3/23/1774
Patrick, Ebenezer			B325	4/15/1775
Patrick, Matthew		1/2 share		9/19/1753
Hopkins, David Jr.			B211	5/15/1774
Patrick, Matthew				
Hopkins, David Jr.			A308	
Patrick, Samuel et al*	Windsor, VT	1 share	£29	5/6/1795
Horton, Hiram	Brandon, Rutland, VT		E47	2/24/1796
Stephen Cady; Benoni Patrick, heirs of Matthew Patrick, Jr.				
Patrick, William*	Ulster, Luzerne, PA	300 A, Lot 32 = 1/2 No. 92 of 600	good cause	6/30/1795
Irwin, James	Athens, Luzerne, PA	Murraysfield Twp	C596	7/6/1795
for Mehitable Bidlack now William Patrick's wf; see 1188				
Patterson, John	Brookfield, Fairfield, CT	1 share	£3.12	2/25/1795
Brown, David	Brookfield, Fairfield, CT		C641	8/9/1795
Patterson, Samuel	Athens, Luzerne, PA	4.5 A	£2.5	9/30/1794
Harris, Jonathan	Athens, Luzerne, PA	Athens Twp btw Patterson & Harris	I228	7/19/1795
Payne, Hiram	Tioga, Luzerne, PA	1/2 share	$250	12/28/1798
Wainship, Timothy	Tioga, Luzerne, PA		H321	8/3/1799
Payne, John	Hanover, Grafton, NH	1/2 share	£20	2/6/1796
Payne, Hiram	Hanover, Grafton, NH		E101	3/1/1796
Payne, John	Sydney, Cape Breton Island,	1/2 share	£20	11/30/1795
Payne, John	Hanover, Grafton, NH		E100	3/1/1796
Payne, John	Hanover, Grafton, NH	1/2 share	£20	10/1/1795
Swift, Charles	Lebanon, Windham, CT		E182	6/7/1796
Pearl, David	Windham	1/2 share	£12.18	5/5/1780
Pearl, James	Willington		C20	5/17/1780
Pearl, James	Stafford, Tolland, CT	1/2 share	£3	3/12/1795
Young, William, Jr.	Windham, Windham, CT		C598	7/10/1795
Pearl, Philip		Pwr Att to locate and layout 1/2 share 1/4 pt		5/6/1795
Young, William Jr.			C600	7/9/1795
Pearl, Phillip	Windham, Windham, CT	1 share	£13	4/24/1775
Pearl, Phineas	Windham, Windham, CT		B338	12/4/1775

grantor grantee notes	grantor residence grantee residence	description location	amount acct bk page	deed date record date
Pearl, Phillip				
Utley, Jonathan			A458	
Pearl, Phineas	Charlestown, Cheshire, NH	1/2 share	love	10/16/1778
Farnam, Ruben	Windham		C8	10/7/1779
Pearl, Timothy	South Hero, Chittenden, VT	2/9 share	$5	2/27/1795
Stoddard, Philo	Woodbury, Litchfield, CT		C631	7/10/1795
Pease, Jonathan		1/2 share No. 287 of 600*		8/3/1795
Thayer, Levi			E339	5/15/1796
except 1st division land on Sugar Creek btw Ulster & Juddsburgh laid out 12/16/1793				
Pease, Joseph		1 share		10/1/1772
Johnson, Job			A438	
Peck, Enos	Pompey, Onondaga, NY	1/2 share & 2/3 of 1/2 share		11/29/1795
Tripp, Joshua	Pompey, Onondaga, NY		F89	8/31/1795
Peck, James	New Haven, New Haven, CT	1 share	val sum	10/28/1773
Cooke, Samuel	New Haven, New Haven, CT		B96	10/29/1773
Peck, James*	New Haven	1 share	$9	12/31/1755
Hinman, Eleazar	New Haven		MB	
pd Thomas Darling				
Peck, Job & Uffoot, Benjamin Jr.	Stafford, Fairfield, CT	Pwr to establish claim	1/3 all land	8/25/1795
Sherwood, Aaron	Stafford, Fairfield, CT		E169	5/31/1796
Peet, Richard*	Bethlehem, Litchfield, CT	1 share	val sum	4/11/1795
Wheeler, Abner	Bethlehem, Litchfield, CT	Watertown Twp*	C621	7/1/1795
son of Richard Peet, OP; 600 A on this right entered in Watertown for John Spalding June 1, 1795				
Peirce, Abel		1/2 share	val con	10/3/1794
Dorrance, Benjamin			E368	4/1/1796
Peirce, Delano & Timeus*	Brooklin, Windham, CT	all right	£12	6/1/1796
Peirce, John	Plainfield, Windham, CT		E274	7/15/1796
sons and heirs of Benjamin Peirce				
Peirce, Ezekiel				
Peirce, John & Timothy			A92	
Peirce, John	Plainfield, Windham, CT	3,840 A (12/50th)	$1,920	8/16/1796
Lee, Daniel	Westerly, Washington, RI	Randolph Twp	F177	7/10/1797
Peirce, John	Plainfield, Windham, CT	960 A (3/50th)	$480	12/8/1796
Mowry, George	Smithfield, Providence, RI	Randolph Twp	F167	5/17/1797
Peirce, Lemuel				
McClure, Thomas			A100	
Peirce, Phineas	Westmoreland, Litchfield, CT	1/2 share	£50	9/22/1774
Vreeland, Garardus/Garet	Warior's Run		I201	4/1/1795
Peirce, Phinehas	Ontario, NY	1/2 share	£16	5/14/1795
Burr, Jonathan	Rensselaer, NY		E332	3/24/1796
Peirce, Phinehas	Ontario, NY	1/2 share	£16	5/14/1795
Burr, Jonathan	Rensselaer, NY		E333	3/24/1796
Peirce & Ransom		1/2 share No. 139 of 400		4/23/1796
Holt, Jacob		Athens Twp	E152	4/25/1796
Pell, John		1/2 share		12/14/1773
Thayer, David			GF	
Pellet, Joseph	Brooklyn, Windham, CT	1/4 share	$36.50	3/10/1797
Pike, Nathan et al	Brooklyn, Windham, CT		H98	6/19/1799
Elijah Fasset & Rufus Parrish				
Pendleton, Benajah		1 share		
Walsworth, William			GL	
Pendleton, Benajah				
Walworth, William			A273	
Pennoyer, John	Hudson, Columbia, NY	400 A of No. 210 of 600	£40	10/16/1786
Barnes, Caesar	Hudson, Columbia, NY		H12	10/30/1798
Perkins, James, estate	Lyme, New London, CT	1 share		6/3/1794
Elliot, William	Saybrook, Middlesex, CT		C351	3/2/1795
John Perkins, adm				
Perkins, John				
Andrus, Benjamin			A330	
Perkins, Zepheniah				
Carpenter, Nathan			A443	

grantor	grantor residence	description	amount	deed date
grantee	grantee residence	location	acct bk page	record date
notes				
Perry, Ben	Wilkesbarre, Luzerne, PA	1 proprietor's right inc. 300 A laid out	£12	6/4/1796
Tuttle, Steph Jr. & Blackman,	Wilkesbarre, Luzerne, PA	Bedford Twp	E301	6/8/1796
Perry, Daniel	Lanesborough, Berkshire, MA	all right	£3.13	2/20/1769
Garnsey, Joseph	Waterbury, New Haven, CT		B160	3/9/1774
Perry, Gideon				
Canfield, Samuel			A67	
Pettibone, Abel	Simsbury, Hartford, CT	1/4 share	£5	4/1/1763
Case, Roger	Simsbury, Hartford, CT		C623	7/1/1795
Pettibone, Giles	Norfolk, Litchfield, CT	1/2 share	£50	9/2/1785
Enos, Joab	New Marlboro, Berkshire, MA		C92	12/14/1785
Pettibone, Isaac				
Frishhnet, Samuel			A470	
Pettibone, Isaac	Norfolk, Litchfield, CT	1/2 share	£6.10	3/27/1763
Lawrence, Gideon	Canaan, Litchfield, CT		F54	4/23/1796
Pettibone, Jonathan	Simsbury, Hartford, CT	Pwr to locate 1/4 share	1/4 land plus costs	1/18/1755
Case, Benjamin	Simsbury, Hartford, CT		B215	5/25/1774
Pettibone, Jonathan	Simsbury, Hartford, CT	1/4 of 1 share	£15	9/12/1755
Humphrey, Charles Jr.	Simsbury, Hartford, CT		E441	10/16/1796
Pettibone, Noah, Jr.		1/4 share		1/1/1773
Pettibone, Noah			GM	
Pettibone, Oliver*	Kingston, Luzerne, PA	1200 A, 3/4 share	£9	1/30/1796
Stephens, Ira Capt.	Kingston, Luzerne, PA		E367	4/1/1796
son and Adm estate Noah Pettibone				
Phelps, Alexander	Hebron, Hartford, CT	1/2 share	£8	3/31/1770
Carver, David	Hebron, Hartford, CT	Susquehanna Purchase	B50	5/11/1772
Phelps, Alexander	Hebron, Hartford, CT	1/2 share	£1.2.6	1/3/1769
Waters, Joseph	Hebron, Hartford, CT		B52	5/11/1773
Phelps, Benajah	Granby, Hartford, CT	150 A, 1/2 undivided Lot 15	$135	12/15/1798
Rockwell, Alexander	Great Barrington, Berkshire,	Murraysfield Twp	H115	11/19/1799
Phelps, David	Simsbury, Hartford, CT	1/2 share or 1/1600 of entire	£10	12/25/1755
Willcockson, William	Simsbury, Hartford, CT		E87	3/5/1796
Phelps, Edward	Litchfield, Litchfield, CT	1/2 share	£1.5	11/11/1773
Royce, Phineas	Waterbury, New Haven, CT		B214	5/25/1774
Phelps, Edward	Litchfield, Litchfield, CT	1/2 share	40s	1/18/1769
Taylor, Sarah, wid	Litchfield, Litchfield, CT		F195	8/2/1797
Phelps, Hezekiah	Simsbury, Hartford, CT	1/2 share	5s	1/24/1755
Willcockson, Amos	Simsbury, Hartford, CT	Susquehanna Purchase	B65	6/4/1773
Phelps, Jesse		1/2 share No. 88 of 400		
Spalding, John			E136	3/29/1796
Phelps, Noah	Simsbury, Hartford, CT	1/2 share	$5	5/19/1795
Hale, George	Catskill, Albany, NY		C379	2/28/1795
Pierce, Abel	Plainfield, Windham, CT	1/2 share	£7	2/7/1774
Kenney, Joseph	Plainfield, Windham, CT		B201	4/6/1774
Pierce, Abel	Plainfield, Windham, CT	1/2 share	£10	7/1/1774
Wattles, John	Lebanon, Windham, CT		B336	2/15/1775
Pierce, Hannah, wife		1/2 share		1/2/1775
Pierce, Timothy			GH	2/1/1777
Pierce, John	Plainfield, Windham, CT	all Joseph Spalding's rights	$50	7/16/1796
Biles, Joseph, surveyor	Tioga	Susquehanna Company land	H38	11/10/1798
Pierce, John*	Plainfield, Windham, CT	388 A	lands in Randolph	3/25/1799
Frink, Mathias	Sterling, Windham, CT	Litchfield Twp	H54	4/16/1799
agent for Litchfield Associates				
Pierce, John	Plainfield, Windham, CT	all Jesse Spalding's rights	$50	7/16/1796
Hitchcock, Joseph		Susquehanna Company land	H37	11/10/1798
Pierce, John*	Plainfield, Windham, CT	640 A, Lot 15; 442 A, Lot 18	$1,040	3/8/1799
William, Isaac 2nd et al	Stonington, New London, CT	Litchfield Twp	H52	4/16/1799
agent for Litchfield Associates; David and Daniel Main				
Pierce, John*	Plainfield, Windham, CT	880 A		5/20/1799
Williams, Isaac et al*	Stonington, New London, CT	Litchfield Twp	H106	10/18/1799
agent for Litchfield Twp associates; David & Daniel Main				
Pierce, Lemuel	Plainfield, Windham, CT	1/2 share	9s	5/13/1774
French, Isaac	Voluntown, Windham, CT		B223	5/14/1774

grantor grantee notes	grantor residence grantee residence	description location	amount acct bk page	deed date record date
Pierce, Phinehas		1/2 share		7/5/1776
Darby, Shadrack			GG	7/28/1776
Pierce, Phinehas		1/2 share		9/25/1773
Lewis, Ethan			GC	
Pierce, Phinehas		1/2 share		1/15/1777
Livingston, Thomas			GG	
Pierce, Phinehas		1/2 share		4/12/1774
Low, Cornelius			GD	6/20/1774
Pierce, Phinehas		1/2 share		3/9/1776
Pasio, Isaiah			GD	12/23/1776
Pierce, Samuel	Plainfield, Windham, CT	1/2 share	40s	1/16/1769
McClure, Thomas	Plainfield, Windham, CT		I53	5/10/1786
Pierpoint, John	New Haven, CT	1/2 share	$35	2/11/1796
Goodrich, Benjamin			E405	9/15/1796
Pinto, Jacob	New Haven	1/2 share		1/1/1796
Goodrich, Benj & Munson, Joshua			E255	7/1/1796
Pitkin, Elisha		16,000 A	$2,000	9/9/1796
Belding, Chester		Hector Twp	E515 - E185	2/17/1797
Pitkin, Elisha	Catskill, Albany, NY	all right	£1,000	2/25/1797
Maxwell, Anthony	Kinderhook, Columbia, NY	Ovid Twp	H282	9/1/1800
Pitkin, Elisha Jr.	E. Hartford, Hartford, CT	1 share	£25	6/24/1795
Kingsbury, Phineas	Granby, Hartford, CT		D27	9/29/1795
Pitkin, Elisha Jr.	East Hartford, Hartford, CT	3 half shares		10/31/1795
McKinstry, Thomas Capt.			E285	6/6/1796
Pitkin, Elisha Jr.	East Hartford, Hartford, CT	1 share		10/31/1795
McKinstry, Thomas Capt			E286	6/6/1796
Pitkin, Elisha Jr.	East Hartford, Hartford, CT	1/2 share		10/31/1795
McKinstry, Thomas Capt			E288	6/6/1796
Pitkin, Elisha Jr.	East Hartford, Hartford, CT	1/2 share		10/31/1794
McKinstry, Thomas Capt			E289	6/6/1796
Pitkin, Elisha Jr.	East Hartford, Hartford, CT	1/2 share		10/31/1795
McKinstry, Thomas Capt			E289	6/6/1796
Pitkin, Elisha Jr.	East Hartford, Hartford, CT	1 share		10/13/1795
McKinstry, Thomas Capt			E290	7/1/1796
Pitts, Samuel	Langersfield, Herkimer, NY	300 A	$500	1/16/1796
Brown, Eli	Germans Flatts, Herkimer, NY	Pleasant Valley Twp	E138	4/13/1796
Pixley, Clark	Owego, Tioga, NY	1/2 share	£20	1/23/1795
Pixley, David	Owego, Tioga, NY		C329	2/20/1795
Pixley, David	Stockbridge, Berkshire, MA	1 share	£11	11/13/1768
Buck, William	Amenia, Dutchess, NY		B242	8/30/1774
Pixley, David	Union, Tioga, NY	1 share		6/9/1796
Wattles, Mason	Union, Tioga, NY		E473	11/26/1796
Pixley, Ephriam	Hillsdale, Columbia, NY	500 A	$1,000	1/5/1796
Bacon, Michael & Samuel	Berkhemsted, Litchfield, CT	Goresburgh. Northumberland, PA	E422	10/11/1796
Pixley, Ephriam	Hillsdale, Columbia, NY	2,000 A (1/8 part)	$3,000	5/24/1796
Brinsmade, Thomas Clark	New Hartford, Litchfield, CT	Nottingham Twp	E312	8/8/1796
Pixley, Ephriam	Hillsdale, Columbia, NY	1/4 township	$6,260	11/3/1795
Bulkley, James	Middletown, Middlesex, CT	Dunkirk Twp	E29	2/10/1796
Pixley, Ephriam	Hillsdale, Columbia, NY	1/8 township	$3,125	11/3/1795
Bulkley, James	Middletown, Middlesex, CT	Mifflin Twp	E35	2/10/1796
Pixley, Ephriam	Hillsdale, Columbia, NY	2000 A (1/8 township)	$3,150	11/3/1795
Bulkley, James	Middletown, Middlesex, CT	Cambridge Twp	E39	2/12/1796
Pixley, Ephriam	Hillsdale, Columbia, NY	2000 A (1/8 township)	$3,125	11/3/1795
Burnham, Ashbel	Middletown, Middlesex, CT	Mifflin Twp	E37	2/12/1796
Pixley, Ephriam	Hillsdale, Columbia, NY	2,000 A	$2,500	1/5/1796
Case, Wm & Billy & Ingham, Isaac		Goresburgh. Northumberland, PA	E423	10/11/1796
Pixley, Ephriam	Hillsdale, Columbia, NY	1/4 township	$6,230	11/3/1795
Clark, Samuel	Middletown, Middlesex, CT	Dunkirk Twp	E27	1/9/1796
Pixley, Ephriam	Hillsdale, Columbia, NY	3/8 township	$10,350	11/3/1795
Clark, Samuel	Middletown, Middlesex, CT	Cambridge Twp	E31	2/10/1796
Pixley, Ephriam	Hillsdale, Columbia, NY	16,000 A	$16,000	5/6/1796
Clark, Samuel & Bulkley, James	Middletown, Middlesex, CT	Alba Twp	E310	8/8/1796

grantor grantee notes	grantor residence grantee residence	description location	amount acct bk page	deed date record date
Pixley, Ephriam	Hillsdale, Columbia, NY	2/3 or 10,666 A in each twp	$28,500	4/20/1796
Clark, Samuel & Bulkley, James	Middletown, Middlesex, CT	Derry & Cabot Twps	E311	8/8/1796
Pixley, Ephriam	Hillsdale, Columbia, NY	16,000 A	$24,000	4/26/1796
Clark, Samuel & Bulkley, James	Middletown, Middlesex, CT	Rochester Twp	E314	5/18/1796
Pixley, Ephriam	Hillsdale, Columbia, NY	16,000 A	$3,000	5/16/1796
Clark, Samuel & Bulkley, James	Middletown, Middlesex, CT	Sharon Twp	E315	5/18/1796
Pixley, Ephriam	Hillsdale, Columbia, NY	4000 A	$3333.33	8/6/1795
Dewey, Stephen	Sheffield, Berkshire, MA	Dunkirk Twp, N.E. 1/4	I274	2/6/1796
Pixley, Ephriam	Hillsdale, Columbia, NY	500 A*	$916.68	1/5/1796
Frazer, George and Loomis, Grove		Goresburgh Twp	E351	8/24/1796
Pixley claims under both PA and CT grants				
Pixley, Ephriam	Hillsdale, Columbia, NY	2000 A*	$3666.72	1/7/1796
Frazer, George & Lewis, Charles	Litchfield, CT	Goresburgh Twp	E349	8/24/1796
Pixley claims under both PA and CT grants				
Pixley, Ephriam	Hillsdale, Columbia, NY	500 A*	$1000	1/7/1796
Hayden, Samuel	Berkhemsted, Litchfield, CT	Goresburgh Twp	E350	8/24/1796
Pixley claims under both PA and CT grants				
Pixley, Ephriam	Hillsdale, Columbia, NY	1/4 Twp	$6,250	11/3/1795
Henshaw, Daniel	Middletown, Middlesex, CT	Mifflin Twp	E33	2/10/1796
Pixley, Ephriam	Hillsdale, Columbia, NY	3750 A	£2000	8/25/1795
Henshaw, Daniel; Bulkeley, James	Middletown, Middlesex, CT	Nottingham Twp	D5	9/15/1795
Pixley, Ephriam	Hillsdale, Columbia, NY	2250 A	£2000	8/25/1795
Henshaw, Daniel; Bulkeley, James	Middletown, Middlesex, CT	Nottingham Twp	D6	9/15/1795
Pixley, Ephriam	Hillsdale, Columbia, NY	1/3 each of 2 townships	$15,000	4/26/1796
Henshaw, Joshua	New Hartford, Litchfield, CT	Derry & Cabot Twps	E308	8/8/1796
Pixley, Ephriam	Hillsdale, Columbia, NY	700 A*	$700	1/7/1796
Phelps, Oliver	Berkhemsted, Litchfield, CT	Goresburgh Twp	E351	8/24/1796
Pixley claims under both PA and CT grants				
Pixley, Ephriam	Hillsdale, Columbia, NY	4000 A	$6,250	11/3/1795
Redfield, Frederick	Middletown, Middlesex, CT	Mifflin Twp	E38	2/12/1796
Pixley, Ephriam	Hillsdale, Columbia, NY	500 A*	$1000	1/7/1796
Smith, Josiah	Winchester, Litchfield, CT	Goresburgh Twp	E349	8/24/1796
Pixley claims under both PA and CT grants				
Pixley, Ephriam	Hillsdale, Columbia, NY	2000 A	$3,125	11/3/1795
Southmayd, Timothy	Middletown, Middlesex, CT	Mifflin Twp	E36	2/12/1796
Pixley, Ephriam	Hillsdale, Columbia, NY	1/8 township	$3,125	11/3/1795
Wright, Joseph	Middletown, Middlesex, CT	Mifflin Twp	E34	2/10/1796
Pixley, John heirs*	Great Barrington, Berkshire,	1 share	£5	4/17/1795
Pixley, David	late of Stockbridge, MA		C554	4/17/1795
Mercy, wid; Hall & Samuel Pixley, Desire & Hugh Humphrey, husband				
Platner, Henry	Claverack, Columbia, NY	16,000 A	£2,000	12/17/1796
Fitch, Peletiah	New York, New York, NY	Milton Twp	E519	2/28/1797
Platner, Henry & Vincent, Charles	Claverack, Columbia, NY	16,000 A	£800	10/5/1795
Chauncey, Worthington G.		Stanford Twp	E530	11/1/1796
Platt, Epenetus	Hempstead, Queens, NY	1 share	£8	8/2/1763
Avery, Samuel	Groton, New London, CT		B239	8/20/1774
Plumb, Joshua	Derby, New Haven, CT	1/2 share	good con	1/26/1795
Person, Isaac	Derby, New Haven, CT		I164	2/16/1795
Plumb, Joshua*	Darby, New Haven, CT	1/2 share*	good cause	1/5/1796
Pope, Robert	Darby, New Haven, CT		E407	9/15/1796
son & heir of Samuel Plumb by Will				
Pond, Moses	Southington, Hartford, CT	1/2 share	val con	8/25/1794
Roberts, Seth	Paris, Herkimer, NY		C639	7/29/1795
Pope, Ansel*	Preston, New London, CT	Pwr Att to claim land		5/30/1796
Peirce, John	Plainfield, Windham, CT	Susquehanna Purchase	E276	7/15/1796
Heir of Seth Pope, OP				
Pope, Robert	Darby, New Haven, CT	1 1/2 shares	$150	6/10/1796
Bryan, Richard	Watertown, Litchfield, CT		E483	11/15/1796
Pope, Robert	Darby, New Haven, CT	5 1/2 shares	$40	2/9/1796
Canfield, Judson	Sharon, Litchfield, CT		E411	9/15/1796
Pope, Robert	Derby, New Haven, CT	3/4 share	£22.10	5/25/1796
Lockwood, Ezra	Watertown, Litchfield, CT		D173	7/2/1796

grantor grantee notes	grantor residence grantee residence	description location	amount acct bk page	deed date record date
Pope, Seth Jr.	Voluntown, Windham, CT	1/2 share	£10	12/9/1773
Pope, Gersham	Plainfield, Windham, CT		B99 - B102	12/13/1773
Porter, Ezekiel, decd.*	Weathersfield, Hartford, CT	1 or more shares	$20	5/12/1794
Hale, George	Catskill, Albany, NY		C371	2/28/1795
Belden [Belding], Ezekiel adm*				
Porter, Gideon	Berlin, New Haven, CT	1 share	$50	1/26/1796
Allyn, John B.	Berlin, Hartford, CT		E142	2/25/1796
Porter, Isaiah	Coventry, Tolland, CT	1/4 share	£6	1/3/1795
Demick, Eliphalet	Mansfield, Windham, CT		I198	4/1/1795
Porter, Joseph estate*	East Windsor, Hartford, CT	1/2 share	£6	11/11/1774
Allen, Levi	Salisbury, Litchfield, CT		B303	1/19/1775
by Nathaniel Porter, heir				
Porter, Thomas	Kent, Litchfield, CT	1/2 share & 35 A settling right	£100	3/13/1786
Hutchinson, John & Austin, Nathl	Sheffield, Berkshire, MA	Wilkes-Barre Twp	C102	9/27/1786
Porter, Thomas		1/2 share		
Stevens, Asa			GE	
Post, Aaron & Hannah*	Granby, Hartford, CT	1 share	£30	3/18/1796
Holt, Jacob	Canaan, Litchfield, CT		F60	4/23/1796
Heirs of Hezekiah Phelps; house fire destroyed books, bonds and other writings				
Post, Eldad	Thetford, Orange, VT	Pwr Attorney 1 share *	1/2 of land	8/18/1795
Strong, Jabin	Glastenbury, Hartford, CT		E67	2/28/1796
this deed refers to Liber A page 349 for deed chain thus is proof that lone Index belongs to lost Liber A				
Post, Jeremiah	Oxford, Rockingham, NH	1/2 share	£5	8/7/1772
Kilborn, Benjamin	Bolton, Hartford, CT		B58	2/11/1773
Potter, John	Huntington, Luzerne, PA	Lot 33, first tier, north half		5/24/1796
Hunlock, Jonathan		Haverill Twp	F151	6/1/1796
Potter has had peaceable possession for five years on 300 A in Haverill. Now will deed N 1/2 to Hunlock who must cover with proprietor right from father and record at own expense				
Powers, David	Newtown, Tioga, NY	1 share except 600 A already located	$75	5/30/1796
Paine, David	Athens, Luzerne, PA		E464	5/21/1796
Powers, Stephen	Woodstock, Windsor, VT	1 share	£8	2/9/1796
Grant, Josiah	Poultney, Rutland, VT		F74	5/24/1796
Pratt, Jacob				
Bingham, Silas			A445	
Pratt, Noah	Danby, Rutland, VT	1,000 A	$1416.66	5/26/1796
Arnold, Nehemiah	Providence, Providence, RI	Springhill Twp	E209	6/20/1796
Pratt, Noah	Danby, Rutland, VT	500 A, 1/32 pt all undivided land	$706.16	5/20/1796
Nash, Robert W.	Foster, Providence, RI	Springhill, Luzerne, PA	F245	2/13/1798
Pratt, Noah	Darby, Hartford, CT	500 A	$708.33	5/20/1796
Smith, Ransford*	Pomfret, Windham, CT	Springhill Twp	H63	4/29/1799
farmer, currier and cordwainer				
Pratt, Noah, merchant	Danby, Rutland, VT	1000 acres	$1416.165	5/30/1796
Thurber, John	Providence, Providence	Springhill Twp	D162	6/20/1796
Prindle, Aaron	New Milford, Fairfield, CT	1/4 share	5s	9/10/1794
Brownson, Isaac	New Milford, Litchfield, CT	New Milford Twp	I121	12/6/1794
Prindle, Aaron	New Fairfield, Fairfield, CT	1 share	£22.12	4/15/1763
Wanzer, Moses	New Fairfield, Fairfield, CT	New Milford Twp	I155	12/6/1794
Prout, John	Wallingford	all shares	val sum	4/6/1772
Thompson, John	Branford, New Haven, CT		B35	9/15/1773
Putnam, Israel	Pomfret, Windham, CT	1 share	£20	2/11/1774
Witter, Joseph Jr.	Preston, New London, CT		C8	9/1/1795
Raab, George	PA	1/2 share	$20	12/21/1773
Aurand, John			B176	3/14/1774
Randall, Joseph Greenfield		1 share		
Pearl, Phillip			A394 - MB	
Randsom [Ransom], Samuel	Westmoreland, Litchfield, CT	1/2 share	£19	7/28/1776
Darby, Shadrick Doct	Westmoreland, Litchfield, CT		F66	4/25/1796
Ransom, George P.*		1/2 share		3/15/1796
Stephens, Ira			E368	4/1/1796
by Will; son of Samuel Ransom; deed fr Lee 11/5/1773				
Ransom, George P(almer)	Luzerne, PA	six half shares*	£25	1/15/1796
Stephens, Ira	Luzerne, PA		E370	4/1/1796
five half shares fr Samuel Ransom, father, & 1/2 share fr George P., son of Samuel				

grantor grantee notes	grantor residence grantee residence	description location	amount acct bk page	deed date record date
Ransom, Samuel	Tioga,NY	300 A, Lot 11 on No. 275 of 400	$45	5/10/1795
Irwin, James	Tioga Point, Luzerne, PA	Murraysfield Twp	E440	10/1/1796
Ransom, Theophilus	Watertown, Litchfield, CT	2/3 township	£1105	6/17/1796
Clark, Samuel	Middletown, Middlesex, CT	Jay Twp	D177	8/9/1796
Rathbone, Anchor	Stonington	Pwr Attorney		5/15/1795
Ells, Cushing	Norwich		CD	9/1/1795
Rathbone, Joshua 3rd, heirs of		1/2 share		5/19/1774
Denison, Joseph 2nd			CB	
deed recorded Stonington, CT, Bk. 9, folio 441				
Rathbun, Daniel	West Stockbridge, Berkshire,	600 A of 1 share	£30	1/23/1795
Baldwin, Samuel	West Stockbridge, Berkshire,	New Milford Twp	C332	2/26/1795
Rathbun, Jacob	Groton, New London, CT	1 share	£10	11/10/1754
Rathbun, Joshua, father	Stonington, New London, CT		C599	7/9/1795
Rathbun, Job	Canaan, Litchfield, CT	1 share, 2000 A	$1,000	11/20/1792
Andrews, Benajah	W Stockbridge, Berkshire, MA	Baldwinsville Twp	H334	5/20/1802
Rathbun, John		1/2 share		9/1/1755
Stark, James			GM	8/29/1775
Rathbun, Joshua	Stonington, New London, CT	1/2 share	£6	3/27/1772
Rathbun, Achors, grandson	Stonington, New London, CT		B48	4/2/1772
Rathbun, Joshua	Stonington, New London, CT	1/2 share	£6	3/27/1772
Rathbun, Joshua 3rd, grandson	Stonington, New London, CT	Susquehanna Purchase	B49	4/2/1772
Rathbun, Valentine	Pittsfield, Berkshire, MA	333.3 A, Lot 10	$300	2/12/1798
Rathbun, Benjamin	Pittsfield, Berkshire, MA	Rathbun Twp	H60	4/17/1799
Rathbun, Valentine	Pittsfield, Berkshire, MA	333.3 A, Lot 10	$300	2/12/1798
Rathbun, James	Pittsfield, Berkshire, MA	Rathbun Twp	H59	4/17/1799
Rathbun, Valentine	Pitsfield, Berkshire, MA	333.3 A, Lot 10	$300	2/12/1798
Rathbun, Saxton	Pitsfield, Berkshire, MA	Rathbun Twp	H58	4/17/1799
Rathbun, Wait	Troy, Rensselaer, NY	1667A: 1000 A, Lot 10; 667 A, Lot	$2000	1/11/1798
Rathbun, Valentine	Pitsfield, Berkshire, MA	Rathbun Twp*	H55	4/17/1799
Col. James Davis of Carlisle agrees to obtain PA title for entire Rathbun Twp				
Rathbun, Wait Jr.	Middletown, Rutland, VT	14,000 A	£748	10/12/1797
Willard, William	Middletown, Rutland, VT	Homerstown Twp	F214	10/25/1797
Rathone, Acors by Ells, Cushing		agent for a Twp survey*	1/2 share	7/20/1795
Throop, Benjamin			C120.1	9/1/1795
for fifteen owners, including Throop, who pay Throop 6s per day for his time and horse; total of 8 shares; A. Rathbone 1/2 share				
Rawse, John	Mansfield CT	1 share	£14	5/24/1771
Frisby, James	Branford, New Haven, CT		D53	11/9/1795
Rawson, Edmund G.	East Haddam, Middlesex, CT	1 share	£3	6/18/1794
Elliot, William	Saybrook, Middlesex, CT		C458	2/21/1795
Ray, James	Great Barrington, Berkshire,	1/4 share	£5	11/8/1773
Thayer, David	New Castle, PA		B144	2/21/1774
Ray, Patrick	Voluntown, Windham, CT	1 share	£30	3/25/1761
Kingsly, Samuel	Bridgewater, Plymouth, MA		C85	6/9/1784
Raynold, Jonathan Jr.	Exeter, Kings, RI	1/2 share	£3	9/18/1773
Raynold, Joseph Jr.	Exeter, Kings, RI		B74	9/21/1773
Raynolds, Benjamin	Exeter, Washington, RI	all right equally	love	3/6/1797
Raynolds, Joseph & Benjamin, sons	Exeter, Washington, RI		H17	11/15/1798
Read, John				
Dorrance, Samuel			A83	
Read, Joshua				
Read, William			A454	
Redington, Nathaniel & Mary*	Richmond, Berkshire, MA	1/2 share	£3	
Benton, Elihu	Guilford, New Haven, CT		D57	11/16/1795
dau of Manns Griswold				
Reed, Beriah, Elle & Phinehas	Windham, Windham, CT	1/2 share except land in Salem Twp	10s	5/2/1795
Larrabee, Lebbeus	Windham, Windham, CT		C606	7/9/1795
Reed, Hezekiah	Kent, Litchfield, CT	300 A	$1,000	6/25/1799
Eastman, Benjamin	Mt Vernon, Prov of Maine, MA	btw Cowanesque R & NY-PA	H77	6/25/1799
Lycoming Co, PA				
Reed, Hezekiah	Kent, Litchfield, CT	2 shares, 4000 A	£250	11/26/1796
Weed, Abm and Comstock, Enoch	Stamford, Fairfield, CT	Reed Twp	H76	6/25/1799

grantor grantee notes	grantor residence grantee residence	description location	amount acct bk page	deed date record date
Reed, James	Horton, Kings, Nova Scotia	1/2 interest in all right*	£10	5/28/1761
Doggett, Micajah	Norwich, New London, CT		E253	7/1/1796
by inheritance from John Reed the Elder				
Reed, John	Salisbury, Litchfield, CT	all right	£15	4/6/1795
King, George & Mills, Eli	Sharon, CT & Amenia, NY		C573	6/22/1795
Reed, Joshua	Windham, Windham, CT	1 1/3 shares*		12/10/1783
Reed, Edith et al*		Susquehanna Purchase	C605	7/9/1795
Joshua Reed heirs: Edith 1/3 share; Beriah 1/2 share; Elle and Phinehas 1/2 share; copy of Will also names Sarah, £4; Ruth £6, Lucy £6				
Reed, Mary et al*	Norwich, New London, CT	1/2 share	£10	7/8/1760
Doggett, Micajah	Norwich, New London, CT		E252	7/1/1796
Heirs of John Reed, the Elder: Mary, Elizabeth, William, Ruth				
Reed, Samuel	East Haddam, Hartford, CT	all rights	£13.10	11/12/1774
Selden, Samuel & Ely, Joseph	Lyme, New London, CT		B277	10/6/1774
Reed, William	Williamsbury, Hampshire, MA	300 A	£10	9/11/1773
Sedgwick, Benjamin	Canaan, Litchfield, CT	Salem Twp	B118	1/12/1774
Reeve, Ebenezer	Norwich, New London, CT	two 1/4 shares	£12	2/8/1796
Tracy, Elisha	Norwich, New London, CT	SP; DP	F29	4/23/1796
Reynold, James				
McNeal, Archibald			A460	
Reynold, Jonathan & Ann	Exeter, Kings, RI	1 share	£4.19	12/12/1771
Reynold, Jonathan Jr.	Exeter, Kings, RI	Susquehanna Purchase	B17	9/18/1773
Reynolds, Jedediah	Lebanon, Windham, CT	1/2 share	£5	2/6/1773
Wattles, John	Lebanon, Windham, CT		B210	4/23/1774
Reynolds, John	Arlington, Bennington, VT	1 share	$50	5/22/1795
Todd, Timothy	Arlington, Bennington, VT		H289	3/31/1801
Reynolds, Joseph, Jr., heirs*		Pwr Att to locate		2/19/1796
Hyde, Ezekiel		Susq and Delaware Purchases	F37	4/23/1796
Enoch, Phoebe, Sarah,and Charles Reynolds, and Abby L. Homedieu				
Rhoades, Obadiah	Voluntown, Windham, CT	1/2 share	love	4/8/1775
Rhoades, John, son	Worthington, Hampshire, MA		B324	4/11/1775
Rhoads/Rhodes, Obadiah	Thorum, Addison, VT	1 share	£10	3/7/1795
Ward, Ichabod	Windham, Windham, CT		E56	2/24/1796
Rhodes, John		1/2 share each fr two deeds*		11/13/1781
Benjamin, Isaac			H85	9/1/1798
8 Apr 1775 & 13 Nov 1781				
Rhodes, Obadiah	Voluntown, Windham, CT	1/2 of 1 share	good causes	11/13/1781
Rhodes, John	Worthington, Hampshire, MA		H85	9/1/1798
Rian, John & Arthur,				
Dorrance, Samuel			A83	
Rice, John		1/4 share		
Ellery, Benjamin			A289 - E480	11/15/1796
Rice, Matthew & Ruth (Yale), wf	Southington, Hartford, CT	1/2 and 1/16 share	$20	11/18/1795
Yale, Thomas	Darby, New Haven, CT		E409	9/15/1796
Rice, Stephen	Canaan, Litchfield, CT	1 share inc. Lot 10, 1st division	£40	9/3/1773
Ransom, John	Canaan, Litchfield, CT	Plymouth Twp	B379	3/26/1778
Rice, Stephen	Canaan, Litchfield, CT	1/2 share	£8	8/5/1773
Sedgwick, Benjamin	Canaan, Litchfield, CT		B117	1/12/1774
Richards, Guy	New London, New London, CT	all right	£20	1/28/1796
Tracy, Elisha	Norwich, New London, CT		F24	4/23/1796
Richards, Guy, Capt., heirs*	New London, New London, CT	all right	$40	1/28/1796
Tracy, Elisha	Norwich, New London, CT		F25	4/23/1796
Guy, Nathaniel, Benjamin Richards; Mary and George D. Avery; Esther Hempsted				
Richards, Jedediah	Norfolk, Litchfield, CT	1/2 share	£3	5/5/1773
Stevens, Safford	Canaan, Litchfield, CT		I8	6/6/1786
Richards, Joseph	Southbury, Litchfield, CT	1 share	val con	9/24/1794
Terrill, Job Jr. & Bostwick, Dimon	New Milford, Litchfield, CT		I148	12/6/1794
Riggs, Miles Jr.	Norfolk, Litchfield, CT	1/2 share	good cause	10/23/1794
Brown, Daniel	Freehold, Albany, NY		C435	2/1/1795
Robbards, Elias	Farmington, Hartford, CT	1/2 share	£10	4/20/1772
Humiston, Noah & Seymore, Abel	Waterbury, Hartford, CT		B167	3/9/1774
Robbins, Moses	Preston, New London, CT	2 shares SP; 1/4 & 1/2 shares DP	£11.5	11/21/1794
Hyde, Elisha	Norwich, New London, CT		I128	12/25/1794

grantor grantee notes	grantor residence grantee residence	description location	amount acct bk page	deed date record date
Robe, Andrew* chr & heirs*	Simsbury, Granby, Woodbury	1 share	£30	3/15/1796
Holt, Jacob	Canaan, Litchfield, CT		F58	4/23/1796
died June or July 1792 age 91; Walter Robe, Asa Case, Elizabeth Robe, Benjamin Farnham att for James Robe, Zerah Phelps, Andrew Robe, Frances Garret				
Roberts, Daniel		1/2 share No. 136 of 400		1/29/1795
Enos, Erasmus		Allensburgh Twp*	E495	12/17/1796
entered on 9/24/1787				
Roberts, Daniel	Athens, Luzerne, PA	300 A	£10	3/3/1795
Parks, Thomas	Athens, Luzerne, PA	Athens Twp	I263	3/3/1795
Roberts, Elias	Kingstown, on Susquehanna	1 share	£20	5/10/1778
Hogeboom, Jeremiah	Lackawany, on Susq. River	Kingstown Twp	F199	8/2/1797
Roberts, Gideon	Bristol, Hartford, CT	1/2 share	delivering a bond	6/20/1794
Smith, Elnathan	Berlin, Hartford, CT		C325	2/20/1795
Roberts, Hezekiah Jr.	Plymouth, Luzerne, PA	300 A of 1/2 share No. 77 of 400	£10	11/20/1795
Barney, Benjamin		Bedford Twp*	F102	9/16/1796
entered on 5/11/1795				
Roberts, Jabez				
Churchill, Benjamin			A86	
Roberts, Seth	Bristol, Hartford, CT	16,000 A	£1800	3/10/1796
Dean, Silas	Stockbridge, Berkshire, MA	Hannibal Twp	E319	8/8/1796
Roberts, Seth	Bristol, Hartford, CT	1,575 A	rest of 1 1/2 shares	10/25/1798
Kason, Adam, George D., Myron	Huntington, Fairfield, CT;	Lewistown Twp	H142	9/14/1799
Roberts, Seth	Bristol, Hartford, CT	12,000 A	$3,000	6/13/1796
Lombard, Roswell, sadler	Stockbridge, Berkshire, MA	Lewistown Twp, 3/4	F184	7/16/1797
Roberts, Seth		1/4 share		8/26/1776
Scott, Obadiah			GM	1/13/1777
Roberts, Seth	Bristol, Hartford, CT	16,000 A	$4,000	5/16/1796
Woodward, Elijah	Watertown, Litchfield, CT	Paris Twp	E162	5/18/1796
Robertson, Archibald	New London, New London, CT	1 1/2 shares	£10	9/3/1794
Elliot, William	Saybrook, Middlesex, CT		C357	3/2/1795
Robertson, Ephriam	Coventry, Windham, CT	1/2 share	£30	2/8/1775
Patten, David	Coventry, Windham, CT		B309	2/7/1775
Robins, Moses/Kezzeiah, wf, heirs*	Voluntown, Preston, Stonington	1/4 share	£5	1/4/1796
Hyde, Elisha & Tracy, Elisha	Norwich, New London, CT		F39	4/23/1796
Samuel, Moses, Lorin, Gillmor Robins of Voluntown; Lot and Betsy Kinne of Preston; Denison and Polly Brown of Stonington				
Robinson, Benjamin	Weathersfield, Windsor, VT	all right	£5	4/10/1795
Bush, Jonathan	Enfield, Hartford, CT		C568	6/22/1795
Robinson, Ebenezer				
Robinson, William			A263	
Robinson, William				
Babcock, Elisha			A268	
Robinson, William	Plainfield, Windham, CT	1 share	£12	9/23/1773
Gray, Samuel	Windham, Windham, CT		B129	9/23/1773
Robinson, William	Plainfield	1 share	£1400	6/2/1779
Norton, Zebulon	Ashueloit Equivalent	Plymouth Twp	C2	9/11/1779
Robinson, William	Plainfield	1 share	£500	6/2/1779
Norton, Zebulon	Ashueloit Equivalent		C3	9/11/1779
Rockwell, Daniel	Cornwallis, Kings, NS	1 share	£50	4/1/1774
Watrous, Walter, carpenter	Horton, Kings, NS		C41	10/10/1774
Rogers, Daniel				4/18/1763
Rogers, Alpheus & Thomas			A288 - C347	
Rogers, David	Saybrook, Middlesex, CT	1/2 share*	£8	9/3/1794
Lester, Eliphalet	Saybrook, Middlesex, CT		D14	9/18/1795
original certificate lost				
Rogers, Jeremiah	Montville, New London, CT	1 share	£100	2/19/1796
Allen, George	Montville, New London, CT		F45	4/23/1796
Rogers, John 2nd	New London, New London, CT	1/4 share	£7.10	4/27/1774
Crouch, William	Groton, New London, CT		B225	7/1/1774
Rogers, Thomas et al*	Montville, New London, CT	1 share	£24	5/10/1795
Olmsted, Zachariah	Colchester, New London, CT		C347	9/1/1795
Alpheus, Asa, James and Jehiel Rogers				
Rogers, Zabdiel	Norwich, New London, CT	1/2 share	$30	10/7/1795
Hyde, Elisha & Tracy, Elisha	Norwich, New London, CT		E40	2/22/1796

grantor grantee notes	grantor residence grantee residence	description location	amount acct bk page	deed date record date
Rogers, Zabdiel				
Wightman, Zerubabbel			A295	
Rood, James	Norfolk, Litchfield, CT	300 A	$300	4/4/1798
Northway, Ozias	New Marlborough, Boston State	Insurance Twp	H323	11/11/1801
Rood, Robert	Goshen, Litchfield, CT	1/2 share	£15	10/28/1780
Beaman, Ebenezer	Kent, Litchfield, CT		E363	9/5/1796
Root, Azariah	Sheffield, Berkshire, MA	1/4 township	$6,250	11/3/1795
Henshaw, Joshua	New Hartford, Litchfield, CT	Dunkirk Twp	E28	2/10/1796
Root, James	Sheffield, Hampshire, MA	1/2 of 1 share	£20	3/8/1768
Hogeboom, Jeremiah	Claverack, Albany, NY		F201	8/2/1797
Root, Jesse	Woodbury, Litchfield, CT	1/8 share	a consideration	9/20/1794
Terril, Job	New Milford, Litchfield, CT	New Milford, Luzerne, PA	I123	12/6/1794
Root, John				
Drake, Nathaniel 3rd			A392	
Root, Jonathan				
Goodman, Samuel			A263	
Root, William*	Hebron, Hartford, CT	1/2 share	£2	4/4/1768
Carver, David	Hebron, Hartford, CT		E59	2/25/1795
pd $1 taxes 2/28/1770; 5/11/1772; decd by 5/23/1772				
Roots, Benajah Garnsey	Rutland, Rutland, VT	1000 A (1/2 share) in square form	$416.66	10/19/1794
Bancroft, Josiah	Cheltendon, Rutland, VT	Sidney Twp, SE Corner	H232	9/10/1800
Rose, Ameriah	Branford, New Haven, CT	all right	$1,645	4/12/1797
Tyler, Peter	Branford, New Haven, CT	Fairfax Twp	F164	4/24/1797
Rose, Timothy				
Foot, Ichabod			A424	
Rose, Timothy	Woodbury, Litchfield, CT	1/4 share	£5	11/29/1760
Frisbie, James	Woodbury, Litchfield, CT		B170	3/9/1774
Roseboom, Jacob	Albany, Albany, NY	1 share	£10	9/10/1796
Hogeboom, Jeremiah	Lackawanna, Westmoreland,		E446	10/25/1796
Rosetter, Samuel	Claverack, Columbia, NY	1/2 twp, eastern part	£800	9/16/1795
Belding, Chester	Claverack, Columbia, NY	Lebanon Twp	E386	9/10/1796
Ross, Daniel		1/2 share		4/4/1795
Irwin, James			E362	
Ross, Jeremiah		1 share		12/7/1772
Parkes, Josiah			GC	2/28/1775
Royce, Mark	Washington, Litchfield, CT	all right	£12	10/26/1795
Winter, Gideon	Bethlehem, Litchfield, CT		E248	7/1/1796
Rude, Stephen	Killingly, Windham, CT	1/2 share, taxes paid	£7	1/13/1775
Gore, Obadiah & Gore, Elijah	Westmoreland & Voluntown,	Ulster Twp	I43	8/17/1786
Rumsey, Benjamin		1/2 share	$4.50	3/1/1754
Bennett, William	Fairfield, Fairfield, CT		C515	4/1/1795
Rumsey, Benjamin Jr., estate*	Fairfield, Fairfield, CT	all right	24s	1/24/1774
Rumsey, David	Fairfield, Fairfield, CT		B154	3/9/1774
Benjamin Rumsey & Mary and Samuel Hendrick of Fairfield; Abigail and Mathias Smith of Bedford, NY; Anne Rumsey of Phillipsburgh, NY				
Rumsey, David	Fairfield, Fairfield, CT	1/2 share each	£10.6	3/3/1774
Hide, Joseph & Nash, Thomas	Fairfield, Fairfield, CT		B155	3/9/1774
Rumsey, David	Fairfield, Fairfield, CT	1/4 share each	£10.6	3/3/1774
Hide, Joseph & Nash, Thomas	Fairfield, Fairfield, CT		C519	5/1/1795
Rundel, William*	New Fairfield, Fairfield, CT	1 share	£20	12/4/1794
Brush, Jonas	New Fairfield, Fairfield, CT		I193	3/29/1795
heir of Joseph Rundel, decd.				
Russel, Dan	Watertown, Luzerne, PA	300 A, Lot 35, plus east 100 A, Lot	$900	9/12/1800
Overton, Thomas	Tioga, Luzerne, PA (now)	Watertown, Luzerne, PA	H238	9/13/1800
Russell, Josiah	Lebanon, Windham, CT	1 share	£50	2/6/1795
Swift, Silas	Lebanon, Windham, CT		I210	4/1/1795
Sabin, Isaac, heirs*	Bozrah, New London, CT	1 share	£100	1/29/1795
Hyde, Elisha; Tracy, Elisha	Norwich, New London, CT		I174	2/22/1795
Capt. Nathan Bingham and Zerviah Sabin, wf; Eunice Sabin				
Sabin, Jesse	Southington, Hartford, CT	Pwr Att 1 share	1/2 land	4/27/1796
Strong, Jabin	Glastonbury, Hartford, CT		E425	9/16/1796
Sabin, Ziba	Lennox, Berkshire, MA	3/4 share	£30	1/24/1795
Stone, Ethan	Sandersfield, Berkshire, MA		C429	2/1/1795

grantor	grantor residence	description	amount	deed date
grantee	grantee residence	location	acct bk page	record date
notes				
Safford, Amos	Beckman Precinct, Dutchess,	1/2 share	£10	4/18/1769
Safford, John			E99	3/1/1796
Safford, David/Mary	Stonington	1/7 share	£6	7/30/1777
Mott, Samuel	Preston		C57	11/11/1782
Safford, Elisha	Gageborough, Berkshire, MA	1/2 share	£12	2/1/1777
Dean, Ezra	West Greenwich, Kent, RI		B369	3/26/1777
Salesbury, Gideon	Luzerne, PA	1 lot drawn in name of Thos Baldwin	£5	4/1/1795
Shaw, Jedediah	Luzerne, PA	Ulster Twp, W side Susq R.	E413	9/14/1796
Salisbury, Gideon		1/2 share, No. 363 of 600*	full consideration	9/3/1795
Calkin, Moses	Luzerne, PA		E331	4/10/1796
177 claims No. 363 to Zera Beach to Moses Calkins				
Salisbury, Gideon	Luzerne Co PA	300 A of 1/2 share No. 377 of 600		9/3/1795
Calkins, Moses		Burlington Twp	I77	9/7/1795
Salisbury, Joseph, cordwainer	Tioga, Luzerne, PA	2/5 of 1/2 share	£50	1/5/1795
Hutchinson, John, trader	Tioga, Luzerne, PA	Bedford Twp	C302	2/28/1795
Salmon, Nathaniel	Springfield, Essex, NJ	1 share inc. Lot 53	£18	8/1/1770
Perkins, John	Hebron, Hartford, CT	Plymouth Twp	B43	1/11/1771
Sanford, Daniel	Newtown, Fairfield, CT	1/2 share	£5.10	10/20/1795
Moseley, William	Woodbury, Litchfield, CT		E404	9/15/1796
Sanford, Jonah	Litchfield, Litchfield, CT	9/10 of 1/2 share	£13.10	2/9/1795
Atwood, Elisha & Judson, Gideon	Woodbury, Litchfield, CT		C628	7/15/1795
Sanford, Oliver	Poultney, Rutland, VT	all right	6s	4/1/1795
Grant, Josiah	Poultney, Rutland, VT		C563	8/9/1795
Sanford, Oliver & Sanford, Jonah	Litchfield, Litchfield, CT	3/4 share	£22.10	2/9/1795
Atwood, Elisha & Judson, Gideon	Woodbury, Litchfield, CT		C629	7/15/1795
Sanford, Philemon & Jerusha wf	Goshen, Litchfield, CT	1/2 share	£7	10/14/1773
Wadham, Noah	New Milford		C106	12/27/1786
Satterlee, Benedict	Athens, Luzerne, PA	300 A: 150 A Lot 41, 150 A	$300	1/3/1800
Satterlee, Elias	Athens, Luzerne, PA	Columbia Twp	H174	1/3/1800
Satterlee, Benedict				
Satterlee, Samuel & Nathaniel			A224	
Satterlee, Benedict	Plymouth Twp	1/2 share	£35	1/5/1774
Spalding, Simon	Kingston Twp		B229	7/8/1774
Satterlee, Daniel	Athens, Luzerne, PA	Lots 34, 47, 49, 300 A each; 2511 A	$3,000	8/23/1799
Satterlee, Elias	Athens, Luzerne, PA	Columbia Twp; Wallingham Twp	H154	12/26/1799
Satterlee, Elias, Physician	Athens, Luzerne, PA	all remaining right; Lot 2	$2,000	3/10/1800
Thayer, Levi, Capt.	Athens, Luzerne, PA	Insurance Twp; Columbia Twp	H279	2/2/1801
Satterlee, Elias, physician	Tioga, Luzerne, PA	all right to land in	$10,000	3/10/1800
Thayer, Levi & Carpenter,	Tioga, Luzerne, PA and	Windsor, Hartford, and Federal	H278	2/2/1801
Satterlee, Elias & Thayer, Levi	Luzerne Co	2000 A	val con	
Carpenter, Comfort & Aborn, Thos		Insurance Twp	H152	12/14/1799
Satterlee, Elisha	Athens, Luzerne, PA	NE 5,000 A, 1/4 twp, reserving 50 A	$3,000	12/27/1799
Satterlee, Elias	Athens, Luzerne, PA	Hamilton Twp	H169	12/30/1799
Satterlee, Elisha		all right	val con	
Satterlee, Elias & Thayer, Levi	Luzerne, PA	Elkfield Twp	H179	1/4/1800
Satterlee, Elisha		300 A	$300	3/25/1796
Satterlee, Samuel		Columbia Twp	E126	3/25/1796
Satterlee, Elisha	Athens	5 A, Lot 40, 2nd Div	val con	3/4/1797
Swift, Samuel		Athens Twp	E520	
Satterlee, Elisha et al	Luzerne, PA	325 A farm lot	£100	9/19/1794
Willcox, Stephen	Luzerne, PA	Towanda Creek	E471	11/25/1796
James Irwin; Lemuel Gaylord; Ira Stephens				
Satterly, Benedict				
Holsted, Josiah & Holley, William			A400	
Sawyer, Daniel		1/2 share No. 139 of 400		6/19/1794
Peirce & Ransom		Athens Twp	E152	4/25/1796
Sawyer, Isaac	Hoosick, Albany, NY	1 share	£18	11/5/1773
Kennedy, Benjamin	Gageborough, Berkshire, MA		B314	3/7/1775
Sawyer, Nathan Sr., estate*	Cornwall, Litchfield, CT	1 share	£20	8/26/1773
Strong, Phillip	Kent, Litchfield, CT		B143	2/17/1774
Samuel, Nathan Jr. and Desire Sawyer, of Middletown, heirs				
Schermehorn, John W.	Stephentown, Rensselaer, NY	2 1/2 shares	£100	3/7/1795
Douglas, Zebulon	Canaan, Columbia, NY		E43	2/23/1796

grantor grantee notes	grantor residence grantee residence	description location	amount acct bk page	deed date record date
Schott, John P.	Wilkesbarre, Luzerne, PA	1 share No150 of 600 ex lots 7, 5,		1/2/1794
Lockwood, Ephriam		Athens Twp	C312	9/2/1795
1st, 2nd, 3rd division lots in that order				
Schott, John Paul		1/2 share		1/2/1795
Lockwood, Ephriam			C330	9/2/1795
Scott, Matthew	Kingsberry, Washington, NY	2,500 A	$700	1/20/1802
Larrabee, Lebbeus	Windham, CT	Trenton Twp	H334	5/20/1802
Scovil, James		Lot 5 of 1/2 share No. 273 of 400		12/1/1794
Franklin, John Col.		Claverack Twp	I191	3/19/1795
Scoville, Champion	Tioga Twp, PA	2 700 A, 2nd div lots		8/18/1795
Morgan, Asa		Juddsburgh Twp	C398	8/23/1795
Scoville, James	Luzerne, PA	part of Lot 5 adj. Scoville*	£50	2/23/1795
Smith, Nathan	Luzerne, PA	Claverack Twp	E296	7/29/1796
76 rods wide and usual lot depth				
Sedgwick, Abraham	Lennox, Berkshire, MA	1/2 share	$40	2/25/1796
Woodbridge, Stephen	Stockbridge, Berkshire, MA		E297 - B217	6/20/1796
Sedgwick, Benjamin	Canaan, Litchfield, CT	1 share inc. Lot 27, 1st div	£28	12/2/1776
Harrison, Steven	Canaan, Litchfield, CT	Huntington Twp	I6	6/6/1786
Sedgwick, Stephen heirs*	Litchfield, Litchfield CT	1/2 share	£12	9/5/1773
Guthrie, Joseph	Kent, Litchfield, CT	Susquehanna Purchase	B17	9/15/1773
Hezekiah and Ann Orton				
Seeley, Abel				
Marsh, Elihu			A75	
Seeley, Ebenezer	New Fairfield	1 share		10/8/1773
Draper, Giddeon	Oblong, Dutchess, NY		MB - E63	2/26/1796
Seeley, Ebenezer	New Fairfield, Fairfield, CT	2 shares	£150	1/9/1775
Squire, Solomon	Alirson, Charlotte, NY		C91	11/3/1785
Seeley, Ephriam				
Gasten, William			A58	
Seeley, Ephriam				
Marsh, Elihu Jr.			A73	
Seely, Bezaleel & Kellsey, Abner	New Town, NY	4 shares No 54, 55, 75, 84 of 600*	5s	10/19/1797
Burroughs, William Y.	Claverack, Columbia, NY		E543	10/24/1797
only 600 A laid out				
Seely, Ephriam	Danby, Charlotte, NY	3 1/2 shares	£52.10	11/8/1773
Kennedy, Benjamin	Gageborough, Berkshire, MA		B315	3/7/1775
Seely, Ephriam	Dutchess, NY	1/2 share	£11.5	9/14/1763
Wright, Kent	New Fairfield		B121	1/5/1774
Seelye, Ebenezer	New Fairfield, Fairfield, CT	1 share	£18.10	5/5/1763
Draper, Gideon	Oblong, Dutchess, NY		B61	10/8/1773
Selby, Brainard	Sanderfield, Berkshire, MA	1/2 share	$100	1/28/1800
Loper, Levi	Sanderfield, Berkshire, MA		H318	7/11/1801
Seldon, Aaron	Sheffield, Hampshire, MA	1/2 share	£10	6/26/1760
Smedley, John	Litchfield, Litchfield, CT		B316	3/7/1775
Seymore, Norman	Hartford, Hartford, CT	1/4 share	£3	11/15/1782
Belden, Simeon	Hartford, Hartford, CT		C73	11/15/1782
Seymore, Timothy	Hartford, Hartford, CT	1/2 share	£3	11/15/1782
Seymore, Norman	Hartford, Hartford, CT		C71	11/15/1782
Seymour, Timothy	Hartford, Hartford, CT	1/4 share annexed to my 1 share*	£10	1/31/1775
Belding, Simeon	Hartford, Hartford, CT		E425	9/16/1796
Simeon Belding and Norman Seymour pd $4 taxes 11/14/1782				
Shaw, Daniel	Canandagua, Ontario, NY	1 share	val con	11/8/1795
Hutchinson, John	Athens, Luzerne, PA	Murraysfield Twp*	E159	5/16/1796
300 A on this right entered in Murraysfield for Simon Spalding				
Shaw, Ichabod		1/2 share, No. 121 of 400		4/12/1794
Gaylord, Edmund			D50	11/6/1795
Shaw, Ichabod		proprietor's right*		6/4/1796
Manville, Ira			E266	7/8/1796
William Reynolds, OP				
Shaw, Jedediah		1 lot drawn in name of Thos Baldwin	$20	9/2/1796
Paine, Clement	Luzerne, PA	Ulster, west side of [Susq] river	E413	9/14/1796

grantor grantee notes	grantor residence grantee residence	description location	amount acct bk page	deed date record date
Shaw, Jedediah		1/2 share, No 279 of 600*		3/5/1795
Paine, David			C318	3/5/1795
except lots in Ulster				
Shaw, John & Shoemaker, Daniel		1/2 share		6/23/1795
Coolbaugh, Moses		Claverack Twp		
Shearlook, Sarah et al*	Great Barrington, Berkshire,	all right	$10	3/22/1796
Wheeler, Preserved	Charlotte, Chittenden, VT		E132	2/28/1796
Sarah Sherlock, wid of Thomas Sherlock; Bliss, Jacob & wf Mary; Willard, David & wf Martha				
Shelden, William	Smithfield, Providence, RI	1/2 share	£13.10	11/15/1774
Mowry, George	Smithfield, Providence, RI		B298	12/28/1774
Shelden, William	Cranston, Providence, RI	1/2 share	$3.50	3/12/1756
Tracy, John	Scituate, Providence, RI		B299	12/28/1774
Sheldon, Aaron	Sheffield, Hampshire, MA	1/2 of 1 share	£6	12/11/1759
Root, James	Sheffield, Hampshire, MA		F200	8/2/1797
Sheldon, Elisha, son and heir*	Sheldon, Chittenden, VT	1 share	$45*	5/22/1795
Douglass, Zebulon	Canaan, Columbia, NY		F67	4/23/1796
of Elisha Sheldon, decd. If title fails, deed and $45.00 to be returned				
Shelton, James Jr.	Huntington, Fairfield, CT	1 share	12s	12/11/1794
Osborn, Elisha	Derby, New Haven, CT		C415	4/4/1795
Shepard, Abraham	Plainfield, Windham, CT	1/2 share	£6	2/16/1786
Shepard, Stephen	Plainfield, Windham, CT		C94	2/21/1786
Shepard, Abraham	Plainfield, Windham, CT	1 share	£70	2/16/1786
Spalding, Simon	Westmoreland, Susq R.		C95	2/21/1786
Shepard, Abraham	Plainfield, Windham, CT	1 share	£40	2/16/1786
Spalding, Simon	Westmoreland, Susq R.		C96 - G	2/21/1786
Shepard, John	Athens, Luzerne, PA	1 whole share right of land*	$50	6/11/1795
Burrough, William Y.	Livingston, Columbia, NY		E431	10/14/1796
2,000 A composed of unlocated parts of several shares				
Shepard, John	Tioga, Luzerne, PA	725 A*	£300	10/28/1796
Burroughs, William Y. and	Livingston, NY	Athens Twp	E453	10/28/1796
Lots No 32 & 34, 3rd div; No. 6, 7 & 9, 4th div				
Shepard, John	Luzerne, PA	Town Lot 9	£3	4/7/1794
Maxwell, Guy	Luzerne, PA	Athens Twp	E119	3/1/1796
6 perches on street and back to Tioga R.				
Shephard, Abraham		1/2 share		2/18/1774
Pierce, Phinehas			GD	
Shephard, Abraham		1/2 share		12/28/1776
Spalding, Simon			GD	
Shephard, Abraham		1/2 share		
Spalding, Simon			GD	
Shephard, John	Tioga Twp, Luzerne, PA	2,300 A; Lot 53*	£1080	5/15/1794
Brown, Daniel Jr.	Freehold, Albany, NY	pitch NW of Athens; Athens Twp	I74	6/6/1794
According to Thos Handy map of Athens town lots				
Shephard, John	Tioga, Luzerne, PA	550 A	$100	10/27/1801
Cornwell, Ashbell	Montgomery, NY	Litchfield Twp	H320	10/27/1801
Shepherd, John	Luzerne Co, PA	300 A, Lot 48	£21	6/26/1795
Backus, Ebenezer	Luzerne Co, PA	Murraysfield Twp	I89	6/27/1795
Shepherd, John	Luzerne Co, PA	300 A, Lot 48	£21	6/26/1795
Backus, Ebenezer	Luzerne Co, PA	Murraysfield Twp	C583	6/27/1795
Shepherd, John	Athens, Luzerne, PA	340 A; 2 undiv shares; 1 meadow lot*	£127. 13. 4	2/25/1795
Livingston, John	Livingston, Columbia, NY	Athens Twp	C552	2/25/1795
2/3 Lots 2 & 3, 4th Div; 4th Div owned by Zera Beach & Justus Gaylord; owned by Justus Gaylord				
Sheppard, Isaac	Plainfield, Windham, CT	1 share	£12	3/7/1769
Spalding, Simon	Plainfield, Windham, CT		B330	6/27/1775
Sheppard, Willard	Gageborough, Berkshire, MA	1 share	£70	3/13/1778
Dean, Ezra	West Greenwich, Kent, RI		B385	4/8/1778
Sheppard, Willard	Gageborough	1/2 share	£18	4/20/1774
Norton, Zebulon	Ashueloit Equivalent		C1	9/11/1779
Sherlock, Thomas				
Hopkins, Dorcas			A259	
Sherlock, Thomas	Great Barrington, Berkshire,	1 share, Lot 10	£25	12/23/1777
Jefford - Tefford, Thomas	New Marlboro, Berkshire, MA	Huntington Twp	I57	7/10/1786

grantor grantee notes	grantor residence grantee residence	description location	amount acct bk page	deed date record date
Sherman, Edmund, heir*	Canaan, Columbia, NY	1 share	£10	2/21/1795
Hunter, Andrew			E382	7/1/1795
of Samuel Hunter, decd.				
Sherman, William and others*	New Haven, New Haven, CT	1/2 share	$30	2/16/1796
Munson, Eneas Jr.	New Haven, New Haven, CT		D171	7/2/1796
Sarah Townsend; Anne Trowbridge; Lemuel Sherman and Phila, wf; Samuel. Cornelia, Abigail Sherman				
Sherwood, Aaron and Assoc.*	Weston, Fairfield, Stratford	16,000 A ex 1980 A heirs of Couch	5s	3/15/1796
Keeler, Timothy Jr.	Litchfield, CT	West Fairfield Twp	E379	9/15/1796
S.B. Sherwood, D. Coley, D. Andrews, Joseph Strong, M. Sherwood, O. Barr, N. Adams, E. Hull, E.. Banks, Jas. Chapman, Josiah Lacey, J. Peck, B. Uffoot				
Sherwood, Daniel Jr.	Fairfield, Fairfield, CT	1/2 share	$25	8/25/1794
Sherwood, Moses	Fairfield, Fairfield, CT		C519	5/1/1795
Sherwood, Levi	Oxford, Tioga, NY	1/2 share	£10	5/22/1795
Irwin, James	Athens, Luzerne, PA		E436	10/1/1796
Sherwood, Moses	Fairfield, Fairfield, CT	1/2 share	£9	4/14/1795
Lacy, Josiah & Burr, Ozias	Fairfield, Fairfield, CT		C517	5/1/1795
Sherwood, Samuel B.	Weston, Fairfield, CT	1/2 share	$25	4/10/1795
Sherwood, Aaron	Fairfield, Fairfield, CT		C515	5/1/1795
Sherwood, Samuel B.	Weston, Fairfield, CT	1/2 share	£9.17	4/17/1795
Sherwood, Aaron	Fairfield, Fairfield, CT		C516	5/1/1795
Sherwood, Stephen	Bedford, Westchester, NY	1/4 share	$100	2/24/1779
Hawley, Gideon	Charlton, Saratoga, NY		H89	8/19/1799
Shoemaker, Daniel				
Weeks, Jonathan			A317	
Shoemaker, Elijah	Kingston	Nicholas Depue's share*	$50	
Jenkins, John	Exeter		F237	1/12/1797
from Manuel Gansals [Gonzales]				
Sill, Shadrack	Seaskill, Albany, NY	16,000 A	$8,000	10/28/1795
King, Apollo, merchant	Chesterfield, Hampshire, MA	Jefferson Twp	F239	11/9/1797
Silsby, Henry	Achworth, Cheshire, NH	1/2 share	£7.10	2/7/1774
Lothrop, Ebenezer	Norwich, New London, CT		B187	3/17/1774
Silsby, Samuel	Ackworth, Cheshire, NH	1/2 share	£15	12/11/1773
Knolton, Thomas	Ashford, Windham, CT		B189	3/17/1774
Silsby, Samuel				
Lasell, James			A12	
Simons, Jacob 3rd	Brandon, Turland, VT	1 share	£20	8/17/1796
Grant, Josiah	Poultney, Rutland, VT		E534	1/1/1797
Simons, Jacob, Cmte		cost of surveying	24s	3/26/1774
Pearl, Philip		Hancock Twp	C600	7/9/1795
Sippio/Scippio, Solomon	Hartford, Cumberland, VT	1/2 share	£45.10	1/4/1780
Bliss, Ebenezer	Lebanon, Grafton, NH		C78	1/1/1783
Sisko, Jacob				
Root, John			A390	
Skiff, Benjamin	Westmoreland, Westmoreland,	1/3 and 1/2 of 1/3 shares	£5	2/25/1777
Eaton, Benjamin	Kent, Litchfield, CT		H86	9/1/1798
Skiff, Benjamin	Westmoreland, Litchfield, CT	1 share	£30	12/6/1775
Swift, Elisha	Westmoreland, Litchfield, CT		B344	2/7/1776
Skiff, Benjamin & Skiff, Stephen	Mohock Dist, Montgomery, NY	Pwr Att to obtain title from PA		8/30/1787
Benjamin, Isaac		Staples Pitch on Wyalusing Creek*	H87	9/1/1798
deed destroyed in late war with Gr. B when Wyoming destroyed				
Skinner, Joseph	Hebron, Hartford, CT*	1 share	£5	4/17/1795
Barrett, Jonathan & Rathburn, Wait	Norwich, Windsor, VT;		C646	8/10/1795
now Lime, Grafton, NH				
Slager, Samuel				
Hooker, James			A413	
Slater, Mary	Waterbury, New Haven, CT	all right	good cause	1/18/1796
Hopkins, Jesse	Waterbury, New Haven, CT		E145	2/25/1796
Slater, Samuel				
Hooker, James			A41	
Sloan, Sturgeon	Hudson, NY	1/2 share No. 37 of 600	£100	8/25/1796
Stoddard, Ashbel	Hudson		F50	5/1/1796
Sluman, Joseph	East Haddam, Hartford, CT	1/2 share	£25	8/9/1769
Mosley, Thomas, doctor	East Haddam, Hartford, CT		B382	4/17/1778

grantor / grantee / notes	grantor residence / grantee residence	description / location	amount / acct bk page	deed date / record date
Smedley, John	Williamstown, Berkshire, MA	1/2 share	£10	11/4/1773
Kennedy, Benjamin	Gageborough, Berkshire, MA		B317	3/7/1775
Smith, Abel		1/2 share		6/22/1774
Porter, Thomas			GE	1/13/1775
Smith, Benjamin	Gloucester, Providence, RI	1/2 share	£30	11/10/1770
Smith, James, Capt	Smithfield, Providence, RI		H303	6/19/1801
Smith, Benjamin	Gloscester, Providence, RI	1/2 share	£150	12/1/1779
Smith, Stephen	Scituate, Providence, RI		D157	6/28/1796
Smith, Charles	Haddam, Middlesex, CT	1/2 share	good causes	8/4/1794
Lester, Eliphalet	Saybrook, Middlesex, CT		D11	9/18/1795
Smith, Charles	Haddam, Middlesex, CT	1/2 share, original certificate lost		
Lester, Eliphalet	Saybrook, Middlesex, CT		D13	9/18/1795
Smith, David	Colchester, Hartford, CT	1/2 share	£10	8/24/1774
Fowler, Dijah	Lebanon, Windham, CT		B252	9/17/1774
Smith, David	Exeter, Luzerne, PA	5 lots, 300 A each*	$750	3/11/1796
Mitchel, Reuben	Glouster, Providence, RI	Smithfield Twp	E235	7/4/1796
choice of all lots for 2 and equal draught with Smith for 3				
Smith, Ebenezer	Brookfield, Fairfield, CT	1/2 share inc. Lot 15	£80	1/12/1795
Ruggles, Eden	Brookfield, Fairfield, CT	Bedford Twp	I217	4/10/1795
Smith, Ebenezer	Brookfield, Fairfield, CT	1/2 share	£6	12/4/1794
Smith, Sherman	Brookfield, Fairfield, CT		I216	4/11/1795
Smith, Elisha		1/2 share		12/12/1768
Smith, James			GD	
Smith, Elisha	Oblong, N.E., Dutchess, NY	1/2 share	£13.10	10/12/1768
Smith, James Jr.	Oblong, N.E., Dutchess, NY		B374	11/2/1777
Smith, Elnathan	Berlin, Hartford, CT	1 share	good cause	6/20/1794
Brown, Daniel	Freehold, Albany, NY		C440	2/21/1795
Smith, Francis	Plainfield, Cheshire, NH	Pwr Att 1 share	1/2 land	8/17/1795
Strong, Jabin	Glastenbury, Hartford, CT		E93	3/5/1796
Smith, Gilbert	Albany, NY	Pwr Att 1 share		7/3/1786
Stephens, Ira	Northumberland, PA	btw Athens and NY border E on	E369	4/1/1796
Smith, John		1 share		4/3/1773
Bennet, Thomas			A345	
Smith, John	Dighton, MA	11,555 A in 5 Twps	$15,000	12/14/1801
Huggins, Zadock	Dorset, VT	see note	H326	12/21/1801
Graham, S part, 4000A; Fullersville, 4000A; Windsor, 2,315A; Ulster 740A bounded by Susq R on E, Isaac Cash S, George Dorrance N; Insurance 500A adj. Ulster and Comfort Carpenter				
Smith, John				
Perkins, Oliver			A34	
Smith, Jonathan	Glocester, Providence, RI	1/2 share	£15	5/9/1777
Blanchard, Joseph	Scituate, Providence, RI		B357	6/15/1777
Smith, Jonathan	Woodbury, Litchfield, CT	1/2 share	val con	4/3/1769
Hollister, Gideon & Judson, David	Woodbury, Litchfield, CT		C60	11/13/1782
Smith, Jonathan		1,000 A, 1/2 share, No 110 of 400*	F277 - C175	
Hunt, Bensle		Harlem Twp		6/1/1798
Smith, Joseph	Norwich, New London, CT	1 share	£2	1/9/1770
Giles, Benjamin			B255	10/4/1774
Smith, Joseph	Plainfield NH	1/2 share	£6	9/28/1770
Smith, Isaac	Plainfield, Windham, CT		B212	5/5/1774
Smith, Joseph	Tioga, Luzerne, PA	1/2 share ex lot in Ulster	£20	10/23/1795
Thayer, Levi	Tioga, Luzerne, PA		E340	5/15/1796
Smith, Joshua	Norwich, New London, CT	1/2 share	£10	3/30/1769
Smith, David	Colchester, Hartford, CT		B252	9/17/1774
Smith, Lemuel Jr., heir*	Plainfield, Windham, CT	1/2 share	£6.16	1/11/1775
Collins, Josiah & Hovey, Nathl Jr.	Windham, Windham, CT		B332	8/7/1775
of Lemuel Smith, father, of Voluntown				
Smith, Lockwood	Sheshequin, Luzerne, PA	1 share except 1st division rights	$28.00	12/17/1795
Bebee, Solomon	Luzerne, PA	[Athens Twp]	E324	4/10/1796
Smith, Nathan	New Windsor, Ulster, NY	1/2 share	£50	5/18/1761
Hollister, Timothy	Ulster, NY		MB - B269	11/11/1774
Smith, Nathan	White Creek, Albany, NY	1/2 share	£20	12/31/1773
Preston, Ebenezer	Dutchess, NY		B120	1/5/1774
Smith, Phineas and wf Hannah	Bristol, Hartford, CT	1/4 share	£4.16	1/1/1796
Allyn, John B. & Smith, Lemuel	Berlin, Hartford, CT		E139	2/25/1796

grantor grantee notes	grantor residence grantee residence	description location	amount acct bk page	deed date record date
Smith, Ransford, tanner and	Foster, Providence, RI	500 A	$1,000	1/18/1799
Smith, Mowry, trader	Gloucester, Providence, RI	Springhill Twp	H65	4/29/1799
Smith, Samuel	Sharon, Litchfield, CT	1/2 share	£7	11/21/1762
Baldwin, Daniel	Sharon, Litchfield, CT		C52	11/11/1782
Smith, Seth	Stonington, New London, CT	1/2 share	$5	2/13/1796
Downer, Joshua	Preston, New London, CT		E242	7/4/1796
Smith, Seth				
Smith, Ephriam			A396	
Smith, Simeon Doct	Sharon, CT	1/2 share No. 208 of 600		2/20/1795
Stoddard, Philo			C571	7/10/1795
Smith, T				1/6/1776
Storey, Benjamin Jr.			GC	
Smith, Thomas	Scituate, Providence, RI	1/2 share	£9	12/12/1774
Smith, Benjamin	Glocester, Providence, RI		B301	12/28/1774
Smith, Timothy		bond		9/25/1773
Pierce, Phinehas			GC	
Smith, William	White Haven, Luzerne, PA	Release 1/2 interest	£1,500	3/14/1795
Sutton, James	Exeter, Luzerne, PA	Suttonfield Twp	E155	5/4/1796
Snell, Thomas			1/2 share	
Fitch, James			A225	
Snell, Thomas Jr.	Woodstock, Windham, CT	1/2 share	£6	8/2/1777
Snell, Joseph	Ashford, Windham, CT		B380	4/3/1778
Snell, Thomas Sr.	Ashford, Windham, CT	1/2 share	£6	4/15/1774
Snell, Thomas	Woodstock, Windham, CT		B223	6/13/1774
Snow, Abraham Jr.	Canterbury, Windham, CT	1/2 share	20s	12/15/1769
Forster, William	Canterbury, Windham, CT		B222	6/8/1774
Soule, Samuel insolvent debtor*	East Greenwich, Kent, RI		15s	7/6/1771
Crary, Archibald	Voluntown, Windham, CT		B78	10/18/1773
administrators Hopkins Cook, Gideon Mumford of East Greenwich, CT and Oliver Arnold of Warwick				
Southward, Samuel	Ulster, Luzerne, PA	Lot 9	£300	4/22/1795
Bingham, Chester	Ulster, Luzerne, PA	Old Sheshequin [Ulster Twp]	C535	5/7/1795
Spafford, Darius	Westmoreland, CT	Lot 44, Div 2	£12	12/21/1777
Spafford, Phinehas	Westmoreland, Westmoreland,	Wilkes Barre Twp	C108	8/14/1787
Spafford, John				
Witter, Josiah			A418	
Spafford, Josiah		1/2 share		4/26/1777
Owens, Daniel			GC	
Spaford, Andrew	Dalton, Berkshire, MA	Pwr to locate 1 share	1/2 land	5/12/1795
Strong, Jabin	Glastenbury, Hartford, CT		E70	2/28/1796
Spalding, Amasa et al	Plainfield, Cheshire, NH	Pwr Att to locate 1 share	1/2 part of land	4/11/1795
Strong, Jabin	Glastonbury, Hartford,CT		E83	3/2/1796
Barzillia Spalding & John Stevens, 3d, heirs of John Spalding of Plainfield, Windham, CT				
Spalding, Edward	Canaan, Litchfield, CT	1/2 share	£100	11/3/1755
Hewet, Richard	Stonington, New London, CT		B86	11/8/1773
Spalding, Jesse	Plainfield, Windham, CT	all rights	£6	5/16/1796
Pierce, John	Plainfield, Windham, CT	Susquehanna Company land	H36	11/10/1798
Spalding, John	Tioga, Luzerne, PA	16,000 A	$8,000	10/28/1795
Bingham, Chester	Tioga, Luzerne, PA	Hexham Twp	E467	11/6/1796
Spalding, John	Tioga, Luzerne, PA	16,000 A	$8,000	10/28/1795
Bingham, Chester	Tioga, Luzerne, PA	Durkee Twp	F76	6/3/1796
Spalding, John		3 1/2 2nd div rights*		9/19/1795
Buck, William			C647	9/19/1795
this deed written on back of deed recorded on C614; 1 Pixley, David B242; 1 Buck, Elijah B247; 1 Buck, William B242; 1/2 Buck, William A66 + 4,900A reverses deed of 3/6/1795				
Spalding, John	Ulster, Luzerne, PA	all right	$16,000	1/3/1800
Satterlee, Elias et al	Athens, PA & Providence, RI	Windsor Twp	H180	1/4/1800
Levi Thayer, Comfort Carpenter				
Spalding, John	Ulster, Luzerne, PA	all right	$16,000	1/3/1800
Satterlee, Elias et al	Athens, PA & Providence, RI	Federal Twp	H181	1/4/1800
Levi Thayer, Comfort Carpenter				
Spalding, John		12,500 A, all of	val con	
Satterlee, Elias & Thayer, Levi	Luzerne, PA	Insurance Twp, location limits size	H152	12/14/1799
Spalding, John	Ulster, Luzerne, PA	all right	$6,000	1/25/1796
Street, Caleb	Catskill, Albany, NY	Newton Twp	D147	6/10/1796

grantor	grantor residence	description	amount	deed date
grantee	grantee residence	location	acct bk page	record date
notes				
Spalding, John	Ulster, Luzerne, PA	300 A, Lot 53	$300	1/3/1800
Thayer, Levi	Athens, Luzerne, PA	Murraysfield Twp	H189	1/6/1800
Spalding, John	Ulster, Luzerne, PA	Part of Lot 14	$40	1/8/1800
Thompson, John	Burlington, NJ	Watertown Twp	H197	1/14/1800
Spalding, John	Luzerne, PA	all right to 4 twps	$40,000	4/10/1795
Wynkoop, William	Tioga, NY	Eden, Bath, Hexham, Durkee Twps	F176	6/27/1797
Spalding, John & Kingsberry,	Ulster, Luzerne, PA	10,666.66 A (2/3 twp)	$10,000	1/3/1800
Thayer, Levi et al	Athens, PA and Providence, RI	Hartford Twp*	H188	1/6/1800
Elias Satterlee, Comfort A. Carpenter				
Spalding, Joseph	Athens, Luzerne, PA	700 A of 2nd division land	$30	9/17/1796
Kingsbury, Phinehas	Granby, Hartford, CT		E428	9/24/1796
after division of Stephen Jenkins 1/2 share				
Spalding, Joseph	Plainfield, Windham, CT	all rights	£6	12/18/1795
Pierce, John	Plainfield, Windham, CT	Susquehanna Company land	H38	11/10/1798
Spalding, Joseph	Tioga, Luzerne, PA	17 A*	$125	9/13/1800
Rice, Wanton	Warwick, Kent, RI	Tioga [Athens], Luzerne, PA	H239	9/13/1800
south part Joseph Spalding land				
Spalding, Joseph	Athens, Luzerne, PA	Lot 13, Third Division	£50	10/26/1794
Spalding, John	Athens, Luzerne, PA	Athens Twp	D174	7/2/1796
Spalding, Oliver	Woodbury, Litchfield, CT	1/2 share	£6.6	4/8/1773
Wheeler, Benjamin	Woodbury, Litchfield, CT		B279	10/31/1774
Spalding, Oliver		1 share		4/3/1773
Wheeler, Benjamin			GJ	11/11/1773
Spalding, Simon		1/2 share		
Bendor, Phillip			GD	
Spalding, Simon		1/2 share		8/13/1775
Carver, Nathaniel			GH	9/15/1775
Spalding, Simon		1/2 share		1/12/1774
Dunkens [Duncan], David			GJ	
Spalding, Simon				
Peirce, Abel			A371	
Spalding, Simon		1/2 share		
Pierce, Phinehas			GD	
Spalding, Simon	Ulster, Luzerne, PA	1,500 A	$1,500	
Thayer, Levi	Athens, Luzerne, PA	Fullersville Twp	H189	1/4/1800
Spalding, William		1400 A 2nd division		
Campbell, James		Juddsburgh Twp, south line of	H118	11/23/1799
surveyed by Spalding for Campbell, see deed for metes and bounds				
Spaulding, Amos	Plainfield, Windham, CT	1/4 share	£6	7/12/1774
Jameson, John	Westmoreland, Litchfield, CT		B230	7/13/1774
Spaulding, Amos	Plainfield, Windham, CT	1/2 share	£12	3/21/1774
Kenney, Joseph	Plainfield, Windham, CT		B200	4/6/1774
Spaulding, Amos				
McGonerell, James			A52	
Spaulding, Edward	Canaan, Litchfield, CT	1/2 share	£100	5/5/1755
Doneghy, John	Canaan, Litchfield, CT		B228	7/6/1774
Spaulding, Joseph	Columbia, Luzerne, PA	300 A of 1/2 share, Lot 29	£120	6/9/1794
Paine, David	Rensselaerville, NY	Columbia Twp	I80	6/16/1794
Spaulding, Phineas	P/Denton, Charlotte, NY	1/2 share	£18	10/13/1773
Elmore, Samuel	Sharon, Litchfield, CT		C103	9/30/1786
Spencer, Caleb		1 share	£70	9/17/1792
Dimock, David			I219	7/8/1795
Spencer, Caleb				
Kilborn, Benjamin			A436	
Spencer, Jared				
Field, Samuel			A32	
Spencer, John		1/4 share		
Bradley, Joel			A5	
Spencer, John				
Paine, William			A6	
Spencer, John Gilbert	Bolton CT	1/2 share	£8	9/24/1770
Lester, Edward	Transcient		B37	1/11/1771

grantor grantee notes	grantor residence grantee residence	description location	amount acct bk page	deed date record date
Spencer, John Golbert				
Goodrich, Craft			A477	
Spencer, John Jr.				
Hebard, Moses			A19	
Spicer, Abel	Groton, New London, CT	1/2 share	£6	12/20/1782
Gore, Robert 2nd	Groton, New London, CT		C353	3/2/1795
Spicer, Capt. Oliver	Groton, New London, CT	1/2 share	10s	3/23/1796
Downer, Joshua	Preston, New London, CT		E242	7/4/1796
Sprague, Joseph & Eunice wf	Wyoming, Northumberland, PA		£15 + 3 gal whisky	4/1/1785
Vanfleet, Joshua			C533	5/1/1795
Sprague, Obadiah	Providence, Providence, RI	1/2 share	taxes on 1 share	2/21/1774
Bryant, Prince, tanner	Providence, Providence, RI		B147	2/24/1774
Sprague, Theodore		1/2 share		
Brewer, Daniel			GL	
Sprague, Theodore		1/2 share		
Brown, Daniel			GH	
Sprague, Theodore		1/4 share		
Dorrance, John			GH	
Sprague, Theodore		1/3 share		9/1/1773
White, Joseph			GH	9/1/1773
Squire, Amasa	Montgomery, Hampshire, MA	all right bought of Oliver Clark	$50	11/1/1796
Hyde, Ezekiel	Norwich, New London, CT		F211	10/21/1797
Squire, Zachariah	Noble Town, Albany, NY	1/2 share	£50	11/29/1779
Hogeboom, Jeremiah	Albany, NY		F271	3/14/1798
St. John, John		100 A		11/14/1794
Baldwin, Waterman			E303	6/20/1796
Stafford, Amos	Plainfield, NH	all right	£9.10	10/15/1773
Cressey, William	Woodbury, Litchfield, CT		B132	1/20/1774
Stage, William & Margaret	Harlem, Luzerne, PA	108 A	5s bond on $80.00	9/3/1797
Harris, Thomas	Harlem, Luzerne, PA	Harlem Twp	F235	12/12/1797
Standiford, John*	Windham, Windham, CT	Pwr Att to locate 1 share; 300A		1/20/1795
Spalding, John	Tioga PA	Watertown Twp	C618	7/1/1795
husband of Jerusha Standiford				
Standley, John				
Hubbard, Watts			A8	
Standley, Noah				
Graham, John			A9	
Standley, Noah				
Standley, Thomas			A16	
Standley, Timothy				
Standley, Gad			A15	
Standly, William	Hartford	1/2 share		
Kilborn, Benjamin*			GK	
Kilborn has pd taxes to 2/11/1773				
Stanley, Gad & Mary	Berlin, Hartford, CT	1 share	2s	1/15/1796
Smith, Lemuel & Allyn, John B.	Berlin, Hartford, CT	Allynsgrove Twp	E149	2/25/1796
Stanley, Thomas	Marietta, Washington, Territory	3/4 share*		10/15/1799
Stanley, Lot, brother	Berlin, Hartford, CT		H209	2/14/1801
1/2 from decd father's estate left to Thomas				
Stanley, Timothy	Berlin, Hartford, CT	3/4 share	£12	1/14/1796
Smith, Lemuel & Allyn, John B.	Berlin, Hartford, CT		E151	9/20/1781
Stanly, Seth, Noah, Adna	Berlin, Hartford, CT	1/2 share	$25	1/18/1796
Smith, Lemuel & Allyn, John B.	Berlin, Hartford, CT	Allynsgrove Twp	E150	9/20/1781
Stanly, William	Tolland, Hartford, CT	1/2 share		12/31/1769
Walden, Jonathan	Tolland, Hartford, CT		D50	11/6/1795
Stanton, Jacob & Jemima, wf	Mummy, Cotton Pct, Ulster, NY	1/2 share	£10	4/8/1773
Whittlesey, David	Kent, Litchfield, CT		B174	3/9/1774
Staple, John	Wilkesbarre, Luzerne, CT	1/2 share	£19	10/27/1773
Layn, John	Middletown, Hartford, CT		C381	2/28/1795
Staples, John		1/2 share		9/9/1772
Judd, Enoch			GK	
Stark, Nathan				
Wightman, Allen			A89	

grantor grantee notes	grantor residence grantee residence	description location	amount acct bk page	deed date record date
Stark, William		1/4 share		
Hinton, George			GD	
Starlin, John	Lyme, New London, CT	1/2 share + 1 settling right	£12	4/14/1772
Harvey, Benjamin	Lyme, New London, CT		B55	9/14/1772
Starr, Josiah	New Milford, Litchfield, CT	Pwr Att to locate, lay, sell 1/2 share*		11/23/1795
Bostwick, Benjamin	Brookfield, Fairfield, CT		D93	12/4/1795
Alexander Stuart OP				
Starr, Josiah	New Milford, Litchfield, CT	Pwr Att to locate, layout, sell 1		11/23/1795
Bostwick, Benjamin	Brookfield, Fairfield, CT		D93	12/4/1795
Thomas Stevens Jr., OP				
Starr, Josiah	New Milford, Litchfield, CT	Pwr Att to locate, layout, sell 1		11/23/1795
Bostwick, Benjamin	Brookfield, Fairfield, CT		D93	12/4/1795
Joseph Hurlbut, OP				
Starr, Josiah	New Milford, Litchfield, CT	Pwr Att to locate, lay, sell 1/3 share*		11/23/1795
Bostwick, Benjamin	Brookfield, Fairfield, CT		D93	12/4/1795
Matthew or Samuel Benedict, OP				
Starr, Josiah	New Milford, Litchfield, CT	Pwr Att to locate, layout, sell 1		11/23/1795
Bostwick, Benjamin	Brookfield, Fairfield, CT		D93	12/4/1795
Ebenezer Baldwin, OP				
Starr, Josiah	New Milford, Litchfield, CT	Pwr Att to locate, layout, sell 1		11/23/1795
Bostwick, Benjamin	Brookfield, Fairfield, CT		D93	12/4/1795
Josiah Starr, OP				
Starr, Josiah	New Milford, Litchfield, CT	Pwr Att to locate, lay, sell 1/3 share*		11/23/1795
Bostwick, Benjamin	Brookfield, Fairfield, CT		D93	12/4/1795
Matthew Benedict, OP				
Starr, Josiah	New Milford, Litchfield, CT	Pwr Att to locate, layout, sell 1		11/23/1795
Bostwick, Benjamin	Brookfield, Fairfield, CT		D93	12/4/1795
Daniel Starr, OP				
Starr, Josiah	New Milford, Litchfield, CT	Pwr Att to locate, layout, sell 1		11/23/1795
Bostwick, Benjamin	Brookfield, Fairfield, CT			
John Wood, OP				
Stearns, Ebenezer Jr.	Lanesborough, Berkshire, MA	1/2 share	£12	5/7/1774
Burg, Seth	Equivalent, Berkshire, MA		B306	1/25/1775
Steavens, Zebulon				
Dean, Jonathan			A113	
Stedman, James				
Fuller, Stephen			A319	
Stedman, James				
Rogers, Josiah			A453	
Stedman, Thomas*	Hampton, Windham, CT	1 share and 1/3 of 1/8th share*	£50	7/8/1801
Larrabee, Lebbeus	Windham, CT		H222	8/6/1801
heir of Ebenezer Griffin				
Stedman, Thomas				
Utley, Joseph & Farnam, Ruben			A385	
Steel, John 2nd	Bethlehem, Litchfield, CT	Pwr Att 2 shares, pay taxes, costs		4/13/1795
Wheeler, Abner	Bethlehem, Litchfield, CT		C620	7/1/1795
Steel, John & Bostwick, Bushnell*		taxes pd by Hutchinson	$1	3/19/1786
Hutchinson, John			I17	3/19/1786
1/2 share each man				
Steel, John & Steel, Elisha	Bethlehem, Litchfield, CT	1/2 share, 300 A	$75	2/4/1795
Shafson, George & Minor		New Milford Twp	D34	10/8/1795
Stephens, Ira		all right except 200 A	$20	2/4/1796
Beebe, Solomon			E542	8/15/1799
Stephens, Ira	Athens, Luzerne, PA	1 A, Lot 38 1st Div	£3	5/24/1791
Hopkins, Stephen	Athens, Luzerne, PA	Athens Twp	E541	
Stephens, Ira			$15	8/31/1795
Rathborn, Wait	Troy, Rensselaer, NY		E367	4/1/1796
Stephens, Jesse	Canaan, Litchfield, CT	1 share	£5	12/3/1768
Buck, Asahel	Amenia, Dutchess, NY		B242	8/30/1774
Stephens, John		1/2 share	val recd	11/26/1794
Teall, Nathan			E302	6/20/1796
Stephens, Peter	Luzerne, PA	Lot 48	£10	5/8/1794
Beebe, Solomon	Luzerne, PA	Murraysfield Twp	I89	6/21/1794

grantor grantee notes	grantor residence grantee residence	description location	amount acct bk page	deed date record date
Stephens, Peter	Luzerne, PA	Lot 48	£10	5/8/1794
Beebe, Solomon	Luzerne, PA	Murraysfield Twp	C583	6/21/1794
Stevens, Cyprian	Plainfield, Windham, CT	1/2 share + settling right of first 200	£12	7/2/1767
Benjamin, Isaac	Plainfield, Windham, CT		B248	9/3/1774
Stevens, David	Number Five, Berkshire, MA	1/2 share	£18	6/2/1774
Halluck, William	Chesterfield, Hampshire, MA		B254	9/20/1774
Stevens, Ebenezer	Westhaven, Rutland, VT	1/4 share	$8 2/3	2/20/1795
Stoddard, Philo	Woodbury, Litchfield, CT		C630	7/15/1795
Stevens, Henry	Canaan, Litchfield, CT	1 share, taxes paid	£16	7/15/1777
Franklin, John	Canaan, Litchfield, CT		I4	6/3/1786
Stevens, Isaac	Pawlett, Rutland, VT	1 share	$6	6/6/1795
Mosely, Nathaniel J.	Pawlett, Rutland, VT		C568	6/20/1795
Stevens, Jesse	Canaan, Litchfield, CT	1/2 share	£4	8/2/1762
Stevens, Simeon	Stonington, New London, CT		B156	3/9/1774
Stevens, John	New Grantham, Chester, NH	Pwr Att 1 share	1/2 land to Strong	4/11/1795
Strong, Jabin	Glastenbury, Hartford, CT		E72	2/29/1796
Stevens, Levi	Castleton, Rutland, VT	3 shares	$180	5/22/1795
Grant, Josiah	Poultney, Rutland, VT	In tract disputed between PA and CT	C561	6/20/1795
Stevens, Levi	Castleton, Rutland, VT	1 share	£12	5/9/1795
Grant, Josiah	Poultney, Rutland, VT		C562	6/20/1795
Stevens, Nehemiah				
Peirce, Abel			A370	
Stevens, Noah	Stillwater, Saratoga, NY	1/2 share	£6	3/21/1795
Janes, Elijah, merchant, et al	Troy, Rensselaer, NY		C128	8/9/1795
James Dole, merchant; Wait Rathbun, innkeeper				
Stevens, Peter	Athens, Luzerne, PA	1/2 share except 300 A		5/6/1795
Shepperd, John		Murraysfield Twp	C369	5/6/1795
Stevens, Safford	Canaan, Litchfield, CT	two half shares	£50	4/11/1795
Backus, Andrew	New York City, NY		I211	4/11/1795
1/2 Jedediah Richards; 1/2 Andrew Stevens				
Stevens, Thomas	Sheffield, Berkshire, MA	1/2 share	£15	11/6/1773
Belknap, Abel	Stillwater, Albany, NY		B158	3/9/1774
Stevens, Thomas	Plainfield, Windham, CT	1/4 share	£3	10/30/1769
Cady, John	Plainfield, Windham, CT		B204	4/6/1774
Stevens, Uriah	Canaan, Litchfield, CT	1 share	£30	5/13/1763
Hopkins, Stephen	Amenia, Dutchess, NY		B255	9/21/1774
Stevens, Zebulon	Canaan, Litchfield, CT	1/2 share	£8	2/19/1776
Sedgwick, Benjamin	Canaan, Litchfield, CT		I8	6/6/1786
Stevens, Zebulon	Canaan, Litchfield, CT	1 share*	£20	10/12/1791
Stevens, Thomas & Jonathan	Hungtington, Luzerne, PA	unlocated	I238	8/18/1795
except 100 A to Joel Sawyer				
Stewart, Thomas				
Hammond, Elnathan			A2	
Stiles, Aaron	Hebron, Hartford, CT	1/3 share	£5	2/23/1769
Carver, David	Hebron, Hartford, CT		E61	2/25/1795
Stiles, Benjamin*	Hebron, Hartford, CT	1/3 share	£5	2/23/1769
Carver, David	Hebron, Hartford, CT		E60	2/25/1795
Amos Stiles, father, pd £6.10 toward Susq Purchase 9/28/1753				
Stiles, Nathan	Lebanon, Windham, CT	1/2 share	£6	5/20/1760
Barber, David	Hebron, Hartford, CT		B77 - GM	5/6/1773
Stocking, Reuben	Chatham, Middlesex, CT	1 share	bond of equal date	9/22/1795
Olcott, Elisha	East Hartford, Hartford, CT		E246	7/1/1796
Stoddard, Ashbel		Pwr Att to locate two half shares*	1/3 part of land	11/20/1796
Gordon, Samuel			F50	5/1/1796
1/2 share No. 205 and 1/2 share No. 37 of 600 bought fr Sturgeon Sloan				
Stoddard, Philo	Woodbury, Litchfield, CT	1/4 share	$15	5/12/1795
Atwood, Elisha & Judson, Gideon	Woodbury, Litchfield, CT		C630	7/15/1795
Stoddard, Philo	Woodbury, Litchfield, CT	2/9 share	$15	5/12/1795
Atwood, Elisha & Judson, Gideon	Woodbury, Litchfield, CT		C630	7/15/1795
Stoddard, Philo		1/2 share No. 202 of 600		2/20/1795
Leavensworth, Asa			C571	7/10/1795
Stoddard, Philo		1/2 share No. 208 of 600		2/20/1795
Leavensworth, Asa			C571	7/10/1795

grantor	grantor residence	description	amount	deed date
grantee	grantee residence	location	acct bk page	record date
notes				
Stoddard, Philo	Woodbury, Litchfield, CT	7 shares*	$440	4/17/1795
Leavensworth, Asa	Watertown, Litchfield, CT		H211	4/10/1800
1 ea. James Woodward, Samuel Brown, James Babcock, Nathan T. Moseley, Sarah and James Babcock, Jonathan Parker; 1/2 ea.				
Archibald Dickson, Stephen Starkweather				
Stoddard, Philo	Woodbury, Litchfield, CT	1 share	$40	5/12/1795
Martin, Reuben	Woodbury, Litchfield, CT		C633	7/10/1795
Stoddard, Philo	Bethlehem, Litchfield, CT	14,000 A	£748	6/19/1797
Rathbun, Wait	Middletown, Rutland, VT	Homerstown Twp	F178	7/14/1797
Stoddard, Solomon				
Hitchcock, John			A464	
Stoder, Mortimer				
Pride, John			A361	
Stone, John	Chesterfield, Hampshire, MA	give up my title*	good cause	10/10/1798
Brown, Daniel		Pittsfield Twp	H204	5/13/1800
assignment on back of deed D. Brown to Barney and Stone, C163				
Stone, John	Chesterfield, Hampshire, MA	16,000 A	$4,000	10/5/1796
Clark, Gamaliel	Stockbridge, Berkshire, MA	Brooklyn Twp	F241	11/9/1797
Stoughton, Daniel	East Windsor, Hartford, CT	all shares	£3.10	11/6/1773
Standiford, Jerusha, dau	Windham, Windham, CT		B90	11/19/1773
Stow, Polly		1/2 share, No. 133 of 400 ex 300 A		10/24/1795
Paine, Clement		Juddsburgh Twp	D24	10/25/1795
Stoyel, Stephen				
Vernon, William			A290	
Streater, John	Sturbridge, Worcester, MA	1 share		6/17/1772
Cheney, Ebenezer*			C440	4/14/1795
a soldier in Gov. Shirley's Regiment 1755				
Street, Caleb	Catskill, Albany, NY	all right, 10 shares already located	diverse consideration	1/25/1796
Spalding, John	Ulster, Luzerne, PA	Federal Twp	E108	3/16/1796
Street, Elnathan Jr.	Wallingford, New Haven, CT	1 share*	£18	9/10/1794
Fowler, William	Guilford		C120	10/1/1794
1/2 Street, Elnathan Sr. & 1/2 Street, Samuel				
Street/Steeter, John				
Cheney, Ebenezer			A435	
Strickland, Jonathan				
Daviss, Comfort			A218	
Strickland, Jonathan				
Wickwire, James			A333	
Strickland, Peter	New London, New London, CT	1/2 share		4/20/1772
Selby, Brainard	Landisfield, Berkshire, MA		C437	2/1/1795
Strickland, Samuel & Amie, wf*	Waterbury, New Haven, CT	1/5 of 2/3 share	£4	6/13/1774
Miner, Christopher	Kent, Litchfield, CT		B318	3/16/1775
Maiden name Cogswell				
Strickland, Stephen		300 A of 1/2 share to be in a 1st div		3/5/1795
Newel, John			I190	3/16/1795
Stricklin, Jonathan		1/2 share		
Wickwire, James			GC	
Strong, Amasa	Warren, Litchfield, CT	Pwr Attorney 1 share	1/4 land	6/25/1795
Strong, Jabin	Glastenbury, Hartford, CT		E69	2/28/1796
Strong, Ebenezer				
Mallery, Abner			A336	
Strong, Jabin	Glastonbury, Hartford, CT	Pwr Att*		11/4/1796
Paine, Clement	Luzerne, PA		E94	3/5/1796
15 whole; 4 half; one 7/8; one 3/4; one 1/4 share & one 200 A; one 930 A tracts				
Strong, Jabin	Glastonbury, Hartford, CT	300 acres, part of 1/2 share	£100	11/3/1795
Schoonover, Christopher	Luzerne Co PA	Athens Twp*	E45 - E418	11/5/1795
east line where Schoonover now lives				
Strong, John	Hebron, Hartford, CT*	all share	12s	4/13/1795
Barrett, Jonathan	Norwich, Windsor, VT		C644	8/10/1795
now Thetford, Orange, VT				
Strong, John	Farmingham, Hartford, CT	1/2 share	£10	6/1/1773
Bull, Samuel	Harwinton, Litchfield, CT		B64	6/2/1773
Strong, John	Lebanon, Windham, CT	1/2 share	20s	2/28/1758
Lomis, Joseph	Lebanon, Windham, CT		E102	3/10/1796

grantor	grantor residence	description	amount	deed date
grantee	grantee residence	location	acct bk page	record date
notes				
Strong, Solomon	Sheffield, Berkshire, CT	1/2 share	£20	2/19/1781
Hogeboom, Jeremiah	Claverack, Albany, NY		F268	3/12/1798
Strong, Solomon	Claverack, Albany, NY	all right	£200	11/11/1783
Hogeboom, Peter	Claverack, Albany, NY	Susquehanna Purchase	E447	10/25/1796
inc. 2 whole & three half shares & Solomon Avery's right in Claverack				
Strong, Solomon		1/2 share		2/17/1776
Strope, Bastion			GL	3/31/1777
Stuffelbeem, Michael	Athens. Luzerne, PA	1/2 share inc. Lot 6, 300 A		3/22/1794
Murray, Noah		Murraysfield Twp	C283	9/7/1795
Summer, Jabez	Stratford, Fairfield, CT	1 share	£8	6/4/1774
Allen, Levi	Salisbury, Litchfield, CT		B256	10/5/1774
Sumner, Edward	Ashford	Pwr Att to obtain land for share		6/14/1795
Chauncey, Worthington G.	Durham, New Haven, CT		C321	2/26/1795
Susq Co		1 share*	$2	7/18/1753
Abbe, John			MB - Deed	
pd Journeying Cmte				
Susq Co		1/2 share	services rendered	3/11/1796
Abbot, Joel	Luzerne, PA		E103	3/11/1796
Susq Co		1 share		7/11/1754
Abbott, Abiel			Deed	
Susq Co		1/2 share	£6	4/12/1769
Adams, David Dr.			C98	8/12/1786
Susq Co		1/2 share*		4/1/1773
Adams, John Junr.			MB	4/1/1773
by Samuel Gray				
Susq Co		1/2 share	$4.50	5/10/1755
Adams, Nathaniel	Fairfield, Fairfield, CT		B125	1/19/1774
Susq Co		1/2 share*	$4.50	5/1/1755
Adams, Nathaniel	Fairfield, CT		RB	
pd Daniel Edwards				
Susq Co		1 share		
Adkins, John Esqr			Deed	
Susq Co		1/2 share of 400, certificate lost		12/2/1796
Alden, Andrew			I231	12/2/1796
Susq Co		1/2 share*		5/1/1754
Alden, Daniel			MB - Deed	
pd S Gray				
Susq Co		1/2 share*		10/20/1761
Alden, Prince			MB	
pd Isaac Tracy				
Susq Co		1/2 share No. 267 of 400*		9/10/1785
Alden, Prince Jr.		Athens Twp	I66	6/10/1786
entered in Athens 5/8/1786				
Susq Co		1 share		7/11/1754
Alden, Seth			Deed	
Susq Co		1/2 share		7/11/1754
Alexander, Joseph			MB	
Susq Co		1/2 share		7/11/1754
Alexander, Joseph			Deed	
Susq Co		1 share	£8	6/24/1761
Allen, David	New Haven, New Haven CT		B101	10/25/1773
Susq Co				
Allen, Humphrey			A240	
Susq Co		1 share	£15	8/21/1773
Allen, Ira	Salisbury		MB - B253	10/5/1774
Susq Co		1 share, 300 A		7/3/1795
Allen, John	late Windham, now Berlin	Bedford Twp	I222	7/3/1795
Susq Co		1 share*		4/7/1763
Allen, John	Windham		MB	
by Jonathan Root				
Susq Co		1 share*		11/20/1754
Allen, Joseph			MB - Deed	
pd Capn Uriah Stevens				

grantor grantee notes	grantor residence grantee residence	description location	amount acct bk page	deed date record date
Susq Co		1 share*	£12	1/20/1775
Allen, Levi	Salisbury, Litchfield, CT		B285	1/20/1775
in right of Nathan Hurlbut				
Susq Co		1 share*	£12	6/1/1778
Allen, Levi	Salisbury, Litchfield, CT		B293	6/1/1778
in right of David Martin of Goshen, decd., who never paid; one of 100 special shares authorized 4/12/1769				
Susq Co		1 share		8/21/1773
Allen, Levi			MB	
Susq Co		1/2 share*	$4.50	7/8/1755
Allen, Nathan	New Haven, New Haven CT		MB - B101	10/25/1773
pd Thomas Darling				
Susq Co		1/2 share*	$4.50	5/1/1755
Allen, Nathan	New Haven		RB	
pd Daniel Edwards				
Susq Co		1/2 of 1 share No. 394 of 600		7/13/1785
Allen, Nathaniel	Catskill, Albany, NY		C285	9/7/1795
Susq Co		1/2 share No. 395 of 600		
Allen, Nathaniel	Catskill, Albany, NY	Burlington Twp	I229	9/6/1795
Susq Co		1/2 share No. 396 of 600		3/13/1794
Allen, Nathaniel	Catskill, Albany, NY	Burlington Twp	I229	9/6/1795
Susq Co		1 share No. 197 of 600		
Allen, Nathaniel	Catskill, Albany, NY		C570	
Susq Co		1/2 share No. 398 of 600		
Allen, Nathaniel	Catskill, Albany, NY		E270	7/6/1796
Susq Co		1/2 share No. 389 of 600		
Allen, Nathaniel	Catskill, Albany, NY		E271	6/6/1796
Susq Co		two whole and twelve half shares		6/5/1794
Allen, Nathaniel	Catskill, Albany, NY	Burlington Twp*	F80 - F85	9/7/1796
2 shares No. 199-200; twelve 1/2 shares No. 378-381, 384-386, 390-392, 399-400 all of the 600 granted at various dates between 6/5/1794 and 8/9/1795				
Susq Co		1 share*	$9	12/31/1755
Allen, Timothy	New Haven		MB	
pd Thomas Darling; Allen in MB but Alling in I158				
Susq Co		1 share*		9/4/1761
Alling, Daniel	New Haven		MB	
pd Daniel Lyman				
Susq Co				10/1/1785
Allington, Thomas			I71	6/13/1794
Susq Co		1/2 share*	$4.50	5/1/1755
Allyn, Henry	Windsor		RB	
pd Daniel Edwards				
Susq Co		1 share		7/11/1754
Anderson, Thomas			Deed	
Susq Co		1 share		7/11/1754
Andrews, John			Deed	
Susq Co		1/2 share		
Andross, John			Deed	
Susq Co		1/2 share*	$4.50	5/1/1755
Andrus, Daniel	Fairfield, CT		RB	
pd Daniel Edwards				
Susq Co		1 share*		11/20/1754
Andrus, Eben/Elier			MB - Deed	
pd Capn Uriah Stevens				
Susq Co				7/18/1753
Andrus, Epaphras			MB	
Susq Co		1 share*		11/20/1754
Andrus, Ephriam			MB - Deed	
pd Capn Uriah Stevens				
Susq Co		1 share*		8/27/1761
Andrus, Joseph			MB	
pd Major Elizer Talcott				
Susq Co		1 share*	$2	7/18/1753
Andrus, William			MB - Deed	
pd Journeying Cmte				

grantor grantee notes	grantor residence grantee residence	description location	amount acct bk page	deed date record date
Susq Co		1/2 share	$4.50	6/12/1755
Andruss, Daniel	Fairfield, Fairfield, CT		B125	1/19/1774
Susq Co		1 share*	$42	1/1/1770
Angar, Fred and Frank, Fred*			E535	3/3/1797
sold in 1770 and recorded in Westmoreland Records page 1158				
Susq Co		1/2 share, or 1,000 A*	£4	2/11/1762
Angel, Jeremiah	Situate, RI	Harlem Twp	B292	6/29/1798
Lots 16, 17, 18 @ 300 A each; Lot 19 @ 100 A				
Susq Co		1 share	£16.5	5/14/1754
Arnold, Benedict, Capt	Norwich, New London, CT		Deed - B26	8/30/1773
Susq Co		1/2 share		7/11/1754
Arnold, Henry			Deed	
Susq Co		1 share*	$50	2/12/1763
Arnold, James*	Warwick, Kent, RI		MB - B341	2/8/1776
son of Elisha Arnold; by Ezra Dean				
Susq Co		1 share		7/11/1754
Arnold, Joseph			Deed - A423	
Susq Co		1 share		7/11/1754
Arthur, Bartholomew			Deed	
Susq Co		1 share		7/11/1754
Ashley, Benjamin	NY		Deed	
Susq Co		1/3 of township	$333	3/12/1799
Ashley, Oliver	Clermont, Cheshire, NH	Victory Twp	H123	11/26/1799
Susq Co		10,667 A	$600	11/25/1799
Ashley, Oliver et al	Clermont, Cheshire, NH;	Victory Twp	H124	11/26/1799
9,967 A Oliver Ashley; 600 A Jeremiah Spencer; 100 A Edward Goodwin				
Susq Co		1/2 share*	taxes pd	12/14/1786
Atherton, Asahel			I34	12/14/1786
bought from Thos Sawyer				
Susq Co		1/2 share, No. 288*		5/24/1794
Atherton, Moses			I235	10/28/1795
Susq Co		1/2 share*	$4.50	5/1/1755
Atwater, John	Cheshire, CT		RB	
pd Daniel Edwards				
Susq Co		1/2 share*	£4	8/16/1761
Austin, David	New Haven, New Haven, CT		MB - B100	10/25/1773
pd Daniel Lyman				
Susq Co		1 share	$5	5/18/1754
Avery, Abner	New London, New London, CT		MB - B129	1/26/1774
Susq Co		1 share	£15	12/1/1762
Avery, Christopher	Norwich, New London, CT		B25	8/30/1773
Susq Co		1/2 share	£4	8/24/1762
Avery, Christopher	Norwich, New London, CT		B26	8/30/1773
Susq Co		1 share*		10/20/1761
Avery, Christopher			MB - A23	
pd Isaac Tracy				
Susq Co		1 share*		10/20/1761
Avery, Christopher Junr			MB	
pd Isaac Tracy				
Susq Co		1/2 share	£4	8/24/1762
Avery, Humphrey	Norwich, New London, CT		B25	8/30/1773
Susq Co		1 share*	£8	9/2/1761
Avery, Humphrey	Winthrop, Suffolk, NY		MB - B83	11/9/1773
pd Isaac Tracy				
Susq Co		1 share*		10/20/1761
Avery, Humphrey			MB - A23	
pd Isaac Tracy				
Susq Co		1 share	£8	8/24/1762
Avery, Humphrey	Norwich		C18	3/16/1780
Susq Co		1 share*		8/24/1762
Avery, Humphrey Esq.			MB - A24	
pd Col. Elizr Talcott				

grantor grantee notes	grantor residence grantee residence	description location	amount acct bk page	deed date record date
Susq Co Avery, Humphrey Esq. *by Isaac Tracy*	 Norwich	1/2 share*	 MB	12/1/1762
Susq Co Avery, Isaac, Samuel & Siball		1 share each	£24 E398	8/27/1762 9/20/1796
Susq Co Avery, James *pd Isaac Tracy*		1 share*	 MB - A25	10/20/1761
Susq Co Avery, Latham, son of Ebenezer *pd Isaac Tracy*	 Groton, New London, CT	1 share*	£8 MB - B83	4/30/1761 11/9/1773
Susq Co Avery, Palmer *by Isaac Tracy*	 Norwich, New London, CT or	1 share*	£15 MB - B24	12/1/1762 8/30/1773
Susq Co Avery, Samuel *pd Isaac Tracy*		1 share*	 MB - A25	10/20/1761
Susq Co Avery, Samuel			 A360	
Susq Co Avery, Siball *by Isaac Tracy*	 Groton, New London, CT	1 share*	£15 MB - E395	12/1/1762 9/20/1796
Susq Co Avery, Solomon Jr. *pd Isaac Tracy*		1 share*	 MB - A25	10/20/1761
Susq Co Avery, Solomon s of Humphrey	 Norwich	1 share	£8 C18	8/24/1762 3/16/1780
Susq Co Avery, Waitstill	 Norwich, New London, CT	1 share	£15 B84	12/1/1762 11/9/1773
Susq Co Avery, William *pd Isaac Tracy*		1 share*	 MB - A24	10/20/1761
Susq Co Ayeres, Daniel		1/2 share No. 233, 300 A Bedford Twp	 I221	10/1/1785 7/3/1795
Susq Co Ayers, Peter			 MB - A361	7/18/1753
Susq Co Aylsworth, Phillip	 Coventry, Kent, RI	1 share	£8 B362	2/11/1762 9/15/1777
Susq Co Ayrault, Daniel Jr. *pd S Gray*	 RI	1 share*	$4 MB - Deed	5/29/1754
Susq Co Backus, Eben Esq. *pd Isaac Tracy*		1 share*	 MB	10/20/1761
Susq Co Backus, Elijah		1 share	 Deed	7/11/1754
Susq Co Backus, John *pd Journeying Cmte*		1 share*	$2 MB - Deed	7/18/1753
Susq Co Backus, John	 Hudson, Columbia, NY	1 share No. 42 of 600	 C571	7/13/1785 7/7/1795
Susq Co Backus, Simon		1 share	 Deed	7/11/1754
Susq Co Bacon, Andrew *pd Capn Uriah Stevens*		1/2 share*	 MB - A463 - Deed	11/20/1754
Susq Co Badcock, Babcock, Joseph *pd Jed Elderkin*		1/2 share*	 MB - Deed	5/1/1754
Susq Co Badcock/Babcock, Oliver		1 share	 Deed	7/11/1754
Susq Co Bailey, Benjamin		1,000 A unlocated lands	services E377	9/14/1796 9/14/1796

grantor grantee notes	grantor residence grantee residence	description location	amount acct bk page	deed date record date
Susq Co Bailey, John Jr.			A483	
Susq Co Baker, James pd Eliphalet Dyer		1/2 share*	MB	12/31/1755 1/15/1762
Susq Co Baker, Jonathan pd S Gray	Ashford	1 share*	$2 MB - Deed	7/18/1753
Susq Co Baker, Joshua Junr pd Eliphalet Dyer		1/2 share*	MB	12/31/1755 1/15/1762
Susq Co Baker, Nathaniel		1 share	Deed	7/11/1754
Susq Co Baldwin, Caleb	Newtown	1 share	$5 Deed - B102	2/11/1754 10/28/1773
Susq Co Baldwin, Capt Ebenezer	Norwich, New London, CT	1/2 share	£7.10 E255	12/13/1773 7/1/1796
Susq Co Baldwin, Daniel by Zachariah Clark	Sharon, Litchfield, CT	1/2 share*	£4 MB - B101	4/29/1773 10/29/1773
Susq Co Baldwin, Ebenezer pd Stephen Gardner; $1 advance money for settling expenses; pd Thomas Darling; should be on Deed	Norwich	1 share*	$5 MB - E255	1/14/1754 7/1/1796
Susq Co Baldwin, Ebenr by Samuel Gray		1/2 share*	MB	
Susq Co Baldwin, Henry		1/2 share No. 336 of 400	E356	10/1/1785 7/20/1796
Susq Co Baldwin, Isaac	Sheola, PA	1/2 share No. 276 of 400	I63	6/13/1786 6/13/1786
Susq Co Baldwin, James pd Thomas Darling	Derby, New Haven, CT	1/2 share*	$4.50 MB	12/31/1755
Susq Co Baldwin, John	Norwich, New London, CT	1 share	$4 Deed - B199	1/14/1754 4/1/1774
Susq Co Baldwin, Michael pd Daniel Edwards	Guilford, CT	1 share*	$9 MB - RB	12/24/1754 12/29/1768
Susq Co Baldwin, Silvanus	New Milford, Litchfield, CT	1/2 share	$4.50 B266	7/14/1755 11/2/1774
Susq Co Baldwin, Stephen pd Daniel Lyman	Guilford, New Haven, CT	1/2 share*	£4 MB - B32	5/6/1761 9/15/1773
Susq Co Baldwin, Thomas	Ulster Twp	1/2 share, No 279 of 600	C318	7/4/1786 3/5/1795
Susq Co Baldwin, Thomas entered 300 A in Abornton Twp	Sheshequin	1/2 share No. 270 of 400*	I64	5/8/1786 6/10/1786
Susq Co Baldwin, Thomas	Sheshequin	1/2 share No. 279 of 600 Ulster Twp	I64	7/4/1786 7/4/1786
Susq Co Baldwin, Waterman entered in Athens 5/10/1786	Athens Twp	1/2 share No. 256 of 400*	I61	9/10/1785 6/10/1786
Susq Co Baldwin, Waterman	Wyoming, PA	1/2 share	E303	11/14/1794 6/20/1796
Susq Co Ball, David			A243	
Susq Co Ballard, Stephen		1 share No. 97 of 600	I276	6/26/1793
Susq Co Ballard, Stephen		1/2 share No. 298 of 600	I276	6/26/1793
Susq Co Ballou, Noah	Cumberland, Providence, RI	1/2 share	£4 B321	7/28/1762 3/22/1775

grantor grantee notes	grantor residence grantee residence	description location	amount acct bk page	deed date record date
Susq Co		1 share*	$9	5/1/1755
Bancroft, Azariah	Schoharry [NY]*		RB	
pd Daniel Edwards; ; late of Stockbridge, MA				
Susq Co		1/2 share*	£1.7	5/1/1756
Bancroft, Ephriam	Windsor		H15	11/20/1798
entered 300 A in Murraysfield Twp by Stephen Tuttle, 1794				
Susq Co		1/2 share	£15*	8/22/1773
Banks, Ebenezer, Capt	Fairfield, Fairfield, CT		B110	12/23/1773
splitting cost of 1 share with Increase Bradley				
Susq Co		1/2 share*		8/27/1761
Banks, John Jr.			MB	
pd Zachariah Clark				
Susq Co				
Banks, Joseph			A239	
Susq Co		1 share*	$2	9/6/1753
Barber, David			MB - Deed	
pd Dewey & Bulkley				
Susq Co		1/2 share*		10/20/1761
Barber, John Rev			MB	
pd Isaac Tracy				
Susq Co		1/2 share*	$4.50	5/1/1755
Barker, Isaac	Branford, CT		RB	
pd Daniel Edwards				
Susq Co		1/2 share	$2.50	3/14/1754
Barker, John	Wallingford, New Haven, CT		Deed - E123	3/1/1796
Susq Co		1 share*	$2	7/18/1753
Barker, Nehemiah, Rev			MB - Deed	
pd Capt John Fitch				
Susq Co		1 share No 193 of 600, Lots 29 & 48		1/20/1792
Barlow, Nathan	Luzerne Co	Putnam Twp	I96	5/26/1794
Susq Co		1 share*	$2	7/18/1753
Barnam, Jehiel			MB - Deed	
pd Journeying Cmte				
Susq Co		1/2 share*		11/20/1754
Barnes, Abel			MB - Deed	
pd Capn Uriah Stevens				
Susq Co		1/2 share	$2.50	3/5/1754
Barnes, Nathaniel	New Haven		Deed - C31	2/2/1782
Susq Co		1 share	$5	3/9/1754
Barnes, Samuel			Deed - C29	2/6/1782
Susq Co		1 share*	$2	9/6/1753
Barnet, Moses			MB - B141 - Deed	2/17/1774
pd S Gray				
Susq Co		1/2 share*	$4.50	5/1/1755
Barr, John	Fairfield, CT		RB	
pd Daniel Edwards				
Susq Co		1 share*	£16.5	5/1/1754
Barton, Rowland			MB - Deed	
pd S Gray				
Susq Co		1/2 share*	£8.2.6	1/9/1754
Bass, Henry			MB - Deed	
pd S Gray				
Susq Co		1/2 share*	$4.50	12/31/1755
Bates, Benjamin	Darby		MB	
pd Thomas Darling				
Susq Co		1 share*	$2	7/18/1753
Bates, Caleb			MB - Deed	
pd Capt John Fitch				
Susq Co			£6.6	4/8/1772
Bates, Jonathan			D10	9/18/1795
Susq Co		1/2 share*		11/20/1754
Baulding, Baldwin, Gideon			MB - Deed	
pd Capn Uriah Stevens				

grantor	grantor residence	description	amount	deed date
grantee	grantee residence	location	acct bk page	record date
notes				
Susq Co		1/2 share No. 39 of 400		9/10/1785
Beach, Abner		Putnam Twp	I34	11/22/1786
Susq Co		1/2 share No. 105 of 400		10/1/1785
Beach, Alexander		Putnam Twp	I34	11/22/1786
Susq Co		1/2 share No. 41 of 400		9/10/1785
Beach, Joseph		Putnam Twp	I33	11/22/1786
Susq Co		1/2 share, No. 362 of 600		2/22/1794
Beach, Zerah	Amenia Precinct, NY		I77	9/7/1795
Susq Co		1/2 share, No. 363 of 600		2/22/1794
Beach, Zerah			I77	
Susq Co		1/2 share*	£4	4/30/1761
Beacher, David	New Haven, New Haven, CT		MB - B31	9/15/1773
by Daniel Lyman				
Susq Co		1 share		7/11/1754
Beacher, Ebenezer			Deed	
Susq Co				
Beal, George Sr.			A405	
Susq Co		1 share*	$9	5/1/1755
Beal, Matthew Sr.			RB	
pd Daniel Edwards				
Susq Co		1 share	$5 on acct.	2/23/1754
Beard, James Jr.	Stratford, Fairfield, CT		B255*	
Minute Book 2:35 references B255				
Susq Co		1 share		7/11/1754
Beardsley, Josiah			Deed	
Susq Co		1 share*		5/1/1754
Beckwith, Stephen			MB - Deed	
pd Jed Elderkin				
Susq Co		1/2 share	£6.6	4/8/1772
Beebee, Samuel	Long Island		D7	9/18/1795
Susq Co		1 share*	$9	12/31/1755
Beers, Nathan	New Haven		MB	
pd Thomas Darling				
Susq Co		1 share*	$2	7/18/1753
Belding, Ezra			MB - Deed	
pd Journeying Cmte				
Susq Co		1/2 share*	$2.50	5/1/1754
Belding, Thomas Jr.	Hartford Co		MB - Deed	
pd Thomas Stantly				
Susq Co		1/2 share		
Bellamy, Aaron			Deed	
Susq Co		1/2 share		
Bellamy, Moses			Deed	
Susq Co		1 share*	$9	5/2/1755
Benedick, Nathan	Danbury		MB	
pd Josiah Starr; certificate given 10/28/1774				
Susq Co		1 share	£8	10/1/1761
Bennet, Cornelius Dr.	Middleborough, Plymouth, MA		C89	9/30/1785
Susq Co		1/2 share, No 269 of 400		9/10/1785
Bennet, Elijah/Elisha			E124 - H285	2/13/1801
Susq Co		1 share		7/11/1754
Bennet, Ephraim			Deed	
Susq Co		1/2 share*	$4.50	7/15/1755
Bennet, Isaac	Preston, New London, CT		MB	1/31/1762
pd Eliphalet Dyer				
Susq Co		1/2 share No. 144 of 400		9/10/1785
Bennet, Jehmael		Athens Twp*	I61	6/10/1786
entered 5/10/1786				
Susq Co		1/2 share No. 72 of 400		9/10/1785
Bennet, Joshua			E266	7/8/1796
Susq Co		1/2 share*		5/1/1754
Bennet, Samuel			MB - Deed	
pd Jed Elderkin				

grantor grantee notes	grantor residence grantee residence	description location	amount acct bk page	deed date record date
Susq Co		1/2 share		9/10/1785
Bennett, Amos			D91 - H256	8/28/1798
Susq Co		1/2 share of 600*		1/15/1794
Bensly, John			I276	
No. not found				
Susq Co		1 share*	$4	1/9/1754
Berry, Nathaniel			MB - Deed	
pd S Gray				
Susq Co		1/2 share		7/11/1754
Bibbins, Ebenezer			MB - Deed	
Susq Co		1/2 share*	$2	1/9/1754
Bicknall, Zachariah			MB - Deed	
pd S Gray				
Susq Co		1 share No. 84 of 600		12/26/1793
Biddleman, Samuel/Baker, Samuel			I276	
Susq Co		300 A of 1/2 share No. 31 of the 400		
Bidlack, James	Athens, Luzerne, PA	Murraysfield Twp	H263	7/1/1795
Susq Co		1 share, No. 92 of 600*		12/25/1794
Bidlack, Sally & Bidlack, Mehitable	Athens, Luzerne, PA	Columbia; Murraysfield Twps	I188	3/19/1795
300 A, Lot 51 for Sally; 300 A, Lot 32 for Mehitable				
Susq Co		1/2 share*		11/20/1754
Bidwell, David			MB - Deed	
pd Capn Uriah Stevens				
Susq Co*		1/2 share	£4	5/1/1772
Bidwell, David Capt	Canaan CT & Stillwater NY		B138	2/2/1774
Samuel Gray, clerk, affidavit: Indians stole Bidwell's pocket book containing Company receipt				
Susq Co		1/2 share	£8.2.6	5/1/1772
Bidwell, David Capt	Canaan CT & Stillwater NY		B138	2/2/1774
Susq Co		1/2 share*	$4.50	5/1/1755
Bidwell, Isaac	Farmingham		RB	
pd Daniel Edwards				
Susq Co		1/2 share*	£3.5	3/13/1754
Bigelow, Asa			MB	
pd Maj. Charles Bulkley; should be on Deed				
Susq Co		1 share*	£6.10	11/20/1754
Bigelow, David			MB	
should be on Deed				
Susq Co		1/2 share*		5/1/1754
Bigelow, David Jr.			MB - Deed	
pd Jed Elderkin				
Susq Co		1/2 share*	£3.5	3/13/1754
Bigelow, John			MB	
pd Maj. Charles Bulkley; should be on Deed				
Susq Co		1/2 share No. 141 of 400		10/1/1785
Bigelow, Oliver		Athens Twp	I60	6/10/1786
entered 5/10/1786				
Susq Co		1/2 share		
Biggs, Miles			Deed	
Susq Co		1/2 share*	$2	1/9/1754
Bill, Benajah			MB - Deed	
pd S Gray				
Susq Co		1 share		7/11/1754
Bill, Ephriam			Deed	
Susq Co		1 share	$5	5/24/1754
Billings, Joseph Jr.	Preston, New London, CT		Deed - B140	2/17/1774
Susq Co		1 share	$5	5/23/1754
Billings, Stephen	Groton, New London, CT		Deed - B36 - E338	5/18/1776
Susq Co		2 shares No. 126 & 127 of 600		12/25/1793
Bingham, Charles			I276	
Susq Co		1,235 A, inc. an island		9/1/1787
Bingham, Chester	Ulster, Luzerne, PA	Ulster Twp	E389	9/14/1796
adj. s of Ulster; this is Chester's home tract				

grantor grantee notes	grantor residence grantee residence	description location	amount acct bk page	deed date record date
Susq Co		1/2 share	$2	1/10/1754
Bingham, Elijah			MB - A347 - B177	3/6/1774
Susq Co		1 share*	$2	7/18/1753
Bingham, Gideon	Canterbury, Windham, CT		MB - Deed	
pd Journeying Cmte				
Susq Co		1 share*		5/1/1754
Bingham, Joseph Jr.			MB - Deed - I50	
pd Jed Elderkin				
Susq Co		1/2 share		7/11/1754
Birch, Joshua			Deed	
Susq Co		1 share		7/11/1754
Birchard, John			Deed	
Susq Co		1 share		7/11/1754
Birchard, John 3rd			Deed	
Susq Co		1 share*		11/20/1754
Bird, James			MB - Deed - F7	
pd Capn Uriah Stevens				
Susq Co		1 share*		11/20/1754
Bird, Joseph Esq. et al*			MB - Deed - A469	
other names not given; pd Capn Uriah Stevens				
Susq Co		1 share*		11/20/1754
Bird, Thomas			MB - Deed - F7	
pd Capn Uriah Stevens				
Susq Co		1/2 share*	£4	8/16/1761
Bishop, Samuel Jr.	New Haven, New Haven CT		MB - B66	6/2/1773
pd Daniel Lyman				
Susq Co		1/2 share*	$4.50	5/1/1755
Blakeslee, Isaac	North Haven, CT		RB	
pd Daniel Edwards				
Susq Co		1 share*	$9	5/1/1755
Blakeslee, John			RB	
pd Daniel Edwards				
Susq Co		1 share*	$5	
Blakesley, James	Waterbury, New Haven, CT		MB	12/28/1768
pd Thomas Seymour				
Susq Co		1/2 share*	$4.50	11/27/1754
Blakesley, Reuben	Waterbury, New Haven, CT		MB	12/28/1768
pd Roger Wolcott Junr				
Susq Co		1/2 share*	$4.50	11/27/1754
Blakesley, Tilly	Waterbury, New Haven, CT		MB	12/28/1768
pd Roger Wolcott Junr				
Susq Co		1/2 share		5/25/1774
Blakesly, Tilly	Waterbury, CT		E406	
Susq Co		1 share		5/1/1754
Bliss, John			Deed	
Susq Co		1 share		7/11/1754
Boles, Thomas			Deed	
Susq Co				
Bolles, John			A302	
Susq Co		1/2 share		6/22/1770
Bolles, John Jr.			A346	
Susq Co		1 share*	£6.10	7/18/1753
Booth, Nathan	Farmington, Hartford, CT		MB - B100 - Deed	10/21/1773
pd S Gray				
Susq Co		1 share		7/11/1754
Boothe, Jonathan			Deed	
Susq Co		1 share No. 43 of 600		7/13/1785
Bortle, John Capt	Claverack NY	Towandee Cr., adj. to	I28	11/29/1786
Susq Co		1 share No. 44 of 600		7/13/1785
Bortle, John Capt	Claverack NY	Towandee Cr.	I28	11/29/1786

grantor grantee notes	grantor residence grantee residence	description location	amount acct bk page	deed date record date
Susq Co Bostick, Bushnel *pd Daniel Edwards*	New Milford, CT	1 share*	$9 RB	5/1/1755
Susq Co Bostick, Joseph *by Zachariah Clark*	Stratford	1/2 share*	MB	4/7/1763
Susq Co Bowen, Benjamin *pd S Gray*	RI	1 share*	£16.5 MB - Deed	5/29/1754
Susq Co Bowen, Jabez Esqr *pd S Gray*	RI	1 share*	£16.5 MB - Deed	5/29/1754
Susq Co Bowen, Penuel		1 share	Deed	7/11/1754
Susq Co Bowen, Samuel *for delivery of $4 to committee on Susq Affair*	Woodstock	receipt*	C50	1/9/1754 10/28/1782
Susq Co Boyington, Robert	Wallingford, New Haven, CT	1 share	$5 Deed - B103	3/5/1754 10/28/1773
Susq Co Bradford, James *pd S Gray*		1 share*	$2 MB - Deed	1/9/1754
Susq Co Bradford, John Capt *pd Eliphalet Dyer*		1/2 share*	MB	12/31/1755 1/15/1762
Susq Co Bradley, Joel *pd Daniel Edwards*	North Haven, CT	1/2 share*	$4.50 RB	5/1/1755
Susq Co Bradly, Increase *splitting cost of 1 share with Ebenezer Banks*	Fairfield, Fairfield, CT	1/2 share	£15* B110	8/22/1773 12/23/1773
Susq Co Bragg, Nicholas	Warwick, RI	1 share	$9 C127	4/12/1795
Susq Co Bragg, Nicholas *by Ezra Dean*	Warwick, RI	1/2 share*	MB	2/19/1763
Susq Co Branch, Thomas Jr.		1 share	Deed	7/11/1754
Susq Co Brayton/Braton, David *by Ezra Dean*	Coventry, Kent, RI	1/2 share*	$25 MB - B112	2/16/1763 12/22/1773
Susq Co Breed, Gershom		1 share	Deed	7/11/1754
Susq Co Brett, Cornelius	Dutchess, NY	1 share	£50 F239	8/30/1762 12/5/1794
Susq Co Briggs, Noah *pd S Gray*		1 share*	$2 MB - B259 - Deed	9/6/1753 10/6/1774
Susq Co Brink, Lambert *should be on Deed*			MB	
Susq Co Brockway, Richard	Great Nine Ptners, Dutchess,	1 share	$40 B247	3/10/1770 8/30/1774
Susq Co Brokaw, Abraham *by Isaac Tripp*		1/2 share*	MB - A319	7/27/1769
Susq Co Brown, Benjamin	Southhold, Suffolk, NY	1 share	£12 C21	6/20/1770 10/17/1780
Susq Co Brown, Beriah	RI	1 share	Deed	7/11/1754
Susq Co Brown, Daniel		1/2 share No. 12 of 400	E271	9/10/1785 6/6/1796

grantor grantee notes	grantor residence grantee residence	description location	amount acct bk page	deed date record date
Susq Co		1/2 share		10/1/1787
Brown, Ezekiel			E429	10/18/1796
Susq Co		300 A. Lot 1 of No. 161 of 400		10/1/1785
Brown, Humphrey		Allensburg Twp	I214	
Susq Co		1/2 share		12/1/1762
Brown, James	Providence, RI		MB	
by Isaac Tracy				
Susq Co		1 share*		12/31/1755
Brown, Samuel			MB - A299	1/15/1762
pd Timothy Woodbridge				
Susq Co		1 share*		4/8/1763
Brown, Samuel	Guilford		MB	
pd Elisha Sheldon				
Susq Co		1 share*		12/31/1755
Brown, Samuel Junr			MB	1/15/1762
pd Timothy Woodbridge				
Susq Co		1/2 share		7/11/1754
Brown, Thomas			Deed	
Susq Co		1/2 share*	$4.50	5/1/1755
Brown, Timothy	Windsor, CT		RB	
pd Daniel Edwards				
Susq Co		1 share*		7/6/1762
Brownson, Roger			MB	
pd Capt Elisha Sheldon				
Susq Co		1 share	£8	3/11/1762
Bruce, Robert	Canaan, Litchfield, CT		B326	2/20/1775
Susq Co		1/2 share*		11/20/1754
Bryant, Jeheil			MB - Deed	
pd Capn Uriah Stevens				
Susq Co		1 share	$40	7/5/1772
Buck, Aholiab	Wilkes Barre Twp		B247	8/30/1774
Susq Co		1 share	$40	7/12/1770
Buck, Asahel	Great Nine Ptners, Dutchess,		B246	8/30/1774
Susq Co		1 share	$40 + $2 tax*	11/5/1772
Buck, Elijah			B247	8/30/1774
equals £15				
Susq Co		1 share		7/11/1754
Buck, Jonathan	NY		Deed	
Susq Co		1 share*	$2	11/14/1753
Buck, William	Grt Nine Partners, Dutchess,		MB - B242 - Deed	8/30/1774
pd Journeying Cmte				
Susq Co		1 share		7/11/1754
Bucklin, John	RI		Deed - E65	
Susq Co		1 share	$5	5/29/1754
Bucklin, Joseph	Coventry, Kent, RI		MB - B317	3/7/1775
Susq Co		1 share*		12/1/1762
Budd, Benjamin	Southhold		MB	
by Isaac Tracy				
Susq Co		1 share		12/1/1762
Budd, John Capt	Southhold		MB	
by Isaac Tracy				
Susq Co		1 share*	£6.10	11/20/1754
Bulkley, Charles			MB	
should be on Deed				
Susq Co		1 share No. 68 of 600		7/13/1785
Bull, David	Hartford, Hartford, CT		C625	7/1/1795
Susq Co		1/2 share		
Bull, David			Deed	
Susq Co		1 share*		8/27/1761
Bull, Isaac			MB	
pd Elisha Sheldon				

grantor grantee notes	grantor residence grantee residence	description location	amount acct bk page	deed date record date
Susq Co		1 share*	£6.10	9/28/1753
Burge, Daniel			MB	
pd Charles Dewey; should be on Deed				
Susq Co		1 share		7/11/1754
Burghart, Hendrick Junr	NY		Deed	
Susq Co		1/2 share of 400, regrant, original lost		6/28/1794
Burnham, Asahel			I97	6/28/1794
Susq Co		1 share*		4/7/1763
Burnham, Elihu	Farmington		MB	
by Jonathan Root				
Susq Co		1 share	£12	2/18/1773
Burnham, Elizur	Glastonbury, Hartford, CT		B166	3/10/1774
Susq Co		1/2 share No. 212 of 400		10/1/1785
Burnham, Kenney		White Haven Twp	I97	6/28/1794
Susq Co		1/2 share		
Burr, Gideon			Deed	
Susq Co		1/2 share	$4.50	5/10/1755
Burr, John 1st	Fairfield, Fairfield, CT		B125	1/19/1774
Susq Co		1 share*	£3.5	3/13/1754
Burt, Joseph			MB - A243	
pd Maj. Charles Bulkley; should be on Deed				
Susq Co		1 share		7/11/1754
Burt, Thomas	RI		Deed	
Susq Co		1 share*		5/1/1754
Butler, Malachi	Windham		MB - Deed	
pd Jed Elderkin				
Susq Co		1 share*	$2	7/18/1753
Cady, Abijah			MB - Deed	
pd S Gray				
Susq Co				7/18/1753
Cady, William			MB	
Susq Co		1/2 share No. 79 of 400		9/10/1785
Cady, Zebulon		Putnam Twp	I32	11/22/1786
Susq Co		1 share*	$9	5/1/1755
Calling, Jonathan	Harwinton, CT		RB	
pd Daniel Edwards				
Susq Co		1/2 share	£4	2/7/1762
Campbell, Charles Jr.	Voluntown, Windham, CT		B259	10/6/1774
Susq Co				
Campbell, Charles Jr.			A94	
Susq Co		1/2 share	£4	2/11/1762
Campbell, Isaac	Voluntown, Windham, CT		B226	7/13/1774
Susq Co		600 A of 1 share No. 93 of 600		6/12/1793
Campbell, James	Tioga, PA	Juddsburgh Twp	H118 - I276	11/23/1799
entered 6/10/1793				
Susq Co		1/2 share		1/9/1754
Campbell, James Jr.			Deed - A93	
Susq Co		1 share	£3.5	1/9/1754
Campbell, John			MB - Deed	
Susq Co		1/2 share		1/9/1754
Campbell, John 3rd			MB	
Susq Co		1/2 share		
Campbell, John 3rd			Deed	
Susq Co		1/2 share*	$4.50	5/1/1755
Canfield, Joseph	New Milford		RB - A66	
pd Daniel Edwards				
Susq Co		1/2 share*	$4.50	5/1/1755
Canfield, Joseph	New Milford, CT		RB	
pd Daniel Edwards				
Susq Co		1/2 share*	$4.50	5/1/1755
Canfield, Samuel	New Milford, CT		RB	
pd Daniel Edwards				

grantor / grantee / notes	grantor residence / grantee residence	description / location	amount / acct bk page	deed date / record date
Susq Co		1 share No.90 of 600 inc Lot 14 Mfld		8/11/1794
Canfield, Seba		Murraysfield & Juddsburgh Twps	I276 - E355	
Susq Co		1/2 share*		12/1/1762
Carew, Samuel	Greenwich		MB	
by Isaac Tracy				
Susq Co		1 share	£12	8/3/1770
Carew, Simeon	Norwich, New London, CT		C80	12/25/1782
Susq Co		1 share	£8	2/12/1763
Cartwin, Samuel	NY		B315	3/7/1775
Susq Co		1 share*		3/31/1786
Cary, Barnabas		Putnam Twp	I32	11/25/1786
originally to be laid out in Muncy Cr. Twp				
Susq Co		1 share as a suffering settler*		12/24/1789
Cary, Eleazer, dec'd, heirs	Putnam	Putnam Twp	E181	
as per records review; entered 6/4/1795, Lot 7				
Susq Co		1/2 share No 1 of 400		9/10/1785
Cary, Nathan		Athens Twp*	I61	6/10/1786
entered on 5/10/1786				
Susq Co		1/2 share	£6	4/25/1770
Case, Caleb			B294 - C625	5/25/1774
Susq Co		1/2 share		7/11/1754
Case, Jacob			MB - Deed	
Susq Co		1/2 share		
Case, James			Deed	
Susq Co		1/2 share*	$2.50	3/13/1754
Case, Joseph			MB - Deed	
pd Thomas Darling				
Susq Co		1/2 share*		4/8/1763
Case, Zacheus	Simsbury		MB - A463	
pd Elisha Sheldon				
Susq Co		1 share*		8/28/1761
Casey, Samuel Esq.			MB	
pd Nathaniel Wales Junr Esq.				
Susq Co		1/2 share		
Casten, Constant			Deed	
Susq Co		1 share*		4/7/1763
Cater, Samuel	Dutchess County		MB	
by Zachariah Clark; Certificate given				
Susq Co		1/2 share No. 170 of the 400		9/10/1785
Center, Jonathan			E66	2/26/1796
Susq Co		1/2 share*	$1	10/2/1753
Chamberlain, John			MB	
pd Charles Dewey; should be on Deed				
Susq Co		1 share*	$4	1/9/1754
Chandler, Samuel Esq.			MB - Deed	
pd S Gray				
Susq Co		1 share*	$4	1/14/1754
Chandler, William Esq.			MB - Deed	
pd S Gray; one half of this share (1000 A) owned by John Chandler. See Whitelaw Papers, Mss 32.				
Susq Co		1/2 share*	£6	1/31/1770
Chapman, Noah	Colchester		MB - D9	9/18/1795
by Gershom Breed				
Susq Co		1/2 share	$4.50	6/12/1755
Chapman, Phineas	Fairfield, Fairfield, CT		B125	1/19/1774
Susq Co		1/2 share*	$4.50	5/1/1755
Chapman, Phinehas	Fairfield, CT		RB	
pd Daniel Edwards				
Susq Co		1/2 share*		2/19/1763
Chase, Abraham	Warwick, RI		MB	
by Ezra Dean				
Susq Co		1 share, No. 56 of 600		
Chase, Benjamin	Hudson, NY		H319	10/26/1802

grantor / grantee / notes	grantor residence / grantee residence	description / location	amount / acct bk page	deed date / record date
Susq Co		4 shares, Nos. 63, 64, 67, 68 of the		
Chase, Benjamin	Hudson		H333	5/21/1802
Susq Co		1 share, No. 55 of 600		
Chase, Benjamin	Hudson, Columbia, NY		H319	10/26/1802
Susq Co		1/2 share	£4	11/6/1762
Chatfield, Josiah			E409	9/15/1796
Susq Co		1/2 share*	$1	7/18/1753
Cheney, Ebenezer	Sturbridge		MB - Deed	
pd S Gray				
Susq Co		1 share*		8/28/1761
Chew, Joseph			MB - A296	
pd Nathaniel Wales Junr Esq.				
Susq Co		1/2 share*	£4	5/6/1761
Chidsey, Joseph	Guilford, New Haven, CT		MB - B32	9/15/1773
pd Danniel Lyman				
Susq Co		1/2 share*	£4	5/6/1761
Chittenden, Daniel Sr.	Guilford, New Haven, CT		MB - B32	9/15/1773
pd Daniel Lyman				
Susq Co		1/2 share	£6.6	4/8/1772
Chittenden, John & Chalker, Daniel			C622	7/1/1795
Susq Co		1 share	$5	5/29/1754
Choate, John			Deed - MB - I42	
Susq Co		1 share*	$5	5/1/1754
Church, Joseph	Hartford Co		MB - Deed	
pd Thomas Stantly				
Susq Co		1/2 share*		11/20/1754
Church, Samuel			MB - Deed	
pd Capn Uriah Stevens				
Susq Co		1/2 share	£6. 6	5/5/1772
Church, Silas			A363 - F49	5/1/1796
Susq Co		1 share*	$2	7/18/1753
Churchel, Giles			MB - Deed	
pd Journeying Cmte				
Susq Co		1 share*		5/20/1773
Churchill, Charles			MB	5/20/1773
by Samuel Gray				
Susq Co		1/2 share*		4/7/1763
Churchill, Jesse	Farmington		MB	
by Jonathan Root				
Susq Co		1 share*	£6.10	7/18/1753
Churchill, William			MB - Deed	
pd S Gray				
Susq Co		1 share*	$9	5/1/1755
Clap, Elijah	Hartford, CT		RB	
pd Daniel Edwards				
Susq Co		1 share*	$9	5/12/1755
Clapp, Elijah	Hartford, Hartford, CT		MB - B233	8/19/1774
pd Daniel Edwards				
Susq Co		1/2 share*	$2	10/9/1753
Clark, John			MB - B161	3/10/1774
should be on Deed				
Susq Co		300 A of 1/2 share No. 295 of 600		7/13/1785
Clark, John	Juddsburgh, PA	Juddsburgh Twp	C397	8/24/1795
laid out 6/26/1793				
Susq Co		1/2 share No. 295 of 600		6/26/1793
Clark, John			I276	
Susq Co		1 share*	$9	12/31/1755
Clark, William	Darby		MB - A243	
pd Thomas Darling				
Susq Co		1 share	$5	2/9/1754
Clark, Zachariah*	Stratford,	New Milford & Granby Twps	Deed - E473	11/28/1796
entered for heirs James, Nathan & Zachariah Clark 11/28/1796, 600 A New Milford, 1400 A Granby				

grantor grantee notes	grantor residence grantee residence	description location	amount acct bk page	deed date record date
Susq Co		1 share	$5	5/4/1754
Clarke, Abel			Deed - D11	9/18/1795
Susq Co		1/2 share*		4/1/1773
Cleaveland, Aaron			MB	4/1/1773
by Samuel Gray				
Susq Co		1 share*		11/20/1754
Cleaveland, Josiah			MB - Deed	
pd Capn Uriah Stevens				
Susq Co		1 share*	£12	7/31/1770
Clements, Jeremiah	Norwich, New London, CT		B235	8/20/1774
Susq Co		1 share*		5/1/1754
Clements, Jeremiah			MB - Deed	
pd Jed Elderkin				
Susq Co		1/2 share*	£4	5/11/1761
Cluckston, John			MB - B153	3/8/1774
pd Zachariah Clark				
Susq Co		1 share*		11/20/1754
Cochran, Samuel			MB - Deed	
pd Capn Uriah Stevens				
Susq Co		1/2 share*	$1	7/18/1753
Cogswell, John			MB - Deed	
pd Capt John Fitch				
Susq Co		1/2 share*	$4.50	5/1/1755
Cole, David	Fairfield, CT		RB	
pd Daniel Edwards				
Susq Co		1 share*	£8	11/9/1762
Cole, David	Farmington		MB	
pd Daniel Lyman				
Susq Co		1/2 share*	$4.50	5/1/1755
Cole, Ebenezer	N Hartford & Hatfield		RB	
pd Daniel Edwards				
Susq Co		1 share*	$9	5/1/1755
Cole, Samuel	Farmington, late Symesbury, CT		RB	
pd Daniel Edwards				
Susq Co		1/2 share*	$1	7/18/1753
Coleburt, John			MB - Deed	
pd Journeying Cmte				
Susq Co		1 share*	$2	7/18/1753
Colegrove, Francis			MB - Deed	
pd S Gray				
Susq Co		1 share*	$2	9/6/1753
Coleman, Niles			MB - Deed	
pd Dewey & Bulkley				
Susq Co		1/2 share		9/10/1785
Coleman, Thomas			I231	9/9/1795
Susq Co		1 share		7/11/1754
Collins, Benjamin			Deed	
Susq Co		1/2 share*	£4	5/6/1761
Collins, Daniel	Guilford, New Haven, CT		MB - B32	9/15/1773
pd Daniel Lyman				
Susq Co		1/2 share*	£4	5/6/1761
Collins, William	Guilford, New Haven, CT		MB - B32	9/15/1773
pd Daniel Lyman				
Susq Co		1 share*		
Colt, Harris wf			A302	
in Arch Turam right [not found]				
Susq Co		1/2 share*		5/1/1754
Colton, Eli			MB - Deed	
pd S Gray				
Susq Co		1 share*	£16.5	5/1/1754
Colvin/Callwell, Benjamin	Coventry, Kent, RI		MB - B291 - Deed	5/25/1774
pd S Gray				

grantor grantee notes	grantor residence grantee residence	description location	amount acct bk page	deed date record date
Susq Co		1/2 share*	$1	7/18/1753
Cone, John			MB - Deed	
pd Journeying Cmte				
Susq Co				
Congdon, Joseph			A302	
Susq Co		1/2 share*		4/23/1773
Convarse, Thomas			MB	4/23/1773
by Samuel Gray				
Susq Co		1 share		7/11/1754
Cook, John			Deed	
Susq Co		1/2 share		7/11/1754
Cook, Richard			MB - Deed	
Susq Co		1/2 share		
Cook, Samuel			A483 - G	
Susq Co		1 share*	£8	5/13/1761
Cooke, Nicholas	Providence, Providence, RI		MB - B233	11/15/1774
pd Isaac Tracy				
Susq Co		1/2 share	$4.50	5/10/1755
Cooley, David	Fairfield, Fairfield, CT		B125	1/19/1774
Susq Co				
Coon, John			A462	
Susq Co				
Cooper, Thomas			A88	
Susq Co		1/2 share		
Cornish, Elisha			Deed	
Susq Co		1 share		7/11/1754
Couch, Thomas			Deed	
Susq Co		1/2 share*	$25	2/12/1763
Cowan, Morgan	Warwick, Kent, RI		MB - B350	2/12/1763
by Ezra Dean				
Susq Co				
Cowels, Ebenezer			A89	
Susq Co		1 share		7/11/1754
Cowles, Josiah			Deed	
Susq Co		1/2 share*	£4	4/11/1761
Craft, Samuel	Pomfret, Windham, CT		MB - B169	3/11/1774
pd Nathaniel Wales Junr Esq.				
Susq Co		1/2 share		7/11/1754
Crandall, Nathaniel			Deed	
Susq Co		1/2 share*	$1	9/30/1753
Crary, Aaron			MB	
pd S Gray				
Susq Co		1/2 share*	$2	1/10/1754
Crary, Aaron			MB - Deed	
pd S Gray; inc $1 tax				
Susq Co		1 share*	$1 on acct. + $2	9/29/1753
Crary, Benjamin	Voluntown, Windham, CT		MB - B211 - Deed	5/15/1774
pd S Gray; amt. inc advance dollar; 2 receipts				
Susq Co		1/2 share*	$2 + 32s 6d	5/24/1754
Crary, Christopher	Voluntown, Windham, CT		MB - B140	2/17/1774
pd S Gray				
Susq Co		1 share		
Crary, Christopher			Deed	
Susq Co		1/2 share*	$1	9/29/1753
Crary, George	Voluntown, Windham, CT		MB - B287	2/3/1775
pd S Gray				
Susq Co		1/2 share*	$2	1/10/1754
Crary, George	Voluntown, Windham, CT		MB - B287 - Deed	2/3/1775
pd S Gray; inc $1 tax				
Susq Co		1/2 share*	$1	9/30/1753
Crary, Oliver	Voluntown, Windham, CT		MB - B290	2/3/1775
pd S Gray				

grantor grantee notes	grantor residence grantee residence	description location	amount acct bk page	deed date record date
Susq Co Crary, Oliver *pd S Gray; inc $1 tax*	Voluntown, Windham, CT	1/2 share*	$2 MB - B290 - Deed	1/10/1754 2/3/1775
Susq Co Crary, Robert Jr. *pd S Gray*	Voluntown, Windham, CT	1 share*	$2 MB - B140 - Deed	9/30/1753 2/17/1774
Susq Co Crary, William *pd S Gray*	Voluntown, Windham, CT	1/2 share*	$1 MB - Deed	7/18/1753
Susq Co Crawford, David *pd Zachariah Clark*		1/2 share*	MB	8/27/1761
Susq Co Culver, Samuel *pd Daniel Edwards*	Guilford & Litchfield	1/2 share*	$4.50 MB - RB	5/1/1755 12/28/1768
Susq Co Culver, Zebulon *pd Daniel Edwards*	Litchfield, CT	1/2 share*	$4.50 MB - RB	5/1/1755 12/28/1768
Susq Co Cunningham, Garwood *pd Thomas Darling*	Woodbury	1 share*	$9 MB	12/31/1755
Susq Co Curtice, Josiah *pd S Gray*		1 share*	£6.10 MB	7/18/1753
Susq Co Curtice, Josiah *pd Thomas Darling*	Stratford	1 share*	$9 MB - Deed	12/31/1755
Susq Co Curtice, Matthew		1 share	Deed	7/11/1754
Susq Co Curtice, Nathan *pd Thomas Darling*	Woodbury	1/2 share*	$4.50 MB	12/31/1755
Susq Co Curtice, Peter		1 share	Deed	7/11/1754
Susq Co Curtice, Samuel *pd Thomas Stantly*	Hartford Co	1/2 share*	$2.50 MB - Deed	5/1/1754
Susq Co Cushman, Nathaniel *pd Jed Elderkin*	Windham	1 share*	MB - Deed	5/1/1754
Susq Co Cutler, Beach			MB	7/18/1753
Susq Co Dana, Jacob	Ashford, Windham, CT	1/2 share	£6.10 MB - B199 - Deed	7/11/1754 4/2/1774
Susq Co Daniels, Nathaniel *pd Jed Elderkin*		1 share*	$2 MB - Deed	9/6/1753
Susq Co Darby, William *by Samuel Gray*	Canterbury	1/2 share*	MB - F63	4/1/1773 12/17/1796
Susq Co Darling, Samuel *pd Thomas Darling*	New Haven	1 share*	$9 MB	12/31/1755
Susq Co Darling, Thomas Esq. *pd Thomas Darling*		1 share*	$9 MB	12/31/1755
Susq Co Darrow, Zadoc	New London	1 share	£12 C42	6/20/1770 5/27/1782
Susq Co Dart, Ebenezer	Middletown	1 share	$9 B262	7/20/1755 10/20/1774
Susq Co Dart, Ebenezer *under vote of 1/6/1768*	Chatham	1 share*	9s E89	4/8/1768 3/4/1796

grantor grantee notes	grantor residence grantee residence	description location	amount acct bk page	deed date record date
Susq Co		300 A		6/18/1799
Dart, Samuel		Smithfield Twp*	H70	6/11/1799
Pitch in Muncy Twp withdrawn and entered in Smithfield, Lot 28				
Susq Co		1 share*	£12	4/6/1770
Dart, William	Bolton, Hartford, CT		MB - B139	2/4/1774
by Ebenr Backus				
Susq Co		1 share		7/11/1754
Davison, Joseph Esqr			Deed	
Susq Co		1/2 share*	$2	7/27/1769
Daviss, Isaac			MB - A318	
by Isaac Tripp				
Susq Co		1/2 share*	$4.50	5/1/1755
Daviss, Samuel	Fairfield, CT		RB	
pd Daniel Edwards				
Susq Co		1/2 share*		11/20/1754
Day, Thomas			MB - Deed	
pd Capn Uriah Stevens				
Susq Co		1 share		2/3/1754
Dean, Elijah			Deed - A402	
Susq Co		1/2 share*	$2.50	1/9/1754
Dean, Ephriam	Taunton		MB - Deed	
pd S Gray				
Susq Co			$2	
Dean, Ezra			A81	
Susq Co		1 share		7/11/1754
Dean, Jabez			Deed	
Susq Co		1 share*		11/20/1754
Dean, John	Salisbury, Litchfield, CT		MB - Deed	
pd Capn Uriah Stevens				
Susq Co		1 share*	$2	7/18/1753
Dean, Josiah Jr.	Cannan		MB - Deed - G	
pd Journeying Cmte				
Susq Co				7/18/1753
Dean, Nathaniel Jr.			MB	
Susq Co		1 share	£3.5	5/29/1754
Dean, Seth			MB - Deed	
Susq Co		1/2 share*	$2.50	1/10/1754
Dean, Simeon	Taunton		MB - Deed	
pd S Gray				
Susq Co		400 A	services rendered	1/27/1796
Decker, Henry		Susquehanna Purchase	E530	1/27/1797
Susq Co		1 share*	$5	2/8/1754
Deforrest, Samuel			Deed - E125	3/1/1796
pd $2 on 11/25/1754				
Susq Co				
Deming, Ebenezer			A38	
Susq Co		1/2 share*	$4.50	5/1/1755
Deming, Ebenezer	Weathersfield, CT		RB	
pd Daniel Edwards				
Susq Co		1 share*		5/20/1773
Deming, Janna			MB	5/20/1773
by Samuel Gray				
Susq Co		1 share	£6.10	10/11/1753
Demming, Gideon	Weathersfield		MB - B303 - Deed	1/17/1775
1/2 share to Amos Bidwell and certificate given, but Amos Bidwell not on Deed as an original proprietor.				
Susq Co		1/2 share*		11/20/1754
Demmon, Hezekiah			MB - Deed	
pd Capn Uriah Stevens				
Susq Co		1 share	£16. 5	5/5/1754
Denison, Joseph	Norwich, New London, CT		B316	3/7/1775
Susq Co		1 share		7/11/1754
Denniss, George			Deed - E330	

grantor grantee notes	grantor residence grantee residence	description location	amount acct bk page	deed date record date
Susq Co		1 share	$5	4/17/1775
Depew, Samuel			B339	11/27/1775
Susq Co		1 share		7/11/1754
DeRidder, Kiliaen	NY		Deed	
Susq Co		1 share*		9/28/1753
Dewey, Charles			MB	
pd Charles Dewey; should be on Deed				
Susq Co		1 share		7/11/1754
Dewey, David			Deed	
Susq Co		1 share*		5/1/1754
Dewey, Noah			MB - Deed	
pd Jed Elderkin				
Susq Co		1 share No. 100 of 600		6/26/1793
Dewitt, Paul			I276	
Susq Co		1 share No. 99 of 600		7/13/1785
Dewitt, William	Tioga Twp, PA		C398 - I276	8/23/1795
Susq Co		8000 A		3/1/1795
Dimock, David	Pittstown, Luzerne, PA	Dimock Pitch*	D82	12/4/1795
btw Exeter and Greenfield Twps				
Susq Co		1 share		7/11/1754
Dimock, Israel			Deed	
Susq Co		1 share*	$2	9/6/1753
Dixon, Barnet			MB - B141 - Deed	2/17/1774
pd S Gray				
Susq Co		1 share*	$2	9/6/1753
Dixon, James Jr.			MB - B141 - Deed	2/17/1774
pd S Gray				
Susq Co		1 share*	$2	7/18/1753
Dixon, John			MB - Deed	
pd Capt John Fitch				
Susq Co		1 share*		12/14/1793
Dixon, John, decd	Voluntown		C540	
Certificate fr Sam Gray: John Dixon was OP of 1 share; he sold 1/2 to son Robert Dixon so heirs entitled to only 1/2 share				
Susq Co		1 share*	$2	7/18/1753
Dixon, Robert			MB - Deed	
pd Capt John Fitch				
Susq Co		1 share No. 98 of 600		6/26/1793
Dobbin, William	Tioga Twp, PA	Juddsburg Twp	E135 - I276	3/29/1796
Susq Co		1/2 share	$4.50	11/20/1754
Dodd, Benjamin	Hartford, Hartford, CT		B291	5/25/1774
Susq Co		1 share		7/11/1754
Dodge, David Jur.			Deed	
Susq Co		1/2 share*		10/20/1761
Dolbeare, George			MB	
pd Isaac Tracy				
Susq Co		1/2 share		7/11/1754
Done, Eleazar			Deed	
Susq Co		1 share	$4	1/9/1754
Dorrance, George	Scituate, Providence, RI		Deed - B376	1/10/1778
Susq Co		1 share*	$4	1/9/1754
Dorrance, Gersham			MB - Deed	
pd S Gray				
Susq Co		1 share*	$2	7/18/1753
Dorrance, John			MB - Deed	
pd S Gray				
Susq Co		1 share	$4	1/9/1754
Dorrance, Michael	Scituate, Providence, RI		Deed - B376	1/13/1778
Susq Co		1 share	$4	1/9/1754
Dorrance, Samuel	Scituate, Providence, RI		Deed - B376	1/13/1778
Susq Co		1 share		
Dorrance, Samuel			Deed	

grantor grantee notes	grantor residence grantee residence	description location	amount acct bk page	deed date record date
Susq Co		1 share*	$2	9/19/1753
Dorrance, Samuel, Rev	Voluntown, Windham, CT		MB - B211	5/15/1774
pd S Gray				
Susq Co		1 share*	$2	7/18/1753
Douglas, Asa			MB - Deed	
pd Journeying Cmte				
Susq Co		1 share*		5/1/1754
Douglas, James			MB - Deed	
pd S Gray				
Susq Co		1/2 share	£8.2.6	2/11/1754
Douglas, Samuel	New Hartford, Litchfield, CT		B82	10/11/1773
Susq Co		1 share*	£8	4/2/1763
Douglas, Samuel	New Hartford, Litchfield, CT		MB - B333	10/7/1775
pd Elisha Sheldon				
Susq Co		1/2 share*		11/20/1754
Douglas, Samuel			MB - Deed	
pd Capn Uriah Stevens				
Susq Co		1/2 share*	$4.50	10/11/1773
Douglas, Samuel	New Hartford, Litchfield, CT		B82	10/11/1773
Susq Co		1/2 share	£6.6	4/8/1772
Douglass, Daniel	Saybrook, Middlesex, CT		C352	3/2/1795
Susq Co		1/2 share*		10/20/1761
Douglass, Daniel			MB	
pd Isaac Tracy				
Susq Co		1 share No 159 of 600		7/13/1785
Douglass, Daniel & Israel	Saybrook, Middlesex, CT		C352	3/2/1795
Susq Co		1 share	£3.5 - $2	12/11/1754
Douglass, James	Voluntown CT		MB - C244	9/2/1799
Susq Co		1/2 share*	$2	1/9/1754
Douglass, Samuel	Voluntown		MB - Deed	
pd S Gray				
Susq Co		1/2 share*	$4.50	5/1/1755
Douglass, Samuel	N. Hartford, CT		RB	
pd Daniel Edwards				
Susq Co				7/18/1753
Douglass, Thomas			MB	
Susq Co		1 share*	$2	7/18/1753
Downer, Richard			MB - Deed	
pd Journeying Cmte				
Susq Co		1 share*	$2	7/18/1753
Downing, David			MB - Deed	
pd S Gray				
Susq Co				
Downing, Perigo & Jonathan			A330	
Susq Co		1 share		7/11/1754
Drake, Asahel			Deed	
Susq Co		1/2 share*		12/6/1789
Drake, Elisha			I34	12/6/1786
taxes pd				
Susq Co		1 share		7/11/1754
Drake, Jacob			Deed	
Susq Co		1 share		7/11/1754
Drake, Jacob Junr			Deed	
Susq Co				
Drake, John*			MB	
should be on Deed				
Susq Co				
Drake, Samuel*			MB	
should be on Deed				
Susq Co		1 share		7/11/1754
Draper, Simeon	RI		Deed	
Susq Co		1 share		7/11/1754
Drown, Samuel	RI		Deed	

grantor grantee notes	grantor residence grantee residence	description location	amount acct bk page	deed date record date
Susq Co Dudley, Jared *by Daniel Lyman*		1/2 share*	MB - B31	1/1/1762 9/15/1773
Susq Co Dudley, Medad *pd Danniel Lyman*	Guilford, New Haven, CT	1/2 share*	£4 MB - B32	5/6/1761 9/15/1773
Susq Co Dudley, Oliver Capt *pd Daniel Edwards*	Guilford, CT	1 share*	$9 MB - RB	12/24/1754 12/29/1768
Susq Co Dunham, James *pd Capn Uriah Stevens*		1 share*	MB - Deed	11/20/1754
Susq Co Dunlap, Joshua *pd S Gray*		1/2 share*	$2 MB - B200 - Deed	1/9/1754 4/5/1774
Susq Co Durkee, Jeremiah			A324	
Susq Co Durkee, John Maj. *pd Isaac Tracy*		1/2 share*	MB - A89	10/20/1761
Susq Co Durkee, Robert			A460	
Susq Co Durkee, William		1/2 share No. 299 of 600	I276	10/12/1793
Susq Co Dyer, Eliphalet *pd Capt John Fitch*		1 share*	$2 MB - Deed	7/18/1753
Susq Co Earl, Benjamin		1/2 share	I98	10/5/1785 5/26/1794
Susq Co Earl, Jeptha		1/2 share No. 81 of 400 Putnam Twp	C325 - I34	9/10/1785 11/22/1786
Susq Co Earl, Joseph		1/2 share No. 104 of 400 Putnam Twp	I32	10/1/1785 12/6/1786
Susq Co Eaton, Joseph *pd Capt John Fitch*		1 share*	$2 MB - Deed	7/18/1753
Susq Co Eddy, John		1/2 share	Deed	7/11/1754
Susq Co Edgerton, John		1 share	Deed	7/11/1754
Susq Co Edwards, Daniel *pd Thomas Stantly*	Hartford Co	1 share*	$5 MB - Deed	5/1/1754
Susq Co Elderkin, Jedediah *pd Capt John Fitch*		1 share*	$2 MB - Deed	7/18/1753
Susq Co Elderkin, John *pd Jed Elderkin*		1 share*	MB - Deed	5/1/1754
Susq Co Elderkin, Joshua *pd Capt John Fitch*		1 share*	$2 MB - Deed	7/18/1753
Susq Co Ellery, Benjamin *pd Major Elizer Talcott*		1/2 share*	MB	8/27/1761
Susq Co Elliot, Christopher	Dover Twp	1 share	£15.5 C28 - E442	1/24/1755 1/16/1786
Susq Co Elliot, Jared *pd Daniel Edwards*		1 share*	$9 (pd $7, owes $2) RB	5/1/1755
Susq Co Elliot, John *pd Thomas Darling*	New Haven	1 share*	$9 MB	12/31/1755

grantor grantee notes	grantor residence grantee residence	description location	amount acct bk page	deed date record date
Susq Co		1 share No. 157 of 600		
Elliot, William	Saybrook, CT		F120	6/6/1796
Susq Co		1 share No. 158 of 600		
Elliot, William	Saybrook, CT		F120	6/6/1796
Susq Co		1/2 share No. 98 of 400*		10/1/1785
Elster, Casper			E64	
pd John Franklin; requires 3 yrs residence				
Susq Co		1 share*		8/27/1761
Elsworth, John			MB	
pd Major Elizer Talcott				
Susq Co		1 share		7/11/1754
Ely, Daniel			Deed	
Susq Co		1/2 share*	$4.50	4/24/1755
Ely, Eunice			MB	12/28/1768
pd Phineas Lyman				
Susq Co		1 share*		11/20/1754
Ely, James			MB	
pd Stephen Gardner; should be on Deed				
Susq Co		1 share		6/1/1775
Ely, Samuel	Lyme, New London, CT		A301	
Susq Co		1/2 share	£6 promissory note	8/24/1770
Emerick, Andrew	West Branch Susq R.		B176	3/14/1774
Susq Co		1 share*		11/20/1754
Emerson, Nathaniel			MB	
pd Stephen Gardner; should be on Deed				
Susq Co		1/2 share*		7/6/1762
Enno, Samuel Junr			MB	
pd Capt Elisha Sheldon				
Susq Co		1/2 share		5/24/1774
Eno, Samuel	Windsor		F2	3/1/1796
Susq Co		1/2 share*	£4	9/3/1761
Eno, Samuel	Windsor		MB	
pd Elisha Sheldon				
Susq Co		1/2 share No 46 of the 400		9/10/1785
Enos, Ebenezer			E438	10/1/1796
Susq Co		1 share*		11/20/1754
Ensign, Eliphalet			MB - Deed	
pd Capn Uriah Stevens				
Susq Co		1/2 share No. 275 of 400		10/1/1785
Evans, Zeba	Murraysfield Twp*		E439	10/1/1796
entered on Lot 11				
Susq Co.		1/2 share No. 322 of the 400		10/1/1785
Evelyn, Frederick			E66	8/27/1774
Susq Co		1/2 share No. 45 of 400		9/10/1785
Evelyn, Frederick Jr.			E65	8/27/1774
Susq Co		1 share*		11/20/1754
Everitt, Josiah Capt			MB - Deed	
pd Capn Uriah Stevens				
Susq Co		1 share		7/11/1754
Everitt, Timothy			Deed	
Susq Co		1 share*	$2	7/18/1753
Ewings, Edward Junr			MB - Deed	
pd S Gray				
Susq Co		1 share*	£13	1/9/1754
Farnam, Zebadiah			MB - B199 - Deed	4/2/1774
pd S Gray				
Susq Co		1/2 share		7/11/1754
Fay, Judah			Deed	
Susq Co		1 share	£8	1/4/1772
Fellows, Abiel	Canaan, Litchfield, CT		B19	6/26/1772
Susq Co		1/2 share*		11/20/1754
Fellows, John			MB - Deed	
pd Capn Uriah Stevens				

grantor grantee notes	grantor residence grantee residence	description location	amount acct bk page	deed date record date
Susq Co Fellows, Joseph *pd Capn Uriah Stevens*		1/2 share*	MB - Deed	11/20/1754
Susq Co Fellows, Nathan			MB	7/18/1753
Susq Co Fellows, Thomas *pd Capn Uriah Stevens*		1/2 share*	MB - Deed	11/20/1754
Susq Co Fellows, William *pd Capn Uriah Stevens*		1 share*	MB - Deed	11/20/1754
Susq Co Fish, John* *should be on Deed*			MB	
Susq Co Fish, Moses *pd S Gray*		1 share*	£13 MB - Deed	1/9/1754
Susq Co Fish, Thomas	Groton, New London, CT	1 share	$5 Deed - B380	5/25/1754 4/1/1778
Susq Co Fitch, Adonajah & Daniel *pd Eliphalet Dyer*		1 share*	MB - A285	12/31/1755 1/15/1762
Susq Co Fitch, Ebenezer		1 share	gratuitous MB - B323	3/17/1775 3/30/1775
Susq Co Fitch, Eleazar Esq. *pd Jed Elderkin*		1 share*	$2 MB - Deed	7/18/1753
Susq Co Fitch, Felch, Ebenezer *entered on Lot 17, 1st Div.*	Huntington PA	1/2 share No. 286 of 600 Columbia Twp*	I95 - I276	11/1/1793 11/30/1793
Susq Co Fitch, Jabez Esq.		1 share	MB - Deed	7/18/1753
Susq Co Fitch, Jabez Jr.			MB	7/18/1753
Susq Co Fitch, John *300 A, see deed for metes & bounds; [I214 and Liber A, Volume 2 conflict over 1/2 or 1 share]*	Luzerne Co PA	1 share No. 186 of 400 Northmoreland Twp	I214	6/21/1795
Susq Co Fitch, John Capt *pd Jed Elderkin*		1 share*	$2 MB - Deed	7/18/1753
Susq Co Fitch, John Jr.		1 share	Deed	
Susq Co Fitch, Jonathan		1/2 share	Deed	
Susq Co Fitch, Samuel *pd Daniel Edwards*	Guilford, CT	1/2 share*	$4.50 MB - RB	12/24/1754 12/29/1768
Susq Co Fitch, William *pd S Gray*		1 share*	$2 MB - Deed	1/9/1754
Susq Co Flagg, Samuel *pd Jed Elderkin; pd $2 tax 1/12/1754; pd the advance $1 but no date*		1 share*	MB - E250 - Deed	5/1/1754
Susq Co Fletcher, Cotton *pd Capn Uriah Stevens*		1/2 share*	MB - Deed	11/20/1754
Susq Co Fletcher, Ebenezer *pd Capn Uriah Stevens*		1 share*	MB - Deed	11/20/1754
Susq Co Follet, Benjamin *pd S Gray*		1/2 share*	£8.2.6 MB - Deed	1/9/1754

grantor grantee notes	grantor residence grantee residence	description location	amount acct bk page	deed date record date
Susq Co		1 share*		5/1/1754
Follet, Joseph	Windham		MB - Deed	
pd Jed Elderkin				
Susq Co		1/2 share*	$2	10/9/1753
Foot, Charles			MB - B161	3/10/1774
should be on Deed				
Susq Co		1 share*	£6.10	10/9/1753
Foot, Daniel			MB	
should be on Deed				
Susq Co		1/2 share	$4.50	12/18/1754
Ford, John	Brentford		D172	7/2/1796
Susq Co		1/2 share*	$4.50	5/1/1755
Ford, John	Branford, CT		RB	
pd Daniel Edwards				
Susq Co		1/2 share*		11/20/1754
Ford, Samuel			MB - Deed	
pd Capn Uriah Stevens				
Susq Co		1 share, No 81 of the 600		11/1/1785
Forsman, Hugh & Robert		Ulster Twp*	H213	5/5/1800
1/2 of the share laid out for Hugh Forsman in Ulster, 1786				
Susq Co		1/2 share*		12/31/1755
Fortune, Jonah			MB	1/15/1762
pd Timothy Woodbridge				
Susq Co		1/2 share No. 300 of 600		
Foster, Abiel	Tioga, PA		I191	3/19/1795
Susq Co		1/2 share No. 300 of the 600		
Foster, Abiel	Tioga, PA		I276	3/19/1795
Susq Co		1/2 share*	£6	4/1/1773
Foster, William	Canterbury, Windham, CT		MB - B227	7/6/1774
by Samuel Gray				
Susq Co		1/2 share*	$4.50	12/24/1754
Fowler, Ebenr Jr. & Culver, Samuel	Guilford & Litchfield		MB - RB	12/29/1768
pd Daniel Edwards				
Susq Co		1/2 share*	£4	4/9/1761
Fowler, Timothy	Guilford, New Haven, CT		MB - B32	9/15/1773
pd Daniel Lyman				
Susq Co		1/2 share	£6	7/31/1770
Fox, Benjamin	New London, New London, CT		C559	6/20/1795
Susq Co		1 share*	$2	7/18/1753
Francis, Elijah			MB - Deed	
pd Journeying Cmte				
Susq Co		1,000 A	services	9/14/1796
Franklin, Arnold		unlocated lands	E377	9/14/1796
Susq Co		1/2 share No. 205 of 400	3 yr residency	10/1/1785
Franklin, Jehiel			C116	2/26/1795
Susq Co		1 share*		11/20/1754
Franklin, John			MB - Deed	
pd Capn Uriah Stevens				
Susq Co		1 share No. 77 of 600		5/1/1786
Franklin, John	Wyoming	Athens Twp	I58	5/20/1786
Susq Co		1 share No. 79 of 600		6/28/1786
Franklin, John	Wyoming	Athens 1/2; White Haven 1/2	I58	7/10/1786
Susq Co		1 share No. 80 of 600		6/28/1786
Franklin, John	Wyoming	Juddsburgh Twp	I58	7/10/1786
Susq Co		1 share	$5	2/8/1754
Franklin, John	Canaan, Litchfield, CT		I189	9/1/1794
Susq Co		1/2 share No. 32 of 400		
Franklin, John	Athens		F252	1/1/1794
Susq Co		1 share, No. 85 of 600		
Franklin, John	Athens	Savannah Twp*	F252	2/28/1795
entered 2000 A, Feb 1795				

grantor grantee notes	grantor residence grantee residence	description location	amount acct bk page	deed date record date
Susq Co		1 share, No. 86 of 600		
Franklin, John	Athens	SavannahTwp*	F252	2/28/1795
entered 2000 A, Feb 1795				
Susq Co		1 share, No. 122 of 600		
Franklin, John et al*	Athens	Beebesburgh & Murraysfield Twps*	H126	11/26/1799
300 A Ira Stephens; 300 A, Lot 40 Samuel McAlhoes; remainder John Franklin				
Susq Co		1/2 share*	$4.50	5/1/1755
Freeman, Capt Nathaniel	Middletown, CT		RB	
pd Daniel Edwards				
Susq Co		1 share		7/11/1754
French, John			Deed	
Susq Co		1/2 share*	$4.50	12/31/1755
French, Samuel	Darby		MB	
pd Thomas Darling				
Susq Co				
French, Solomon			A401	
Susq Co		1 share	$2	1/11/1754
Frink, Elias			MB - Deed	
Susq Co		1/2 share*	£6:10	1/9/1754
Frink, Elias, Jr.			MB - Deed	
pd S Gray				
Susq Co		1/2 share	£4	12/12/1754
Frisbie, Daniel	Branford, New Haven, CT		B31	9/15/1773
Susq Co		1/2 share*	£4	4/24/1761
Frisbie, James	Branford, New Haven, CT		MB - B171	3/9/1774
pd Daniel Lyman				
Susq Co		1/2 share*	$4.50	5/1/1755
Frisbye, Daniel	Branford & Hartford, CT		RB	
pd Daniel Edwards				
Susq Co		1/2 share	$4.50	5/15/1755
Frotheringham, Ebenezer			E341	6/15/1796
Susq Co		1/2 share*	$4.50	5/1/1755
Frothingham, Ebenezer	Weathersfield, CT		RB	
pd Daniel Edwards				
Susq Co		1 share No. 132 of 600		12/25/1793
Fuller, John & Marshall, Josiah			I276	9/15/1796
Susq Co		1 share		7/11/1754
Fuller, Stephen			Deed	
Susq Co		1 share*		5/1/1754
Gale, Benjamin			MB - Deed	
pd Jed Elderkin				
Susq Co		1 share	$3	7/11/1754
Gallop, Isaac	Volentown		Deed	
Susq Co		1/2 share*		10/20/1761
Gallop, Nathan			MB	
pd Isaac Tracy				
Susq Co		1/2 share*	£4	4/25/1761
Gallop, William	Groton, New London, CT		MB - B173	3/9/1774
pd Isaac Tracy				
Susq Co		1 share*	£15	12/1/1762
Gallup, William	Groton, New London, CT		MB - B241	8/20/1774
by Isaac Tracy				
Susq Co		1 share	$4.	1/5/1754
Gardiner, Ephriam	Stonington, New London, CT		B355	4/4/1777
Susq Co		1 share	$9	3/10/1755
Gardner, Benoni	Exeter, Kings, RI		B167	3/10/1774
Susq Co		1 share*		6/23/1761
Gardner, Christian Capt			MB - A90	
pd Nathaniel Wales, Junr, Esq.				
Susq Co		1 share		7/11/1754
Gardner, Ephriam			Deed	

grantor grantee notes	grantor residence grantee residence	description location	amount acct bk page	deed date record date
Susq Co		1 share*	£8	6/23/1761
Gardner, John Capt	James Town, RI		MB - B224	6/29/1774
pd Nathaniel Wales, Junr, Esq.				
Susq Co		1 share*		12/1/1762
Gardner, John Hon Esq.	Newport		MB	
by Isaac Tracy				
Susq Co		1 share*	$2	10/8/1753
Gardner, Jonathan			MB - B241 - Deed	8/28/1774
pd S Gray				
Susq Co		1 share*	$2	10/8/1753
Gardner, Stephen			MB - B241 - Deed	8/28/1774
pd S Gray				
Susq Co		1 share*	$2	10/8/1753
Gardner, Stephen Jr.			MB - B241 - Deed	8/28/1774
pd S Gray				
Susq Co		1/2 share of 400		7/13/1785
Garner, Lebbeus			C199	12/5/1794
Susq Co		1 share	£16. 5	1/29/1754
Garnsey, Ebenezer	Woodbury, Litchfield, CT		B377	3/13/1778
Susq Co		1 share No. 113 of 600		12/25/1793
Garskill, Silas & Jonathan	Union, NY		E329 - I276	4/10/1796
Susq Co		1 share	£15	5/1/1754
Gaston, Alexander	Voluntown, Windham, CT		B106	12/15/1773
Susq Co		1 share*	£9.15	5/1/1754
Gaston, Alexander			MB - Deed	
pd S Gray				
Susq Co		1 share*	$2	9/6/1753
Gaston, John			MB - B224 - Deed	6/14/1774
pd S Gray				
Susq Co		1/2 share No 166 of 400		
Gaylord, Ambrose			E329	4/10/1795
Susq Co		1/2 share No. 86 of 400		9/10/1785
Gaylord, Justin Jr.		Athens Twp*	I65	6/10/1786
entered 6/1/1786				
Susq Co		1/2 share*	£4	4/26/1761
Geer, Amos	Norwich, New London, CT		MB - B83	11/5/1773
pd Isaac Tracy				
Susq Co		1 share	$9	5/1/1755
Geer, Ebenezer	Groton, New London, CT		B259	
Susq Co		1/2 share	$4.50	5/1/1755
Geer [Gere], Robert			B83	11/5/1773
Susq Co		1/2 share	£8.5	5/29/1754
Geers, Benjamin	Groton, New London, CT		Deed - B381	4/9/1778
Susq Co		1/2 share	£8.5	5/29/1754
Geers, Jacob	Groton, New London, CT		Deed - B381	4/9/1778
Susq Co		1 share		7/11/1754
Gennings, Jonathan			Deed	
Susq Co		1/2 share	$4.50	6/12/1755
Gennings/Jennings, Joshua	Fairfield, Fairfield, CT		B110	12/23/1773
Susq Co		1 share*	$5	11/21/1754
Gerauld, Duty			MB - B89	11/23/1773
should be on Deed				
Susq Co				
Gilbert, Samuel			A51	
Susq Co		1 share*	£16. 5	1/9/1754
Gilbert/Gilbrett, Noah			MB - A327 - Deed	
pd S Gray				
Susq Co		1 share		7/11/1754
Giles, Benjamin			Deed	
Susq Co		1 share		7/11/1754
Giles, Thomas			Deed	

grantor grantee notes	grantor residence grantee residence	description location	amount acct bk page	deed date record date
Susq Co		1 share*	£8	4/29/1761
Giles, Thomas	Groton, New London, CT		MB - I179	2/22/1795
pd Isaac Tracy				
Susq Co		1 share	£16.5	5/13/1754
Giles, Thomas	Groton, New London, CT		I179	2/22/1795
Susq Co				
Gillet, John			A486	
Susq Co		1/2 share*	$4.50	5/1/1755
Ginnings, Joshua	Fairfield, CT		RB	
pd Daniel Edwards				
Susq Co		1 share	£12	8/3/1770
Glover, Grover	Long Island		C44	12/5/1782
Susq Co				
Goalden/Golden, Pierce*			MB	
should be on Deed				
Susq Co		1 share*		11/4/1762
Goldsmith, Benjamin	Goshen, NY		MB	
by Daniel Lyman; also by Zachary Clark; also Uriah Stevens				
Susq Co		1 share*	£15	3/4/1763
Goldsmith, Benjamin	Goshen		MB	12/28/1768
pd Uriah Stevens				
Susq Co		1 share*		11/4/1762
Goldsmith, Richard	Goshen, NY		MB	
by Daniel Lyman; also by Zachary Clark; also Uriah Stevens				
Susq Co		1 share*	£15	3/4/1763
Goldsmith, Richard	Goshen		MB	12/28/1768
pd Uriah Stevens				
Susq Co		1 share*		11/4/1762
Goldsmith, Richard Junr			MB	
by Daniel Lyman				
Susq Co		1 share*	£15	3/4/1763
Goldsmith, Susanah, Ann & Abigail	Goshen, NY		MB	12/28/1768
pd Uriah Stevens; also by Lyman & Clark				
Susq Co		1 share*		11/20/1754
Gooden, Eleazar			MB - Deed	
pd Capn Uriah Stevens				
Susq Co		1 share		
Gooden, Samuel			Deed	
Susq Co				
Goodman, Samuel			A482	
Susq Co		1/2 share*		7/27/1761
Goodrich, John			MB	
pd Major Elizer Talcott				
Susq Co		1 share*	$5	5/1/1754
Goodwin, Daniel	Hartford Co		MB - Deed	
pd Thomas Stantly				
Susq Co		1/2 share*	$4.50	5/1/1755
Goodyear, Theop	New Haven		RB	
pd Daniel Edwards				
Susq Co		1/2 share*	$4.50	7/8/1755
Goodyear, Theophilus	New Haven, New Haven CT		MB - B101	10/25/1773
pd Thomas Darling				
Susq Co		1 share*		8/28/1761
Gordon, George			MB	
pd Nathaniel Wales Junr Esq.				
Susq Co				7/18/1753
Gordon, Robert			MB	
Susq Co		1 share	£8	4/15/1771
Gordon, Samuel	Voluntown, Windham, CT		B376	1/13/1778
Susq Co		1/2 share*		11/20/1754
Gordon, Samuel			MB - Deed	
pd Capn Uriah Stevens				

Susquehanna Company Proprietors

grantor grantee notes	grantor residence grantee residence	description location	amount acct bk page	deed date record date
Susq Co		1 share*		8/28/1761
Gordon, Samuel			MB	
pd Nathaniel Wales Junr Esq.				
Susq Co		1/2 share*		2/19/1763
Gordon, Samuel	Warwick, RI		MB	
by Ezra Dean				
Susq Co		1/2 share		9/10/1785
Gore, Avery		Ulster Twp	I44	8/17/1786
Susq Co		1/2 share No. 241 of 400		9/10/1785
Gore, John			C584	6/28/1795
Susq Co		1 share		7/11/1754
Gore, Obadiah			Deed	
Susq Co		1 share*		5/1/1754
Gore, Samuel			MB - Deed	
pd Jed Elderkin				
Susq Co		1/2 share		9/10/1785
Gore, Samuel		Ulster Twp	E96	3/1/1796
Susq Co		1/2 share	£4	5/22/1762
Gorton, Othniel	Warwick, Kent, RI		B211	5/15/1774
Susq Co		1/2 share	$25	2/12/1763
Gorton, Samuel	Warwick, Kent, RI		B341	2/8/1776
Susq Co				7/18/1753
Gots, Daniel			MB	
Susq Co				7/18/1753
Gould, John			MB	
Susq Co		1 share*	$9	12/31/1755
Graham, Andrew	Woodbury		MB	
pd Thomas Darling				
Susq Co		1 share*		11/20/1754
Gransey, Ebenezer			MB - Deed	
pd Capn Uriah Stevens				
Susq Co		1 share*		11/20/1754
Gransey, Peter			MB - Deed	
pd Capn Uriah Stevens				
Susq Co		1/2 share*		8/27/1761
Grant, Ezekiel			MB	
pd Major Elizer Talcott				
Susq Co		1 share		7/11/1754
Grant, John			Deed	
Susq Co		1 share		7/11/1754
Grant, Solomon			Deed	
Susq Co		1/2 share*	£6	4/13/1769
Gray, Ebenezer Jr.			MB - B77	10/15/1773
by Samuel Gray				
Susq Co		1/2 share*		11/4/1762
Gray, Jonathan			MB	
by Daniel Lyman				
Susq Co		1 share*	$2	7/18/1753
Gray, Samuel Esq.			MB - A461 - Deed	
pd Capt John Fitch				
Susq Co		1/2 share*	£6.6	4/16/1773
Gray, Samuel Jr.			MB - B76	6/21/1773
by Samuel Gray				
Susq Co		1/2 share*	£6.6	4/16/1773
Gray, Thomas			MB - B76	6/21/1773
by Samuel Gray				
Susq Co		1 share*		11/20/1754
Green, Benjamin			MB - Deed	
pd Capn Uriah Stevens				
Susq Co		1/2 share*		2/19/1763
Green, Benjamin	Warwick, RI		MB	
by Ezra Dean				

grantor grantee notes	grantor residence grantee residence	description location	amount acct bk page	deed date record date
Susq Co		1/2 share*	$25	2/16/1763
Green, Jabez*			MB - B341	2/8/1776
son of James of Warwick, Kent, RI, by Ezra Dean				
Susq Co		1/2 share	£4	7/8/1762
Green, John, Forge Master	Coventry, Kent, RI		H229	8/21/1800
Susq Co		1/2 share*	$25	2/16/1763
Green, John, Forge Master	Coventry, Kent, RI		MB - H229	8/21/1800
by Ezra Dean; entered in Warwick 1774, but falling out of the Purchase was reentered in Smithfield for Lodowick Green, 300A				
Susq Co		1 share		5/29/1772
Green, Nathaniel			GG	
Susq Co		1/2 share*		12/1/1762
Green, Nathaniel	Warwick		MB	
by Isaac Tracy				
Susq Co		1 share*		11/4/1762
Green, Nathaniel & Joseph			MB - A286	
pd Daniel Lyman				
Susq Co		1/2 share*	$25	2/16/1763
Green, Paul	North Kingston, Kings, RI		MB - B341	2/8/1776
by Ezra Dean				
Susq Co		1/2 share*	£6.6	5/5/1772
Green, Timothy	New London, New London, CT		MB - B158	3/9/1774
by Samuel Gray				
Susq Co		1/2 share*		4/1/1773
Green, Timothy			MB	4/1/1773
for compensation of debts; by Samuel Gray				
Susq Co		1/2 share*	$25	2/16/1763
Greene, David	Warwick, Kent, RI		MB - B341	2/8/1776
by Ezra Dean				
Susq Co		1 share*		2/19/1763
Greene, Job	Warwick, RI		MB - A244	
by Ezra Dean				
Susq Co		1 share*		2/19/1763
Greene, Joshua	North Kingston, RI		MB - A244	
by Ezra Dean				
Susq Co				
Greene, Nathaniel			A30	
Susq Co		1 share		
Griffen, Ebenezer			Deed	
Susq Co		1 share	£13	1/1/1754
Griffin, Ebenezer			B198	3/19/1774
Susq Co		1/2 share*	$4.50	12/31/1755
Griffin, John	Darby		MB	
pd Thomas Darling				
Susq Co		1 share		7/11/1754
Griswold, Abel			Deed	
Susq Co		1 share*	$2	7/18/1753
Griswold, David			MB - Deed	
pd Journeying Cmte				
Susq Co		1 share*	$2	7/18/1753
Griswold, Elijah			MB - Deed	
pd Journeying Cmte				
Susq Co		1/2 share*	$4.50	5/1/1755
Griswold, George	Windsor, CT		RB	
pd Daniel Edwards				
Susq Co		1 share*	$9	5/1/1755
Griswold, Gideon			RB	
pd Daniel Edwards				
Susq Co				7/18/1753
Griswold, Gideon			MB	
Susq Co		1 share*	$5	1/12/1754
Griswold, Joseph			MB	
pd Stephen Gardner; should be on Deed				

grantor grantee notes	grantor residence grantee residence	description location	amount acct bk page	deed date record date
Susq Co		1/2 share*	$2.50	5/1/1754
Griswold, Josiah Capt.	Hartford Co		MB - Deed	
pd Thomas Stantly				
Susq Co		1/2 share*	£4	5/6/1761
Griswold, Manns	Guilford, New Haven, CT		MB - B32	9/15/1773
pd Danniel Lyman				
Susq Co		1/2 share*	$4.50	5/1/1755
Griswold, Noah	Windsor, CT		RB	
pd Daniel Edwards				
Susq Co		1 share*	$2	10/8/1753
Grosvenor, Ebenezer	Pomfret, Windham, CT		MB - B19	9/25/1773
pd S Gray				
Susq Co		1 share		
Grosvenor, Ebenezer			Deed	
Susq Co		1 share*	$2	10/8/1753
Grosvenor, John Cap't	Pomfret, Windham, CT		MB - B19 - Deed	9/25/1773
pd S Gray				
Susq Co		1 share		7/11/1754
Grover, Ebenezer Jr.			Deed	
Susq Co		1/2 share*		10/20/1761
Guild, Samuel			MB - A223	
pd Isaac Tracy				
Susq Co		1 share*		11/20/1754
Guitteau, Francis			MB - Deed	
pd Capn Uriah Stevens				
Susq Co		1 share*		11/20/1754
Guitteau, Joshua			MB - Deed	
pd Capn Uriah Stevens				
Susq Co		1/2 share*	$4.50	12/31/1755
Gunn, Abel	Darby		MB	
pd Thomas Darling				
Susq Co				
Gunsaulus/Gonzales, Emanuel*			MB	
should be on Deed				
Susq Co		1 share*		6/4/1766
Gwynne, Howell Esq.	Garth, England		MB	
by John Gardiner, Esq.				
Susq Co		1 share		7/11/1754
Hale, Elisha			Deed	
Susq Co		1 share*	$5	5/1/1754
Hale, Jonathan	Hartford Co		MB - Deed	
pd Thomas Stantly				
Susq Co				7/18/1753
Hall, John			MB	
Susq Co		1 share		7/11/1754
Hall, Jonathan			Deed	
Susq Co		1/2 share No. 59 0f 400		3/22/1787
Hall, William			I162	9/10/1785
Susq Co		1/2 share No. 91 of 400		9/10/1785
Halsted, Richard			I63	6/10/1786
Susq Co		1 share		7/11/1754
Hamilton, Jonathan	RI		Deed	
Susq Co		1 share*	£6.10	11/20/1754
Hamilton, Solomon			MB	
should be on Deed				
Susq Co		1/2 share*		11/20/1754
Hannas, James			MB - Deed	
pd Capn Uriah Stevens				
Susq Co		1 share		
Hannis, Robert			Deed	
Susq Co		1/2 share*	$1	10/8/1753
Harden, Abraham			MB - B241 - Deed	8/28/1774
pd S Gray				

grantor grantee notes	grantor residence grantee residence	description location	amount acct bk page	deed date record date
Susq Co		1 share*	$2	10/8/1753
Harden, Stephen			MB - B241 - Deed	8/28/1774
pd S Gray				
Susq Co			MB	
Hardey, Samuel*				
should be on Deed				
Susq Co		1 share*		10/20/1761
Harrington, Jeremiah			MB	
pd Isaac Tracy				
Susq Co		1 share No 187 of the 600		7/13/1785
Harris, Alpheus			D50	11/6/1795
Susq Co		1 share		7/11/1754
Harris, Charles	RI		Deed	
Susq Co		1/2 share No. 235 of the 400		9/10/1785
Harris, Charles		Allensburgh Twp	E366	4/1/1796
entered 9/24/1787				
Susq Co		1/2 share*	$1	9/28/1753
Harris, Ephriam			MB	
pd Stephen Gardner; should be on Deed				
Susq Co		1/2 share*		2/19/1763
Harris, Jedediah	Cranston, RI		MB	
by Ezra Dean				
Susq Co		1/2 share*	£6.10	9/28/1753
Harris, Lebius			MB	
should be on Deed				
Susq Co		1 share*	$2	1/9/1754
Harriss, Jonathan			MB - Deed	
pd Capt John Fitch				
Susq Co		1/2 share*	$2.50	5/1/1754
Hart, John	Hartford Co		MB - Deed	
pd Thomas Stantly				
Susq Co		1/2 share		7/11/1754
Haskell, Gideon			Deed	
Susq Co		1 share		7/11/1754
Hatch, Barnabas			Deed	
Susq Co		1/2 share	$21	11/7/1772
Hatch, Jethro & Esbon			B307	2/9/1775
Susq Co			A50	
Hatch, John				
Susq Co		1/2 share*		10/20/1761
Haugton, James			MB	
pd Isaac Tracy				
Susq Co		1 share	$5	7/11/1754
Hawley, Francis	Stratford, Fairfield, CT		Deed - E278	6/8/1796
Susq Co		1/2 share*		9/4/1761
Hawley, Stephen	New Milford		MB	
pd Daniel Lyman				
Susq Co		1 share*		2/21/1754
Haynes, Joseph			MB	
should be on Deed				
Susq Co		1/2 share*	$4.50	5/1/1755
Hazard, John	Fairfield, CT		RB	
pd Daniel Edwards				
Susq Co		1/2 share*	£8.2.6	1/9/1754
Hazen, Joseph			MB - Deed	
pd S Gray				
Susq Co		1/2 share	$4.50	5/10/1755
Hazzard, John	Fairfield, Fairfield, CT		B125	1/19/1774
Susq Co		1 share		7/11/1754
Hazzard, Robert Esq.	RI		Deed	
Susq Co		1 share*		4/8/1763
Hazzard, Stephen	South Kingston, Washington, RI		MB - H108	9/19/1800
by Ezra Dean				

grantor	grantor residence	description	amount	deed date
grantee	grantee residence	location	acct bk page	record date
notes				
Susq Co		1 share	£12	4/14/1773
Hazzen, William Howlett	Norwich, New London, CT		B346	4/14/1773
Susq Co		1 share*	£6	7/18/1753
Heard, Thomas			MB	
pd S Gray				
Susq Co		1/2 share No. 76 of 400		9/10/1785
Heath, Thomas			I221	7/4/1795
Susq Co		1/2 share, all taxes paid	$2	1/10/1754
Hebard/Hibbard, Paul	Windham, Windham, CT		Deed - C582	6/20/1795
Susq Co		1 share*	£6.10	11/20/1754
Helms, Silas			MB	
should be on Deed				
Susq Co		1 share*		5/1/1754
Hende, Barzilla			MB - Deed	
pd Jed Elderkin				
Susq Co		1/2 share*	£4 in Bills of Credit	4/1/1763
Henderson, James	New Hartford		MB - B123	1/20/1774
pd Elisha Sheldon				
Susq Co		1 share*		11/20/1754
Hensdell, Jacob Capt			MB - Deed	
pd Capn Uriah Stevens				
Susq Co		1 share		7/11/1754
Hensdell, John			Deed	
Susq Co		6,000 A	sufficient vouchers	11/22/1796
Henshaw, Daniel	Middletown, CT	Mendee Twp	E467	11/22/1796
Susq Co		1 share		7/11/1754
Henshaw, Daniel*	PA		Deed	
corrected to James Handshaw				
Susq Co		replacement crtf for 1/2 share of 600		10/21/1794
Hervey, Thomas		Murraysfield Twp	E338	5/15/1796
Susq Co		1 share*	$2	9/5/1753
Hewets/Hewitt, Henry			MB - B140 - Deed	2/17/1774
pd Capt John Fitch				
Susq Co		1 share	£8	8/29/1762
Hewit/Hewett, Walter	Canaan		Deed - C126	8/9/1795
Susq Co		1/2 share*		5/1/1754
Hibbard, Gideon	Windham		MB - Deed	
pd Jed Elderkin				
Susq Co		1/2 share*		5/1/1754
Hibbard/Hebard, Zebulon			MB - Deed	
pd Jed Elderkin				
Susq Co		1/2 share*	$4.50	7/15/1755
Hichcox, Samuel			MB	
pd Thomas Darling				
Susq Co		1/2 share*		4/7/1763
Hide, Abijah	Darbe		MB	
by Zachariah Clark				
Susq Co		1 share*	$4	1/10/1754
Hide, Caleb, Capt	Lebanon, Windham, CT		MB - Deed - B383	11/12/1778
pd Jed Elderkin				
Susq Co		1 share		7/11/1754
Hide, Daniel			Deed	
Susq Co		1 share*	£8	6/13/1761
Hide, Eliakim			MB - E283	6/8/1796
pd Zachariah Clark				
Susq Co		1 share*		5/1/1754
Hide, Elijah	Windham		MB - Deed	
pd Jed Elderkin				
Susq Co				7/18/1753
Hide, Ephriam			MB	
Susq Co		1 share		7/11/1754
Hide, James			Deed	

grantor grantee notes	grantor residence grantee residence	description location	amount acct bk page	deed date record date
Susq Co		1/2 share*	$2	1/9/1754
Hide, Nathaniel			MB - Deed	
pd S Gray				
Susq Co		1/2 share, No. 122 of 400		9/10/1785
Hide/Hyde, William		Athens Twp*	E436	10/1/1796
entered 300 A, 1786				
Susq Co		1/2 share*	$4.50	5/1/1755
Hill, Andrew	Fairfield, CT		RB	
pd Daniel Edwards				
Susq Co		1 share*	$9	5/1/1755
Hill, Thomas, Esqr	Fairfield, CT		RB	
pd Daniel Edwards				
Susq Co		1/2 share*	$4.50	5/1/1755
Hill, Thomas Jr.	Fairfield, CT		RB	
pd Daniel Edwards				
Susq Co		1/2 share	£6	4/8/1772
Hill, William	Saybrook, New London, CT		B291	5/25/1774
Susq Co		1 share*		5/21/1796
Hillhouse, William	New Haven, CT		F153	5/21/1796
as per Company meeting Tioga 2/18/1795				
Susq Co		1 share*	$9	1/30/1755
Hills, Col. Jonathan	Hartford, CT		MB - RB	12/28/1768
pd Daniel Edwards				
Susq Co		1 share	$4	1/21/1754
Hinckley, Gershom	Stonington		B282	12/21/1774
Susq Co		1 share		7/11/1754
Hinkly/Hinckley, Gershom			Deed	
Susq Co		1/2 share		7/11/1754
Hinman, Alexander			Deed	
Susq Co		1 share*	$9	12/31/1755
Hinman, Samuel	Woodbury		MB	
pd Thomas Darling				
Susq Co		1 share*	$9	12/31/1755
Hinman, Truman	Woodbury		MB	
pd Thomas Darling				
Susq Co		1 share		7/11/1754
Hinman, Wate			Deed	
Susq Co		1/2 share*	$4.50	12/31/1755
Hitchcock, Amos	New Haven		MB	
pd Thomas Darling				
Susq Co		1 share*	$9	5/1/1755
Hitchcock, Benjamin	Cheshire, CT		RB	
pd Daniel Edwards				
Susq Co		1 share*		3/24/1763
Hitchcock & Brownshon*			MB	
John & Josiah; pd Zachariah Clark				
Susq Co		1/2 share*	$4.50	5/1/1755
Hitchcock, Caleb	North Haven, CT		RB	
pd Daniel Edwards				
Susq Co		1 share		7/11/1754
Hogeboom, Jeremiah	NY		Deed	
Susq Co		1 share		7/11/1754
Holden, Phineas			Deed	
Susq Co		1 share		12/6/1786
Hollenback, John	Wyoming		I17	12/6/1786
Susq Co		1 share	£12	6/18/1770
Hollenback, Matthew			B356	4/5/1777
Susq Co		1 share*		7/27/1767
Hollister, Charles			MB	
by Elizer Talcott				
Susq Co		1/2 share*		8/27/1761
Hollister, Elisha			MB	
pd Major Elizer Talcott				

grantor grantee notes	grantor residence grantee residence	description location	amount acct bk page	deed date record date
Susq Co		1/2 share		6/21/1774
Hollister, Elisha Capt			I54	
Susq Co		1/2 share*		8/27/1761
Hollister, Ephriam			MB	
pd Major Elizer Talcott				
Susq Co	Hartford, Hartford, CT	1/2 share	£6	5/15/1772
Hollister, John			MB - B94	11/4/1773
Susq Co		1/2 share*		7/27/1767
Hollister, Nathaniel			MB	
by Elizur Talcott				
Susq Co		1 share*	£8	8/20/1762
Hollister, Solomon, William & Asa	Glastonbury		MB - B268	11/11/1774
pd Zachariah Clark				
Susq Co		1 share*	£8	8/20/1762
Hollister, Timothy Capt	Glastonbury		MB - B268	1/12/1774
pd Zachariah Clark				
Susq Co		1 share*	£8	8/20/1762
Hollister, Timothy Jr. & Isaac	Glastonbury		MB - B268	1/12/1774
pd Zachariah Clark				
Susq Co		1 share*		11/20/1754
Holmes, John Capt			MB - Deed	
pd Capn Uriah Stevens				
Susq Co		1 share		
Holt, Paul			Deed	
Susq Co		1 share*		11/20/1754
Hooker, Hezekiah Esqr.			MB - Deed	
pd Capn Uriah Stevens; also on Deed under 1/2 share				
Susq Co		1 share	$5	2/6/1754
Hooker, Roger			B307 [sic 308]	2/6/1775
Susq Co		1 share*	$5	5/1/1754
Hooker, Roger	Hartford Co		MB - Deed	
pd Thomas Stantly				
Susq Co		160 A*		11/8/1799
Hopkins, Timothy		Haverill Twp, adj.	H111	11/8/1799
survey by Benjamin Newberry west of mouth of Shickshinny Cr. near Fishing Cr.; see Harvey: 812				
Susq Co		1 share*	$2	9/16/1753
Horsford, Daniel			MB - Deed	
pd Journeying Cmte				
Susq Co		1 share*	$2	9/16/1753
Horsford, Josiah			MB - Deed	
pd Journeying Cmte				
Susq Co		1 share*	$5	5/1/1754
Horsmore, Thomas	Hartford Co		MB - Deed	
pd Thomas Stantly				
Susq Co		1 share*	$2	9/16/1753
Hough, John			MB - Deed	
pd Journeying Cmte				
Susq Co		1 share*	£16.5.0	1/9/1754
Hovey, Nathaniel			MB - Deed	
pd S Gray				
Susq Co				7/18/1753
How, James			MB	
Susq Co		1 share		7/11/1754
How, Samuel			Deed	
Susq Co				
Howard, James			A397	
Susq Co		1 share*	$2	9/26/1753
Howard, John			MB - B320 - Deed	3/22/1775
pd S Gray				
Susq Co				7/18/1753
Howard, Joseph			MB	

grantor grantee notes	grantor residence grantee residence	description location	amount acct bk page	deed date record date
Susq Co		1 share*	$5	5/29/1754
Howard, Martin Esq.	RI		MB - Deed	
pd S Gray				
Susq Co		1 share	$4	1/9/1754
Howard, Thomas	late of Mansfield*		Deed - C51	12/10/1782
now living north of Union				
Susq Co				
Howard, William			A327	
Susq Co		1/2 share of 600 [Number not found]		6/26/1793
Howey, Thomas			I276	
Susq Co			£8	1/7/1762
Hoxsey, Zebulon			GH	3/7/1778
Susq Co		1/2 share	£6.10 + £1.12.6	1/22/1754
Hoy, Jedediah	Ashford, Windham, CT		B222	6/7/1774
Susq Co		1 share*		11/4/1762
Hubbard, Daniel	Boston		MB - A31	
pd Daniel Lyman				
Susq Co		1/2 share*	$4.50	12/31/1755
Hubbard, Daniel	New Haven		MB	
pd Thomas Darling				
Susq Co		1/2 share*		11/4/1762
Hubbard, Leverrett Junr	Boston		MB	
pd Daniel Lyman				
Susq Co				
Hubbard, Nathaniel			A291	
Susq Co		1 share*		11/4/1762
Hubbard, William	Boston		MB - A31	
pd Daniel Lyman				
Susq Co		1 share*		5/1/1754
Hubbard/Hulbart, Joseph			MB	
pd Jed Elderkin				
Susq Co		1/2 share		
Hughes, John			Deed	
Susq Co		1 share		
Hulbart, Joseph			Deed	
Susq Co		1/2 share		
Hulbert, Samuel			Deed	
Susq Co		1/4 share		8/28/1770
Huling, Mark			GH	
present by John Durkee, Cmte				
Susq Co		1 share	$5 on acct.	2/22/1754
Hull, Cornelius	Fairfield, Fairfield, CT		Deed - B109	12/23/1773
Susq Co		1/2 share	$4.50	6/12/1755
Hull, Eliphalet	Fairfield, Fairfield, CT		B109	12/23/1773
Susq Co		1/2 share*	$4.50	5/1/1755
Hull, Eliphalet	Fairfield, CT		RB	
pd Daniel Edwards				
Susq Co		1/2 share	$4.50	6/12/1755
Hull, Jedediah	Fairfield, Fairfield, CT		B109	12/23/1773
Susq Co		1/2 share*	$4.50	5/1/1755
Hull, Jedediah	Fairfield, CT		RB	
pd Daniel Edwards				
Susq Co		1/2 share*	$4.50	12/31/1755
Hull, Joseph	Darby		MB	
pd Thomas Darling				
Susq Co		1 share*	$9	12/31/1755
Humervile, Benjamin	New Haven		MB	
pd Thomas Darling				
Susq Co		1 share*	$9	12/31/1755
Humphrey, Daniel	Darby		MB	
pd Thomas Darling				

grantor / grantee / notes	grantor residence / grantee residence	description / location	amount / acct bk page	deed date / record date
Susq Co		1 share*	$5	5/1/1754
Humphrey, Hezekiah	Hartford Co		MB - Deed	
pd Thomas Stantly				
Susq Co		1 share*	$5	5/1/1754
Humphrey, John	Hartford Co		MB - Deed	
pd Thomas Stantly				
Susq Co		1 share*	$5	5/1/1754
Humphrey, Jonathan	Hartford Co		MB - Deed	
pd Thomas Stantly				
Susq Co		1/2 share		
Humphries, Thomas			A100 - Deed	
Susq Co		1/2 share		
Humphry, Oliver			Deed	
Susq Co		1 share*	£15	2/26/1763
Hungerford, Benjamin	Farmington, Hartford, CT		MB - B377	2/25/1778
by Jonathan Root				
Susq Co		1/2 share*		4/7/1763
Hungerford, Jacob & Jesse Gallard	Farmington		MB	
by Jonathan Root				
Susq Co		1 share		7/11/1754
Hunn, Samuel			Deed	
Susq Co				
Hunt, Benjamin			A64	
Susq Co		1 share*	$2	9/6/1753
Hunter, John			MB - Deed	
pd S Gray				
Susq Co		1 share*	$2	9/6/1753
Hunter, Robert			MB - B259 - Deed	10/6/1774
pd S Gray				
Susq Co		1 share	$4	1/9/1754
Hunter, Samuel	Voluntown, Windham, CT		Deed - B259	10/6/1774
Susq Co			$2	12/11/1754
Hunter, Samuel	Voluntown, Windham, CT		E382	7/1/1795
Susq Co		1/2 share*	$2	1/10/1754
Huntington, Hezekiah			MB - B275 - Deed	11/14/1774
on Deed twice				
Susq Co		1 share	sundry services	7/7/1773
Huntington, Samuel	Norwich		E364	9/6/1796
Susq Co		1 share*	$2	9/26/1753
Huntington, Sarah, wid Col. Jabez			MB - Deed	
pd Capt John Fitch				
Susq Co		1 share		7/11/1754
Huntington, Simon			Deed	
Susq Co				
Huntington, Solomon			A215	
Susq Co		1 share		1/1/1774
Hurlbert, Simeon			GH	
Susq Co				
Hurlbut, Buttoloph G.			A363	
Susq Co		1/2 share		10/1/1785
Hurlbut, John		Athens Twp	I60	6/10/1786
entered 5/10/1786				
Susq Co			£8	8/17/1762
Hurlbut, Nathan	Sharon, Litchfield, CT		B149	3/8/1774
Susq Co		1 share*	£15	3/5/1763
Hurlbut, Nathan			MB - B294	5/25/1774
by Uriah Stevens				
Susq Co		1 share*	£15	3/4/1763
Hurlbut, Nathan	Alford, Berkshire, MA		MB - B295	5/25/1774
by Uriah Stevens				
Susq Co		9,600 A*		8/29/1774
Hurlbut, Stephen*		New Groton Twp	F94	9/13/1796

agent for 30 proprietors; entire township was in same proportion for the 30 proprietors as a township for 50 proprietors, i.e. 300 A x 30 + 900 A for public use

grantor grantee notes	grantor residence grantee residence	description location	amount acct bk page	deed date record date
Susq Co		1 share*		10/20/1761
Hurlbutt, Joseph			MB	
pd Isaac Tracy				
Susq Co		1/2 share*		
Hurlbutt, Joseph Capt			MB	
by Gershom Breed				
Susq Co		1/2 share*		
Hurlbutt, Joseph Junr			MB	
by Samuel Gray				
Susq Co		1 share		5/25/1774
Hurlbutt, Nathan	Alford, Berkshire, MA		E97	3/1/1796
Susq Co		1 share*	$4	1/9/1754
Huston, William	Voluntown CT		MB - Deed - C244	9/2/1799
pd S Gray				
Susq Co		1 share*		11/20/1754
Hutchinson, Samuel Esq.			MB - Deed	
pd Capn Uriah Stevens; name corrected from John in Deed as per MB				
Susq Co		200 acres*		1/1/1787
Hyde, John	Newport, Luzerne, PA		E271	6/6/1796
granted 1786 or 1787; certified 1/15/1794				
Susq Co		1/2 share	$4.50	7/14/1754
Ingraham, Medes	New Haven		E411	9/15/1796
Susq Co		1/2 share No. 174 of 400		7/13/1785
Inman, Edward		Graham Twp*	C341	3/10/1795
1000 A entered 3/4/1795				
Susq Co		1/2 share No. 139 of 400		10/1/1785
Jackays/Jackways/Jacques,		Athens Twp	E152	4/25/1796
Susq Co		1/2 share*		11/20/1754
Jackson, Samuel			MB - Deed	
pd Capn Uriah Stevens				
Susq Co		1 share*	$2	9/16/1753
Jackson, William			MB - Deed	
pd Capt John Fitch				
Susq Co		1 share*	£15	3/3/1763
Jearom, William	Farmington, Hartford, CT		MB - B379	3/13/1778
by Jonathan Root				
Susq Co		1/2 share*		4/7/1763
Jearom, Zerubabel	Farmington		MB - A241	
by Jonathan Root				
Susq Co		1/2 share*		4/7/1763
Jearome, Timothy Junr	Farmington		MB	
by Jonathan Root				
Susq Co		1/2 share No 258 of 600		1/13/1786
Jenkins, Benjamin	Wyoming PA	Putnam Twp	I32	11/22/1786
Susq Co		1 share*	$2	10/8/1753
Jenkins, John			MB - B241 - Deed	8/28/1774
pd S Gray				
Susq Co		6400 A		12/1/1795
Jenkins, John	Luzerne Co, PA	Jenkin's Pitch	E1	12/1/1795
Susq Co		1 share		7/11/1754
Jenkins, Stephen			Deed	
Susq Co		1/2 share	£6	6/20/1770
Jerom, Benjamin	New London, New London, CT		D33	10/6/1795
Susq Co				7/18/1753
Jewell, Thomas			MB	
Susq Co		1 share*		10/20/1761
Jewet, David Rev			MB	
pd Isaac Tracy				
Susq Co		1/2 share*		7/6/1762
Johnson, David of NJ			MB	
pd Capt Elisha Sheldon				

grantor grantee notes	grantor residence grantee residence	description location	amount acct bk page	deed date record date
Susq Co		1 share*		11/20/1754
Johnson, Elijah			MB	
pd Stephen Gardner; should be on Deed				
Susq Co		1/2 share No. 227 of 400		9/10/1785
Johnson, Jehoida			I192	3/19/1795
Susq Co		1/2 share	£12	4/19/1773
Johnson, John			B21	4/19/1773
Susq Co		1 share*	£16:5:0	1/9/1754
Johnson, John Jr.	Lebanon, Windham, CT		MB - Deed - B25	8/30/1773
pd S Gray				
Susq Co		2 shares*		6/15/1794
Johnson, Solomon		Muncey Creek; Cabbanashana	I190	3/19/1795
found not convenient to settle [on W Br] so both shares to be relocated anywhere in SP				
Susq Co		1 share*		7/6/1762
Johnson, Stephen Rev			MB	
pd Capt Elisha Sheldon				
Susq Co		1/2 share		6/17/1786
Johnson, Turner			E366	4/1/1796
Susq Co				
Johnson, William			A60	
Susq Co		1 share*		9/18/1777
Jones, Benjamin			I70	1/22/1794
signed by Nathan Denison				
Susq Co		1/2 share		8/25/1770
Jones, Benjamin			I199	4/1/1795
Susq Co		1/2 share No. 80 of 600		9/10/1785
Jones, Daniel Earl		Putnam Twp	I33	12/6/1786
Susq Co		1 share*	$4 + $1 taxes	11/20/1754
Jones, Jabez	Colchester		MB - E486	11/15/1796
pd Stephen Gardner; should be on Deed				
Susq Co		1 share*		11/20/1754
Jones, James			MB	
pd Stephen Gardner; should be on Deed				
Susq Co		1 share*		12/31/1755
Jones, Josiah Junr			MB	
pd Timothy Woodbridge				
Susq Co		1 share No. 120 of 600		12/5/1793
Jones, Justus	Tunkhannock District, PA		H15 - I276	11/17/1798
Susq Co		1/2 share No 131 of 400		9/10/1785
Jones, Nathan			I218	6/22/1795
Susq Co		1 share*		5/1/1754
Jones, Thomas			MB - Deed	
pd S Gray				
Susq Co		1 share	$4	2/15/1754
Jordan, Miles	Voluntown, Windham, CT		Deed - B296	6/21/1774
Susq Co		1 share*	$2	9/16/1753
Judd, John			MB - Deed	
pd Journeying Cmte				
Susq Co		1 share*	£6.10	7/18/1753
Judd, Phinehas			MB - Deed	
pd S Gray				
Susq Co		1/2 share*		4/23/1773
Judd, William			MB	4/23/1773
by Samuel Gray				
Susq Co		1 share		7/11/1754
Judson, Agur			Deed	
Susq Co		1 share	$5	2/18/1754
Judson, Ephriam	Stratford, Fairfield, CT		Deed - E279	6/8/1796
Susq Co		1/2 share*	$2.50	5/1/1754
Judson, Peter	Hartford Co		MB - Deed	
pd Thomas Stantly				
Susq Co				7/18/1753
Kagwin, James			MB	

grantor	grantor residence	description	amount	deed date
grantee	grantee residence	location	acct bk page	record date
notes				
Susq Co		1 share*	$2	9/16/1753
Kagwin, John			MB - Deed	
pd S Gray				
Susq Co		1 share*	$2	9/6/1753
Kasson, Adam	Coventry, Kent, RI		MB - F5 - Deed	
pd Capt John Fitch; pd $2 taxes 5/1/1769				
Susq Co		1 share*	$2	9/6/1753
Kasson, Archibald			MB - Deed	
pd Capt John Fitch				
Susq Co		1 share*	£6.10 = $2	9/16/1753
Kasson, James	Woodbury	New Milford Twp*	MB - E162 - Deed	5/17/1796
pd Journeying Cmte either 9/16/1753 or 10/12/ 1753; entered 600 A in New Milford, 1795 for heirs: 1105				
Susq Co		1 share*	$2	9/6/1753
Kasson, Samuel			MB - Deed	
pd Capt John Fitch				
Susq Co		1 share*		12/31/1755
Kellog, Amos			MB - A483	1/15/1762
pd Timothy Woodbridge				
Susq Co		1/2 share*	$4.50	5/1/1755
Kellog, Daniel	Branford & Hartford, CT		RB	
pd Daniel Edwards				
Susq Co				7/18/1753
Kellog, Stephen			MB	
Susq Co		1 share*	$9	5/1/1755
Kellogg, Abraham	Hartford, now		RB	
pd Daniel Edwards				
Susq Co		1/2 share*	£3.5	9/28/1753
Kellogg, Daniel			MB	
pd Charles Dewey; should be on Deed				
Susq Co		1/2 share No. 89 of 400		9/10/1785
Kellogg, Eldad			I62	6/10/1786
Susq Co		1 share*		11/20/1754
Kellogg, John			MB	
pd Stephen Gardner; should be on Deed				
Susq Co		1 share	$2	2/13/1754
Kellogg, John	Colchester		E62	2/25/1795
Susq Co		1/2 share No. 88 of 400		
Kellogg, Josiah			E136	3/29/1796
Susq Co		1 share	$5	5/29/1754
Kenady/Kennedy, Robert	Norwich		Deed - B275 - E290	6/6/1796
Susq Co		1 share*	$2	9/21/1754
Kennedy, Hugh Jr.			MB - B107 - Deed	12/14/1773
pd S Gray				
Susq Co		1 share*	$2	9/16/1753
Kenney, Gideon			MB - Deed	
pd Capt John Fitch				
Susq Co		1 share*	$2	9/16/1753
Kenney, Jeremiah			MB - Deed	
pd Capt John Fitch				
Susq Co		1 share*	$2	9/16/1753
Kenney, John	Voluntown, Windham, CT		MB - Deed	
pd Capt John Fitch				
Susq Co		1/2 share No. 284 of 400		9/10/1785
Kenney, Joseph	Ulster Twp		I12	8/19/1786
Susq Co		1/2 share		5/1/1786
Kenney, Joshua	Allensburg & New Barrington		E262	8/14/1798
entered 300 A, Lot 21, 2/15/1787; entered 700 A, New Barrington 5/1/1798 - withdrawn in favor of John Bradshaw on Lot 21 see E263				
Susq Co		1 share*	$2	9/16/1753
Kenney, Moses			MB - Deed	
pd Capt John Fitch				
Susq Co		1 share*	$2	9/16/1753
Kenney, Nathan			MB - Deed	
pd Capt John Fitch				

grantor grantee notes	grantor residence grantee residence	description location	amount acct bk page	deed date record date
Susq Co		1 share*	$2	9/16/1753
Kenney, Spencer			MB - Deed	
pd Capt John Fitch				
Susq Co		1/2 share No. 146 of 400		4/3/1787
Kenney, Thomas	Wyoming	White Haven Twp	I35	4/3/1787
Susq Co		1 share*	$2	9/16/1753
Kenney, Thomas Jr.			MB - Deed	
pd Capt John Fitch				
Susq Co		1 share*	$2	9/16/1753
Kent, Seth			MB - Deed	
pd Journeying Cmte				
Susq Co		1/2 share*	£3.5	3/13/1754
Killborn, Benjamin			MB	
pd Maj Charles Bulkley				
Susq Co		1/2 share	$2.50	6/8/1754
Killey, Nathan			B296	5/27/1774
Susq Co		1 share		7/11/1754
Kimball, Jacob			Deed	
Susq Co		1 share		7/11/1754
King, David	MA		Deed	
Susq Co				
Kingsbury, Jabez			A244	
Susq Co		1/2 share	$2	9/5/1753
Kinne, Gideon			B140	2/17/1774
Susq Co		1/2 share	$2	9/5/1753
Kinne, Jeremiah			B140	2/17/1774
Susq Co		1/2 share	$2	9/5/1753
Kinne, John			B140	2/17/1774
Susq Co		1/2 share	$2	9/5/1753
Kinne, Moses			B140	2/17/1774
Susq Co		1/2 share	$2	9/5/1753
Kinne, Nathan			B140	2/17/1774
Susq Co		1/2 share	$2	9/5/1753
Kinne, Spencer			B140	2/17/1774
Susq Co		1/2 share	$2	9/5/1753
Kinne, Thomas Jr.			B140	2/17/1774
Susq Co		1 share	$5	3/11/1754
Kirtland, Constant	Wallingford, New Haven, CT		Deed - B32	9/15/1773
pd Thomas Darling				
Susq Co		1 share	£8	1/1/1762
Knap, Ebenezer	Canaan, Litchfield, CT		I189	9/1/1794
Susq Co		1 share*	£8	1/1/1762
Knap, Ezra			MB	
pd Uriah Stevens				
Susq Co		1 share	$40	10/2/1769
Kneff, Christian			E168	5/25/1796
Susq Co		1 share		
Knolton, Daniel			Deed	
Susq Co		1 share*	$2	10/8/1753
Kyle, Joseph			MB	
pd Capt John Fitch				
Susq Co		1 share		
Kyle, Joseph			Deed	
Susq Co		1 share		7/11/1754
Laboree, John			Deed	
Susq Co				7/13/1772
Lampher, Isaac			GL	
Susq Co				
Lampshire, Isaac			A436	
Susq Co		1 share	$5	6/5/1754
Lancton, Jonathan	Farmington, Hartford, CT		Deed - B15 - C422	9/20/1781

grantor grantee notes	grantor residence grantee residence	description location	amount acct bk page	deed date record date
Susq Co		1 share*	£8	11/1/1762
Landon, David	Guilford, New Haven, CT		MB - B33	9/15/1773
pd Elisha Sheldon & recorded in MB 4/8/1763				
Susq Co		1 share*		4/8/1763
Landon, Jared	Southhold		MB	
pd Elisha Sheldon				
Susq Co		1 share*		4/8/1763
Landon, Nathan	South Haven		MB	
pd Elisha Sheldon				
Susq Co		1 share*		4/8/1763
Landon, Samuel	Southhold		MB	
pd Elisha Sheldon				
Susq Co		1/2 share*		12/1/1762
Landon, Samuel	Southhold		MB	
by Isaac Tracy				
Susq Co		1 share*		7/11/1754
Lansing, Abraham	NY		Deed	
Susq Co		1 share*	$2	9/16/1753
Larnard, Ebenezer			MB - Deed	
pd S Gray				
Susq Co		1 share	$2	9/22/1753
Larned, Ebenezer	Killingly, Windham, CT		B162	3/9/1774
Susq Co				
Larrabe,---			A353	
Susq Co		1/2 share*	£6.10	1/9/1754
Larrabe, John			MB - Deed	
pd S Gray				
Susq Co		1 share		7/11/1754
Latham, Daniel			Deed - E395	
Susq Co		1/2 share	£6.6	5/7/1773
Lathrop, Zachariah	Norwich, New London, CT		I176	2/22/1795
Susq Co		1 share*	£6.10	10/9/1753
Latimore, Jonathan			MB	
should be on Deed				
Susq Co		1 share		11/20/1754
Lawrence, Daniel Capt	RI		Deed	
Susq Co		1/2 share*	£8	11/20/1754
Lawrence, Gideon	Canaan		MB - F55 - Deed	4/23/1796
pd Capn Uriah Stevens				
Susq Co		1/2 share	£4	1/1/1762
Lawrence, Gideon	Canaan, Litchfield, CT		F54	4/23/1796
Susq Co		1 share*		5/1/1754
Lawrence, Isaac			MB - Deed	
pd Jed Elderkin				
Susq Co				7/18/1753
Lawrence, Thomas			MB	
Susq Co		1 share		7/11/1754
Leach, Ebenezer Capt			Deed	
Susq Co		1 share*	$2	7/18/1753
Leavenworth, John			MB - Deed	
pd S Gray				
Susq Co		1 share*		6/4/1766
Leavey, John Augustine, Attorney	England		MB	
by John Gardiner Esq.				
Susq Co		1 share		7/11/1754
Lee, Benjamin			Deed	
Susq Co		1/2 share No. 287 of 600*		12/16/1793
Lee, Ebenezer	Ulster Twp	Ebenezer Lee Pitch	I69 - I276	12/16/1793
recorded on both 400 and 600 lists in Liber A, Volume 2, but 600 is correct as per I276 list of 600				
Susq Co		1,000 A (1/16 part)		10/4/1796
Lee, Ebenezer & Simeon		Mendee Twp	E492	10/4/1796

grantor grantee notes	grantor residence grantee residence	description location	amount acct bk page	deed date record date
Susq Co		1 share*	$2	9/16/1753
Lee, Isaac			MB - Deed	
pd Journeying Cmte				
Susq Co		1 share*		11/20/1754
Lee, Samuel Doctr			MB - Deed	
pd Capn Uriah Stevens				
Susq Co		1 share*	$2	9/16/1753
Lee, Stephen			MB - A87 - Deed	
pd Journeying Cmte				
Susq Co		1 share*		11/4/1762
Lee, Stephen			MB	
by Daniel Lyman				
Susq Co		1/2 share*	£4	6/29/1762
LeHommedieu, Ezra	Southhold, NY		MB - B26	8/30/1773
by Isaac Tracy				
Susq Co		1 share*		8/28/1761
Leonard, David			MB	
pd Nathaniel Wales Junr Esq.				
Susq Co		1/2 share	£6.6	2/15/1773
Lester, Eliphalet			C111 - C356	8/19/1788
Susq Co		1/2 share		
Levinsworth, John			Deed	
Susq Co		1/2 share		7/11/1754
Levinsworth, Mark			Deed	
Susq Co				
Levore, William			MB	
should be on Deed				
Susq Co		1/2 share No. 294 of 600		12/25/1793
Lewis, Benjamin	Union, NY		E330 - I276	
Susq Co		1/2 share*		11/20/1754
Lewis, Ebenezer			MB - Deed	
pd Capn Uriah Stevens				
Susq Co		1 share		7/11/1754
Lewis, Edmund Junr			Deed	
Susq Co				7/18/1753
Lewis, Jonathan			MB	
Susq Co		1 share		7/11/1754
Lewis, Josiah Junr			Deed	
Susq Co		1/2 share	$2.50	5/1/1754
Lewis, Nehemiah	Hartford Co		MB - Deed	
Susq Co		1/2 share*	$2.50	5/1/1754
Lewis, Phineas	Hartford Co		MB - Deed	
pd Thomas Stantly				
Susq Co		1 share*	$5	11/20/1754
Lewis, Thomas			MB	
Attorney claims receipt; should be on Deed				
Susq Co		1/2 share*		8/28/1761
Lilly, Silas			MB	
pd Nathaniel Wales Junr Esq.				
Susq Co		1/2 share*	£4	5/5/1761
Linley, Jonathan	Branford, New Haven, CT		MB - B380	4/1/1778
pd Daniel Lyman				
Susq Co		1 share	$5	5/25/1754
Lippet/Lippitt, Joseph			Deed - B341	2/8/1776
Susq Co		1/2 share*		11/20/1754
Little/Lylly, Thomas, Doc			MB - Deed	
pd Capn Uriah Stevens; Lylly in Indian Deed, but Little as grantor				
Susq Co		1 share		7/11/1754
Livingworth, James			Deed	
Susq Co		1 share*		6/4/1766
Lloyd, Herbert, Sir, Baronet	England		MB	
by John Gardiner, Esq.				

grantor grantee notes	grantor residence grantee residence	description location	amount acct bk page	deed date record date
Susq Co		1/2 share*	$2.50	5/1/1754
Lockwood, James	Hartford Co		MB - Deed	
pd Thomas Stantly				
Susq Co		1/2 share replacement certificate		1/24/1795
Lomis/Loomis, Richard	Kingston		F56	4/23/1795
Susq Co		1 share*	$9	5/1/1755
Loomis, Ctriah			RB	
pd Daniel Edwards				
Susq Co		1 share*		
Loomis, Ezra	Bolton		MB	
by Ebenr Backus				
Susq Co		1/2 share*		5/1/1754
Loomis, Nathaniel			MB - Deed	
pd S Gray				
Susq Co		1 share*	$9	5/1/1755
Loomis, Odiah			RB	
pd Daniel Edwards				
Susq Co		1/2 share*	$4.50	5/1/1755
Loomis, Timothy	Windsor		RB	
pd Daniel Edwards				
Susq Co				
Loomiss, Ebenezer			A100	
Susq Co				
Loomiss, Obediah & Uriah			A240	
Susq Co		1/2 share		
Loomiss, Seth			Deed	
Susq Co				
Loomiss, Timothy			A240	
Susq Co		1 share No. 82 of 600		11/24/1786
Loop, Peter Capt	Columbia Co., NY	Standing Stone Twp	I28	11/24/1786
entered 1/2 of share on Lot 11				
Susq Co		1/2 share*		10/20/1761
Lothrop, Azariah			MB	
pd Isaac Tracy				
Susq Co		1 share*		5/1/1754
Lothrop, Daniel			MB - Deed	
pd Jed Elderkin				
Susq Co		1/2 share*		4/1/1773
Lothrop, Ebenezer Jr.			MB - A382	4/1/1773
by Samuel Gray				
Susq Co		1 share		7/11/1754
Lothrop, William			Deed	
Susq Co		1/2 share*		4/1/1773
Lothrop, Zachariah			MB - A482	4/1/1773
by Samuel Gray				
Susq Co				7/18/1753
Lothrup, Rufus			MB	
Susq Co		1 share*		8/27/1761
Loveland, John			MB	
pd Major Elizer Talcott				
Susq Co		1/2 share*		11/4/1762
Luddington, Elisha			MB	
by Daniel Lyman				
Susq Co				7/18/1753
Lush, David			MB	
Susq Co		1 share		7/11/1754
Lydius, Baltsaser	NY		Deed	
Susq Co		1 share*	gratis	5/16/1796
Lyman, Mary wf of Medad, decd.	New Haven, New Haven, CT		H223	11/26/1799
deed states share is reimbursement for £5.19.4 spent by Lymans on food/drink for 20 proprietors meeting 40 years ago (1756) & room/board for Co Reps Jenkins and Clapp 23 years ago (1773)				
Susq Co		1 share*	$5	1/9/1754
Lyman, Phinehas Esq.			MB - Deed	
pd S Gray				

grantor grantee notes	grantor residence grantee residence	description location	amount acct bk page	deed date record date
Susq Co		1 share*	£8	5/11/1761
Lyon, Ebenezer Jr.			MB - B109	12/23/1773
pd Zachariah Clark				
Susq Co		1 share	£70	3/29/1763
Mabe, Peter	Dutchess, NY		H252	10/1/1800
Susq Co				
Macannale, Patrick			MB	
should be on Deed				
Susq Co				
Macdole, Jonathan			MB	
should be on Deed				
Susq Co		1 share*		4/7/1763
Mallet, Peter	Stratford		MB	
by Zachariah Clark				
Susq Co		1/2 share*	£3.5	9/28/1753
Man, Nathan			MB	
should be on Deed				
Susq Co		1/2 share		
Manly, William			Deed	
Susq Co		1/2 share		
Manly, William Junr			Deed	
Susq Co		1 share*	$2	9/28/1753
Manning, John Jr.			MB - Deed	
pd Journeying Cmte				
Susq Co				
Mansfield, Richard			A67	
Susq Co		1/2 share*	$4.50	12/31/1755
Mansfield, Richard	Darby		MB	
pd Thomas Darling				
Susq Co		1 share*	$9	12/31/1755
Mansfield, Saml/Allen, Stephen Co.			MB	
pd Thomas Darling				
Susq Co		1 share*	$2	9/28/1753
Mansfield, Thomas			MB - Deed	
pd Capt John Fitch				
Susq Co		1000 A	services rendered	7/6/1796
Manville, Ira			E266	7/8/1796
Susq Co		1/2 share*	£6	9/9/1769
Manwaring, David	New London, New London, CT		MB - C99	3/17/1787
by Samuel Gray				
Susq Co		1 share*		11/20/1754
Marsh, Ebenezer Esq., Maj.			MB - Deed	
pd Capn Uriah Stevens				
Susq Co		1 share*		3/24/1763
Marsh, Elihu Junr			MB	
pd Zachariah Clark				
Susq Co		1/2 share*		11/20/1754
Marsh, Job			MB - Deed	
pd Capn Uriah Stevens				
Susq Co		1 share*		3/24/1763
Marsh, William			MB	
pd Zachariah Clark				
Susq Co		1/2 share No. 329 of 400		10/1/1785
Marshall, Josiah			I167	2/21/1795
Susq Co		1 share*	$9	5/1/1755
Marshall, Noah	Torrington, CT		RB	
pd Daniel Edwards				
Susq Co		1 share*		4/7/1763
Marshall, Seth	Farmington		MB	
by Jonathan Root				
Susq Co		1 share*		11/16/1762
Marvin, David			MB	
by Uriah Stevens				

grantor grantee notes	grantor residence grantee residence	description location	amount acct bk page	deed date record date
Susq Co Mason, Jeremiah *should be on Deed*		1 share*	£6.10 MB	11/20/1754
Susq Co Mason, Jeremiah Jr. *should be on Deed*		1 share*	£6.10 MB	11/20/1754
Susq Co Mather, Richard *pd Isaac Tracy*		1/2 share*	MB	10/20/1761
Susq Co Matterson, Israel	Johnston, RI	1/2 share	£4 B263	5/22/1762 11/4/1774
Susq Co Matterson, Thomas	Coventry, Kent, RI	1/2 share	$4.50 B362	5/8/1775 5/8/1775
Susq Co Matterson, Thomas	RI	1 share	A309	
Susq Co Matterson, Thomas Jr.	Scituate, Providence, RI	1/2 share	£4 B263	5/22/1762 11/4/1774
Susq Co Matthews, Peter		1/4 share	GD	
Susq Co Matthewson, Betsy *for suffering at Wyoming in contest between PA and CT claimants in 1783 and for her attachment to the cause of the CT claim; 150 A already laid out*	Athens	300 A of 1 share No. 124 of 600* Columbia Twp	I192	3/19/1795
Susq Co Matthewson, Elisha *entered 5/10/1786*		1/2 share No. 242 of 400 Athens Twp*	I62	9/10/1785 6/10/1786
Susq Co Mattison, Thomas *pd John Fitch*	East Greenage, RI	1 share*	$5 Deed - B211	5/29/1754 5/15/1774
Susq Co May, Hezekiah *pd Thomas Stantly; 6s taxes pd on 1/4 share 3/1/1770*	Weathersfield	1/2 share*	$2.50 MB - F2/3 - Deed	5/1/1754
Susq Co May, Samuel *pd Thomas Stantly*	Hartford Co	1/2 share*	$2.50 MB - Deed	5/1/1754
Susq Co McClure, Thomas			A218	
Susq Co McDowal, Daniel *entered 5/8/1786*	Tioga, PA	1/2 share No 269 of 600 Athens Twp*	I63	5/8/1786 7/3/1786
Susq Co McFarland, Samuel *pd S Gray*		1 share*	$2 MB - B141 - Deed	9/6/1753 2/17/1774
Susq Co McKinstry, John, Col.		16,000 A Derry Twp	sufficient vouchers C168	2/24/1795 2/24/1795
Susq Co McLean, James		1 share No. 96 of 600	I276	6/26/1793
Susq Co McNeil, Alexander *pd Daniel Edwards*	Litchfield, CT	1/2 share*	$4.50 MB - RB	5/1/1755 12/28/1768
Susq Co McNeil, Archibald *pd Daniel Edwards*	Litchfield, CT	1/2 share*	$4.50 MB - RB	5/1/1755 12/28/1768
Susq Co Meeker, Amos		1/2 share, No. 133 of 400	D24	10/1/1785 9/24/1795
Susq Co Meigs, Jehiel	Guilford, New Haven, CT	1 share	$9 B101	11/20/1754 10/28/1773
Susq Co Meloy, Edward *pd Daniel Lyman*	New Haven, New Haven, CT	1/2 share*	£4 MB - B32	4/29/1761 9/15/1773
Susq Co Merrell, Joseph 2nd *pd Elisha Sheldon*	New Hartford, Litchfield, CT	1 share*	£8 MB - B80	4/2/1773 10/11/1773

grantor	grantor residence	description	amount	deed date
grantee	grantee residence	location	acct bk page	record date
notes				
Susq Co		1/2 share*	$4.50	5/1/1755
Merril, Abraham	Hartford & Windsor		MB - RB	12/28/1768
pd Daniel Edwards				
Susq Co		1/2 share*	£4	
Merriman, Eben	Farmington		MB	12/28/1768
pd Daniel Lyman				
Susq Co				
Metcalf, Andrew			A279	
Susq Co		1/2 share*	$4.50	12/31/1755
Miles, Jonathan	Darby		MB	
pd Thomas Darling				
Susq Co		1 share	special services	1/12/1770
Miller, Abraham	Delaware River		H49	1/10/1799
Susq Co		1 share*	$2	9/16/1753
Miller, Gann			MB - GM - Deed	
pd S Gray; taxes pd to 11/20/1773				
Susq Co		1 share No. 95 of 600		5/11/1793
Miller, Johnson		Johnson Miller Pitch	I68 - I276	5/30/1793
Susq Co				7/18/1753
Miller, Peter			MB	
Susq Co		1/2 share No. 164 [sic. 116] of 400*		11/26/1799
Millet, John	Athens, Luzerne, PA		H126	11/26/1799
certificate lost, but list of 400 in Liber A, Volume 2 assigns No. 116 to John Millet				
Susq Co		1 share		7/11/1754
Milliner, Rachel			Deed	
Susq Co		1 share	$5	2/18/1754
Mills, Elisha	Stratford		Deed	6/8/1796
Susq Co		1/2 share		12/6/1754
Mills, Elisha/Elijah			MB	
Susq Co		1 share		7/11/1754
Mills, Jedediah			Deed	
Susq Co		1/2 share	$2.50	6/8/1754
Mills, Peletiah			B296	5/27/1774
Susq Co		1 share*	$5	5/1/1754
Mills, Peletiah	Hartford Co		MB - Deed	
pd Thomas Stantly				
Susq Co		1/2 share*	$4.50	12/31/1755
Mills, Philo	Derby, New Haven, CT		MB	
pd Thomas Darling				
Susq Co		1/2 share		10/1/1786
Mills, Reuben			E362	
Susq Co		1/2 share*		8/27/1761
Mills, Treat			MB	
pd Zachariah Clark				
Susq Co		one suffering right*		6/12/1793
Minard, George		any proprietor's township	E271	
in lieu of right in Wilkesbarre; certified one of the first 200 and had right in Wilkesbarre, but lost right due to absence				
Susq Co		1 share		7/11/1754
Miner, Daniel			Deed	
Susq Co		1 share	£16.5	2/25/1754
Miner, Henry	Stonington, New London, CT		E347	8/24/1796
Susq Co		1 share*		11/20/1754
Minor, John			MB - Deed	
pd Capn Uriah Stevens				
Susq Co		1 share*	$2	9/28/1753
Minor, Manasseth			MB - Deed	
pd S Gray				
Susq Co		1/2 share*	$4.50	5/1/1755
Mire, Ebenezer	Farmingham & Hartford, CT		RB	
pd Daniel Edwards				
Susq Co		1/2 share*	£4	5/25/1761
Mitchel, John	Woodbury, Litchfield, CT		MB - B126	1/18/1774
pd Elisha Sheldon				

grantor grantee notes	grantor residence grantee residence	description location	amount acct bk page	deed date record date
Susq Co		1/2 share*	£4	12/28/1761
Mitchel, John Jr.	Woodbury, Litchfield, CT		MB - B127	1/18/1774
pd Capt Elisha Sheldon				
Susq Co		1 share No. 32 of 600		9/28/1786
Moder, John Jay A.	New York City, NY		E166	5/14/1796
Susq Co		1 share*	$2	9/28/1753
Moffet, Joseph	Sturbridge MA		MB - B118 - Deed	3/9/1774
pd S Gray				
Susq Co		1 share	$5	5/29/1754
Moffet, Thomas	Killingly		B282	12/22/1774
Susq Co		1 share		7/11/1754
Moffitt, Doctor			Deed	
Susq Co		1 share*	$2	9/16/1753
Montgomery, James	Voluntown, Windham, CT		MB - Deed	
pd S Gray				
Susq Co		1 share*	$2	9/16/1753
Montgomery, John			MB - Deed	
pd S Gray				
Susq Co		1 share	$40	5/4/1770
Montgomery, John			E77	3/2/1796
Susq Co		1 share*	$2	9/6/1753
Montgomery, John Jr.			MB - Deed	
pd S Gray				
Susq Co		1/2 share*	$4.50	5/1/1755
Moor, Simeon	Windsor, CT		RB	
pd Daniel Edwards				
Susq Co		1/2 share each*	$9	2/5/1755
Moore, Simeon & Griswold,	Windsor		E238	7/21/1796
taxes paid on behalf of Simeon Moore 1774 and by Benjamin Moore 5/28/1796				
Susq Co		1/2 share	$4.50	6/12/1755
Morehouse, Nathan	Fairfield, Fairfield, CT		B125	1/19/1774
Susq Co		1/2 share*	$4.50	5/1/1755
Morehouse, Nathan	Fairfield, CT		RB	
pd Daniel Edwards				
Susq Co		1 share		7/11/1754
Morey, Jonathan	RI		Deed	
Susq Co		1/2 share*	£4	5/2/1761
Morgan, Daniel, Capt	Preston, New London, CT		MB - F35	4/23/1796
pd Isaac Tracy; pd taxes for self and Col. Lydius 4/5/1768; 3/1/1770				
Susq Co		1 share, No 167 of 600*		7/13/1785
Morgan, John	Hartford, Hartford, CT		C105	12/27/1786
by William Judd				
Susq Co		1 share*		6/4/1766
Morgan, Morriel	England		MB	
by John Gardiner Esq.				
Susq Co		10,800 of 16,000 A	sufficient vouchers	3/1/1795
Morgan, Nathaniel	Reading, Fairfield, CT	Granby Twp	E164	5/20/1796
Susq Co		1 share	£12	4/8/1772
Morgan, Theophilus	Killingworth CT		C43	5/27/1782
Susq Co		1/2 share*		10/20/1761
Morgan, William			MB	
pd Isaac Tracy				
Susq Co		1/2 share*		11/20/1754
Morris, James			MB - Deed	
pd Capn Uriah Stevens				
Susq Co		1 share	$5	2/20/1754
Morriss, Daniel	Fairfield, Fairfield, CT		Deed - B109	12/23/1773
Susq Co		1 share*	$5	5/1/1754
Moseley, Abner	Hartford Co		MB - Deed	
pd Thomas Stantly				
Susq Co		1 share*		11/20/1754
Moseley, Increase Esq.			MB - Deed	
pd Capn Uriah Stevens				

grantor grantee notes	grantor residence grantee residence	description location	amount acct bk page	deed date record date
Susq Co		1 share		7/11/1754
Mosely, Isaac			Deed	
Susq Co		1/2 share		
Moses, Caleb			Deed	
Susq Co		1/2 share		7/11/1754
Moses, Timothy			MB - Deed	
Susq Co		1 share*	$9	5/1/1755
Mosher or Mosley, Eleazar	Lyme		RB	
pd Daniel Edwards				
Susq Co		1 share*	$9	12/31/1755
Moss, Solomon	New Haven		MB	
pd Thomas Darling				
Susq Co		1 share*	$2	9/29/1753
Mott, Edward	Voluntown, Windham, CT		MB - B140 - Deed	2/17/1774
pd S Gray				
Susq Co				7/18/1753
Moulton, Samuel			MB	
Susq Co		1 share*		3/24/1763
Mullener, Peter & William			MB	
pd Zachariah Clark				
Susq Co		1/2 share*	$4.50	5/1/1755
Nash, Jonathan	Fairfield, CT		RB - B125	1/19/1774
pd Daniel Edwards				
Susq Co		1 share*		7/27/1769
Nesbit, James			MB	
by Isaac Tripp				
Susq Co		1/2 share No [blank]		9/10/1785
Nesbitt, Abraham		Athens Twp*	I60	6/10/1786
entered 5/10/1786				
Susq Co		1 share		7/11/1754
Newcomb, Benjamin			Deed	
Susq Co		1 share*		5/1/1754
Newcombe, Obadiah			MB - Deed	
pd Jed Elderkin				
Susq Co		1/2 share		7/11/1754
Newell, Eliphalet			Deed	
Susq Co		1 share		7/11/1754
Newton, Jesse			Deed	
Susq Co		1 share*	$5	1/12/1754
Newton, John	Colchester, Hartford, CT		MB - B285	1/15/1775
1/2 Newton, John; 1/2 Morgan, John				
Susq Co		1 share	$9	1/22/1755
Nichols, Benjamin	Newport RI		C595	7/8/1795
Susq Co		1 share	$5	5/17/1754
Nichols, Jonathan Esq.	RI		Deed - B373	10/9/1777
Susq Co		1/2 share*	£4	7/27/1761
Northrup, Isaac	New Milford, Litchfield, CT		MB - B15	9/20/1781
pd Daniel Lyman				
Susq Co		1/2 share*	$4.50	5/1/1755
Norton, Ebenezer	Guilford, CT		RB	
pd Daniel Edwards				
Susq Co				
Norton, Issacher			A412	
Susq Co		1 share		7/11/1754
Norton, Jedediah			Deed	
Susq Co		1/2 share*		
Norton, Lott			Deed - MB	
should be 1 share				
Susq Co		1/2 share*	$4.50	5/1/1755
Norton, Reuben	Guilford, CT		RB	
pd Daniel Edwards				
Susq Co		1/2 share	$9	2/26/1755
Norton, Rubin & Edward, bros	Guilford, New Haven, CT		B22	9/15/1773

grantor grantee notes	grantor residence grantee residence	description location	amount acct bk page	deed date record date
Susq Co		1/2 share*		11/20/1754
Norton, Samuel			MB - Deed	
pd Capn Uriah Stevens				
Susq Co		1 share*		11/20/1754
Norton, Seth			MB - Deed	
pd Capn Uriah Stevens				
Susq Co		1 share*		4/7/1763
Noys, William Junr	Groton		MB	
by Zachariah Clark				
Susq Co		1/2 share*	$4.50	5/1/1755
Ogden, Humphrey	Fairfield, CT		RB - B125	
pd Daniel Edwards				
Susq Co		1 share*	$2	9/6/1753
Olcott, Josiah			MB - E249 - Deed	
pd Journeying Cmte: pd $2 tax 11/23/1753				
Susq Co		1/2 share	discharge of debt*	6/2/1773
Olcott, Nathaniel	Hartford, Hartford, CT		B213	5/11/1774
Susq Co owed £6.7.6 to Lazarus & William Stewart and five others, 1771				
Susq Co		1 share	$9	
Olcott, Thomas	New Hartford		F87	9/15/1796
Susq Co		1/2 share	promissory note	8/29/1770
Old, Daniel & Isaiah			B176	3/12/1774
Susq Co		1/2 share*	$4.50	5/1/1755
Old, Thomas	N Hartford & Hatfield		RB	
pd Daniel Edwards				
Susq Co		1 share*	£8	5/9/1761
Olmsted, John	Colchester, New London, CT		MB - C341	9/1/1795
pd Major Elizer Talcott				
Susq Co		1 share No. 56 of 2nd 600		
Olney, Joseph	Hudson, Columbia, NY	Litchfield Twp*	H35	9/11/1799
entered 600 A, 21 Feb 1795				
Susq Co		1 share*		11/20/1754
Orten, Lemuel			A335 - Deed	
pd Capn Uriah Stevens				
Susq Co		1 share*		11/20/1754
Orten, Samuel			MB - Deed	
pd Capn Uriah Stevens				
Susq Co		1 share*		11/20/1754
Orton, Azariah			MB - Deed	
pd Capn Uriah Stevens				
Susq Co		1/2 share*		11/20/1754
Orton, Hezekiah			MB - A239 - Deed	
pd Capn Uriah Stevens				
Susq Co		1/2 share*		8/27/1761
Orton, Hezekiah			MB	
pd Elisha Sheldon				
Susq Co		1 share*		8/27/1761
Orton, John			MB	
pd Elisha Sheldon				
Susq Co		1/2 share	£4	5/4/1761
Osborn, Jeremiah	New Haven, New Haven, CT		B100	10/21/1773
Susq Co		1/2 share*		10/21/1773
Osborne, Jonathan Junr	New Haven		MB - E345	6/15/1796
by Daniel Lyman; all taxes pd				
Susq Co		1/2 share of the 400		2/21/1795
Ossencup, Jacob			C447	2/21/1795
Susq Co		2,500 A		3/20/1795
Ousterhout, Gideon	Luzerne, PA	Ousterhout Pitch	D151	6/15/1796
Susq Co		1 share		11/20/1754
Overton, Azariah			MB	
Susq Co		1/2 share*		12/1/1762
Overton, John	Southhold		MB	
by Isaac Tracy				

grantor	grantor residence	description	amount	deed date
grantee	grantee residence	location	acct bk page	record date
notes				
Susq Co		1/2 share	£6	7/31/1770
Owen, John	New London CT		C51	11/8/1782
Susq Co		1 share*		5/1/1754
Palmater, Joseph			MB - Deed	
pd Jed Elderkin				
Susq Co		1/2 share No. 296 of 600		6/26/1793
Palmelee [Parmelee], Abraham			I276	
Susq Co		1 share	£8	9/20/1762
Palmer, Abel			B135	2/2/1774
Susq Co		1/2 share*		10/20/1761
Palmer, Abijah			MB	
pd Isaac Tracy				
Susq Co		1 share		7/11/1754
Palmer, Christopher			Deed	
Susq Co		1/2 share, heirs certified*		4/1/1795
Palmer, Daniel	Voluntown, Windham, CT		C604 - A84	
legal heirs: Elisha Palmer, Joseph Palmer, Benjamin Palmer, Freeborn Palmer, Huldah Palmer, Margaret Palmer all of Voluntown				
Susq Co		1/2 share		7/11/1754
Palmer, David			Deed	
Susq Co		1 share*		11/20/1754
Palmer, George			MB - Deed	
pd Capn Uriah Stevens				
Susq Co		1/2 share		7/11/1754
Parish, Oliver			Deed	
Susq Co				7/18/1753
Park, John			MB	
Susq Co		Lot 53, 300 A		12/12/1796
Park, Moses	Ulster	Murraysfield Twp	E528	12/14/1796
Susq Co		1 share	$2	1/10/1754
Parke, Benjamin	Voluntown, Windham, CT		MB - B104 - Deed	12/13/1773
Susq Co		1/2 share	$2	1/9/1754
Parke, Benjamin Jr.	Voluntown, Windham, CT		MB - B211 - Deed	5/15/1774
Susq Co		1/2 share	$4.50	12/27/1754
Parke, Joseph	Voluntown, Windham, CT		B104	12/13/1773
Susq Co		1 share*	$2	7/18/1753
Parke, Nathan			MB	
pd Journeying Cmte				
Susq Co		1 share*	$9	12/31/1755
Parker, James	New Haven		MB	
pd Thomas Darling				
Susq Co		1/2 share*		5/1/1754
Parkes, Benajah			MB - Deed	
pd S Gray				
Susq Co		1 share No. 87 of 2nd 600 inc 600 A		4/3/1787
Parkes, Darius & Kerney, William	Kingston, Wyoming, PA	Parkes/Kerney Pitch	I45	4/3/1787
Susq Co		1/2 share		7/11/1754
Parkes, Josiah			Deed	
Susq Co		1 share		
Parkes, Nathan			Deed	
Susq Co		1 share		5/1/1754
Parkes, Nathaniel			Deed	
Susq Co		1 share*	$2	7/18/1753
Parkes, Robert			MB - Deed	
pd Journeying Cmte				
Susq Co		1 share*	$2	7/18/1753
Parkes, William			MB - Deed	
pd S Gray				
Susq Co		1 share		11/20/1754
Parkhurst, Joseph	Plainfield		MB	
Susq Co		1 share	£8	1/4/1762
Parks, Nehemiah	Plainfield, Windham, CT		B81	10/11/1773

grantor / grantee / notes	grantor residence / grantee residence	description / location	amount / acct bk page	deed date / record date
Susq Co		1/2 share*		9/4/1761
Parmeley, Hezekiah Junr	New Haven		MB	
by Daniel Lyman				
Susq Co		1 share*		11/20/1754
Parmeley, Thomas			MB - Deed	
pd Capn Uriah Stevens				
Susq Co		1 share*		12/31/1755
Parson, Elihu			MB	1/15/1762
pd Timothy Woodbridge				
Susq Co		1 share		7/11/1754
Pason, Nathan			Deed	
Susq Co		1 share		7/11/1754
Paterson, John			Deed	
Susq Co		1 share*	$2	9/16/1753
Patrick, Jacob			MB - Deed	
pd Capt John Fitch				
Susq Co		1 share*		12/14/1773
Patrick, Jacob	Voluntown	Northmoreland & Braintrim Twps*	I225	4/1/1795
entered 1/2 Northmoreland, 8/4/1775; 1/2 Braintrim, 1777				
Susq Co		1 share*	$2	9/19/1753
Patrick, Matthew			MB - B211 - Deed	5/15/1774
pd S Gray				
Susq Co		1 share*	$2	1/9/1754
Patrick, Matthew Jr.			MB - Deed	
pd S Gray				
Susq Co		1 share*	$9	4/24/1755
Pease, Joseph			MB	12/28/1768
pd Phineas Lyman				
Susq Co		1 share*		11/20/1754
Peat, Richard			MB - Deed	
pd Capn Uriah Stevens				
Susq Co		1 share*	$9	12/31/1755
Peck, James	New Haven		MB	
pd Thomas Darling				
Susq Co		1 share	£12	5/5/1769
Peckham, Phillip	New Port, RI		B224	6/29/1774
Susq Co				7/18/1753
Peirce, Abel			MB	
Susq Co				
Peirce, Amos			A488	
Susq Co		1 share*	$2	7/18/1753
Peirce, Ezekiel Esq.			MB - Deed	
pd Capt John Fitch				
Susq Co				7/18/1753
Peirce, Lemuel			MB	
Susq Co		1/2 share*	$25	2/12/1763
Peirce, Samuel	Warwick, RI		MB - B247	11/26/1774
by Ezra Dean				
Susq Co		1/2 share	$4.50	6/12/1755
Penfield, Peter	Fairfield, Fairfield, CT		C526	5/1/1795
Susq Co		1/2 share*	$4.50	5/1/1755
Penfield, Peter	Fairfield, CT		RB	12/28/1768
pd Daniel Edwards				
Susq Co		1/2 share*	$2	1/8/1754
Perkins, James			MB	
pd Stephen Gardner; should be on Deed				
Susq Co				
Perkins, John			A337	
Susq Co		1/2 share*		11/20/1754
Perkins, John			MB - Deed	
pd Capn Uriah Stevens				

grantor grantee notes	grantor residence grantee residence	description location	amount acct bk page	deed date record date
Susq Co		1 share*		8/28/1761
Perkins, Zephaniah			MB - A443	
pd Nathaniel Wales Junr Esq.				
Susq Co		1 share*		11/20/1754
Perry, Daniel			MB - Deed	
pd Capn Uriah Stevens				
Susq Co				
Perry, Gideon			A67	
Susq Co		1/2 share*	$4.50	12/31/1755
Perry, Gideon	Darby		MB	
pd Thomas Darling				
Susq Co				
Persons, Samuel Holden			A486	
Susq Co		1/2 share*		
Petebone, Abel			Deed	
Susq Co		1/2 share		7/11/1754
Petebone, Abram			Deed	
Susq Co		1/2 share		
Petebone, Giles			Deed	
Susq Co		1/2 share		
Petebone, Isaac			Deed	
Susq Co		1 share*	$5	5/1/1754
Pettibone, Jonathan	Hartford Co		MB - Deed	
pd Thomas Stantly				
Susq Co		1 share*	$2	9/6/1753
Phelps, Alexander			MB - Deed	
pd Dewey & Bulkley				
Susq Co		1 share*	$5	5/1/1754
Phelps, David	Symsbury		MB - Deed	
pd Thomas Stantly				
Susq Co		1 share*	$9	5/1/1755
Phelps, Edward Col.	Litchfield, CT		MB - RB	12/28/1768
pd Daniel Edwards				
Susq Co		1/2 share*	$4.50	5/1/1755
Phelps, Edward Jr.	Litchfield, CT		MB - RB	
pd Daniel Edwards				
Susq Co		1 share*	$5	5/1/1754
Phelps, Hezekiah	Hartford Co		MB - Deed	
pd Thomas Stantly				
Susq Co				
Phelps, Noah			A486	
Susq Co		1 share*	$2	9/16/1753
Phillips, Joseph			MB - Deed	
pd Capt John Fitch				
Susq Co		1 share*	$2	9/16/1753
Pierce, Benjamin Jr.	Scituate		MB - Deed	
pd S Gray				
Susq Co		13,444 A		11/19/1798
Pierce, John	Plainfield, Windham, CT	Litchfield Twp, part of	H33	11/20/1798
Susq Co		1 share*	$2	1/9/1754
Pierce, Thomas			MB - Deed	
pd S Gray				
Susq Co		1/2 share*	£4	8/15/1761
Pierpont, John	New Haven, CT		MB - E405	9/15/1796
pd Daniel Lyman				
Susq Co		1/2 share*	$4.50	12/31/1755
Pinto, Jacob	New Haven		MB - E255	7/1/1796
pd Thomas Darling; E255 gives 7/9/1755				
Susq Co		1/2 share	$4.50	7/9/1755
Pinto, Jacob	New Haven		E255	7/1/1796
Susq Co		1 share*	$5	5/1/1754
Pitkin, William Jr. Esq.	Hartford Co		MB - Deed	
pd Thomas Stantly				

grantor grantee notes	grantor residence grantee residence	description location	amount acct bk page	deed date record date
Susq Co		1 share*	$9	1/20/1755
Pixley, David	Grt Nine Partners, Dutchess,		MB - B242	8/30/1774
pd Timothy Woodbridge				
Susq Co		1 share*		12/31/1755
Pixley, John			MB	1/15/1762
pd Timothy Woodbridge				
Susq Co		1/2 share No. 6 of 400		9/10/1785
Platner, John		Athens Twp	I65	6/10/1786
entered 5/8/1786				
Susq Co		1 share	£8	8/24/1762
Platt, Epenetus	Hempstead, Queens, NY		B239	8/20/1774
Susq Co		1/2 share*	$4.50	12/31/1755
Plum, Samuel	Darby		MB	
pd Thomas Darling				
Susq Co		1/2 share	$4.50	6/14/1755
Plumb, Samuel	Darby, New Haven, CT		E407	9/15/1796
Susq Co		1 share*	$2	9/6/1753
Pomeroy, Benjamin			MB - Deed	
pd Dewey & Bulkley				
Susq Co		1/2 share*		9/4/1761
Pond, Aaron	New Haven		MB	
pd Daniel Lyman				
Susq Co		1 share	£8	2/7/1762
Pope, Seth Jr.			B99	12/8/1773
Susq Co		1/2 share*	$2.50	5/1/1754
Porter, Ezekiel Doctr.	Hartford Co		MB - Deed	
pd Thomas Stantly				
Susq Co		1/2 share*		8/27/1761
Porter, Gideon			MB	
pd Major Elizer Talcott				
Susq Co		1/2 share	$4.50	11/20/1754
Porter, Joseph	Windsor, Hartford, CT		B303	1/20/1775
Susq Co		1/2 share*	$4.50	5/1/1755
Porter, Joseph	Hartford & Windsor		RB	
pd Daniel Edwards				
Susq Co		1/2 share*		11/20/1754
Porter, Thomas			MB - Deed	
pd Capn Uriah Stevens				
Susq Co				
Potter, John			A60	
Susq Co		1 share*		6/4/1766
Powell, William, Attorney at Law	England		MB	
by John Gardiner Esq.				
Susq Co		1 share*		4/7/1763
Prendal, Aaron	New Fairfield		MB	
by Zachariah Clark				
Susq Co		1 share	$5	5/24/1754
Pride, Hubbard	Norwich, New London, CT		Deed - B149	3/8/1774
Susq Co				7/18/1753
Putnam, Israel			MB	
Susq Co		1/2 share*	$20	7/31/1769
Raab, George	Wilkes Barre		B176	3/14/1774
Susq Co		1 share*	$2	7/18/1753
Randal, Joseph Greenfield			MB - A394	
pd John Smith Esqr				
Susq Co		1 share		7/11/1754
Randall, Job Esq.	RI		Deed	
Susq Co		1 share		7/11/1754
Randall, Jonathan Esq.	RI		Deed	
Susq Co		1 share		7/11/1754
Randsome, Joshua			Deed	

grantor grantee notes	grantor residence grantee residence	description location	amount acct bk page	deed date record date
Susq Co		1/2 share No. 211 of 400		9/10/1785
Ransom, William		Columbia Twp*	E369	4/1/1796
entered Lot 34, 12/25/1793				
Susq Co		1 share	£50	8/26/1768
Rapalye, Garret	New York, NY		B130	1/20/1774
Susq Co		1 share		
Rathbone, John			Deed	
Susq Co		1 share*		2/23/1795
Rathbone, Wait	Stonington CT & Troy NY	Columbia Twp	C104	2/27/1795
1 share now worth 2000 A which equals 300 A Lot 36 Columbia + 1700 A anywhere else				
Susq Co			$9	2/25/1761
Rawson, Grindel Rev.			MB	
Susq Co				7/18/1753
Ray, Patrick			MB	
Susq Co		1/2 share		
Read, John			Deed	
Susq Co		1 share*	$2	1/10/1754
Read, John Junr*	Norwich, New London, CT		Deed - B151	3/8/1774
John Read twice on Deed but no Junr				
Susq Co		1/2 share		
Read, Joshua			Deed	
Susq Co		1/2 share		5/1/1754
Read/Reed, Joshua	Windham		MB	
Susq Co		1 share*	$5	1/26/1754
Reed, John	Northampton		B232 - H343	8/9/1774
taxes pd thru 3/31/1774; entered in Northampton 9/7/1774 [not a Susq Co twp]				
Susq Co		1/2 share*	£6.10	1/10/1754
Reed, Joshua	Windham		MB - C605	7/9/1795
pd Jed Elderkin				
Susq Co		1 share*	$4	1/8/1754
Reed, Samuel	Colchester, Hartford, CT		MB - B275	12/20/1774
pd Stephen Gardner; should be on Deed				
Susq Co		1 1/2 share*		
Renehid[?], John			MB	
by Ebenr Backus				
Susq Co		1/2 share*		8/27/1761
Reynolds, Hames			MB	
pd Elisha Sheldon				
Susq Co		1 share		7/11/1754
Reynolds, John	RI		Deed	
Susq Co		1 share		7/11/1754
Reynolds, John Jr.	RI		Deed	
Susq Co		1 share		7/11/1754
Reynolds, Jonathan	RI		Deed	
Susq Co				
Reynolds, William			A82	
Susq Co		1 share*	$2	7/18/1753
Rhodes, Obadiah Jr.			MB - Deed	
pd S Gray				
Susq Co		1 share		7/11/1754
Rhumsey, Benjamin Junr			Deed	
Susq Co		1/2 share*	$2	1/9/1754
Rice/Royce, John			MB - Deed	
pd S Gray				
Susq Co		1/2 share*		7/26/1769
Richards, Guy			MB	
by Eliphalet Dyer				
Susq Co		1/2 share*		7/26/1769
Richards, Guy, Jr.			MB	
by Eliphalet Dyer				
Susq Co		1 share*		11/20/1754
Richards, Jedediah			MB - Deed	
pd Capn Uriah Stevens				

grantor grantee notes	grantor residence grantee residence	description location	amount acct bk page	deed date record date
Susq Co		1/2 share*	$4.50	12/24/1754
Richards, John	Guilford, CT		MB - RB	12/29/1768
pd Daniel Edwards				
Susq Co		1 share*	$9	12/31/1755
Riggs, John	Darby		MB	
pd Thomas Darling				
Susq Co		1 share*	$5	5/1/1754
Robe, Andrew	Hartford Co		MB - Deed	
pd Thomas Stantly				
Susq Co		1/2 share No. 136 of 400		9/10/1785
Roberts, Daniel		Allensburgh Twp*	E495	12/17/1796
entered 9/24/1787				
Susq Co		1 share*	£15	3/22/1763
Roberts, Elias	Farmington, Hartford, CT		MB - B377	3/13/1778
by Jonathan Root				
Susq Co		1/2 share No. 77 of 400		9/10/1785
Roberts, Hezekiah Jr.		Bedford Twp*	F102	9/16/1796
entered 300 A 5/11/1795				
Susq Co		1/2 share*		4/7/1763
Roberts, Jabez & Thomas Cooper	Farmington		MB - A88	
by Jonathan Root				
Susq Co		1/2 share No. 155 of 400		9/10/1785
Roberts, Moses		Allenborough Twp*	I66	
entered Allenborough 9/29/1787; reentered on pitch N Athens on Susq R, 300A 6/18/1791				
Susq Co		1 share No. 88 of 2nd 600		7/1/1794
Roberts, Seth	Paris, NY		C582 - I277	6/20/1795
Susq Co		1/2 share	£6	7/15/1769
Robertson, Ephriam	Coventry, Windham, CT		B105	12/15/1773
Susq Co		1 share*	£6	7/18/1753
Robinson, Ebenezer			MB	
pd S Gray				
Susq Co		1 share	$5	8/23/1773
Robinson, Eliakim			B33	9/15/1773
Susq Co		1/2 share		
Robinson, Ephriam			Deed	
Susq Co		1 share		7/11/1754
Robinson, Josiah			Deed	
Susq Co		1 share		7/11/1754
Rockwell, Daniel			Deed	
Susq Co		1 share*		2/1/1755
Rogers, Daniel			MB - A288 - C347	1/15/1762
pd Eliphalet Dyer				
Susq Co		1/2 share*		10/20/1761
Rogers, Theophilus			MB	
pd Isaac Tracy				
Susq Co		1 share*		10/20/1761
Rogers, Zabdiel			MB - A295	
pd Isaac Tracy				
Susq Co		1 share		3/9/1774
Rogers, Zabdiel	Norwich		CA	
Susq Co		1 share*	£6.10	11/20/1754
Root, Jonathan			MB	
should be on Deed				
Susq Co		1/2 share*	$4.50	5/1/1755
Root, Jonathan	Farmingham		RB	
pd Daniel Edwards				
Susq Co		1/2 share*	£3.5	9/28/1753
Root, William			MB	
pd Charles Dewey; should be on Deed				
Susq Co		1 share		7/11/1754
Rosa, John	NY		Deed	
Susq Co		1 share	$9	12/24/1754
Rose, Jacob	Branford, New Haven, CT		B31	9/15/1773

grantor grantee notes	grantor residence grantee residence	description location	amount acct bk page	deed date record date
Susq Co		1 share*		11/20/1754
Rose, Timothy			MB - Deed	
pd Capn Uriah Stevens				
Susq Co		1 share		7/11/1754
Roseboom, Jacob	NY		Deed	
Susq Co		1 share*		11/20/1754
Roser/Raser, Dennis			MB	
should be on Deed				
Susq Co		1 share*	$9	5/1/1755
Ross, Jacob	Branford, CT		RB	
pd Daniel Edwards				
Susq Co		1 share*	$2	7/18/1753
Ross, Jeremiah			MB - Deed - A95 -	
pd S Gray				
Susq Co		1/2 share		4/12/1773
Ross, Jeremiah			GD	
Susq Co		1/2 share	£4	5/6/1761
Rossiter, Theophilus, Esq.	Guilford, New Haven, CT		MB - B32	9/15/1773
pd Daniel Lyman				
Susq Co		1 share*		11/16/1762
Rothbone, Amos			MB	4/9/1763
by Uriah Stevens				
Susq Co		1 share		7/11/1754
Rothbone, Daniel			Deed	
Susq Co		1 share		7/11/1754
Rothbone, Jacob			Deed	
Susq Co		1 share*		11/16/1762
Rothbone, Job			MB	4/9/1763
by Uriah Stevens				
Susq Co		1 share*		11/20/1754
Rothbone, John			MB - Deed	
pd Capn Uriah Stevens; on Deed as John				
Susq Co		1 share*		11/20/1754
Rothbone, Joshua			MB - Deed	
pd Capn Uriah Stevens				
Susq Co		1 share		7/11/1754
Rothbone, Valentine			Deed	
Susq Co		1 share*	$2	7/18/1753
Rude, Stephen			MB - Deed	
pd S Gray				
Susq Co				7/18/1753
Russel, Josiah			MB	
Susq Co		1 share		7/11/1754
Sabin, Isaac Jr.			Deed	
Susq Co		1/2 share No. 377 of 600		9/3/1795
Salisbury, Gideon	Luzerne Co PA		I77	9/7/1795
Susq Co		Receipt		
Salmon, Nathaniel			A11	
Susq Co				
Salmon, Nathaniel			A279	
Susq Co		1/2 share, 1,000 A	£4	5/22/1762
Salsbury, William*	Scituate, RI	Harlem Twp	F237	12/12/1797
for heirs of Wm Salsbury				
Susq Co		1 share*		11/20/1754
Sanford, Oliver			MB	
pd Capn Uriah Stevens				
Susq Co		1 share		
Sanford, Oliver			Deed	
Susq Co		1/2 share*	$1	9/6/1753
Sanger, Jonathan	Ashford		MB - Deed	
pd S Gray				
Susq Co		1/2 share	services rendered	12/25/1799
Satterlee, Benedict			H174	12/27/1799

grantor	grantor residence	description	amount	deed date
grantee	grantee residence	location	acct bk page	record date
notes				
Susq Co		1 share No. 91 of 600		12/25/1794
Satterlee, Daniel & Franklin, Billa		Columbia Twp*	I188	3/17/1795
300 A, Lot No 47				
Susq Co		1/2 share No. 260 of 400		1/19/1786
Satterlee, Elisha Capt	Wyoming, PA	Standing Stone Twp*	E97	3/1/1796
entered Lot 20, 7/10/1786				
Susq Co		1 share No. 111 of 600		3/30/1799
Satterlee, Samuel	Athens, PA		H41	3/30/1799
Susq Co		1 share*		5/1/1754
Sawyer, Isaac			MB - Deed	
pd Jed Elderkin				
Susq Co		1 share No. 150 of 600*		1/10/1786
Schott, John Paul		Athens Twp	C342	9/2/1795
entered 1/2 of share in Athens 1/2/1787				
Susq Co		1 share	$4	4/12/1754
Scovell, Elisha	Colchester, Hartford, CT		B199	4/1/1774
Susq Co		1 share*		7/11/1754
Scovil, Elisha	Colchester		MB - Deed - I195	
taxes pd thru 3/1/1774				
Susq Co		1/2 share No. 273 of 400		6/1/1786
Scovil, James	Salisbury, CT		I191	3/19/1795
Susq Co		1 share, No 2 of the 600		12/6/1796
Scovill, James	Exeter, Luzerne, PA		E492	12/6/1796
Susq Co		1/2 share*		4/23/1773
Sedgwick, Abraham			MB	4/23/1773
by Samuel Gray				
Susq Co		1/2 share*	$4.50	5/1/1755
Sedgwick, Stephen	Farmingham & Hartford, CT		RB	
pd Daniel Edwards				
Susq Co		1 share*		4/7/1763
Seeley, Abel	New Fairfield		MB	
by Zachariah Clark				
Susq Co		1 share, No. 154 of 600		3/2/1787
Seeley, Barzilla Esq.	Minising CT [PA]		I37	3/2/1787
Susq Co		1 share*		4/7/1763
Seeley, Benjamin	New Fairfield		MB	
by Zachariah Clark				
Susq Co		1 share		10/8/1773
Seeley, Ebenezer	New Fairfield		E63	
Susq Co		1 share*		4/7/1763
Seeley, Ebenezer	New Fairfield		MB	
by Zachariah Clark				
Susq Co		1 share*		4/7/1763
Seeley, Ephriam	New Fairfield		MB	
by Zachariah Clark				
Susq Co		1 share*	$5	5/1/1754
Seymore, Thomas Capt	Hartford Co		MB - Deed	
pd Thomas Stantly				
Susq Co		1 share*	$5	5/1/1754
Seymore, Timothy	Hartford Co		MB - Deed	
pd Thomas Stantly				
Susq Co		1 share*	$9	5/1/1755
Seymour, David	Hartford, CT		RB	
pd Daniel Edwards				
Susq Co		1/2 share, No 121 of 400		10/1/1795
Shaw, Ichabod			D50	11/6/1795
Susq Co		1/2 share of 400		10/1/1785
Shaw, Jeremiah			E97	
Susq Co		1/2 share	7s 6d	1/2/1770
Shearlock, Thomas	Dover		E133	2/28/1796
Susq Co		1 share*	£16.5	1/27/1755
Shearlock, Thomas	Dover		E133	2/28/1796
pd Capt Nathaniel Barry				

grantor grantee notes	grantor residence grantee residence	description location	amount acct bk page	deed date record date
Susq Co		1 share		7/11/1754
Sheffield, Benjamin	RI		Deed	
Susq Co		1 share		7/11/1754
Shelden, Aaron	NY		Deed	
Susq Co		1 share*		11/20/1754
Shelden, Elisha Capt			MB	
pd Capn Uriah Stevens				
Susq Co		1 share		
Sheldon, Elisha			Deed	
Susq Co		1 share		2/27/1754
Sheldon, Isaac			Deed - A295	
Susq Co		1 share		7/11/1754
Sheldon, William	RI		Deed	
Susq Co		1/2 share*	$4.50	12/31/1755
Shelton, James	Stratford		MB	
pd Thomas Darling				
Susq Co		1/2 share*	$4.50	12/31/1755
Shelton, Samuel	Stratford		MB	
pd Thomas Darling				
Susq Co		1/2 share*		8/27/1761
Shelton, Thadeus			MB	
pd Zachariah Clark				
Susq Co		1 share*	$2	9/6/1753
Shepard, Isaac			MB - Deed	
pd Capt John Fitch				
Susq Co		1 share, No 1 of the 600*		12/6/1796
Shepard, John	Tioga, Luzerne, PA		E492 - E548	12/6/1796
as per Meeting of 2/18/1795; not found in Liber A, Volume 2				
Susq Co		1 share No. 3 of the 600		12/6/1796
Shepard, John	Tioga		E548	12/6/1796
not found in Liber A, Volume 2				
Susq Co		1 share		7/18/1753
Shepard, Jonas Jr.			MB - Deed	
Susq Co		1 share of the 600*		
Shephard, John	Athens, PA		H264	10/27/1800
this right disproved by order of the Commissioners				
Susq Co		1/2 share No. 285 of 400		9/10/1785
Shepherd, John	Ulster Twp	I12	8/19/1786
Susq Co		1 share*	£13	1/9/1754
Sheppard, Josias			MB	
pd S Gray				
Susq Co		1/2 share*	$4.50	12/31/1755
Sherman, James	New Haven		MB	
pd Thomas Darling				
Susq Co		1 share	40s	2/22/1754
Sherwood, Daniel	Fairfield, Fairfield, CT		Deed - B109	12/23/1773
Susq Co		1/2 share No 279 of the 400		10/1/1785
Sherwood, Levi			E436	10/1/1796
Susq Co		1 share	$9	5/10/1755
Sherwood, Samuel	Fairfield, Fairfield, CT		B125	1/19/1774
Susq Co		1/2 share No. 297 of 600*		12/25/1793
Shifflebeem, Michael			C283 - I276	9/7/1795
not found in Liber A, Volume 2				
Susq Co		1 share*	$2	9/6/1753
Shoemaker, Benjamin	PA		MB - Deed	
pd Journeying Cmte				
Susq Co		1 share*	$2	9/6/1753
Shoemaker, Daniel	PA		MB - Deed	
pd Journeying Cmte				
Susq Co		1/2 share No. 263 of 400		2/23/1786
Shoemaker, Daniel & Shaw, John	Northampton, PA		I219	6/23/1795

grantor grantee notes	grantor residence grantee residence	description location	amount acct bk page	deed date record date
Susq Co		300 A*		4/20/1797
Shoemaker, Elijah		Susq R and Buttermilk Falls Cr.	F55	4/28/1798
surveyed before Revolutionary War but original certificate lost so Commissioners reapproved				
Susq Co		1/2 share No. 234 of 2nd 600		
Showfalt, Philip	Claverack, NY	Rutland Twp*	I118	12/17/1794
entered 700 A Rutland; reentered in Alba 12/5/1800				
Susq Co		1 share*		4/7/1763
Sill, Elijah	New Fairfield		MB	
by Zachariah Clark				
Susq Co		1/2 share*		8/28/1761
Silsby, Henry Capt			MB - A219	
pd Nathaniel Wales Junr Esq.				
Susq Co		1 share*	$2	9/6/1753
Silsby, Samuel			MB - Deed	
pd Journeying Cmte				
Susq Co		1/2 share		
Simons, Jacob			Deed	
Susq Co		1/2 share*		5/1/1754
Simons, Jacob 3rd			MB - Deed	
pd Jed Elderkin				
Susq Co		1/2 share	$2	1/10/1754
Simons, Jeduthan			Deed - B200	4/6/1774
Susq Co		1/2 share*		11/20/1754
Sisco, Jacob			MB - Deed	
pd Capn Uriah Stevens				
Susq Co		1 share*		5/1/1754
Skiff, Joseph			MB - Deed	
pd Jed Elderkin				
Susq Co		1 share*		7/18/1753
Skinner, Joseph	PA		MB - Deed	
pd S Gray				
Susq Co		1 share*	£6.10	7/18/1753
Skinner, Stephen			MB - Deed	
pd S Gray				
Susq Co		1 share*		11/20/1754
Slaughter, Samuel			MB - Deed	
pd Capn Uriah Stevens				
Susq Co		1/2 share	$4.50	5/8/1775
Slocum, Jonathan	Coventry, Kent, RI		B362	5/8/1775
Susq Co				
Slocum, Jonathan			A309	
Susq Co		1/2 share	£4	5/22/1762
Smith, Benjamin	Glocester, Providence, RI		MB - B302	12/28/1774
Susq Co		1/2 share		4/8/1772
Smith, Charles	Haddam, Middlesex, CT		D11	9/18/1795
Susq Co		1 share*	$2	9/6/1753
Smith, Ebenezer			MB - Deed	
pd Journeying Cmte				
Susq Co		1 share*	$2	9/6/1753
Smith, Ebenezer Jr.			MB - Deed	
pd Journeying Cmte				
Susq Co				7/18/1753
Smith, Francis 3rd			MB	
Susq Co		1 share*	$2	9/6/1753
Smith, John Esq.			MB - Deed	
pd Capt John Fitch				
Susq Co		1/2 share	£4	5/22/1762
Smith, Jonathan	Glocester, Providence, RI		B298	12/28/1774
Susq Co		1 share*		11/20/1754
Smith, Jonathan			MB - Deed	
pd Capn Uriah Stevens				

grantor grantee notes	grantor residence grantee residence	description location	amount acct bk page	deed date record date
Susq Co		1/2 share No 110 of 400*		8/25/1785
Smith, Jonathan	Lyme		F277	6/1/1798
must arrive in Wyoming by 10/1/1785 and not leave for 3 yrs				
Susq Co		1 share*	$2	9/6/1753
Smith, Joseph Jr.			MB - Deed	
pd Journeying Cmte				
Susq Co		1/2 share*	$2	1/1/1754
Smith, Joshua	Colchester, Hartford, CT		MB - B281	12/17/1774
should be on Deed				
Susq Co		1 share*	$2	9/6/1753
Smith, Lemuel			MB - Deed	
pd S Gray				
Susq Co		1 share	$40	3/5/1771
Smith, Lockwood	Grt Nine Partners, Dutchess,		B247	8/30/1774
Susq Co		1/2 share No. 109 of 400		8/25/1786
Smith, Martin	Colchester, Litchfield, CT	Martin Smith Pitch	I59	11/4/1786
Susq Co		1/2 share*	$4.50	5/1/1755
Smith, Merrit	Fairfield, CT		RB	
pd Daniel Edwards				
Susq Co		1 share		3/24/1763
Smith, Nathan			MB	
Susq Co		1 share		
Smith, Seth			Deed	
Susq Co		1 share*	$5	11/20/1754
Smith, Seth & Ephriam	Stonington		MB - B279	2/3/1775
1/2 share each				
Susq Co		1/2 share No. 202 of 600		7/13/1785
Smith, Simeon Doct	Sharon, CT		C571	7/10/1795
Susq Co		1/2 share No. 208 of 600		7/13/1785
Smith, Simeon Doct	Sharon, CT		C571	7/10/1795
Susq Co		1/2 share*	£4	4/24/1761
Smith, Stephen	New Haven, New Haven, CT		MB - B31	9/15/1773
pd Daniel Lyman				
Susq Co		1/2 share No. 117 of 400		10/1/1785
Smith, William		William Smith Pitch	I224	5/10/1794
Susq Co		1 share*	$2	9/6/1753
Snell, Thomas			MB - Deed	
pd Capt John Fitch				
Susq Co		1/2 share*	$2.50	1/10/1754
Snow, Abraham Jr.	Windham, Windham, CT		MB - B222 - Deed	6/8/1774
pd Capt John Fitch				
Susq Co				
Soals, Samuel			A90	
Susq Co		1 share		7/11/1754
Sommers, Jabez			Deed	
Susq Co		1 share*		4/7/1763
Soul, Timothy	Dutchess County		MB	
by Zachariah Clark				
Susq Co		1/2 share	£10	8/24/1775
Spafford, Darius	Windham	Northmoreland Twp	F86	9/15/1796
Susq Co		1/2 share*		5/20/1773
Spafford, Darius			MB	5/20/1773
by Samuel Gray				
Susq Co		1 share	£8	6/26/1762
Spalding, Amos	Plainfield, Windham, CT		B200	4/6/1774
Susq Co		1/2 share		7/11/1754
Spalding, Curtice			Deed	
Susq Co		1 share*		11/20/1754
Spalding, Edward			MB - Deed	
pd Capn Uriah Stevens				
Susq Co				7/18/1753
Spalding, Ezekiel			MB	

grantor grantee notes	grantor residence grantee residence	description location	amount acct bk page	deed date record date
Susq Co		1 share*	$2	9/6/1753
Spalding, Jesse			MB - Deed	
pd Capt John Fitch				
Susq Co		1/2 share No. 283 of 400		9/10/1785
Spalding, John		Ulster Twp*	I12	8/19/1786
300 A				
Susq Co				7/18/1753
Spalding, John			MB	
Susq Co		1/2 share		7/11/1754
Spalding, Joseph			Deed	
Susq Co		1/2 share No. 277 of 400		7/21/1786
Spalding, Joseph Capt	Wyoming	Ulster Twp*	I12	8/19/1786
300 A				
Susq Co		1 share*	$42	6/30/1772
Spalding, Oliver	Woodberry		GJ	
Receipt recorded Town Book of Wilkes Barre, p.1313				
Susq Co		1/2 share No. 278 of 400		8/19/1786
Spalding, Simon Capt		Ulster Twp*	I11	8/19/1786
300 A				
Susq Co		1/2 share No. 282 of 400		9/10/1785
Spalding, Simon Capt		Ulster Twp*	I11	8/19/1786
300 A				
Susq Co		1/2 share	£6	8/27/1770
Speedy, William	West Branch Susq R.		B176	3/14/1774
Susq Co		1/2 share		
Spencer, John			Deed	
Susq Co		1 share*		
Spencer, John Gilbert	Bolton		MB	
by Samuel Gray				
Susq Co		1 share*		5/1/1754
Spencer, John Jr.	Windham		MB - Deed	
pd Jed Elderkin				
Susq Co		1 share	$5	5/13/1754
Spicer, Oliver	Groton, New London, CT		Deed - B166	3/10/1774
Susq Co		1 share*	$9	5/1/1755
Sprague, Obadiah	Providence, Providence, RI		B147	2/24/1774
recorded Providence, RI: Bk. 15, page 1				
Susq Co		100 acres*		9/25/1787
St.John, John		Susquehanna Purchase	E302	6/20/1796
by Company vote 12/26/1786				
Susq Co		1 share		7/11/1754
Stafford, Amos	RI		Deed	
Susq Co		1 share		7/11/1754
Stafford, Amos Jr.	RI		Deed	
Susq Co		1 share	£6. 10	10/11/1753
Standly, John	Farmington, Hartford, CT		B305	1/20/1775
Susq Co		1/2 share*	$4.50	5/1/1755
Stanly, Samuel	Hartford, CT		RB	
pd Daniel Edwards				
Susq Co				7/18/1753
Stantly, Gadd			MB	
Susq Co		1 share*	$2	9/6/1753
Stantly, John			MB - Deed	
pd Journeying Cmte				
Susq Co		1 share*	$2	9/6/1753
Stantly, Noah			MB - Deed	
pd Journeying Cmte				
Susq Co		1/2 share	$4.50	1/22/1755
Stantly, Samuel	Hartford		C11	10/1/1779
Susq Co		1 share	$2	1/9/1754
Stantly, Thomas			MB - Deed	

grantor grantee notes	grantor residence grantee residence	description location	amount acct bk page	deed date record date
Susq Co		1 share*	$2	9/6/1753
Stantly, Timothy			MB - Deed	
pd Journeying Cmte				
Susq Co		1 share*	$5	5/1/1754
Stantly, William	Hartford Co		MB - Deed	
pd Thomas Stantly				
Susq Co		1 share		7/11/1754
Stark, Christopher			Deed	
Susq Co		1 share*	$9	5/1/1755
Starr, Comfort	Danbury, CT		RB	
pd Daniel Edwards				
Susq Co		1 share*	$9	5/2/1755
Starr, Daniel	Danbury		MB	
pd Josiah Starr				
Susq Co		1 share*	$9	5/1/1755
Starr, Josiah Capt	Danbury, CT		RB	
pd Daniel Edwards				
Susq Co		1/2 share*		11/20/1754
Steal, Elisha			MB - Deed	
pd Capn Uriah Stevens				
Susq Co		1/2 share*		11/20/1754
Steal, John			MB - Deed	
pd Capn Uriah Stevens				
Susq Co		1/2 share*	$1	9/6/1753
Steal, Thomas			MB - Deed	
pd Journeying Cmte				
Susq Co				7/18/1753
Steavens, Cyprian			MB - B230	
Susq Co		1/2 share	£4	9/25/1762
Steavens, Lucy	Canaan, Litchfield, CT		B135	2/2/1774
Susq Co		1 share		7/11/1754
Stedman, James			Deed	
Susq Co		1 share		7/11/1754
Stedman, Thomas			Deed	
Susq Co		1 share	£13	1/11/1794
Stedman, Thomas	Windham, CT		H222	8/6/1801
Susq Co		1 share*	$2	9/6/1753
Stephens, Andrew			MB - Deed	
pd Journeying Cmte				
Susq Co		1 share*	$2	9/6/1753
Stephens, Benjamin			MB - Deed	
pd Journeying Cmte				
Susq Co		1 share		7/11/1754
Stephens, Henry			Deed	
Susq Co		2000 A, No. 123 of 2nd 600		11/26/1799
Stephens, Ira		Beebesburgh Twp	H125	11/26/1799
Susq Co		1 share No. 131 of 600		11/26/1799
Stephens, Ira and Thayer, Levi	Athens, Luzerne, PA	Beebesburgh Twp	H125	11/26/1799
Susq Co		1 share*		11/20/1754
Stephens, Jedediah			MB - E369 - Deed	
pd Capn Uriah Stevens; taxes "paid by services done to said Company by Nathan Stevens who was slain in Defense of the right of the Settler's." Dated Wilkesbarre March 15 1787" signed John Franklin				
Susq Co		1/2 share		
Stephens, Jesse			Deed	
Susq Co		1 share*	$2	9/6/1753
Stephens, John			MB - Deed	
pd Capt John Fitch				
Susq Co		1/2 share		9/10/1785
Stephens, John			E302	6/20/1796
Susq Co		1 share*	$2	9/6/1753
Stephens, Nehemiah			MB - Deed	
pd Journeying Cmte				

grantor grantee notes	grantor residence grantee residence	description location	amount acct bk page	deed date record date
Susq Co		1 share*		11/20/1754
Stephens, Noah			MB - Deed	
pd Capn Uriah Stevens				
Susq Co		1 share*		11/20/1754
Stephens, Thomas			MB - Deed	
pd Capn Uriah Stevens; on Deed twice				
Susq Co		1 share		7/11/1754
Stephens, Thomas Junr			Deed	
Susq Co		1 share*		11/20/1754
Stephens, Zebulon			MB - A443 - Deed	
pd Capn Uriah Stevens				
Susq Co		1 share*	$2	9/6/1753
Stephens/Stevens, Uriah Capt			MB - Deed	
pd Journeying Cmte, on Deed twice				
Susq Co		1/2 share*	$4.50	5/1/1755
Stergis, Samuel	Fairfield, CT		RB	
pd Daniel Edwards				
Susq Co		1/2 share No. 83 of 400		9/10/1785
Stevens, Ira		Athens Twp	I62	6/10/1786
entered 5/10/1786				
Susq Co		1/2 share*		11/20/1754
Stevens, Jesse			MB - Deed	
pd Capn Uriah Stevens				
Susq Co		1/2 share No. 305 of 600		12/25/1794
Stevens, Peter	Athens, Luzerne, PA	Murraysfield Twp*	C368 - I195	4/4/1795
300 A				
Susq Co		1/2 share*		
Stewart, Charles			MB	
by Ebenr Backus				
Susq Co		1/2 share*		11/4/1762
Stewart, Henry	Blanford, Boston Government		MB	
pd Daniel Lyman				
Susq Co		1/2 share*		11/4/1762
Stewart, Samuel	Palmer, Boston Government		MB	
pd Daniel Lyman				
Susq Co		1 share*	$2	9/6/1753
Stewart, Thomas			MB - Deed	
pd S Gray				
Susq Co		1 share	$40	
Stewart, William			B290	5/24/1774
Susq Co		1/2 share	£6	3/27/1774
Stewart, William			B290	5/24/1774
Susq Co		1/2 share	£6. 6	1/15/1773
Stewart, William			B290	5/24/1774
Susq Co		1 share*	£6.10	9/28/1753
Stiles, Amos			MB	
pd Charles Dewey; should be on Deed				
Susq Co		1/2 share		
Stiles, Ezra			Deed	
Susq Co		1/2 share*	$4.50	5/1/1755
Stirgis, Daniel Jr.	Fairfield, CT		RB	
pd Daniel Edwards				
Susq Co		1 share	$9	7/28/1755
Stocking, Capt George	Chatham, Middlesex, CT		E246	7/1/1796
Susq Co		1 share*	$2	9/6/1753
Stoddard, Solomon			MB - Deed	
pd Journeying Cmte				
Susq Co		1/2 share*	£4	5/6/1761
Stone, Nathaniel	Guilford, New Haven, CT		MB - B32	9/15/1773
pd Danniel Lyman				
Susq Co		1 share*		11/20/1754
Stone or Storey, Silas			MB - Deed	
pd Capn Uriah Stevens				

grantor / grantee / notes	grantor residence / grantee residence	description / location	amount / acct bk page	deed date / record date
Susq Co		1 share*	£8.2.6 + $2.50	1/9/1754
Stoughton, Daniel			MB - Deed	
pd S Gray				
Susq Co		1 share		7/11/1754
Stoughton, Samuel, Lemuel			Deed	
Susq Co		1 share*	£6	7/18/1753
Stoyel, Stephen			MB - A320	
pd John Smith Esqr				
Susq Co		1 share*	$2	9/6/1753
Streater, Thomas, John	Sturbridge		MB - Deed	
pd S Gray; incorrectly Thomas in Deed				
Susq Co		1 share	$5	3/5/1754
Street, Elnathan & Catlin, Constant*	Wallingford, New Haven, CT		Deed - B33	9/15/1773
purchased 1 share together				
Susq Co		1 share		7/11/1754
Street, John			MB	
Susq Co		1/2 share*		9/4/1761
Street, Samuel	Wallingford		MB	
pd Daniel Lyman				
Susq Co		1/2 share	£6.6	4/20/1772
Strickland, Peter	New London, New London, CT		C437	2/1/1795
Susq Co		1 share		7/11/1754
Stricklin, Jonathan			Deed	
Susq Co		1/2 share*	$4.50	12/31/1755
Strong, Ebenezer	Woodbury		MB	
pd Thomas Darling				
Susq Co		1 share*		5/1/1754
Strong, John	Lebanon		MB - Deed	
pd Jed Elderkin				
Susq Co		1/2 share*	$2.50	5/1/1754
Strong, John	Hartford Co		MB - Deed	
pd Thomas Stantly				
Susq Co		1/2 share*	$2	1/9/1754
Stuart/Stewart, Alexander			MB - Deed	
pd S Gray				
Susq Co		1/2 share	$4.50	5/12/1755
Sturges, Daniel Jr.	Fairfield, Fairfield, CT		B109	12/23/1773
Susq Co		1 share	$5	2/22/1754
Summer, Jabez	Stratford, Fairfield, CT		B125	1/19/1774
Susq Co		1 share*		4/7/1763
Summers, David	Stratford		MB	
by Zachariah Clark				
Susq Co		1 share*		12/5/1782
Summers, Jabez			C330*	
see also Westmoreland Records Liber A, page 128				
Susq Co		1 share	£8	4/1/1774
Swan, Isaac & Amos	Kent, Litchfield, CT		B337	10/7/1775
Susq Co		1 share		7/16/1772
Swetland, Luke			GJ	
Susq Co		1 share*		5/1/1754
Swetland, Peter			MB - Deed	
pd S Gray				
Susq Co		1 share		7/11/1754
Swetland, William			Deed	
Susq Co		1 share*		8/27/1761
Swift, Elisha			MB - A252	
pd Elisha Sheldon				
Susq Co		1 share*	$9	5/1/1755
Swift, Jabez	Kent, CT		RB	
pd Daniel Edwards				
Susq Co		1/2 share No. 84 of 400		9/10/1785
Swift, John		Athens Twp	I65	6/10/1786
entered 5/8/1786				

grantor grantee notes	grantor residence grantee residence	description location	amount acct bk page	deed date record date
Susq Co Swift, Reuben		1 share	Deed	7/11/1754
Susq Co Symmons, John *by John Gardiner Esq.*	England	1 share*	MB	6/4/1766
Susq Co Talcot, Eben *pd Daniel Edwards*	Weathersfield, late of	1/2 share*	$4.50 RB	5/1/1755
Susq Co Talcott, Elizer	CT	1 share	Deed	7/11/1754
Susq Co Talcott, Israel *pd Major Elizer Talcott*		1/2 share*	MB	8/27/1761
Susq Co Talcott, Josiah *pd Major Elizer Talcott*		1 share*	MB	8/27/1761
Susq Co Talcott, Matthew *pd Thomas Stantly*	Hartford Co	1 share*	$5 MB - Deed	5/1/1754
Susq Co Talcott, Samuel *by Talcott, Samuel of Hartford*	Glastenbury	1 share*	$5 D16 - Deed	2/11/1754 9/18/1795
Susq Co Talcott, Samuel Col. *pd Thomas Stantly*	Glastonbury, Hartford, CT	1 share*	$5 MB - Deed	5/1/1754
Susq Co Taylor, Ebenezer Jr. *pd Elisha Sheldon*		1/2 share*	MB	8/27/1761
Susq Co Taylor, Ephriam		1 share	$5 MB	11/20/1754
Susq Co Taylor, Joseph *pd Capt John Fitch; on Deed twice*		1 share*	$2 MB - Deed	1/9/1754
Susq Co Taylor, Joseph		1 share	Deed	
Susq Co Taylor, Lemuel *pd Journeying Cmte*		1 share*	$2 MB - Deed	7/18/1753
Susq Co Taylor, Philip		1 share	$2 MB	10/8/1753
Susq Co Taylor, Thomas *pd Josiah Starr; certificate given May 1774*	Danbury	1 share*	$9 MB	5/2/1755
Susq Co Terrey, John *tax pd on right of Banks Bennet*	Halifax, VT	copy of receipt*	$2 E375	12/24/1782 9/13/1796
Susq Co Thomas, Ebenezer *pd Isaac Tracy*		1/2 share*	MB	10/20/1761
Susq Co Thompson, Abraham *pd Thomas Darling; should be on Deed*		1 share*	$5 MB	5/3/1754
Susq Co Thompson, Benjamin		1 share	$5 Deed - B147	5/22/1754 2/24/1774
Susq Co Thompson, John	Branford, New Haven, CT	1 share	£12. 12 B291	5/14/1772 5/25/1774
Susq Co Thornton, Richard *pd Stephen Gardner*	RI	1 share*	$5 Deed - E361	11/20/1754 6/1/1796
Susq Co Tiffany, Consider *pd Stephen Gardner; should be on Deed*		1 share*	MB	11/20/1754

grantor grantee notes	grantor residence grantee residence	description location	amount acct bk page	deed date record date
Susq Co		1 share*	$4	1/8/1754
Tiphany/Tiffany, Ebenezer			MB	
pd Stephen Gardner; should be on Deed				
Susq Co		1/2 share*	$4.50	5/1/1755
Todd, Hezekiah	North Haven, CT		RB	
pd Daniel Edwards				
Susq Co		1/2 share*		8/27/1761
Tomlinson, Beach			MB	
pd Zachariah Clark				
Susq Co				
Tomlinson, Henry			A51	
Susq Co				
Tomlinson, Samuel			A241	
Susq Co		1/2 share*	£4	6/16/1761
Tomlinson, Zachariah Junr			MB - E475	11/28/1796
pd Zachariah Clark				
Susq Co		1 share*	$9	12/31/1755
Tomlison, Ager	Darby		MB	
pd Thomas Darling				
Susq Co		1/2 share*	$4.50	12/31/1755
Tomlison, Samuel	Darby		MB	
pd Thomas Darling				
Susq Co				
Tracy, Andrew Jr.			A364	
Susq Co		1 share		7/11/1754
Tracy, Elisha			Deed	
Susq Co		1 share		7/11/1754
Tracy, Isaac			Deed	
Susq Co		1 share		7/11/1754
Tracy, Isaac Jr.			Deed	
Susq Co		1/2 share		11/20/1754
Tracy, James			MB	
Susq Co		1 share		7/11/1754
Tracy, Joseph Jr.			Deed	
Susq Co				7/18/1753
Tracy, Phineas			MB	
Susq Co		1 share*	$4	1/9/1754
Tracy, Prince			MB - Deed	
pd S Gray				
Susq Co		1 share		7/11/1754
Tracy, Samuel			Deed	
Susq Co		1/2 share*	$4.50	12/31/1755
Treadwell, Hezekiah	Stratford		MB	
pd Thomas Darling				
Susq Co		3,200 A*		8/14/1773
Trumbull, Jonathan and Company*		Trumble & Co.	F92	8/31/1796
Jonathan Trumbull 1100 A, Major John Durkee, Vine Elderkin, Ebenezer Gray, Junr., Andrew French, Capt Ebenezer Backus, 425 A each as a replacement for their right in Kingston				
Susq Co		1 share		7/7/1773
Trumbull, Jonathan, Honbl., Esq.			F32	4/23/1796
Susq Co		1 share	£12.12	7/12/1773
Trumbull, Jonathan Jr.	Lebanon CT		C442	2/21/1795
Susq Co				
Trumbull, Joseph			A487	
Susq Co		1/2 share No. 82 of 400		9/10/1785
Tubbs, Enos		Putnam Twp	I33	12/6/1786
Susq Co		1 share*	$2	10/8/1753
Tubbs, Simon			MB - B241 - Deed	8/28/1774
pd S Gray				
Susq Co		1 share*		11/20/1754
Turner, Daniel			MB - Deed	
pd Capn Uriah Stevens				

grantor grantee notes	grantor residence grantee residence	description location	amount acct bk page	deed date record date
Susq Co Turner, Phillip *pd Journeying Cmte*		1 share*	$2 MB - Deed	7/18/1753
Susq Co Tuttle, David *recorded 1770*			A363 - D8	
Susq Co Tuttle, Oliver *by Jonathan Root*	Farmington	1/2 share*	MB	4/7/1763
Susq Co Tuttle, Stephen *entered 300 A, 1799*	Fishkill, NY	1/2 share No. 268 of 600 Murraysfield Twp*	I59	6/1/1786 5/1/1786
Susq Co Tyler, Ephriam *pd Samuel Adams*		1 share*	$5 MB - A318	7/11/1754
Susq Co Underwood, Israel & Isaac, son *pd John Smith Esqr*	Plainfield, Windham, CT	1 share*	$2 MB - B206	10/1/1753 4/7/1774
Susq Co Van Fleet, Abraham *certificate dated 12/26/1786; approved 6/19/1787*		200 A* Van Fleet Pitch	E105	6/19/1786 3/1/1796
Susq Co Van Fleet, Joshua *entered 9/24/1787*		1/2 share No. 32 of 400 Allensborough Twp	I67	9/10/1785 6/18/1791
Susq Co Vancamp, Isaac			A321	
Susq Co Vanduzen, Isaac *pd Timothy Woodbridge in 1755; entered in MB Jan 1762*		1 share*	$9 MB - F190	5/28/1755 7/19/1796
Susq Co Veits, John *pd Thomas Stantly*	Hartford Co	1 share*	$5 MB - Deed	5/1/1754
Susq Co Vial, Peter *pd Elisha Sheldon*	Guilford	1 share*	MB	4/8/1763
Susq Co Waddous, Noah	New Milford, Litchfield, CT	1 share	£12.12 B90	4/22/1773 11/23/1773
Susq Co Wadham, Noah, Rev.		1 share	$42 C105	4/1/1772 12/27/1786
Susq Co Wadsworth, William Capt *pd Thomas Stantly*	Farmington, Hartford,	1/2 share*	$2.50 MB - E49 - Deed	5/1/1754
Susq Co Wadsworth, William, decd.*	Farmington, Hartford, CT	1 share, certified owner, all taxes	E49	6/1/1775
Susq Co Wager, Barnet *700 A, later removed to Alba*	Claverack, NY	1/2 share No. 231 of 400 Rutland Twp*	I118	12/17/1794
Susq Co Wait, John Capt *pd S Gray*		1 share*	£16.5 MB - Deed	5/1/1754
Susq Co Wakeman, E B Jr. *pd Daniel Edwards*	Fairfield, CT	1/2 share*	$4.50 RB	5/1/1755
Susq Co Wakeman, Ebenezer Jr.	Fairfield, Fairfield, CT	1/2 share	$4.50 B125	6/12/1755 1/19/1774
Susq Co Wakeman, Gideon	Fairfield, Fairfield, CT	1/2 share	$4.50 B110	6/12/1755 12/23/1773
Susq Co Wakeman, Gideon *pd Daniel Edwards*	Fairfield, CT	1/2 share*	$4.50 RB	5/1/1755
Susq Co Wakeman, John Jr. *pd Daniel Edwards*	Fairfield, CT	1/2 share*	$4.50 RB	5/1/1755

grantor	grantor residence	description	amount	deed date
grantee	grantee residence	location	acct bk page	record date
notes				
Susq Co		1 share*	$4.50*	5/10/1755
Wakeman, Joseph			B125	1/19/1774
pd $36 for self and 7 other subscribers, under date 5/10/1755. See other entries, B125				
Susq Co		1/2 share	$4.50	6/12/1755
Wakeman, Joseph Jr.	Fairfield, Fairfield, CT		B110	12/23/1773
Susq Co		1 share		7/11/1754
Wakeman, Josiah			Deed	
Susq Co		1 share		7/11/1754
Wakeman, Stephen Junr			Deed	
Susq Co		1 share*	$2	9/6/1753
Walden, Joseph			MB - Deed	
pd Capt John Fitch				
Susq Co		1 share		7/11/1754
Waldow, Edward			Deed	
Susq Co		1 share*	£16.5	1/14/1754
Wales, Nathaniel Esq.			MB - A339 - Deed	
pd S Gray				
Susq Co		1 share*	$2	1/9/1754
Wales, Nathaniel Jr.			MB - Deed	
pd S Gray				
Susq Co		1 share		7/11/1754
Walker, Eliakim	RI		Deed - B232	8/9/1774
Susq Co		1 share*	$5	1/26/1754
Walker, Elnathan	Dighton, MA		Deed - B232 - H344	8/9/1774
taxes pd to 8/9/1774; H344 recorded 8/27/1802				
Susq Co		1 share	$5	2/9/1754
Walker, Robert			B326	2/20/1775
Susq Co		1 share*		11/20/1754
Walker, Robert			MB - Deed	
pd Capn Uriah Stevens				
Susq Co		1 share No. 94 of 600		6/12/1793
Wallace, Samuel	Ulster, PA	Juddsboro Twp*	E158 - I276	5/7/1796
Lot 3 & 4, 300 A each				
Susq Co		1 share		7/11/1754
Wallworth, Thomas			Deed	
Susq Co		1/2 share*		
Walsworth, Charles			MB	
pd by Gershom Breed				
Susq Co		1 share		7/11/1754
Walworth, Samuel			Deed	
Susq Co		1 share	$7	5/16/1754
Walworth, Thomas	Groton		I220	7/8/1795
Susq Co		1/2 share*	£4	5/6/1761
Ward, Edmund	Guilford, New Haven, CT		MB - B32 - E187	9/15/1773
pd Daniel Lyman				
Susq Co		1 share		7/11/1754
Ward, Macock			Deed	
Susq Co		1 share*	$2	9/6/1753
Warner, Isaac			MB - Deed	
pd Capt John Fitch				
Susq Co		1 share*	£16.5	1/9/1754
Warner, Nathaniel			MB - Deed	
pd S Gray				
Susq Co		1/2 share*	$1	1/9/1754
Warner, Thomas	Ashford		MB - C599 - Deed	
pd Journeying Cmte; taxes pd to 3/8/1774				
Susq Co		1 share	£3.5	5/29/1754
Warren, Joseph			MB - Deed	
Susq Co		1/2 share	$4.50	6/1/1755
Washburn, Abisha			B358	6/19/1777
Susq Co		1/2 share	$4.50	6/1/1755
Washburn, Robert	Plainfield		C40	4/12/1782

grantor grantee notes	grantor residence grantee residence	description location	amount acct bk page	deed date record date
Susq Co		1 share		7/11/1754
Waterman, Asa			Deed	
Susq Co		1 share		7/11/1754
Waterman, Zebulon			Deed	
Susq Co		1 share*	$2	9/6/1753
Waters, David			MB- Deed	
pd S Gray				
Susq Co		1/2 share No. 163 of 400		9/10/1795
Waters, Walter			C200	2/28/1795
Susq Co		1 share*		7/11/1754
Watson, Ebenezer			Deed - E249	
taxes pd 11/21/1754; 3/24/1768				
Susq Co		1 share*		11/20/1754
Watson, Levi			MB - Deed	
pd Capn Uriah Stevens				
Susq Co		1 share*		11/20/1754
Watson, Thomas			MB - Deed	
pd Capn Uriah Stevens				
Susq Co		1 share		7/11/1754
Wealder, Jonathan			Deed	
Susq Co		1/2 share		7/18/1753
Webb, John			MB - Deed	
Susq Co		1/2 share*	$2.50	5/1/1754
Webb, Joseph	Hartford Co		MB - Deed	
pd Thomas Stantly				
Susq Co		1/2 share*	£6:10	1/14/1754
Webb, Samuel Jr.			MB - Deed	
pd S Gray				
Susq Co		1/2 share*		8/28/1761
Webster, Ashabel			MB	
pd Nathaniel Wales Junr Esq.				
Susq Co		1 share		7/11/1754
Webster, John			Deed	
Susq Co		1 share		7/11/1754
Webster, Noah			Deed	
Susq Co		1 share*		4/1/1773
Weeks, Holland			MB - A105	4/1/1773
by Samuel Gray				
Susq Co		1 share*	£8	2/12/1763
Weeks, Jonathan	Fairfield Co CT		MB - B314	3/7/1775
by Zachariah Clark				
Susq Co				
Welch, Jeremiah			A234	
Susq Co				
Welles, Amos			A423	
Susq Co		1 share*	£6.10	7/18/1753
Welles, Ichabod			MB - Deed	
pd S Gray				
Susq Co		1 share*	$5	5/1/1754
Welles, Joseph Doctr	Hartford Co		MB - Deed	
pd Thomas Stantly				
Susq Co		1 share*	$5	5/1/1754
Welles, Samuel Capt	Hartford Co		MB - H107 - Deed	
pd Thomas Stantly				
Susq Co		1 share		7/11/1754
Welles, Samuel Junr			Deed	
Susq Co		1 share	$5	2/12/1754
Welles, Thomas Esq.	Hartford Co		MB - Deed	
Susq Co				
Wells, James			A423	
Susq Co		1 share*		7/11/1754
Wells, John			Deed - E287	6/6/1796
certified E287 on 9/18/1795				

grantor grantee notes	grantor residence grantee residence	description location	amount acct bk page	deed date record date
Susq Co Wells, John		1/2 share	Deed	
Susq Co Wells, Silas, William		1 share	Deed	7/11/1754
Susq Co Wells, Thomas		1/2 share	Deed - A65	7/11/1754
Susq Co Wells, Thomas		1 share	Deed	
Susq Co Wells, Thomas Capt. *pd Thomas Stantly*	Hartford Co	1/2 share*	$2.50 MB	5/1/1754
Susq Co Wentworth, Benjamin		1 share	MB - Deed	7/11/1754
Susq Co Westbrook, Richard *Liber A, Volume 2*		1/2 share No. 13 of 400* Standing Stone Twp	3 yr residency C110	9/10/1785 9/10/1785
Susq Co Westbruck, Anthony *should be on Deed*			MB	
Susq Co Wheeler, Caleb *pd Capn Uriah Stevens*		1/2 share*	MB - Deed	11/20/1754
Susq Co Wheeler, Joseph *should be on Deed*		1 share*	MB	12/5/1753
Susq Co Wheelock, John* *president of Dartmouth College in New Hampshire*		1/2 share No. 213 of 600	E102	3/1/1796
Susq Co Whipple, David & Jeremiah			A64	
Susq Co White, Eben Rev. *pd Josiah Starr*	Danbury	1 share*	$9 MB	5/2/1755 12/28/1768
Susq Co Whitelsey, Eliphalet *pd Journeying Cmte*		1 share*	$2 MB	7/18/1753
Susq Co Whiting, Gamaliel			A66	
Susq Co Whiting, Nathan *taxes pd 6/1/1797*	New Haven	1 share*	$9 F238	5/1/1755 6/1/1797
Susq Co Whiting, William *pd Journeying Cmte*		1 share*	$2 MB - Deed - A227	9/6/1753
Susq Co Whitman, Eleazar *pd Roger Wolcott Junr Esqr*	Bridgewater	1 share*	$9 MB	12/7/1758
Susq Co Whitney, David Capt Esq. *pd Capn Uriah Stevens*		1 share*	MB - Deed	11/20/1754
Susq Co Whitney, John *pd Stephen Gardner; should be on Deed*	East Haddam, Hartford, CT	1 share*	$5 MB - B261	5/15/1754 10/13/1774
Susq Co Whitney, Joshua *pd Capn Uriah Stevens*		1 share*	MB - Deed	11/20/1754
Susq Co Whitney, Tarbel *pd Capn Uriah Stevens*		1 share*	MB - Deed	11/20/1754
Susq Co Whitney, William *pd Jed Elderkin*		1 share*	MB - Deed	5/1/1754

grantor grantee notes	grantor residence grantee residence	description location	amount acct bk page	deed date record date
Susq Co Whiton, Elijah			A215	
Susq Co Whittlesey, Eliphalet *pd Journeying Cmte*		1 share*	$2 MB - Deed	8/24/1753
Susq Co Wight, Joseph		1 share	MB	7/11/1754
Susq Co Wilcox, Stephen *see also Barnet Wager as grantee and grantor of No. 231 of the 400*		1/2 share No. 231 of the 400*	E437	10/1/1785 10/1/1796
Susq Co Wiley, James *pd S Gray*		1 share*	$2 MB - B259 - Deed	9/6/1753 10/6/1774
Susq Co Wiley, John Jr. *pd S Gray*		1 share*	$2 MB - Deed	9/6/1753
Susq Co Wiley, Thomas *pd Capt John Fitch*		1 share*	$2 MB - Deed	9/6/1753
Susq Co Wiley/Wyley, Hugh	Voluntown, Windham, CT	1 share	$2 MB, Deed, A315,	1/9/1754 11/26/1774
Susq Co Wiley/Wyley, Hugh Jr. *pd S Gray*		1 share*	MB - Deed - B201	5/1/1754
Susq Co Wilkinson, Philip *pd S Gray*	RI	1 share*	$4 MB - Deed	5/29/1754
Susq Co Wilkinson, Philip Capt	RI	1 share	MB	7/11/1754
Susq Co Willard, Elias	Hartford	1/2 share	$4.50 C11	1/22/1755 10/1/1779
Susq Co Willard, Jonathan		1 share	Deed	7/11/1754
Susq Co Willcocks, Daniel *pd Capn Uriah Stevens*		1 share*	MB - Deed	11/20/1754
Susq Co Willey, Allen		1 share	Deed	7/11/1754
Susq Co Williams, Ebenezer *pd Stephen Gardner*		1 share*	MB - Deed - E232	7/11/1754 1/15/1762
Susq Co Williams, Elisha Col. *pd Thomas Stantly*	Hartford Co	1 share*	$5 MB - Deed	5/1/1754
Susq Co Williams, Elisha Jr. *pd Thomas Stantly*	Hartford Co	1/2 share*	$2.50 MB - Deed	5/1/1754
Susq Co Williams, Ezekiel *pd Thomas Stantly*	Hartford Co	1 share*	$5 MB - Deed	5/1/1754
Susq Co Williams, Henry Esq. *by John Gardiner Esq.*	Crickhowell, England	1 share*	MB	6/4/1766
Susq Co Williams, John *pd Timothy Woodbridge in 1755*	Sheffield	1 share*	$9 MB - Deed - F10	7/11/1754 1/15/1762
Susq Co Williams, John		150 A John Williams Pitch	F104	3/1/1795 9/17/1796
Susq Co Williams, Nathaniel			MB	7/18/1753
Susq Co Williams, Thomas *pd Capn Uriah Stevens*		1 share*	MB - E234 - Deed	11/20/1754

grantor grantee notes	grantor residence grantee residence	description location	amount acct bk page	deed date record date
Susq Co		1 share*		1/1/1769
Williams, Thomas			MB - F86	9/19/1796
date is "sometime in 1769"				
Susq Co		1/2 share*		
Williams, Thomas Dr.			MB	
by Samuel Gray				
Susq Co		1/2 share*		12/31/1755
Williams, Warham			MB	1/15/1762
pd Timothy Woodbridge				
Susq Co		1 share*	$2	9/6/1753
Williams, William	Colchester		MB - Deed	
pd S Gray				
Susq Co		1/2 share No. 232 of 400		10/1/1785
Williams, William Jr.		Putnam Twp	I33	12/14/1786
Susq Co		1/2 share*	$4.50	5/1/1755
Williard, Elias	Hartford, CT		RB	
pd Daniel Edwards				
Susq Co		1 share		5/1/1754
Wills/Wells, Joshua			MB - Deed	
Susq Co		1 share		7/11/1754
Willson, James			Deed	
Susq Co		1 share, No 128 of 600*		
Wilson, Noah	Addison, VT		H256	11/6/1801
not listed in Liber A, Volume 2				
Susq Co		1 share*		11/20/1754
Wincott, Robert			MB - Deed	
pd Capn Uriah Stevens				
Susq Co		1 share*	$5	2/22/1754
Wing, John	Dartmouth, Bristol, MA		Deed - H344	
Susq Co		1 share*	$5	2/22/1754
Wing, John Junr	Dartmouth, Bristol, MA		Deed - H344	
Susq Co		1 share*		6/4/1766
Wingfield, George	England		MB	
by John Gardiner Esq.				
Susq Co		1 share*	$5	5/1/1754
Wolcott, Alexander	Hartford Co		MB - Deed	
pd Thomas Stantly				
Susq Co		1 share*		11/20/1754
Wolcott, Oliver Capt			MB - Deed	
pd Capn Uriah Stevens				
Susq Co		1 share*		5/1/1754
Wolcott, Roger Jr. Esq.			MB - Deed	
pd Jed Elderkin				
Susq Co		1/2 share No. .291 of 600*	services rendered	4/5/1794
Wolcott, Silas		Murraysfield Twp*	I276 - E510	2/18/1797
entered 6/12/1796 on Lot 39; not listed Liber A, Volume 2				
Susq Co		1 share	$5	1/29/1754
Wolley, Allen			B89	11/11/1782
Susq Co		1 share		7/11/1754
Wood, John			Deed	
Susq Co		1/2 share	£6	4/12/1770
Wood, Josiah	Wilkes Barre		B263	10/29/1774
Susq Co		1 share		7/11/1754
Woodbridge, Ashbel	CT		Deed	
Susq Co		1 share*		10/20/1761
Woodbridge, Dudley			MB	
pd Isaac Tracy				
Susq Co		1 share		7/11/1754
Woodbridge, Joseph	NY		Deed	
Susq Co		1/2 share*		10/20/1761
Woodbridge, Paul			MB	
pd Isaac Tracy				

grantor grantee notes	grantor residence grantee residence	description location	amount acct bk page	deed date record date
Susq Co		1 share*	$5	5/1/1754
Woodbridge, Russel	Hartford Co		MB - Deed	
pd Thomas Stantly				
Susq Co		1 share	gratis	1/10/1754
Woodbridge, Timothy	Stockbridge, MA		MB - Deed	
Susq Co		1/2 share	$4.50	7/10/1773
Woodhouse, Josiah	Hew Haven, New Haven, CT		B100	10/25/1773
Susq Co		1/2 share*	$4.50	12/31/1755
Woodhouse, Josiah	New Haven		MB	
pd Thomas Darling				
Susq Co		1/2 share		10/1/1785
Woodward, David			C315	3/9/1795
Susq Co		1 share*	$2	1/9/1754
Woodworth, Isaac			MB - Deed	
pd Journeying Cmte				
Susq Co		1/2 share	20s	10/12/1769
Woolf, Mitchell			B290	5/24/1774
Susq Co		1/2 share		9/10/1785
Woolley, John	Allensburgh Twp*		E97	3/1/1796
entered 9/24/1787				
Susq Co		1/2 share*	$4.50	12/31/1755
Wooster, Daniel	Darby		MB	
pd Thomas Darling				
Susq Co		1 share*	$9	12/31/1755
Wooster, David	New Haven		MB - E258	
pd Thomas Darling				
Susq Co		1/2 share*	$4.50	12/31/1755
Wooster, Henry	Darby		MB	
pd Thomas Darling				
Susq Co		1/2 share*	$4.50	12/31/1755
Wooster, John	Darby		MB	
pd Thomas Darling				
Susq Co		1/2 share*	$4.50	12/31/1755
Wooster, Samuel	Darby		MB	
pd Thomas Darling				
Susq Co		1/2 share*		11/20/1754
Wough, John			MB - Deed	
pd Capn Uriah Stevens				
Susq Co		1 share*	$2	7/18/1753
Wright, Eben			MB	
pd Capt John Fitch				
Susq Co		1 share*	$2	8/24/1753
Wright, Ebenezer Jr.	Mansfield		MB - B248 - Deed	4/1/1769
pd Capn John Fitch				
Susq Co		1 share		7/11/1754
Wright, Joseph			Deed	
Susq Co		1 share*	$2	8/24/1753
Wright, Judah			MB - Deed	
pd Journeying Cmte				
Susq Co		1/2 share*	$2	1/14/1754
Wright, Seth			MB - Deed	
pd S Gray				
Susq Co		1/2 share No. 293 of 400		12/4/1792
Wyeth, Joseph	Claverack NY	Claverack Twp*	I67	12/7/1792
entered 320 A				
Susq Co		1/2 share No. 30 of 600		12/4/1792
Wyeth, Joshua			I276	
Susq Co			$2 on acct.	9/6/1753
Wyley, John Jr.			B259	10/6/1774
Susq Co				
Wylie, Hugh			A315	

grantor	grantor residence	description	amount	deed date
grantee	grantee residence	location	acct bk page	record date
notes				
Susq Co		1 share*	$5	5/1/1754
Wyllys, George	Hartford Co		MB - Deed	
pd Thomas Stantly				
Susq Co		1 share*		8/27/1761
Yale, Benjamin			MB	
pd Elisha Sheldon				
Susq Co		1/2 share*		11/4/1762
Yale, Enos			MB	
by Daniel Lyman				
Susq Co		1/2 share	£4	11/22/1762
Yale, Job	Wallingford, New Haven, CT		C407	4/4/1795
Susq Co		1/2 share*	£4	11/22/1762
Yale, Job			MB	
pd Daniel Lyman				
Susq Co		1/2 share*		11/4/1762
Yale, Ozias			MB	
by Daniel Lyman				
Susq Co		1/2 share*		11/4/1762
Yale, Stephen			MB	
by Daniel Lyman				
Susq Co		1 share*	£8	11/3/1762
Yale, Thomas	Farmington		MB	
pd Daniel Lyman				
Susq Co		1/2 share*		5/1/1754
Young, John			MB - Deed	
pd Jed Elderkin				
Susq Co		1/2 share*		12/1/1762
Young, Thomas	Southhold		MB	
by Isaac Tracy				
Sutton, James	Exeter, Luzerne, PA	16,000 A	$4,000	4/20/1796
Hammond, Elisha & Hitchcock, Jas	Chenango, Tioga, NY	Suttonfield Twp	E156	5/4/1796
Sutton, William	Braintrim, Luzerne, PA	5,300 A	$442	2/17/1797
Hammond, Elisha and Cooper,	Ulster, Luzerne, PA	Suttonfield Twp	H110	11/1/1797
Swan, Amos	Kent, Litchfield, CT	1/2 share	Good cause	4/30/1765
Parks, William	Plainfield, Windham, CT		B82	10/11/1773
Swan, Isaac	Kent, Litchfield, CT		£80	4/10/1767
Parke, William	Plainfield, Windham, CT		B337	10/7/1775
Sweeting, Eliphalet*	Orwell, Rutland, VT	all right	£3	2/28/1795
Stoddard, Philo	Woodbury, Litchfield, CT	Susquehanna Purchase	C632	7/10/1795
purchased of Eliphalet Briggs [no record of either person other than this, but Briggs may be son of Noah, OP]				
Sweetland, Peter				
Post, Eldad			A348	
Sweetland, Peter	Hebron, Hartford, CT	1/2 share	£13	4/23/1770
Root, Jonathan	Hebron, Hartford, CT		B46	5/23/1772
Swetland, Caleb		1/4 share		10/4/1773
Millard, Thomas			GM	11/23/1773
Swetland, William	Hebron Hartford, CT	1/2 right	£30	8/23/1774
Babcock, Robert	Coventry, Windham, CT		C50	10/28/1782
Swetland, William heir*	Burlington, Otsego, NY	all right	$7.50	5/12/1796
Grant, Josiah	Poultney, Rutland, VT		F73	5/24/1796
Charles Brown, grandson, son of dau Hannah; other dau Lydia				
Swift, Charles	Lebanon, Windham, CT	1/2 share	£20	1/14/1799
Payne, John	Westfield, MA		H269	11/12/1800
Swift, Elisha				
Gould, Hezekiah			A251	
Swift, John	Ontario, NY	the ten acre lot	$20	5/6/1794
Spalding, Joseph	Luzerne, PA	Athens Twp	F168	5/24/1797
Swift, John	Ontario, NY	700 A 2nd division land*	£10	7/21/1796
Stephens, Ira	Luzerne, PA		E371	8/1/1796
1/2 share "after division"				
Swift, Ruben				
Hodgkiss, Samuel			A287	

grantor	grantor residence	description	amount	deed date
grantee	grantee residence	location	acct bk page	record date
notes				
Taber, Job & Mary*	New London, New London, CT	all right	£10	1/28/1796
Tracy, Elisha	Norwich, New London, CT	First Delaware Company	F25	4/23/1796
chr. & heirs of Joseph Hurlbut, Jr. , decd.				
Talcott, Elizur	Glastonbury, Hartford, CT	1 or more shares	$20	5/19/1794
Hale, George	Catskill, Albany, NY		C368	2/28/1795
Talcott, Samuel	Hartford, Hartford, CT	2 shares	£18	11/19/1794
Selby, Brainard	Sandisfield, Berkshire, MA		C432	2/1/1795
Talcott, William & Gad*	Hebron, Tolland, CT	Pwr Att to locate 1 share	1/2 the lands*	4/23/1795
Hale, George	Catskill, Albany, NY		D16	9/18/1795
sons & heirs of Samuel Talcott; within 3 mos. of location				
Talmage, James, Col.	Stanford, Dutchess, NY	2 Twps 16,000 A each	£1,100	9/24/1795
Platner, Henry & Vincent, Charles	Claverack, Columbia, NY	Stanford and Milton Twps	F243	1/23/1798
Taylor, Ebenezer		1/4 share		
Moseley, Increase			A405	
Taylor, John & Deborah, wf, heir*		Pwr Att to locate 2 shares	1/3 of 2 shares	
Gordon, Samuel			F53	5/1/1796
of Jonathan Buck and Aholiab Buck				
Taylor, Joseph, decd	Colchester	1/2 share		5/11/1772
Carver, David	Hebron, Hartford, CT		E62	2/25/1795
Taylor, Joseph, decd.*	Hartland, Litchfield, CT	1 share*	£2.5	2/3/1769
Phelps, Alexander	Hebron, Hartford, CT		B50	5/11/1772
affidavit from Joseph Waters of Hebron, adm. that he sold at auction on 6/6/1768 Taylor's 1 share to Alexander Phelps				
Taylor, Joseph, decd.	Colchester	1/2 share		5/11/1772
Waters, Joseph	Hebron, Hartford, CT		E62	2/25/1795
Taylor, Lemuel	Stillwater, Saratoga, NY	2 shares	£26.2	4/3/1795
Janes, Elijah et al	Troy, Rensselaer, NY		C642	8/9/1795
James Dole, Wait Rathbun				
Taylor, Thomas	Danbury, Fairfield, CT	1/4 share	13s 6d	5/12/1774
Taylor, David	Danbury, Fairfield, CT		B214	5/18/1774
Taylor, Thomas	Danbury, Fairfield, CT	1/2 share	£1.7	5/4/1774
Taylor, Joseph	Danbury, Fairfield, CT		B221	5/18/1774
Taylor, Zebulon*	Litchfield, Litchfield, CT	1/2 share	good cause	5/27/1782
Strong, Solomon, Capt	Claverack, Albany, NY		F196	8/2/1797
heir of Sarah Taylor, decd mother; Zebulon Taylor appt. adm 6/10/1777 by Oliver Woolcutt, Judge of the Court of Probate, Litchfield District, copy E196-97				
Taylor, Zebulon Jr.	Litchfield, Litchfield, CT	1/3 share	£5	5/27/1782
Bradley, Abraham	Litchfield, Litchfield, CT		C74	11/13/1782
Teall, Nathan		1/2 share		1/20/1795
Hinchman, Joseph			E302	6/20/1796
Tennant, Caleb	Ashford, Windham, CT	1/2 share	£11	4/20/1775
Knowlton, Abraham	Ashford, Windham, CT		B345	3/27/1776
Terrel, Job		1 share	£30	1/11/1796
Starr, Josiah		New Milford Twp	E127	3/1/1796
Terril, George	Newtown, Fairfield, CT	1/6 share	£2.2	1/12/1781
Northrop, Isaac	Newtown, Fairfield, CT		C24	3/29/1781
Terrill, Job	New Milford, Litchfield, CT	1/2 share except 300 A New Milford	$21	9/14/1796
Paine, Clement			E412	9/14/1796
Terrill, Job & Bostwick, Dimon	New Milford, Litchfield, CT	1 share except 300 A New Milford		9/14/1796
Paine, Clement			E412	9/14/1796
Terrill, Job & Brownson, Isaac	New Milford, CT & Luzerne,	2,000 A	2 proprietors rights	1/6/1797
Canfield, Joseph, heirs		Footsburgh Twp	F179	7/17/1797
Terrill, Job Jr.	New Milford, Litchfield, CT	1 share	$83	11/4/1796
Canfield, Judson		Canfield Twp	E509	
entered 1,000 A, 11/7/1796				
Thayer, David	New Castle, PA	1/4 share	£8	11/24/1773
Backus, Sylvanus	Windham, Windham, CT		B145	2/21/1774
Thayer, David		1/2 share		12/13/1773
Benjamin, William			GG	1/9/1775
Thayer, David		1/2 share		12/29/1774
Cover, Nathaniel			GC	1/24/1775
Thayer, David				1/5/1774
Inman, Elijah			GC	1/25/1775
Thayer, David		1/2 share		10/14/1774
Inman, Elijah			GF	12/15/1774

grantor grantee notes	grantor residence grantee residence	description location	amount acct bk page	deed date record date
Thayer, David		1/2 share		2/15/1775
Smith, William H,			GC	2/17/1775
Thayer, Levi	Athens, Luzerne, PA	500 A undivided	$500	4/9/1800
Aborn, Lowrey	Providence, RI	Suttonfield Twp	H301	6/9/1801
Thayer, Levi	Luzerne, PA	3,200 A: Lots 1-4, 6-7, 10-11	$3,200	5/9/1800
Bowen, Uriah	Rehobeth	Fairfield Twp	H274	2/6/1801
Thayer, Levi	Athens, Luzerne, PA	11,300 A*	$2,000	6/3/1800
Bowen, Uriah	Rehobeth, Bristol, MA	Jenkin's' Gore, & 2 Twps*	H275	2/6/1801
2,500 A Jenkin's Gore; 4,000 A Windsor; 4,800 A in 16 Lots in Bachelor's Adventure				
Thayer, Levi	Luzerne, PA	306 A	$306	5/16/1800
Brown, Uriel	Rehobeth, Bristol, MA	Durkee Twp	H253	9/30/1800
Thayer, Levi	Athens, Luzerne, PA	4,033 A*	$3,900	6/2/1800
Brown, Uriel	Rehobeth, Bristol, MA	4 Townships*	H254	9/30/1800
900 A Insurance; 800 A Graham; 800 A Fullersville, 1,533 A Windsor;				
Thayer, Levi	Athens, Luzerne, PA	867 A	$1083	5/24/1800
Brown, William	Dighton, Bristol, MA	Bachelor's Adventure, near or part	H249	9/22/1800
E by Claverack, S by Bloomingdale, W by a gore lying E of Juddsburg, N by a line parallel to S boundary				
Thayer, Levi	Luzerne, PA	300 A, Lot 36	$300	3/15/1800
Burlingham, Enoch	Johnstown, Providence, RI	Watertown Twp	H227	7/2/1800
Thayer, Levi	Luzerne, PA	800 A, 2 Lots, 9 and 13	$800	3/13/1800
Carpenter, Asahel	Rehobeth, Bristol, MA	Fairfield Twp	H244	9/20/1800
Thayer, Levi	Athens, Luzerne, PA	150 A	$100	12/20/1799
Chatty, John	Providence, Providence, RI	Durkee Twp	H196	1/4/1800
Thayer, Levi	Athens, Luzerne, PA	150 A, 1/2 Lot 32	$150	9/21/1796
Cook, Zenas	West Britain, Hartford, CT	Watertown Twp	E459	11/9/1796
Thayer, Levi	Athens, Luzerne, PA	200 A, S part Lot 53	$700	11/4/1796
Cornell, Thomas	Philipstown, Dutchess, NY	Watertown Twp	E459	11/4/1796
Thayer, Levi	Athens, Luzerne, PA	1,400 A*	£660	11/4/1796
Curtiss, Daniel Jr.	Chatham, Columbia, NY	Watertown Twp	H299	6/3/1801
Lots 40, 44, 45, 300 A each and 200 A of the west of Lot 34				
Thayer, Levi	Luzerne, PA	300 A, undivided	$300	5/16/1800
Dean, Samuel	Dighton, Bristol, MA	Durkee Twp	H248	9/22/1800
Thayer, Levi	Athens, Luzerne, PA	1,850 A*	$1,850	10/24/1799
Fenner, Arthur	Providence, Providence, RI	Durkee Twp	H173	12/30/1799
along west line of Athens				
Thayer, Levi	Athens, Luzerne, PA	1,000 A common and undivided	$1,000	8/14/1802
Forbes, Elisha	Kingsberry, Washington, NY	Susquehanna Purchase	H345	8/20/1802
Thayer, Levi	Athens, Luzerne, PA	3,000 A*	$2,500	2/5/1802
Forbes, Elisha	Kingsberry, Washington, NY	Durkee Twp	H345	8/20/1802
adj. Athens Twp				
Thayer, Levi	Luzerne, PA	300 A, Lot 50	$450	5/5/1800
Foster, Ebenezer	Providence, RI	Watertown Twp	H250	9/22/1800
Thayer, Levi	Luzerne, PA	2,500 A*	div con	5/23/1796
Grant, Josiah	VT		E340	5/25/1796
on rights as ff: 400 A Stephen Billings; 700 A Ebenezer Lee No. 287; 700 A Joseph Smith, Tioga; 700 A Joseph Arnold; 50 A Thomas Hervey				
Thayer, Levi	Athens, Luzerne, PA	1000 A	$1,000	8/14/1802
Lyon, Asa	Northumberland, Saratoga, NY	Luzerne, PA	H346	8/20/1802
Thayer, Levi	Tioga, Luzerne, PA	Lot 47, 300 A	$260	8/27/1795
Murphy, John	Tioga, Luzerne, PA	Watertown Twp	E364	8/30/1796
Thayer, Levi	Tioga, Luzerne, PA	300 A. Lot 14	$300	6/22/1795
Parker, Hezekiah & Samuel, bros	Tioga, Luzerne, PA	Watertown Twp	C589	6/30/1795
actually dated 6/31/1795 but computer will not record that date				
Thayer, Levi	Tioga, Luzerne, PA	300 A, Lot 39	$868	9/12/1800
Parks, Thomas	Tioga, Luzerne, PA (now)	Watertown, Luzerne, PA	H236	9/13/1800
Thayer, Levi	Athens, Luzerne, PA	600 A	$600	12/30/1799
Peckham, James et al*	Providence, Providence, RI	Durkee Twp	H170	12/30/1799
James Peckham, house wright; Wilber Paul, cooper; Jonathan French, painter; James Larcher, hatter, tenants in common				
Thayer, Levi	Athens, Luzerne, PA	150 A, Lot 32	$150	10/25/1799
Sergeant, Joseph, & Gowdy, Chas	Mansfield, and Windham, CT	Watertown Twp	H242	9/20/1800
Thayer, Levi	Athens, Luzerne, PA	16,000 A	$16,000	5/12/1800
Smith, John	Dighton, MA	Bloomfield Twp	H305	6/24/1801
Thayer, Levi	Athens, Luzerne, PA	2,325 A ex 1st lots of present settlers	$2,325	5/16/1800
Smith, John	Dighton, Bristol, MA	Windsor Twp	H307	6/24/1801

grantor grantee notes	grantor residence grantee residence	description location	amount acct bk page	deed date record date
Thayer, Levi	Athens, Luzerne, PA	500 A	$800	5/28/1800
Smith, John	Dighton, Bristol, MA	Insurance Twp	H307	6/24/1801
Thayer, Levi	Athens, Luzerne, PA	4,000 A undivided	$4,000	5/15/1800
Smith, John	Dighton, Bristol, MA	Fullersville Twp	H308	6/24/1801
Thayer, Levi	Athens, Luzerne, PA	840 A with exceptions*	$1,500	5/29/1800
Smith, John, Clerk	Dighton, Bristol, MA	Ulster Twp	H309	6/24/1801
exceptions: 141 A of SE corner sold to Solomon Tracy; 1/2 a grindstone Lodge discovered to be on the premises with 1/2 of the profits thereof				
Thayer, Levi	Athens, Luzerne, PA	4,000 A, south 1/4	$4,000	
Smith, John, Clerk	Dighton, Bristol, MA	Graham Twp	H310	
Thayer, Levi	Athens, Luzerne, PA	300 A Lot 46	$300	9/1/1796
Terrill, Joel	Athens, Luzerne, PA	Watertown Twp	E420	9/23/1796
Thayer, Levi	Athens, Luzerne, PA	300 A	$600	10/10/1801
Underhill, Isaac, Capt.	Dorset, Bennington, VT	Durkee Twp adj. Jas Lasher on the N	H325	12/21/1801
Thayer, Levi	Athens, Luzerne, PA	100 A	$100	10/28/1801
Weaver, Richard	Clarenden, Rutland, VT	Durkee Twp	H326	12/11/1801
Thayer, Levi	Athens, Luzerne, PA	496 A, Lot 25	$600	5/16/1800
Whitmarsh, Rufus	Dighton, Bristol, MA	Fairfield Twp	H247	9/22/1800
Thayer, Levi	Luzerne, PA	320 A, Lot 24	$300	5/15/1800
Winslow, Job	Dighton, Bristol, MA	Smithfield Twp	H245	9/22/1800
Thayer, Levi	Athens, Luzerne, PA	160 A in common and undivided	$150	5/16/1800
Winslow, Job	Dighton, Bristol, MA	Durkee Twp	H246	5/22/1800
Thayer, Levi	Athens, Luzerne, PA	1/2 share, 1,000 A	$500	3/20/1801
Wright, Cyprian	Swanzy, Cheshire, NH	Susquehanna Purchase	H286	3/20/1801
Thayer, Levi & Nathan	Tioga, Luzerne, PA	300 A, Lot 37	$300	6/20/1796
Moon, Silas	New Cornwall, Orange, NY	Watertown Twp	E207	6/20/1796
Thayer, Levi & Nathan	Tioga Twp, Luzerne Co, PA	300 A, Lot 25	$300	6/22/1795
Towner, Elijah & son Enoch	Tioga Twp, Luzerne Co, PA	Watertown Twp	C587	6/30/1795
actually dated 6/31/1795 but computer will not record that date				
Thayer, Levi & Satterlee, Elias	Athens, Luzerne, PA	1,000 A	$1,000	10/16/1798
Aborn, Thomas	Warwick, Kent, RI	Insurance Twp	H134	11/30/1799
Thayer, Levi & Satterlee, Elias	Athens, Luzerne, PA	1,000 A E - W parallel with north	$1,000	10/16/1799
Carpenter, Comfort A., Dr.	Providence, Providence, RI	Insurance Twp	H151	11/30/1799
Thayer, Levi & Thayer, Nathan	Tioga, Luzerne, PA	Lot 8	$300	12/8/1795
Hodgkiss, Samuel et al	Bristol, Hartford, CT	Watertown Twp	D123	12/9/1795
Lynde Phelps; John Ward				
Thayer, Nathan	Athens, Luzerne, PA	4,000 A	$4,000	8/30/1796
Thayer, Levi	Athens, Luzerne, PA	Watertown Twp, SE 1/4	E432	9/6/1796
Thayer, Nathan	Athens, Luzerne, PA	700 A remaining on 1/2 share*	$700	3/19/1801
Whitcomb, Nathan	Swansey, Cheshire, NH	Susquehanna Purchase	H287	3/20/1801
Nathan Thayer reserved 300 A for lot 39, Murraysfield				
Thayer, Polly Howbut	Athens, Luzerne, PA	300 A	$450	12/30/1799
Thayer, Levi	Athens, Luzerne, PA	Juddsborough Twp	H175	1/1/1800
Thomas, Charles				
Canfield, Thomas			A49	
Thomas, Charles				
Hunt, John			A52	
Thomas, Ebenezer, Simeon,	Norwich, New London, CT	all right except share in Berlin Twp	£30	11/24/1794
Hyde, Elisha; Tracy, Elisha	Norwich, New London, CT		I143	12/25/1794
heirs and chr of Ebenezer Thomas, the Elder decd.				
Thomas, Joseph	Tioga, NY	1/2 share except 300 A*	$10	4/7/1795
Shepard, John	Tioga, Luzerne, PA	Susquehanna Purchase	E325	4/10/1796
laid in a gore btw Athens and NY line on E side Tioga Br [renamed Chemung R.]				
Thomas Post Jr.		to survey	$3	2/10/1774
Post, Eldad		Brookhaven Twp	E68	2/28/1796
Thomas, Samuel	Newtown, Fairfield	1 share	val con	12/6/1773
Griswould, Elijah	Nobletown, Oblong, NY		E356	7/20/1796
Thompson, Abraham et al	New Haven, New Haven, CT	1 share	$80	12/28/1795
Munson, Joshua	Canaan, Litchfield, CT		E251	7/1/1796
Isaac, Jacob, Nathaniel Fitch & Mary, wf, all heirs and chr. Abraham Thompson, Sr.				
Thompson, John	Branford, New Haven, CT	1 1/2 share	£50	6/19/1777
Morris, Amos	New Haven		C26	7/6/1782
Thompson, John	Brentford, New Haven, CT	1/2 share	£8	3/23/1773
Munson, Walter Dr.	New Haven, New Haven, CT	Yaletown Twp	D41	10/26/1795

grantor grantee notes	grantor residence grantee residence	description location	amount acct bk page	deed date record date
Thomson, Caleb		all right except 300 A	val recd	6/8/1796
Beebe, Solomon		Burlington Twp	E331	4/10/1796
Thornton, Richard	Providence, Providence, Rhode	1/5 share	£10	1/6/1755
Carpenter, Israel	Providence, Providence, Rhode		E357	6/1/1796
Thornton, Richard	Providence, Providence, Rhode	1/5 share	£10	1/6/1755
Clemance, Thomas	Providence, Providence, Rhode		E359	6/1/1796
Thornton, Richard	Providence, Providence, Rhode	1/5 share	£10	1/6/1755
Harris, Christopher	Providence, Providence, Rhode		E358	6/1/1796
Thornton, Richard	Providence, Providence, Rhode	1/5 share	£10	1/6/1755
Sheldon, Edward	Providence, Providence, Rhode		E360	6/1/1796
Throop, Benjamin		agent for a Twp survey	2 shares	7/20/1795
Throop, Benjamin			C120-1	9/1/1795
Throop, Benjamin		agent for a Twp survey		7/20/1795
Throop, Benjamin			C120.1	9/1/1795
for fifteen owners, including Throop, who pay Throop 6s per day for his time and horse; total of 8 shares; B. Throop 2 shares				
Thurber, John 2nd	Providence, Providence, RI	1,000 A	$1,000	9/12/1799
Tifft, Daniel	Providence, Providence, RI	Springhill Twp	H266	11/1/1800
Tibballs, Thomas Jr.& Sr.	Norfolk, Litchfield, CT	1 3/4 shares	£10	7/26/1794
Brown, Daniel	Freehold, Albany, NY		C478	2/1/1795
Tiffany, Consider	Hartland, Litchfield, CT	1/2 share	40s	12/28/1773
Hopkins, William	Harwinton, Litchfield, CT		B215	2/25/1774
Tiffany, Consider Sr.	Lyme, New London, CT	1 share	£50	12/18/1754
Tiffany, Consider Jr.	Lyme, New London, CT		B322	3/29/1775
Tiffany, Ebenezer	Lyme, New London, CT	1/2 share	£3	10/15/1773
Colt, Harris Capt	Lyme, New London, CT		C453	2/21/1795
Tiffany, Ebenezer	Lyme, New London, CT	1/2 share	£3	3/10/1794
Elliot, William	Saybrook, Middlesex, CT		C457	2/21/1795
Tiffany, Isaiah	West Stockbridge, Berkshire,	Pwr Att*		5/7/1796
Baldwin, Samuel Dr.	West Stockbridge, Berkshire,		D4	8/9/1796
to execute deeds to Samuel Clark, James Bulkley, Joshua Henshaw on their fulfilling a contract with Ebenezer Center				
Tiffany, Isaiah	West Stockbridge, Berkshire,	750 A	$750	4/23/1796
Brinsmade, Thomas C.	New Hartford, Litchfield, CT	Ralpho Twp	D1	8/9/1796
Tiffany, Isaiah	West Stockbridge, Berkshire,	2000 A	$2000	3/25/1796
Brinsmade, Thomas C.	New Hartford, Litchfield, CT	Ralpho Twp	D2	8/9/1796
Tiffany, Isaiah	West Stockbridge, Berkshire,	16,000 acres	$16,000	5/6/1796
Clark, Samuel & Bulkley, James	Middletown, Middlesex, CT	Gilead Twp	E306	8/8/1796
Tiffany, Isaiah	West Stockbridge, Berkshire,	4000 acres	$4,000	3/25/1796
Henshaw, Joshua	New Hartford, Litchfield, CT	Ralpho Twp	E305	8/8/1796
Tiffany, Isaiah	West Stockbridge, Berkshire,	500 A*	$500	4/2/1796
McGanigal, James *undivided*	New Hartford, Litchfield, CT	Ralpho Twp	D168	7/5/1796
Tiffany, Isaiah & Baldwin, Samuel	W Stockbridge, Berkshire, MA	16,000 A	$20	5/24/1796
Clark, Samuel & Bulkley, James	Middletown, Middlesex, CT	Walsingham Twp	D178	8/9/1796
Tiffany, Isaiah & Baldwin, Samuel	West Stockbridge, Berkshire,	16,000 A	$20,000	6/6/1796
Henshaw, Joshua	New Hartford, Litchfield, CT	Burretsfield Twp	E316	6/8/1796
Tiffany, Isaiah & Baldwin, Samuel	West Stockbridge, Berkshire,	8,000 A	$5,000	2/1/1797
Lombard, Roswell, saddler	Stockbridge, Berkshire, MA	Armenia Twp	F181	7/16/1797
Tiffany, Isaiah & Whiting, William	W Stkbridge, MA & Canaan	7,900 A	$11,000	4/15/1796
Beardsley, John et al* *Daniel Rose, Jr., Peter Tyler, Jr.*	Branford, New Haven, CT	Fairfax Twp	F162	4/24/1797
Tinker, Edward	New London, CT	1 share*	£10	9/3/1794
Lester, Eliphalet	Saybrook, Middlesex, CT		D12	9/18/1795
son lost share when went to settle with Samuel Jackson. Jackson was killed in war and papers lost.				
Todd, Timothy		2,000 A	$100	5/11/1800
Wilson, Isaac			H206	6/10/1800
Tomlinson, Henry				
Thomas, Charles			A51	
Tomlinson, Henry Sr.	Derby, New Haven, CT	1 share	val sum	3/21/1795
Plumb, Joseph	Huntington, Fairfield, CT		C578	6/19/1795
heir & Ex Henry Tomlinson, Jr.; see C578 for copy of 1778 Henry Tomlinson Sr. Will				
Tomlinson, Zachariah		1/2 share, 300 A; 700 A		
Curtiss, Elihu* *conveying deed not produced*		New Milford Twp; Millsberry Twp	E475	11/28/1796

grantor / grantee / notes	grantor residence / grantee residence	description / location	amount / acct bk page	deed date / record date
Torrey, John	Granville, Washington, NY	1/2 share	£8	5/4/1795
Grant, Josiah	Poultney, Rutland, VT		C559	6/20/1795
Tozer, Samuel Jr. estate	Colchester	1/2 share	£20	5/13/1778
Tainter, John	Colchester		C39	5/31/1778
Tracy, Andrew*	Norwich, New London, CT	1/2 share	£20	12/10/1794
Tracy, Elisha	Norwich, New London, CT		I182	2/22/1795
son & heir of Isaac Tracy of Norwich, OP				
Tracy, Andrew	Norwich, New London, CT	Pwr Attorney	1/2 of receipts or	11/21/1794
Tracy, Elisha	Norwich, New London, CT		E42	2/22/1796
Tracy, Andrew Jr.				
Clements, Jeremiah			A364	
Tracy, Charlotte, Polly, Deborah*	Norwich, New London, CT	all right	£30	12/11/1794
Tracy, Elisha	Norwich, New London, CT		I197	4/1/1795
heirs of Dr. Elisha Tracy, Sr.				
Tracy, Elisha	Norwich, New London, CT	300 A, Lot 7	£10	10/22/1795
Baldwin, Simeon	New Haven, New Haven, CT	Bachelor's Adventure Twp	H49	1/8/1799
Tracy, Elisha	Norwich, New London, CT	150 A, 1/2 Lot 29	£10	2/11/1796
Breed, John, Esq.*	Norwich, New London, CT	Bachelor's Adventure Twp	H142	9/14/1799
and other heirs of Gershom Breed, Esq.				
Tracy, Elisha	Norwich, New London, CT	1/2 share	£5	7/3/1770
Clements, Jeremiah	Norwich, New London, CT		B236	8/20/1774
Tracy, Elisha	Norwich, New London, CT	1/2 of 30 lots + lot 8*	$1	12/7/1796
Kingsberry, Joseph	Tioga	Bachelor's Adventure Twp	H183	1/3/1800
1/2 of lots 4-5, 9-10, 12-15, 18, 19, 21, 29, 33-36, 38, 44-46, 48-54, 56-58 + all lot 8, 300A each				
Tracy, Elisha & Hyde, Elisha*	Norwich, New London, CT	all land laid out since 2/24/1795*	5s	5/9/1795
Brown, Daniel Jr.	New Durham, Albany, NY		E120 - E508	3/1/1796
joint proprietors on shares of John Bliss, Joseph Griswold, Abel Griswold, Ebenezer Thomas, Jesse Birchard, Lemuel Gardner				
Tracy, Isaac	Norwich	1 1/4 share		1/14/1775
Tyler, Hannah*	Norwich		C12	9/1/1795
dau of Isaac Tracy and wf Rev. John Tyler				
Tracy, John	Scituate, Providence, RI	1/2 share	£100	7/16/1756
Smith, Thomas	Scituate, Providence, RI		B300	12/28/1774
Tracy, Mehitable	Canterbury, Windham, CT	1 share	£10	1/1/1795
Dorrance, Samuel	Windham, Windham, CT		C393	2/22/1795
Tracy, Philemon et al*	Norwich, New London, CT	1 share	£30	12/10/1794
Tracy, Elisha	Norwich, New London, CT		I147	12/25/1794
Charlotte, Polly, & Deborah, all heirs of Phinehas Tracy				
Tracy, Prince	Windham, Windham, CT	1 share	£1.10	1/20/1795
Larrabee, Lebbeus	Windham, Windham, CT		C346	2/27/1795
Trapp, Caleb et al*	Norwich, New London, CT	1 share	$5	1/23/1796
Downer, Joshua	Preston, New London, CT		E242	7/4/1796
Edward Tracy & Azubah wf of Preston, all chr. to Jonathan Jennings, late of Preston, decd.				
Tripp, Isaac				
Tripp, Henry Dow			A109	
Tripp, Isaac	Warwick, Kent, RI	1/4 share	£4.10	8/13/1770
Tripp, Job Jr.	Scituate, Providence, RI		B139	2/9/1774
Tripp, Isaac Jr.	Warwick, Kent, RI	1/2 share + 1 lot*	£40	9/22/1776
Aborn, Samuel	Pawtucket, Kent, RI	Putnam Twp	B349	11/12/1776
lot adj. to Dr. Bowen of Providence				
Tripp, Joshua	Pompey, Onondaga, NY	Pwr Att*	1/3 land	9/5/1796
Hill, Charles	Cazenovia, Herkimer, NY		F91	8/31/1796
to locate share purchased of Elias Benjamin and Enos Peck				
Trowbridge, Oliver	Freehold, Albany, NY	16,000 A	£2000	10/22/1795
Whitaker, Ephraim	Hudson, Columbia, NY	Homerstown Twp	E355	7/20/1796
Trowbridge, Samuel	New Fairfield, Fairfield, CT	1/4 share	£6.5	4/29/1763
Stevens, Ebenezer Jr.	New Fairfield, Fairfield, CT		C629	7/15/1795
Trumbull, David*	Lebanon, Windham, CT	Pwr Att*		2/16/1796
Hyde, Ezekiel	Norwich, New London, CT		F33	4/23/1796
Exec for estate of His Excellency, Jonathan Trumbull, decd.; 1 share Ebenezer Fitch, 1 share Jonathan Trumbull, Esq., 1 share brother Joseph Trumbull, decd				
Trumbull, Jonathan Jr.	Lebanon CT	1 share		9/21/1794
Backus, Ebenezer	Tioga		C442	2/21/1795
Tubbs, Enos	Seneca, Ontario, NY	1/2 share		3/7/1794
Bartell, Peter Jr.	Ontario, NY		C315	3/9/1795

grantor	grantor residence	description	amount	deed date
grantee	grantee residence	location	acct bk page	record date
notes				
Tucker, John	Stockbridge, Berkshire, MA	250 A	$40	9/2/1797
Curtiss, Abel	Stockbridge, Berkshire, MA	Lovisa Twp	F225	11/1/1797
Tucker, John	Stockbridge, Berkshire, MA	1,000 A	$200	9/2/1797
Curtiss, Iram	Stockbridge, Berkshire, MA	Lovisa Twp	F223	11/1/1797
Tucker, John	Stockbridge, Berkshire, MA	Pwr Att*		9/24/1796
Holt, Jacob	Canaan, Litchfield, CT		F195	7/19/1797
to locate 1/2 share from Sanford Holmes				
Tucker, John	Stockbridge, Berkshire, MA	1,000 A	$200	9/2/1797
Judd, Ozias	Stockbridge, Berkshire, MA	Lovisa Twp	F226	11/1/1797
Tucker, John	Stockbridge, Berkshire, MA	2,500 A	$200	9/2/1797
Lombard, Roswell, saddler	Stockbridge, Berkshire, MA	Lovisa Twp	F221	11/1/1797
Turner, Philip	Norwich, New London, CT	350 A	£5	11/6/1794
Tracy, Elijah Capt	Norwich CT	Bedford Twp	I110	12/6/1794
Turner, Philip	Norwich, New London, CT	1 share	$40	11/6/1794
Tracy, Elisha	Norwich, New London, CT		I196	4/1/1795
Turner, Samuel*	Newmansboro, Berkshire, MA	1/7th share	$60	1/28/1800
Knap, Zadoch	Northumberland, Saratoga, NY		H207	2/8/1800
heir of Daniel Turner, decd				
Turner, Seth	Catskill, Albany, NY	16,000 A	£1,600	1/9/1796
Buckley, Eliphalet	Colchester, New London, CT	Millsbury Twp	F18	
Turner, Seth	Catskill, Albany, NY	16,000 A	5s	8/25/1795
Goodrich, Elihu Chauncey	Claverack, Columbia, NY	Nankin Twp	F136	11/12/1796
Turner, Seth	Catskill, Albany, NY	16,000 A	5s	8/25/1795
Goodrich, Elihu Chauncey	Claverack, Columbia, NY	Calcutta Twp	F139	11/12/1796
Tuthill, Rufus	Plumb Island, Suffolk, NY	1/2 share	£12	10/29/1773
Robertson, Patrick	New London, New London, CT		C360	3/2/1795
Tuttle, Daniel	Long Island, Suffield, NY	1 share	£12	8/25/1794
Lester, Eliphalet	New London, New London, CT		A363 - D7	9/18/1795
Note comment by David Paine, clerk, on D7: "This is a record of an assignment written on back of certificate recorded in 1770 in Liber A, page 363."				
Tuttle, Daniel	Long Island, Suffield, NY	1 share	£17	8/25/1794
Lester, Eliphalet	New London		D9	9/18/1795
Tuttle, Henry and Strope, Isaac	Claverack, Luzerne, PA	Lot 19 with full iron mining rights*	£7.10 yr rent*	11/12/1794
Draper, Amos	Union, Tioga, NY	Claverack Twp	D35	10/20/1795
received £100 for 19/20ths rent on 30 Nov 1794; Wisocks Great Marsh, NW side Wisocks Cr., contains bed of iron ore				
Tuttle, Joseph	Sandgate, Bennington, VT	3 shares	£24	4/11/1795
Janes, Elijah et al*	Troy, Rensselaer, NY		C643	8/9/1795
James Dole, merchant; Wait Rathbun, innkeeper				
Tuttle, Oliver				
Munson, Obediah			A395	
Tyler, Caleb		agent for a Twp survey*	1 share	7/20/1795
Throop, Benjamin			C120.1	9/1/1795
for fifteen owners, including Throop, who pay Throop 6s per day for his time and horse; total of 8 shares; C. Tyler 1 share				
Tyler, Ephriam				
Weeks, Jonathan			A316	
Tyler, John		agent for a Twp survey*		7/20/1795
Throop, Benjamin			C120.1	9/1/1795
for fifteen owners, including Throop, who pay Throop 6s per day for his time and horse; total of 8 shares; J. Tyler 1/4 share				
Tyler, Peter Jr. et al*	Branford, New Haven, CT	2,000 A	$1,200	4/25/1796
Tyler, Peter & Rose, Ameriah	Branford, New Haven, CT	Fairfax Twp	F165	4/24/1797
John Beardsley; Daniel Rose, Jr.				
Tyler, Peter Jr. & Rose, Daniel	Branford, New Haven, CT	5,900 A	$6,580	10/19/1796
Tyler, Peter & Rose, Ameriah	Branford, New Haven, CT	Fairfax Twp	F164	4/24/1797
Tyler, Samuel, merchant	Norwich, New London, CT	300 A, Lot 31	$200	6/20/1799
Tyler, Pascal P, late partner,	Norwich, New London, CT	[Smithfield Twp]	H140	9/14/1799
Underwood, Isaac	Plainfield, Windham, CT	1/4 share	£10	1/1/1771
Pellet, Joseph	Plainfield, Windham, CT		B39	1/11/1771
Underwood, Israel	Plainfield, Windham, CT	1/2 share	£20	1/1/1771
Underwood, Isaac, son	Plainfield, Windham, CT		B37	1/11/1771
Underwood, Israel	Plainfield, Windham, CT	1/2 share	£20	10/31/1782
Underwood, Timothy, son	Plainfield, Windham, CT		C615	7/1/1795
Underwood, Timothy	Plainfield, Windham, CT	all right*		1/12/1795
Spalding, John	Ulster, Luzerne, PA	Susquehanna Purchase	C616	7/1/1795
300 A on this right for Spalding in Watertown Twp, June 1, 1795				

grantor grantee notes	grantor residence grantee residence	description location	amount acct bk page	deed date record date
Usher, Hezekiah	East Haddam, Middlesex, CT	1 share	£3	3/10/1794
Elliot, William	Saybrook, Middlesex, CT		C454	2/21/1795
Utley, John				
Staples, John			A458	
Utley, John	Windham CT	1/2 share	£6	4/2/1773
Utley, Joseph			B40	4/2/1773
Van Rensselaer, Henry J.	Hudson, Columbia, NY	8,000 A	£600	10/14/1795
Goodrich, Elihu Chauncey	Claverack, Columbia, NY	Hudson Twp	F127	11/12/1796
Van Rensselaer, Henry J.	Hudson, Columbia, NY	16,000 A	£1200	10/14/1795
Goodrich, Elihu Chauncey	Claverack, Columbia, NY	Stockbridge Twp	F144	11/12/1796
Van Rensselaer, John H.		all within mentioned lands*	£702	1/20/1795
Lefferts, Leffert, merchant	New York City		F149	11/12/1796
none mentioned, but probably the 2350 A from Chester Bingham				
Vanduzen, Abraham & Jacob*	Great Barrington, Berkshire,	1 share, release interest in	$60	5/14/1796
Vanduzen, Isaac*	Great Barrington, Berkshire,		F190	7/19/1796
heirs of Isaac Vanduzen, decd.				
Vanduzen, Isaac	Great Barrington, Berkshire,	Pwr Att to locate 1 share		5/4/1796
Tucker, John	Stockbridge, Berkshire, MA		F192	7/19/1796
Vanfleet, Joshua		1/2 share 1st division	$5	2/27/1796
Beebe, Solomon		Athens Twp	I260	8/15/1799
deed written 1776 but considered to be an error; see I261				
Vanfleet, Joshua		1/2 share		2/21/1795
Beebe, Solomon			C447	2/21/1795
Vanfleet, Joshua	Wyoming, Northumberland, PA	1/4 share	£3.10	6/9/1785
Howell, Josiah			C531	5/1/1795
VanFleet, Joshua	Athens, Luzerne Co PA	Lot 41, 326 A	£134.9	12/1/1794
Livingston, John	Livingston, Columbia, NY	Athens Twp	C545	4/1/1795
Vanfleet, Joshua	Athens, Luzerne, PA	1/2 share, Lot 1	£26	6/11/1795
Shepard, John	Tioga, Luzerne, PA	Murraysfield Twp	E326	4/10/1796
Veets, John	Simsbury, Hartford, CT	1/2 share	20s	12/21/1754
Forward, Abel	Simsbury, Hartford, CT		I157	2/19/1795
Vial, Peter				
LeHommedieu, Ezra			A299	
Viets, Hezekiah P.	Athens PA	1/2 share	$100	2/21/1795
Platt, Daniel	Kinderhook, Albany Co NY		C196	2/28/1795
Vincent, Charles		2 Twps, 16,000 A each	£55£	11/23/1796
Platner, Henry		Stanford & Milton Twp	F244	1/23/1798
Visscher, Sebastian, Attorney	Albany, Albany, NY	16,000 A	£1,600	8/23/1796
Goodrich, Elihu Chauncey		Albany Twp	E472	11/20/1796
Vreeland, Michael, heir to Garret		1/2 share	val recd	12/26/1801
Blakeslee, Ephriam		Sullivan Twp	H332	10/15/1802
Wadsworth, Asahel*	Farmington, Hartford, CT	1/2 share	£3	10/29/1795
Henshaw, Daniel	Middletown, Middlesex, CT		E49	2/24/1796
heir of William Wadsworth				
Wager, Barnet	Claverack, NY	1/2 share No. 231 of 400		
Segar, Henry		Enfield Twp	I118	12/17/1794
entered 300 A Enfield; 700 A in Rutland reentered in Alba 12/5/1800				
Wainwright, David	Great Barrington, Berkshire,	1/2 share	£22	1/20/1779
Hogeboom, Jeremiah	Claverack, Albany, NY		F275	3/19/1798
Wakeman, Banks	Fairfield, Fairfield, CT	all right	20s	6/12/1795
Wakeman, Jessup	Fairfield, Fairfield, CT		E169	5/31/1796
Wakeman, Ebenezer	Fairfield, Fairfield, CT	1/2 share	$20	3/29/1796
Banks, Ebenezer	Fairfield, Fairfield, CT		E170	5/31/1796
Wakeman, Gideon	Bedford, NY	1/2 share	$25	10/17/1794
Sherwood, Samuel B.	Weston, Fairfield, CT		C525	5/1/1795
Wakeman, Joseph	Fairfield, CT	1/2 share	$40	3/20/1797
Bradley, Walter		Augusta Twp, part laid out in	H1	10/13/1798
Wakeman, Joseph et al*	Fairfield, Fairfield, CT	1/2 share	$10	10/18/1794
Sherwood, Moses	Fairfield, Fairfield CT		C522	5/1/1795
Hezekiah; Thomas & Abigail Davis, heirs of Joseph Wakeman				
Walcott, Nathaniel	Burlington, Otsego, NY	Pwr Att for 1/2 share	1/2 of 1/2 share	5/19/1796
Grant, Josiah	Poultney, Rutland, VT		F72	5/24/1796

grantor grantee notes	grantor residence grantee residence	description location	amount acct bk page	deed date record date
Walden, Jonathan				
French, John			A216	
Waldo, Edward	Canterbury CT	1/2 share	love	10/20/1781
Johnson, Alfred, grandson	Plainfield	Warwick Twp	C25	10/20/1781
Waldo, Zachariah	Canterbury, Windham, CT	1 share	£20	12/10/1794
Tracy, Elisha	Norwich, New London, CT	Cabot Twp	I135	12/25/1794
Wales, Elisha	Arlington, Bennington, VT	1 share	$50	11/11/1798
Todd, Timothy	Arlington, Bennington, VT		H290	3/31/1801
Wales, Nathaniel				
Manning, Stephen			A309	
Wales, Nathaniel	Windham, Windham, CT	1/2 share	£6.6	4/10/1773
Wales, Jonathan, son	Windham, Windham, CT		B69	4/10/1773
Wales, Nathaniel				
Wales, Nathaniel 3rd			A228	
Wales, Nathaniel 3rd	Windham, Windham, CT	1 share	£30	1/2/1771
Perkins, John	Hebron, Hartford, CT	Kingston Twp*	B44	1/11/1771
Twp of 40 proprietors				
Wales, Nathaniel Jr.	Windham, Windham, CT	1/2 share	15s	12/13/1794
Chauncey, Worthington G.	Durham, New Haven, CT		C443	2/21/1795
Walker, Edward		1/2 share		4/26/1777
Davis, Urian			GC	
Walker, Edward	Gageborough, Berkshire, MA	1/2 share, pitched	£30	1/31/1775
Hayward, Caleb	Lebanon, Windham, CT	Brookhaven Twp	B319	3/22/1775
Walker, Eliakim heir*	Taunton, Bristol, MA	Pwr Att to locate 1 share		1/15/1795
Dorrance, Samuel & Ward,	Windham, Windham, CT		C397	2/22/1795
and adm, Eliakim Walker, father, of Taunton, Bristol, MA				
Walker, Elnathan	Woodstock, Windham, CT	all rights	£4.16	2/6/1770
Bolles, David	Ashford, Windham, CT		C581	6/20/1795
Walker, Robert	formerly Canaan	1 share	£100	4/23/1782
Bruce, Robert	Salem, Westchester, NY		C84	4/28/1783
Walker, William	Lenox, Berkshire, MA	1/2 share	£30	4/14/1795
Pixley, David	Chenango, NY		E65	2/26/1796
Wall, Henry	North Kingstown, Kings, RI	1 share	£42	9/20/1776
Aborn, Samuel	Warwick, Kent, RI		B349	10/1/1776
Wallace, Uriah*	North Salem, West Chester, NY	12,000 A	$2,700*	8/23/1796
Baldwin, Samuel	West Stockbridge, Berkshire,	Hexham Twp	E465	11/6/1796
Reverse deed titled Baldwin to Wallace. If Baldwin meets conditions of 5 payments in set amounts on set dates, the deed Baldwin to Wallace, is null and void.				
Waller, Nathan	Wilkesbarre, Luzerne, PA	1/2 share	$20	12/8/1794
Baldwin, Waterman	Pittstown, Luzerne, PA		E303	6/20/1796
Wallis, Moses and Abigail	Jerico, NY	all right	$20	9/30/1799
Knap, David	NY		H109	10/30/1799
Walsworth, Charles	Groton, New London, CT	1/2 share	£6	9/8/1770
Lester, Eliphalet	New London, New London, CT		C361	3/2/1795
Walsworth, William		1 share		
Goss, William			GL	
Walsworth, William				
Hallam, Nicholas			A354	
Walworth, Nathan	Barnard Town, MA	1/2 share	£8	6/24/1775
Walworth, Elijah, heirs*	Groton, New London, CT		B343	2/14/1776
Abigail, Mary, Nathan				
Wanzer, Abraham	New Fairfield, Fairfield, CT	3/4 share	10s	9/10/1794
Brownson, Isaac	New Milford, Litchfield, CT	New Milford Twp	I153	12/6/1794
Wanzer, Moses	New Fairfield, Fairfield, CT	1/4 share	£5.5	12/12/1765
Prindle, Aaron	New Fairfield, Fairfield, CT	New Fairfield Twp	I156	12/6/1794
Ward, Edmund	Guilford, New Haven, CT	1/2 share	£20	3/12/1774
Caldwell, Nathaniel	Guilford, New Haven, CT		E187	6/9/1796
Ward, Hacock				
Atwater, Enos			A261	
Ward, William	New Marlboro, Berkshire, MA	1/2 share	£18	3/1/1775
Whitney, Josiah	Canaan, Litchfield, CT		B373	7/14/1777
Warner, Eleazer*	Ashford, Windham, CT	Pwr Att to locate and lay out rights		5/8/1795
Young, William	Windham, Windham, CT		C599	7/15/1795
heir of Thomas Warner, OP				

grantor grantee notes	grantor residence grantee residence	description location	amount acct bk page	deed date record date
Warner, Isaac				
Bingham, Elijah			A29	
Warner, Nathaniel				
Follet, Benjamin			A45	
Warren, Moses	Equalcut, Berkshire, MA	1/2 share	30s	10/29/1773
Bradford, William	Canterbury, Windham, CT		B284	1/10/1775
Warren, Moses	Lyme	1/2 share	£3	9/3/1794
Ely, Elisha	Saybrook		C115	10/1/1794
Washborn, Robert	Manior Levington, Albany, NY	1/2 share	£30	2/11/1778
Beach, Barnabas	Amenia, Dutchess, NY		C40	4/12/1782
Washburn, Abisha	Salisbury, Litchfield, CT	1/2 share	£16.6	2/10/1775
Beach, Barnabas	Grt Nine Partners, Dutchess,		B358	6/19/1777
Washburn, Jacob & Isbell, Nathan	Lenox, Berkshire, MA	1/3 of 1/2 share	$1,333.33	10/17/1795
Williams, Ebenezer	Stockbridge, Berkshire, MA	Hancock Twp	F228	11/1/1797
Washburn, Joseph	New Braintree, Worcester, MA	1/2 share	£5	3/10/1775
Allen, Levi	Salisbury, Litchfield, CT		E224	7/2/1796
Waterhouse, Saml & Harris,	Saybrook, Middlesex, CT	300 A, Lot 34	$150	8/21/1798
Canfield, Joel Jr.	Saybrook, Middlesex, CT	ElysiumTwp	H20	11/27/1798
Waterhouse, Samuel	Saybrook, Middlesex, CT	300 A, Lot 10	£25	6/12/1798
Southworth, Martin	Saybrook, Middlesex, CT	Elysium Twp	H21	11/27/1798
Waterman, Asa, father	Norwich, New London, CT	1/2 share	£5	5/30/1769
Waterman, Thomas, son	Norwich, New London, CT		I140	12/25/1794
Waterman, Erastus et al*	Norwich, New London, CT	1/2 share	£30	12/10/1794
Hyde, Elisha	Norwich, New London, CT		I146	12/25/1794
Eben Backus; Eben & Eunice Waterman, all heirs of Thomas Waterman				
Waterman, Sarah*	Colchester, New London, CT	1 share	£3	7/7/1794
Elliot, William	Saybrook, Middlesex, CT		C452	2/21/1795
and Gurdon Hamilton, adms. for Zebulon Waterman, Jr., late of Colchester, decd., and heir of Zebulon Waterman Sr., decd.				
Waters, David	Killingly, Windham, CT	1/2 share	£4	6/21/1763
Howard, Isaac	Situate, Providence, RI		H287	3/19/1801
Waters, David	Falmouth, MA	1/2 of 1 share	£30	3/20/1778
Leavins, John	Killingly, Windham, CT		C70	12/9/1782
Waters, Sarah & Rhoda*	Westmoreland PA & Bozrah,	1/2 share	£3	9/9/1794
Elloit, William	Saybrook, Middlesex, CT		C448	2/21/1795
heirs and sisters of Elihu Waters, decd.				
Waters, Walter Jr.	Newtown, Tioga Co NY	1/2 share	$50	2/21/1795
Platt, Daniel	Kinderhook, Albany Co NY	Columbia Twp	C198	2/28/1795
Watson, Levi & Watson, Cyprian	New Hartford, Litchfield, CT	1/2 share	£2.2	10/30/1762
Case, Daniel	Simsbury, Hartford, CT		I257	12/4/1795
Watson, Thomas	New Hartford, Litchfield, CT	1/2 share	$3.50	5/5/1755
Case, Daniel	Simsbury, Hartford, CT		I256	12/4/1795
Webb, John				
Denison, Nathan			A101	
Webb, John	Windham, Windham, CT	1/2 share	£10	12/27/1794
Dorrance, Samuel	Windham, Windham, CT		C392	2/22/1795
Webb, Ruben	Waterbury, New Haven, CT	Right No. 14	good cause	10/14/1773
Lassly, James	Woodbury, Litchfield, CT	Hanover Twp	B98	12/8/1773
Webb, Samuel	Windham, Windham, CT	Pwr Att for Susq Co rights		5/30/1795
Hebard, Jonathan	Windham, Windham, CT		C582	6/20/1795
Webster, Ashabel		1/2 share		8/28/1761
Paine, John			MB	
Webster, Moses				
Moseley, Peabody			A274	
Webster, Nathaniel				
Payne, John			A253	
Webster, Noah				
Loomis, Thomas Jr.			A14	
Week, Thomas	Wilkesbarre. Luzerne, PA	1/2 share except 300 A laid out	£60	1/27/1794
Farnham, Ebenezer	Wilkesbarre. Luzerne, PA		F98	9/15/1796
Weeks, Holland	Pomfret, Windham, CT	1/2 share	£7	12/2/1773
Weeks, Ebenezer	New London, New London, CT		B146	2/9/1774
Weeks, Jonathan				
Weeks, Philip & Thomas			A317	

grantor	grantor residence	description	amount	deed date
grantee	grantee residence	location	acct bk page	record date
notes				
Weissman, Peter		1/2 of No. 31 of the 600		10/1/1786
Bortle, John	Claverack NY	Towandee Cr.	I28	11/24/1786
Weitman, Abraham			$2	8/6/1776
Sluman, Joseph			B197	3/28/1774
Welch, David	Litchfield, Litchfield, CT	two 1/2 shares	$100	6/2/1796
Wadsworth, Elijah	Litchfield, Litchfield, CT		E223	7/2/1796
Welch, Jeremiah				
Parish, Zebulon & Spafford, John			A284	
Welch, Jeremiah				
Welch, Elijah			A229	
Welles, Jonathan	Glastonbury	1 share	£10	5/10/1773
Burnham, Elizar	Glastonbury		C37	2/28/1782
Welles, William	Glastonbury, Hartford, CT	1 share	£12	6/9/1773
Burnham, Elizur	Glastonbury, Hartford, CT		B273	11/11/1774
Wells, Amos	Colchester, New London, CT	all shares	£30	2/5/1795
Dorrance, Gershom	Windham, Windham, CT		C536	5/7/1795
Wells, James & Elias*	Stratford, Fairfield, CT	Agent to estab 1 share	1/3 part	4/11/1795
Sherwood, Aaron	Fairfield, Fairfield, CT		C528	5/1/1795
heirs and exec of Thomas Wells, certified by Robert Walker, Judge of Probate				
Wells, John	Glastonbury, Hartford, CT	1/2 share	val con	5/12/1794
Hale, George	Catskill, Albany, NY		C375	2/28/1795
Wells, John	East Hartford, Hartford, CT	1 share	£3	10/7/1794
Pitkin, Elisha Jr.	East Hartford, Hartford, CT		E287	6/6/1796
Wells, John	Colchester, New London, CT	1 share		8/25/1794
Turner, Seth	New Haven, New Haven, CT		C291	3/4/1795
Wells, John & Wells, Jonathan*	East Hartford, Hartford, CT	all the original right	£3	10/7/1794
Pitkin, Elisha Jr.	East Hartford, Hartford, CT		E286 - H108	6/6/1796
adms estate Samuel Wells, Jr.; third son, Samuel Wells, devised all land to brothers John and Jonathan				
Wells, Joseph	Cambridge, Washington, NY	1 share	$5	5/20/1795
Eager, George	Cambridge, Washington, NY		C555	5/20/1795
Wells, Joseph Jr., Ex, heir*	Stratford, Fairfield, CT	1 share	£3	4/10/1795
Peck, Job & Uffoot, Benjamin Jr.	Stratford, Fairfield, CT		C527	5/1/1795
of Joseph Wells, attest by Probate Judge				
Wells, Samuel Jr. et al	Stratford, Fairfield, CT	establish 1 share	1/3 share	4/16/1795
Sherwood, Aaron	Fairfield, Fairfield, CT		C529	5/1/1795
*William Fairchild and Hannah, wf, * heirs of Abijah Wells*				
Wentworth, Benjamin, decd		1 share		
Wentworth, Jared, by will*	Norwich CT		E227	7/2/1796
before 20 Jan 1775				
Wentworth, Jared				
Johnson, Daniel	Farmingham		A88	
West, Clement & Prudence	Exeter, Wyoming, PA	150 A, 1/2 Lot. 20	£42	7/4/1786
Daily, Samuel	Exeter, Wyoming, PA	Exeter Twp	I52	7/15/1786
West, William	Scituate, Providence, RI	all right	£155 in silver	1/24/1795
West, William Jr.	Scituate, Providence, RI	Susquehanna Company lands	D157	6/19/1796
Westbrook, Leonard	Tioga, Luzerne, PA	1/2 share, Lot 31	£30	12/25/1794
Hutchinson, John	Tioga, Luzerne, PA	Columbia Twp	C308	2/28/1795
Wheeler, Abner	Bethlehem, Litchfield, CT	10 whole shares; three half shares*	val sum	11/2/1795
Goodrich, Benjamin	Canaan, Litchfield, CT		E254	7/1/1796
Saml Rose, Eben Norton, John Patterson, Richard Peat , John Montgomery, William Buck, Arch Kasson, Saml Norton, Nehm Lewis, Saml Osborne; Tim Everett; John Curtiss, Eben Lewis				
Wheeler, Abner	Bethlehem, Litchfield, CT	Pwr to locate & sell land*	1/3 all land	5/4/1795
Spalding, John		Watertown Twp	C622	7/1/1795
OP's: S. Rose 1, J. Patterson1, R. Peet1, J. Montgomery1, Wm Buck,1 Arch Kasson1, Abner Wheeler, 2; Robt Gordon1/2, Robt Hannah 1/2; J. Steel 2, 2/3 to be returned to him				
Wheeler, Benjamin	Woodbury, Litchfield, CT	1/4 share	£2	1/8/1774
Moseley, Abner	Woodbury, Litchfield, CT		B280	10/31/1774
Wheeler, Ephriam	Stillwater, Saratoga, NY	1/4 share	16s	4/1/1795
Janes, Elijah, merchant et al*	Troy, Rensselaer, NY		C126	7/9/1795
James Dole, merchant; Wait Rathbun, innkeeper				
Wheeler, John	Bethlehem, Litchfield, CT	2000 A. 1 share		7/1/1794
Terrill, Job Jr.	New Milford, Litchfield, CT	New Milford Twp	C337	2/26/1795
Wheeler, Joseph				
Tripp, Isaac			A324	

grantor grantee notes	grantor residence grantee residence	description location	amount acct bk page	deed date record date
Wheeler, Nathaniel		1 share		
Nichols, Robert			GN	
Wheeler, Reuben	Poultney, Rutland, VT	500 A undivided	£37.10	4/22/1802
Ward, Elshia	Poultney, Rutland, VT	Addison Twp	H342	8/19/1802
Wheeler, Walter	Ulster, Luzerne, PA	500 A undivided	$1,000	12/21/1799
Thayer, Levi	Athens, Luzerne, PA	Suttonfield Twp	H157	12/26/1799
Wheeler, William	Rhinebeck, Dutchess, NY	3 ctfts: No. 53, 59, 60 of the 600*	£50	12/24/1794
Ely, John, Col.	Saybrook, Middlesex, CT		D138	3/2/1795
dated 1/13/1785, Hartford				
Whitaker, Ephriam	Hudson, Columbia, NY	16,000 A	$8000	8/31/1795
Hunt, Thomas	Stockbridge, Berkshire, MA	Richmond Twp	D71	12/4/1795
Whitaker, Ephriam	Hudson, Columbia, NY	16,000 A	$8,000	7/20/1795
Paine, David	Tioga Point, Luzerne, PA	Roxbury Twp	C496	9/7/1795
Whitaker, Ephriam Jr.	Hudson, NY	16,000 A	$6,000	12/4/1795
Moseley, Nathaniel T.	Pawlett, Rutland, VT	Homerstown Twp	F215	10/25/1797
White, Jeremiah	Owego, Tioga, NY	1/2 share of the 400, No. not recd	£5	2/13/1795
Pixley, David	Owego, Tioga, NY		C553	2/13/1795
White, Jeremiah		1/2 share*	val con	10/17/1795
Pixley, David	Owago		E66	2/26/1796
granted to Jeremiah White for services rendered in 1784				
White, Joseph Moss et al*	Danbury, Fairfield, CT (sons);	1 share	£12	11/2/1794
Smith, Ebenezer	Brookfield, Fairfield, CT		I215	4/11/1795
Ebenezer R., Thomas P.& Mary White; Amelia Lloyd, heirs of Rev. Ebenezer White				
White, Solomon	Hudson, Columbia, NY	1/2 share	£1600	11/18/1795
Fowler, Daniel	Bethlehem, Berkshire, MA	Eastham Twp	E458	10/31/1796
White, William				
Day, Benjamin			A451	
White, William, heir	Simbridge, Orange, VT	1 share	£15	4/21/1796
Hill, Charles,	Lebanon, Grafton, NH		F90	8/31/1796
Whitelsey, Eliphalet	Kent, Litchfield, CT	1/2 share	£12	10/27/1773
Whitelsey, Martin	Kent, Litchfield, CT		C32	2/18/1782
Whiting, Gameliel		1/2 share		
Buck, William			A66	
Whiting, William	Norwich, New London, CT			4/19/1774
Tenant, Caleb	Ashford, CT		A256	
Whitman, Zerubabbel				
Lothrop, Cyprian			A106	
Whitmarsh, Samuel*				3/28/1795
Lee, Ebenezer H. and Simeon			E490	10/4/1796
see Westmoreland Records, The Town book, page 770-771, Microfilm Roll 1				
Whitmore, Josiah		1/2 share		
Bullard, Josiah			GH	
Whitney, James	Canniserauger, Ontario, NY	1/2 share 1st div*	$2	11/2/1795
Vanfleet, Joshua		Athens Twp	I261	12/3/1795
East side Susq R.				
Whitney, John		1 share	£100	6/23/1774
Peirce, Moses			B261	10/13/1774
Whitney, Joshua				
Dean, Ezra			A81	
Whitney, Joshua		1 share		3/31/1774
Taylor, Lemuel			GF	
Whitney, Joshua		1/2 share		3/31/1774
Taylor, Lemuel			GG	
Whitney, Joshua heirs*	Plainfield, Windham, CT	1 share	£20	8/26/1774
Fellows, Abiel	Canaan, Litchfield, CT		I19	1/1/1795
Asa & Abigail Bacon; Lemuel & Mary Kingsbury; David & Huldah Whitney; Joshua Whitney, 2nd; Josiah Whitney				
Whitney, Joshua heirs*	Canaan, Litchfield, CT;	1 1/2 shares	£70	2/24/1781
Kingsberry, Lemuel	Canaan, Litchfield, CT		H218	10/19/1799
Joshua Whitney, 2nd, Josiah, David, Amy all of Canaan; Asa Bacon & Abigail wf, Canterbury; Elias Palmer & Huldah, wf., Stillwater, Albany, NY				
Whitney, Josiah	Canaan, Litchfield, CT	1/2 share inc. 100 A	£1000	4/29/1780
Fellows, Ezra	Sheffield, Berkshire, MA	Brinton on Fishing Creek	I29	11/25/1786
Whitney, Tarbel				
Kingsbury, Stephen			A272	

grantor grantee notes	grantor residence grantee residence	description location	amount acct bk page	deed date record date
Whiton, Elijah	Ashford, Windham, CT	1/2 share	£6	4/9/1773
Bullock, Nathan	Ashford, Windham, CT		B97	10/28/1773
Whittelsey, Eliphalet	Kent, Litchfield, CT	1/4 share	£10	11/12/1773
Starkweather, Stephen	Kent, Litchfield, CT		B166	3/8/1774
Whittemore, Josiah		1 share		7/6/1772
Bullard, Josiah			GH	1/5/1775
Whittlesey, Chauncey	New Haven, New Haven, CT	1/2 share	£10	3/30/1774
Allen, Levi	Salisbury, Litchfield, CT		B258	10/5/1774
Whittlesey, David	Kent, Litchfield, CT	1/4 share	£6	9/27/1773
Guthrie, Joseph	Kent, Litchfield, CT		B171	3/9/1774
Whittlesey, Eliphalet				
Whittlesey, Asaph			A475	
Whittlesey, John		all right		1/16/1796
Terrel, Job		Susquehanna Purchase	E127	3/1/1796
Whittlesey, Martin et al		2/3 of 6 half shares		11/9/1793
York, Lucretia		Braintrim Twp*	I167	
entered 6/1/1780				
Wickwin, James		1/2 share		3/21/1770
Utley, Nathan & Abbot, John Jr.			GC	2/17/1775
Wickwire, James	East Haddam, Middlesex, CT	Pwr Attorney to locate 2 half shares*	1/4 land to Strong	2/25/1795
Strong, Jabin	Glastenbury, Hartford, CT		E70	2/29/1796
James Wickwire pd $2 taxes on 1/2 share Jonathan Stricklin 3/1/1775 and $1 plus note for 18s for taxes on Elnathan Walker 1/2 share 3/1/1770				
Wickwire, James				
Utley, Nathaniel			A334	
Wight, Joseph	Preston, New London, CT	1 share	£1200	11/19/1794
Tracy, Elisha	Norwich, New London, CT	Cabot Twp	I131	12/25/1794
Wightman, Allen*	Bozrah, New London, CT			2/13/1796
			E232	7/1/1796
pp. 230-231 missing from original; only this last portion of deed survives on p. 232				
Wightman, Zerubabel	Norwich, New London, CT	1/2/share	£6	3/26/1770
Woodworth, Benjamin	Norwich, New London, CT		B44	10/1/1773
Wilcocks, Daniel	Simsbury, Hartford, CT	1/2 share	£10	12/6/1773
Forward, Joseph	Simsbury, Hartford, CT		B293	5/25/1774
Wilcox, Elijah	Simsbury, Hartford, CT	Pwr Att to survey and locate 1/2	1/2 surveyed land	1/16/1795
Ballard, Stephen et al*	Judsborough, Luzerne, PA		C622	7/1/1795
Samuel C. Chamberlain of Colebrook, Litchfield, CT				
Wilcox, Stephen		1/2 share No. 231 of the 400*		
Irwin, James			E437	10/1/1796
except 300 A sold to Daniel Ross 9/5/1796				
Wiley, James*	Stephenstown, NY	all right	£40	8/31/1796
Wiley, Simeon*	Great Bend of the Susquehanna		E381	9/15/1796
also spelled Wylley				
Wiley, John & Abraham	East Haddam, Middlesex, CT	1 share	$50	11/15/1794
Selby, Brainard	Landisfield, Berkshire, MA		C434	2/1/1795
Willcox, Symorris	Ulster, Luzerne, PA	300 A	£75	12/1/1796
Rood, James	Norfolk, CT	Insurance Twp	E501	1/3/1797
Willerd, Dubartius		2/4 share		7/14/1774
Shawes, Thomas			GD	8/20/1774
Williams, Ebenezer	Northridge, Berkshire, MA	1,675 A out of 1/3 of 1/2 share	$837	10/17/1795
Robinson, Levi et al*	Lee, MA	Hancock Twp	E469	11/10/1796
Jesse Clark, John Yale				
Williams, Elisha		1/2 share		
Deming, Ebenezer Jr.			A38	
Williams, Elisha	Stonington, New London, CT	1 1/2 share	24s	11/6/1794
Kingsbury, Joseph	Enfield, Hartford, CT		C150	2/24/1795
Williams, Ezekiel	Weathersfield, Hartford, CT	1 share	$20	5/13/1794
Hale, George	Catskill, Albany, NY		C384	2/28/1795
Williams, John*	Great Barrington, Berkshire,	3/4 share	£11.5	11/6/1794
Brown, Sanford	Sanderfield, Hampshire, MA		F10	3/1/1796
son & heir of old John				
Williams, John	Groton	1 share	18s	6/28/1794
Fowler, Reuben	Killingworth, Middlesex, CT		C118	10/1/1794

grantor	grantor residence	description	amount	deed date
grantee	grantee residence	location	acct bk page	record date
notes				
Williams, John	Sharon, Litchfield, CT	all right	£9	4/4/1795
King, George & Mills, Eli	Sharon, Litchfield, CT &		C574	6/22/1795
Williams, Nathaniel	Lebanon, Windham, CT	1 share	£3	1/30/1795
Larrabee, Libbeus	Windham, Windham, CT		C348	2/27/1795
Williams, Thomas	Waterbury, New Haven, CT	all right	good cause	1/1/1796
Hopkins, Jesse	Waterbury, New Haven, CT		E146	2/25/1796
Williams. Thomas		1 share		
Matthews, Henry*			F87	9/19/1796
orig name Gameliel Maltar, assignment written in German				
Williams, Thomas	Lebanon, Windham, CT	Pwr Att to recover 1/2 share		2/18/1796
Throop, Benjamin	Bozrah, New London, CT		E234	
Williams, Thomas, Ex*	Norwich, New London, CT	Pwr Att to recover 1 share*		6/3/1796
Throop, Benjamin	Bozrah, New London, CT		E232	7/1/1796
estate & property of father Ebenezer Williams, decd.; taxes paid				
Williams, William	Colchester, Hartford, CT	1 share	£10	3/23/1774
Ackley, Joseph	East Haddam, Hartford, CT		B194	3/24/1774
Wilson, James				
Tripp, Isaac			A104	
Winchester, Andrew	Canterbury	1/2 share	£150	11/26/1779
Winchester, Amariah	Kent, Litchfield, CT		C6	12/27/1779
Winders, William	Lansingburgh, NY	Rights of John H. & Beleazer Lydius	$200	2/16/1796
Wheeler, Preserved	Charlotte, Chittenden, VT		E130	3/28/1796
Winship, Jabez	New London	1 share	£46	3/2/1780
Fitch, Shared	Norwich		C15	3/7/1780
Winter, Gideon	Bethlehem, Litchfield, CT	1 share	$70	10/30/1795
Wheeler, Abner	Bethlehem, Litchfield, CT		E253	7/1/1796
Wise, Samuel P.	Watertown, Litchfield, CT	Pwr Att to locate 1, 1/4 & 1/8 shares		10/18/1796
Bryan, Richard	Watertown, Litchfield, CT		E481	11/15/1796
Witham, Joshua				
Chapman, Edmond			A473	
Witter, Joseph	Patridgeville, Berkshire, MA	Agent		4/15/1795
Crary, Oliver	Preston, New London, CT		C9	9/1/1795
Witter, Joseph	Partridgefield, Berkshire, MA	1 share	$100	2/1/1796
Ryxbe, Moses	Washington, Berkshire, MA	Throopsburgh Twp, pt; rest unlocated	E236	7/4/1796
Witter, Josiah	Preston, New London, CT	1/4 share	$20	3/31/1774
Avery, Jabez	Norwich, New London, CT		B209	4/20/1774
Witter, Josiah	Preston, New London, CT	1/4 settling right	£6	3/3/1774
Belleu, Peter	Preston, New London, CT		B192	3/22/1774
Wolcott, Oliver*	Litchfield, Litchfield, CT	all right	affection for son	1/30/1796
Wolcott, Frederick	Litchfield, Litchfield, CT		E401	9/15/1796
$2.00 taxes pd 11/24/1754				
Wolcott, Roger	East Hartford, Hartford, CT	1/2 of 1 share*	£10	10/20/1797
Drake, Nathaniel Jr.	East Windsor, Hartford, CT		F266	3/12/1798
other half sold to Wolcott "some years ago"				
Wolcott, Silas		1/2 share, Lot 39	$30	8/27/1796
Thayer, Nathan		Murraysfield Twp	E510	2/18/1797
Wolcutt, Silas	Tioga, Luzerne, PA	Lot 39; 300 A	£100	1/22/1796
Dutcher, Christopher	Tioga, Luzerne, PA	Murraysfield Twp	E167	3/24/1796
Wolf, Mitchell		1/2 share	value recd	5/26/1770
Bachman, Michael			B290	5/24/1774
Wood, John				
Gore, Obadiah			A428	
Wood, Josiah	Lebanon, Windham, CT	1/2 share	£15	12/29/1774
McClure, Thomas	Westmoreland, Litchfield, CT		B302	12/29/1774
Wood, Nathaniel	Hillsdale, Columbia, NY	640 A	$426.66	12/5/1795
Chapin, Jason	Wilbraham, Hampshire, MA	Cumberland Twp, 1/25	E443	10/24/1796
Wood, Nathaniel	Lowden, Berkshire, MA	4,000 A	$2,000	8/1/1796
Fowler, Daniel	Bethlehem, Berkshire, MA	Litchfield Twp	E455	10/31/1796
25 Lots of 160 A each as ff: 3-7, 14-18, 23-27, 34-5, 38-40, 46-7, 55-6, 65				
Wood, Nathaniel	Hillsdale, Columbia, NY	1,000 A	$5,000	1/6/1796
Gillet, Aaron	Westfield, Hampshire, MA	Halstead Twp, SE corner*	E22	2/9/1796
subj. to an equal division with current proprietors Elijah Wood and Noble Sashet				

grantor grantee notes	grantor residence grantee residence	description location	amount acct bk page	deed date record date
Wood, Nathaniel	Hillsdale, Columbia, NY	320 A, Lots 21, 22	$300	4/22/1796
King, Asaph	Wilbraham, Hampshire, MA	Litchfield, Luzerne, PA	E450	10/25/1796
Woodbridge, Ashbel	East Hartford, Hartford, CT	1 share	£3	4/16/1795
Pitkin Jr., Elisha	East Hartford, Hartford, CT		E247	7/1/1796
Woodbridge, Deodat	East Hartford, Hartford, CT	1/2 share	£10	9/16/1795
Pitkin, Elisha Jr.	East Hartford, Hartford, CT		E289	6/6/1796
Woodbridge, Jahleel, heir*	Stockbridge, Berkshire, MA	1 share	£30	2/26/1796
Woodbridge, Stephen	Washington, Berkshire, MA		E290	6/20/1796
Joseph Woodbridge, decd.; no taxes owed as of 9/8/1774; see E300 for affidavit re heirs of Joseph Woodbridge				
Woodbridge, Russell	Hartford, Hartford, CT	1/2 share	1/2 costs on 1 share	1/30/1760
Olmsted, William	Hartford, Hartford, CT		B218	5/24/1774
Woodbridge, Samuel et al*	Hartland, Litchfield, CT	all rights	£12	5/11/1774
Burnam, Elizur	Glastonbury, Hartford, CT	Susquehanna Purchase	B356	4/9/1777
Theodore, of Hartland; Timothy of Colchester, Hartford, CT; Howell, Elizabeth, William of Glastonbury, Plainfield, CT				
Woodbridge, Timothy	Stockbridge, Berkshire, MA	1 share		1/1/1760
Hays, David			GH	
Woodbridge, Timothy	Stockbridge, Berkshire, MA	1/2 share	£8	8/25/1773
Heath, Bartholomew	Noble Town, Albany, NY		B151	3/8/1774
Woodbridge, Timothy	Stockbridge, Berkshire, MA	1 share		
Wheeler, Nicholas			GN	
Woodbridge, William	Vergennes, Addison, VT	1 share	5s	2/16/1796
Morgan, Sylvia	Northbridge, Berkshire, MA		E74	3/1/1796
Woodward, David		1/2 share, No. 70 of 400		3/18/1794
Bartell, Peter			C315	3/9/1795
Woodward, Elijah	Watertown, Litchfield. CT	16,000 A	$8,000	5/7/1796
Bulkley, Joshua et al		Paris Twp	E313	8/8/1796
Samuel Clark; Joshua Henshaw				
Woodward, Samuel	Canterbury, Windham, CT	1/2 share	£3	7/3/1767
Stevens, Cyprian			B230	7/23/1774
Woodworth, Benjamin	Norwich, New London, CT	1/4 share	£6	10/20/1773
Dean, James	Lebanon, Windham, CT		B92	11/30/1773
Woodworth, Benjamin	Mount Pelia, Orange, VT	1/2 share	£100	
Throop, Benjamin	Bozrah, New London, CT		CA	
Woodworth, Jabez	Norwich, New London, CT	1/2 share	£12	10/20/1773
Dean, James	Lebanon, Windham, CT		B93	11/30/1773
Woolcut, Roger				
Drake, Nathaniel Jr.			A392	
Wooster, Ephriam*	Huntington, Fairfield, CT	all right	good cause	12/13/1794
Pope, Robert	Derby, New Haven, CT		C420	4/4/1795
and Elizabeth A. Mills, wf				
Wooster. Henry	Derby, New Haven, CT	Pwr Att to locate 1 share	1/2 share	8/12/1794
Towsey, Zerah	Freehold, Albany, NY		C382	2/28/1795
Wooster, Mary		1 share	$20	12/31/1795
Goodrich, Benj & Munson, Joshua			E258	7/1/1796
Wooster, Thomas*	New York	all rght of late Gen'l David Wooster,	$25	12/7/1795
Wooster, Mary & Ogden, Mary	New Haven, New Haven, CT		E257	7/1/1796
formerly of New Haven				
Worster, Samuel				
Northrup, Abraham			A75	
Worthington, Elias/Isham, Joseph*	Colchester, Hartford, CT	1/2 share	£12	12/21/1773
Fitch, Lemuel	Colchester, Hartford, CT		B113	1/3/1774
trustees for John Clarke, insolvent debtor				
Worthington, William	Catskill, Albany, NY	all right	$10,500	10/14/1796
Bingham, Chester	Tioga, Luzerne, PA	Durkee Twp	H158	12/13/1799
except 1,200 A to Jacob Radcliff of Poughkeepsie, Dutchess, NY and 1,000 A to Peletiah Pierce of Sharon, Litchfield, CT				
Worthington, William	Catskill, Albany, NY	1000 A	£100	4/22/1796
Peirce, Peletiah	Sharon, Litchfield, CT	Durkee Twp	E387	9/19/1796
Worthington, William	New Haven CT	1/2 share No. 175 of 600		1/22/1795
Turner, Seth			C217	2/28/1795
Worthington, William	New Haven, New Haven CT	all right*		1/22/1795
Turner, Seth	New Haven, New Haven CT		C299	3/4/1795
William Cook, OP				

grantor grantee notes	grantor residence grantee residence	description location	amount acct bk page	deed date record date
Wright, Charles et al*	Lebanon, Windham, CT	1/2 share	£9	1/5/1795
Holmes, Sanford	Woodstock, Windham, CT		C582	6/20/1795
Joel Wright, bro, heir and adm of Capt Seth Wright, father, decd.				
Wright, Ebenezer Jr.	Mansfield, Windham, CT	1 share		2/5/1754
Orcutt, John	Mansfield, Windham, CT		B248	4/1/1769
Wright, Ezekiel	Saybrook, Middlesex, CT	1/2 share	£3	9/1/1794
Elliot, William	Saybrook, Middlesex, CT		C355	3/2/1795
Wright, Reuben	Berlin, Hartford, CT	1/2 share	£6	1/29/1796
Smith, Lemuel & Allyn, John B.	Berlin, Hartford, CT		E149	2/25/1796
Wright, Samuel	Hebron, Tolland, CT	1/2 share	£10	1/23/1795
Swift, Silas	Lebanon, Windham, CT		I203	4/1/1795
Wyllys, George*		Public Notice*		12/4/1792
All persons			C470	2/22/1795
Secretary of State, Connecticut; take Doct Jabez Adams' Letters of Attorney seriously; they were signed by valid JPs Constant Southworth and Experience Storrs.				
Wyllys, Samuel, William &	Hartford, Hartford, CT	1 share	$50	6/8/1796
Mason, Jeremiah	Lebanon, Windham, CT		E236	7/4/1796
Wynkoop, William	Tioga, NY	2 Townships	$20,000	6/27/1797
Spalding, John	Ulster, Luzerne, PA	Hexham and Durkee Twps	F218	7/10/1797
Wynkoop, William	Tioga Co NY	4000 A	not mentioned	7/11/1795
Wood, Nathaniel	Hillsdale, Columbia, NY	Hexham Twp, 1/4	E23	2/9/1796
Wynkoop, William	Tioga Co NY	8,000 A	$4,500	6/27/1795
Wood, William	Hillsdale, Columbia, NY	Cato Twp, 1/2	E18	2/9/1796
Wynkoop, William	Tioga Co NY	16,000 A	£3,200	8/5/1795
Wood, William	Hillsdale, Columbia, NY	Sullivan Twp	E20	2/9/1796
Wynkoop, William	Chemung, Tioga, NY	3 1/2 2nd division rights*		3/5/1796
Wynkoop, Benjamin	Chemung, Tioga, NY		E166	3/1/1796
1 Pixley, David B242; 1 Buck, Elijah B247; 1 Buck, William B242; 1/2 Buck, William A66 + 4,900A reverses deed of 3/6/1795, see C614; see C647; D33				
Wynkoop, William	Chemung, Tioga, NY	1 share		3/5/1796
Wynkoop, Benjamin	Chemung, Tioga, NY		E167	5/20/1796
Wynkoop, William	Chemung, Tioga, NY	16,000 A	$110	7/22/1799
Wynkoop, Benjamin	Chemung, Tioga, NY	Ottertown Twp	H272	11/21/1799
Wynkoop, Wm and Spelman,	Chemung, Tioga, NY	8,000 A	£400	9/15/1796
Satterlee, Elisha & Bingham,		Greenfield Twp, 1/2	E461	11/6/1796
Wynkoop, Wm & Dorrance, Benj	Chemung, Tioga, NY &	2700 A	£300	10/31/1794
Rossetter/Rositer, Benjamin		Brooklyn Twp	I119	12/8/1794
Brooklyn Twp, but description fits Lebanon or E of Lebanon,. Not clear how Wynkoop & Dorrance became owners.				
Yale, Benjamin Jr.	Pauling Town, Dutchess, NY	1/2 share (inc. one pitch in high	good cause	3/13/1795
Craft, Edward	Derby, New Haven, CT		C410	4/4/1795
laid out by Capt Enos Atwater 3/5/1774				
Yale, Benjamin, son of Benjamin	Pauling, Dutchess, NY	1 share	£1.4	3/13/1795
Yale, Thomas	Darby, New Haven, CT		E410	9/15/1796
Yale, Benjamin Sr.	Wallingford, New Haven, CT	2 shares, 1/2 to each child	love	4/5/1770
Yale, Benj Jr, Uriah, Lydia, Ruth,			C407	4/4/1795
Yale, Enos	Unedilla, Otsego, NY	1/2 share	£10	6/11/1796
Bush, Jonathan	Franklin, Otsego, NY		E509	1/21/1797
Yale, Job	Cheshire, New Haven, CT	1/2 share	£10.10	1/5/1795
Kimberly, Israel; Kimberly, Liberty	Derby, New Haven, CT		C408	4/4/1795
Yale, Job	Wallingford, New Haven, CT	1/2 share	£8	4/4/1772
Yale, Noah	Wallingford, New Haven, CT		B220	5/26/1774
Yale, Thomas	Farmington	1 share	some consideration	11/2/1767
Hungerford, Benjamin			MB	12/28/1768
Yale, Thomas et al*	Darby, New Haven, CT	2 shares	good cause	2/8/1796
Pope, Robert	Darby, New Haven, CT		E408	9/15/1796
Israel & Liberty Kimberly				
Yale, Thomas & Yale, Benjamin	Derby, New Haven, CT	1/2 share/all rights*	good cause	3/23/1795
Kimberly, Liberty	Derby, New Haven, CT		C405 - C406	4/4/1795
inc 1/4 in high tree laid out by Capt Enos Atwater 9/29/1774				
Yarington, Abel	Wilkesbarre, Luzerne, PA	1/2 share	$30	11/23/1795
Irwin, James	Luzerne, PA		E439	10/1/1796
except town lot, meadow lot and 100 A lot in Athens				
Yarrington, Abel	Wyoming, PA	1/2 Town Lot 31, 1 7/8 A	£15	5/3/1786
Franklin, John	Wyoming	Wilkesbarre Twp	I51	12/1/1786

grantor grantee notes	grantor residence grantee residence	description location	amount acct bk page	deed date record date
Yong, William	Windham, Windham, CT	1 share	£40	3/28/1774
Huntington, Hezekiah	Windham, Windham, CT		C319	2/26/1795
York, Lucretia		2/3 of six 1/2 shares, i.e. 2 shares		
York, Minor		Braintrim Twp	I167	
recorded in Luzerne county records				
York, Minor		2/3 of six 1/2 shares, i.e. 2 shares	val con	11/9/1793
Gordon, Samuel		Braintrim Twp	I167	2/21/1795
Young, David				
Murdock, Dan			A277	

Made in the USA
Coppell, TX
16 August 2021